12/07

FOUR
STARS
OF
VALOR

FOUR STARS

OF

VALOR

THE COMBAT HISTORY OF
THE 505TH PARACHUTE
INFANTRY REGIMENT
IN WORLD WAR II

PHIL NORDYKE

ZENITH PRESS

First published in 2006 by MBI Publishing Company LLC and Zenith Press, an imprint of MBI Publishing Company, Galtier Plaza, Suite 200, 380 Jackson Street, St. Paul, MN 55101-3885 USA

Library of Congress Cataloging-in-Publication Data

Nordyke, Phil.
    Four stars of valor : the combat history of the 505th Parachute Infantry Regiment in World War II / Phil Nordyke.
        p. cm.
    Includes bibliographical references and index.
    ISBN-13: 978-0-7603-2664-0 (hbk.)
    ISBN-10: 0-7603-2664-9 (hbk.)
    1. United States. Army. Parachute Infantry Regiment, 505th. 2. World War, 1939–1945—Regimental histories—United States. 3. World War, 1939–1945—Campaigns—Western Front. I. Title.
D769.348505th .N67 2006
940.54'1273—dc22

Zenith Press titles are also available at discounts in bulk quantity for industrial or sales-promotional use. For details write to Special Sales Manager at MBI Publishing Company, Galtier Plaza, Suite 200, 380 Jackson Street, St. Paul, MN 55101-3885 USA.

To find out more about our books, join us online at www.zenithpress.com.

ISBN-13: 978-0-7603-2664-9
ISBN-10: 0-7603- 2664-0

Designer: LeAnn Kuhlmann
Printed in the United States of America

On the front cover: The 2nd Battalion, 505th Parachute Infantry Regiment, jump into Holland during Operation Market Garden, September 17, 1944.—*Photograph by William H. Jenks, courtesy of the 82nd Airborne Division War Memorial Museum*

CONTENTS

Acknowledgements 6

Introduction 8

CHAPTER 1   "As Tough And Intelligent A Group Of Fighting Men As Ever Pulled On Jump Boots" 10

CHAPTER 2   "If You Fell Out, You Were Dismissed From The Regiment" 25

CHAPTER 3   "Africa Was A Living Hell" 41

CHAPTER 4   "The Eyes of the World Are Upon You. The Hopes And Prayers Of Every American Go With You." 57

CHAPTER 5   "A Blazing Hell Of Mortar, Artillery, And Small Arms Fire" 79

CHAPTER 6   "The Italians Were Something Less Than Enthused About Fighting" 95

CHAPTER 7   "A Scene I Would Carry With Me Always" 116

CHAPTER 8   "An Irresistible Force That Nothing Could Stop" 134

CHAPTER 9   "A Small Unit Performance That Has Seldom Been Equaled" 155

CHAPTER 10   "The 82nd Airborne Division's Undiscovered World War II Equivalent Of Sergeant Alvin C. York" 178

CHAPTER 11   "I Would Rather Have A Platoon Of Those Men Than A Battalion Of Regular Infantry" 196

CHAPTER 12   "The Sky Is Full Of Silk" 222

CHAPTER 13   "All Of The Men Worshipped Him" 243

CHAPTER 14   "You Fired Fast And Straight Or You Were Dead" 258

CHAPTER 15   "We Were Not Going To Pull Back ... If They Take Us Back, They're Going To Have To Carry Us Back" 284

CHAPTER 16   "Boy, I Feel Sorry For The First Germans Those Guys Get Ahold Of" 307

CHAPTER 17   "The Krauts Are All Around Us" 327

CHAPTER 18   "The Company I Came to Know and Love No Longer Existed" 349

CHAPTER 19   "Is This Armageddon?" 378

CHAPTER 20   "Fugitives From The Laws Of Averages" 395

EPILOGUE   "Invisible Pathfinders" 414

Notes 418

Bibliography 453

Index To Maps 465

Index 466

ACKNOWLEDGMENTS

I am indebted to many individuals and groups for their direct and indirect contributions to the completion of this project. First, I want to thank my family, particularly my wife, Nancy, for her understanding during my long hours of work, doing jobs around the house that should be my responsibility, as well as editing and proofreading. My sons, Jason and Robert, as well as my daughter, Amy, have been supportive, despite the time my writing has taken away from activities with each of them.

My heartfelt thanks go to my literary agent, Ms. Gayle Wurst, Princeton International Agency for the Arts, who did a superb job of promoting the book project and negotiating on my behalf.

Mr. Richard Kane, one of the most respected editors in military publishing, deserves much credit and my sincere appreciation for having faith in my ability to write a regimental history. Tom Kailbourn did a great job of copy editing the book and getting it in shape for publication.

Phil Schwartzberg, the cartographer at Meridian Mapping, Minneapolis, Minnesota, produces the best maps in the business and I owe him my thanks for his superb work.

The research materials for the book came from several repositories and archives. I am indebted to a number of wonderful people who provided help in obtaining the information. The Cornelius Ryan Archives at Ohio University in Athens, Ohio, was a wealth of veterans' accounts and documents relating to the Normandy and Holland campaigns. I want to thank Doug McCabe, Curator of Manuscripts, Robert E. and Jean R. Mahn Center for Archives and Special Collections, the Alden Library, Ohio University, for providing the large volume of materials referenced in this book.

I want to recognize and thank Martin K. A. Morgan, noted author, historian, and curator at the Eisenhower Center in New Orleans, Louisiana, who provided copies of oral history transcripts and written accounts from the center's archives.

I want to extend my gratitude to Dr. John Duvall, Museums Chief, and Betty Rucker, Collections Manager, who opened up the Ridgway–Gavin Archives at The 82nd Airborne Division War Memorial Museum at Fort Bragg, North Carolina, a rich source of primary documents for this book.

Ericka L. Loze, Librarian, Donovan Research Library, Fort Benning, Georgia, provided monographs of 505th Parachute Infantry Regiment veterans from the library's massive collection. I owe her much.

Guy LoFaro and Normand E. Thomas were kind enough to locate and send materials from the U.S. Military History Institute and the U.S. Army Center of Military History, saving me a great deal of time and expense.

I appreciate very much the after-action report of the 307th Airborne Engineer Battalion in Normandy, provided by Brian Siddall.

My thanks to Father G. Thuring and Frank van den Bergh with the Liberation Museum in Groesbeek, Holland. They provided much information about the campaign in Holland. Their books and expertise helped correct several errors in my understanding of the battle for the Nijmegen bridges.

The veterans of the 505th RCT Association deserve the greatest credit and appreciation for making this book possible. I must begin by acknowledging the early support of the late Lieutenant General Jack Norton and Colonel Mark Alexander, as well as Colonel Ed Sayre. They encouraged and inspired me to write this book.

I owe an enormous debt to 505th PIR veteran Don Lassen and his *Static Line* magazine for so much of the contact information of the 505th RCT veterans.

There were individuals with each unit who helped me with contact information, who provided entrées to others in their units, and who provided information about the units. The names are too numerous to mention without invariably omitting to thank one or more. To the more than five hundred veterans, friends, and families of the 505th RCT who contributed to the book, I owe the greatest appreciation. This book would not have been possible without the first person accounts of the veterans of the regimental combat team.

In some cases, I have made minor changes to some of the personal accounts, correcting grammatical and spelling errors, rearranged sentences to put the action in chronological order, or to omit repetitive or irrelevant information in long quotes, and to have consistency in unit designations, equipment, and other items. However, the first person accounts are always true to the veterans' original words.

It is to all of the officers and men who served with the legendary 505th Regimental Combat Team during World War II that this book is dedicated.

INTRODUCTION

This is the remarkable story of the only parachute regiment to make four combat jumps, and one of the greatest fighting forces ever assembled. It was an incredible collection of men from many backgrounds, with many individual talents and skills, attracted by the adventure and danger of being a paratrooper.

From the rigorous selection process of the parachute school at Fort Benning to the grueling training in the heat of the Frying Pan, Alabama Area, and North Africa—only the most physically fit, mentally strong, and highly motivated of those who volunteered, remained with the regiment. Under the command of one of the pioneers of airborne warfare and one of World War II's greatest commanders, James M. Gavin, the 505th Parachute Infantry Regiment (PIR) was arguably the toughest, best-trained regiment that the United States Army has ever fielded. General Matthew B. Ridgway, who commanded both the 82nd Airborne Division and the XVIII Airborne Corps, which included the 101st and 17th Airborne Divisions, stated, "I have no doubt that, based on its record, the 505 was the best parachute regiment to come out of World War II." [1]

Gavin's paratroopers made the first regimental combat jump in U.S. Army history, spearheading the invasion of Sicily. There, despite being badly scattered, they fought the powerful Hermann Göring Panzer Division to a standstill.

Barely two months later, they made a second parachute jump at Salerno, Italy, along with the 504th Parachute Infantry Regiment, saving the beachhead. The regiment led the drive north where it captured Naples, the first city in Europe liberated by Allied forces.

Eight months later, the regiment parachuted into Normandy, France, in the predawn hours of June 6, 1944—some of the first Allied soldiers to land on Hitler's fortress Europe. Thanks to the great work of the unit's pathfinders, the 505th PIR was the only regiment to land on and close to their drop zone. There they liberated the first town in France, Ste.-Mère-Église, and held it against overwhelming numbers of enemy armor and infantry, preventing a counterattack on the forces landing at Utah Beach. The regiment spent thirty-three days in Normandy, spearheading the drive toward the port of Cherbourg, the severing of the Cotentin Peninsula at St.-Sauveur-le-Vicomte, and the capture of strategic hills near La Haye-du-Puits.

In little more than sixty days, the regiment made its fourth combat jump in fourteen months, when it spearheaded the Allied invasion of Holland, jumping in daytime, fifty-three miles behind German lines to provide a corridor for the British Second Army's drive to the Rhine River. Together with the 504th PIR's famed "Devils in Baggy Pants," the regiment captured the massive highway bridge at Nijmegen. They fought for fifty-four days in Holland before being withdrawn to France for replacements and reorganization.

When powerful German armored forces broke through the American lines in the Ardennes, the regiment, without proper clothing, equipment, and training for winter fighting, rushed to Belgium and fought to a standstill Germany's two best equipped, most powerful SS panzer divisions. The 505th then counterattacked during the worst winter conditions in Europe in fifty years, driving the enemy back to their own border and piercing the Siegfried Line.

They stood guard on the Rhine River and made an assault crossing of the Elbe River in the closing days of the war in Europe, preventing Soviet occupation of Denmark, and assisted in the capture of an entire German army.

During six campaigns in the Mediterranean and European Theaters of Operations, their courage and fighting prowess became legendary. By the end of the war in Europe, most of the regiment's veterans wore Purple Heart medals, many with one or more oak leaf clusters, and decorations for valor.

Supported by the paratroopers of Company B, 307th Airborne Engineer Battalion; the 456th Parachute Field Artillery Battalion; and elements of the glider-borne 80th Airborne Antiaircraft (Antitank) Battalion, the men of this great regimental combat team participated in some of the heaviest combat of World War II, yet were never defeated in battle. Their exploits on battlefields will long shine in U.S. military history—Biazzo Ridge, Ste.-Mère-Église, Nijmegen, Trois Ponts.

This is not only the story of the 505th Regimental Combat Team's great feats of arms on the battlefield. It is the story of close combat, devotion to duty, remarkable courage, and tremendous sacrifice—told as only frontline combat infantrymen can.

CHAPTER 1

"As Tough And Intelligent A Group Of Fighting Men As Ever Pulled On Jump Boots"

The seeds of the elite 505th Parachute Infantry Regiment were sown during the Great Depression, when most of the young men who would fill its ranks grew up poor, enduring the bitter hardships of the economic conditions of that time. They learned at a young age the meaning of self-reliance, hard work, and personal responsibility. They developed mental and physical toughness, independence, and willingness to take risks that would carry over in their attitudes toward military service and would distinguish them from the average soldier during World War II. Fred F. Caravelli was a twelve-year-old kid growing up in New Jersey when the Depression struck. "My father passed away when everything was bad in 1929, so my mother, my brother, and I had to move to Philadelphia to live with my grandmother. We went from Haddonfield, New Jersey, which was a really rich town to south Philadelphia, which was quite a change. I got out of high school in the tenth grade because there was no use in me going . . . I couldn't go to college. That's when I went to work in a clothing factory." [1]

Frank A. Bilich was born in Chicago, Illinois, the second of three sons of Croatian immigrants. "We moved to a Croatian neighborhood, attended a Croatian church and school, and basically we spoke Croatian in almost everything we did, until I was nine years old, when we moved out of the neighborhood. I spoke Italian, too, because the neighborhood we lived in was basically Croatian and Italian.

"At that time, it was the Depression and nobody had any money. My mother had a hard time raising three kids, because my dad had already gone. She had three boys, so we were on relief. I had been a sick boy from the time I was a kid. I had rheumatic fever, I had heart problems, and so did my younger brother. As a result, the doctors told me not to do anything. Well, being a boy, I did exactly what they told me not to do. I did all of the running and playing baseball.

"The first year of high school was just making acquaintances and meeting people. I got to like high school pretty well. I didn't have much trouble with my classes, and I thought I was a pretty good student. The third year while summer vacation was on, one of the fellows told me that the local bakery, which was the A&P Bakery, was hiring part-time help. I had a newspaper stand with my buddy to try to bring in some money to help my mother. When the opportunity came, I went there for an interview.

"The guy said, 'How old are you?'

"I said, 'Sixteen.'

"He said, 'You're kind of young to be looking for a part-time job.'

"I explained the situation to him and he said, 'Well, we can use you on Fridays and maybe Saturdays,' which would be twelve hours each night. So that's how I started that summer, which was my third year of high school. I started working Fridays and Saturdays, twelve hours.

"When the school term began again, he called me in and said that he could use me another night, maybe two during the week, and could I fit it in with my schedule. It was on the graveyard shift from eleven to seven.

"So I said, 'Sure.' So I started working Wednesday, Fridays, and Saturdays eleven to seven." 2

Near the end of his junior year, Bilich was approached about running for class president for the upcoming school year. "I didn't really want the job, but one of the girls came up to me and said, 'Why don't you take the president of the senior class next year?'

"I said, 'I'm too busy working, and what would I have to do?'

'Then about two weeks later she came back and said, 'How about vice president? We need somebody.'

"So I said, 'I don't think I could get elected.' In two days there were posters all over the school; 'Be bright. Vote right. Frank Bilich for vice president.' I had a good buddy of mine that ran my campaign. They took over the campaign and I won.

"Both in grammar school and high school I had wonderful teachers; people that were really on the ball and cared for us. My teacher that taught public speaking, Mrs. Kathleen B. Rigby, wrote to all of the boys who went into the service all during the war." 3

By his senior year, Bilich was working full time at the bakery. "I was working five nights a week, eleven that night to seven in the morning, punching the clock, walking a block home, having a bite to eat, catch the street car and go to school. I would usually get there about 8:00 or 8:15. My first class was a quarter to nine. The last year I would go to class from about nine o'clock to about two, come home, do homework, take a little nap, and then go back to work. It was a rewarding experience." 4

Bilich and his brothers were friends with some of the older guys in the neighborhood. "We kind of looked up to those guys. These guys were eight, ten years older than us. John Rabig lived two doors away from me. He was playing for the Ramblers, which was a softball team that played in the Windy City League. We got to be real good friends. He was real good to us. He was like a bunch of fellows in the neighborhood, and couldn't get a job; so he joined the CCC camp, the Civilian Conservation Corps. They were paid something like twenty dollars per month. They wore Army uniforms and were under the control of the U.S. Army. They built parks and recreation centers. It was a job created to get people off of the streets." 5

Ronald Snyder also grew up poor and needed to earn money to support himself and the family. "In 1939, as a sixteen-year-old high school student, I enlisted in the

Pennsylvania National Guard, of course, claiming to be eighteen years of age. The weekly drills and summer encampments were lots of fun. However, during the winter of 1940–41, the government declared a national emergency and federalized the National Guard for one year's active duty. And, even though I was only a seventeen-year-old high school senior, I found myself in the regular army." 6

Edwin Sayre grew up working hard on his father's dairy farm on the edge of the oil boom town of Breckenridge, Texas. Sayre played halfback on the great Breckenridge football teams while in high school. "The day I got to be seventeen years old, I was old enough to go into the National Guard. We had a new National Guard [Company of the 36th Infantry Division] coming to Breckenridge. Believe it or not, we were glad to get into this [unit]. It kind of broke the monotony of our seven day [work week] and gave us something else to do. That National Guard Company got sent for two weeks' training down on the Texas coast. You got to sleep until 5:00 every morning. I thought, 'Boy, I have it made.' Besides that, we didn't work at all on Sundays and I could go down and loll around on the beach. It was really a two-week vacation, and we got a dollar a day for it, plus room and board. Now, the showers didn't have any heat and a few things like that.

"My initial thought when I joined was I would learn to be a cook. I enjoyed the discipline.

"My mentor was a first lieutenant named Bob Mahaffey. He said, 'You really should start taking this correspondence course to be a second lieutenant.'

"So I signed up for what they called the ten series. When you completed the ten series you were theoretically qualified to be a second lieutenant. When you completed the twenty series you were qualified to be a first lieutenant. And when you completed the thirty series you were qualified to be a captain.

"At the time we were called to active duty in 1940, I had just about completed the thirty series. By the time we got down there [to Camp Bowie in Brownwood, Texas] and saw this terrible shortage of officers, they invited the four hundred senior officers to take competitive examinations to be second lieutenants.

"I went in and looked at that examination, and it was right out of the correspondence course. I had done all of this correspondence and sent in all of my lessons, got them back corrected, and resubmitted them correctly. It was a two-hour examination, and I finished it in about forty minutes, and that gave me time to go back and check it." 7

Sayre passed the exam easily with a high score. "Unfortunately, the colonel didn't want any of us to [out]rank the sergeant major, and he didn't do too well on the test. He barely squeezed into the top forty. He didn't get made a second lieutenant until about two weeks after the rest of us had made it." 8

Another young man who came up through the ranks of the U.S. Army during the Great Depression was James Maurice Gavin, born in Brooklyn, New York, to poor Irish immigrants, who both died when he was very young. He was raised in poverty by foster parents, Martin and Mary Gavin, in the coal mining town of Mount Carmel, Pennsylvania. As a young schoolboy, Gavin sold newspapers in the morning and evenings to help support the family. By the time he was eleven years old he had two paper routes of his own and sold other out-of-town newspapers locally. Gavin's foster parents forced him to drop out of school after the eighth grade in order to work full time to help support the family.

Young Gavin realized that the key to escaping poverty was an education. At age seventeen, he left Mount Carmel and moved to New York City, where he discovered that he could obtain an education while serving in the military. Gavin lied about his age and joined the U.S. Army as a private. Subsequently, he took competitive examinations to enter an army preparatory school for the U.S. Military Academy at West Point, then won an appointment and entered West Point at age eighteen in 1925.

Gavin read extensively about the subject of military history and studied the science of military operations and tactics, to the point where, upon graduation in 1929, he was assigned as an instructor of military tactics at West Point. At the outbreak of World War II in Europe, Gavin "became deeply interested in the Germans' conquest of Europe and their use of a new arm—parachute-glider troops—and I taught as many classes as possible in the new and evolving tactics that could be learned from the European war. I had access to many of the original documents relating to the German airborne operations in Holland. I also read avidly the reports from our military attaché in Cairo, Colonel Bonner Fellers, on the German parachute and glider operations in Crete. The whole concept of vertical envelopment was an exciting one, and it would seem to offer us a new dimension of tactics if we entered the war." [9]

Captain Gavin requested a transfer to the fledgling U.S. Army airborne program, but was denied the transfer by the superintendent of West Point. However, he used connections in the War Department to obtain a transfer. He arrived at Fort Benning in August 1941, to take parachute training. After graduating from the parachute school, Captain Gavin was assigned to command Company C, 503rd Parachute Infantry Battalion (PIB).

When General Omar N. Bradley toured Fort Benning in late 1941, he inspected the new paratroopers, whom he described as "a breed apart—the toughest, best trained infantry I had ever seen." [10]

Lieutenant Colonel Bill Lee, commanding the new airborne forces, quickly discovered the brilliant young captain and moved Gavin up to his staff as plans and training officer. Gavin wrote the very first manual of the U.S. Army's airborne doctrine, entitled *The Employment of Airborne Forces*. "My new job, as Plans and Training Officer, gave me an exciting opportunity to experiment and develop new techniques for large-scale parachute-glider operations.

"The problems were without precedent. Individuals had to be capable of fighting at once against any opposition they met on landing. Although every effort was being made to develop the communications and techniques to permit battalions, companies, and platoons to organize promptly, we had to train our individuals to fight for hours and days, if necessary, without being part of a formal organization. Equipment had to be lightweight and readily transportable. Weapons had to be hand-carried. This meant that larger weapons had to be broken down into individual loads, such as mortars and parachute-dropped artillery. Finally, since entry into combat was to take place in the midst of the enemy, a new scheme for issuing combat orders and coordinating the efforts of all the troops had to be developed. All these problems brought into sharp focus the most important problem of all—how to train the individual paratrooper.

"We sought to train the paratroopers to the highest peak of individual pride and skill. It was at this time that the use of nameplates was adopted, the purpose being to emphasize the importance of an individual's personality and reputation. To the soldiers of another generation, it seemed to suggest too little discipline and too much initiative given to individual soldiers. We were willing to take a chance that this would not have a disrupting effect on larger formations.

"It did not. Aside from the impact of this type of training on the airborne formations themselves, it had tremendous significance to the army as a whole. The morale of the airborne units soared, especially after their first combat, when they could see for themselves the results of their training." [11]

In December 1941, Gavin was promoted to the rank of major. "In the spring of 1942 Brigadier General William Lee and I, as his Plans and Training Officer, went to Washington to discuss the creation of our first airborne division. The Washington staff seemed rather skeptical about the whole idea. However, after some discussion it was agreed that we could start the organization of an airborne division provided certain stipulations were met. The division had to be one that had already completed basic training, and it could not be a regular Army or National Guard division; the States would not want the National Guard made airborne. It was also stipulated that the division should be one that was stationed where flying weather was generally good and near one or more airfields. The one division that met all these requirements was the 82nd Division at Camp Claiborne, Louisiana." [12]

Elmo Bell grew up poor in Mississippi, where he learned carpentry skills from his father that helped him find steady work right out of high school in 1941 prior to America's entry into World War II. "After the defense buildup started, I started working as a carpenter at the various Army posts. The first place I worked was Camp Shelby." [13]

His work brought him into contact with the soldiers there and those training at Fort Polk, Louisiana, in the months prior to the Japanese attack on Pearl Harbor. By that time Bell "had developed a bad attitude toward the army. I had the idea that most of the soldiers were draftees, that they were not motivated, that they were not in the service because they wanted to be, but because they were drafted. And I had frequent altercations with them." [14]

Paul Nunan was at home listening to the radio on the afternoon of December 7, 1941. "The news came over the radio that Pearl Harbor had been bombed with great loss of life. I'm afraid I got a little bit emotional about that.

"I was working in the steel mill at the time, and I thought about trying to enlist. I didn't know whether I would pass the eye test or not. I ran into a couple of people who were paratroopers and I talked to them and wound up volunteering for the paratroop outfit." [15]

Most young Americans seethed with anger over the sneak attack by the Japanese. Young men from all over the United States immediately flooded recruitment offices to join the fight. Berge Avadanian "wanted to inflict as much violence on the enemy as possible." [16]

Charles "Chuck" Copping was working on a ranch near his birthplace of Glendive, Montana, when Pearl Harbor was bombed. "We were out gathering horses on the morning and afternoon of December 7th. We got back to the ranch house and they told us about Pearl Harbor. We immediately threw our saddles, our clothes, and bridles in the car and went to town." [17]

The following morning in Glendive, Copping ran into a couple of his buddies. "We had a three-way discussion about Pearl Harbor. We wanted to kick the hell out of the Germans and the Japanese. I said, 'Let's go down and talk to the recruiting sergeant.'

"We had a recruiting office in the basement of the post office. We all went down there and caught the recruiting sergeant. We told him that we wanted to join the army and wanted to leave that night.

"He looked at his watch and he said, 'Well, it's eleven thirty. You go have lunch and then come back, and we'll take care of signing you up.'

"I said, 'If you've got to have lunch, go ahead. We'll go to Miles City and join the army; but we're leaving tonight.'

"He said, 'Forget lunch.'" [18]

Copping and his two buddies and their parents signed the papers later that day for the three young men. They left that night by train for the induction center at Butte, Montana.

Anthony Antoniou was a high school student in Astoria, New York, who had emmigrated with his parents in 1939 from the Mediterranean island of Cyprus. Fortunately, because Cyprus had been under British control, Antoniou spoke and read English. He was only seventeen years old when the Japanese attacked Pearl Harbor and therefore needed his father's signature on a permission form in order to enlist. "I wanted to get away from my stepmother. I went to my father. I gave him the paper to sign. I told him I wanted to borrow some books from the library. He couldn't read English that well, and he signed it." [19]

The next day, Antoniou's father found out that his son had joined the army and was leaving for the induction center. "When he saw me, he started cursing." [20]

The reasons men volunteered for the airborne were varied, but the most common themes were the excitement of flying, serving in an elite unit, extra money, and escape from units with poor morale and leadership.

On the evening of December 7, 1941, high school senior Howard C. Goodson was "with a couple of friends of mine at Luther Morgan's service station in Brownwood, Texas, when it came over on the radio. A couple of us there got all excited and said, 'Man, now we can go into the service.'

"I found out I was too young, by a couple of months, but my mother fixed it up for me where I could go into the service. I wanted to get into the air force. They weren't taking everyone at the time, and they started talking about paratroopers.

"I said, 'No way.'

"They said, 'Come back next week.'

"My buddy and I came back the next week and they didn't have any openings for the air force.

"The third week was the same thing, and I told my buddy, 'Well, I think I'm going ahead and joining the paratroopers.' He backed out and I joined." [21]

Once America entered the war, Elmo Bell could have avoided military service with a deferment, because he held a defense-related job. "But I didn't want the stigma of being a draft dodger, and so I decided to enlist in the Marine Corps. But while I was looking for the recruiting office, I ran into the army recruiter and asked directions. He told me that he would take me to the marine recruiting office, but he had to drop off the mail at his office first. He told me it was block out of the way, and we'd walk by there and have a cup of coffee, and then he'd take me to the marine recruiter. Well, over the cup of coffee, he asked me why I chose the marines. I told him, and he couldn't argue with my logic.

"And then he asked me if I'd ever heard of the parachute troops, and I hadn't. And he told me that that was the elite of the armed forces; that they wore special uniforms, had more rigid physical requirements, plus physical fitness testing, and that they collected an extra fifty dollars per month hazardous duty pay. That really got my attention, because I had been making good money in defense work; I had earned good money since I was in high school. I knew that on twenty-one dollars a month that it was going to be a tight squeeze. So I decided to go that route, and we completed the enlistment form. He sent me to a doctor for a physical, and when I came back, he called the doctor or the doctor called and told him that I had passed the physical." [22]

That night, Bell told his best friend what he had done, and he decided to join Bell in volunteering for the airborne. After his friend passed the physical exam, they took the oath of enlistment and were sent by bus to a reception center at Camp Shelby, Mississippi, where they were issued uniforms. A few days later they were shipped to Camp Wheeler, Georgia, for basic training. "I was terribly disappointed and disturbed with basic training. They wanted a bunch of soldiers that were a bunch a sheep; they'd just follow the leader without ever thinking for themselves or questioning anything. Most of the trainees were draftees; they didn't want to be there. Their heart was not in the job, and they did as little as they could. They dodged all the duties and took a get-by attitude, and I was terribly disturbed because there was no opportunity for individuals to distinguish themselves." [23]

After joining the army, Marty Cuccio was assigned as a medic at a stateside army hospital. "I was dissatisfied working in a hospital. Everything was dull. I didn't like it.

"A friend said, 'Come on, let's volunteer [for the airborne].'

"I said, 'Yeah, go ahead, let's volunteer.'"[24]

Private Ronald Snyder found himself serving in an engineer unit with the 28th Infantry Division at the time of the attack on Pearl Harbor. "I didn't want to spend the war in an engineering unit because of the desired adventure and excitement [of combat]. So, I volunteered for the parachute troops."[25]

Private Howard Goodson, who had volunteered to become a paratrooper when he enlisted, was taking basic training at Camp Roberts, California, when "instructors from Fort Benning came down and put us through all kinds of physical work to see if we were able to go into the airborne. Luckily, I passed it. About 80 percent of us made it, because all of us were in pretty darn good shape. They put us on a troop train. Everyone that was going to Fort Benning was on this troop train. We stopped in a lot of places I had never seen. It took us about five days to get to Fort Benning."[26]

Every enlisted man and non-commissioned officer above the rank of private who volunteered for parachute school had to agree to a reduction in rank to private as a condition of acceptance to the school. Officers were treated no differently than privates upon entering jump school until they graduated or washed out.

Parachute school at Fort Benning, Georgia, was a four-week course, broken into four one-week stages. The first, "A" Stage, was designed to separate the paratroopers from the men. Upon arrival, Private Allan C. Barger and the other candidates were each issued jump boots and coveralls. "We immediately became infatuated with our boots and constantly competed with each other for the best shine. Considering we were competing mostly with Texans with their saddle soap and whiskey spit, it was not a fair battle."[27]

On Monday morning of the first day of "A" Stage, Private Frank Miale assembled with his class at 5:00 a.m. The class ran two courses of one mile each, followed by calisthenics for a half-hour before breakfast. Afterward, Miale and his class assembled in a large hangar-type building, where they were addressed by one of the instructors, Lieutenant Bill Chappell, who would become a legend in the annals of the airborne school. "A real muscular guy stood at the front of the group and said, 'I'm called Flash Gordon, and you'll get to know me as the meanest, toughest son of a bitch this side of anywhere that you've ever been and you've ever had the misfortune to meet. I know you're going to hate my guts, but I don't really give a rat's ass because you guys don't amount to more than a piece of shit to me. I want all of you fart-faces on the ground and on your stomachs and I want you to give me ten pushups."[28]

After the class performed the ten pushups, Miale listened as the instructor told them, "To make sure you guys are always paying attention, I'm going to holler: 'JAB!' and when I do, I want to hear only one thud as you punch your chests. God help anyone I catch with a late thud. That's just the preliminaries; I want you to meet my sergeants who will be in charge of your training and riding your asses to be assured you learn everything there is to know."[29]

After each instructor stepped in front of the class and called out his last name, "Flash Gordon" then continued, "These are my disciples, and on a scale of one to ten on toughness, they'll rank a solid ten. You can't hide anything from them, and they will make sure you don't get away with 'diddley-squat.' They have but one goal in life, and that is to make sure you all are as miserable as all hell while you're learning. If any of you think I'm kidding and you don't want to put up with this shit any longer, just step forward now and you can save the government a slew of money by not wasting our time training a bunch of gutless bastards." [30]

Private Miale and his class stood motionless as "Flash Gordon" paused momentarily. "No one moved a muscle and most accepted quietly the psychological implications without being aware that they had unknowingly picked up the gauntlet.

"'JAB!' One hundred forty-some-odd fists hit their chests in unison." [31]

Flash Gordon had their attention.

Private W. A. Jones' initial impression of the instructors was that "they were the meanest son of a guns in the world. I still think so. I was afraid of them.

"The first week, every time my left foot hit the ground I said, 'What in the hell am I doing here?' Because you ran everywhere you went, you didn't walk. They told you that you were going to forget how to walk; and you did. The first week was strictly physical training . . . eight, nine hours a day. Everywhere you went, you ran. You climbed ropes. You had to be able at the end of the week to climb a rope thirty-five feet high; climb up and then to hold it until they told you, and then come down. You had to be able to do a minimum of thirty pushups and a five-mile run. There were certain things you had to do. If you didn't, you were out." [32]

Like all new volunteers at the parachute school, Private Jones did an endless number of pushups at the whims of the instructors. "I don't care what you did. 'Give me ten.' 'Give me twenty.' They could meet you on the street and not like the way you were walking." [33]

Most trainees, like Private Howard C. Anderson, quickly learned the lessons. "Full gear or stripped for a shower, you ran and if you were caught walking, you were ordered down on your belly and gave the 'almighty deity' who was looking out for you one hundred pushups. Never smart-mouth the man and ask which arm you were supposed to do this or that with, or you could end up doing one-arm pushups." [34]

Private Elmo Bell quickly adapted to the tough physical training of "A" Stage. "Immediately after reveille formation, we'd do a two-mile run. And then we'd come back for the breakfast meal, and immediately following that, we'd go through a period of calisthenics. Then we would pair off for judo training.

"During this stage, there was extensive physical fitness testing that we had to undergo. You had to do a required number of pull-ups, pushups, sit-ups, knee-bends, and quite a broad spectrum of physical events to qualify. If you failed to measure up in any of these events, you were disqualified—your school training was terminated." [35]

Private Bill Dunfee soon realized that "A" Stage "was an all-out effort to 'washout' all but the most determined. The regimen was constant physical exercise, calisthenics, and double time. While in ranks you were at attention, parade rest, or double timing in place. Pushups were given as punishment at the slightest provocation. You had the added pressure of knowing an instructor could wash you out at any time, and for any reason. Rope climbing and tumbling exercises were repeated over, and over again. This was to build upper body strength and taught body control on landing. During this week when you sat for instructions, which was rare, you sat upright as near as possible to attention. When standing there were only two acceptable positions, at attention or parade rest—you dared not lean on anything. Your hands were at your side or locked behind your back at all times. You did not wipe your brow or scratch your butt, without being instructed to do more pushups. In retrospect, I realize the instructors had their orders to make it tough on us, but some seemed to take a sadistic joy in taking it out on the few guys that were having the most trouble. Our one pleasure in life was daydreaming about catching that bastard in town and teaching him some manners. It was July in Georgia and very hot—we had men pass out in ranks from heat exhaustion. If you made an effort to help the fallen man, you were instructed to 'Leave him lay, soldier, he ain't dead.'

"The men in my class that were washed out or quit for whatever reason were transferred immediately. When we returned to barracks they and their belongings were gone." [36]

On Thursday of their "A" Stage, Private Miale and his class were climbing thirty-five-foot ropes fastened to steel girders at the top of the hangar-type building. "After about an hour of struggling, Flash Gordon said, 'What's the matter with you guys? I can piss up that rope faster than you boneheads can climb it.'

"He then proceeded to climb, using only his hands and made everyone feel like idiots. He was as agile as a monkey." [37]

Private Dunfee found that the second week of jump school was even tougher. "'B' Stage was a continuation of all the exercises, calisthenics and double time of 'A' Stage. The tumbling exercises were elevated onto two-foot, three-foot and four-foot platforms. On these platforms you took the position of 'tumblers at ease.' On command, you jumped to the ground, simulating a downward pull on the risers, and tumbled forward, or to one side or the other, per instructions. After we became proficient at landing forward, we jumped off backward and simulated a landing coming in backward. In parachute school, you learn by doing. We were taught hand-to-hand combat and judo—the goal was to kill a man silently. Bayonet and knife training was emphasized, and the silent kill was constantly impressed on us. The area we trained in was a sawdust-covered field, with about an inch of sawdust covering the baked Georgia clay. We were ordered on numerous occasions not to spit in the sawdust. Those dumb enough to ask what to do with the sawdust they got in their mouth were told to swallow it. The officers in our class received no special favors. There was a lieutenant colonel in my group who was caught spitting sawdust out, after being dumped in a judo class. The instructor had him dance around on one leg reciting 'I will not spit in the sawdust' over and over again for some period of time. Rank has no privilege at parachute school.

"We were suspended in a parachute harness that was attached to a circular pipe ring that was four or five feet in diameter. This taught us to guide the parachute while descending by pulling down on the risers. By pulling down on the right hand or left hand risers, you could slip the chute to the right or left. By pulling down on the front or rear risers, you could slip forward or backward. By pulling down on one riser only, the parachute would turn slowly. If you were landing backward, you could put your right arm behind your head and grasp the left riser, and with your left hand grasp the right riser and pull with both hands. This action would turn you and the harness 180 degrees, and you would land moving forward." [38]

Through "A" and "B" Stages, most of the men who dropped out did so because of the physical exertion. Now, during "C" Stage, the courage of each man would be tested on towers designed to simulate various aspects of a parachute drop.

Private David V. Bowman and most troopers agreed that "the worst beast of all—the ogre that washed out more would-be parachutists than any one of the monsters to which we were exposed—the thirty-four-foot tower. This was a shed in which the floor was raised to thirty-four feet above the ground and the inside built as closely as feasible to the inside of a C-47, the plane we'd be jumping out of. In it was a steel cable running end to end, and attached to it was a static line twelve feet long, comparable to the one attached to the apex of our chutes. The purpose of this unit was to train us in the proper exiting procedures—that we keep our heads down and our bodies upright. What made this training aid so intimidating, I guess, is that it was so close and yet so far from the ground. They may have arrived at the figure of 'thirty-four-feet' after a long period of research showed it to be the optimum height to inspire the greatest fear. Or, the height may have been simply an arbitrary decision. At any rate, most agreed that it was much harder to jump from that than from a plane at fifteen hundred to two thousand feet above the ground." [39]

Private Chester Harrington, who had worked as a medical technician in an army hospital before volunteering to become a paratrooper, somehow reached down and summoned the courage to execute the instructor's commands on the thirty-four-foot tower. "You stood in the door, just like an airplane door at thirty-four feet in the air. You stepped off the platform just like you stepped out of the plane door and you dropped about sixteen feet until that [canvas strap] caught you. You rolled down the cable to the lower end. There was an automatic 'trip' and you dropped down about twelve to fifteen feet to the ground. You learned to hit on your feet and roll." [40]

Private W. A. Jones almost washed out because of the thirty-four-foot tower. "I came very near quitting. I don't know what it was, but I was just scared to death of those towers, and I still am. I froze in the [mockup] door; they had to 'help' me out the first two or three times. I wouldn't have gone out if the instructor, Sergeant Swetish, hadn't pushed me." [41]

The next towers were the two-hundred-fifty-foot towers, which Private Howard Goodson found to be exciting, because they simulated an actual parachute jump. "'A' tower was a chair. Two guys went up in this chair all the way up to the top, and all of a sudden they released you real quick and scared the heck out of you, but brought you back down.

"'B' tower was when they strapped you in an actual harness, and you were alone, and they took you up and released you, and you fell and came back down.

"The third tower was really scary. That was the one where most of the guys [who quit] got out; they couldn't take it. The guys [who dropped out] wouldn't even go up; they fell out." [42]

This tower was an experience that Private Dunfee would never forget. "Individually we were placed in a parachute harness, then laid on our stomachs on the ground. The harness was then suspended from the back and you were raised about fifty feet in the air looking straight down. There was a ["D" ring attached to a] ripcord on your left breast. You were then ordered to pull the ["D" ring to release the] ripcord, count to three thousand slowly in multiples of one thousand at a time and hang unto the ["D" ring]. When you pulled the ["D" ring], you went into a free fall for about twenty feet, then you came to a bone jarring stop. If you remembered to count and hang onto the ["D" ring], they let you down; if not, you did it all over again." [43]

For Private Goodson, the fourth tower was the most enjoyable aspect of his training by that point in the course. "The last tower was the best. An actual parachute was hooked up, and when you reached the top, it automatically released you. You were floating along like a regular parachute. The instructor was down below with a bullhorn, and they taught you how to pull on your risers to guide you down. Then you had to land exactly right. They always taught you to land on the balls of your feet and either go over your left shoulder or right shoulder and make a roll. If it was really windy you had to try to get up and run around behind your chute and collapse it, or it would really drag you." [44]

On Friday of "C" Stage, each trainee learned to pack a parachute that he would use the following Monday for his first qualifying jump. It made for restless nights for many trainees, silently wondering if they had packed their parachutes properly.

The fourth and last week, during "D" Stage, the trainees made five qualifying jumps from a C-47 aircraft. By this point in the course, trainees such as Private Dunfee were the survivors of some of the most physically and mentally demanding training conducted by the United States military at that time. "The exercises, calisthenics, and double time continued. However, morale was excellent, because we could see the light at the end of the tunnel. The most exciting part of this week was in making five jumps in five days. We had stars in our eyes looking forward to the ten-day furloughs we were promised on completing our training. We usually jumped in the mornings and packed our chutes in the afternoon for the jump the following day.

"A critique was held daily by the instructors to point out any real or imagined goofs we had made. We enjoyed these ass chewings, because as each day went by we were that much closer to graduating. We could dream that special dream of getting a particular instructor in Columbus, Georgia, and teaching him some manners.

"I will mention, too, that anytime prior to your fifth jump, you may quit without prejudice. Once you make five jumps and are qualified, it's a court-martial offense to refuse to jump. Refusing in combat is considered cowardice in the face of the enemy.

"A personal note: I had never been in an airplane prior to my joining the army. I made ten or twelve parachute jumps before landing in an airplane. At age nineteen, I was willing to try anything; the extra fifty dollars a month hazardous duty pay was an added incentive." [45]

After three weeks of training, most of the men had become buddies with another trainee. On Monday of "D" Stage, Private Goodson and his buddy were assigned to the same plane for their first qualifying jump. Goodson's buddy was "a guy by the name of Jack Hale; he was about twelve years older than me. We met on the train coming in. Luckily, I got assigned with him. He and I were real close. They put us on the plane in alphabetical order and Jack Hale ended up on the second string and I ended up the first man to go out the door. It was the easiest jump I ever made." [46]

As Private Allan Barger was waiting to make his first qualifying jump, he noticed a problem with the first trainee in line to jump. "Our student acting company commander was in the first stick, and as he was going out we were all surprised to see him 'freeze' in the door and fight against making the jump. The jumpmaster helped him out, and I remember seeing him hanging by his fingers before he finally let go. That was kind of scary." [47]

When Barger's turn came he went out the door without any trouble. "Then, suddenly the chute opened and I was swinging pleasantly in the breeze. It was exhilarating. It was the pleasantest sensation. Then I had to stabilize the chute and get ready to land. That, I did in proper order, and as I rolled up my chute I had this great feeling come over me. I felt like I could lick five men my own size. It was like a special drug. Everyone experienced it and it stayed with us for the rest of the day." [48]

The following day, Barger watched the same trainee who had struggled the previous day. "He did the same thing, so he was washed out—no wings. This was quite odd, for he was just as anxious as the rest of us to jump. We felt bad about that, for we all admired him anyway." [49]

On his third qualifying jump, Private Otis Sampson, who had been a member of the U.S. Army's horse cavalry years before, badly injured his right ankle when he attempted to land standing up. "I happened to land close to the 'meat wagon' (ambulance). The medic came running over to me and asked, 'You all right?'

"'O.K.' was my answer, as I tried not to show pain.

"'Let me see you jump up and down,' he ordered.

"I did as he asked, with the weight of my body on my left foot; I did fool the medic, but not myself. I marched to the sheds that evening in great pain and packed my chute, but the next morning, the injured foot would not bear my weight. 'Oh God, I'm going to miss out on graduating with my class.' There was no way of kidding myself; I was hurting. I limped to the infirmary, where I soaked the foot in a whirlpool of hot water. Several times that day I repeated the treatment, praying to God it would be all right tomorrow.

"The next day, I was at the packing sheds drawing my chute to make my fourth jump. I sweated that one out, but it [was] a good landing. Returning to the packing sheds, I tried to draw another chute to make my fifth jump, but I was told I didn't need to make another, I had already qualified. It felt good to know that someone had kept close track of me." [50]

On Saturday, after making their qualifying jumps, trainees attended graduation ceremonies, where they proudly wore their jump boots, shined to a mirror finish, with their uniform pant legs bloused. Each received a certificate, and shiny new silver wings were pinned on his chest. Every officer and enlisted man who graduated from Fort Benning's Parachute School was proud to be part of an elite fraternity—U.S. Army paratroopers.

The new paratroopers could for the first time wear their jump boots outside the training area. For new paratroopers like Private Paul D. Nunan, "The boots were a big ego booster." [51]

The U.S. Army began an experiment on February 24, 1942, to develop a parachute artillery unit that could support the parachute infantry units forming. Lieutenant Joseph D. Harris was selected as the commanding officer (CO), and Lieutenant Carl E. Thain as the executive officer (XO) of the Parachute Test Battery. Thain was just out of the hospital, having suffered a concussion in a horse riding accident. "One hundred ninety-nine enlisted men and four second lieutenants from the 'Animal Area' (97th, 99th, and 4th Field Artillery Pack Mule Battalions of Fort Bragg)—all volunteers—were sent by truck convoy to Fort Benning, Georgia, to test the feasibility of dropping a 75mm pack howitzer, with a section of men, from a C-47 and putting it into action on the ground.

"The infantry class number 16 was being trained at the time, and the artillery became 16-A, and was trained as a unit—both officers and men. We received our wings April 17, 1942.

"We proceeded to train as an artillery unit, while some, with the help of the Rock Island Arsenal personnel, devised means to package the several pieces of the howitzer to be dropped from six pods, under the belly of a C-47, and kicked out the door. Different methods of packing, dropping, and assembling were tested by battery personnel until a standard method was agreed upon." [52]

In June of 1942, a cadre of commissioned and non-commissioned officers from the Airborne Command, the 503rd PIB, the 502nd PIR, and the 504th PIR were formed to begin the formation and training of a new parachute infantry regiment. Most of the NCOs and officers from the Airborne Command would transfer out as new units formed, while most of the others would remain with the regiment. Captain Benjamin H. Vandervoort, who had been the parachute training officer at the school prior to America's entry into World War II, was assigned as the commander of Company F for the cadre of the as yet to be formed 505th Parachute Infantry Regiment. He was very impressed with the quality of the enlisted men who were assigned to the regiment. "All of the enlisted men were double volunteers—not draftees. Called to arms by Pearl Harbor, they had volunteered for the Army and again for the paratroops. Screened, tested, and jump qualified by the parachute school, they were the top of the line of America's citizen soldiers. Many would have been in college except for the war. The goal of the regimental cadre was to train them into as tough and intelligent a group of fighting men as ever pulled on jump boots." [53]

CHAPTER 2

"If You Fell Out,
You Were Dismissed From the Regiment"

The 505th Parachute Infantry Regiment was born in the crucible of the blazing Georgia summer heat and humidity at the "Frying Pan" area of Fort Benning. The regiment was activated on June 25, 1942, and its first commander, young Lieutenant Colonel James M. Gavin, took command on July 6, 1942.

As classes graduated from the parachute school, almost all of the new paratroopers were sent directly to the 505th PIR at the Frying Pan. The first graduates assigned to the regiment filled the ranks of the 1st Battalion, commanded by Major Arthur F. "Hardnose" Gorham. Each battalion had a battalion headquarters, a headquarters company, and three rifle companies. Captain Amelio D. Palluconi, a member of the cadre, was the first commander of Company A. Company B was under the command of a Captain John H. Sanders, also one of the cadre. The first commander of Company C was Lieutenant Michael Conlon.

Private Cecil E. Prine was among those first troopers assigned to the regiment. "My class filled up the 504 and nineteen of us, me included, were assigned to B Company, 505. Not very much was accomplished in the Frying Pan area. We were awaiting additional troopers to fill the company and regiment. Training there was daily calisthenics, close order drill, and running—quite often around the airfield to build strength." [1]

The vast majority of these new paratroopers were privates and lieutenants. The cadre generally assigned most of them initially to one of the rifle companies. A rifle company's table of organization at that time totaled 119 men and eight officers. Each company was composed of a company headquarters and three rifle platoons. Each rifle platoon consisted of a platoon headquarters, two twelve-man rifle squads, and a mortar squad. The cadre selected those who had previous military experience or exhibited natural leadership qualities as acting corporals and sergeants. Private Prine soon learned that the leadership abilities of the acting non-coms varied significantly. "[Private First Class Harvill W.] Lazenby was the one that I thought would be a real combat leader, and he was. Staff Sergeant [James Elmo] Jones turned out to be great, but never showed it in training. First Sergeant [Joseph V.] O'Donnell was loud and full of hot air and turned out to be a dud." [2]

Newly arrived lieutenants with prior military duty as an officer were usually assigned as platoon leaders, while those without prior experience or with less seniority as an officer were assigned as assistant platoon leaders.

When Captain Walter F. Winton, Jr. reported to the regiment, Gavin told him that "in this outfit an officer is the first man out of the airplane and the last man in the chow line." [3]

As the military records of the newly assigned officers and enlisted men arrived, the cadre reviewed them for those with needed skills. Some had graduated from the army's demolition or communications schools. The cadre sought many other skills acquired primarily in civilian life, such as typing, clerical, industrial sewing, photography, mechanical or topographic drawing, telephone switchboard and line operations, and foreign language skills (especially German and Italian). Enlisted men who had been medical and dental technicians, carpenters, gunsmiths, cooks, truck drivers, and vehicle mechanics were also needed to fill out the regiment's table of organization. These officers and men were assigned to headquarters and headquarters companies at the regimental and battalion levels, as well as the regiment's service company.

Each of the three parachute infantry battalions had a headquarters and a headquarters company to support its operations. Captain Winton was assigned as the first commander of Headquarters Company, 1st Battalion. The battalion headquarters companies each had a company headquarters platoon, a communications platoon, a light machine gun platoon, and an 81mm mortar platoon.

Lieutenant Dean McCandless graduated from jump school on July 25, 1942, and was assigned as the communications officer with Headquarters Company, 1st Battalion. Shortly after he arrived, McCandless reported to Major Gorham's office. "As I stood at attention, he said, 'Lieutenant, I don't know much about communications, but our communications section is going to be the best one in this man's army. Do you understand me?'

"I said, 'Yes, sir.'

"We were not authorized to have a code table to teach Morse code, but we scrounged parts from here and there, and made one for ourselves. Soon, even our wiremen could send and receive Morse code. One of my men, Ott Carpenter, had been in the artillery and knew semaphore. So we made some semaphore flags and Ott taught us how to use them. Nonetheless, Major Gorham was 'on my case' a lot—or at least I thought so. He always saw things as needing to be improved. Now, I think it was his way of pushing all of us to do our best." [4]

While at the Frying Pan, there was a lot of shuffling among the acting NCOs and new officers as some exceeded expectations, while others didn't meet them. Some officers and NCOs bonded and worked together well, while others who clashed were shifted to try to find the right slots. Still others failed and were demoted, or sometimes transferred out of the regiment.

Lieutenant Edwin M. Sayre, who previously had been a lieutenant with the 36th Infantry Division, was the executive officer of Company B. "We had some little headquarters buildings; they were little one-board-thick buildings. One day I was inside and there were soldiers in the shade on the other side. They were talking about how hard it was to get a pass. One guy said, 'It isn't hard to get a pass. It's very simple. You just go see any of the platoon sergeants or the first sergeant and tell him that you want a pass. When you tell him that, he will say, "Gosh, I wish I had enough money to go on a pass. If I knew somebody I could borrow ten dollars from, I could give you a pass and I could go with you.'"

"The ones that really wanted a pass would give him ten dollars and they got their passes. Well, I may have been a little naïve, but I didn't really think this was a way to run a business. So, I went to the company commander and I said, 'Your first sergeant and your three platoon sergeants are selling passes.'

"He said, 'What the hell are you talking about, Sayre?'

"And I told him.

"He said, 'Well forget it. You know, I brought those people with me as cadre from the 503rd. They're damned good NCOs. I'll tell them to let up on that stuff. You just forget it.'

"'O.K.'

"And he went on two weeks' leave. As soon as he went out that door, I went over to see the battalion commander. I said, 'Major Gorham, these guys are selling passes and I think they ought to be busted to privates.'

"He said, 'Aren't you the acting company commander? Well, do whatever needs to be done.'

"So I just went over and told the first sergeant and the three platoon sergeants, 'You're busted, you're now privates.'

"And in about two weeks, here comes the company commander, and of course, the [former] sergeants ran to tell the company commander what a stupid ass I was. I've read the leadership book, too. It says don't make critical decisions while the commander is not present; and this obviously was a rather critical decision. But, from my point of view I gave him an opportunity to do the right thing and he didn't do it.

"So he said, 'You come with me; I'm getting rid of you right now. We're going to Major Gorham's office.'

"We went in his office and he said, 'Major Gorham, I want Sayre out of B Company, and I really would like to see him clear out of this battalion. He just doesn't understand anything about the army. He doesn't understand that you're not supposed to make critical decisions when the company commander is not there.'

"Major Gorham said, 'Well, you don't have to worry about him being in B Company. . . . I'm moving him to A Company. A Company has got some real problems, and Sayre may be the person who can straighten them out.'

"Then he called in the [Company A] company commander and said, 'You're relieved. You have the highest court-martial rate and the highest AWOL [absent without leave] rate in the regiment, and I'm not going to put up with it.'

"I got the people together and I told them to start with, 'I'm glad to be in A Company. I think we've got a lot of good people here. But, this AWOL and court-martial thing has got to stop. You're not going to get court-martialed anymore. We're going to have company punishment. Now, this company punishment is fairly simple. If you want to take three days' AWOL, just know one thing. Every hour of training you are gone, you're going to have to make it up on your own time. The training will start right after supper each evening.'

"We had seven officers, and each one of us took them one evening per week. We took them for four hours' training. They had to have a full pack and they had to march twelve miles and march back. It was a hard, hard night.

"But, the courts-martial and the need for them disappeared quite rapidly. As they weren't AWOL, they didn't need to be court-martialed. So, we corrected both the court-martials and the AWOLs in a fairly short time.

"I was also fortunate that Lieutenant [Mike] Chester was in B Company and he came over to regiment and said, 'Can I come over to A Company?' And Major Gorham let him come over to A Company. I had some great officers, but probably the most outstanding was Mike Chester; he was a great officer, a great athlete, and a great leader. He was a lot of help to me.

"[Lieutenant] Harold Case had been in the regular army, and was at Pearl Harbor at the time of the attack, so we already had one combat veteran in our outfit. He was a good officer, and his platoon won every contest they had for platoons, because he was a great leader.

"My own first sergeant was about as bad it gets. His solution to everything was, 'I'll court-martial you; I'll court-martial you.' So I asked for him to be transferred to some other place. I made a young man named [Patrick F.] Grace [the first sergeant], he was about five foot six and about one hundred fifty pounds; but he was a ball of dynamite, an amateur boxer. I told them that this is your new first sergeant, Sergeant Grace. He was quiet, but he let the people know. When he told them to do something and they didn't do it, he didn't say, 'I'm going to court-martial you,' He said, 'I'll meet you at the back of the building.' It didn't take but about two sessions of those. As small as he was, I think he must have been a semi-pro as a boxer, because he took them all. Sergeant Grace was a great help to me." 5

Captain Edwin M. Sayre had been commanding Company A for a short time when the commander of the 1st Battalion, Major Arthur Gorham, came into his tent.

"He said, 'Lieutenant Sayre, I've got a new officer for you. This is [Francis J.] Joe Meyers. He's completed the Infantry School, is a graduate of the [U.S.] Military Academy, and he'll be in A Company.'

"My heart fell a mile. I thought they're not sending a West Point officer in here to be an executive officer to an old farm boy. They're sending him here to be the company commander. So I thought I was lost.

"We had a jump that night. It was Lieutenant Meyers' first night jump and he was very happy, having come through it fine. So he decided to go over to the [officers] club and celebrate a little bit. But he celebrated all night long. In the meantime, I went to bed at a normal time.

"I got [awakened] about 5:00 in the morning with someone piddling [urinating] right on me. There stood Lieutenant Meyers and he said, 'They tell me that you're a hot shot company commander. Well this is what I think about you.'

"I woke up out of my daze enough to find out that he was 'piddling' on me. I jumped out and hit him so hard that I knocked him out the front door of the tent and all the way into the street. Then I ran out to kill him, but he was lying there unconscious, so I didn't have to do anything.

"I thought, 'I wonder what in the world is going to happen now, because they're going to find out that I really assaulted him. There wasn't any doubt that I did it.' I went over to the company just like I always did. And where's my new lieutenant? He didn't show up. Nobody told me what happened to him or anything else. He was just transferred to another battalion. He wasn't made a company commander either. So I said, 'Somebody may replace me, but he's not going to be the guy.'" 6

THE 2ND BATTALION WAS FORMED UNDER the command of Captain Frederick S. Wright. Captain William A. Bolton initially commanded Company D, with Captain James E. McGinity commanding Company E, Captain Benjamin H. Vandervoort serving as the first commander of Company F, and Captain Robert L. Fleet, Headquarters Company commander.

One officer that most of the troopers of the 2nd Battalion never liked was Captain Edward C. Krause, who became the second commanding officer of Company D. Krause soon had the nickname of "Cannonball" for his fiery temper and tough-talking demeanor. Private First Class Paul Nunan, with Company D, called Krause "a poor man's George Patton. . . . He was a real wiz-bang, that guy. Krause was real gung ho." 7

Krause was soon promoted to executive officer of the 2nd Battalion. There, he became well known to everyone in the battalion for his tirades. Private John P. Cages, with Company E, discovered that the dog owned by the 2nd Battalion commander, Captain James Gray, a large boxer named Max, was afraid of Krause. "Max would not come out when Krause was outside with his big mouth hollering. Max would lie down and cover his ears." 8

One morning, Private Dave Bowman, with Company D, was in his tar-paper housing, getting ready for the day's training. "I had trouble preparing my gear in the prescribed manner—and while all the other men were in formation ready to march, I was still struggling with my gear. As I finished and turned to join the troops, I was shocked to see standing outside the door at the bottom of the steps the battalion [executive officer], Captain Krause, glowering. A staccato of questions and butt-chewing followed. The worrisome part of it for me was that the captain had a reputation of manhandling those who defied the rules.

"I had to pass that officer to reach my platoon, and with his reputation in mind, I knew I would not—could not—allow him to strike or push me around without defending myself. Yet, I knew doing that, even in self-defense, could get me in big trouble. Recognizing there was nothing else I could do, I walked down the steps, three or four of them, saying to myself, 'Don't touch me. I just hope he doesn't touch me.'

I reached the last step and then the ground; he backed off and I went by him. As I made a dash toward my platoon, now on the march, I heard the threatening words from my rear, 'If I ever catch you in there again, I'll kick your ass all the way . . .'

"Well, Captain Krause never got the opportunity to kick my ass all the way to . . . From that time on, I prepared my gear the night before." [9]

Upon joining the regiment, Lieutenant Frank P. Woosley was assigned as a platoon leader with Company E. A few days later, Woosley was introduced to another young lieutenant newly assigned to the company. "When I met Lieutenant Wray, he said to me, 'My name is Waverly Wright Wray, but just call me Charlie.' He had a Mississippi drawl. We wondered a little about Charlie. He had a soft face, maybe a little heavy, read his Bible daily, and did not drink, smoke, or chase women. He was not quite our picture of a real paratroop hero." [10]

Staff Sergeant Charlie D. Turner, a member of the cadre, was the platoon sergeant of the 1st Platoon, Company D. "The infantry soldiers finished jump school full of pride and thought erroneously that they had it made. The cadre for the regiment met each group behind regimental headquarters as they detrucked with their barracks bags. They were formed in a platoon, with all baggage, and given double time march with all their luggage" [11]

Private Otis Sampson was assigned to Company E. Like other new paratroopers, Sampson had heard all about this training area prior to graduation from jump school: "'Wait until they get you out in the "Frying Pan" area!' we were told by troopers who had previously been through the mill. 'That is where they will initiate you fellows.' I looked forward to this 'hell hole,' as it was described. I felt it would toughen us for the combat days ahead. And, as others before us, we too started our training in the 'Frying Pan.' A place well named when the burning sun bore down.

"Our Company E was assigned Captain McGinity, a West Point [graduate]. By his talk and actions, I felt we had a captain who wanted to make our company one to be proud of.

"One of our first training problems was a night compass course in groups of four. We took off; a small light a good distance away was our destination. Henry Bly, Victor Schmidt, Edmund Rosowski and I made up our team. This kind of game was right up our alley; as a boy my father taught me how to use the stars, especially the North Star. It was a clear night.

"During the course when in a heavily wooded area, I had been looking up through the leafed branches of the high trees, keeping contact with the North Star, counting my steps also trying to make time. Then, with no warning, I found myself in space, falling; I relaxed to take the sudden stop and landed in a sandy dry creek bed and was not hurt. I waited to let the others of the group experience the thrill; a thud to the right of me and then another. I waited for the third and it never came. I turned and looked up. The dark form of Henry Bly stood on the edge of the bank, looking down. He had been following and must have wondered what happened when we all disappeared from his view. Our group won that problem by a large margin; for this accomplishment, we were all made acting non-coms.

"Shortly after the compass course, I saw the acting non-coms' names on the billboard. I had been made sergeant of the 1st Platoon mortar squad." [12]

MAJOR HERBERT F. BATCHELLER, A WEST POINT GRADUATE, was the first commander of the 3rd Battalion. His company commanders were Captain Patrick J. Gibbons, Jr., Company G; Captain Fredric L. Mill, Company H; Lieutenant Willard R. "Bill" Follmer, Company I; and Captain Leolus L. Wall, Headquarters Company.

Second Lieutenant Jack R. Isaacs had come to Fort Benning as a sergeant and graduated from Officer's Candidate School, the Infantry School, then Parachute School at age nineteen. "I then applied for and attended the army's demolition school at Fort Benning, Georgia, and in August of 1942 was assigned to G Company, 505th Parachute Infantry, in the Frying Pan area. Being the youngest and least ranking second lieutenant in the company, I was assigned as the assistant platoon leader of the 3rd Rifle Platoon." [13] Such was the caliber of the young officers joining the regiment.

Most of the young lieutenants impressed their men with their leadership. Private Harry J. Buffone and the other men in his Company I platoon admired and respected their platoon leader, Lieutenant George Clark. "The men in the 3rd Platoon would follow him to hell and back, just like they would for Colonel Gavin." [14]

LIEUTENANT COLONEL GAVIN'S INITIAL STAFF included Lieutenant Colonel Orin D. Haugen, executive officer; Captain Robert H. Miller, S-1 (adjutant); Captain Arthur B. "Barney" Oldfield, an already famous Hollywood press agent, S-2 (intelligence) and responsible for the regiment's publicity; and Major Edward A. Zaj, S-4 (supply).

The regimental headquarters company supported the regimental staff. It consisted of a headquarters, an operations section, an intelligence section, a communications platoon, and a demolition platoon made up of a headquarters and three battalion demolition sections.

Private Robert W. Gillette was assigned to the intelligence section. "My MOS [military occupational specialty] was officially cartographer. Map reading and map handling was a function of the S-2 and S-3, so that was the basis for my assignment. I had completed two years of college engineering and had done drafting and basic engineering work in power and [also] telephone work. Our special S-2 training was in map reading, aerial photography and photo interpretation. Our first [regimental headquarters] company commander was Captain [Julius H.] Scruggs. We considered him a mental case and thus not proud of our association. He soon disappeared—probably reassigned elsewhere. Our first sergeant was Elmer Ward, a great guy, who later became [regimental] sergeant major." [15]

Private Gillette was soon promoted to sergeant, and became the first regimental intelligence section leader and held that job throughout the war.

The regimental headquarters communications platoon's first commander was Lieutenant John H. Boyd. Captain David E. Thomas, the regimental surgeon, commanded the regiment's medical detachment from the 307th Airborne Medical Company. It was organized to support the three infantry battalions, with a headquarters and three sections, one of which was attached to each battalion.

During the summer of 1942, Captain Thomas was sent overseas on a temporary assignment. "I spent six weeks with a small group in England comparing our methods with theirs, and resulting in changes in chute packing methods and landing techniques which markedly reduced opening shock and landing injuries to ankles and shoulders——a most productive TDY [temporary duty] trip. I returned a major and found myself posted to the 505 PIR, commanded by Lieutenant Colonel soon to be Colonel Jimmy Gavin. Jimmy from the start put his imprint on the 505. He was a soldier's soldier, always on top of the training and in the field with the troops every day. Soldiers could empathize with him. I can remember walking down a company street behind a couple of young troopers and Jimmy was ahead of us.

"One of these young guys said to the other one, 'I'd follow that guy through hell.' What he didn't know was, that was exactly where Jimmy was going to lead them!" [16]

The regiment was supported by a service company, which was composed of company headquarters, a regimental headquarters platoon, a parachute maintenance and supply platoon, and a transportation platoon. The regimental headquarters platoon was composed of a staff section, a regimental supply section, and three battalion supply sections. The regimental personnel officer, who reported to the S-1, led the staff section.

On August 15, 1942, the 307th Engineer Battalion at Camp Claiborne, Louisiana, was redesignated the 307th Airborne Engineer Battalion, and Companies B and C were replaced by newly formed parachute-qualified companies. Company B would support the 505th PIR as part of the regimental combat team. Private Cornelius J. "Neil" Droogan was assigned to Company B. "I wasn't happy about going to the 307th—I wanted to stay in the infantry. Lieutenant [David G.] Connally and Lieutenant [Edward P.] Whalen were good leaders. The sergeants were not trained for the infantry—they were engineers." [17]

On August 29, 1942, the 505th PIR moved across the Chattahoochee River to Camp Billy Mitchell, but known to everyone as the Alabama Area. Gavin initiated a training regimen at the Alabama Area that was "just about as tough and demanding as we could make it. The troopers responded well." [18]

Private Berge Avadanian, who served with Headquarters Company, 2nd Battalion, described the Alabama Area as "miserable, unsanitary, hot, humid, insects, [and] heat rash. The stench of the latrines was so unbearable I started wearing my gasmask until it was ordered removed.

"Harsh training hardened even the weakest. Colonel Gavin led us on the toughest forced marches (twenty-five to thirty miles)." [19]

If anyone fell out during a march or run for anything other than an injury such as a broken ankle, he shipped out the following day. This winnowed out men who had made it through parachute school, but not in good enough physical condition or mentally tough enough for the long, tortuous hikes and runs.

To Private William Blank with Company G, the training seemed to be almost continuous. "The 3rd Battalion had a daily retreat parade regardless of what training had been done that day. My first night jump was my 13th. We lost a couple of troopers who slipped out of their chutes over a blacktop road and were killed. They had mistaken the road for the Chattahoochee River, which was between us and Lawson Field at Fort Benning." [20]

Gavin was promoted to colonel in September, as he continued to hone the 505th to a razor's edge. Major Herb Batcheller was promoted to lieutenant colonel and replaced Lieutenant Colonel Orin Haugen as the regimental executive officer. Captain Ed "Cannonball" Krause replaced Batcheller as the 3rd Battalion commander. Captain James Gray took command of the 2nd Battalion.

AS THE 505TH PIR WAS SWEATING IN THE ALABAMA AREA, the Parachute Test Battery completed its work at Fort Benning. Lieutenant Carl Thain and the other three officers and 112 men had pioneered the development of airborne artillery. "In September 1942, the Test Battery was moved back to Fort Bragg to become the cadre for the 456th Parachute Field Artillery Battalion, and subsequently sent cadres to other parachute field artillery battalions." [21]

The U.S. Army's first parachute artillery battalion, the 456th, was activated on September 24, 1942, under the command of Lieutenant Colonel Harrison B. Harden, Jr.

WHILE IN THE ALABAMA AREA, the 505th PIR held a competition to determine the best squad. Private First Class Paul Nunan, a member of the 2nd Squad, 3rd Platoon, Company D, recalled, "We had a sergeant, Tommy Thompson—an old army man who at one time had been the middleweight boxing champion of Fort Benning. He was our squad leader in the Alabama Area. He determined the 2nd Squad of the 3rd Platoon was going to enter that competition, and not only were we going to enter it, we were going to win it.

"It involved a full field inspection, to see that you had your name and serial number on all of your clothing. Then we made a jump in the Alabama Area, close to the Chattahoochee River, and it was a combat exercise. We had to execute a live fire attack on the 'enemy.'

"We had to go through a swamp up to your armpits with a few [water] moccasin snakes, and arrived on the objective, which had silhouette targets, and had a live fire exercise.

"Lo and behold, we won it. We received a certificate from Colonel Gavin.

"The *Static Line*, which was our regimental newspaper, had an article written with the headline, 'D Company squad wins—Regimental boxing champion, Sergeant Tommy Thompson, has acquired another "champ" title; but this time, he shares the honors with the men of his squad. He and his men, representing D Company, walked off with top honors in the regimental squad problem competition held recently. All members of the squad will be presented with a special insignia, to be worn on their blouse sleeve. Also, Captain Krause announces that all privates of the squad will be "decorated" with a PFC stripe. Roll call of the champion squad—Sergeant Thompson, Corporal [Joseph J.] Ketz, PFCs [David M.] Sheffler, [Paul D.] Nunan, Privates [Glenn C.] Swarts, [Fred A.] Chaudion, [Roy A.]

Stark, [Clarence C.] Sigler, [Raymond D.] Smithson, [Frank E.] Cobb, [Herbert J.] Buffalo Boy, and [Frank] Schneider.'" 22

Despite daily five-mile runs, long marches with full gear, intense physical training in hand-to-hand combat, weapons training, and tactical problems, the young paratroopers still had the energy to get into trouble during weekend passes. One night, six troopers from the 505th PIR were drinking at a roadhouse in Phenix City, Alabama, when they got into a fistfight with the locals. Sergeant Tommy Thompson, with Company D, was one of the regiment's boxing champions, and was more than the civilians could handle. They pulled knives and straight razors, cutting Private Gasper Lucero, with Company D, on the back with a straight razor, leaving a wound a foot long and three-quarters of an inch wide. His wound required hospitalization. The other five troopers made it back to the Alabama Area and told their buddies what had occurred. Furious, a large group of troopers decided to go back to Cotton's Fish Camp that Friday night and tear the roadhouse apart. Word of the raid leaked out and a squad of Alabama state troopers and a military police contingent were waiting. As the paratroopers approached the roadhouse, they ran into the state police and MPs. Some troopers tried to take on the police, who were armed with billy clubs. Others, realizing they would be in trouble if arrested, bolted from the scene. Twenty-seven troopers were taken into custody and delivered to the guardhouse at Fort Benning, where they spent the night. Gavin went to the provost marshal the following morning to convince him to release them. Gavin told him that the punishment the troopers would receive would be far harsher than any they would receive in confinement. After obtaining the release of his troopers, Gavin issued an order for the entire regiment to fall out with full gear and weapons, including .30-caliber machine guns, as well as 60mm and 81mm mortars. He then led the regiment on what Private First Class Norbert P. Beach with Company H would call "a twenty-four-hour forced march, which covered fifty-four miles. Quite a few people dropped out." 23

The march was naturally hardest on the heavy-weapons crews. Company E platoon leader Lieutenant Frank Woosley noticed that "the light machine gunners were complaining. There was no way to carry a light machine gun that it did not hurt. [They are] heavy and all sharp edges." 24

A short time later, Woosley saw the powerfully built, two-hundred-fifty-pound Lieutenant Waverly Wray do something that amazed him and just about everyone in the company who witnessed it. "'Charlie' said, 'John Brown,' which was his harshest expletive. He took both guns from the gunners in the platoon that he was in and carried one on each shoulder until the next break. This seemed impossible. Then he walked up and down the road, where the platoon lay in the ditch during the break, with the guns still on his shoulders, and carried them until the following break. We did not wonder about Charlie anymore. We all knew we had a man among us." 25

Private John P. Cages, with Company E, had just joined the regiment at the Alabama Area a few days before the punishment march. "If you fell out, you were dismissed from the regiment very soon. One hundred nine men were eight-balled out of the regiment [the following] morning. Hell had already started in the 505." [26]

Private First Class Norbert Beach, with Company H, was exhausted the next afternoon when the regiment arrived back at the encampment at the Alabama Area. He could hardly believe his eyes when "some people got on their Class A uniforms and were heading back into town. Colonel Gavin made the remark that those able to do this must be some tough son-of-a-guns." [27]

In late January 1943, the 505th received orders to move to Camp Hoffman, North Carolina, and on February 7 it moved there by train.

On February 12, 1943, the 326th Glider Infantry Regiment was officially transferred to the newly forming 13th Airborne Division. The 505th Parachute Infantry Regiment was transferred to the 82nd Airborne Division to replace it. At Camp Hoffman, the 505th PIR was joined by supporting units to form the 505th Regimental Combat Team. The U.S. Army's regimental combat team organization was designed to provide a more or less self-sufficient fighting force—an infantry regiment with supporting artillery, engineer, and medical units. The 456th Parachute Field Artillery Battalion's 75mm pack howitzers would provide the heavy firepower. Company B, 307th Airborne Engineer Battalion, would provide engineering support; and the 307th Airborne Medical Company supported each unit with medical detachments.

AFTER SEVEN MONTHS UNDER COLONEL GAVIN, the regiment was in superb physical condition from training that had included obstacle courses, jujitsu, hand-to-hand combat, and long marches with full gear, weapons, and ammunition. Because Gavin had literally written the book on airborne operations, he thoroughly schooled the regiment in rapid assembly after a night jump, the best methods to pack equipment bundles, etcetera. His high expectations of his non-commissioned and commissioned officers weeded out most of the weak and fostered extremely close bonds among one another and their enlisted men. Every man in the regiment was a reflection of Gavin's leadership. There was intense unit pride and loyalty, especially to Gavin, which rose above even the other parachute regiments. By the time the 505th joined the 82nd Airborne Division, it was likely the best parachute regiment in the U.S. Army.

Private John Cages had joined the army in November 1941, at age fifteen. One night, Cages accompanied a buddy to a hangout frequented by soldiers stationed at or near Fort Bragg. "Private James R. Harris and I went to the Town Pump early one Friday night. I was only seventeen at that time and did not drink. Harris and I had fried chicken—he had a beer and I had milk. Soon we heard that there was going to be a showdown with the MP [military police] from Fort Bragg that night. I told Harris I did not want to get involved in what was going to happen, so I took an early bus back to Bragg.

"The 504 and 505 were not going to be harassed or bullied by the MP from Bragg anymore, and about 9:00 p.m., all hell broke out. MPs [were armed] with clubs and .45-caliber weapons—heads were cracked on both sides, and Private Powell from F Company was shot in the fleshy part of the thigh, between the knee and hip. The next day there were some sad looking troopers in the battalion. Colonel Reuben H. Tucker [commanding officer of the 504th PIR] and Colonel James Gavin made arrangements that from now on, airborne troopers would have their own MPs wherever they went." [28]

ON MARCH 30, 1943, THE ENTIRE 505TH PARACHUTE INFANTRY REGIMENT made U.S. Army history when it flew from Pope Field, adjacent to Fort Bragg, to make the first mass parachute jump at Fort Jackson, near Camden, South Carolina. It was an unforgettable day for Private Irvin W. "Turk" Seelye, with Company E. "The planes flew for eighty minutes at an altitude of two hundred feet. As we approached the DZ [drop zone], the planes abruptly climbed to nine hundred feet. It was an awesome sight to see so many troopers bailing out and floating to earth. I landed in a plowed field near a grammar school. The kids ran out of the building to see all of the excitement." [29]

Private Berge Avadanian, with the S-2 section of Headquarters Company, 2nd Battalion, was assigned to photograph the jump. "I took pictures from a plane, of the vast formation with an aerial camera. I'll never forget the thrill of such a vast air drop . . . and proud to be a part of it." [30]

As the 1st Battalion serial approached the drop zone, Private First Class Harvill W. Lazenby, with Company B, was standing near the open door as the stick prepared to jump. "Lieutenant [James M.] Irvin was standing in the door, [Private Charles S.] McBride was right up against Jim, and I was jammed up next to McBride. I remember the tip of the wing of the plane next to us coming through the door. Irvin ducked down as well as McBride. I can still see the light on the wingtip. The planes rocked apart, the wingtip reversed and cleared the door, and man, we left in a hurry." [31]

In one of the Company A planes, Private David R. "Dave" Bullington was jumping seventeenth with the company medic, Private Kelly Byars, jumping as the last man in the stick as number nineteen. As the green light came on, Bullington shuffled toward the door close behind the others in his stick. After he exited the plane, he felt the shock of his parachute opening. When Bullington looked up to check his canopy, he saw a C-47 and its propellers cutting a swath through several troopers. "One of the planes stalled and came down through a group of troopers. It was the most awful noise: the plane sounded like somebody beating on a tin roof with a 2x4, going down through that stick. It cut [Byars'] parachute off. But, he opened his reserve."

Private Mark Rupaner, with Company B, had just landed and looked up and saw that "men were hit by the airplane's propellers. There were pieces coming down."

Bodies and body parts hit the ground with sickening thuds. Private First Class Lazenby was horrified at the sight of "a jump boot complete with foot lying on the ground."

Bullington landed seconds later—"right by the first sergeant of C Company. Of course, he was dead. I got out of my chute and went the other way. It killed three men. At that time they were slowing the planes to ninety knots [for the jump]. They decided [ninety knots] was a little slow and stalled [the plane]. Old Byars said, 'I'll never jump again.' But he did. He went all the way."

Private Cecil Prine, with Company B, saw "a sergeant of B Company, who jumped with a movie camera running and was killed while filming the jump. I went over to where he was lying on the ground, camera still running. An officer directed me to leave and took his camera—I never knew what happened to it." 32

Even though each paratrooper knew that parachuting from airplanes was dangerous, this horrible accident, witnessed by so many, brought home the grim reality of that danger. But it was too late for any of them to quit. Any refusal to jump after the fifth qualifying jump was a court-martial offense.

After landing on the drop zone, each company assembled and moved to designated objectives simulating the capture of bridges, crossroads, and other points. Company G had the mission to "hold" the bridge over the Catawba River. Private Bill Blank was assigned to one of the roadblocks. "We stopped all cars to search and asked if they had anything to drink. Most did, and this made for a nice night. We pooled our money and I hitched a ride to a Camden restaurant for sandwiches. When I arrived it seemed as though all of the regiment was there. I enjoyed the food and hitched a ride back."

Lieutenant Robert A. Fielder reported to the 505th at Fort Bragg in mid-April and "was sent to Captain Bob Kirkwood, [3rd] Battalion headquarters company commander. It so happened that there was a meeting of company NCOs, and I remember standing, silently staring, while Kirkwood introduced me as the communications officer. They looked tough, competent, proud, and in excellent physical condition. Many were from the Pennsylvania coal mines. Kirkwood took me under his wing and helped me through the transition of a green lieutenant. He was a good company commander—very fair, evenhanded, and well liked. While he smoked a cigar, he would say with a grin, 'Even with instructions, you guys couldn't find your way out of a telephone booth.'" 33

Shortly before the regiment left Fort Bragg, there was a tragic incident. Private Bill Blank found out that his unit, Company G, was assigned a new commander. "Our company had about thirty-two AWOLs, and the company commander was replaced with Lieutenant [Francis J. "Joe"] Meyers, a West Pointer. It was believed some discipline could be restored by him. The AWOLs were rounded up and made to pitch tents outside the barracks. An armed guard was placed over them and instructed to shoot if they tried to leave. A Company G man was on guard, and just before 'lights out,' he shot and killed two of them. The man who shot them was later transferred to the parachute engineers, and Lieutenant Meyers received one of his several demotions." 34

Captain Robert Franco replaced Major Dave Thomas, who had broken a leg in a practice jump, as regimental surgeon. Franco had only two medical officers (MOs) under his command until shortly before the 505th RCT was scheduled to be shipped overseas. "Suddenly, we went from two MOs to eight. Because of changes in doctor recruiting at that time, I entered as a first lieutenant, and they started as captains. All or most of these men outranked me. We needed a day or so for the new men to wash their hands and change their socks—but when those were done, [Lewis A.] Lew Smith was the new regimental surgeon, [Daniel B.] McIlvoy was second ranked, and I was allowed to stay as assistant regimental surgeon. In the rush of the last days at Bragg, we settled on the following: 1st Battalion, Carl [R.] Comstock, battalion surgeon, and Gordon [C.] Stenhouse, assistant battalion surgeon; 2nd Battalion, Lester Stein, battalion surgeon, and Kurt [B.] Klee, assistant; 3rd Battalion, McIlvoy, battalion surgeon, and Lee F. Scarborough, assistant. In addition, we were lucky to have two regimental dentists [Captains Alexander P. 'Pete' Suer and Domat L. Savoie]." [35]

In mid-April the regiment began preparing for overseas deployment. This movement was made in strict secrecy, because the army didn't want the Germans to know that an elite airborne division was being moved overseas. Private James Elmo Jones, with Company B, was told that everyone was to eliminate all items that would identify them as paratroopers. This included "removing patches and all identification from uniforms, hiding polished jump boots, [and] using ordinary infantry leggings, much to everyone's disgust. Jump wings couldn't be worn. Cameras and diaries were to be mailed home." Even the special chinstraps were to be tucked inside of their helmets. They were issued standard combat boots and leggings for the journey.

Private Turk Seelye, with Company E, was ready for the adventure that awaited. "Our personal belongings were placed in A and B barracks bags. We carried our combat gear. On April 20, 1943, we boarded trucks that took us to the Fort Bragg railroad station, where we boarded troop trains for Camp Edwards, Massachusetts. Twenty-four hours later, we were at Camp Edwards. We stayed at this camp for one week. On April 28, we boarded trains to the New York Port of Embarkation." [36]

Sergeant Bob Gillette, with regimental headquarters company, deduced that "from our clothing and our point of departure, it was fairly clear that we were not going to the Pacific Theater.

"Leaving the Port of New York on the USS *Monterey*, converted to a troop ship, I got my first-ever glimpse of the Statue of Liberty. Our transport joined a very large convoy of ships with major naval protection.

"There was not enough bunk space below deck, so I was happy to volunteer to sleep on deck. The one unforeseen disadvantage was that at dawn, the sailors gleefully called out, 'Clean sweep-down, fore and aft,' and thirty seconds (at the most) later, turned on the fire hoses. Reveille was never as effective." [37]

Private Berge Avadanian, with Headquarters Company, 2nd Battalion, looked out at the massive convoy, "seeing destroyers and other naval craft, we felt strong, safe, and confident.

"The food was awful and mess lines seemed around the clock. Bunks were four high. Numerous inspections—boat drills—for exercise we climbed the rope ladders up the mast." [38]

Private Seelye spent his time "reading, talking, playing cards, and watching the ships in the huge convoy move about. Rumor had us going to all parts of the world. Meals were served two times each day. We ate standing upright at long tables. These were not gourmet meals. [We took] salt water showers." [39]

Staff Sergeant Joseph I. O'Jibway, with Company B, found that in addition to the poor quality of the food, they couldn't easily choose the foods they wanted to eat and those they wanted to avoid, because of the way it was served. "They just stacked all the different foods all together in your mess kit and the last thing on your mess kit was ice cream." [40]

Like most of the men, Company G trooper Private Bill Blank didn't know the destination of the convoy. "We eventually learned our destination was North Africa. On the way to Africa we were instructed on all of the dos and don'ts of conduct when we were exposed to the Arabs and their customs."

On board the ships of the convoy were EGB 447 and 448, attached to fill the ranks when units lost men injured or killed in training and jump accidents, or from disease. EGB was the army acronym for replacement battalions. These officers and men were already qualified paratroopers, many having come from other units just forming in the United States. Some were veterans of the harsh training at Camp Toccoa, Georgia. Most EGBers were not happy about being assigned to these replacement battalions, and sarcastically commented that EGB stood for "Excess Government Baggage." The paratroopers of the 82nd Airborne Division called them "Easy Going Bastards."

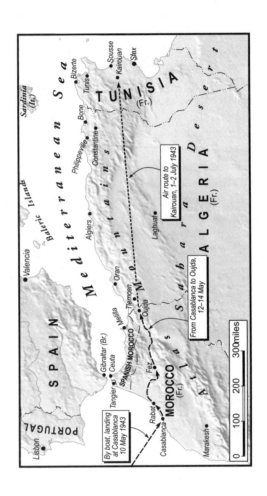

CHAPTER 3

"Africa Was A Living Hell"

On the morning of May 10, 1943, the *Monterey* pulled into the port of Casablanca, French Morocco. The 1st Battalion communications officer, Lieutenant Dean McCandless, was not impressed. "Casablanca could be smelled before it could be seen." [1]

After docking, the regiment disembarked, and as the troopers were waiting to move out, Arabs descended upon them, begging for food and cigarettes, selling trinkets, and trying to buy mattress covers. The regiment then marched through Casablanca to Camp Don Passage on the outskirts of the city. For almost all of the officers and men, such as Private Wilton H. Johnson, with Headquarters Company, 2nd Battalion, "Casablanca seemed like a different world. The Arabs were so different from anyone I had experienced." [2]

On May 12, 1943, the entire 82nd Airborne Division began moving to its training base near the small town of Oujda, French Morocco, located near the border with Spanish Morocco, more than three hundred miles away. Some units were transported by slow-moving trains, with troopers riding in blazing hot passenger cars and 40 & 8s (boxcars that held forty men or eight horses). Others rode in the backs of 2 1/2-ton trucks, moving in long convoys over rough and dust-choked roads. The lucky flew by C-47 aircraft.

Company E trooper Private Turk Seelye rode in a passenger car of one of the troop trains. "The ride was a hot and dirty one. We ate K-rations and tried to sleep on the hard wooden seats. There were no toilet facilities. On the way, the train passed other trains carrying German and Italian POWs. At various stops, we had our first glimpses of Arab towns—not impressive." [3]

On May 15, the truck convoys carrying part of the regiment arrived near Oujda. Lieutenant Bob Fielder, communications officer with Headquarters Company, 3rd Battalion, described Oujda as "a dirty little Arab town located a few miles west of the Algerian border and about thirty miles south of the Mediterranean Sea." [4]

The area had previously been a sparse wheat field, and now only the short stalks, sand, and rocks remained. General Ridgway had intentionally selected the area near Oujda with its intense heat to toughen the troopers. "We had picked, on purpose, land that was not in use for grazing or agricultural purposes. We trained in a fiery furnace, where the hot wind carried a fine dust that clogged the nostrils, burned the eyes, and cut into the throat like an abrasive." [5]

Private Dave Bowman, with Company D, arrived at the bivouac site after a long train ride in a 40 & 8 boxcar. "Our company was assigned a particular area, which was further broken down into platoon and squad areas. The individual soldier had one-half of a pup tent, so we were paired, and two men lived in this pup tent. We were instructed to dig a trench around the tent to keep water out of the floor when it rained. Now, you can imagine how much good a trench would do on level ground when a torrential downpour came with accompanying wind—and this occurred more than just a couple of times while we were there."

The officers' quarters were not much better, as Lieutenant Fielder quickly discovered. "We encamped in four-man tents and unrolled our sleeping bags on the sand . . . in mid-morning the wind would start to blow, covering our bedding rolls and equipment with sand. The bivouac area soon acquired the name of 'the dust bowl.'" [6]

Shortly after getting settled in the division's new bivouac near Oujda, Colonel Gavin was ordered to report to General Ridgway. "General Ridgway called myself and Colonel Tucker up to orient us on our probable combat task. It had been directed by the G.H.Q., and was to be known as 'Husky' and was to be executed July 10th. It contemplated the seizure of Sicily. The 505th C.T. was to spearhead the amphibious landing of the 1st or 45th Divisions. Our jump was to take place in moonlight the night of July 9th, 11:30 p.m. The exact mission was yet an issue. From an analysis of the probable missions it was clear that the effort would be a very risky one and a costly one." [7]

On May 15 and 16, Gavin conducted briefings on Operation Husky for his battalion commanders and Lieutenant Colonel Harrison Harden, the commanding officer of the 456th Parachute Field Artillery Battalion. Gavin and his staff spent the following week developing operational plans for the mission. On May 24, Gavin made a reconnaissance of the area around Oujda in a Piper Cub aircraft to find ground that approximated the terrain in Sicily for use in rehearsals of the Husky mission.

While near Oujda, four factors would affect the training and conditioning of the regimental combat team for the upcoming invasion: water, food, disease, and the heat. The critical nature of each of these factors soon became very apparent to Private Dave Bowman. "We continued the training, very much as before—physical exercises, night problems, assaults, defense, and other such military exercises and maneuvers. When we started out in this desert—or, I guess more precisely, semi-desert—in the morning, we had with us only one canteen of water, and this was to last us through our whole day of exertion in the heat. 'Water discipline,' they called it. Occasionally, they would bring a Lister bag full of water, well heated in the desert sun—but this was rare.

"Equally painful to me was the skimpy amount of food we were allowed while there. But this may have been of minor importance to most, considering that many contracted malaria and yellow jaundice, and I think we all got dysentery at some time or another." [8]

The amount, taste, and temperature of the water for most troopers, like EGB Private William H. Tucker, was difficult to overcome. "We got our water from fifty-gallon Lister bags filled with chlorinated water standing in the sun. I never got a cool drink of water. We were allowed a half canteen per day per man to shave and wash. Many times during my stay at Oujda, I swore fervently I would give ten dollars for a glass of cold water, cold beer, or cold anything." [9]

Corporal Harry Buffone, with Company I, and some of the troopers of the regiment used an ancient method to cool the water, only somewhat though. "We covered a sock over our canteens, hung it in the middle of the pup tents that were open at both ends. The air blowing through cooled the water enough to be drinkable." [10]

One of the major complaints of just about all of the troopers was the food. Private Berg Avadanian, with Headquarters Company, 2nd Battalion, described the food served while at Oujda as "very bland, but at least nourishing—scrambled eggs made with powdered eggs, never fully mixed, so we ate powder. Powdered lemon juice—strong coffee with powdered milk. The bread was not bad, but the butter was substitute.

"We could see hamburgers grilling on the grills, but it was only an illusion—they were awful salmon patties. Spam was a regular fare—I hated it! It and the SOS (shit on a shingle)—chipped beef on toast was often on the 'menu.' Powdered mashed potatoes and lousy beans would occasionally appear. Our cooks were called 'belly robbers.'

"Chef Sergeant [Clarence W.] 'Tudy' Hayhurst, a real nice guy, was in charge of the field kitchen.

"One night, my buddy, John Everhardy, and I stole a five-pound can of tuna from the cooks. We ate it all the next day in the heat. I hate tuna fish! I haven't eaten canned tuna since Oujda!" [11]

Private Cecil Prine, with Company B, had a much lower opinion of the quality of the food. "I really don't know what that slop was they called food—it ruined my stomach to this day." [12]

Private Bill Blank, with Company G, felt that the contamination of the food was worse than its quality. "Our kitchens were set up outdoors, and the mess line was the same. Every day at meal time a dust storm would blow right down the mess line and the food would be full of dirt." [13]

Even the rations eaten in the field were inundated with sand. Private W. A. "Arnold" Jones, with Headquarters Company, 2nd Battalion, had been in the CCC prior to the war and was used to eating food outdoors—but this was different. "You could hardly eat the dirt off of the C-rations." [14] He heard some of his fellow troopers sarcastically say, "Well, it gave the C-rations a flavor." [15]

For troopers like Private Russell McConnell, with Company H, dirt in the food was only one of the miseries at chow time. "You take a bite of bread or anything, yellow jackets and hornets would land on it and you'd have to brush them off. They were almost in your mouth. It was absolute misery." [16]

As the 505th RCT prepared for a night combat jump in a location known to only a few officers and men in the division, the medical detachment from the 307th

Airborne Medical Company was already at war, fighting disease. Each doctor who served with the 505th RCT medical detachment was a paratrooper who had undergone the same grueling rigors as everyone else. Every one of them had graduated from jump school; most of them had endured the Frying Pan and the Alabama Area, and now were undergoing the same hardships at Oujda. Each considered himself a member of the 505th RCT, not the 307th Airborne Medical Company.

First malaria, then dysentery struck many of the troopers. Private Tucker was one of the few troopers who developed an allergic reaction to the Atabrine tablets, taken daily to prevent malaria. "It was compulsory to take Atabrine tablets. An officer stood at the end of the chow line and watched while we each swallowed a pill. After I took the medicine a second time, I became violently ill. Life was at a low premium, so no one paid much attention to me. In my spasm and agony, I had to drag myself four hundred yards to the aid station.

"I was not alone. Two or three were there. We were taken to the hospital, and for approximately ten or twelve hours, I had steady dry heaves. I was told I had nearly died. There was nothing that could be done for me. I had a severe allergy, and I had to pull myself through. I rejoined my company a day or so later, but I never took another Atabrine tablet and wound up getting malaria." [17]

Private Russell McConnell, with Company H, was one of the unfortunate troopers stricken with dysentery, "throwing up, urinating, everything all at once. Every one of us had dysentery. The Captain [John Norton] said, 'Well, you're not cleaning your mess gear. I haven't got it.' The next day he had it." [18]

Even with the many cases of malaria and dysentery, the primary health problem remained, according to Captain Daniel B. "Doc" McIlvoy, Jr., the 3rd Battalion surgeon, "diarrhea, which everyone had. This was not just an enlisted men's disease; we all had it." [19]

The training, initially conducted during the day, took a great toll in heat exhaustion and rapid weight loss—further exacerbated by the limited calories from the diet, the rationed water, and dehydration resulting from disease. The medical staff advised that if the training in the heat of the day continued, the troopers would be unfit for combat in a few weeks. So beginning on May 23, the early mornings were used for physical conditioning, while training was conducted primarily at night.

That created another problem: the heat of the day made it very difficult getting comfortable enough to sleep. Private Turk Seelye found that "placing straw in a mattress cover made sleeping a bit more comfortable. Scorpions and ants were always around, as were flies." [20]

Night training was conducted at both the individual and unit levels. Private First Class Elmo Bell, with Company C, noted that the individual exercises concentrated on "hand-to-hand combat and bayonet training." [21]

Live fire assaults on buildings, using live hand grenades, were conducted on the night of May 25. Every activity associated with combat operations after a night jump was simulated, such as assembly of units in darkness; recovery of bundles containing crew-served weapons, ammunition, medical supplies, and rations; establishment of communications among units and commanders; and night movements by compass. Private Avadanian participated in both battalion-level and small-unit exercises, such as "attacking 'enemy' atop a range of mountains at least twenty-five miles distant. We returned by mid-morning to seek shade and sleep in our pup tents.

"One night I, with the five man S-2 team, were blindfolded, given a compass, a map, and basic rations, flown in a C-47 for a half-hour flight, and dropped. By noon the next day, we found our way back—thanks to sighting aircraft rising from the field on the horizon." 22

Battalion-level night exercises helped each unit, such as Lieutenant Dean McCandless' 1st Battalion communications section, improve their proficiency in night operations. "We deployed everyone in a scattered fashion, as we expected to be when we jumped in combat. At a predetermined time we rushed to our scattered equipment bundles, then to our positions on terrain selected to be similar to that of Sicily. My wire parties ran lines from our battalion switchboard to the telephone of each company. Once hooked up and able to communicate with the companies, I reported this to Lieutenant Colonel Gorham [the battalion commander]. On his telephone order, the companies were to launch their assault." 23

It was important before the 505th RCT went into combat that each man and medic know what to do if wounded or injured. The 3rd Battalion surgeon, Captain Doc McIlvoy, and the other doctors developed procedures for virtually every circumstance. "For training parachute infantrymen and parachute medical men, casualties were divided into four categories: wounded or injured, non-ambulatory and alone; wounded or injured, ambulatory and alone; wounded or injured, isolated with medical personnel; and wounded or injured, with attack units. Training was based on these classifications, thereby requiring that the infantryman be thoroughly familiar with his aid packet, that he see demonstrated repeatedly what he should do with almost every conceivable wound; how to use his bandages and his morphine; and how to conceal and protect his wounded body until picked up by friendly or enemy troops. These men received daily training by medical officers, medical aid men, and their own company officers in this particular phase for several weeks prior to the Sicily jump. It paid dividends. To this training, many a man owes his life.

"Under the second classification, training consisted mainly of treating minor wounds and securing himself in a safe place until he could be contacted by friendly troops.

"Wounded, isolated with medical aid men or officers were to be cared for as usual by the medical personnel in the way he best knew how. In addition, should wounded be in an installation, [the medic] was instructed to plaster the building with Geneva Red Cross flags and await contact with friendly forces.

"Under the fourth classification, the wounded or injured with an attack unit, with unit personnel, the training was primarily [for the] medical unit only. We saw that every aid man had thorough training in giving plasma, giving first aid to any type of wound, and could control bleeding of any controllable type. After weeks of this, it became obvious to an aid man that any fool who could grip a nut with pliers could stop bleeding blood vessels with a hemostat.

"There was a morale boosting factor (and God knows everyone needed it then) when we gave the troops a general discussion of wounds, types of treatment, etcetera. The main factors we tried to bring out were that the majority would be nonfatal and could be adequately cared for by themselves or by available medical personnel for several days without any alteration of the end result." [24]

While training in Oujda, the 82nd Airborne Division was under the command of the General Mark Clark's U.S. Fifth Army. However, during the invasion of Sicily, the division would fight as part of the U.S. Seventh Army, led by the already legendary General George S. Patton. On May 19, the division conducted a review for Clark.

The 52nd Troop Carrier Wing, assigned to carry the 505th RCT serials into Sicily, received very little training in night operations despite the efforts of the commander, Brigadier General Hal Clark. The C-47 flight crews had not received training in the United States in close-formation night flying prior to deployment to North Africa. The airfields around Oujda, from which the 52nd Troop Carrier Wing would conduct practice drops with the 82nd, were not completed until May 25, 1943. The 52nd was not ready for training operations with the 82nd Airborne Division until June 1. There just had not been enough time to conduct the training to prepare the troop carrier flight crews for the Sicily night jump. General Clark developed a combat formation for the Sicily drop of nine planes flying in a V-of-Vs configuration. Nine planes would carry a company of paratroopers. Each V-of-V would fly one behind the next about a minute and a half apart. Four or five nine-plane formations would make up a serial. A serial would carry a parachute battalion. The serials would follow each other at ten-minute intervals. This formation would become standard in future airborne operations, although the intervals between serials would later be reduced.

On June 3, the division held a review for Generals Patton, Clark, and Bradley, as well as a number of foreign generals and dignitaries. The review included a parachute jump by the 1st Battalion in full combat gear, code-named Operation Eyewash. [25] The battalion flew in thirty-six planes, with another three used to drop a "resupply." The camouflaged T-7 parachute canopy was employed for the first time. High winds made the landings very hard—twenty-two were hospitalized with jump injuries—three seriously, including Lieutenant John E. Samsel, with Headquarters Company, with a concussion; Lieutenant Wilbert H. Robbins, Jr., with Company C, a leg gash; and Sergeant Louis L. Handfield, with Company B, a back injury.

The regimental combat team began practice jumps on June 5, when the 3rd Battalion made a jump, in spite of a thirty-mile-an-hour wind. Strong surface winds pitched some troopers over as they landed, breaking legs and hips. Staff Sergeant Phillip O. Mattson, with Company G, broke both legs so seriously that he was also sent back to the United States, along with a number of others.

Private Howard Goodson, with Company I, was carrying hand grenades in the front pockets of his jumpsuit pants. "As you got close to the ground, it was really windy. It took me, swung me up and slammed me down on the ground. I hit with those hand grenades in my pockets. I was purple and blue." [26]

Company H trooper Private Richard E. "Pat" Reid's landing was typical. "There was terrible downdraft and almost everyone came in hard and actually bounced when they hit the ground. I know that I came in and bounced several times. After I hit, I lay there a few moments feeling spots on my body to be sure I had no broken bones. After my examination I decided I was okay. I got up and started to assemble with my company. The first person I came to was one of my company's lieutenants. He was lying on the ground, I'm sure as much from disappointment as from hurting. He lay there, moaning and saying, 'I bent my collarbone. I bent my collarbone.'

"I looked at him and could see that his shoulder was sticking straight up. I said, 'Sir, it looks to me like you broke your collarbone.'

"He said, 'No, damn it. It's bent. I was in a car wreck in the States and had my right collarbone replaced with a silver one.' He was disappointed because he knew he would have to return to the States and he wanted to stay with his outfit." [27] The battalion reported to Gavin that it had fifty-three hospital cases as a result of the jump.

The Regimental Headquarters Company made a practice jump on June 7, with six hospitalized and one fatality—Private Gilbert C. Smith, who suffered a "streamer" when his parachute failed to open. With injuries mounting, Gavin decided to limit practice jumps to "as little as necessary and yet accomplish our training objectives." [28]

On June 9 and 10, Operation Dodger was conducted. Battery A, 456th Parachute Field Artillery Battalion and the 1st Battalion's jumpmasters and equipment bundles were dropped at 10:00 p.m. into a simulated drop pattern of the battalion, already in position on the ground around the drop zone. At 11:30 p.m., Battery C, 456th Parachute Field Artillery Battalion, and the 3rd Battalion's jumpmasters and equipment bundles were dropped into the drop pattern area of the battalion, also already on the ground. The purpose of the exercise was to give the artillery crews a practice jump, but more importantly an opportunity to recover bundles and assemble their 75mm howitzers. Additionally, the drops by the jumpmasters gave the troop carrier squadrons the opportunity to practice formation flying and navigation, as well as interaction between jumpmasters and aircrews. The drop pattern of the jumpmasters provided a way to gauge the accuracy of the drop, with minimal exposure to further injuries. The drops of the two battalions' equipment bundles were used to practice recovery immediately after a night jump. For the first time, luminous buttons were attached to the equipment bundles, and there was experimentation with metal "crickets," which Gavin indicated "seem very good." [29]

After the jumps on the night of June 9, the two battalions moved two miles in darkness along the Naima Wadi to defensive positions, then moved another six miles on the wadi on June 10, to simulate an attack, using full combat ammunition loads. On the night of June 11–12, Gavin; Major Charles W. Kouns, the commander of the 3rd Battalion, 504th, and Major Krause, the commanding officer of the 3rd Battalion, 505th, made a reconnaissance flight over the drop zones in RAF Mosquito bombers. On June 12, Lieutenant Colonel Gorham left Oujda to perform a reconnaissance of the same type.

Sergeant Bob Gillette, with the regimental S-2 section, received copies of the aerial reconnaissance photos from Gavin's mission. "My section constructed an elaborate sand table of the primary objective, the 'Y' in the road northeast of Gela. We had many photos of pillboxes, but the deadly effect of an occupied pillbox didn't sink in until we were in Sicily." [30]

One night, Sergeant Bill Blank, with Company G, was guarding the tent where a sand table was set up. "To my delight, I saw Colonel Gavin coming toward this tent. In order to have some fun and to let him know it was being guarded, I let him get close; I clicked the safety off on the rifle and commanded him to halt. He came to an abrupt halt and I let him proceed after giving the proper password. He knew that he would be shot if he didn't comply. He taught us well." [31]

With aerial reconnaissance photos of the objectives, Gavin had full-scale replicas constructed of the fortifications at each objective. Pillboxes, trenches, blockhouses, and barbed-wire obstacles were of the type and location of the same fortifications at each objective. Assaults were rehearsed repetitively against these fortifications using live ammunition.

The 1st and 2nd Battalions, supported by two platoons of Company B, 307th Airborne Engineer Battalion, had the objective of assaulting and capturing the fortifications defending the crossroads at Objective "Y." Private First Class Harvill Lazenby, a squad leader with Company B, 505th PIR, would later learn that the training "was to simulate the mission in Sicily—taking the fortifications at the 'Y,' which were pillboxes—wired-in strong points. Bangalore torpedoes were used to cut wire, while live fire was used to 'pin down the enemy.'" [32]

It was during these live-fire rehearsals that Private Neil Droogan, with Company B, 307th Airborne Engineer Battalion, learned how they would breech the fortifications they would encounter at Objective "Y." "Johnnie Davis and I would put a mock Bangalore torpedo under the barbed wire of the pillbox, light it, and run back. Thirty seconds later, it would blow up and Al Mayer would take a satchel charge and throw it into the mock pillbox." [33]

On the night of June 14, a full-dress rehearsal code-named Operation Pirate began with a night jump by battalion staffs, company commanders, and platoon leaders. The drop was scattered. The following night, the ground portion of the operation, night organization of a defensive area, was conducted. A critique of the operation held the following evening at the Paris Theater in Oujda emphasized the poor performance of Major James Gray's 2nd Battalion. The following day, Major Gray flew to Kairouan, Tunisia' to inspect the airfields. Gavin considered him AWOL for not having informed him, although Gray would claim upon his return that he told Captain Alfred W. Ireland, the regimental adjutant, of his plans.

Gavin conducted a review of the 505th RCT on June 18, and two U.S. Navy ensigns reported for jump training. They would provide the 505th RCT with liaison fire control with naval ships during the invasion. On June 21, Gavin gave the key personnel a big-picture orientation of Operation Husky. The next day, Gavin relieved Gray as battalion commander and replaced him with the 2nd Battalion executive officer, Major Mark J. Alexander. Gavin transferred the man he felt was one of his best company commanders, Captain John "Jack" Norton, the CO of Company H, to replace Alexander as executive officer. It was a bitter disappointment for Norton, who wanted to lead the company he had trained into combat. The original Company H commanding officer, Captain Fredric L. Mill, replaced Norton. Lieutenant Neal L. McRoberts was also transferred on June 22, from 1st Battalion S-2 to commanding officer of Company F.

On June 24, 1943, General Ridgway ordered the 82nd Airborne Division to move to its staging area for Operation Husky. "After six weeks in this dusty, wind-swept hell hole, we moved up to Kairouan, in central Tunisia, the jump-off point for Sicily." [34]

Again, the troopers boarded trains with 40 & 8 boxcars, 2 1/2-ton trucks, and C-47s for the journey. Lieutenant Jim Coyle, with Company E, was one of the lucky troopers to make the trip in a C-47. "We broke camp and flew to another unbearably hot area outside of the city of Kairouan in Tunisia. The crew chief on my plane said that the controller at the airfield told him it was 120° F on the field when we landed! We bivouacked in pup tents in this area, and within a few days, briefings began for what we knew was a combat jump. We were never told exactly where we were going during the briefings, but the maps that were issued had Italian names on them." [35]

As if the misery in Oujda hadn't been bad enough, Kairouan's unrelenting heat and a logistics problem conspired to continue to make it almost unbearable for the division. General Ridgway was at least able to use orchards near the airfields for bivouac areas for his troopers. "In the shade of the pear and almond trees, we took what refuge we could from the searing heat, but for those who had to work in the Quonset huts, there was no escape. It was like living and working inside a stove. There was always a wind, at times the hot sirocco, blowing off the desert like the breath of hell, and at midday the thermometer sometimes stood at one hundred twenty-six degrees. For the first time our supply system broke down, and for one long stretch we lived almost exclusively on marmalade and Spam." [36]

However, some troopers like Private W. A. Jones, thought Kairouan, even with the heat, was much better than Oujda. "That was a good move. They put us in a big olive grove. We were under some shade. That was just like moving into a nice hotel." [37] Plus, Kairouan was close enough to the Mediterranean Sea to receive a relatively nice, cool breeze in the evenings.

The 505th Regimental Combat Team's mission was to spearhead the invasion of Sicily and prevent enemy reserves from attacking the beach landed forces by blocking key roads and disrupting enemy communications. The regimental combat team would jump the night before the beach landings in an area east and northeast of Gela and south of Niscemi, to protect the landings of the U.S. 1st and 45th Infantry Divisions.

The 456th Parachute Field Artillery Battalion, commanded by Lieutenant Colonel Harrison Harden, would provide the artillery support for the combat team. Company B, 307th Airborne Engineer Battalion, commanded by Captain William H. Johnson, would assist in the assault on the enemy pillboxes. A detachment of the 82nd Airborne Signal Company, commanded by Lieutenant Edward Kacyainski, would assist in establishing communications with the 1st and 45th Infantry Divisions, and a detachment of the 307th Airborne Medical Company, commanded by Staff Sergeant Jack M. Bartley, would assist the 505th PIR medical detachment with medical evacuations.

The 3rd Battalion, 504th PIR, commanded by Lieutenant Colonel Charles Kouns, would be attached to the 505th RCT for the initial operation, would land on DZ "Q" on the northern end of the airhead and block the road south from Niscemi. The 1st and 2nd Battalions of the 505th, with Batteries A and B, 456th PFA Battalion, would jump on DZ "S" and capture Objective "Y," a key road junction.

The 3rd Battalion less Company I, Regimental Headquarters and Headquarters Company, Service Company, together with Headquarters Battery and Batteries C and D, 456th, would land on DZ "T" and capture the high ground to the south of Objective Y. Company I would land southeast of the 3rd Battalion drop zone to capture and block another road junction and light a bonfire to act as a beacon for the 1st Infantry Division's beach landing.

A regimental demolition section would jump five miles southeast of the main landings on Drop Zone "X," would prepare the road and rail bridges over the Acate River for demolition, and would blow the bridges if attacked in strength. The 505th RCT would be attached to the 1st Infantry Division through D+1 and would assist with the capture of the airfield at Ponte Olivo.

The 52nd Troop Carrier Wing's five groups would carry the 505th Regimental Combat Team into Sicily. The 61st Group would carry the attached 3rd Battalion, 504th, and lead the other serials into Sicily; the second serial would be the 314th Group carrying the 3rd Battalion; followed by the 313th Group with the 1st Battalion. The 316th Group would transport regimental headquarters in the next serial, and the 64th Group would transport the 2nd Battalion in the last serial.

After arriving in Kairouan, Major Mark Alexander, CO of the 2nd Battalion, met with commanders of the 64th Troop Carrier Group, Colonel John Cerny, the CO, and his XO (executive officer), Lieutenant Colonel Tommy Thompson. Major Alexander had just one request: "No matter where they dropped us, they would make every effort to drop us all together, that we would have the opportunity to organize and fight as a battalion." [38]

Captain Willard "Bill" Follmer, the commander of Company I, had just landed after the flight from Oujda with his company. "Somebody came to me as I got out of the plane and said that Krause wanted me and the other company commanders to come over to the area where they were doing the planning." [39]

Captain Follmer was assigned the detached special mission of reducing a pill-box complex at a road junction and lighting a bonfire on a hill overlooking the landing beaches near the town of Gela that would act as a beacon for the 1st Infantry Division. The drop zone was near Lake Biviere, with a narrow valley and steep ridges running through the area. Follmer listened intently as he was briefed on the company's assignment. "There was a mission that [Major Krause] wanted me to do. There was an area where I was to go in just with my company alone, and the main thing he felt about the whole thing was to set this fire at two o'clock in the morning. Have somebody that I was sure would do it. That's why I got [Lieutenant George] Clark. [Krause] gave me two photographs that were rather blurred. It wasn't really totally effective, but it was good enough for me to make a guideline for where I was going to go." [40]

As Follmer studied the photos, he saw that it would be difficult to drop his entire company into the narrow valley and mentioned that he planned to discuss it with the troop carrier pilot commanding the nine planes which would transport his men. "I said, 'I'm going to look into this,' and he said, 'No, don't see the pilots.' I thought I shouldn't salute this guy, but I did and didn't say a word and walked off." [41]

Back at the Alabama Area, Follmer had been assigned to drop breakfast by parachute to the battalion, which was located in a small clearing in the middle of some tall pine trees. "It was that prior deal of putting the food on the ground at breakfast time for the battalion that alerted to me to all of the things you've got to look into. The pilots were new and not as well trained, and I knew that they had dumped people in the wrong places. Recognizing that, I just said I'm waiting until dark." [42]

Shortly after dark, Follmer slipped out of his tent, moved through the olive grove where his company was bivouacked, crossed through a cactus hedge, and walked the considerable distance to the tents and planes of the air corps group that would carry the 3rd Battalion. On the way, he thought about Major Krause's order not to talk to the pilots. But Follmer was putting the mission ahead of his own well-being. "In the back of my mind, was when you go ahead and do something you're told not to do, it's a court martial possibility." [43]

Follmer was able to locate the tent of the lieutenant colonel commanding the group. "I said, 'I'm assigned to this position of going in first with a group of men at this area on this map. I would like to know [the pilot's name] and where he is, and I'd like to have permission to talk to him.' He turned me over to a sergeant. The sergeant gave me everything I wanted. The man's name he gave me was [Captain William R.] Bommar. He was more concerned about whether I was waking this guy up.

"When I got to the tent, I begged their pardon because three or four were lying down. I introduced myself to Bommar and he said, 'I heard you would probably see me.' That raised my imagination. 'Who said that to him?'

"He got out a flashlight and we looked at this thing and he had studied this. Apparently, the group leader had told him he was going to have this special job. He was as well prepared as I was, plus he was just the right kind of guy.

"The first thing was so I wouldn't get tangled up with the rest of the four nine-plane formations, I asked him, 'Can you please be the last group of nine planes in the serial?'" [44]

After studying the aerial photos and the map, Follmer determined that he would need to drop his company into a narrow valley with steep ridges on both sides. The standard nine-plane V-of-Vs formation would result in a wide drop pattern for the nine planes carrying Follmer's company. Follmer asked Bommar to fly in three three-plane Vees, one behind the other. "We looked up the coast on the map and we saw a river, I believe it was the Acate River, coming down to the [sea]. That was significant on a half moon night. Then as you came along you would begin to see the beginning of a small inland lake almost running parallel with the coast, then a railroad and a road. They would be almost consecutive. If you would turn properly, where the vee of the valley started to allow you inland, you could see all of those things." [45]

A white house, only visible from the right side of the cockpit when flying up the valley, would serve as the landmark for the drop. Follmer made a final request that Bommar sit on the right side of the cockpit. "The only little close scrap we had was when I asked him about that house on the side of the hill that we saw in the photograph.

"He says, 'Sir, I don't sit on the right side.'

"I said, 'Would you mind doing it for us, just this once? So you would be the man who would judge when you should give the dome light on, give us the green light, and that all of these guys be stacked up behind you and not over the ocean. Be sure they're inland.' I knew that white house was far enough inland that we would all land on the spot we were supposed to be.

"As soon as he studied this thing for a while and had thought it out, he said, 'Yes sir.'" [46]

With the plan for the drop worked out to their mutual satisfaction, Follmer thanked Bommar and left to return to his tent, convinced that whatever personal risk he ran, he had put the accomplishment of the mission above his own well-being.

On July 6, the 505th RCT celebrated its first anniversary with a barbecue. Three steers were purchased from the Arabs, and someone in the regiment miraculously located and scrounged enough beer for each man in the regiment to have at least a canteen cup of the delicious liquid. This was as close to heaven as Sergeant Otis Sampson, with Company E, could get while in North Africa. "Some old steer who had lived through much of the past history of early Africa finally found himself barbecued as a special treat for the 505th. It was special. Not counting the real steaks, we also had beer, and if the cards were played right, one was able to slip back into line now and again, which some of them did. It was a good party." [47]

Two days later, the officers and men of the regimental combat team were driven in shuttles a few miles away, where they took their first showers since arriving in North Africa. Private Avadanian, with Headquarters Company, 2nd

Battalion, greatly enjoyed the refreshment. "They were overhead fifty-five gallon drums with holes, under which we walked, uniform and all. It was great! We were dry in minutes." [48]

Some troopers, like Private First Class Russell W. Brown, with Company F, also got to take a dip in the Mediterranean Sea. "It was good just to sit in the water." [49]

On July 7 and 8, briefings were conducted to inform each trooper of his company or platoon's mission. Private Howard Goodson, with the 2nd Platoon, Company I, was briefed by his platoon leader regarding their assignment, although the destination was not revealed. "Lieutenant [George] Clark took some of us down to an area where they had a sand table, told us exactly where we were supposed to jump and what we were supposed to do. We were supposed to go up this mountain at the western end of the lake and set a fire with whatever we could find . . . something that would really glow. The reason we did this was the 16th Infantry Regiment of the 1st Division was supposed to come through our area." [50]

Private First Class Douglas M. Bailey was a member of Battery B, 456th Parachute Field Artillery Battalion. "They had a Quonset hut set up with a sand table, and we would go in groups and a lieutenant with a pointer would point out different targets that we would take out." [51]

Before dawn on the morning of the jump, Sergeant Bill Dunfee, with Company I, awoke the troopers in his squad. "July 9th started with an early breakfast, and we were then issued a basic combat load of ammo, grenades, and rations. We were issued two items that were unique to the Sicily operation, being Mae West life preservers and gas masks." [52]

Each trooper was issued all of the equipment, weapons, ammunition, and food to be self-sufficient for several days. The typical combat load carried by each paratrooper included a main parachute, plus a reserve parachute. Each carried his personal weapon, ammunition, and grenades; typically an M1 rifle, 168 rounds of .30-caliber ammunition, four fragmentation grenades, one smoke grenade, plus a bayonet, trench knife, and switchblade jump knife. Along with their jumpsuit, each wore a helmet, gloves, silk escape map and compass sown inside their jumpsuit, wristwatch, combat harness, and carried a handkerchief. Extra clothes included two pairs of socks and one pair of under shorts. Each was issued a musette bag that held a mess kit, one "K" and one "D" ration, toothbrush, tooth powder, safety razor with five blades, one bar of soap, pencil, paper, ten packs of Camel cigarettes, matches, cigarette lighter, and Halazone tablets for water purification. And finally, each load included a thirty-foot rope, blanket, shelter half, gas mask, entrenching tool, two first aid kits, and a canteen filled with water. Most carried extra .30-caliber machine gun ammunition or other special items. Officers and NCOs carried a .45-caliber pistol with ammunition. Including the main and reserve parachutes, the average load would weigh around eighty to ninety pounds.

Crew-served weapons (60mm mortars, 81mm mortars, .30-caliber machine guns, bazookas, and 75mm pack howitzers) and ammunition, extra small arms ammunition, medical supplies, demolition materials (Composition C, fuses, blasting caps, detonators), and communications gear (radios, wire, switchboards) previously packed in equipment bundles were attached underneath the fuselages of the C-47s, and the release mechanisms tested.

Private First Class Doug Bailey, with Battery B, 456th Parachute Field Artillery Battalion, helped load the bundles on his plane. "We loaded the 75mm howitzer in six bundles underneath the plane and had a door load of a padded box, containing the sight and breech block and a bundle of the two wheels [of the howitzer] strapped together." [53]

As the equipment bundles were being loaded underneath and into the planes, Private Dave Bowman, saw one of the Company D platoon leaders, Lieutenant Waverly Wray, approaching. "Three men from the air corps were struggling on the tarmac to load one of our equipment bundles onto the plane. Wray was walking by at the time and observed them for a moment, then picked the [bundle] up and hefted it inside, much to the amazement of the men. As he walked away, one of the men exclaimed, 'Geez, all you paratroopers that strong?'

"'Well, no—as much as we'd like that image, we're not.' He was strong, even for a paratrooper. He was an unusually strong man. I suppose he could, without exaggeration, be called 'powerful.'" [54]

Lieutenant Robert M. Piper was the assistant regimental adjutant. "Final briefings were held to reassure each man of his part in the overall plan. Invasion armbands, which bore the American flag, were issued to be worn by all personnel on their right arms, and strips of white cloth, which were to be worn on the left arm for night identification purposes, were also issued. Individual parachutes were issued and left in the planes for use that night.

"Pilot-jumpmaster conferences were held later in the day, at which time the complete air force and airborne plans for the drop were discussed. It was important that all airborne personnel knew the type of formation to be flown, checkpoints, air support, and air force instructions concerning the actual drop. It was at these conferences that all questions were answered and the air force–airborne team understood their mutual mission. It was at these conferences, also, that the airborne troop leaders found out that the objective area, which they knew so well, was located in Sicily.

"During the afternoon, the men dressed for combat. And after the evening meal, company commanders gave final briefings." [55]

Major Mark Alexander gathered the men and officers of his 2nd Battalion for a final talk that evening. Private Berge Avadanian admired Alexander. "He was truly a great leader—he filled us with confidence. He was tough, yet considerate. I feel I owe my life to his leadership." [56]

During the briefings, the paratroopers had been told that enemy opposition would consist of elements of the Italian army and a few German technicians. The Italian army had a poor reputation after being consistently defeated by the British and American forces in North Africa. So, the paratroopers were confident that they could easily handle anything that the Italians threw at them.

General Ridgway was confident his paratroopers would make a good account of themselves in their first combat. "By the takeoff time for Sicily, the men were so lean and tough, so mean and mad, that they would have jumped into the fires of torment just to get out of Africa. . . Gavin had done a prodigious job preparing for that attack, and we were ready, right down to the last round of ammunition." [57]

What no one in the 82nd Airborne Division knew was that the German Hermann Göring Fallschirm Panzer and 15th Panzer Grenadier Divisions were in Sicily. The top secret British Ultra machine, decoding encrypted German military communications, had revealed the presence of these powerful German units in Sicily. Ultra had been used to successfully break the German Enigma code, thought by the Germans to be totally safe from enemy decoding. This allowed the Allies to learn of enemy dispositions and plans without their knowledge. Protecting the secrecy of the existence of Ulta was paramount to the Allies, so therefore no Allied units involved in the invasion of Sicily were informed of the presence of the two German divisions.

This troubled General Omar Bradley, one of the few U.S. generals with the security clearance to know of the existence of Ultra and its information. "Owing to the extreme secrecy of Ultra, we were not allowed to pass this information on to the lower echelons or include it in our circulated intelligence summaries. If we were asked if there were Germans on the island, we had to lie and say, 'There may be a few technicians.' This was a cruel deception on our own forces, but necessary in order to protect the secrets of Ultra." [58]

The Hermann Göring Fallschirm Division was a Luftwaffe unit made up of paratroopers (fallschirmjägers) that was in the process of evolving into a panzer division. Although it was understrength, the division had significant armored elements, with more than 131 tanks and assault guns (including a company of seventeen Mark VI Tiger I tanks), armored artillery, and reconnaissance units with many half-tracks and flak-wagons. Most dangerous of all, the division was deployed just north of the 505th RCT's drop zones. It was in a perfect position to drive the U.S. 1st and 45th Infantry Divisions' beach landings back into the Mediterranean Sea.

A couple of hours prior to takeoff, Colonel Gavin stood on top of his jeep and spoke to his men. Private W. A. "Arnold" Jones, with the 81mm Mortar Platoon, Headquarters Company, 2nd Battalion, heard him tell the assembled men: "'Remember, you came over here to cause that SOB to die for his country, not to die for yours. He is no dummy; they're smart people. You've got to work just a little bit harder at staying alive than he does, if you want to go back home.' He told us, 'Look at the guy on your left. Look at the guy on your right. They're your friends. But, if you don't go in there saying, "I will take that so-and-so out. He's not going to get me," then you're not coming back. Some of you are not going to be with me tomorrow.'" [59]

To Company H paratrooper Private Russell McConnell, it didn't matter where they jumped or who opposed them. "Africa was a living hell. We knew that Sicily couldn't be any worse. We were looking forward to it. By the time we were ready to go to Sicily, we were more than glad to go." [60]

CHAPTER 4

"The Eyes Of The World Are Upon You. The Hopes And Prayers Of Every American Go With You."

Sergeant Bill Dunfee, with Company I, had waited through the interminable heat of the long North African day with the same type of anxious tension as athletes develop before a big game. "We had an early supper and at 1600 hours trucks carried each group to their C-47s that were manned by the 52nd Troop Carrier Wing. After the equipment bundles were checked and loaded, we crawled under the wing in the shade and relaxed. At this time we were given the password, being 'George-Marshall' and told our destination by a mimeographed note given to each of us from Gavin." [1]

> Soldiers of The 505th Combat Team
> Tonight you embark upon a combat mission for which our people and the free people of the world have been waiting for two years. You will spearhead the landing of the American Force upon the island of Sicily. Every preparation has been made to eliminate the element of chance. You have been given the means to do the job and you are backed by the largest assemblage of air power in the world's history. The eyes of the world are upon you. The hopes and prayers of every American go with you. Since it is our first fight at night you must use the countersign and avoid firing on each other. The bayonet is the night fighter's best weapon. Conserve your water and ammunition. The term American Parachutist has become synonymous with courage of a high order. Let us carry the fight to the enemy and make the American Parachutist feared and respected through all his ranks. Attack violently. Destroy him wherever found. Good landing, good fight, and good luck.
> Colonel Gavin
> Commanding

As Private Turk Seelye, with Company E, sat in his plane, there was little conversation. "No one knew what to expect or what was about to happen. Each was nervous and frightened." [2]

The C-47 carrying Captain Ed Sayre, the commanding officer of Company A, waited its turn to take off. "At 1930 hours 9 July 1943, the first of 226 planes carrying the paratroops began taking off from the dispersal airdromes." [3]

After what seemed like an eternity, Sayre's plane began to taxi out onto the dirt runway, then revved both engines as the pilot applied the brake, and finally began rolling down the rough airstrip. Sayre could see other planes in the distance lifting off from other runways in the Kairouan area, joining the planes already in the air.

Finally, after a long wait as the other serials took off, Private Berge Avadanian, with Headquarters Company, 2nd Battalion, could feel his plane taxi to the end of the runway, then turn and begin powering up the engines. "The takeoff was without flaw—lots of dust, and it seemed all planes were soon airborne.

"There was a lot of chatter among troopers.

"'How the hell am I going to take a leak or a dump?'

"'What a relief to get out of A-rab country.'

"'I wonder what Axis Sally looks like.'

"'Does anyone still have a German propaganda (surrender) leaflet?' (No one did.)" [4]

After takeoff, Sergeant Otis Sampson, commanding the 60mm mortar squad of the 1st Platoon, Company E, looked out of the door of his C-47. "The sunset was beautiful as we climbed in a wide circle to gain altitude; below the shadows had lengthened and turned to darkness. In flock formation of three, we had joined the long line of planes and disappeared into the night out over a darkening sea. . . .

"The troopers had settled down, and I supposed their thoughts were much the same as mine. There was much of my past life I wanted to think over and put in place; it would be a long four hours, the time we were told it took before crossing the Sicilian coast over our destination. 'Plenty of time to reminisce,' I thought." [5]

As the 3rd Battalion serial flew east over the Mediterranean Sea, Sergeant Bill Dunfee, with Company I, felt the plane begin to be buffeted by a powerful thirty-five mile an hour headwind. "The air corps was ordered to fly the mission two hundred feet above the water to avoid detection by enemy radio directional finders. The pilots were as green as ourselves, and navigation at the time was pretty primitive. They established a heading and flew it for x number of minutes and made their turns as indicated to another heading. This did not take into account the thirty-five miles per hour gale we were experiencing. Consequently the flights became separated, and many missed the checkpoints of the small island of Linosa and the larger island of Malta." [6]

Standing in the door of his plane, Captain Sayre glanced at his watch and noticed that something was amiss. "The first thought that all was not going just as planned came when the Island of Malta was not sighted on schedule. At about the time the planes should have passed over Malta, the formation ran into heavy headwinds and then began breaking up into small groups. The nine-plane formation carrying the battalion commander's group and the 1st and 2nd Platoons and Company Headquarters of Company A managed to stay together." [7]

Major Edward "Cannonball" Krause's 3rd Battalion was the second serial into Sicily, ten minutes behind the 3rd Battalion, 504th serial. However, because of the winds encountered earlier, the pilot of the lead aircraft of the serial didn't recognize any landmarks that he should have seen by that time on the flight plan.

Lieutenant Raymond A. Grossman, with Battery C, 456th PFA Battalion, which was part of the 3rd Battalion serial, was the jumpmaster on his plane. As the planes crossed the coast of Sicily, Grossman watched enemy antiaircraft fire rise up to meet them. "We stood up and hooked up and were ready to jump. Then the column took a big turn, went back out to sea. We were standing up for the better part on an hour and were drenched with sweat. Hitting that outside cool air was a real pleasure. I landed on loose soil in an olive grove." [8]

As the jumpmaster on his plane gave the command to stand in the door, the stick's "pusher," Sergeant Raymond F. Hart, with Company H, watched everyone in the stick press against the man to his front. "The wind was very strong, and as I went out, I was a long way from our bundles, as the pilots sped up to get away from the ack-ack and small-arms fire. I landed hard, but safely, in a field of small trees (olive trees, I believe) with tomatoes between the tree rows. I joined some fellow troopers, and we started in search of our equipment bundles. We managed to get twenty-three or so troopers including our CO, Lieutenant [Roy H.] Smith, and assistant platoon leader, Lieutenant [Arthur T.] Laird. There was sporadic small-arms firing in the distance as we moved to our mission, securing roads leading to the beach landings." [9]

After landing, Corporal Norbert Beach set out to find his Company H buddies in the moonlit night. Beach linked up with "Sergeant [Archie J.] Brandt, Private [Robert S.] Ballard, and two more privates. No one knew where we were, so we moved toward the beach. We came to a country road, and Sergeant Brandt decided to put two men on each side of the road. He would go out and see if he could find more troops, or [find out] where we were.

"As he came back, one of our own men shot him in the chest. We gave him first aid and decided to wait till daylight." [10]

Sergeant Bill Blank's Company G stick landed in an olive grove, "somewhere south of Biazzo Ridge. It was a good jump—we landed close together. We gathered up what equipment we could find. It included a machine gun and mortar. After a short time, we got together with Lieutenant [Jack] Isaacs and some other troopers and moved out to the northeast. We did not encounter any opposition until daylight, when we came upon a farmhouse occupied by Italian soldiers. They opened fire and after a brief skirmish, they surrendered.

"We took them prisoner and moved out in the direction where we crossed the road just north of Biazzo Ridge and proceeded to a hill a short distance in sight of Biazzo Ridge. While crossing a grape vineyard, a German fighter plane came down very low across us—but he must have had his mind on the ships lying just offshore, since he didn't try to harass us. We proceeded to the hill just ahead and set up our defensive position. We had a commanding view of the sea and the road below. Later, we were joined by a group from the 45th Infantry Division." [11]

Lieutenant Ray Grossman landed near Vittoria and quickly found most of Battery C. "We were a three-gun battery because our fourth section plane ditched offshore and the crew came in by rubber dinghy. I think we had most of the battery together by early morning. The guns were moved by hand, using the harnesses for the gunners. We had three howitzers. We went into the town of Vittoria. No opposition except one sniper, and we fired a 75mm into the bell tower and silenced him. Then we started for Gela. We had picked up two small Italian personnel carriers and a couple of donkeys to help pull the guns. It was a ragtag-looking outfit going down the road." [12]

Flying at the rear of the 3rd Battalion serial was Company I in three trailing three-plane Vs, as Captain Follmer and Captain Bommar had agreed. Sergeant Bill Dunfee was the assistant jumpmaster of the stick. "Since my squad was jumping from Captain Follmer's plane, I was put at the end of the line, being the last man out. I was concerned when Follmer put one of the new men between me and the rest of my squad. We had a direct order from Major Krause to shoot any man that refused to jump. This presented an interesting problem, since had it occurred, my M1 was in a canvas container under my reserve chute. During most of the flight, Captain Follmer was spending his time up front with the pilot. I recall asking him if he had them headed in the right direction; he grinned and nodded yes.

"As we approached Sicily and for reasons unknown to this day, the rest of the 3rd Battalion flight turned back out to sea, subsequently returning to be dropped on the wrong DZ. Pilot Bommar and Captain Follmer, seeing the Acate River in the distance, were satisfied we were on a proper course, and the I Company flight proceeded toward Sicily. As we crossed the coastline, Follmer told me to pass the word back to 'Stand up, hook up and check equipment.' This done, we sounded off equipment check, starting with me and moving toward the door. At about this time we were over Lake Biviere, [and] Captain Follmer moving by me said, 'About five minutes,' and moved on back to his position at the door. Being crowded when we stood up and hooked up, it was necessary for me to step through the bulkhead into the radio operator's area.

"At this point I noticed the new man in front of me had sat down. I told him to stand up and he started giving me conversation and I made it very clear to him in four-letter words that he damned well better stand back up. I had noticed the green light had been on for some time when Captain Follmer yelled, 'Let's go!' and we started moving toward the door. For whatever reason, the man in front of me went past the door into the tail section of the plane. I grabbed his backpack and pulled him back to the door. He started to back off again, so I grabbed the sides of the door opening and pulled us both out. I had no more than felt the shock of the parachute opening, when I was going through pine trees, hitting the ground going downhill. Getting down so fast, my thought was as I hit the ground, I've had a malfunction (partial opening), but I was able to get up, get rid of the parachute harness, get my equipment together, and move out. Being unable to find the man who went out ahead of me, I assumed he hit the ground ahead of me and could be dead. Starting back the way we flew in to 'roll up the stick,' I couldn't find anyone and spent the night searching for my company. Since I had no idea how far the plane had traveled during the mix-up at the door, my assumption was that I had landed over the crest of a mountain beyond the valley we were to land in." [13]

As Follmer's chute deployed, a strong wind caught him. "I saw the other side of the valley coming up . . . before I could get anything flat to land on. I thought I'd be smart and lower my right leg so I could take [the side of the ridge] on a tilt. The right leg just snapped right away. Then I started crawling, trying to find somebody. There was quite a bit of crawling down the hill. I heard a rustle in some bushes down by the roadside. I was down by the road by then. I yelled, 'George.'

"There was a 'Marshall.' Out comes [Private] John [J. "Scotty"] Hough.

"We went on and gradually picked up more men, while I was riding on John's back. We were heading for where I told the men that my headquarters would be . . . up on this hill near Gela . . . if they needed anything that was where to go, and where to bring prisoners.

"I said, 'I think I can get up and walk.'

"And John said, 'You better not.'

"I started [to stand] up a little bit and slide, and he promptly picked me up and carried me up that hill that would rise to where we put the headquarters. The head-quarters group went up ahead of me, to this farmhouse where John Hough had told them there was a mule. John wanted to get some relief [from carrying Follmer with a full equipment load on his back]. One guy banged against the front door with the butt of his rifle and said, 'American . . . American.'

"All of the lights came on and the farmer came out. The men said, 'We want your mule.' They brought him out and John hoisted me aboard practically by himself.

"We went on up that road and started to go up the hill again. By the time we got to the top of the hill, all of the men were there, and they circled me, and I said, 'Let's not get so close here.'

"I began to hear some firing coming from what looked like a pillbox, but later turned out to be a bathroom for the Italians that were supposed to defend that place. The officer who got there first, Lieutenant [Joseph W.] Vandevegt, tried to rouse all of those Italians and get them out of there. They all tried to hide behind a shower curtain and didn't realize that their legs showed. One guy let go with a Tommy gun and put a couple of rows of shots down there, and they came out in a hurry. We had quite a few prisoners to take care of.

"I recall two pillboxes at the crossroads. I had a man drop on top of one of them, and the Italians came out. And there wasn't anyone in the other pillbox." [14]

Corporal Harry Buffone was in Follmer's stick and landed on the tile roof of a farmhouse. "One leg went through the roof up to my crotch, and it was the bed-room of the tenants. I assumed it was a large room, because it sounded like about twenty-five people—adults and children. I can imagine with one leg sticking down through the roof, there was a lot of screaming. I could understand enough Italian to hear a lot of 'mama mia' and 'the end of the world has come,' etcetera, etcetera.

"A gust of wind filled my chute and dragged me across the roof and, falling about six to eight feet from the roof, I had a lot of scratches and cuts." [15]

After landing, Company I trooper Private Howard "Goody" Goodson found the trooper who had jumped behind him, Private Joe Patrick. Goodson and his buddy began to climb the hill overlooking the 1st Division landing beach. "We knew what our mission was. Joe was with Lieutenant Clark's platoon. We eventually wound our way up this mountain and ran into different guys and ended up with a group of seven or eight of us. We found this farmhouse right at the western end of this lake, and we set the barn and the haystacks on fire." [16]

By 2:00 a.m., Company I had accomplished all of its initial objectives: eliminating the opposition at the pillboxes at the crossroads, setting up a perimeter defense of the crossroads, and lighting a bonfire to mark the landing beach for the 1st Infantry Division. Due to brilliant planning and cooperation between Captains Follmer and Bommar, and flawless execution, Company I was the only company in the 505th Regimental Combat Team to land largely on the intended drop zone. The only exception was one planeload jumped by Lieutenant Walter B. Kroener, which landed far inland. Most of the 3rd Battalion landed far to the southeast of their drop zone, between the towns of Scoglitti and Vittoria.

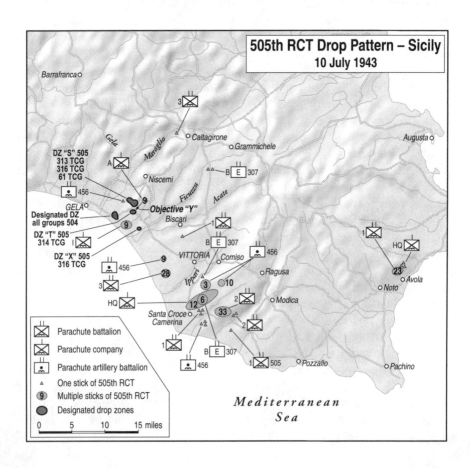

TEN MINUTES BEHIND THE 3RD BATTALION SERIAL was Lieutenant Colonel Gorham's 1st Battalion serial. As several planes containing Company C troopers approached Avola, on the east coast, Private Arnold G. "Dutch" Nagel was getting anxious to get out of the plane. "The planes rocked back and forth because antiaircraft shells were exploding around them. When the pilot turned the red light on, we stood and hooked up. Some troopers lost their footing before they jumped, and because of the weight and bulk we were carrying, we had to help them back to their feet. When he turned the green light on, we jumped! I made my first combat jump and landed safely. I landed sixty miles from where I was supposed to be, but I was alive—now, I just needed to stay alive and find some fellow troopers." [17]

Sergeant Michael Vuletich was pushing the stick as his planeload of Company B troopers began jumping. "We had a trooper who refused to jump and froze in the door of the plane. We missed the drop zone as a consequence. The co-pilot came from the front of the plane and said, 'You know what my orders are,' pointing a Tommy gun at me. I informed him we would jump and to circle around. In the meantime, a couple of troopers beat on the refusal and he pulled back and ran to the rear of the plane. The plane circled again and we jumped—but it was too late for the plane. The delay gave the enemy time to shoot the plane down in flames with the plane's crew and refusal personnel." [18]

Staff Sergeant Joe O'Jibway, and his planeload of Company B troopers landed nearly sixty miles off course on a hill above the British invasion beaches. "I found eighteen men and 1st Lieutenant [Fred W.] Johnson. We were not fired on upon landing. We got in a ditch and Sergeant [Michael] Petrillo talked to some of the locals.

"Every curve in the road had an Italian gun emplacement. We weren't allowed to shoot until daylight. We had a bazooka and lots of hand grenades. We blew them up on the way down the hill." [19]

O'Jibway and the small band of paratroopers moved down to meet the British, who had landed earlier that morning. "We had 115 Italian prisoners. The British were getting ready to bury two of our paratroopers who had been captured and executed—one was [Company C trooper, Corporal Howard S.] Owens." [20]

The only significant portion of the 1st Battalion to land near the planned drop zone was the nine planes carrying Captain Ed Sayre's Company A, as well as some troopers with Headquarters, 1st Battalion. However, as the nine planes approached the coast of Sicily, Sayre knew something wasn't right. "At the time when the planes were supposed to be nearing the drop zone, antiaircraft fire could be seen coming up on the left side of the planes. This could only mean one thing: the planes were coming in on the wrong side of the island. The flight commander realized this, and the formation was turned back out to sea in order to make another attempt to find the correct drop zone. After about an hour, a lake, which was the final checkpoint, was sighted. The planes turned over the lake in the direction to bring them over the drop zone in about two minutes. After proceeding about one minute and a half, the formation met heavy antiaircraft fire and began breaking up. One minute later the green 'go' light was given, and the parachutists left the planes.

"I led my group out and a few seconds later disentangled myself from my parachute in a vineyard on the side of a very steep hill. Because of losing so much time in trying to find the drop zone, it was now very dark, and no one could see over a few feet. About six machine guns which had been firing on the planes as the men jumped, had now lowered their fire and were traversing back and forth over the area in which the troops had landed. Due to the rough terrain and the fact that the guns were firing tracer ammunition, which could be seen coming, the fire caused the troops very little trouble." [21]

Private Dave Bullington was a scout/sniper with Company A and had slept on the flight over. "The .03-A3 Springfield rifle was jumped in a bundle. I jumped the sight in the musette bag, and I was also armed with a folding-stock carbine. The fellow in front of me, a buddy of mine, Orval Hartman from Texas, fixed his [belly] band on his M1 rifle. He didn't put it in a Griswold container like he was supposed to. He fixed the bayonet and went out the door with his rifle at high port and you know what happened—he lost that rifle.

"When I went out the door it was lit up like the Fourth of July. The red tracers looked like it was a couple or three miles down near the beach. They didn't even come close to the plane I was in. Somebody was sure shooting at something. We must have jumped at about three or four hundred feet, because I stepped out of the plane and it seemed like I oscillated a couple of times and I was on the ground. I know there were three planeloads that jumped there, because I could see three planes going across the top of the hill in a vee.

"I went about a hundred or two yards back the direction we came in and found the bundle easily. I got my .03 out, and about that time Hartman came up and said he lost his rifle, and I gave him my carbine and some of the ammunition I had." [22]

After landing, Captain Sayre began getting his Company A troopers assembled. "My group seemed to be scattered over an area of several hundred yards. About an hour was consumed in getting this group and their equipment together. During this time, none of the other planes which were supposed to land in the same area as Company A had landed, so the [SCR-]536 radios were opened in an attempt to contact other elements of Company A. The 1st and 2nd Platoon leaders were soon contacted, but they did not know where they were in relation to my position. They were told to listen for three rapid shots from an M1 rifle and tell us if they heard them. They did hear the shots. They were given orders to make every effort to recover their crew-served weapons and ammunition from the bundles dropped by the planes and then to assemble at my position.

"About 0230, I went on a reconnaissance to see if I could determine the exact positions of the machine guns which had continued firing from the time the troops had jumped. The positions of the guns were easily located because of the tracers being fired. During the reconnaissance, the battalion executive officer [Major Walter Winton] was contacted. I requested permission to attack the machine guns and it was given.

"While the communications sergeant waited at the spot on which the platoon was to assemble, I took twelve men and moved out to attack the machine guns. The men were divided into two-man teams. Each team was to crawl as far as possible to their assigned gun and pull the pin on their hand grenades. When I threw my grenade, all other teams were to throw at the same time. If, after the grenades exploded, it looked as if there were too many enemy for the men to overcome, they were to immediately withdraw to a rendezvous point in an unoccupied trench about one hundred yards from the machine gun positions.

"With the pop of the fuse on the first grenade, the teams threw their grenades. By the light of the grenades thrown and by about twenty [grenades] that the enemy threw back, it could be seen that the troops were attacking not dug-in machine guns as supposed, but heavy concrete and stone pillboxes. A very hasty withdrawal to the rendezvous point was made. One man was slightly wounded, but none lost.

"The group then returned to the company assembly point. By 0500 hours, about forty-five men from the 1st and 2nd Platoons had assembled. They had been able to recover two 60mm mortars with fifty rounds of ammunition and three light machine guns with two thousand rounds for each gun." [23]

THE REGIMENTAL HEADQUARTERS SERIAL was the next into Sicily. Sergeant Bob Gillette was assigned to the stick that included Colonel Gavin and Major Benjamin H. Vandervoort, the regimental S-3. As Sergeant Gillette followed Gavin out of the door, he felt a terrific opening shock as his parachute deployed. Then Gillette noticed something else wasn't right. "It seemed to me that we were dropped much higher than expected and at a much higher speed than we wanted. While descending, in the light of flares fired from the ground, I could see many other chutes in the air. Once [I was] on the ground, they all seemed to have disappeared, and there was nothing but silence and aloneness until one by one, contact was made over what seemed to be a long, long time.

"I was in the early group assembled with Colonel Gavin. It wasn't until [we were] on the ground and partially assembled that we knew we had been seriously misdropped. At one time, an hour or two after landing, there were possibly thirty to forty of us together." [24]

Gillette and the regimental headquarters group moved quietly through the moonlit darkness, when suddenly hand signals were passed back to halt. "Under a regime of silence, we rested at the side of the trail while the leaders were trying to determine our location. When the front of the column restarted, there was a break in the chain of contact, and the remainder of the group, of which I was a part, was not alerted. This was just one of our early learning experiences." [25]

The regimental headquarters group that had left Gillette and the others behind in the darkness consisted of Colonel Gavin; Captain Al Ireland, the S-1; Major Vandervoort; and about twenty men.

Almost as soon as he landed, Private John J. Gallo, a clerk with regimental headquarters, was challenged. "But due to poor hearing and fright, I didn't hear a word.

I snapped to real quick when this GI leaped at me with his M1 rifle and bayonet. I was lucky enough to convey the password [countersign] and have him lower his weapon." [26]

Headquarters Battery and Battery D, 456th Parachute Field Artillery Battalion, were part of the regimental headquarters serial. Lieutenant Richard S. Aiken, a forward observer with Battery D, landed near Ragusa. "We gathered about fifteen paratroopers. Colonel [Harrison] Harden, 456th CO, took command of our small group, and we moved out looking for our fellow troopers. We came upon a fortified railroad station, where I and two troopers attacked the pillbox. I was shot in the head, and was probably taken by German soldiers to a hospital in Ragusa. Later, I was evacuated to the beachhead and back to Africa for more treatment." [27]

THE 2ND BATTALION SERIAL WAS THE LAST ONE INTO SICILY. Major Mark Alexander, the commanding officer, was standing in the door looking at the beautiful blue water of the Mediterranean Sea below, which shone in the moonlight as the armada approached the coast of Sicily. "The red light came on—we hooked up and prepared to jump. The green light came on and I was still looking down at the Mediterranean. Of course, the men tried to push me out the door, and after fighting them off I went forward and cussed out [Lieutenant Colonel Tommy] Thompson. His reply was simply that the copilot was nervous and had gotten in too much of a hurry.

"We received considerable tracer fire as we finally crossed the coast. We were to have dropped on a ground elevation of 120 meters, but instead, were dropped on an elevation of 200 to 250 meters." [28]

Private Berge Avadanian and his stick of Headquarters Company, 2nd Battalion troopers had a different experience. "When we approached the Sicily shoreline and [began receiving] antiaircraft fire, I believe the pilot rose way above the formation to evade ground fire. When the green light went on, I could see planes below and behind. When we exited and the chutes opened, I swore other planes would fly through our chutes. On landing in a hilly area, among olive trees, I was unhurt.

"The first person I met could not remember the countersign to my 'George!' He blurted out 'Washington!' It had to be one of ours—it was Dr. Lester Stein, battalion surgeon. Next one, I believe was Private [Thomas J.] Michaud. Going toward a coastal pillbox, I ran into Lieutenant Eugene Doerfler [2nd Battalion S-2 officer] and others." [29]

Private Turk Seelye, with Company E, just wanted to get out his plane. "Some of the troopers became ill and vomited. The steel floor of the plane was slippery. We jumped at about four hundred feet." [30]

Private First Class Doug Bailey and the troopers on his plane hadn't put their parachutes on before takeoff. "My Battery B [456th Parachute Field Artillery Battalion] jumped with the 2nd Battalion of the 505 Parachute Infantry Regiment. When we were about a half hour from the coast of Sicily, the crew chief of the plane came back and told us it was time to chute up. This was a nervous time for all—slipping where the air sick guys puked on the floor—it was dark, the plane jerking around, and we had to get all the straps and harness over all our stuff. It was our first combat—I guess we were a little nervous.

"The pilots missed our drop zone by about twenty miles, and gave us the green light over an area of pillboxes, rock walls, and trees. I don't think we were over 250 to 300 feet when we jumped. We also jumped with our guns unloaded and had little tin crickets for identification." [31]

Private Dave Bowman, an assistant machine gunner with Company D, was carrying a box of machine gun ammunition, which an officer and an NCO had strapped to the front of his reserve chute shortly before takeoff from Kairouan. "When I left the door, my body was supposed to retain the upright position. But, because of the extra load on my chest, I began tipping over, headfirst. As the chute opened, the suspension lines grabbed my left ankle, and when the inevitable opening shock came, I thought my knee had been pulled from the socket. That was bad enough, but potentially worse was yet to come, as I was now going down headfirst. I frantically worked to untangle the lines from my foot and eventually managed to do so and assume the proper landing position, just as I hit one of the Siciliano's ubiquitous stone walls. After hitting that wall, I rolled over it and landed in a ditch by the side of a dirt road, where machine gun bullets were flying by.

"I have no idea what they were firing at, but apparently it was not me, since they could easily have scored a hit, had they seen me. After the passage of a long period of time struggling with my harness, I finally freed myself of it. Then, by hugging the low wall, [I] reached its top and rolled over to the other side with the box of ammo still attached to my chest. Here, with greater leisure and less anxiety, I removed the box—and now, with this spectacular baptism of fire still in my mind, I prepared to join my unit." [32]

After landing, Private First Class Russ Brown, with Company F, found the other troopers with his mortar squad, but they were unable to locate the equipment bundle containing their 60mm mortar. "We were in an olive grove, and a native Sicilian came and invited the squad to his home. He made spaghetti for the squad. He made the spaghetti in large black pots hung over a fire. It was good to get a hot meal." [33]

Lieutenant James J. Coyle was Lieutenant Waverly W. Wray's assistant platoon leader, with the 1st Platoon, Company E. Coyle was making only his seventh jump. "The red light came on—I was barely able to get the men's static lines hooked up to the cable in the plane and get an equipment check before we crossed the coast of Sicily. The green light came on and we jumped into the dark.

"It seemed that my chute had only been deployed about ten seconds when I hit the ground. While it is difficult to judge altitude at night, I am certain that my planeload was jumped at no more than four hundred feet. No one in the 1st Platoon was injured, however, and we were able to assemble and locate our equipment bundles quickly.

"The mission of the 1st Platoon was to set out a roadblock about two miles north of the DZ to prevent the enemy forces from moving to the beach at Gela, where the 1st Division was to land in the morning. We moved out with Wray in the lead and myself bringing up the rear, which is where Wray always placed me. In this case it was fortunate that he did.

"We had observed an antiaircraft beacon light, which we assumed was on an airfield indicated on our maps as north of Gela. This would be an aid in moving cross country, as there were no roads that would take us to our objective. The moon was now bright, but it was rough going at times, because we seemed to hit a stone wall, which we had to climb over, every two hundred yards or so. After an hour, the column halted and the men sat down for a break.

"After about fifteen minutes had passed and we had not moved out again, I went to the head of the column—or what was left of it! When Wray had moved out after the break, half of the platoon had moved out with him—but about half way back in the column, a couple of men had fallen asleep and never saw the front half of the column move on.

"I got the men awake and on their feet and started after the rest of the platoon. I led the men for another half hour over the stone walls and was finally becoming concerned about locating Wray and the rest of the platoon, when I was challenged and found them covering us with their weapons from behind a stone wall. Lieutenant Wray had reached a road which appeared to be the objective, and we set up our roadblock and waited until dawn." [34]

As Major Alexander and his headquarters company landed, they received immediate heavy fire from very close range. "Our battalion headquarters company dropped on a concentration of five pillboxes and wire. Lieutenant (Dr.) [Kurt B.] Klee unfortunately landed in the wire to the east of the larger pillbox and was killed immediately. Corporal Fred Freeland [Company D] got hung up in the same area and played dead until we took the pillboxes later in the morning. My battalion XO, Captain John Norton, had an interesting experience. 'George'-'Marshall' was our sign and countersign. In the dark of early D-Day, in trying to locate other members of the battalion, he approached what appeared to be a house, heard low voices, called out, 'George' and some Italian voice called back, 'George, hell!' and nearly shot his head off with a machine gun. Norton later learned that he had approached one of the pillboxes." [35]

Through the darkness and into the dawn's light, Major Mark Alexander and his 2nd Battalion worked to knock out the pillbox complex that he and his men had landed among. "We had a good fight in the early hours of the morning. The two large pillboxes gave us considerable resistance. With Lieutenant [William T.] Wilson directing the fire of his light machine guns into the apertures and Lieutenant [Ivey K.] Connell directing mortar fire, we attacked and cleared out the large domed pillbox of about forty feet in diameter. In the meantime, we were receiving heavy fire from the smaller, two story pillbox. Lieutenant [John D.] Sprinkle [the executive officer of Company D] led the gallant attack on this pillbox later in the morning." [36]

Sprinkle tried to single-handedly knock out that pillbox, but was hit in the head and killed by crossfire from a machine gun in another pillbox. Major Alexander watched as his men assaulted and knocked out the pillbox "by throwing grenades through the fire ports and a door at ground level.

"By about 10:00 a.m. we had cleared out the five pillboxes and were pretty well organized. I could see some enemy armor and trucks on a road about one-half mile north of us, but they chose not to attack. I was faced with the decision of whether to stay there and fight or move toward the regimental objective.

"In the early morning we had accounted for about four hundred men; by 10:00 a.m. we had assembled about four hundred seventy-five men. By 11:00 a.m. we had most of the battalion, plus twenty-one men from the 456th Parachute Field Artillery with Lieutenant Colonel Harrison Harden, Jr., and one 75mm howitzer and thirty rounds of ammunition. My adjutant, Lieutenant Clyde Russell, gave me a strength report at about 12:00 on D-Day, and our total strength was 536 men inclusive of the 21 from the 456th.

"On the coast and one-half mile south of our landing area, we had spotted an extensive coastal artillery fortification, at the village of Marina di Ragusa. We attacked from the north and rear. We placed a few rounds of 75mm howitzer into the fortification and without much trouble captured most of the artillery company defending the fortification. We disabled the guns by throwing the breech blocks and other weapons into the sea. By this time it was late in the day, and we took a perimeter defense position to the north and west of Marina di Ragusa." 37

Lieutenant Jim Coyle was at the Company E roadblock established by Lieutenant Waverly Wray earlier, as the morning sun rose. "No Germans or Italian soldiers showed up. There were no houses or civilians around to question as to our exact location, but everything indicated that we were in the right spot or close to it. About 0900 hours, a runner from Headquarters Company arrived to inform us that we had dropped at Marina di Ragusa, about twenty miles east of Gela! Wray and I couldn't believe it, as everything looked so right. (I later learned that the beacon we had seen was at the Comiso airfield, not the airfield north of Gela as we had thought.)

"We rejoined the company outside of Marina di Ragusa." 38

AT SUNRISE SERGEANT BOB GILLETTE, the regimental communications NCO, found himself "in a group of about fifteen along with Captain Johnson of the 307 Engineers. We later connected with a small group led by Lieutenant [Harold] Swingler at a crossroads pillbox, (by then abandoned) where Swingler conducted a brief service while we buried (temporarily) three Regimental Headquarters Company men KIA, probably during the night in front of that pillbox. Those three were [Private David J.] McKeown, [Jr.,] [Private First Class Thomas D.] Adams, and [Private William J.] Kerrigan. This was south of Vittoria, probably in the vicinity of Santa Croce Camerina." 39

As the first rays of sunlight began to appear, Captain Ed Sayre, commanding Company A, was able to assess what he and his small group of paratroopers faced. "It could now be seen that the pillboxes attacked during the night were surrounding a large, two-story stone house which had been converted into a garrison. It was decided to reattack the position immediately in order that it might be taken before the enemy could bring up reinforcements.

"The plan of attack was for the 1st Platoon and Company Headquarters to attack from the front and the 2nd Platoon to attack from the right flank. All rifle grenadiers and the rocket launcher would accompany me. The two mortars were to take up positions in battery some four hundred yards from the pillboxes. They were to be controlled by relayed voice commands. The mortars were to fire first on the pillboxes and, on order, shift to the stone house. The 2nd Platoon was to place heavy fire on the pillboxes, keeping the vents covered until they could be assaulted by the 1st Platoon with the rifle grenadiers and rocket launcher.

"All troops were able to get within one hundred yards of positions due to the unoccupied trenches which led almost up to the pillboxes. At 0530 hours, the 1st Platoon and Company Headquarters were able to bring effective fire with the rifle grenades and rocket launcher on the pillboxes, which were then assaulted with hand grenades and taken." [40]

Private Dave Bullington and "a fellow by the name of Anderson worked our way around to the back of the house. We could hear machine guns firing there. There were two outbuildings behind the house, and right behind them the ground sloped off rather abruptly . . . three or four feet. We could crawl on our hands and knees and not be seen. We got around to the back where we could look between those buildings and see the back door of the house. About the time we stuck our heads up, a grenade landed right in front of me. I saw it coming . . . I ducked, but didn't duck soon enough. A little piece got me in the neck. The next one went way over me. I thought, 'That old boy has got a pretty good arm.' Later, I found it wasn't his arm at all: he had a grenade launcher in the back door of that house. I went back the way I came. I heard Captain Sayre say, 'Fix bayonets. Give me five more rounds on that mortar and we're going in.' That was the first thing I heard him say. I didn't even know he was there. It was the second try before I got [the bayonet] on [the rifle]. I guess I was a little shaky after being hit by that grenade." [41]

Captain Sayre led his men forward as they assaulted the stone house. "The machine guns in the pillboxes were now turned on the enemy troops who were firing from the first and second story of the garrison. Under cover of this heavy fire, the 1st Platoon gained the side of the building and began tossing grenades in the windows. The heavy doors on the building were blown down with rocket launcher fire, and more grenades were tossed in." [42]

Bullington "went straight up over that bank [of dirt] toward one of the outbuildings, and Captain Sayre came in from the other direction and we met there at the corner. He told me to put a grenade into the outbuilding right across from him. It wasn't but about fifteen feet. The opening wasn't very big, and [the grenade] kind of hung up on the roof, and when it did [go in] I got out of there fast. I ducked around the building." [43]

After the grenades thrown through the windows had exploded, Sayre heard the enemy "yelling that they would surrender. The ones able to walk were rounded up. They included about forty Italians and ten Germans. During the attack, four of the parachutists had been wounded, one seriously and three slightly." [44] Sayre and his men had killed fifteen enemy soldiers during the assault.

Meanwhile, Bullington, at the back of the house, decided to go in and clear the building. "The back door of that house was open. As soon as you went in the door, there was a room off to the right that had a bench running along the wall. There were about a half a dozen Italians in there, sitting and lying down. I guess some mortar fragments got them; it looked like they were wounded and bleeding. I knew there were some people upstairs, because they had fired. I went on upstairs and thought that Sayre was behind me, but it was [William A.] 'Wild' Bill Harris. We got several of them out of a room." [45]

After a couple of his men interrogated the prisoners, Sayre learned "that the Germans were an outpost from a combat team of the Hermann Göring Panzer Division, which was only about two miles away. An attack was expected very soon, so a hasty reorganization was made and all around defense was set up. The garrison contained nearly 500,000 rounds of machine gun ammunition and twenty machine guns. All of these were utilized in the defense. While the organization for the defense was going on, the battalion commander, Lieutenant Colonel [Arthur] Gorham, came in with about thirty men, including the two battalion surgeons. They were carrying several men who had been seriously wounded.

"Colonel Gorham ordered the troops to continue to consolidate the position, since it commanded the road leading from Niscemi to the beaches. He also ordered a patrol to be sent to the drop zone to obtain information as to the strength of enemy there as well as in fortifications around the road, which it was our mission to capture.

"At 0700 hours, a German armored column was seen about four thousand yards away coming from Niscemi. It was preceded by a point of two motorcycles and a Volkswagen. The point was allowed to get into the position and was fired on. All of its personnel were killed or captured. The armored column stopped when they heard the firing.

"Within about thirty minutes, two companies of enemy troops were seen moving across the open ground to the front toward our position. When they were within about two hundred yards of the positions, they were fired on by all of the twenty machine guns. Most of the enemy were pinned down and killed. But the few who did manage to escape evidently informed the German armored unit of our positions, for shortly thereafter a mobile 88[mm gun] moved to a position on a hill just out of range of any weapon the parachutists had and began shelling the position.

"The patrol sent out to reconnoiter the drop zone had now returned with the news that there were no enemy there. But, about twenty Italians armed with heavy machine guns were holding a fortified position, surrounded by several rows of barbed wire, around the road junction [that] it was our mission to capture.

"Colonel Gorham moved the troops toward the drop zone with the prisoners carrying the wounded, leaving one officer and a squad of men to cover the withdrawal. When the troops had reached the next terrain feature to the rear, the squad withdrew under covering fire. As the troops continued to move to the drop zone area, German tanks could be heard coming around our right flank. Shortly after the tanks were heard, the troops also heard several rounds of rocket launcher fire." [46]

The paratroopers firing at those tanks were a squad from Company A, led by Sergeant Tim Dyas. "As the sounds of battle were nearby, I headed my group towards them, for this is why we jumped. A small hill appeared in front of us, so I headed my group that way. The bazooka team of Pat Sheridan and John Wroblewski went around the hill to be on the roadside. As we came atop the hill, a German tank roared up the [other] side of it. As [it did so,] we ran down the side of the hill near the road. Training paid off, for we were able to avoid any tank fire.

"As we hugged the side of the almost vertical hill, Sergeant John Dixon reported to me that the bazooka team had knocked out the two German tanks we could see on the road to our left. He told me that the first bazooka shot hit the turret of the first tank, killing the officer who was looking ahead not aware of the presence of our group.

"Shortly after the tanks were knocked out, German hand grenades came over the crest of the hill, as I ordered our men to throw our grenades up over the crest at the Germans. This type of warfare went on for about two to three hours before a German tank bypassed the two burning ones and turned its [75mm] gun on us. As soon as I saw this I knew we had no chance, so I ordered our men to surrender as I threw down my weapon. This has haunted me all my life, but intellectually I knew I was right.

"As we came down from the hill, German grenadiers approached with fingers on the triggers of their weapons, and I fully expected we'd be shot. Fortunately for us, they were good soldiers, and a good soldier does not kill an unarmed enemy. We were then moved off and eventually up to Germany as POWs for some twenty-three months. I returned home weighing eighty-five pounds." [47]

DURING THE DARKNESS, ALL BUT THREE of the twenty or so troopers with Colonel Gavin, Captain Ireland, and Major Vandervoort had become separated. Following a trooper who was acting as lead scout, Gavin led his small group across the Sicilian countryside in the direction he believed would take them to their objective. "Suddenly, as we came over the crest of high ground, there was a burst of small arms fire. We hit the ground. There was a sickening thud of near misses kicking up dirt in my face. I reacted instinctively as I had been taught in the infiltration course by hugging closely to the ground. In no time I realized that I would not continue to live doing that; I had to shoot back. I started firing my carbine, and it jammed. I looked to Vandervoort about six feet to my left; he was having the same trouble." [48]

As he was working to get his jammed carbine working, Gavin suddenly saw an Italian officer appear only fifty feet away, looking at him through the branches of an olive tree. "Captain Ireland gave him the first squirt from his Tommy gun, and he went down like a rag doll. I began to fire my carbine single-shot. The leading trooper, who had gone down in the first fusillade, writhed and rolled over. He appeared to be dead, practically in the enemy position. Their fire increased, and there was a loud explosion like that of a mortar shell. I decided that there was at least a platoon of enemy and that our best prospects were to try to work around it. I yelled to Vandervoort, Ireland, and the troopers to start moving back while I covered. It worked. We had a close call and nothing to show for it but casualties, and our prospects were not very bright." 49

During the predawn darkness of July 10, Lieutenant Dean McCandless, the 1st Battalion communications officer, had managed to find only one of his men, Sergeant Ott Carpenter. They had climbed to the top of a hill and had dug in. As the sun came up, Lieutenant McCandless looked out through a hedge next to the road where they had dug in and could see the "invasion fleet several miles east of us, a beautiful sight." 50

A short time later, McCandless heard a strange, low, roaring sound that grew louder and louder. It was "our own Navy shooting over our heads—those big shells sounding almost like a freight train going over!" 51

Early that morning, a landing craft brought General Ridgway and his aide, Captain Don Faith, ashore on the 1st Infantry Division's beach. Together they immediately set out for the command post (CP) of General Terry Allen, the commanding officer of the 1st Division. There, Ridgway learned from Allen that reconnaissance elements of the 1st Division moving inland had reported that they had not found any paratroopers, nor were his communications sections successful in reaching any paratroopers via radio. It was very disturbing, and Ridgway decided to set out on foot with Faith and a couple of bodyguards that Allen insisted he take along to try to find his paratroopers on his own.

JUST BEFORE DAWN, AFTER LANDING IN THE BRITISH ZONE, Private First Class Elmo Bell, with Company C, heard a trooper begging for help. "I [slung] my rifle and started walking in the direction of the voice. I walked down to the person, and it turned out to be a member of my platoon, an Italian boy named [Private First Class Michael A.] Scambelluri. Scambelluri was fully conscious and very lucid. He described in detail how he had landed in the courtyard of a small Italian army garrison, and he had been captured before he got out of his chute. The captors carried him into the garrison commander, and the commander was interrogating him. In the course of the interrogation, Mike started answering in Italian. Mike was born in Italy and came over to the states as a small child. The garrison commander was highly incensed when he found Scambelluri was a native Italian, and he accused him of being a traitor to his homeland. He directed the two enlisted men who had brought him in, to take him out in the courtyard, shoot him, and bury him.

"They carried him out and backed him against the wall, and one of them emptied a little Beretta .32-caliber pistol into his stomach area, and Mike slumped down by the wall. Then they took his hand grenades and got on the other side of the wall and tossed his hand grenades over, and one of his grenades rolled up in his crotch and exploded. As soon as Mike explained what happened, and I saw the nature of his wounds, the bullet holes in his belly and everything, I gave him a shot of morphine. I didn't realize that Scambelluri had already injected himself, and he wasn't feeling a lot of pain. That's the reason he was perfectly conscious and cognizant of everything that had happened." [52]

About that time, four or five other troopers who had been hiding in some nearby bushes joined Bell. Together they rigged a litter from a piece of a parachute that Bell had cut from an equipment bundle and two poles. They carried Scambelluri back to an olive orchard as it was getting daylight. As he was attending to the badly wounded trooper, Bell noticed a small group approaching. "Two troopers came in with an Italian POW, and they asked Scambelluri if he had seen this one at the garrison. Scambelluri indicated that he was one of the two who carried him out and shot him. He said he was the one who shot him in the belly with a pistol. So they carried this Italian soldier out and had him dig a grave and shot him and buried him. Then a half hour later, I guess someone came in with another one. Scam identified him as being the second of the two enlisted men, and they asked if he had anything to do with his being wounded.

"Scambelluri didn't know of any, said, 'He didn't shoot the gun.' He didn't know who threw the grenades, but he wasn't involved unless he threw the grenades.

"And they said, 'Well, did he do anything to stop the other one?'

"And he said, 'No, he didn't.'

"So they carried him out and shot him, too.

"We covered [Scambelluri] with this piece of parachute to protect him from the flies, and he could reach down in his crotch and just get a handful of, like, hamburger meat and throw it aside. And it became obvious that if he didn't get medical attention soon, that he couldn't possibly make it. And the only medical attention that I could think of was on the beach." [53]

Bell got Scambelluri evacuated to a British hospital ship offshore. A couple of days later, the ship was hit and sunk by German aircraft. Scambelluri miraculously escaped and wound up in a hospital in Tripoli. *Star and Stripes* got word of this story and dubbed Scambelluri "Iron Mike." Because of the terrible damage done to his digestive system by the wounds, Iron Mike slowly dropped from his weight of 180 pounds to 87 pounds when he died a few months later. His death made three-inch headlines in the *Stars and Stripes*, "Iron Mike Dies."

Another trooper on that hospital ship was Private Joseph Gironda, with Company E. Gironda had fractured his right ankle in two places upon landing in the British sector. "Upon seeing that the hospital ship was sinking, although two other airborne men and I had splints on our legs, we managed to throw a raft overboard. We dived behind it and got on it. We got away from the ship by paddling with our hands. In the shadow of the night, we were picked up by a British destroyer. The following day, they transferred us to Tripoli." [54]

Lieutenant Gus L. Sanders, a platoon leader with Company C, who had landed in the British zone, was shot by an Italian soldier during the first morning. "I was shot through the lung—it stung like fire, as if a hot needle went through my body. But I did not have much real pain. My men could not find a medic, and when they got one, he was shot—so I almost died from loss of blood. Were it not for the British, I would be a dead duck. I will always be grateful to Montgomery's Eighth Army for taking care of me, as well as English doctors and nurses. They are tops in my book." [55]

Despite being horribly misdropped, paratroopers individually and in small groups, though badly outnumbered, were wreaking havoc on the Italian and German reinforcements moving toward the beach landings. They laid impromptu ambushes and formed roadblocks, which held up the counterattacking forces during the critical first hours when beach landings are always most vulnerable.

About noon, from his position dug in on a hill, Lieutenant Dean McCandless, with the Headquarters Company, 1st Battalion, heard the low rumble of engines and the squeaking sound of bogey wheels and tank treads. "Several German tanks came clanking up our road and stopped just opposite us. I was peeking up at the German tank commander as he looked across toward our invasion fleet. Thank God, he never looked down, and they soon clanked on." [56]

The tanks were part of the Western Kampfgruppe of the Hermann Göring Panzer Division. It consisted of two panzer battalions: approximately ninety Mark III (twenty-three tons) and Mark IV tanks (twenty-five tons, with a high-velocity, long-barrel 75mm main gun), two armored artillery battalions, one armored reconnaissance battalion (less one company), and one armored engineer battalion (less one company). The lead elements of this powerful German armored force had tangled with Captain Sayre's two Company A platoons. Then two of their tanks had been knocked out and the force held up for several hours by Sergeant Tim Dyas' Company A troopers when the kampfgruppe attempted to move around the flank of Sayre's position. After overwhelming Dyas and his men, the kampfgruppe continued to move south toward the beaches.

The heroic fight by Dyas and his squad against the tanks had enabled Sayre and his men to continue to move toward Objective "Y." As Sayre led his men south, he kept hearing tanks in the distance to the west. "When the drop zone was reached, the troops could see heavy naval gunfire landing about two hundred yards in front of the enemy fortified position. This fire was apparently being directed by a naval plane that was circling overhead. At this time, a German fighter plane appeared and shot down the naval plane. However, the fire continued to land in front of the enemy positions. The fire could not be brought directly onto the positions because of high ground protecting them.

"Company A took up positions about one thousand yards from the pillboxes, and we told one of the prisoners to go to the pillboxes to tell them that the paratroops were controlling the heavy gunfire and if they did not immediately surrender, the fire would be placed on them. The prisoner was evidently an eloquent speaker, for in a very few minutes after he entered the first pillbox, all occupants of the three pillboxes in the area came out with their hands up.

"Company A took over the pillboxes at 1045 hours, and none too soon, for within a few minutes four German tanks approached from the north. When the troopers in the pillboxes fired on them with machine guns, they withdrew. At 1130 hours, scouts from the 2nd Battalion of the 16th Infantry, 1st Division, contacted the troopers. The prisoners and wounded were evacuated through the 1st Division, and I, through the 1st Division communication channels, was able to inform General Ridgway of our position and actions." [57]

This was the first communication that Ridgway had with any of his paratroopers since the operation commenced. It was a huge relief, but still didn't calm his concern that the bulk of Gavin's troopers had been wiped out, or badly misdropped, or both.

After notifying Ridgway of the capture of Objective "Y," Sayre met with the battalion commander whose men had linked up with his force earlier. "The two platoons from Company A and the battalion command group were now attached to the 2nd Battalion of the 16th Infantry, commanded by Lieutenant Colonel [Joseph] Crawford. We started forward against the enemy who had been pursuing us. Colonel Crawford was very apprehensive of the attack because he had only one 57mm gun for defense against the German armor, which seemed to be concentrating to the front. The battalion was able to advance only one mile in the face of light resistance before being given orders to dig in for the night.

"About half of the [2nd] battalion [16th Infantry] was made up of new replacements who had joined the battalion only a few weeks before to replace casualties suffered in the African campaign. The noncommissioned officers did a wonderful job at all times in keeping them down when under fire and getting them on the move again as the attack continued." [58]

For his courage and exceptional leadership in capturing the regimental objective that morning with fewer than one hundred men, Captain Ed Sayre was later awarded the Distinguished Service Cross, the country's second highest decoration for valor.

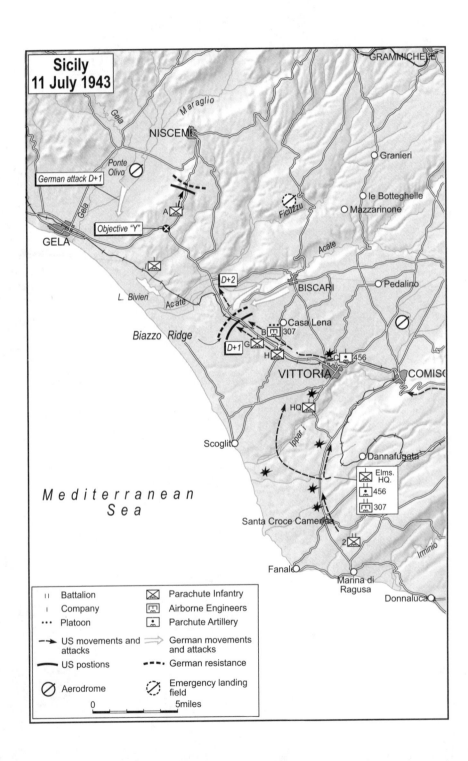

Sicily
11 July 1943

GRAMMICHELE

Maraglio

Gela

NISCEMI

Granieri

Ponte
Olivo

German attack D+1

le Botteghelle

Ficuzzu

Mazzarinone

A

Objective "Y"

GELA

Acate

L. Bivieri

Acate

D+2

BISCARI

Pedalino

Biazzo Ridge

Casa Lena

B   307

D+1   G

H

C   456

VITTORIA

COMISO

HQ

Scoglit

Ippari

Dannafugata

Elms.
HQ.

456

307

M e d i t e r r a n e a n
S e a

Santa Croce Camerina

2

Irminio

Fanale

Marina di
Ragusa

Donnaluca

ıı	Battalion	
ı	Company	
⋯	Platoon	

Parachute Infantry

Airborne Engineers

Parchute Artillery

US movements and
attacks

German movements
and attacks

US postions

German resistance

Aerodrome

Emergency landing
field

0   5miles

CHAPTER 5

"A Blazing Hell Of Mortar, Artillery, And Small Arms Fire"

B y the afternoon of July 10, the Hermann Göring Panzer Division's Eastern Kampfgruppe began to move south toward the left and right flanks of the U.S. 45th Infantry Division's beachhead. This powerful armored force consisted of the 1st Panzer Grenadier Regiment, one armored artillery battalion, and one heavy panzer company, consisting of seventeen Mark VI Tiger I tanks each weighing sixty tons and mounting an 88mm main gun.

Late on the afternoon of July 10, General Ridgway found his first paratroopers. Captain Bill Follmer, the Company I commander, was sitting on the edge of his foxhole trying to alleviate the pain of his badly broken ankle as Ridgway approached. Follmer struggled to his feet and saluted. "[General Ridgway] had a talk with me and he said, 'Well you've got to get up and get around.'

"I said, 'Yes I do.'

"He was mainly interested in, 'Where is everybody else?' Luckily my men that I had sent out had found remnants of different organizations on both sides [of his company].

"He was headed toward where Sayre and 'Hardnose' [Gorham] were around the airport. That's the afternoon on which they gave the order to bring more planes and parachutists up that direction. That's the first time I knew they were up there." [1]

AT DUSK ON JULY 10, CAPTAIN SAYRE approached the commander of the 2nd Battalion, 16th Infantry Regiment, to whom his company was temporarily attached. "I asked for and received permission to take a patrol to the front to see if any wounded paratroopers in the area could be picked up. The patrol moved out just after dark with eight men. When we had advanced about one-half mile in front of the battalion's positions, we were met by heavy machine gun fire which stopped our advance and forced us to crawl several hundred yards to reach cover in an old dry stream bed about five feet deep. As the men were sitting in the stream bed catching their breath, an enemy patrol jumped in with us. The enemy were as surprised as the paratroops. I had picked up an extra pistol from one of my officers who had been killed, and now started firing at the enemy not actually struggling with my own men, with two guns. The superior ability of the American parachutists was now in its best element, and the enemy who came in hand-to-hand combat with us were soon on the ground. Three were captured, one killed, and the other six men of the patrol escaped in the darkness. When the patrol arrived back at the 2nd battalion CP with our prisoners, we were told to prepare for a dawn attack on Hill 41 about one-half mile to the front.

"The attack jumped off shortly after daylight with the parachutists leading. The battalion was on the objective within an hour after meeting only light enemy resistance. We had been on the hill for about an hour when we were hit by a heavy German tank attack. Six tanks were coming directly toward the battalion positions and about twenty more hitting the 26th Infantry about four hundred yards to the battalion's rear and left flank. The rawness of the replacements of the 2nd Battalion now became evident for the first time. When most of them saw the tanks coming, they jumped from their foxholes and started running to the rear. About one-third of that battalion and all of the parachutists stuck to their positions. The tanks were soon on top of the battalion positions. The troops were fighting back desperately with rocket launchers, rifle grenades, machine guns, rifles, pistols, and throwing hand grenades. One of the tanks was knocked out by Colonel Gorham with a rocket launcher. Two officers of the 2nd Battalion managed to get a 57mm gun, which had been deserted by its crew, into action. They also knocked out a tank. When this tank was knocked out, the remaining tanks withdrew to the battalion's left flank. The desperate fighting of the American troops denied them the only covered route of approach to the beaches of the 1st Division. As the tanks could not take the covered route, they continued to the left flank and pushed on toward the beaches.

"In order to get to the beaches, the tanks were forced to cross a wide-open flat piece of terrain about three miles from the beaches. As the tanks started across this open ground, they were taken under fire by U.S. Navy destroyers in the landing area of the 1st Division. When the smoke cleared away, more than fifteen of the enemy's heavy tanks had been knocked out and the others forced to withdraw.

"Because the 2nd Battalion now only had about two hundred men, Colonel Crawford decided to withdraw to a hill about five hundred yards to the rear. This hill was almost inaccessible to tanks and gave the battalion a chance to round up their men and reorganize. Many of the men who ran had abandoned crew-served weapons, and these all had to be redistributed. The parachutists had picked up six Browning Automatic Rifles and were happy to have them." [2]

BY DAWN ON JULY 11, SOUTHEAST OF THE FIGHTING that was taking place around Gela and Niscemi, Colonel Gavin's small group had made it to Vittoria after moving all night. There, Gavin, Major Ben Vandervoort, and Captain Al Ireland borrowed a jeep and drove west to look for the regiment. A couple of miles west of town, Gavin found Major Krause and a couple hundred of his men sitting on the edges of their foxholes in a tomato field beside the road. Krause told Gavin that he was getting the battalion reorganized. Gavin ordered him to move his battalion west toward Gela. Gavin, Vandervoort, and Ireland then left, driving west along the highway to Gela. About two miles down the road, Gavin found "a group of forty men of L Company, 180th Infantry, and twenty parachutists." [3]

Gavin ordered the paratroopers—Company B, 307th engineers, under the command of Lieutenant Ben L. Wechsler—to move west as well. Gavin drove a little less than a mile west "to the railroad station one mile east of Biazzo Ridge, where a point reconnaissance was made. At this point, a German officer and private suddenly came around the corner in a motorcycle and were captured. They made no effort to resist capture and appeared to be quite disgusted with the lack of resistance being offered by the Italian troops, but refused to give any information regarding their own troops." [4]

Gavin sent Vandervoort back down the road to expedite the arrival of Krause's battalion, then to find the 45th Division CP to get a message to the 1st and 82nd Divisions of his plan to advance west toward Gela. Meanwhile, Gavin awaited the arrival of the twenty paratroopers that he had found a couple of miles back. "Just ahead was a ridge, about half a mile away and perhaps a hundred feet high. The slope to the top was gradual. On both sides of the road were olive trees and beneath them tall brown and yellow grass, burnt by the hot Sicilian summer sun. The firing from the ridge increased. I told Lieutenant Wechsler to deploy his platoon on the right and to move on to seize the ridge.

"We moved forward. I was with Wechsler, and in a few hundred yards the fire became intense. As we neared the top of the ridge, there was a rain of leaves and branches as bullets tore through the trees, and there was a buzzing like the sound of swarms of bees. A few moments later Wechsler was hit and fell. Some troopers were hit; others continued to crawl forward. Soon we were pinned down by heavy small arms fire, but so far nothing else.

"I made my way back to the railroad crossing, and in about twenty minutes Major [William] Hagen [Hagan, III] joined me. He was the Battalion Executive Officer for the 3rd Battalion. He said the battalion was coming up. I asked where Cannonball [Krause] was, and he said that he had gone back to the 45th Division to tell them what was going on. I ordered Hagen [Hagan] to have the troops drop their packs and get ready to attack the Germans on the ridge as soon as they came up. By that time, we had picked up a platoon of the 45th Division that happened to be there, part of a company from the 180th Infantry. There was also a sailor or two who had come ashore in the amphibious landings. We grabbed them also." [5]

Gavin was unaware at the time that a powerful German force was fighting the 180th Infantry Regiment west of the ridge and south of the highway and had deployed a screening force of infantry on the ridge as flank protection. His small force was unknowingly attacking the flank of powerful elements of the Eastern Kampfgruppe of the Hermann Göring Division.

A short time later, Company G arrived and was ordered to attack the ridge. As the company swept across the ground in front of the ridge, pinned-down engineers and headquarters troopers jumped to their feet and joined them in the assault up the eastern slope. Company G trooper Sergeant Bill Bishop saw the Germans pulling back from the crest as they came up the eastern slope of Biazzo Ridge. "It didn't take too long to capture it." [6]

As his paratroopers reached the top of the ridge, Gavin stopped to direct the deployment of 3rd Battalion troopers who were coming up the road from the east. "The attack went off as planned, and the infantry reached the top of the ridge and continued to attack down the far side. As they went over the top of the ridge, the fire became intense. We were going to have a very serious situation on our hands. This was not a patrol or platoon action. Mortar and artillery fire began to fall on the ridge, and there was considerable machine gun fire." [7]

Immediately afterward, German infantry counterattacked and pushed the thin line of paratroopers back over the crest of the ridge. Just as the Germans reached the crest, Sergeant Bishop saw Company H coming up the ridge behind him. The Germans "were at the crest of this hill. It amounted to a bayonet fight. They ordered us to fix bayonets and I said, 'Oh Lord, help me.'" [8]

Private Russell McConnell, with Company H, heard the order to fix bayonets. As he seated his bayonet on his M1, McConnell could hear the click of other razor sharp bayonets being seated on rifle barrels around him. "You could hear the German tanks milling about. All of a sudden they told us to charge up, and we all started running up over the ridge." [9]

As Sergeant Bishop was waiting for the command to charge up and over the crest, "H Company came through us, since we had fought up to the crest of the hill, and they went over and engaged in a bayonet fight . . . and that was a bloody, terrible looking sight. I didn't see it, but we could hear it. We saw it when we followed H Company . . . just mangled up bodies. [The Germans] had quite a few killed, and they pulled out." [10]

For McConnell and the Company H troopers, the hand-to-hand combat was terrifying and bloody, but thankfully brief. "The whole fight didn't seem to last too long until we drove them off. They were shooting at us, and we were shooting back at them. I saw dead Germans, but I don't know whether I hit anyone. And then everything quieted down.

"One of the sergeants said, 'Grab that pair of binoculars.' This German had been shot dead. They caught on the back of his helmet and I'm pulling them off and I finally got them away from him." [11]

The 3rd Battalion kept pursuing the German survivors down the western slope of Biazzo Ridge. As they reached the bottom of the ridge, other German infantry was getting ready to launch another counterattack; this time with tanks. As Lieutenant Bob Fielder, the 3rd Battalion communications officer, came over the ridge, he looked down and "saw one of our troopers draped over the limb of a tree, quite dead. Suddenly it started . . . unmistakable ripping noises that were bursts from a rapid-fire German machine gun. Having never heard the sound of 1,200 rounds per minute, I thought, 'What was that?' But it took only a minute or two to figure it out. It was impossible to distinguish a single burst.

"Running down the embankment from the ridge with the others, I lay prone there most of the day. Initially, the Germans fired [white] phosphorous shells that started to burn the foliage and grass, but proved ineffectual." [12]

When those white phosphorous mortar rounds began hitting, Private First Class Cloid Wigle, with Company H, tried to dig in. "This ridge was a hard place to dig a foxhole, and I finally dug a slit trench. It was hard shale, and with extra hard work I finally got it about twenty inches deep, when I saw the tank." [13]

It was the most terrifying thing Wigle had ever seen, a German Mark VI Tiger I tank. "We had no idea the Germans [we had attacked] had tanks, let alone Tiger tanks. I saw the tank rotate its gun towards me and I jumped into the hole." [14]

The tank's 88mm main gun fired at Wigle. The shell hit an oak tree about twelve feet behind him, obliterating it and blowing Wigle out of his shallow trench as shrapnel buzzed overhead, with splinters and pieces of jagged wood raining down all around him. Wigle jumped back into his slit trench and hugged the bottom as the Tiger tank came up the slope toward his hole. "It ran over [the top of] me and twisted [its treads] over the hole. I think I lost consciousness for a short period. I was completely covered with dirt." [15]

Sergeant Bill Bishop hadn't had enough time to dig a slit trench when one of the Mark VI tanks came up the gentle slope toward him, suddenly stopping close by. "Me and a fellow named [Henry D.] Duke Boswell were lying within two or three feet of the tank treads in a small ditch. They would shoot at a single man with the 88s they had on those tanks. They killed a bunch of people with that 88. They ran over one man's legs. Of course, he died from shock. His name was [Sergeant] Gerald Ludlam.

"We had two bazooka men [Earl H. Wright and Private Kenneth L. Harris] and they knocked the track off the first tank that pulled out of this little village. The second tank came around the disabled tank and luckily he jammed the turret and so he withdrew. The third tank saw what was happening and he too withdrew. Bazooka men were in great peril because the first thing they would try to knock out was the bazooka men." [16]

Private McConnell watched the Company H bazooka team of Private Leland "Chief" Laye and Corporal Warren "Pappy" Lyons, the oldest guy in the company, out in front of the line, stalking the tanks. Then, suddenly McConnell saw the turret of the tank rotate toward the bazooka team. "They just turned that 88 on them and blew them to hell. These two guys both got killed. They never had a chance." [17]

Another H Company trooper, Private Richard E. "Pat" Reid, was with another Company H bazooka team out in front, crawling up and trying to get into position to get a good shot at one of the tanks. "J. D. [Private James D.] Long and I were together. He was packing a bazooka. We spotted a German tank, and believing everything you were told in training, we thought we would be able to disable the tank with what equipment we were carrying.

"As we were running toward the tank, the turret swung around and they fired at J. D. They hit him dead center. They then started turning the turret in my direction. I dove behind a tree, its trunk at least two and one-half feet in diameter. When they fired, they hit the tree about three feet above the ground, cutting it completely in two. The next thing I remember is trying to stop the flow of blood from my right arm or shoulder. I couldn't do it, so I thought it best if I could get to the aid station on my own. I knew where it was because we had come by it when we first got to Biazzo Ridge." [18]

A machine gunner on one of the Tiger tanks spotted Lieutenant Fielder lying as flat as he could get in the grass. "The Tiger tank got me in its sights, traversed its machine gun, fired a burst, then traversed three or four clicks and fired another burst. The first burst stitched up the ground inches from me on one side, while the next burst stitched up the ground inches from me on the other side. Any lesser clicks, traversing from left to right would have cut me in two." [19]

As the Mark VI tanks ran low on ammunition they would back up and return to their ammunition carriers in the distance and then come back to continue to inflict their terror on the all-but-helpless troopers.

As the tank that had tried to crush him pulled back, Private First Class Wigle, still covered with dirt in the bottom of his shallow slit trench, heard the voices of his buddies as they crawled up to check on him. "When the other guys found me, I was kind of out of my head and had blood in my ears. My mouth and nose were full of dirt. I sure thought my war was going to be a short one when I saw that tank. If I hadn't been persistent in digging in that shale, I probably would have had it." [20]

With all of Krause's available infantry fighting on the ridge, Colonel Gavin had no ready reserve, and he was justifiably concerned about the next move the Germans might make. "I was worried about being enveloped on the right; some of the 45th Infantry Division should have been down on the left toward the beaches, but the right was wide open, and so far I had no one I could send out to protect that flank. If the German column was coming from Biscari, the tactical logic would have suggested that they bypass me on the right and attack me from the rear. At that time I had a few engineers I kept in reserve, and two 81mm mortars." [21]

Gavin was unaware that a group of about sixty-five troopers led by Captain James E. McGinity, the Company G commander, were occupying a hill about a mile north of Biazzo Ridge, which discouraged a German attack around his right flank. Nevertheless, the situation remained very precarious. As Gavin worked on trying to scrape out a hole for protection against mortar fire, "the first wounded began to crawl back over the ridge. They all told the same story. They fired their bazookas at the front plate of German tanks, and then the tanks swiveled their huge 88mm guns at them and fired at individual infantrymen. By this time the tanks could be heard, although I could not see any because of the smoke and dust and the cover of vegetation. [Major] Hagan came in, walking and holding his thigh, which had been badly torn by fire. Cannonball had gone forward to command the attack.

"It did not seem to be getting anywhere, however, as the German fire increased in intensity and our wounded were coming back in greater numbers. The first German prisoners also came back. They said they were from the Hermann Göring Parachute Panzer Division. I remember one of them asking if we had fought the Japanese in the Pacific; he said he asked because the paratroopers had fought so hard." [22]

The battle was reaching a critical stage, and Gavin fed troops into the thin line as they arrived in small groups. Lieutenant Harvey Ziegler, with Service Company, arrived during the late morning with about fifty desperately needed troopers. Gavin didn't have much in the way of heavy weapons to stop a determined attack by the Germans. "I went back a few hundred yards to check the 81mm mortars and to see what other troopers had joined us. A few had. Lieutenant [Robert L.] May had been hit by mortar fragments. I talked to the crews of the two pack 75mm artillery pieces and told them we were going to stay on the ridge no matter what happened. We agreed that they should stay concealed and engage the less heavily armored underbellies of the tanks when they appeared at the top of the rise. It was a dangerous tactic, but the only thing we could do, and tanks are vulnerable in that position. I was determined that if the tanks overran us we would stay and fight the infantry." [23]

Captain Al Ireland, the regimental S-1, told Gavin that someone ought to go get help from the 45th Division. Gavin thought it was a great idea and sent Ireland off to get that help. Ireland took off on foot, but later commandeered a bicycle and rode east on the road to Vittoria looking for the 45th Division CP. Meanwhile, German tanks continued to pound Gavin's troopers.

Lieutenant Ray Grossman, with Battery C, 456th PFA Battalion, was hearing from the wounded troopers coming back over the east side of the ridge "that a Tiger tank was in the area and kicking the hell out of our troopers. I was next to the 2nd Section, so Sergeant [Joseph N.] Thomas, the section crew, and I rolled the gun up to the top of the ridge. I don't think it was over seventy-five feet high and some thirty-five feet across the top. Captain [Raymond M.] Crossman [the battery commander] had his glasses on the target." [24]

Gavin watched the crew set up the gun. "The crew of our 75mm [commanded by Lieutenant William H. Loren and Sergeant Thomas] were on their knees and lying down, with the gun loaded and ready to fire. Suddenly there was a tremendous explosion in front of the gun. The tank had fired and hit the ground just in front of the gun, knocking the troopers like tenpins in all directions. I was standing just to the left rear, watching the action, and I was knocked down, too. . . . The troopers got up and ran off like startled quail. A second later they realized, to their embarrassment, what they were doing, and they ran back to the gun." [25]

Looking through his binoculars, Lieutenant Grossman had a perfect view as the crew prepared to fire their 75mm howitzer. "Captain Crossman was beside the gun to direct fire. My first look across the smoky valley through the tops of a few trees showed a big tank. I watched the first round, which looked low to me. I was right behind the gun, so [I was] following the projectile with my glasses. It looked real slow, around 1,050 feet per second. In the haste and excitement, nobody rode the trail of the gun, so it had a long recoil. The wheel hit the gunner in the chest, and he did a somersault. He came up like a cat and scratched his way back to the gun. The next round, a crewmember rode the trail, so [there was] not much recoil.

"I busied myself checking ammo, crewman on the trail, etc. and didn't follow the rest of the rounds through my glasses. About this time, I caught the white flash of an exploding shell just to our left and behind us. I assume it came from the tank and just missed us. Smoke started coming up around the tank, and we got off the ridge. It didn't take long, and I can't say how many rounds were expended. Lots of adrenaline was flowing, and [we were] cheering like we had just scored a touchdown. If machine gun fire was coming in our direction, I don't remember, although we were sure exposed." [26]

In the distance, Gavin looked for signs of the Mark VI tank. "In the smoke and dust the tank backed out of sight. That was the last we saw of it. To my amazement, none of the gun crew was hurt. Tanks began to work their way forward off to our left, coming directly up through the vineyard. Although the tank we fired at had backed up, I got the impression that the tank activity was increasing and that we were facing a pretty heavy attack that would come over the ridge at any moment. . . .

"Two troopers came from my left rear in an Italian [tracked] personnel carrier. They were equipped with rifles and wanted to go over the top of the ridge to engage the Germans. I suggested that they not do it, warning them they would be knocked out, but they insisted they could take care of themselves. They added that they wanted to 'scare the Krauts' into thinking that we too had armor.

"They had hardly gotten over the top of the ridge when a direct hit exploded the vehicle in flames. All the next day it was still there, smoking, with two skeletons in the front seat, one of them with a direct hit through his body, the trooper on the driver's side." [27]

The driver of the vehicle, Corporal Lewis W. Baldwin, with Battery C, 456th Parachute Field Artillery Battalion, was later posthumously awarded the Distinguished Service Cross.

Private First Class Murray Goldman, a medic with 3rd Battalion, arrived at the aid station on the reverse slope of Biazzo Ridge in the middle of heavy fighting. "I found the entire area under intense mortar, small-arms, and high-velocity artillery fire. However, the aid station was functioning, and about twenty to thirty wounded were collected and being treated in a defiladed area in an olive orchard. Captain McIlvoy [3rd Battalion surgeon] was present and had procured an Italian truck, which was marked with a Geneva cross.

"A runner appeared and excitedly reported that there were very many wounded up ahead, and exposed to enemy fire. The captain never hesitated. He jumped into the driver's seat of the vehicle and asked for two volunteers to accompany him, as he knew the mission was extremely hazardous. Private First Class Marvin L. Crosley and I were the first aboard and we were off. We drove into the fire swept area searching the fields on both sides of the road for our wounded. Making a turn in the road, we came face to face with a German Mark VI tank." [28]

Captain McIlvoy attempted to turn the truck around, but instead drove it off the road and into the ditch. McIlvoy had difficulty operating the gear shift, which was on his left. "It was a right-hand-drive truck. They shot out the windshield with a machine gun. One of the boys got off and ran back to the aid station. Goldman stayed with me. I got my foot caught between the brake and the clutch trying to get out, and he actually got me released." [29]

Goldman took cover behind a concrete road marker. "We were immediately machine gunned by fire from the tank and several other positions on our flank. The concrete road marker that I was lying behind received a direct hit, and [the] concussion stunned me. I looked up and saw the captain and cried out that I had been hit.

"The captain started toward me and was himself hit in the back by a mortar fragment. Nevertheless, he helped me to my feet, and we both started back. We had proceeded about twenty yards when the truck we had used was blown to bits by a direct hit by cannon fire from the tank.

"The captain helped me back to the aid station and continued throughout the day and far into the night to supervise the collection, treatment, and evacuation of every wounded man in that entire area.

"We had no transportation, our medical supplies were only what we brought in by air and carried for the most part on our persons; yet no wounded man failed to be evacuated to the rear within a short time after being wounded." [30]

Sergeant Raymond F. Hart, with Company H, and a group of troopers were moving west along the Vittoria-Gela road east of Biazzo Ridge when they heard heavy gunfire in the distance. "We could hear a good battle in progress, and as we double-timed up the road, we came upon a war correspondent named John 'Beaver' Thompson. He said, 'They really need you up there,' and off we went, running until we came to the CP. Major Krause gave us orders to deploy on the military crest of the left flank. The road went up between a hill on the left with farm buildings on the left rear and olive trees with grapevines waist high between the rows.

"Firing was intense—bullets cracking and whistling all around us as Lieutenant [Arthur T.] Laird started up the hill, and we were in a skirmish line beside him. I was directly behind him ten or twelve feet or so when he was hit. I decided to go through the farmhouse area to our left and back around the hill, which provided us some cover from the direct frontal firing.

"We got to the military crest of the hill on the left flank, with no other troopers hit and started to dig in. I crawled to the crest of the hill and could see the battle going on below. Shortly after this, we saw nine or ten German soldiers with machine guns over their shoulders coming right at us. We were still digging in, but most of us saw them before they saw us, and we cut loose with everything we had, killing three and wounding several. We captured the rest." [31]

It looked as though the German tanks and supporting infantry might break through the thinly spread line of grimy, dirty, thirsty paratroopers. Still pinned down on the western slope of Biazzo Ridge, Lieutenant Bob Fielder, with Headquarters Company, 3rd Battalion, heard the word being passed around to pull back. "We were told to come back to the top of the ridge. There we saw 'Cannonball' Krause fire a bazooka, the shell bouncing off the tank harmlessly." [32]

Gavin expected German tanks to crest the ridge at any moment. "By this time all of the [rocket] launchers except three had been destroyed and the tanks were within fifty yards of the Combat Team Command Post." [33]

Just as it appeared the Germans might overrun their positions, Gavin saw a group of men coming up the eastern slope of the ridge. It was Captain Ireland, who brought with him forward observer liaison teams for a battalion of 155mm guns from the 45th Division and for navy destroyers. Gavin quickly briefed the officers, and together they tried to get a fix on just where they were located, so that they wouldn't have rounds from heavy artillery and five-inch naval guns landing on Gavin and his men instead of the enemy. The navy ensign calculated their position using the intersection of the railroad and the Vittoria-Gela road, then asked for a smoke round, which came in momentarily and impacted near the buildings where one of the Tiger tanks was positioned. He then ordered the destroyers to fire for effect. The liaison officer for the 155mm battalion also called in a barrage on the same grid coordinates.

For the first time since the fighting began that morning, Gavin could breathe a little easier. He was grateful to Captain Ireland and the two liaison teams. "They did splendid work and at about three o'clock were firing upon known German assembly areas and positions. The 45th Division also sent up two 57mm antitank guns. The attacking forces withdrew and appeared to be regrouping and reorganizing about one thousand yards to a mile in front of the ridge." [34]

Even though the German infantry had pulled back, two enemy snipers had remained hidden behind a wall to suppress any movement. Sergeant Bill Bishop kept his men down in the grass to conceal them. "If you moved around, you were sticking your neck way out, because those German snipers would get you. We had Lieutenants [Ivan F.] Woods and [Jack R.] Isaacs—they decided to get in closer to knock out the snipers. I overheard what they were saying.

"They said, 'You reckon they're going to hit us?'

"The other said, 'I don't know, but let's cross one another to confuse them'—hit and roll." [35]

Bishop watched the two lieutenants make short rushes, hit the ground, crawl, and get closer, as the two snipers kept firing at them. "Both were slightly wounded, but they managed to get those two snipers." [36]

On the left flank, Sergeant Raymond Hart, with Company H, used the brief respite to do a weapons and ammunition check. "We had a .30-caliber machine gun with ammo, [but] no tripod, a bazooka with no ammo, several carbines, some twenty grenades and .30-caliber rifles, one .45-caliber Tommy gun, plus German machine guns with ammo taken from the prisoners.

"We were expecting a counterattack after the tanks pulled back. I directed Corporal Danny Mason and company supply sergeant Alex Smith to take the prisoners back to the CP and give this report to Major Krause that we had no officers, etc." [37]

Gavin now had enough heavy firepower to make it an even fight. But soon, troopers who had "marched to the sound of the guns" were arriving, giving Gavin the manpower he needed to contemplate a counterattack to drive the Germans from the field. "In about an hour I heard that more troopers were coming, and at six o'clock I heard that Lieutenant Harold H. Swingler and quite a few troopers from Regimental Headquarters Company were on the road. Swingler had been a former intercollegiate boxing champion; he was a tough combat soldier. He arrived about seven o'clock. In his wake appeared half a dozen of our own Sherman tanks. All the troopers cheered loud and long; it was a very dramatic moment. The Germans must have heard the cheering, although they did not know then what it was about. They soon found out. . . .

"By now no more wounded were coming back. A heavy pall of dust and acrid smoke covered the battlefield. I decided it was time to counterattack. I wanted to destroy the German force in front of us and to recover our dead and wounded. I felt that if I could do this and at the same time secure the ridge, I would be in good shape for whatever came next—probably a German attack against our defenses at daylight, with us having the advantage of holding the ridge. Our attack jumped off on schedule; regimental clerks, cooks, truck drivers, everyone who could carry a rifle or carbine was in the attack." [38]

Just before the scheduled attack at 8:30 p.m., Technician Fifth Grade Jerome V. "Jerry" Huth, a member of the regimental communications section, could see a Mark VI Tiger I tank down the hill in front of him. "The tank had come up the road through a little cut. He had a command of the whole field. We were ordered to make an attack down the hill just before sunset. We made a line across the top of the hill. I remember we all hesitated a moment." [39]

Sergeant Frank M. Miale, with Company B, 307th Airborne Engineer Battalion, had somehow survived the initial assault, the German counterattacks, the constant shelling, and the terrifying Tiger tanks. He now rose up with the other surviving troopers and began to "walk into a blazing hell of mortar, artillery, and small arms fire. We could hardly see one another for the dust and smoke." [40]

Huth also jumped to his feet and started forward. "[Jack] Ospital and I went down the hill together. Two radio guys, [Technician Fifth Grade] George Banta and [Private First Class] Dick Symonds, got a hold of a bazooka. They were on the left side and I was on the right side. They crept up to within twenty yards [of the Tiger tank] and they fired the bazooka and took out the right track. They were both awarded the Bronze Star." [41]

After Banta and Symonds disabled the tank, the German crew remained in the tank, hosing down anything that moved. Huth and the other troopers nearby could only stay low and hope that the tank didn't spot them. "I was under a grapevine. There was concealment, but no cover. The Tiger kept spraying machine gun bullets over our heads. He either didn't know we were there or couldn't depress his gun because of the position of the tank." [42]

Drawn by the sounds of the firing and explosions, another group from Company B, 307th Airborne Engineer Battalion, led by Lieutenant James A. "Jim" Rightley, arrived on the eastern slope of Biazzo Ridge as the paratroopers made their assault down the western slope. "My group and I were told to drop what packs we had and join in the attack. Saw my first trooper killed; he was right next to me . . . his head was nearly blown off. There were at least three engineer officers on the ridge that day . . . Lieutenant Wechsler; Second Lieutenant Warren [A.] Riffle, killed on the ridge . . . he was my assistant platoon commander; and I." [43]

Lieutenant Harold "Swede" Swingler moved down the western side of the ridge near the road, where he saw an incredible sight: the crew of one of the Mark VI Tiger tanks standing outside of their tank, between it and a dirt embankment at the side of the road. They were talking among themselves as if they were participating in a field exercise. Swingler slipped quietly to a position a few yards away and then pulled the pin on a fragmentation grenade and tossed it into the middle of the crew, killing all of them. He had single-handedly captured the division's first Tiger tank.

Despite the storm of lead and shrapnel from German machine guns, small arms, mortars, and the main guns of the Tiger tanks, the thin line of dirty, sweating, tired paratroopers relentlessly drove the German infantry back, overrunning their machine gun squads and mortar crews. As darkness fell, Gavin's troopers had finally driven elements of the numerically superior Hermann Göring Division from the field after a vicious, day-long struggle. Gavin could see the Germans withdrawing "in apparent confusion, leaving many dead and wounded and considerable equipment of all types. Four tanks were believed to have been knocked out, although all but one were recovered by the Germans during the night." [44]

As darkness fell, Captain McIlvoy worked to get the wounded evacuated. "Captain Pete Suer had taken over an ambulance from the 45th Division, and we used that to evacuate men to the seacoast and to the navy. We had around forty-five killed and 150 wounded. Father [Matthew J.] Connelly and Reverend George [B.] Wood were quite busy consoling the men as well as burying the dead, and when they had the opportunity, also served as litter bearers and did their share of bandaging up the wounded." [45]

ON THE EVENING OF JULY 11, LIEUTENANT MCCANDLESS and Sergeant Ott Carpenter found their way to the 1st Battalion command post. Lieutenant McCandless was expecting to get chewed out by Lieutenant Colonel Gorham for showing up so late. "Instead, Colonel Gorham greeted me like a long lost son!

"That evening he asked me if I could establish an outpost. I was pleased to be asked and assured him that I'd been in the infantry longer than communications. He gave me a bazooka team and machine gun squad. We established the outpost a hundred yards or so on our right flank, and took turns keeping watch, uneventfully throughout the night." [46]

Late that night, the 52nd Troop Carrier Wing, carrying the 504th RCT less the 3rd Battalion, in 144 C-47s, flew a similar route as the 505th RCT two nights before. The drop zone was the Farello airport behind the 1st Infantry Division's positions. Major Mark Alexander and his battalion were moving west toward Gela when the 504th RCT serials approached. "We of the 2nd Battalion saw from our strung out position along the coastal road, two German bombers come in and bomb the naval fleet. About two minutes later, at the same altitude and from the same direction the 504th came in over the naval fleet. The Navy gunners just continued shooting and downed twenty-three of our C-47s carrying the 504th Parachute Infantry Regiment [Combat Team]. From where we were on the coastal road, we could see the Allied white markings on our C-47s. Even the 45th Division got in on the shooting." [47]

The soldiers of the 45th Infantry Division, new to combat, thought the planes were carrying German paratroopers. Sergeant Raymond Hart, with Company H, and his men watching from Biazzo Ridge could see "troopers jumping out of burning planes. Needless to say, we felt like we had just lost the war. More than one man cried that night." [48]

The disastrous friendly fire incident had cost the 504th RCT 81 killed, 16 missing, and 132 wounded. An estimated sixty aircrew of the 52nd Troop Carrier Wing were killed and another thirty wounded.

AT 2:00 A.M. ON THE MORNING OF JULY 12, Captain Ed Sayre, the commanding officer of Company A, reported to the CP of the 2nd Battalion, 16th Infantry Regiment, 1st Infantry Division, to which his company was still attached. "Orders were received to retake Hill 41 immediately. Colonel Crawford issued the order of attack to jump off at 0300 hours. The battalion would attack in a column of companies with the paratroopers leading. The column of companies formation was necessary because of the difficulty of control in the extreme darkness. Direction in the attack was to be maintained by following an old German wire line, which led to Hill 41. I picked up the wire and moved out with a platoon to my right and left in platoon column. The heavy weapons company and battalion commander followed closely behind. No fire was received until the parachutists were almost on top of the hill. Machine guns then opened up on us. Due to the steepness of the hill, none of the machine gun fire was hitting A Company, but the heavy weapons company was receiving heavy casualties. Colonel Crawford was also hit and had to be evacuated. The two machine guns of the enemy on top of the hill were soon knocked out and the battalion began to reorganize on the hill. There were many enemy trenches and emplacements, and these were utilized to the fullest extent in the defense.

"At dawn that morning, it could be seen that the 2nd Battalion was in a very bad position. During the night, Germans tanks had moved between us and the rear leaving us completely surrounded.

"At 0700 hours the first tank attack came. Several Mark IVs and one Mark VI were heading toward the battalion's position with the Mark VI leading." [49]

As the German armored attack hit Hill 41, a group of 1st Battalion headquarters personnel led by Colonel Gorham arrived on the hill to the left of Sayre's position. Lieutenant Dean McCandless, the 1st Battalion communications officer, was with this group. "We were climbing a small hill when all of a sudden there was a lot of shooting in front and to our right. A few paces later, we could see over the crest of the hill and there was a German Tiger tank in the valley to our right, some two hundred yards away. We were all prone in a second! It seemed like everyone was shooting at that tank and that it had been disabled somehow. Colonel Gorham motioned us to keep down while he crept ahead.

"He was either on the crest of the hill or a bit on the forward slope when he knelt and raised the bazooka that he was carrying. Within seconds there was a tremendous explosion right there and Colonel Gorham was down. Lieutenant [Dr. Carl R.] Comstock jumped up and ran to his side. There was a second tremendous explosion, and Lieutenant Comstock was down. I then ran to them. The Tiger tank did not fire at us again.

"At first, I thought they were dead. Colonel Gorham had no pulse, was not breathing, and had a large triangular hole in the center of his forehead. He was dead. [50]

"Lieutenant Comstock had a terrible long gash obliquely across his face, so that his nose and lips were lying on one side of his face. But, he was alive, but in great distress.

"I asked Corporal [Thomas H.] Higgins to go get a jeep in a hurry, even if he had to steal it. In the meantime, I gave Lieutenant Comstock a syrette of morphine, even though he tried to protest through his shattered face.

"In a very short time Higgins was back with a jeep. (I never asked where he got it.) We all loaded Comstock onto the jeep and rushed him back to the hospital on the beach. Higgins and Williams then returned with the jeep and recovered Colonel Gorham's body.

"Why Colonel Gorham took the chances he took we'll never know. I'd never seen him fire a bazooka, and he did not fire it that day. We were well out of bazooka range at any rate. He was a brave and aggressive leader. Such leaders get right up close to the action and take chances." [51]

Captain Sayre, unaware of Lieutenant Colonel Gorham's death, could see the German tanks moving relentlessly toward his positions. "It was almost exactly like the attack in the same spot on the previous morning except for one very important factor: the 2nd Battalion had a battalion of 155s supporting us. The forward observer called for fire. The first salvo landed on the Mark VI Tiger tank, fifty yards from the main line of resistance. The fire then began to land among the other tanks and they were forced to withdraw.

"In the meantime, elements of the 2nd Armored Division were in direct contact with the German armor between the 2nd Battalion and our rear. Our troops were treated to a grandstand spectacle of German and American armor fighting it out in the valley below. While the Germans were engaged to the front, a section of Sherman tanks managed to get directly on their flank and opened fire before they were observed. Several German tanks were knocked out and the others forced to withdraw. Three times during the day the German tanks started toward the position of the 2nd Battalion, but each time were driven back by artillery fire." [52]

Major Walter Winton, the executive officer, took command of the 1st Battalion after Lieutenant Colonel Gorham was killed.

As of daybreak on July 12, General Ridgway had not been able to contact Colonel Gavin or the 505th command post since coming ashore at 7:30 a.m. on July

10. His landing party had set up a division command post three miles southeast of Gela, about a mile from the coast. Ridgway sent a report at 7:55 a.m. to Seventh Army Headquarters that stated, "No formed element of Combat Team 505 under my control. Expect some today, based on 1st Division reports. Elements of Combat Team 504 dribbling in. At present one battery 75 pack howitzer and equivalent of one infantry company available for use . . . Am concentrating all efforts on reorganization." [53]

That morning on Biazzo Ridge, the 505th and German dead from the previous day's fighting were buried. As Sergeant Fredrick W. Randall, with Company H, moved out west on the highway toward Gela with the other survivors of the fighting at Biazzo Ridge, he saw graves being dug in the orchard to the right of the road. "Sergeant [Tony] Castillo, 1st Sergeant of G Company, was in charge of the burial detail. He was a Pueblo Indian from Colorado. German POWs were digging graves, and Castillo gave them a rough time." [54]

In the Company H column, Private Russell McConnell could see the fresh graves and the covered bodies where so many of his buddies were now being buried. "When we marched past where their graves were, that's when it really hit. We had lost some of our closest friends." [55]

Private Turk Seelye, with Company E, had largely missed the combat after landing in Sicily. As he marched past the site of the battle, Seelye saw "my first dead American G.I.s—ten uniformed men of the 505 were lying in a row awaiting burial." [56]

Captain Daniel "Doc" McIlvoy watched the two regimental chaplains as they personally helped bury the dead, as well as conducted a short ceremony for every individual buried. "Father Connelly and Chaplain Wood buried sixty-seven on Biazzo Ridge. These great men can never secure the credit they so rightly deserve." [57]

Lieutenant Bob Fielder, 3rd Battalion communications officer, was one of the lucky troopers who rode in a jeep because of the heavy SCR-300 radios his section operated. A short distance after a bend in the road Fielder saw "the very grim sight of dead paratroopers hanging from trees. A part of a stick of troopers [from the 504th] had been dropped the night before along the road on top of elements of Germans who cut them down." [58]

At about 5:00 p.m. on July 12, Captain Ed Sayre was once again ordered to lead Company A forward in yet another attack. "The battalion received orders from [16th Infantry] Regimental Headquarters to prepare to attack a ridge three thousand yards to our front. We were to be supported by a platoon of Sherman tanks. The battalion was to move forward to a line of departure three hundred yards to our front, and moved out as soon as the tanks arrived.

"All but one of the tanks were knocked out by long-range 88 fire before they reached the line of departure, so the attack was delayed until the next morning.

"The captain who was now commanding the 2nd Battalion pulled the parachutists out of the line and brought us back to the battalion CP, where we were allowed to get our first real rest since we had jumped three nights before. With artillery fire landing around them all night, the men slept like they were home in a nice warm bed until awakened at 0400 hours the next morning to prepare for the attack on the ridge to our front. With a heavy artillery barrage preceding us, the battalion moved out, two companies on line, parachutists and the heavy weapons company on their open right flank and the reserve company following the left company and protecting that flank. Machine gun fire, which had been coming from the ridge, stopped as the artillery fire began landing on the ridge. The battalion moved to the ridge, receiving no fire from there, but a few scattered sniper rounds from a ridge farther to the front.

"When the battalion reached the ridge, the enemy had pulled out, leaving behind a mobile 88 and several of its crew dead nearby. Regimental headquarters was notified that the ridge was taken. The battalion was given orders to pursue the enemy closely and to take the town of Niscemi if possible.

"The battalion moved forward without resistance, except for long-range sniper fire, until we reached the hill overlooking the town. The battalion commander now called for five men from each company to volunteer for a twenty-man patrol to enter the town. No volunteers were found.

"The paratroopers were much fresher than the other men of the battalion due to our good rest the night before, so we were ordered to enter the town. There was one machine gun firing from long range as we entered the outskirts of the town, but it withdrew as soon as fired upon. The parachutists now stopped and the battalion passed through us to take up defensive positions on the other side of town. At this time we received orders from Headquarters, 16th Infantry, that we were relieved from the 16th Infantry and would be returning to an area near Gela where the 505th Parachute Infantry was reassembling." [59]

CHAPTER 6

"The Italians Were Something Less Than Enthused About Fighting"

At 9:00 a.m. on July 13, Colonel Gavin, with about twelve hundred men under his command, reported to General Ridgway at the division command post. The 505th RCT reorganized over the next few days and moved out at 6:00 a.m. on July 17, following the 504th RCT west, where the division relieved the U.S. 39th Infantry Division near Realmonte on July 18. The following morning at 3:00 a.m., with the 504th PIR in the lead, the division began an advance along the coast toward Trapani.

At 9:30 a.m. on July 21, the 505th took the lead, with the 2nd Battalion passing through the 504th at Tumminello, marched to Santa Margherita, occupying it by 11:40 a.m., then pushed on to capture Bellice by 3:00 p.m.—a total of twenty-three miles, without food or a resupply of water.

A platoon from Company G marched west to take the town of Montevago, while Company I moved east from Santa Margherita to capture Sambuca. Sergeant Bill Dunfee was a squad leader with Company I. "The combat team moved up the west coast of Sicily. This was accomplished by leap-frogging the battalions, first one then another leading the way. Although I Company had accomplished its mission with dispatch, we were on Krause's shit list, since we had not participated at Biazzo Ridge. Consequently, when the 3rd Battalion was in the lead position, I Company was out in front. In fairness, I'm sure at that time I Company had the fewest casualties. I'm sure it was obvious to those on high that the Germans were sacrificing the Italian Army to fight a delaying action. This allowed them to evacuate most of their units across the Strait of Messina into Italy. The Germans did have to abandon huge quantities of materiel. The Italians were something less than enthused about fighting, and gave up after a token effort of defense. This was of little comfort to our wounded, and frustrating to those of us that had to take them prisoner." [1]

The next day, the division maintained its positions, while patrolling to the north and east. On the morning of July 23, the 3rd Battalion was ordered to move immediately to seize Trapani, which lay on the northwest coast of Sicily. The battalion moved out from Montevago by truck at 11:30 a.m., driving through territory not previously cleared by Allied troops. As the convoy rolled through the towns of Partanna, Santa Ninfa, and Salemi, the citizenry lined the road, welcoming the troopers as liberators and throwing such delicacies as fruit, bread, and chocolate to the passing truck-borne troopers. It seemed that the locals had appropriated food stocks left behind by the retreating Italian army.

Once again, Company I was in the lead. Sergeant Dunfee enjoyed the ride and the hospitality from the civilians along the way after marching so many miles during the last week. Outside of Trapani the convoy halted and Dunfee ordered his squad out of the back of the truck. Dunfee could see in the distance enemy roadblocks and mines on the road leading into Trapani. "It was an Italian naval and marine base, and we were not real sure of the number of defenders to expect. We had formed up at the edge of an olive grove looking out on a plain that was about a mile to the foothills overlooking the harbor." 2

The remainder of the 3rd Battalion arrived shortly, and Sergeant Bill Blank, with Company G, deployed his squad for an assault. "Just outside of town we unloaded for the assault on the town, and they fired a few rounds of artillery at us without too much effect. We fixed bayonets and went toward the town. We crossed an open area used for an airport and expected the worst, since there was no cover." 3

Simultaneously, Company I moved out from the olive grove to attack. As they did, Sergeant Dunfee heard incoming artillery. "On hearing incoming mail, we would hit the deck and move forward after the explosions. Hearing incoming rounds, we had just hit the deck, when Major Krause drove up in his jeep. He had not heard the incoming rounds and started giving us hell. As luck would have it, at this very moment two rounds bracketed his jeep, and to quote from that era: 'He hauled ass out of there.' We continued forward under constant but moderate artillery fire. When we started up the hill the artillery ceased, and mortar rounds took over. Small-arms fire was quite intense, but we had ample cover in the form of large rock formations.

"As we neared the crest we were ordered to fix bayonets. We continued our advance, and the mortar fire became only an occasional round, and the rifle fire diminished. In short order, white flags appeared, and for these Italians the war was over. I had observed two Italian soldiers disappear into what appeared to be a hole in the ground. Being so close to Trapani, it was probably a homemade air raid shelter. I called [Corporal Harry] Buffone forward, knowing he spoke Italian, and told him to tell the ten people in the cave to come out, or we were coming in shooting. About this time one of the men came up with the pin pulled on a fragmentation grenade. Having heard women and children crying in the cave, I told him not to use it. What was funny to me at the time was, he had discarded the pin and couldn't find it. I told Buff, 'Let's get the hell out of here before he drops the damned thing.' The balance of our stay on Sicily was spent rounding up and guarding POWs." 4

Miraculously, the 3rd Battalion captured the town with only one casualty, a bazooka loader who was accidentally burned by the back blast from the bazooka as it was fired. General Ridgway arrived in town and dictated a surrender document to the Italian commander for the Trapani district, Admiral Alberto Manfredi. It required that all resistance cease immediately; that all Italian military stocks of food, ammunition, and supplies be preserved; and that Ridgway's troopers be permitted to post guards on all military property.

That same day, Major Mark Alexander received a promotion to lieutenant colonel. A few days later, Alexander and his 2nd Battalion were bivouacked in an olive orchard at a village near Trapani. "I had a battalion headquarters tent and an improvised desk of two boxes and some boards. Two of our demolition men came to my tent and asked the adjutant if they could speak to the colonel privately. I said O.K., and invited them into the tent.

"Their story was that they had gotten drunk on native wine the night before and had blown a small bank vault at the village. They took a box of jewelry and Italian money, which they sat on my desk. They asked if I would give it back and not let anyone know what they had done. I agreed, as I did not want the details of a court-martial anymore than they did. However, I fined each one a month's pay and restricted each to hard labor for a week, such as the company commander should provide. I told the company commander of the incident, and he agreed to my decision to keep the incident quiet, as we had a war on, and didn't want to waste time on a court-marshal.

"Not two hours later, after I finished with the demolition men, two AMGOT/ [Allied Military Government of the Occupied Territories] officers came to me and said a small bank had been blown in the village the night before. They had some leads that indicated the perpetrators probably came from my battalion. I asked them if I could get a return of the stolen articles, would they drop the hunt. They readily agreed. I pulled the box from under my desk and sat it in front of them. Their eyes opened wide, they checked the contents of the box, thanked me, and departed. For some time after, I checked the behavior of the two demolition men. They were both good soldiers." [5]

With the invasion of Sicily, the 505th RCT had conducted the first regimental-sized combat jump in U.S. Army history. Although the drops were badly scattered, the paratroopers had engaged elements of the Hermann Göring Division, 15th Panzer Grenadier Division, the Italian 4th Livorno Division, the Italian 54th Napoli Division, and the Italian 206th Coastal Division. The aggressive fighting by small, isolated groups of paratroopers had cleared defenders from the beach areas, delayed counterattacking armored and motorized forces, and caused the Germans and Italians to estimate their numbers to be far in excess of the actual size of the forces.

General Kurt Student, commander of all German parachute forces, would later state, "The Allied airborne operation in Sicily was decisive despite widely scattered drops, which must be expected in a night landing. It is my opinion that if it had not been for the airborne forces blocking the Hermann Göring Panzer Division from reaching the beachhead, that division would have driven the initial seaborne forces back into the sea. I attribute the entire success of the Allied Sicilian operation to the delaying of German reserves until sufficient forces had been landed by sea to resist the counterattacks by our defending forces." [6]

ON JULY 29, 1943, GENERAL RIDGWAY received notification from Fifth Army Headquarters that the 82nd Airborne Division would conduct an airborne operation as part of an amphibious landing scheduled for September 9, in the Bay of Salerno on the western coast above the toe of the Italian boot. Ridgway and some of the division staff flew to Fifth Army Headquarters on August 2 to discuss the operational plan. General Mark Clark's new airborne planner was Major William P. Yarborough, whom Ridgway had relieved shortly after the Sicily campaign for allowing his men to be ambushed at the Tumminello Pass.

Yarborough's plan called for Ridgway's two parachute regiments to drop north of the Sorrento Mountains to block the north end of the passes, preventing two German panzer divisions in the Naples area from reinforcing the defenders of the Bay of Salerno. Ridgway got Clark's assurance that he would get at least three weeks of training for the 504th and 505th to work with the troop carrier forces. Ridgway was wary of Yarborough's abilities and intentions. After the meeting, he assigned Brigadier General Maxwell Taylor, division artillery commander, as a liaison to General Eisenhower's headquarters in Algiers, in order to keep an eye on Yarborough.

The accuracy of night parachute drops needed drastic improvement, but there was little time to devise and test methods to do so. A pathfinder concept was conceived, whereby a small group of paratroopers would jump twenty to thirty minutes before the main forces and employ newly developed electronic gear to guide the main forces to the drop zones and special light beacons to mark the drop zones. The initial training was conducted at the airfield at Comiso, Sicily. The primary electronic gear consisted of a transmitter device, called a Rebecca, mounted in sixteen special pathfinder C-47s, and a responder homing beacon, called a Eureka, used by the pathfinders on the ground. Communications specialists from the 504th, 505th, and the attached 2nd Battalion, 509th PIR, were selected for Rebecca-Eureka training, thus becoming the original U.S. Army pathfinders.

One of those chosen was Technician Fifth Grade Jerry Huth, with Regimental Headquarters Company. "They selected half a dozen guys—Lieutenant [Albert V.] Konar headed it up. The Eureka was a set which all pathfinders used. You set up a beam on the ground. The aircraft were tuned to that frequency and they followed the beam. There were only about five days [that] we had to do the training. We were put at a separate airport. There were a British sergeant and an officer, I believe they came out of the U.K. to train us. The burly British sergeant did all of the training on the Rebecca-Eureka." [7]

Because Ridgway's parachute forces were still in Sicily performing occupation duties and the troop carrier forces were located in the Kairouan, Tunisia, area, no joint training could take place until the parachute elements of Ridgway's forces could return to Kairouan. In addition, the 504th and 505th RCTs had to integrate approximately one thousand replacements for the casualties incurred during the Sicily campaign. After training in Kairouan, the plan was for the troop carrier forces and Ridgway's parachute elements to move to the closer airfields in Sicily a few days prior to the operation.

On August 18, formal orders arrived for the operation, code-named Giant I, which by this time had become even more ambitious. The plan now called for the 504th and 505th RCTs to jump northwest of Naples near the Volturno River, even farther away from the landings at Salerno.

With only twenty-four trucks available to the division, the regimental combat team's troops, weapons, and equipment were moved by shuttles to airfields and returned to Kairouan on August 19 and 20, where training began immediately. Officers were shifted around to fill vacancies created by casualties. Lieutenant Waverly Wray was transferred from Company E to Company D, as its executive officer. Lieutenant David Packard, an original 505th officer who missed the Sicily jump because he had been in the hospital, took command of Wray's 1st Platoon of Company E.

When Lieutenant Colonel Mark Alexander attended the briefing for Giant I, he had serious concerns about dropping "northwest of Naples and approximately forty miles from the nearest proposed Allied beach landing, south of Naples in the vicinity of Salerno. My 2nd Battalion was to have jumped on the banks of the Volturno River near the villages of Arnone and Conchello. Relief of airborne units by ground force elements of the Fifth Army could not be expected for several days." [8]

On August 26, the USO brought Bob Hope and Frances Langford to Kairouan to perform for the men of the division. When Bob Hope said, "It is great to be here with the boys of the 82nd Division," many of the 505th troopers shouted, "No! . . . 505! . . . 505!"

Lieutenant Ray Grossman, with Battery C, 456th Parachute Field Artillery Battalion, thoroughly enjoyed the show. "I was an admirer of Bob Hope before the war. On that day, we sat on our helmets in the sand and he kept us in stitches for over an hour, with mostly one-liners." [9]

On the night of August 28–29, a test of the electronic equipment and lights planned for pathfinder operations was conducted near the town of Enfidaville, Tunisia. Specially selected and trained aircrews flying the sixteen C-47 pathfinder aircraft outfitted with Rebeccas were able to pick up the Eureka beacon about twenty miles out and were effectively guided to the location of the equipment. Testing of a high-frequency radio beacon called 5G that was susceptible to jamming determined that it was not as effective as the Rebecca-Eureka gear. Aldis lamps and krypton lights, supposedly capable of being visible from twenty-five miles away, were used to mark the location and were deemed satisfactory in the test.

A second test was conducted on the night of August 30, this time using a small number of paratroopers to actually jump on the drop zone where the equipment was located. The test resulted in an extrapolation that if a mass jump had been executed, more than ninety percent of the paratroopers would have landed within a mile of the drop zone, a huge improvement over the Sicily jump.

On September 2, Giant I was cancelled, and new orders were issued for a parachute drop near Rome. A few days later, Lieutenant Colonel Alexander attended another secret briefing, where he was informed that the operation had been cancelled and replaced by a jump near Rome. "The proposal had many problems, and we battalion commanders of the 505th Parachute Regiment were relieved when the plan was cancelled. We had not had time for adequate training, and the transport of supplies by air and ground forces would not be adequate for days or weeks of defense of the proposed objective. After a great deal of preparation, the show was cancelled and replaced with a plan for airborne operations in the Rome area, Giant II. The revision called for a drop by the 82nd Airborne Division near and on three airfields east and north of Rome in conjunction with Italian forces in the area." [10]

The parachute elements of the 505th RCT were flown from Kairouan to Sicily on September 5, to prepare for the coming operation. They were bivouacked at three airfields—Regimental Headquarters and Headquarters Company and the 3rd Battalion at Castelvetrano, the 2nd Battalion at Comiso, and the 1st Battalion together with Company B, 307th Airborne Engineer Battalion, at Barizzo.

THE NEW ITALIAN GOVERNMENT, IN SECRET TALKS with General Eisenhower, had agreed to surrender and join the Allies, just prior to the amphibious landings at Salerno. The jump near Rome was part of an arrangement to protect the Italian government from German reprisals once the surrender was announced. The jump was dependent upon support from the Italian army to seize and hold airfields near Rome, provide transport for the 82nd Airborne Division once it arrived, and fight alongside the division until linkup with Allied forces occurred.

Ridgway was highly skeptical of the arrangement and obtained permission from Eisenhower to send General Maxwell Taylor secretly to meet with the Italian government in Rome, to determine the commitment and capability to hold up their end of the deal. Just before the operation was scheduled to commence, Taylor sent a coded message that the Italians couldn't provide logistical support, nor security for the airfields, so Operation Giant II was cancelled.

Like everyone in the division, Lieutenant Colonel Alexander was relieved when he learned that the mission was cancelled. "Several of us knowing the background, by this time had no confidence in the airborne planners at Fifth Army. It would have been a suicide operation with three German armored divisions within twenty miles of Rome." [11]

With Giant II cancelled, the 82nd wasted no time in getting in whatever training they could before their next operation. The 505th's new S-3, Captain Jack Norton, was assigned to get the three newly formed pathfinder teams organized, trained, and prepared at the airfield at Agrigento, Sicily. Norton spent the next week "further familiarizing the teams with the equipment: nomenclature, operation, and method of wearing same. Men actually became proficient at setting up the equipment blindfolded in a few minutes.

"Each [Eureka] set weighed about fifty-one pounds fitted into a compact container known as a leg pack, jumped on one man. Two men were required to work each set: one to jump with the equipment, and the other to assist in setting up and provide a safety factor for operation." [12]

At 3:30 a.m. on September 9, the U.S. Fifth Army, under General Mark Clark, began amphibious landings in the Bay of Salerno. Initially the landings were successful, but large numbers of German reinforcements arrived over the next several days to oppose the Allied force. At dawn on September 12, the Germans launched a massive counterattack, supported by armor, which succeeded in breaking through the lines of the U.S. 36th and 45th Infantry Divisions. The following day, the Germans continued their assault, threatening to drive all the way to the beaches. General Clark desperately sent a message to General Ridgway, asking for help to save the beachhead from being overrun. That night, the 504th RCT, less the 3rd Battalion, took off from airfields in Sicily and dropped inside Americans lines at the beachhead near Paestum.

The following night, September 14, the parachute elements of the 505th RCT prepared to take off to further reinforce the beachhead, also jumping near Paestum. Three C-47 aircraft would carry the 505th pathfinder team ahead of the main force. The first plane's stick would consist of Colonel Gavin, jumpmaster; Lieutenant Colonel Charles Billingslea, pathfinder commander; Lieutenant Albert Konar, 505th team leader with the Eureka set; Corporal George F. Huston, assistant Eureka operator; Corporal Joseph Fitzgerald, Regimental Headquarters Company; two men equipped with flashlights to mark the drop zone if needed; and two riflemen with Company B, 307th Airborne Engineer Battalion.

The jumpmaster of the second plane was Lieutenant Patrick D. Mulcahy; Technician Fifth Grade Jerry Huth, Eureka operator; Corporal Leo T. Girodo, assistant Eureka operator, all with Regimental Headquarters Company; and the same light and security teams as in the first plane. Huth was carrying the backup Eureka. "Both of us were wearing our separate systems strapped to our left legs in quick release leg bags, so that the system would not be separated from the operator, and the weight of the system hitting the ground twenty feet before we did would relieve us of the additional body shock.

"Strict instructions had been given, and thermite grenades were [to be] jumped to insure that if there was a question of capture, we were to melt the system so that no one would be able to identify it." [13]

Captain Jack Norton was the jumpmaster on the third plane. His stick included Lieutenant Claiborne Cooperider, with Service Company, in charge of the light teams, along with the same light and security teams as the other two planes.

At 9:00 p.m., Norton climbed aboard his plane, and a short time later it began rolling down the runway at the Agrigento airfield. Norton felt the nose lift up, then the wheels, as the plane became airborne. "Our planes flew in a close 'V' formation at an altitude from six thousand to seven thousand feet along the prescribed course until a few miles off the coast of Italy. It was evident at the time that the navigation of the lead plane would largely govern the results of the pathfinder work. We crossed the coastline at about one thousand feet and jumped at seven hundred feet. There wasn't any wind. The chutes came straight down near the center of the DZ. Groups assembled without difficulty and without casualty. In three minutes Lieutenant

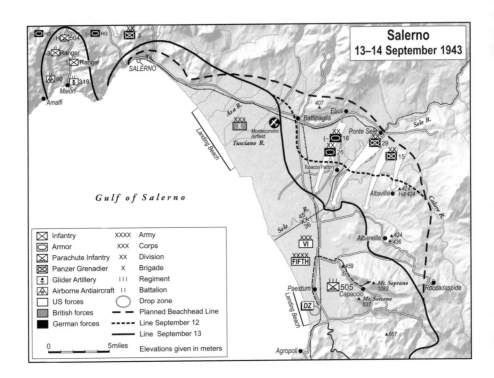

Konar's set was in operation. Corporal [T/5] Huth, standing by, had his set ready for operation. The flashlights were not needed, as the gasoline sand fire signals were operating in good order." 14

The thirty-six planes carrying the 3rd Battalion took off late at 10:40 p.m. from Castelvetrano, Sicily. The nine planes of the Regimental Headquarters and Headquarters Company serial followed the 3rd Battalion, leaving from Castelvetrano. The thirty-six-plane 2nd Battalion serial was airborne at 11:20 p.m. from Comiso, Sicily, while nine planes transporting Company B, 307th Airborne Engineer Battalion, left the airfield at Barizzo, Sicily, at 11:30 p.m. The 1st Battalion serial of thirty-six C-47s was the last serial, lifting off at 1:00 a.m. from Barizzo.

At 1:10 a.m. the 3rd Battalion serial appeared over the drop zone near Paestum. Sergeant Bill Blank, with Company G, was concerned that if they were misdropped, it could be far deadlier than in Sicily. "At the briefing, we were warned that jumping too soon would land us in the sea and too late would land us in among the Germans. Our flight was proceeding without difficulty until we approached the DZ. When the red light came on, we stood in the door, ready to go. The red light went out, and the plane went into a steep climb, and it seemed we flew for several minutes before we got the green light and jumped. As we came down, we could see all of these foxholes—we were certain we were among the Germans. After crawling around for a while, we found they were abandoned foxholes, so we gathered up our equipment and moved out to find the rest of the company. No resistance was met on the drop zone." [15]

The Regimental Headquarters and Headquarters Company serial jumped ten minutes later at 1:20 a.m., and the 2nd Battalion at 1:30 a.m. Company D radioman, Technician Fourth Grade Allan Barger, stepped into the darkness, a couple of seconds later felt the opening shock of his parachute deploying, checked his canopy, and then looked down to see what was below him. "We couldn't miss the drop zone this time, as it was lit up by a fiery cross burning in its center." [16]

Company B, 307th Airborne Engineer Battalion, jumped at 1:40 a.m., and the 1st Battalion at 2:55 a.m. One plane, carrying jumpmaster Lieutenant Jack Tallerday's stick of Company C troopers, had an engine hit by antiaircraft fire. The paratroopers and the C-47's crew all bailed out safely and landed in the British zone, near the town of Battipaglia. Because of a problem, two other planes never took off, and four others became separated from their formations and returned to Sicily with their paratroopers still aboard.

The work of the pathfinder teams had paid huge dividends. Captain Norton couldn't have asked for a better operation. "The battalion jump patterns were extremely small, and all personnel and equipment were assembled in a remarkably short period of time . . . no battalion taking more than sixty minutes to assemble. Jump casualties were extremely light.

"The marking of the DZ was satisfactory from the standpoint of results achieved and the situation of jumping behind our own lines. It is believed, however, that under normal circumstances krypton lights or Aldis lamps would be more practical from the security viewpoint. Smoke pots as used consisted of gasoline and sand, and threw off a considerable flame.

"Plane recognition was accomplished with amber lights on the underside of the wings. The lights were easily visible from the ground. Plane formations flew directly over friendly ships in the harbor at Paestum, and also over shore installations. Previous instructions with the additional aid of amber recognition lights were most necessary and no doubt helped prevent a reoccurrence of the disaster that had met the second lift in the Sicilian operation two months previous." [17]

After the regiment assembled, it was transported by truck to the Mount Soprano area, where it dug in and was placed in corps reserve behind the frontline. The 1st Battalion took part in screening the right flank of an attack by the 1st and 2nd Battalions, 504th PIR, on the night of September 16–17, to capture the towns of Albanella and Altavilla, along with three hills that dominated the area east of the beachhead. The regiment spent the next ten days in reserve.

The 505th PIR and Company B, 307th Airborne Engineer Battalion, were moved by truck to the beach at Paestum on the afternoon of September 27. The 3rd Battalion was moved by LCI (landing craft infantry) from Paetsum to Maiori and then trucked to the Chiunzi Pass area. There, the battalion dismounted and moved through the frontline positions of the Rangers and the 504th shortly before nightfall to secure a highway tunnel during a driving rainstorm. The rest of the 505th RCT moved by LCI to Maiori on September 28, and the following day by truck to catch the 3rd Battalion. On the morning of September 28, the 3rd Battalion began a push through the mountains toward the open plain south of Naples, twenty miles to the northwest. The next morning, with the 3rd Battalion in the lead, the division moved across the plains toward Naples, fighting German rear-guard actions and occupying Castellammare di Stabia that evening.

The 3rd Battalion continued to lead the swift advance past Pompeii and Mount Vesuvius the following day against token resistance. That evening, the regiment was attached to the British 23rd Armoured Brigade for the final push into Naples the next day.

On October 1, the 505th approached the outskirts of Naples, where it halted, while elements of the British 23rd Armoured Brigade made a reconnaissance of the city. After an order was passed to the city's police chief to clear the streets, Gavin led the way into Naples in a jeep to act as a guide for the column, followed by Generals Clark and Ridgway riding in a half-track, with the 3rd Battalion in trucks following immediately behind.

As the 3rd Battalion drove into the city, Sergeant Bill Blank, with Company G, could hear firing in the distance. "We moved into Naples without too much difficulty and set up a defensive perimeter at Garibaldi Square. We closed off the square to prevent a congregation of civilians. There was spasmodic shooting from the rooftops by what the civilians said were diehard Fascists. Thousands of people came to the square. Most of them had weapons, which they promptly turned in. We broke the rifles in half and made a pile of them.

"The town was pretty much destroyed, including the public water system and everything useful. This was done by the Germans on their way out of town. G Company spent the night in a bombed out railroad station. The next day we moved to a bombed out theater where we were organized into patrol groups. My group was assigned to the area near the docks, which by this time was beginning to unload supplies. Our biggest problem was controlling the bread lines at bakeries, where there was a limited amount of bread being produced due to the limited supplies." [18]

Shortly after entering Naples, Major Ed "Cannonball" Krause, commanding officer of the 3rd Battalion, took an American flag he carried with him to the post office, where on behalf of the 82nd Airborne Division he raised the Stars and Stripes over the first major city liberated in Europe. A couple of hours later, Krause was told that the Germans were planning to blow up a reservoir that supplied much of the city's drinking water. Krause ordered Lieutenant Harvey J. Zeigler, the Company H executive officer, to take a platoon and move to the reservoir without delay. Zeigler and his men found the reservoir already destroyed, but local citizens told him of another reservoir close by, which they found to be intact. Zeigler immediately deployed his platoon to guard the reservoir.

A short time later, Zeigler received word from other local citizens that German engineers had mined a bridge on the only road leading north out of Naples. Taking four troopers with him, Zeigler moved two miles through an area not yet cleared of the enemy and found the bridge, guarded by a few Germans and a Mark IV tank. His small group drove off the enemy force and the tank and established a defensive perimeter on the far side. Zeigler sent one man to get help from the 307th Airborne Engineer Battalion, and held their small bridgehead during the night while the engineers removed the demolition charge wired to the bridge supports, thus saving it.

During the regiment's occupation of Naples, Major Ben Vandervoort heard about an incident that would become a cartoon by Bill Mauldin in *Stars and Stripes*. "When we jumped into Salerno in September 1943, our jump boots were wearing out. There were no replacements because the boots, issued exclusively to the airborne, were being short-stopped in the supply lines. In Naples, the 3rd Battalion, 505, was billeted near the harbor docks. In those days, parachute boots were as sacred to the paratroopers as their wings. Quartermaster Corps longshoremen and Supply Corps officers showed up wearing shiny new jump boots. That did it! The 3rd Battalion troopers took the boots off their 'chairborne' feet and left them . . . without any shoes. Outraged, officers in their stocking feet stormed into the battalion command post. The only sympathy they got there was an interrogation by the battalion duty officer. 'Where did you get your jump boots?' In the rear echelons, the word went around: If you weren't jump qualified, don't take your boots to town. The flow of parachute boots to the 82nd Airborne began immediately." [19]

On the morning of October 4, Colonel Gavin received an order attaching the regiment to the British 23rd Armoured Brigade. Leaving the 3rd Battalion to occupy the regiment's sector in Naples, Gavin dispatched the 2nd Battalion immediately and gave an order for the 1st Battalion to be ready to move out the following morning. Lieutenant Colonel Alexander moved his battalion to the Capuccini airfield, where it loaded onto British trucks and was driven to an area south of the town of Villa Literno. "We arrived at about 1800 hours with the mission to drive to the Volturno River, about fifteen miles to the northwest, to save five canal bridges in route to the Volturno River and the village of Arnone on the southwest bank of the river. The bridges were essential to the movement of the armored brigade and eventual crossing of the Volturno River.

"Rather than wait until morning, I directed two platoons of about twenty-four men each to move out as fast as possible in the dark to take the first two bridges. Each platoon had a light machine gun and a bazooka team. The battalion followed in column on both sides of the road." [20]

The 2nd Platoon of Company F, followed by the 1st Platoon, led the battalion as it approached the first canal bridge, which it took without incident. Private Spencer F. Wurst and the 3rd Platoon were following the two lead platoons toward the second bridge. Wurst had been busted from sergeant to private in Sicily, when somebody tossed an empty wine bottle into his slit trench while he was away, and the commanding officer assumed Wurst had drunk the wine. "As Company F approached the bridge towards midnight, the point discovered it was already partially destroyed. Suddenly, two, or maybe three, German machine guns took us under fire from across the canal. It wasn't a split second before we were all in the ditch with tracers whizzing two or three feet over us. Fortunately for us, they were shooting high. Their guns were close, positioned forward, from twenty-five to fifty yards off to the left and right of the road, and they really poured it onto us." [21]

Lieutenant Colonel Alexander was walking along the road with the battalion, just behind Company F. "The leading platoons had alerted the Germans as we heard fire fighting ahead of us. As we marched along on this very dark night the Germans let loose on the battalion, with tracer machine gun fire skipping down the concrete road ahead of us. Of course, both columns of men on both sides of the road took a dive into the ditches on the roadside. It was so dark that we did not know there was a five-foot concrete ditch on the right side of the road. First, I heard thuds and banging as the men on the right side of the road hit the concrete bottom; then moans and curses. When daylight came I could see cut and bruised faces from the dive to the bottom of the concrete-lined ditch on the right." [22]

Up ahead, the German machine gun fire ceased and Company F moved forward in the dark. Private Wurst was told that the company was going to dig in for the night and continue the attack at dawn. "The 2nd Platoon, on point, dug in on the south side of the bridge. The 1st and 3rd Platoons went into all-around circular positions and dug in, the 1st Platoon moving off to the left of the road, and the 3rd Platoon, which was mine, moving to the right a couple hundred yards. Sergeant [John W.] Gore ordered us to string out and dig individual foxholes. I was critical of this because I thought we should pair off. Soldiers performed much better when they had someone with them, and in two-man fighting positions, we could also take turns sleeping. But that night, no one got any sleep; we all remained 100 percent alert, waiting to attack at first light.

"At the break of dawn on October 5, a tremendous firefight broke out in the 2nd Platoon's area, close to the road, by the bridge. The canal was about twenty feet across, and the Germans were still in position on the other side, or had moved back in undetected through the night. Our platoon was close enough to hear the fight, but not close enough to participate in it. The 2nd Platoon lost a number of men, and so did the Germans, who didn't hold us up too long." [23]

Early on October 5, the 1st Battalion was trucked from Naples to Villa Literno, where it dismounted and moved up to cover the flanks and rear of the 2nd Battalion. At 5:30 a.m., Company D took over the attack and moved north on the road to Arnone and the third canal bridge. Company D moved about 300 yards before strong enemy forces positioned to its left front held up the attack. Company E was brought up on the left flank of Company D and advanced toward the German positions. Sergeant Victor M. Schmidt expected the Germans to open up on Company E at any moment. "The terrain ahead of us was flat farmland with a canal alongside the gravel road, and we were walking in a staggered column. About two miles in the distance, a ridge of hills rose up sharply from the plain. We could see a few buildings with our binoculars.

"When we came within about one and a half miles of these buildings, the Germans opened up at us in a steady crossfire with their machine guns. All of us immediately jumped down into the canal, which had a gentle slope, so we didn't have to wade in the water, and it made good cover.

"The Germans had placed barbed wire across this canal about every one hundred feet, so that we had to come out of the canal on the run, jump around the wire and back into the canal again to escape getting hit. In addition to this barbed wire, they had laid some [Teller] mine booby traps along the canal.

"At the head of the column was the 1st Platoon, then 2nd Platoon, and then 3rd. I was with 2nd Platoon, with the mortar squad. When word was passed from the head of the column that I was wanted up front immediately, I assumed that they had captured some Germans and wanted me to question them. (I spoke a little German.)

"I was moving along at a fast trot, passing the guys coming up from the canal to get around the barbed wire, and word came back to watch for this booby trap across our path. I saw the wire across the path about twenty feet away, in front of a trooper named [Private First Class Louis H.] Garrett. I shouted out to him to look out for it. I don't know why, but he turned around and looked at me as I was running toward him—at the same time, he tripped over the wire—it was about six inches above the ground, stretched across our path.

"As he did this, I was about ten feet from him. I dived to my right, toward the canal, and I was in the water when the mine exploded. For some reason, I was watching him as I jumped, and it was like slow motion. It blasted him into the air and I saw a piece of shrapnel tear away about an inch and a half of his face—from behind his right ear, through his hair, and across his chest.

"He fell along the canal embankment on his face. By this time, I had landed headfirst down the embankment, too. I started to get up, but my left foot felt as if someone had run a red hot poker through it. I could see a hole in the top of my boot, with blood running from it.

"I got on my hands and knees to get to Garrett, but by this time our company medic, [Private First Class Clyde F.] Knox, had come up to help me. I told him to take care of Garrett first, as he was badly hurt. While he was occupied with Garrett, I pulled off my jump boot and found a clean hole in my foot. I wrapped a bandage around it and went to Garrett and the medic (Knox). I could see wounds all over Garrett, mostly on his back—he was really hurting.

"About an hour after Garrett and I were hit, a jeep with stretchers came and took us to first aid. From there, we went by ambulance to the hospital in Naples. Garrett died later [November 21, 1943]. His liver and other vital organs were saturated with shrapnel—he was about twenty years old." [24]

Company E continued to advance, forcing the Germans on the left flank to withdraw. Private Berge Avadanian, with the 2nd Battalion S-2 section, up front with the rifle companies, caught a ride on a jeep driven by Lieutenant Richard M.

Janney, with Regimental Headquarters Company, to deliver intelligence information to the battalion command post. "There were three of us, including one wounded. Our communications corporal, Francis August of Worcester, Massachusetts, pleaded for a ride on the jeep—he needed more wire. I gave him my passenger side seat, while I mounted the rear spare tire.

"That jeep didn't get fifty feet—it was blown up by a Teller mine—all three were killed. I was the lucky one on the spare tire, who was uninjured. August lay ten feet from me—dead—he saved my life by hitching that ride." [25]

Lieutenant Colonel Alexander kept his battalion moving rapidly toward the third bridge. "The Germans had blown about half of the bridge, but other than for intermittent German machine gun fire from a farmhouse about one hundred yards to the right, we could cross between bursts of fire, and I led my men across. About this time D Company, which I had moving parallel to the road about one hundred yards to our right flank, took the farmhouse and silenced the machine gun.

"Ahead of us about one-third mile, I could see Germans retreating north on the road. I brought forward an 81mm mortar, and they had a good shoot, very accurate, as they could see their targets. The Germans moved out fast ahead of us and left a horse-drawn wagonload of ammunition and guns, plus a 35mm antitank gun. We drove forward rapidly, took the fourth and fifth canal bridges, and set down for the night to attacking the village of Arnone and the railroad yard the next morning.

"A Company of the 1st Battalion under command of Captain Ed Sayre had been attached to my 2nd Battalion in our advance. Captain Sayre had tripped a wired mine and was severely injured. A Company was still held back in reserve.

"The last three miles of our drive we had straddled the road, with the railroad running along parallel and about one hundred yards to our left; the railroad and road converging at Arnone." [26]

Lieutenant Colonel Alexander's plan of attack for the morning of October 6, was for Company E, led by Captain Talton W. "Woody" Long, to capture the railroad yard; Company F, led by Captain Neal McRoberts, to seize the village of Arnone; Company D to screen the right flank of the attack; and with Company A in reserve.

The 1st and 2nd Platoons of Company F, together with the light machine gun platoon and 81mm mortar platoon of Headquarters Company, 2nd Battalion, moved into the town unopposed, except for harassing artillery fire coming from across the Volturno River. Arnone was situated between two bends in the river, which prevented friendly forces from securing the flanks of any force occupying the village. To secure the flanks, Company F was ordered to put a platoon across the river to establish a bridgehead. The 1st Platoon, Company F, moved out of the village, crossed a levee, and prepared to cross the river. Private First Class Russ Brown was a member of the 1st Platoon's 60mm mortar squad. "The 1st Platoon was about to try to cross the Volturno River, but was met with heavy machine gun and small arms fire." [27]

The 1st Platoon was ordered to withdraw over the dike and move back into the town. Just as they crossed the dike going back into the town, Private First Class Daryle

Whitfield heard the unmistakable sound of a mortar firing in the distance. "We hit the ground and the shell landed up in town. We got up and starting moving a little further, and they fired again. We hit the ground again, and [the shell] hit down next to the river. After it went off, we got up and started to move again, and they fired another round. That time, when we hit the ground, the shell landed right in the middle of a boy's back, about ten or twelve feet behind me. It killed him [Private First Class Frank J. Nowinski] [and] wounded me, Sergeant [Arthur L.] Gregory, and another guy. It hit me in my right hip, my left leg, my neck had a big chunk of steel in it, and all up and down my back. My neck was burning so, that I hollered for the medic. When he got to me, I asked him to get that piece of metal out of my neck. I was lying on my stomach, and he had his knee on my shoulder and one on my hip. He grabbed that piece of metal and it burned his hand, so he got his handkerchief out and wrapped it up and tried to pull it out. He said, 'I can't get it out.'

"I said, 'Man, you've got to get it out—it's burning the hell out of me.' He finally managed to jerk it, and it came out." [28]

As they were getting shelled, Private First Class Brown and his mortar squad quickly set up and started returning fire. "For every round we fired, we got many [fired] back.

"I saw Ed Slavin and three other troopers tear out a door [and] use it for a stretcher for [Private] Francis Malay, who later died." [29]

As the enemy artillery and mortar fire from across the river subsided, a company of German infantry attacked the town from the west, supported by a battalion firing from the north side of the river. The 3rd Platoon, which had not yet been committed, received orders to move to the left flank of the 1st and 2nd Platoons. Private Wurst and the platoon moved forward, taking advantage of whatever cover was available until they reached the town. "We passed through our company CP, a partially open, shed-like building that served as a collection point for the wounded and dead. We saw their bloodied bodies lying in the wide dirt courtyard as we passed.

"We deployed to the left of the company position, where it was reported that the Germans were attempting to counterattack. To do this, the enemy had to recross the Volturno River, and Company F's left flank was exposed.

Sergeant Gore broke down our location into individual areas, We were about to get some on-the-job training in how to fight in a built up area." [30]

As Company F was being attacked, Company E moved into the railroad yard to clear the enemy company from F Company's flank, with the 1st Platoon led by Lieutenant David L. Packard at the point. Sergeant Julius Axman was the acting platoon sergeant. "The 1st Platoon advanced to the railroad yard on the right bank, climbing the twelve-foot elevation to the yard's level. We had scouts out—[Private First Class Ben N.] Popilsky, [Private Thomas J.] Burke, and [Corporal Edward B.] Carpus; [Private Alvin E.] Hart was also a lead man. Lieutenant Packard led the main body up the right side. I was directly behind Lieutenant Packard. The 1st Platoon squad leader, Sergeant [Edward G.] Bartunek, was on the left flank, Corporal Carpus had the 1st Squad, but was also acting as scout.

"When we reached the rear of the second railroad car, the Krauts opened up on us from both sides and the front. We all hit the dirt, and when I looked up, Lieutenant Packard was in a standing position and firing his Thompson. I yelled for him to get down, which he did. He gave me an order to take five men and circle around to the left; the fire was intense as I moved to the rear." [31]

As the Germans hit the point of the platoon from three sides, Corporal Carpus glanced over as the two scouts, "Ben Popilsky and Tom Burke dashed to my right." Carpus then heard Packard say something like, "'Let me get them!' He stepped out to the front of a car and took a burst of burp gun fire. As he fell he said to me, 'Put me under the car!' No luck, he was already dead." [32]

As the burst hit Lieutenant Packard, Private Earl W. Boling dove for cover between a set of tracks. "As I hit the dirt I called, 'Medic!' to try to get medical aid for the lieutenant. As I was lying between the rails of one set of tracks, I rolled over to get between two sets of tracks where I was not quite as exposed to enemy fire. Every time I attempted to move I was coming under automatic weapons fire, with tracers and other bullets hitting the rails a few inches from my face. I finally spotted the gunner on a railroad signal tower and returned fire until he fell from the tower." [33]

Once behind cover, Private John Keller tried to figure out what to do next. "[Corporal] Jack Francis was in a shell hole about twenty feet northeast of where I was positioned. I could hear him trying to raise E Company to our rear. He was saying, 'E Company, can you hear me?!' and repeated it several times, then commented, 'Damn, the batteries must be dead!'" [34]

As Sergeant Axman and five men began moving toward the rear to hit the flank of the Germans, he ran into the assistant platoon leader, who ordered him to cover the right flank instead. "We were quite fortunate to have a little cover, as railroad ties were piled up along the bank about twelve inches high in places. I crawled to a position where I could observe a bunker and alternate positions where heavy fire was coming from. Captain Long and the rest of the company were completely cut off from us." [35]

Sergeant Otis Sampson and his mortar squad were bringing up the rear of the 1st Platoon column, hauling their 60mm mortar and heavy load of ammunition. "The sound of machine gun and rifle fire broke out forward of us; freight cars obstructed our view. I brought the squad to a halt and gave the signal to 'Get down!'

"'Nothing unusual about running into opposition . . . knock it out and continue on,' were my thoughts as I lazily lay there taking advantage of the rest.

"[Private] Jack Hill, Captain Long's runner, came running around the back of a freight car that sat just to the left of us. There was a serious expression on his face as he said, 'Hey, Sarge, Lieutenant Packard has been killed and the platoon is pinned down! And nothing is being done!'

"My first thought, 'I've got to get to the front!'

"Turning to [Private First Class Harry G.] Pickels, I said, 'Take over!'

"'Let's get the hell up front. Jack, lead the way!'

"Hill took off at a run and I followed. We worked our way to the left of the yard and ended up at the left front of a freight car. Dense foliage was on our left. 'Jerry' was in control, and I knew something had to be done and fast.

"'Cover my back!' I quickly said to Hill, and I saw his long legs take off for the rear to position himself.

"'If I can only hold them up long enough for the platoon to get organized,' I thought, and dashed forward, well out in front along the tracks that were barren of cars, and went down firing at two helmeted Germans that were sighting in on me. The bullets were whizzing by. . . . My helmet interfered with my sighting. With one sweep of my right hand I knocked it off. I tried my best to get one or two shots off at a time to save ammunition and to have more control of the Tommy [gun]. . . .

"I know I wasn't short on targets as I silenced one gun after another. I was getting very tired; the sweat was rolling off of me." 36

During a lull in the firing, Sampson quickly moved behind an embankment to his left, near a switch box. "A burst of burp gun fire shattered the branches just forward of my head. I had moved too close to the top edge of the bank, which was clear of foliage from where I lay to about a hundred feet up the tracks. I had encountered some opposition from that forward growth; a machine gun, that had the open [rail] yard for its field of fire. I did think at the time, if it was the one we had been warned about, it was on the left. About a five-foot bank ran at left angle to the higher railroad yard and continued on out into the flat lands for a couple of hundred yards or more, starting just forward of me. I saw the heads and shoulders of two helmeted soldiers using the bank's top to support their machine pistols. I was zeroed in at a range of about fifty feet at eleven o'clock. Picking the one on the right, I figured he was the one that had missed me. I knew I wouldn't have a second chance, and I made sure of my first; his face just disappeared. On his right, the soldier had ducked down, but came right back up and got the first burst in, which again just cleared my head. A couple of quick shots and he too picked up some .45 slugs; his face just disappeared too. A third one appeared just to the right side of the last—a quick burst sent him to the protection of the bank; I doubted if I had hit him." 37

Sampson ducked down behind the embankment and quickly did an ammo check. "I checked my inserted clip to see if I had enough rounds in it for another possible shoot-out. I counted eight, and reached for another [clip]. There wasn't any! Frantically, I searched, with the thought, 'I couldn't be out of them!' I scanned the area thinking, 'I must have lost them in the commotion I had gone through,' but I saw no full ones. . . . A feeling of panic seized me. . . . I had gone through most all of my ammunition; I must have been fighting longer than I thought. Time had stood still.

"I hadn't thought of myself. I just happened to be in the right place at the right time; the enemy's control over the front had to be stopped. . . . How I accomplished the job is simple. I just wasn't hit. Now I had little to fight back with if more Jerries popped up. I was licked. . . . I needed help! 'Mortar fire!' I yelled, repeating the command and giving the short range and direction to get mortar fire behind that bank.

"A Jerry crawled the near bank and tried to take me out with a concussion grenade. It landed a little to my right rear. I glanced its way when it hit and saw a funnel-shaped form shoot upward from the explosion. Just glad it had not been a potato masher.

"Like a prayer answered from heaven, a mortar shell exploded about twenty feet back of the bank where the two Germans had been killed—a perfect round. I looked around, amazed at the short time it took to put the mortar in action. The sight that met my eyes will go to my grave with me, for there was [Corporal] Pickels and [Private Roy L.] Watts right out in the open at about four o'clock from where I lay, facing north with the side of the freight car for a background. Pickels had a squinted face as he sighted in the M4 sights with a look of expecting to feel the impact of bullets. But it didn't interfere with the work cut out for him. Watts sat on the ground, his legs crossed under him to the right of the mortar, a shell in hand, ready to feed another to the tube as soon as he received the command. The mortar tube looked almost vertical; utility wires dominated the area above. It was a worry that some may be hit. I felt proud of those two men. I did not intend for them to come forward as they did, but to set up in a protected position. They knew there was only one way to get the job done quickly. My voice must have told them I was in trouble. They were willing to sacrifice their lives to help me and the rest of the platoon when help was so badly needed. . . .

"A large German soldier, in a lumbering run, tried to escape to the rear of the five-foot bank to get away from the bursting shells. Carefully I took aim to be sure of preserving my precious last rounds. I let one off—as if hit in the head by a sledgehammer, he went down. I put another one into him to be sure. Another tried his luck, but with the same results. A third started, but changed his mind, knowing the fate of the first two. They were trying for the protective coverage of the foliage to their rear along the railroad bank.

"I had but a few rounds left when [Private] John Burdge came running up from the rear between a freight car and the foliage, his long BAR in his hands.

"'Where are they?' he excitedly asked, ready to do battle.

"'Set up your rifle here,' I said, picking out a suitable spot forward of the switch box, 'one will be coming out at the end of that bank.'

"'Are you sure?' he asked, after a short wait.

"'Yes, I'm quite sure. He knows he will be picked off if he tries it from here; he will be coming out soon.' I encouraged him.

"I recalled the scared look in the eyes of the third man as they met mine when he returned to the safety of the bank. One more step or two before turning back and he too, would have died with his buddies. I figured he would use the protection of the bank until he came to its end and then try again for the rear and seek the heavy brush farther back on the railroad bank.

"As I predicted, he came out at its end and started his run, only he had not figured on a BAR coming into the picture. (The small arms weapon most feared by the Germans, on account of its accuracy.)

"'Take your time and squeeze it off—no hurry,' I softly said. 'The first shot kicked up a little dirt [near] his heels.'

"I coached, as if we were back on a firing range in the States. Burdge fired his second shot and the German lunged forward and down.

"'Good shot!' I commanded, 'Throw another shot into him just to be sure.'" 38

Sergeant Sampson had been instrumental in knocking out several German positions on the left or west side of the railroad yard. Private Tom Burke had crawled between the railroad tracks under intense automatic weapons fire and had killed a German machine gun crew with grenades. Individual acts such as these turned the tide. Finally, Corporal Jack Francis got the radio working again. "I was trying to get Captain Long on the radio to relay a range for the British artillery that was backing us up." 39

Captain Long received the call for help from his 1st Platoon. "I was south of the railroad station and east of the railroad a bit. I double-timed the reserve platoon (2nd Platoon) up to the railroad station. I jumped a ditch, moving to the east a little to use the station building as cover. [Private] Dave Comly, a runner, who was second behind me, was hit while in the air jumping the ditch; his death was instant. I always thought the shot came from a sniper in the station building." 40

Sergeant Sampson was still near the embankment west of the railroad tracks when the 2nd Platoon arrived. "I heard [Private Dennis] O'Loughlin's voice behind me.

"'Do you want some mortar fire up there?'

"Looking back down I saw him, loaded down with the mortar and a bag of ammunition, not counting the rest of his equipment.

"'Where in the hell did you come from?' I asked, wondering at the time what a 2nd Platoon man was doing up with the 1st.

"'Captain Long sent me up. I've lost my men and the lieutenant trying to get through, but I've got the mortar and some ammunition.'

"'Yes, let's give them a few rounds.'

"O'Loughlin's mortar fire itself helped to keep Jerry held down. He was set up at the bottom of the V-shaped ditch just to my rear. . . .

"O'Loughlin was a good man to have around, cool and steady. It was the first time I had worked with him in action—it wouldn't be the last." 41

After being pinned down for a short time, Captain Long arrived with the rest of the 2nd Platoon. "I next recall being up in the station area and to the left (west) of some railroad cars. There was some machine gun and rifle fire coming from the left front—it seemed to be coming from a grown-up area of foliage just west of the railroad tracks. I recall calling for artillery fire and trying to adjust by reference to pre-designated concentrations. I don't think the salvo did much good except scare them off. I know I was pretty upset when I was told that we had used up our allocation." 42

However, the short British artillery barrage had forced the German company in the railroad yard and west of Arnone to withdraw across the river over a footbridge that was still intact.

As darkness closed in, Lieutenant Colonel Alexander left a few outposts in Arnone and the rail yard and pulled Companies E and F back to better defensive positions, anticipating a possible counterattack by the German battalion across the river. Alexander moved up Company A on the left flank of Company E and had them dig in for the night.

Alexander called back to his command post to get medical treatment for the wounded who had been evacuated from Arnone and the railroad yard. "We had twenty-four or twenty-five wounded and sheltered under a culvert, but no doctor. I got on the field telephone and told one of our doctors that we needed him at the forward aid station. He insisted that I should take [the wounded] back to him at the rear CP. I told him we had no transportation and also that the road had not been cleared of mines. [The doctor] argued, and I told him to come forward or I would come back there and kick his ass all the way forward.

"He did not arrive, so I headed back to the rear to get him. I looked down the road and there he comes, medical bag across his shoulder, a white bandage around his head (helmet on top), and limping. I said, 'What happened to you?'

"He said, 'You go to hell!' and continued to walk toward the forward aid station and the wounded.

"I said, 'O.K.' He was going in the right direction, so what more could I say?

"I went down the road a little farther and met Dr. Franco [another of the battalion's doctors] and asked him what happened. [Franco] said he was watching the ambulance head toward our forward positions when it hit a mine and blew up in the air, coming down in a pile of junk. He then said he ran to the site. He was standing there looking at what was left of the ambulance when a voice called out, 'Don't just stand there you dummy! Get me out from under here!' Franco said he pulled [the doctor] out, bandaged his head, and off he went, headed for the front. The ambulance driver had been killed." [43]

When Captain Franco saw the ambulance hit the mine, he could hardly believe anyone survived. "The visual effect was stupendous. The whole vehicle rose ten or twelve feet, a wheel leaving every few feet, reached the top of its rise, slowly turned over, and landed flat on its top." [44]

Captain George B. Wood, the regiment's Protestant chaplain, took a few volunteers with him the next morning and recovered the bodies of Lieutenant Packard and the others killed the previous day in Arnone and the railroad yard. That same morning, Lieutenant Colonel Alexander reported to General H. R. Arkwright, commander of the British 23rd Armoured Brigade, that the 505th had captured all five bridges, as ordered. That night, the regiment was relieved from attachment and trucked the following day back to Naples.

After the return to Naples, Lieutenant Theodore L. "Pete" Peterson took command of the 1st Platoon, Company E, replacing Lieutenant Packard, who had been killed in action. Captain Long was transferred to take command of Regimental Headquarters Company, and Captain Clyde Russell, the 2nd Battalion adjutant, took command of Company E. A lieutenant from regiment was assigned to command Company A, but he didn't work out; so Lieutenants Mike Chester and Harold Case effectively ran Company A.

In Naples on October 7, a powerful time bomb left behind a false wall in the main post office building by the retreating Germans exploded, killing or wounding upward of one hundred people, primarily civilians. The 307th Airborne Engineer Battalion immediately began searching for, finding, and disarming any other time bombs and booby traps.

The following Sunday morning, October 10, many of the troopers were sleeping late in various public buildings in Naples where they were been billeted. General Ridgway was attending a church service when he heard the sound of a huge explosion in the distance. Ridgway and his aide left the church and found the location of the explosion—an Italian army barracks housing Company B, 307th Airborne Engineer Battalion. "I will never forget the tragic sight. Arms and legs of American soldiers, killed in their sleep, were sticking pitifully out of the rubble on the second floor. We were never able to establish definitely whether some of the engineers' own demolitions went off by accident. I still believe, though, that it was the result of a German booby trap." [45]

Technician Fifth Grade Thomas C. Goins was asleep on the third floor of the building when it exploded. "I was buried under concrete and dust—bar steel all over me. I thought I was buried alive. After it settled down, I was still on the third floor—my bed, the only full bed left on the third floor. I was able to get out. I was in shock." [46]

Lieutenant James Rightley, the platoon leader of the 1st Platoon, Company B, 307th Airborne Engineer Battalion, was away from the barracks when it exploded. "I had been ordered to take some men and check out a building for explosives. We were doing this when the blast occurred. The 1st Platoon was hit hard by the explosion." [47] Although Rightley lost twenty-three of his men killed, three miraculously survived, though severely wounded.

Sergeant Frank M. Miale had lost many of his friends in the explosion. "The irony of it all was that some of the men were out looking for demolitions under other buildings, while ours was the one to suffer the fate that we wanted to prevent in others. The loss of these men can never be replaced, nor can the memory of the men who died there ever be forgotten by we who knew and cherished their friendship." [48]

CHAPTER 7

"A Scene I Would Carry With Me Always"

G eneral Ridgway conducted a ceremony to mark the promotion of Colonel Gavin to brigadier general and assistant division commander on the day of the explosion in the barracks of the 307th Airborne Engineer Battalion. General Eisenhower had assigned Brigadier General Maxwell Taylor, the temporary assistant division commander after the death of General Charles L. Keerans, Jr., the job of liaison with the Italian government. Gavin had officially received the promotion a few days earlier, October 5, 1943. "I hated to leave the 505th, since I had been through so much combat with it, but it would still be in the division with me. General Ridgway arranged for a brief star-pinning ceremony in front of the Questura, the city police station, which we had been using as headquarters." [1]

The executive officer, Lieutenant Colonel Herbert Batcheller, assumed command of the regiment, while Lieutenant Colonel Alexander, commanding officer of the 2nd Battalion, moved to regimental executive officer, and Major Benjamin H. Vandervoort took command of the 2nd Battalion.

IN MID-NOVEMBER 1943, GENERAL JIM GAVIN was temporarily detached from duty with the 82nd Airborne Division at the request of General Eisenhower, becoming the senior airborne advisor to the COSSAC (Chief Of Staff, Supreme Allied Command) organization, which was responsible for planning the cross-channel invasion of France. The code name for the invasion was Operation Overlord. Prior to Gavin's departure, Ridgway briefed him on the mission and assured him that he would be returned to the division in time to participate in the operation.

The 456th Parachute Field Artillery Battalion, less Batteries C and D, left North Africa on November 17, to join the 504th RCT for combat in Italy. Batteries C and D left by ship eleven days later to join the division.

On November 18, 1943, the division left Italy for an undisclosed destination, with the 505th PIR aboard the USS *Frederick Funston*, the 307th Airborne Engineer Battalion on board the USS *Joseph T. Dickman*, and the 80th Airborne Antiaircraft (Antitank) Battalion on the USS *Thomas Jefferson*.

Lieutenant Bob Fielder, who had transferred to Regimental Headquarters Company as assistant communications officer, found the *Frederick Funston*'s accommodations to his liking. "The ship was a large attack transport that carried the entire regiment and had its own landing barges. Bunkrooms were fairly spacious, heads and fresh water were numerous and functioned well. Mess halls were cafeteria style, with sit-down tables with probably the best food that the regiment had experienced since arriving overseas—but I had yellow jaundice, my skin was true to the name, and the sight of food made me nauseous. I stayed in a two-tiered bunk most of the time, watching everyone play innumerable card games.

"On November 22, the *Funston* dropped anchor in the Oran Harbor, Algeria, for a week while a convoy was assembled. I did manage to struggle to the mess hall for Thanksgiving, eating little or no food. We upped anchor on the 29, and on 1 December, with a lousy storm, queasy stomachs, and Axis Sally bidding us goodbye, we passed through the Strait of Gibraltar. Later, out in the Atlantic, there was the occasional sound of depth charges going off at night, causing the bulkhead to reverberate slightly. Down in the hold, it made me feel a little nervous.

"On December 9, we dropped anchor at Belfast, Northern Ireland, and were trucked east to Cookstown, some forty miles distant. After the barren, brown, hot countries of the Mediterranean, the green Emerald Isle was truly a paradise." [2]

After debarking, the 505th PIR was trucked to their new bivouac at Cookstown, while the 307th Airborne Engineer Battalion was billeted at Garvaugh; the 80th Airborne Antiaircraft (Antitank) Battalion was housed at Kilrea; Battery C, 456th Parachute Field Artillery Battalion, at Castle Dawson; and Battery D at Cookstown. The men and most of the officers were housed in Quonset huts.

To Lieutenant Ray Grossman, with Battery C, 456th PFA Battalion, Northern Ireland was the closest thing he had found to heaven since leaving the States. "They had whiskey, fish and chips, and people you could talk to. The mornings were cold and foggy up until two in the afternoon. We stayed in Quonset huts and tried to stay warm." [3]

Private Berge Avadanian, with the 2nd Battalion S-2 section, found Ireland delightful, despite the poor weather. "It was a wonderful, refreshing change—friendly people, happy children, pretty girls, passes, and dances at Ulster Hall in Belfast." [4]

As the regimental combat team's first Christmas overseas approached, many became homesick for their loved ones. Lieutenant Fielder and others celebrated Christmas by attending Protestant and Catholic church services. "Chaplain [Matthew J.] Connelly said midnight Mass in a decorated mess tent with Majors Frederick Kellam and James McGinity acting as altar boys." [5]

MANY NEW REPLACEMENTS JOINED THE REGIMENT in Northern Ireland. Like all officers, Lieutenant Jim Coyle, an assistant platoon leader with Company E, worked with the non-commissioned officers to integrate them. "Training them and the veterans in the company was restricted to road marches and athletics, because all of the open areas were planted farmland.

"We did travel to a range at Strawberry Hill, near Lough Neagh, where the men had an opportunity to 'zero in' their rifles and fire the company weapons, including machine guns and mortars. While there, we ran obstacle courses and dug foxholes, which we occupied while tanks were driven over us to prove it was safe. This made a change from our normal routine.

"The men were given three-day passes and furloughs while in [Northern] Ireland, and there was a problem in connection with men staying absent without leave. The AWOL rate took a sharp upward curve, due to the fact that the Irish girls were the first English-speaking females the men had seen in almost a year. [Captain] Clyde Russell, who had a very good sense of humor, called it 'Belfast Fever' and told the men at one formation that they weren't 'fighters,' they were 'lovers.'" 6

MEANWHILE, PREPARATIONS IN ENGLAND were ramping up for the coming cross-channel invasion. To replace the 504th PIR, which was still fighting at the Anzio beachhead in Italy, the 507th and 508th PIRs were attached to the division for the upcoming invasion of Normandy. The airborne plan was very aggressive—the 82nd Airborne Division would land near St.-Sauveur-le-Vicomte to cut the western side of the Cotentin Peninsula, while the 101st Airborne Division would land near Ste.-Marie-du-Mont and open the causeways behind Utah Beach. The beach-landed forces would then drive west across the peninsula to link up with the 82nd Airborne.

General Gavin was released from his duties as the senior airborne advisor to the COSSAC staff on February 6, 1944. Upon Gavin's return to the division, General Ridgway assigned him the responsibility for all 82nd Airborne parachute forces for the upcoming operation. Gavin immediately went to work preparing them for their missions. "I concentrated all my energies on planning, training the troops, and studying avidly the German defenses and the daily air photo coverage we were getting of our operational areas." 7

Regimental missions were assigned during February. The 505th would jump just west of St.-Sauveur-le-Vicomte, capture the town and the bridges over the Douve River, and send patrols to the south of Prairies Marécageuses. The 507th would land to the north of Hill 110 near Hills 71 and 82 and would defend against a German attack from the north. The 508th would drop astride Hill 110, consolidate its position, and move south and west to intercept German forces that would try to reinforce those on the Cotentin Peninsula.

On February 13, the 505th PIR moved by ship from Northern Ireland to Scotland and from there, boarded a troop train to their pre-invasion base, Camp Quorn, in the town of Quorndon, Leicestershire, England, near Loughborough. Batteries C and D, 456th Parachute Field Artillery Battalion, were billeted at Husbands Bosworth, south of the city of Leicester. The 80th Airborne Antiaircraft (Antitank) Battalion was quartered at Oadby, on the outskirts of Leicester, southeast of the city. The 307th Airborne Engineer Battalion was housed at Burbage, southwest of Leicester.

Like most troopers of the 505th PIR, Private Berge Avadanian absolutely enjoyed the regiment's new surroundings—"loved the people, passes to Leicester, Sunday chicken dinners, the pubs, and the Red Cross Club.

"We began our first days with bad trouble with our black American servicemen, who were well established with white girls at the Red Cross Club. After several serious fights, higher command was forced to detour blacks away from airborne unit towns." 8

Private First Class Turk Seelye, with Company E, found the tents crowded and poorly heated, but otherwise enjoyed the time spent off duty. "The free time was devoted to playing darts, playing cards and dice, and drinking beer in the pubs, like the Pig and Whistle." 9

On February 20, Major Wagner J. D'Alessio was promoted to lieutenant colonel and took command of Batteries C and D of the 456th Parachute Field Artillery Battalion. Lieutenant Harold R. Thain was Battery D's executive officer. "Quite suddenly one day, we junior officers learned that Colonel Harden had been relieved and replaced by Colonel D'Alessio—rumors 'why' abounded." 10

Under Lieutenant Colonel D'Alessio, the 456th Parachute Field Artillery Battalion immediately began to reconstitute the full battalion around a cadre from the two existing batteries. Most of the personnel from Battery D became cadre for Battery B, under the command of Thain's brother, Captain Carl E. Thain. Lieutenant Harold Thain admitted that serving as the executive officer in a battery that his brother commanded "was a rather sticky arrangement, but we remained friends. We had many new replacements, just arrived from the States, but a cadre of seasoned NCOs, particularly sergeants. We did intensive gun drill, and finally qualified by division artillery as a firing battery, at a live firing range on the moors near Birmingham. Carl moved to battalion S-3, promoted to major, and I became Battery B CO, promoted to captain." 11

Over the next several months, the ranks of the regimental combat team were brought up to strength as veterans returned from hospitals. Returning officers filled vacancies for which they were qualified. The commanding officer of the 1st Battalion, Major Walter Winton, re-injured his leg and was transferred to division, replaced by Major Frederick C. A. Kellam. Captain James E. McGinity, the commanding officer of Company G, was promoted to major and assigned as executive officer of the 1st Battalion. Upon his return after being hospitalized for pneumonia, the regimental adjutant, Captain Bill Follmer, was assigned to command Company G. Captain Bob Piper took Follmer's job as regimental adjutant. Captain Harold H. "Swede" Swingler, released from the hospital, took command of Company I. Lieutenant John J. "Red" Dolan was transferred from Company I to command Company A.

More replacements arrived during late February and March, and the veterans for the most part welcomed them and helped them integrate into their assigned units. Private Gordon Pryne was assigned to Company A. "They were a great bunch—I knew when I got there, right away. The officers were all swell. Everybody was great. The company commander [Lieutenant] Dolan called me in and talked to me. He asked me what training I had had. He was nice guy.

"My sergeant was Oscar Queen, from Texas; he was a good sergeant." 12

As the training began in earnest, it soon became apparent that Lieutenant Colonel Herbert Batcheller was not the right officer to command the regiment. Lieutenant Bob Fielder was at the regimental command post during a large field exercise when General Gavin walked in unannounced. "I was close enough to hear him ask questions about the disposition of the regiment's three battalions. Batcheller really didn't know." [13]

On March 21, Batcheller was relieved and sent to the 508th to command the 1st Battalion. The next day, Lieutenant Colonel William E. Ekman, the executive officer of the 508th, took command of the 505th.

Captain Robert M. Piper, the regimental adjutant, would later learn that Colonel Ekman "came from a relatively poor family in St. Louis; his father had been a strong man in a circus. He wanted to go to West Point, and he got there by enlisting in the army and through competitive exams, received an appointment to 'The Point.'" [14]

Ekman certainly had his work cut out for him. Batcheller had allowed discipline to decline while the regiment was in Northern Ireland. Now it would be up to an officer who hadn't yet seen combat and was new to the regiment to restore discipline among the tough combat veterans.

Ekman assembled the regiment shortly after taking command to introduce himself and communicate his expectations of the regiment. His began his speech with a stumble when he told them that it was an honor to take command of the 508th. He quickly corrected himself, but the mistake drew catcalls, boos, whistles, and laughs from the packed crowd.

Nevertheless, Ekman took it in stride and delivered a fine speech, discussing the discipline problems: AWOLs, race trouble, improper saluting, disobedience of orders, stealing, and venereal disease. He told the officers and men that he couldn't keep them from doing the wrong things, but he could make it damned hard on the ones who were caught. He indicated that he would make their stay in the camp more enjoyable by providing more entertainment, such as movies, a game room, donuts, and a reading room. His demeanor was one of a reasonable and fair man, who had high standards that he expected them to meet.

Most of the men and officers accepted Ekman's changes. Over the next couple of weeks, Ekman dealt with the troublemakers. He resorted to a highly effective form of persuasion on those few problem troopers: telling them that they would be shipped to a "leg" unit. This quickly achieved the desired results, convincing any of the fence-sitters to also comply. The respect for Lieutenant Colonel Ekman began to grow among the officers and men of the regiment.

The regimental combat team began hard training for the cross-channel invasion under Gavin's and Ekman's leadership. Staff Sergeant Bob Gillette was the non-com in charge of the regimental S-2 section. "Training in Quorn was probably the most intense since we had left the States. Early-morning five-mile runs were the ritual five or six days a week. Live ammunition exercises were practiced." [15]

The live-fire training was not without danger. Staff Sergeant Russ Brown was the squad leader of the 60mm Mortar Squad, 1st Platoon, Company F. "The mortar squad went to the Bradgate Park mortar range near Leicester to train. My squad and Lieutenant [John H.] Dodd were on a hillside observing fire on targets to our front. The 2nd Platoon mortar squad had their mortar set up behind us in a small depression and did the firing. It was during this firing [that] a short round, I believe the fins may have come off [the shell] . . . hit us and sent six plus myself to the hospital. I was hit in the left leg above the knee." [16]

Private First Class Norris S. White, a replacement, was assigned as an ammo bearer in the 1st Battalion's 81mm mortar platoon. "We did training problems daily—gun setup races to see which squad was the fastest—nighttime compass training." [17]

A few weeks after training began in England, the regimental S-2 told Sergeant Gillette that he would be assisting in the planning of the upcoming operation. "Captain [Patrick] Gibbons was my S-2 officer. He immediately obtained clearance for me to the War Room, where the regimental planning was to be done. This effectively removed me from company training activities until D-Day. I was able to bring in several men for specific work, but the planning separated me from the [S-2] section for days at a time.

"We did construct a sand table, not of sand, but of cardboard cut out along contour lines and then covered with papier-mâché. Don Adrianson and Nick Kastrantas were the major players on that work. This was centered on our initial target, Hill 131 near St.-Sauveur-le-Vicomte." [18]

The S-2 and S-3 sections of each battalion worked in the regiment's War Room to assist in preparing briefing materials, unit orders, etcetera. Private Berge Avadanian, with the 2nd Battalion S-2 section, was assigned to review aerial photos of the drop zone. "The DZ was near the town of St.-Sauveur-le-Vicomte, about fifteen miles inland from the beach landings. I worked on a large (sand table-type) mockup of the drop zones. The table area contours were made of papier-mâché instead of sand. It was about a ten-feet-by-five-feet-by-ten-inches-deep box with little buildings, etc.

"When I needed supplies in the city of Leicester for the War Room, I was accompanied by guards to prevent leaks." [19]

THE REGIMENT POSTED A NOTICE, requesting volunteers for a special unit—the details of the unit's mission were not provided. Private First Class Chuck Copping, with Company C, showed up to volunteer for the unit. "A lot of us talked about it. They put the notification out that the next morning they wanted anybody that wanted to be in the special unit to be there. The next morning, there were about twelve hundred guys there.

"The guy in charge said, 'There's way too many, we just need a few. Everybody just go on back to your company areas and we'll have a get together.'

"The rumor was that they were after a suicide squad. [Private First Class Jasper] Bowman and I thought they put out that rumor to get rid of a lot of the people who wanted to be a part of the unit. We went back the next day, and Bowman and I both got picked." [20]

The men selected were assigned to three battalion pathfinder teams—the 1st Battalion team commanded by Lieutenant Michael C. Chester, with Company A; the 2nd Battalion team, led by Lieutenant James J. "J. J." Smith, with Company E; and the 3rd Battalion team, under the command of Lieutenant Albert V. Konar, with Headquarters Company, 3rd Battalion.

One of the men selected for the 1st Battalion team was Sergeant James Elmo Jones, with Company B. "We were taken from our companies and put on detached service with the IX Troop Carrier Command stationed at North Witham near Grantham, where we did all of our practice jumps learning to operate the equipment.

"We usually jumped fifteen men to a team. We used seven for the lights, one for the ADF [automatic direction finder], and one for the Eureka radio, plus some additional men to guard the perimeter to keep the enemy from slipping up on us and killing us while we were trying to operate the equipment.

"We were put into a barbed wire enclosure with guards walking the outside perimeter. We were not allowed to go on pass, go into towns. They treated us royally inside that compound. There was always a keg of beer in the corner of the compound. The food was absolutely excellent; steak, eggs, and everything that we hadn't had all during the war. We remained in this compound for approximately six weeks and during that time had some very important visitors . . . General Eisenhower, General Matthew B. Ridgway, General Bradley, and of course General Gavin, along with a lot of British dignitaries.

"I think the unique part of the whole situation was that we had rooms that had mats on the floor that you could walk on as if you were walking over the terrain [of the intended drop area]. It had every bridge, road, most of the houses, railroads, etcetera, clearly to scale on these mats, although there were no names of towns and not enough of the seashore showing to give us a clue as to where we might be jumping. We only knew that it would not be long until we left that compound." [21]

LIEUTENANT BOB FIELDER, WITH REGIMENTAL HEADQUARTERS COMPANY, noticed that a particular emphasis was placed on antitank training. "The airborne landings during an invasion are initially vulnerable to tanks and continue to be so. In training, to prove we could survive, we were required to dig foxholes and crouch down, then a tank would run over us. I took great pains to insure a deep hole and then curled up on the bottom. To offset the vulnerability of tanks, the British introduced Gammon grenades. Made of plastic composition C with a detonator inserted, the grenade was wrapped in a cloth about the size of a hardball. When thrown, the grenade explodes on impact, with an affinity to cut through armor." [22]

In early May, Lieutenant Jack Isaacs, a platoon leader with Company G, knew that the date for the greatest amphibious and airborne invasion in history must be getting close. "We intensified our small-unit training. We began to study French phrases, most of which didn't stick with us. We started studying sand tables and aerial photos of our intended objective, the location of which was unknown.

"The aerial photos were quite revealing, indicating the Germans on our intended target had prepared foxholes of their own. My platoon's objective was to seize those foxholes and use them to defend against a counterattack, which would probably come once we were on the ground." [23]

About a week before the division moved to the airfields, the drop zones were moved east, to areas slightly west of the Merderet River and west of Ste.-Mère-Église. This change was due to the detection of the German 91st Airlanding Division, which had recently arrived on the Cotentin Peninsula. This specially trained anti-airborne unit had moved into the area around Hill 110 and was headquartered at St.-Sauveur-le-Vicomte. It was working to turn all fields that were large enough for glider landings into deathtraps. The 82nd Airborne had been just days away from parachuting directly on top of a German division specifically trained to counter such operations.

New orders were issued for the 82nd Airborne Division to "land astride the Merderet River. Seize, clear, and secure the general area within its zone. Capture Ste.-Mère-Église, seize and secure crossings of the Merderet River at La Fière and Chef-du-Pont, and establish a bridgehead covering these two crossings. Seize and destroy the crossings of the Douve River at Beuzeville-la-Bastille and Ètienville. Protect the northwest flank of the VII Corps within the division zone, and be prepared to advance west on corps order to the line of the Douve north of its junction with the Prairies Marécageuses." [24]

General Ridgway assigned the most critical objective to the 505th PIR. "The 505 was the only parachute regiment in the division (or the whole Allied airborne effort for that matter) with combat experience, slated for the Normandy operation, and accordingly I assigned it the most important task—the capture and retention of Ste.-Mère-Église." [25] The town was a key crossroads and chokepoint in the road network for enemy forces counterattacking Utah Beach from the west or north portions of the Cotentin Peninsula.

On May 29, the 505th RCT moved to the airfields. The 1st Battalion, Regimental Headquarters and Headquarters Company, and one platoon of Company B, 307th Airborne Engineer Battalion, were sealed in at Spanhoe airfield. The 2nd Battalion, 3rd Battalion, and a section with Battery C, 456th Parachute Field Artillery Battalion, were staged at Cottesmore airfield.

Shortly after arriving at the airfields, each unit conducted briefings of the operation. Captain Hubert S. Bass, commanding Company F, attended the 2nd Battalion briefing. "Lieutenant Colonel Vandervoort called a company commanders' meeting to brief us on our mission—Lieutenant [William E.] Schmees, commanding Headquarters Company; Captain [Clyde R.] Russell, E Company; Lieutenant [Taylor G.] Smith, D Company; and Captain Bass, F Company. This was it—we had received our combat orders. We knew how and where we were going, but not sure when. Morale was better now that our missions and objectives were known—our men were trained fighters who desired to close with the enemy. Captain [William J.] Harris, the battalion S-3, issued plane assignments." [26]

After briefings by their respective battalion commanders and staffs, the company commanders conducted briefings for their platoon leaders. During the platoon leader briefings, Lieutenant Jim Coyle, with Company E, learned of both the regimental and battalion missions. "E Company was to set up roadblocks at

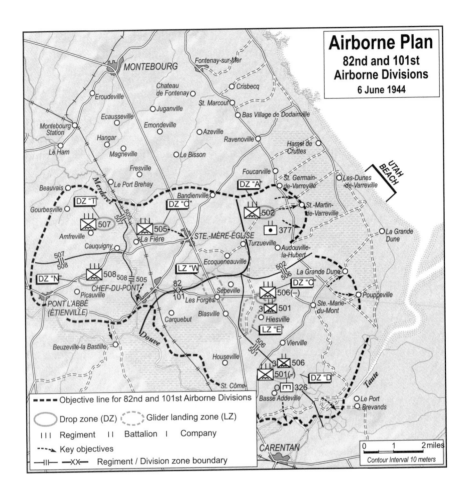

Neuville-au-Plain, a small town north of Ste.-Mère-Église. Ste.-Mère-Église was a main road junction, which the German reserves would have to use in order to attack the 4th Division, which was landing on the beaches east of our objectives. Third Battalion was to take Ste.-Mère-Église. Second Battalion, including our company, was to protect Ste.-Mère-Église from attack from the north by holding Neuville-au-Plain. We were briefed on our mission on large scale maps of the area and low-level aerial photos of the town of Neuville-au-Plain." 27

The platoon leaders then conducted briefings of their respective platoons, so that each trooper knew the mission of his platoon, company, battalion, and regiment. The amount of detail given to the troopers was extraordinary. This was the first such briefing for Private Ernest R. DePaolantonio, a member of a forward observer team with Battery A, 456th Parachute Field Artillery Battalion. The 456th PFA Battalion, less a two-gun section of Battery C, would land by sea at Utah Beach. "We had a sandbox which detailed the town of Ste.-Mère-Église. It also detailed our drop zones, Utah Beach, hedgerows, and swamps—whatever was on the ground, the sand tables mapped it out.

"On a whole, my buddies and I felt ready to go and prepared. Still, we were scared of the uncertainty of the outcome. We talked about it and went over every detail our entire waking hours." 28

Sergeant Roy O. King, with Company D, felt that the sand tables were of great benefit. "I personally thought they were great. The briefings were concise and more clear with the tables." 29

For many of the men in the regiment, this would be their third combat jump. The briefings were routine for them by now. At the briefing Private First Class Bill Tucker and his Company I platoon attended, they were gathered around a sand table as "the briefing officer explained the mission to us, and it seemed very clear as we looked at the mock-up and aerial photographs. The principal mission of our battalion was to seize the town of Ste.-Mère-Église. One of our missions in Ste.-Mère-Église was to attack and destroy the headquarters of the German commander in the area. There weren't many questions. Everything seemed pretty clear cut, and everyone had a sense of confidence that the people higher up knew what they were doing. I had fewer fears about invading Normandy than I had sweating out some practice jumps. It was all like being part of one big machine. We felt strong and confident about what we could do, and we had no thought of failure.

"Our strength of purpose and acceptance of duties ahead were without question due to our real respect for the division's leadership. Pride in the division was above everything, without really saying so. The talk we had been given by General Ridgway probably had the most to do with it, in the sense that he had given us a feeling of unqualified involvement in a tremendous task that was grinding ahead like a juggernaut and had to be done.

"After the briefings, we had two more talks. General Gavin told us again in his quiet, businesslike way that we were well equipped, well trained, and ready to do the job with a minimum of casualties. He said that at the outset in our area we would outnumber the Germans we fought. He was low key in his comments, as always, and sort of reeked of his confidence in us.

"We had the usual dramatic speech by [Lieutenant Colonel] Krause. It had a lot of effect. The point of his speech was when he held up the American flag he always had [with him]. He said, 'This flag was the first American flag to fly over Gela, Sicily, and the first American flag to be raised over Naples. Tomorrow morning, I will be sitting in the mayor's office in Ste.-Mère-Église, and this flag will be flying over that office.' [Lieutenant Colonel] Krause's speech was stirring, because the United States flag was a powerful symbol to us of our pride, sense of duty, and determination." 30

Major Ben Vandervoort, an original member of the 505th PIR, had watched the metamorphosis of the regiment through two campaigns. "When we left Italy the regiment was lean, mean, and battle smart. Whatever job the 505 was given, the lieutenants and NCOs made it work. They led like respected older brothers in a fraternity.

Their emphasis was on self-discipline, rather than discipline applied from above. With never a doubt as to who was in charge, they shared foxholes, rations, hazards, and hopes with their troopers." [31]

He had confidence that the regiment would defeat whatever opposition awaited it in Normandy, because there was "mutual faith" among the troopers that "every other man would do his job in combat or die trying. Within the mutual faith, all competed to make the play to win the game. That faith and competitive spirit welded the regiment into a rough, tough, winning combat team." [32]

Lieutenant Gus L. Sanders, a platoon leader with Company C, knew that the Normandy invasion would be costly, but in the end, the regiment would prevail. "As paratroopers, we were trained to expect the worst—we had been in combat twice before and knew we could overcome anything. We were a highly trained bunch, who knew we were good. The I.Q. was as high, or higher, than any outfit. The spirit of the entire division under the able leadership of General Gavin and General Ridgway was such that we would take on anything against big odds, and most of the time, come out on top." [33]

Technical Sergeant Ronald Snyder was a platoon sergeant with Company G and had made two combat jumps with the regiment. "On June 4, we were fed a sumptuous meal, which we jokingly referred to as a 'last supper' or being 'fattened up for the kill.' However, inclement weather forced a twenty-four hour postponement, and we spent the time honing and re-honing trench knives and bayonets, and cleaning and oiling our weapons." [34]

Veterans like Private Berge Avadanian "tried to joke, especially with the young replacements, who had not experienced combat in Sicily and Italy." [35]

Unfortunately, the operation was postponed because of high winds, high tides, and rain in Normandy. The following morning, the weather improved enough for the operation to be scheduled for the following night of June 5–6.

That evening, the regiment repeated the same process of getting ready for the operation. Again, the troopers were treated to a great meal. Private Ken Russell, a new replacement with Company F, got his plate of food from the mess serving line and looked for a place to sit. "The air force always had good food, and they gave us what you might say was the 'Last Supper.' I recall at that 'Last Supper' a fellow by the name of [Lee G.] Graves, who was in the company, who was a very devout, religious man. He'd always sit down at the end of the table by himself, you know. I do recall at the dinner that evening that there was something within me that wanted to be close to Graves, because he had something I didn't have. He was a devout, religious man, and I got my tray of food, and I went down, and I asked him, 'Graves, may I sit here with you?'

"He said, 'Yes.'

"I said, 'Well, may I share in your blessing?' He was aghast, because I had never done that before. None of us had. Of course, we looked at him as a weirdo. I guess it was something that we sensed—danger. I didn't want to press it. But that was the first time I ever wanted to even sit close to Graves, because he would always pray." [36]

Another man in Russell's platoon who was deeply religious was Private Charles Blankenship. Russell admired him. "He was a devout, religious fellow, nineteen years old at the time. His father was a Baptist minister. He was the only man that went to Regimental Headquarters and asked to take his tithe out of his meager army earnings. Blankenship, he was a nice guy. I guess he knew I was nervous. He was nervous too, but he made me feel good.

"He said to me, 'Well Russell, I'm the tough guy in the unit. I'll be around a long time. In fact, Russell, I'll tell you what I'm going to do. I'm going to raise the chickens to pick the grass off of your grave.'

"He was trying to cheer me up, I guess." 37

After dinner, Sergeant Ron Snyder and his Company G platoon "gathered up our weapons and equipment, assembled in predetermined eighteen-man sticks, and walked onto the airfield to find our assigned plane, which was identified by a large chalk numeral. Here our chutes were piled, and we began the difficult, laborious process of fitting, fastening, suspending, and placing countless items of ammo, mines, weapons, rations, clothing, and tools; then got the parachutes on and strapped over all this gear.

"I was assigned to jump number eighteen position, referred to as the 'pusher.' But, my platoon leader requested that I jump number three, so I'd land close to him and assist him on the assembly at the drop zone. Also, I would release the six equipment bundles which were fastened underneath the plane. These cargo bundles were identified by various colored chutes—red for ammo, white for water and rations, blue for machine guns and mortars, and green for communications equipment. The bundle release was controlled from six toggle switches near the exit door. Customarily, we would obtain a wooden tongue depressor from the medic and tape this to the top of the six switches, so they could release all of the bundles at one time—one swift move and they were off." 38

Waiting to load up, some of the paratroopers engaged in horseplay. Private First Class Charles H. Miller, with Company D, and his buddy engaged in a "wrestling match while we were waiting to get on the plane to go to France. Of course, I got whipped, because he was a big guy. [Private First Class George J.] Rajner had been a weightlifter, in fact.

"He always said, 'If you think this is a war, you ought to see my mother-in-law and me. That's a war.' He wouldn't buy insurance, he wouldn't take the GI insurance, because he said, 'If I die, she'll get it.'" 39

On the evening of June 5, Company E pathfinder Private Dennis O'Loughlin, a member of the 2nd Battalion team, readied himself for the jump, even though he had a broken hand in a bandage. "Whether to make the jump or not with my broken hand was left up to me. They knew damned well I would jump. Told 'em if I could get that cast cut off my hand and a tight bandage put on it so I could use my fingers a little, I thought I could make it." 40

Private O'Loughlin and the other pathfinders were taken to a building where "they sprayed us all we wanted with green paint and handed us burnt cork to rub on our faces and hands. Then we were taken to the plane that was to take us in and lined up and had our picture taken along with the plane crew. We all got copies later." [41]

As darkness approached, the pathfinders put on their parachutes and strapped on their weapons, equipment, and special pathfinder electronic, radio, and light equipment. Private First Class Chuck Copping, a Company C pathfinder, was carrying one of the lights. "It was a tripod—there were three legs to it. The light that fit on the socket was louvered and had a form cut around the light that directed the light upward. We had a car battery tied to one leg, and the tripod and light tied to the other leg." [42]

Private First Class Ralph Stout, Jr., with Company B, also a member of the light team, estimated that he was carrying at least ninety pounds of gear. "We were pretty well loaded down. At that time, I was just a little runt. I weighed about one hundred twenty-five pounds." [43]

The heavily loaded pathfinders then began boarding their planes. They would be the first men to land in Nazi-occupied France a few short hours away.

Shortly before every man with the parachute elements of the 505th RCT boarded his plane, he received a letter from Allied Supreme Commander General Dwight Eisenhower that read:

Supreme Headquarters Allied Expeditionary Force

Soldiers, Sailors and Airmen of the Allied Expeditionary Force!
You are about to embark upon the Great Crusade, toward which we have striven these many months. The eyes of the world are upon you. The hopes and prayers of liberty-loving people everywhere march with you. In company with our brave Allies and brothers-in-arms on other Fronts, you will bring about the destruction of the German war machine, the elimination of Nazi tyranny over the oppressed peoples of Europe, and security for ourselves in a free world.
Your task will not be an easy one. Your enemy is well trained, well equipped and battle-hardened. He will fight savagely.
But this is the year 1944! Much has happened since the Nazi triumphs of 1940–41. The United Nations have inflicted upon the Germans great defeats, in open battle, man-to-man. Our air offensive has seriously reduced their strength in the air and their capacity to wage war on the ground. Our Home Fronts have given us an overwhelming superiority in weapons and munitions of war, and placed at our disposal great reserves of trained fighting men. The tide has turned! The free men of the world are marching together to Victory!
I have full confidence in your courage, devotion to duty and skill in battle. We will accept nothing less than full Victory!
Good luck! And let us beseech the blessing of Almighty God upon this great and noble undertaking.
Dwight D. Eisenhower

SERGEANT NORBERT BEACH WAS a communications NCO with Company H. "I jumped with full equipment, plus a 300S radio, so I had a difficult time getting up the steps into the plane and had to have help." [44]

As Company I trooper, Private First Class Bill Tucker walked to his plane, he looked around. "Countless C-47 aircraft were all over the field. They were scattered, so it seemed impossible to count them. There were single files of bent-over men marching quietly in all directions with their parachutes to board different aircraft. A beautiful sunset was the backdrop for the scene, and you could hear the constant beat and roar of aircraft engines." [45]

As his C-47 slowly rolled down the taxiway at the Spanhoe airfield, part of the seemingly endless line of planes of the mightiest airborne armada in history, Private Arthur B. "Dutch" Schultz, with Company C, sat quietly, alone with his thoughts, when suddenly he heard a muffled blast. "There was a terrible explosion down the line in one of the airplanes. One of these Gammon grenades accidentally went off and set the plane on fire and killed four of the troopers that were with Headquarters Company, 1st Battalion [Private First Class Robert L. Leaky, Private Pete Vah, Corporal Kenneth A. Vaught, and Private Eddie O. Meelberg (who died later that night)]. In fact, everyone was wounded or injured except [Sergeant Melvin J.] Fryer." [46] Fryer, not wanting to be left behind, found a seat on another plane carrying his company, and would be killed in action on June 18.

At airfields all over southern England, C-47s carrying the finest of American and British youth—paratroopers of the 82nd, 101st, and British 6th Airborne Divisions—taxied to the runways. Private First Class Tucker "got a good look out the window as the pilot revved the engines and held the brakes for our takeoff. What I saw was without question a scene I would carry with me always. Along each side of the runway were literally hundreds of people lined up two and three deep. United States and RAF ground personnel, British army girls, cooks, and bakers—and no one moved. They just stared at our plane.

"Without moving, they seemed to offer a profound salute—and perhaps a blessing or prayer. We could feel—I know I could—the spirit of all those people with us as the pilot released the brakes and the plane surged forward." [47]

At approximately 10:30 p.m., the nine planes carrying the 82nd pathfinder teams began lifting off from their airfield at North Witham, bound for Normandy. As his plane climbed into the darkening sky, Company B pathfinder Sergeant James Elmo Jones looked down the aisle at the other handpicked men of the 1st Battalion team. "Some of the pathfinders in the plane had their faces blackened. I did not put anything on my face. I felt if I was going to die, I wanted to die looking normal. Since this was my third combat jump, I won't say that it was any easier, because it certainly was not. We felt that this would probably be the biggest campaign of our lives." [48]

With the pathfinder teams leading the way, the huge formation of 378 aircraft carrying the parachute element of the 82nd Airborne swept onward in mile upon mile of nine-plane waves arrayed in V-of-V formations. The nine-plane waves were grouped in thirty-six- to forty-five-plane serials carrying a battalion. The 2nd Battalion serial was in the lead, followed by the 3rd Battalion, and then the 1st Battalion serial, which included Regimental Headquarters and Headquarters Company.

Captain Hubert Bass, commanding Company F, looked at his watch; it was almost midnight. "At 2349 hours, 5 June 1944, our flight was to rendezvous in the vicinity of Coventry, England. My thoughts while I was sitting near the plane's door were about our mission, our plans, wondering what kind of reception we would get from the Germans during the drop." [49]

Sitting near the door inside his plane, pathfinder Sergeant James Elmo Jones looked out the door at the lengthening shadows. "As it got dark when we left the coast of England, still with a long way to fly, everyone was quiet. No one was joking, no conversations were being carried on, just the constant hum of the engines. The C-47 with its door off [gave me] the ability to look out at sea and watch the water . . . watching the ships on the Channel as we flew over the top.

"In the plane, some of the men had upset stomachs because of the tension and nerves. Some men could not speak. I was so afraid that I would be the same way that I said a prayer again that I had said on the previous two combat jumps. It was simple and it was this: 'Lord thy will be done. But if I'm to die, please help me die like a man.' And then everything seemed to be O.K." [50]

Looking out the door for checkpoints, Captain Bass glanced at his watch once again. "Just forty-nine minutes have passed since we left Coventry; seems like an eternity. I kept thinking of a saying I once heard. 'A coward dies many times before his death, but the valiant tastes the sting of death only once.'

"Some of the troopers in the plane had their eyes closed as if they were sleeping, others were just staring, someone would look at his watch occasionally, loosen or tighten a harness buckle. Those were brave men and [it was] a wonderful comfort to be on their team. There were several checkpoints between Coventry and the English coast. However, I was watching for the coastline, checkpoint 'Flatbush.' Then a destroyer in the Channel . . . a submarine, at which point we [would] change our flight direction towards the Cherbourg Peninsula, [and] Guernsey Island would be on our right.

"Lieutenant [James J.] Smith was on detached service to division headquarters. He was in command of our pathfinder group. Our success of hitting our drop zone depended on his group." [51]

Sergeant James Elmo Jones, with the 1st Battalion pathfinder team, noticed that "as we approached the drop zone, the area was obscured by low clouds. As tracer bullets from the Germans came through the clouds, you could see them light up the sky. We were all standing, and had been since we hit the coast. The equipment was extremely heavy. We were getting very tired, and the only thing we wanted was to get out." [52]

Jones stood near the door waiting for the green light as the C-47 began "a shallow dive at a very high speed. Bullets were hitting the plane as if it could fall from the sky at any time. The cloud cover was still on us, and the plane was still going down.

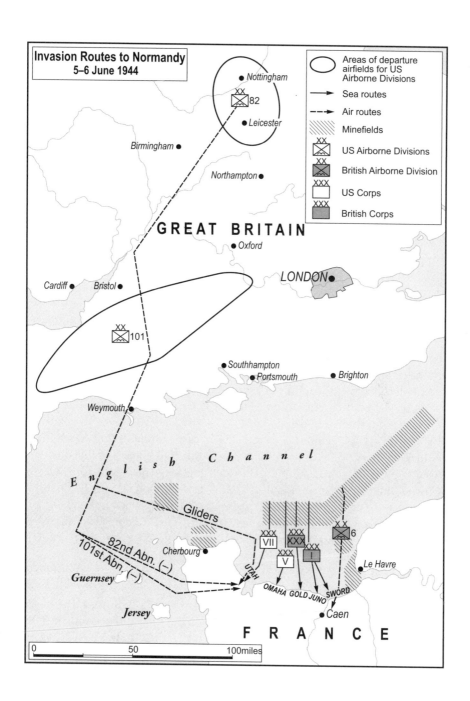

Invasion Routes to Normandy
5–6 June 1944

Areas of departure airfields for US Airborne Divisions

Sea routes

Air routes

Minefields

US Airborne Divisions

British Airborne Division

US Corps

British Corps

Nottingham

82

Leicester

Birmingham

Northampton

GREAT BRITAIN

Oxford

Cardiff   Bristol

LONDON

101

Southhampton
Portsmouth   Brighton

Weymouth

English Channel

Gliders

101st Abn. (–)
82nd Abn. (–)

Cherbourg

Guernsey

Jersey

UTAH

VII

V

XXX

6

OMAHA GOLD JUNO SWORD

Le Havre

Caen

FRANCE

0   50   100 miles

We finally broke through the clouds. We were right on top of the trees. The green light came on and we jumped.

"Lieutenant [Mike] Chester [Company A] was the first man and I was second, behind him. On the short ride down after my parachute opened, I could hear firing all around me. I looked down, and after having looked at the maps back in England, showing the countryside, I saw the trees coming up and I honestly could see the field that we had practiced so many times looking at and landing on.

"By the time my chute opened and I could look up at the canopy, my feet hit the ground. I landed in the middle of a field. Landing was very hard. But, I had learned many jumps before to try not to tumble with so much equipment, because it was an impossibility, and almost without exception, a leg or arm would be broken. So, I simply pulled up my feet, tried to land as much as I could on the equipment, and my parachute settled over my head. And the first thing that I thought, without even trying to get out of my parachute, was 'damn, I just cracked the Atlantic Wall.'" [53]

The 82nd Airborne pathfinder teams jumped on time at 1:21 a.m. The three 505th pathfinder teams were the only ones dropped together on the proper drop zone. The 2nd Battalion serial, consisting of thirty-six C-47 aircraft, was only about thirty minutes away from Drop Zone "O," when the pathfinders jumped.

The drop zone consisted of three large fields west of Ste.-Mère-Église, just north of the main road that led to the La Fière Causeway. The 3rd Battalion pathfinders were to mark the easternmost field closest to Ste.-Mère-Église for the 3rd Battalion, whose mission was to capture the town. The 2nd Battalion pathfinder team was to mark the center field for the 2nd Battalion, which would move north of Ste.-Mère-Église to block the main road from Cherbourg. The 1st Battalion team would mark the western field, which was closest to the La Fière and Chef-du-Pont Causeways, the objectives for the 1st Battalion.

The 2nd Battalion pathfinder team had the least amount of time to set up their equipment, as the 2nd Battalion serial was only thirty minutes from the drop zone. Upon landing, Company E pathfinder Private First Class Anthony J. "Tony" DeMayo quickly assembled his rifle and looked around in the moonlight for familiar landmarks to determine if he had landed in the correct field. "Back in England in the War Room, when we were briefed, we were told that the DZ consisted of three fields surrounded by hedgerows. On the edge of the center field, we were told to look for a barn and a haystack.

"As I got up to get out of my harness, lo and behold, off to the edge of the field was the haystack and the barn—I was surprised.

"Our mission was to get a set of seven lights to form a 'T' and a radar, to send out a code for the 2nd Battalion planes to beam in on. After this equipment was set up, the radar man was to start sending out his code, immediately. The light men, of which I was one, were to leave the lights off and take cover until we heard the sound of the first planes. The rest of the men set up a defense of the DZ." [54]

In the field on the western end of the drop zone, designated for the 1st Battalion, Company C pathfinder Private First Class Chuck Copping found

Lieutenant Mike Chester, the 1st Battalion team commander. "He scattered the security around the perimeter, he told [Private Bob] Murphy where to put that radar, and the light men took off from Murphy, and we formed a team with four going up and three across the top. We wanted to be set up in the right direction." 55

Company A pathfinder Private Bob Murphy removed the forty-pound Eureka chest pack from his harness. "I immediately took the radar out of the container, along with the antenna, and completed the setup. Within ten minutes, we had the radar sending out a Morse code signal, which is the letter 'R'—di-dah-dit." 56

Sergeant Jones was in charge of getting the 1st Battalion light team positioned. "I got the direction of the wind and lined up the 'T' so that the seven men could go out with their lights. I took my ADF (automatic direction finder), got it out of the kit, turned it on, and started assembling it. With the antenna up, it could reach (without obstructions in its way) up to fifty to seventy-five miles. I was trying to get the maximum distance with it.

"The Eureka radio was the other half of the Rebecca radio that was installed in the airplane. It was for pinpoint accuracy on dropping the troops for assembly. The ADF signal went further and the planes picked it up first. The ADF and the radar were picked up some twenty-five to thirty-five miles out over the English Channel." 57

AS HIS PLANE FLEW ACROSS THE ENGLISH CHANNEL, Technical Sergeant Buffalo Boy Canoe, with Company D, looked down the aisle at the other troopers— "some of the group in deep thought, some praying, some trying to hold a conversation, others reading old letters, a few with big tears of fear—which we all had. My thought was what will it feel like to be hit in the sky and if I would ever see my dear ones." 58

As the sky train passed over the English Channel, Private Dutch Schultz, with Company C, was engrossed, reciting the Catholic rosaries. "Once in a while though, I looked around and I saw a number of the old timers sleeping and catching catnaps or whatever. But not me—I was praying." 59

As the 3rd Battalion serial passed over the English Channel, Sergeant Bill Bishop, with Company G, who was jumping number two, could see the awesome spectacle of the massive Allied fleet below. "I hung in the door and I just marveled at all of the ships in the sea and all of the aircraft overhead, headed in one direction." 60

CHAPTER 8

"An Irresistible Force
That Nothing Could Stop"

T
he field where the three 505th pathfinder teams were set up was now silent. Company E pathfinder Private First Class Anthony J. DeMayo crouched near a hedgerow with other pathfinders as the anxious minutes ticked by. "At this point the only sound was an occasional rattle of the equipment. We were told that it would be about thirty minutes from our drop to the drop of the main body. It felt like thirty hours. Then, off in the distance we heard the sound of the first plane motors.

"At this point, the other light men and I went out and turned on the lights and headed back for cover, because we surely thought this would be it, with the field lit up. But still, no sound except for the sound of the planes, which were getting louder all the time." [1]

In the lead plane of the 82nd Airborne Division parachute element was Lieutenant Colonel Benjamin H. Vandervoort, the 2nd Battalion, 505th commander. "The mass and magnitude of the coordinated motion gave one the sensation of being part of an irresistible force that nothing could stop. As we came in over the Normandy coast we stood up and hooked up, ready to jump. Isolated fires were blazing on the ground below. Imagination told us they were aircraft already shot down. We ran into a cloudbank and as we came out of the clouds, I could see our aircraft had begun to scatter. Flak in large volumes was coming up from Ste.-Mère-Église. Our planes were flying too high and too fast." [2]

As the 2nd Battalion serial emerged from the clouds, the sky erupted with German antiaircraft and small arms fire. Multicolored tracers from 20mm antiaircraft guns and machine guns crisscrossed, rising up to meet the oncoming planes, as flak bursts from 88mm antiaircraft guns lit up the sky.

In one of the nine Company F planes, Captain Hubert Bass was watching for the landmarks and the lights marking the drop zone as he called out the commands they all knew by heart. "'Stand up and hook up! . . . Check equipment! . . . Stand in the door!' I don't believe I could be heard—maybe they read my lips. Every man tightened up, pushing towards the door.

"Where were Smith's lights? I began to get worried. It was dark; clouds kept flying past, blocking vision of the ground. Our coded light was color green.

"We could pass beyond our DZ without knowing. The following planes would see us jump. We had to hit our DZ. I was determined [to jump] when we crossed the second river, which was the Merderet and last reference point. To hesitate would put us within seconds of the coast. Where in the hell are those pathfinder lights?" [3]

Vandervoort was "standing in the open door ready to go—checking off the landmarks (highways, railroads, bodies of water) we had memorized during our pre-invasion briefings and studies. Suddenly the green light was turned on. I knew where we were, and the signal was premature. The crew chief standing by me could communicate with the pilot over the intercom. I told him to tell them to turn 'the G.D. thing off' and wait and come down to the proper altitude and speed. The green light went out. We continued to fly as before." [4]

Unfortunately, the troopers in three planes carrying Lieutenant Bill Meddaugh and his 2nd Platoon, Company E, jumped when their pilots prematurely turned on the green lights in their planes. "I was in the lead plane of the three-plane group to the right. In this position, I was able to see the lead three-plane group and the group to its left, very clearly. Suddenly, the three-plane group at the point of the V banked sharply to the left—so sharply that the group to its left had to pull up sharply to avoid a midair collision. In doing so, the three planes scattered. I knew at that instant that our company formation was destroyed.

"With a quick flash, I recalled the jump I made in the Sicilian invasion, where I landed sixty miles away from my DZ. 'Here we go again,' I said to myself. At that instant, I saw the equipment bundles sweep by underneath the plane. The pilot had salvoed the load too early. I swore to myself and saw the green light flash on. No time to think—automatically—'Let's go!' I stepped out and waited for the opening shock. It came—hard. Our jumping speed was too fast. I hung on and hit hard. I was in France and alive.

"My platoon was dropped about three miles from the planned drop zone. We were isolated with various other scattered elements of the 507 and 508 Regiments." [5]

As Bass stood in the door he watched the last landmark, the Merderet River, pass beneath his plane. In the distance he could see a fire burning in Ste.-Mère-Église. "Suddenly, as if in answer to thousands of prayers, the clouds opened up and I saw lights on the ground formed in a 'T' with a green light at the bottom of the stem. Good old Smith." [6]

As the first nine planes of the thirty-six-plane 2nd Battalion serial approached the lights of the drop zone, Lieutenant Colonel Vandervoort "told the crew chief to tell the pilot to pass the jump signal back to the trailing aircraft. The green light came on again and out we went." [7]

Standing by the ADF in the field below, pathfinder Sergeant James Elmo Jones watched the awesome spectacle above as C-47s carrying the regiment "flew directly over us and started dropping their serials right on top of the lights." [8] He saw brief glimpses of paratroopers coming out of the planes as German searchlights swept the sky and flashes of light from exploding shells momentarily illuminated the waves of aircraft moving east across the peninsula.

The plane carrying Vandervoort was flying too fast, and his chute opened with a tremendous shock. "It tore off my musette bag and snapped blinding flashes in front of my eyes. We were too high (perhaps three thousand feet) and drifted away from our drop zone. As I came down I selected a small field with a clump of brush in the center and slipped my chute toward the shadows of the brush to be able to conceal myself while getting out of my harness.

"I landed on about a forty-five degree slope—hit hard and felt my ankle snap and knew at once it was broken. I got out of my chute in the shadows. I was alone—and crawled over to one corner of the hedgerows surrounding the field. The ankle hurt and I shot myself in the leg with a morphine syrette carried in our paratrooper's first-aid kit." [9]

Sergeant Russ Brown, with Company F, was standing in the door looking for landmarks and the "T." The jumpmaster on Brown's plane was an extra lieutenant, not assigned to his company, whom he didn't know. "I saw the lit 'T' and said, 'Lieutenant, stand up and hook up.' We jumped and it took a long time to hit the ground, because we jumped very high. I never saw a green light and wonder if the mortar squad of the 2nd Platoon got a late green light." [10]

As the plane carrying paratroopers with the 60mm Mortar Squad, 2nd Platoon, Company F, began to jump, it was apparent they had overshot the drop zone. With everyone anxious to exit the plane, Private Ken Russell felt his entire stick pushing for the door. "As we left the plane we had flak, machine gun fire, and everything else all the way down, because we were sitting targets." [11]

After his parachute deployed, Russell saw that his stick was jumping right over a town where a large fire was engulfing one of the buildings near the town square, lighting up the whole area. The bell in the church steeple was ringing. The French townspeople were in the square fighting the fire, filling buckets at a water pump in the square, passing them from person to person, and throwing the water on the raging inferno. The German garrison stood below, fully armed in the town square, overseeing the firefighting.

As he floated down, Russell watched a terrifying spectacle unfold. "I saw something I never want to see in my life. I looked to my right, I saw a guy, and instantaneously, there was just an empty parachute coming down. A shell of some kind must have hit one of his Gammon grenades. He was blown away.

"I was trying to hide behind my reserve chute, because you could hear the shells hitting. We were all sitting ducks coming down.

"One guy landed in the fire. I heard him scream one time before he hit the fire. . . . I saw him land in the fire. It was heat from the fire that was drawing all these parachutes in towards the fire.

"I could feel shells hitting the parachute. When I hit the roof [of the church], a couple of my suspension lines, or maybe more, went around the church steeple and I slid off the roof. I was hanging on the edge of the roof on the right side of the church." [12]

Private John Steele also landed on the edge of the roof. "I was trying to dodge the burning building and didn't see the steeple. I actually hit the roof of the church and then my chute caught on the steeple.

"There was furious fighting going on all around the church." 13

Moments after his risers suspended him from the roof, Private Russell watched his mortar squad leader, Sergeant John P. Ray, land. "He missed the edge of the church; he hit in front of the church. Sergeant Ray landed after we did, a split second, I would say.

"I'll never forget, a red haired German soldier came around from behind the church to shoot Steele and me, who were still hanging there. As he came around, he shot Ray in the stomach. Sergeant Ray, while dying in agony, got his .45 out, and as this German soldier started turning around to us, he shot the German soldier in the back of the head and killed him. It was an agonizing death that Ray went through.

"I was scared to death. I finally got to my trench knife. It was carried down on your right jump boot. I cut my risers, threw my knife away, and fell to the ground. I looked up and I knew I couldn't do anything. I thought he [Private Steele] was dead. The only Americans that I saw there were dead, and it was our [Company F] men, you know. Most our stick were killed. Lieutenant [Harold O.] Cadish [and Privates] H. T. Bryant and Laddie Tlapa landed on telephone poles down the street. It was like they were crucified there. Charles Blankenship was in a tree. [Private Ernest R.] Blanchard landed in a tree, and he got so excited, he got his trench knife out to cut his risers and cut one of his fingers off and didn't know it until he was down.

"I didn't see anyone else around, so I dashed across the street, and the machine gun fire was knocking up pieces of earth all around me. I ran over into a grove of trees. I wasn't completely out of town. I was the loneliest man in the world—strange country—just a boy, really. I should have been in high school rather than in a strange country. I think my class was graduating that night.

"There were planes still coming over bringing jumpers in. I almost ran into a flak gun in the grove of trees, shooting our men. I was scared to death. I got my Gammon grenade out, and I threw the grenade in on it. There was a huge explosion. The gun stopped firing. I ran up this field a little ways, and I saw a bicycle come down the road. I knew it couldn't have been an American. I had to take care of the guy on the bicycle. I went two hundred or three hundred yards back to my left in the area where I was at, because I didn't know what else would be coming down this road. I found a guy from the 101st Airborne Division. So we went down the hedgerow and we found another guy from the 82nd. He was from the 507th, I believe. He had a broken leg. Well, we finally found several guys there.

"One of the guys said, 'Well, what are we going to do?'

"I said, 'Well, we've got to get back into Ste.-Mère-Église.' So we came back into Ste.-Mère-Église, and there was [gun]fire all around the area." 14

A German searchlight scanning the sky found the plane carrying Lieutenant Roper Peddicord's Company E stick. Sergeant Cullen Clark, Jr., was jumping third and could see out the door. "As soon as the searchlight picked us up and then went ahead of us, we could see the lines of tracers coming up from the ground. They looked like they were coming right in the door, but curved like a thin line of fire and hit the tail of the airplane. We were all hooked up and ready to jump, but the pilot started zigzagging, and the plane engines sounded like they were going to tear off from the plane. We got away from the searchlight, and Lieutenant Peddicord jumped, then we all followed him.

"Lieutenant Peddicord and I landed quite close together, and I recall [him] saying, 'Clark, this makes three times we have jumped in combat, and all three times we have landed close together. Now, let's start killing Germans.'

"Lieutenant Peddicord informed the planeload of men who had jumped with us 'that the pilot apparently dropped us in the wrong spot. And all I know is that we are in France some place with German soldiers all around us, but we must find Ste.-Mère-Église and join the rest of our platoon and E Company.'" [15]

Lieutenant James J. Coyle, the assistant platoon leader of Company E's 1st Platoon, landed on the drop zone without a problem. "The first man I encountered was our battalion commander, Lieutenant Colonel Benjamin Vandervoort. He asked me if I had found my medical aid man, but I told him I was alone. At the time, he did not mention that he was injured, but he had broken his ankle on the jump. He ordered me to continue to locate my men." [16]

The combination of heavy equipment loads and some C-47s traveling faster than they should have resulted in some troopers experiencing a terrible opening shock from their chutes deploying, blown-out panels in their canopies, equipment torn off, and rough landings. Private George Jacobus, with Company E, was one such trooper, landing northeast of Ste.-Mère-Église. "Out the door—the worst opening shock ever. I looked at the canopy—I had blown three panels and was dropping fast. We were high—at least fifteen hundred to eighteen hundred feet. As the ground began to come into focus, so did a German machine gun nest on my right. There appeared to be a small building to my left. With all my strength, I pulled on the risers to go left away from the machine gun nest. I did, and slammed into the building like a ton of bricks, and on the ground, on my back. Something had hit my left eye.

"I knew in an instant that I had broken my left leg. It was eerie, as I lay amidst the tangled shroud lines and wriggled out of my chute. Then the pain in the left leg became a reality. It hurt like hell. Suddenly, after quite some time, there was another trooper from another airborne unit. He was big enough to pick me up by the armpits and drag me over to be propped up against a tree." [17]

After getting out of his chute, Vandervoort took out his Very pistol and loaded it with a flare. "I then began to shoot up the green flares that were the visual assembly signal for my battalion. Troop-carrying aircraft continued to pass overhead. A bundle containing ammunition came down without its chute and exploded about fifty yards in front of where I sat." [18]

Descending almost on top of that bundle was Company D trooper Sergeant Roy King. "I was fascinated by the sight of the tracers flying around everywhere, when I saw a huge explosion blossom directly below me." [19]

As he looked at the explosion, King suddenly saw something else flash below him. It was "a plane between me and the ground. No, it was not in trouble; I was!

"I was above the stream of airplanes that had just dropped their troopers and equipment. My immediate concern was that I could be chopped to pieces by the propellers of the oncoming planes. [I was] trying furiously to turn and face the oncoming planes in order to be able to see how to safely maneuver through them. I dropped safely through them in spite of my near-hysterical struggles." 20

As Private First Class Charles Miller, with Company D, went out the door of his C-47, he "was awed by the sight. You could just see everything. It was fantastic. It looked like a great big Fourth of July celebration. The whole sky was lit up like a big show. There was Ste.-Mère-Église down below on fire." 21

As D Company trooper Private First Class Donald E. Ellis descended, he saw cows in the field below. "I slipped trying to miss this cow, and I slid off her back, and I fractured one leg. So I was crawling around and hobbling around as best I could. That was the closest time to death I ever had. I was standing talking to a couple of other guys, and all of a sudden out of nowhere [came] a bullet, right by my head. Man, I scooted out of there." 22

Private First Class Robert M. Robinson, with Headquarters Company, 2nd Battalion, landed alone in a small field. "My M1 rifle was stowed in the Griswold case in three parts, so I was quite unarmed, except for my trench knife strapped to my jump boot. The first thing I saw were several creatures charging at me from the shadows. All I could see were white faces, and this unnerved me quite a bit. But when I realized that these creatures were cattle, I was really worried. Being a city dweller, I was afraid of being kicked or bitten, so I quickly cut myself free of my parachute and beat a hasty retreat from the field, with my 'adversaries' in hot pursuit." 23

The 2nd Battalion surgeon, Captain Lyle B. Putnam, came upon Lieutenant Colonel Vandervoort about an hour after landing. "I located him near a small farmhouse. He was seated with a rain cape over him reading a map by flashlight. He recognized me, and calling me close, quietly asked that I take a look at his ankle with as little demonstration as possible. His ankle was obviously broken; luckily a simple rather than a compound fracture. He insisted on replacing his jump boot, laced it tightly, formed a makeshift crutch from a stick, and moved with the outfit as an equal and a leader without complaint." 24

THE SERIAL CARRYING THE 3RD BATTALION SERIAL was five minutes behind the 2nd Battalion serial. Lieutenant Jack Isaacs, a platoon leader with Company G, was standing in the door of his C-47. This was his third combat jump. "As the 3rd Platoon leader, I had the left 'V' of three planes.

"Unfortunately, as we approached the coast we hit a rather dense fog bank, forcing some evasive action on the part of the pilots in order that they didn't run into other planes. I knew that my flight of three planes was veering to the left or the north, and that I would probably be off target.

"Breaking free of the fog, some three or four miles inland, I saw no other planes. There were a few floating clouds. There was a good amount of German antiaircraft fire, light machine gun, 20mm, and some 88mm high explosive stuff. Whether you looked north or south or east or west, you could see plenty of antiaircraft fire.

"The red light came on at approximately the right time for the drop. When the green light came on, seeing that I was over land, and it made no difference where I was over land, it was my duty to take the stick of sixteen jumpers out. This I did upon receiving the green light from the pilot.

"I landed without event. And, getting out of my equipment, of course I set out to 'roll up the stick' and find my men, any men that I could . . . take command of them and move to our objective.

"I began to hear one of those crickets, and following the sound of that cricket, I came upon a man who was badly injured. The Germans had staked out the large fields in Normandy to prevent glider landings. They had set poles in the ground, about the size of one of our own telephone poles—not that high, but maybe ten to twelve feet off the ground. They looked like large pencils sticking in the ground. Unfortunately, this man had landed right on one of those poles and had broken his leg about midway between the knee and the hip.

"He had a severe fracture of the thigh there, was in great pain, was effectively out of the fighting, and could do nothing at all. There was no way I could take him with me. Each man carried a first aid kit, which contained morphine. I took his morphine, gave him a shot of morphine, took his rifle, put his bayonet on it, stuck it in the ground, put his helmet on top of the butt of the rifle. This was somewhat of a universal symbol that a man was out of action and certainly did not intend to fight. Then I went on about trying to find additional men." [25]

When Sergeant Ron Snyder, with Company G, moved toward the door, he hit switches controlling the equipment bundles. "I misplaced my footwork and exited the door with poor body position. I was head down and facing the sky when my chute opened. The opening shock was tremendous—it took my breath. But, recovery was fast when I saw the curtain of silver tracers moving towards me. I could see fires burning in the town, and I clearly heard the church bells. And now, the tracers were ripping my canopy. But I was spared when I dropped behind the shadow of the roof line and slammed into a cow pasture like a sack of cement.

"Quickly, I scrambled out of my harness and found Lieutenant [Travis] Orman, and we began rounding up our platoon." [26]

After getting out of his chute, Corporal Wheatley T. "Chris" Christensen, with Company G, who had jumped last in his stick, started moving back to the west looking for the others. "My stick must have been scattered in three or four small fields. At this time we were being introduced to the Normandy hedgerows. You would pick up two or three men in this field and have to find an opening to get out. The next field you [would] have the same problem, but the opening [was] in another location. To add to this confusion, there was no set pattern to these fields. Those crickets we had been issued were now being put to good use.

"After getting to the end of the stick, I was told Lieutenant [Robert K.] Ringwald, our assistant platoon leader and jumpmaster, wanted to see me. Both he and Sergeant [James R.] Yates were down and hurt bad. He had a broken back, and Yates had two broken legs. We were fortunate in one respect: that they were close together, so we didn't have to move them very far to get them side by side. Removing their equipment and making them as comfortable as possible, after first placing their canteens and first aid kits within easy reach, I had the unpleasant duty of telling them we were going to have to leave them. This they both understood, and we wished each other the best of luck. They were both good people." 27

Captain Bill Follmer, the Company G commander, severely broke his right hip and leg upon landing. Lieutenant Ivan F. Woods, the executive officer, took command of the company.

After landing alone, Private Jack Hillman, with Company I, found a wealth of weapons and ammunition nearby. "I was fortunate to come upon a bundle, and quickly opening it, obtained a light machine gun with two canisters of ammo, and a bazooka with eight rounds. Attaching the tripod to my canteen, locking a belt of ammo in the light machine gun, slinging the bazooka with ammo over my shoulder with my rifle, I proceeded towards my destination, alone and scared to death." 28

Jumping with the 3rd Battalion were two 75mm howitzers and crews with Battery C, 456th Parachute Field Artillery Battalion. Lieutenant Clarence W. McKelvey was the jumpmaster for one of the two planes. "We had gotten the red light from the pilot, which meant for us to stand up and hook up and get ready to go. Sergeant [Joseph] Thomas and I were squatting down by the door looking at the ground, trying to pick up the pathfinder marks. We had a door bundle, and one of the men was behind the door bundle. The plan was for the door bundle [and the man] to go—then our gunner corporal would go, Corporal [James] Bates—then I would go—and the rest of the stick would go, with Sergeant Thomas clicking off the belly bundles. He would then go—the bundles going at the same time.

"When the machine gun fire hit the plane, the pilot jerked the plane over on the left side. All of us went flying on our butts. The door bundle and the man with the door bundle—they went out the door.

"When he righted the plane, we all stood up again, and the crew chief was hollering, 'Go! Go! Go!—You've got the green light!'

"I grabbed him by the chest and threw him to the back of the airplane, cussing him out a little bit, saying, 'We're not over the drop zone. The pilot jerked the airplane and threw us all down.'

"By this time Corporal Bates was in the door, and Sergeant Thomas and I were in the door again looking for the marks, when the pilot jerked the plane again. Corporal Bates flew out the door—I flew out the door—head first, ass over teacups. We didn't know how high we were, but I felt three things in succession—my helmet popped off my head, I felt my chute open, and I looked down and there was the ground.

"I hit the ground. We didn't have quick-release chutes. So I was lying on my back, trying to get all these straps unhooked. Finally, it dawned on me—I've got a trench knife on my right leg. So I got that and I was sawing on the straps to get out, and I heard this voice saying, 'Who are you?'

"I looked up and here was this round thing sticking right in front of my forehead. It looked at the time to be about four inches in diameter. It turned out to be a .30-caliber carbine and a young boy from the 101st.

"I stammered, 'I'm an American—get that damned thing out of my face!' So he helped me out of my straps, and I stood up. About this time Corporal Bates came running across the field with my helmet—though he had lost his.

"A machine gun opened fire across the field. So, the three of us started running toward the hedgerow. We dove into the hedgerow, and I got hung up with my feet dangling in the air. I had a new rubberized gas mask on my left hip and leg, and a .45 pistol on my right hip, as well as a walkie-talkie radio on which I was supposed to contact [Lieutenant] Ray Grossman once we hit the ground. I finally got down into the ditch, and two things I discarded—the gas mask and the radio, because I couldn't get it to work.

"We found several other guys in this ditch. We saw some buildings to our left, and we started moving down this hedgerow toward these buildings—being aware that the machine gun was to our right in the field—firing at us. We got to this little crossroads—just two dirt roads—[where] there were two barns and two houses. When we got to the crossroads, I got out my flashlight and map, trying to figure out where we were. None of us knew.

"The machine gun opened up again. So, we all hit the dirt, crawled behind the buildings—then decided that we had to do something about that machine gun or somebody was going to get hurt. It was decided that I would stay at the corner of the building with the flashlight. A couple of guys would run across the road to the back of the houses. A couple of guys would go the other way and try to sneak around behind the machine gun nest and put it out of commission. I was supposed to shine the flashlight and let them fire at me. We were getting all ready to do this when suddenly, the kid from the 101st who had helped me out of my harness came running up the road hollering, 'I got him!'

"Well, we had heard two explosions a little bit before that. He had gone back there and thrown a couple of grenades in behind the barricade where the machine gun nest was set up. We had no more trouble with that." 29

Lieutenant Ray Grossman was the jumpmaster for the other Battery C gun. "Our pilot put that C-47 down on the deck when we hit France and then was trying to take evasive action. The green light went on, and we threw out the first door load. The pilot tipped the plane to the right and put me and the first man in the stick on the floor. When we got straightened out and jumped, the door load couldn't be found until noon the next day. We gathered up around forty troopers from all outfits and headed for Ste.-Mère-Église. I am guessing we were three miles from our DZ." 30

THE 1ST BATTALION SERIAL CAME IN approximately five minutes behind the 3rd Battalion. As the serial emerged from the cloudbank, it was hit by heavy anti-aircraft fire.

Staff Sergeant Joseph I. O'Jibway, a platoon sergeant with Company B, was the jumpmaster of his stick. "Our pilot, upon hitting the fogbank, turned to the left sharply, to avoid other planes. I had to hold two guys on my back and myself from falling out. I don't know how off course he got—we were hooking up at the time of the sharp turn.

"When we came out of it, he straightened up. I saw three planes on fire up ahead and much tracer fire. Then the green light came on, so we jumped with the plane going 150 miles per hour, five hundred feet off the ground. We hit so hard, the landing was sideways—I was almost knocked out, and my left leg was badly injured." [31]

In addition to his heavy combat load and M1 rifle in a Griswold case, Sergeant Harvill Lazenby, a squad leader with Company B, was carrying a double-barreled, twelve-gauge shotgun and a Colt .38 Special. Lazenby wanted to be able to defend himself as soon as he hit the ground. "The planes went in all directions when the flak started. We jumped around four hundred feet and we were taking a hit when we jumped. Because this was my third combat jump, I jumped with the shotgun in my hand. I landed in a sunken field alone, got out of my chute, made contact later with [Lieutenant James] Irvin, and we began to pick up guys from all units. We were between Montebourg Station and Ste.-Mère-Église." [32]

The plane carrying Private Dutch Schultz, a young replacement with Company C, was taking evasive action. "There was a lot of rocking and rolling. I remember looking out the window, and I thought I saw sparks coming out of one of the engines. I turned to one the veterans and I said, 'Look at those sparks coming out of the engines.'

"And he looked at me and said, 'Sparks, hell—that's flak—that's ack-ack.' That was the first awareness I had that things weren't going to be merely like a practice jump, and that was also the reason for all this rocking and rolling." [33]

Sergeant Elmo Bell and a stick of Company C troopers had just hooked up when "one engine of our plane was hit by several 20mm shells, and it knocked out this engine. The plane banked over sharply and literally dropped for a couple of hundred feet. This sudden maneuver caused everyone to fall into the aisle in one big tangle. The pilot did a tremendous job of recovering control of the plane. He even got the engine restarted, although the engine vibrated terribly. Undoubtedly, there was a bent propeller or there was something that caused the engine to vibrate to the point that there was fear among the troopers that the engine would tear loose and be separated from the plane.

"We lost altitude—we were down to treetop level, and with everyone tangled up in the floor. The jumpmaster was the first sergeant, Herman Zeitner, commonly called 'Zeke,' [who] was thrown back into the tail section. I was the number two man in the stick, and I fell in front of the door so that as soon as I was able to get to my feet, I was in the doorway. I got to my feet intending to jump—and when I looked out we were skimming the treetops. And then, as others started getting to their feet, everyone was interested in getting out of the plane, because it was obviously crippled, and no one knew whether it was losing or gaining altitude. But we were too low, and I was holding [on] the door[way], trying to hold the troopers back, and I was shouting, 'No! No! No!'

"Zeitner finally got to his feet and got to the door and he, too, saw the situation, and we locked arms. Each one [of us] was holding on to each side of the door, with our arms locked in the middle, trying to hold the rest of the troops back. I finally realized that we were saying, 'No!' and above the sound of the engines, that sounded like 'Go!' We then started say, 'Stop! Stop!' And finally, the message got through that we were too low, and the troopers in the rear stopped struggling and pushing, trying to get out the door.

"Zeitner told me to watch the ground and to give him the signal as soon it was high enough to jump. I imagined that three hundred feet would be about the absolute minimum for a safe drop. After a few minutes, it was apparent that we were gaining altitude, very slowly. I could tell that we were definitely gaining altitude, but I thought we were still too low to drop. I turned to Zeitner to tell him that we were gaining altitude, and when I called his name, he went out the door. Well, realizing that my calling his name had triggered his jump, I jumped too—and of course, the rest of the stick followed me out.

"We all landed safely, and Zeitner described the landing—he said that his chute popped open, and in the same instant, his butt hit the ground. He said it was that close. All of the stick members agreed.

"Surprisingly, the stick assembled in a matter of two or three minutes, because we [had jumped] so low that there was no opportunity for the stick to disperse or to scatter. We were all within a few hundred yards of each other. It was the easiest assembly that I ever experienced in combat." [34]

As the flak and machine gun fire increased, Company C trooper Private John E. Wasner waited for the jump sequence to begin. "The red light lit and then Lieutenant [Wilbert H.] Robbins said, 'Stand up—hook up—check equipment. As I looked out, I saw tracers rising from the ground a little distance away, plus bursts of antiaircraft explosions. Suddenly, a loud explosion shook the plane and we felt turbulence. Lieutenant Robbins jumped and I stepped back, although the red light was still on.

"Panic had set in some of the paratroopers' minds, because they thought we were going to crash after being hit by flak, and they were yelling, 'Go! Go! Go!' In the meantime, the green light went on, the signal to jump. I needed no green light. So out I went. As I floated down to earth, it looked like a Fourth of July fireworks display for miles.

"I landed hard on my left foot at an unbalanced, angled position. Then I felt a terrific pain and moaned. My first thought was to get out of my chute. In my haste to get out of my chute, I cut my musette bag straps, plus the chute straps with my 'Jim Bowie' knife. I was scared stiff.

"I heard crickets all around me in the hedgerows area where I had landed. Four other paratroopers landed in the immediate area and were helping one of them hobble towards me. They were from B Company. I told them I had hurt or broke my left leg. They told me [Private Francis A.] Schuler also was injured and had hurt his hip very badly. I was told to stay there with Schuler, and they would see if they could get a medic to fix us up." [35]

As Private John J. Walsh, with Company C, came down, a German machine gunner zeroed in on him. "I thought the Jerry gunner was going to shoot my feet off—tracers just missing. I slipped away, but he kept right at me." [36] Moments later, Walsh landed, without being hit.

Private Gordon Pryne with Company A was close enough to the door of the C-47 that he could see out. "As I was looking out the door, I could see tracers going by. I thought, 'Oh brother, I hope they don't hit the plane.'

"I landed out in a cow pasture." [37]

Shortly after landing, Lieutenant Jack Tallerday, with Company C, gathered six or seven of his men and began moving down a hedgerow. "It was a partial moonlight night, and the hedgerow was about ten feet high, thin foliage with a bank of dirt at the base about three feet high. After going a short distance, we heard, as well as observed, a group of men approaching from the opposite direction, but on the other side of the hedgerow. We stopped and I pinched my 'cricket.' We used this to indicate our presence to other men in our unit. After I pinched my cricket the second time, we heard what we thought to be a reply, as the sound was similar.

"As our two groups of men approached each other, at a distance of five yards, it was quite evident by the configuration of their steel helmets that they were enemies. I believe the Germans realized this too. However, both of us, being surprised as well as frightened, continued to walk forward. As we passed, neither group spoke, and till this day why neither of our groups didn't shoot or kill the others, I don't know. It was like two ships passing in the night. You can be sure that we were more cautious during the next four hours of darkness that night, to the extent that we got into several small firefights. We shot first and asked questions later." [38]

Two planes in the 1st Battalion serial carried the 3rd Platoon, Company B, 307th Airborne Engineer Battalion. After landing, Private Neil Droogan found his platoon leader and some of the other members of the 3rd Platoon, and a few stragglers from the 101st Airborne. They moved out toward the platoon objective— removal of enemy demolition charges from the La Fière bridge—when Droogan heard machine gun fire up ahead. He then saw a veteran member of the platoon make a fatal mistake usually committed by replacements—acquiring a souvenir. "[Private John J.] O'Neill killed a German officer coming out of the building. He ran to get the German's Luger. Fire from the second floor killed O'Neill. We all fired at the building and killed the Germans." [39]

The 1st Battalion serial included nine planes carrying Regimental Headquarters and Headquarters Company. The regiment's executive officer, Lieutenant Colonel Mark Alexander, stood in the door of his C-47 looking for landmarks through the cloud cover. "When we hit the coast of the peninsula, we went into a scattered formation of clouds; the cloud cover broke up the aircraft formations. As we progressed across the peninsula at an elevation of about twelve hundred feet, I had occasional glimpses of the ground, and I was eventually sure that we had over flown the DZ. However, I did not want to jump without the green light, as there might be other planes below and behind us. Finally, we got the green light, going at excessive speed, and we bailed out.

"We landed about three and a half or four miles northwest of Ste.-Mère-Église. I landed on a stump in a clearing near a farmhouse. The stock of my carbine hit the stump first, slammed up into my chin and cut a half-inch gash in my jaw. This was a lightly forested area. I rounded up about twenty of my jump stick and with Captain [Patrick] Gibbons (Regimental S-2) who spoke a little French, and talking with the family in the farmhouse, we figured out where we were—or thought we were.

"We picked up all the equipment we could find and headed for Ste.-Mère-Église. In route, we gathered a few more men who had been dispersed and eventually joined with about fifty men and Major Kellam from the 1st Battalion, who were headed in the same direction—having also been dropped to the northwest of their objective, which was the bridge at La Fière." [40]

After he landed and got out of his harness, Captain George B. Wood, one of the regimental chaplains, couldn't see or hear anyone else in the area. "We were supplied with 'crickets' to snap when we hit the ground in order to locate each other for assembly. I was alone in a field surrounded by hedgerows, snapping my cricket, when Captain [William J.] Harris came up behind me and said, 'Stop that damn noise.'" [41]

Lieutenant Colonel Ekman landed about two miles north of the drop zone and had a particularly bad landing. "I was knocked out and came to with everyone gone. It was dark, of course, and I found myself in the middle of a herd of cattle. Due to my difficulty in walking for the next several days, I am sure I landed astride a cow. I caught up with my staff about an hour later moving in the direction of our selected [CP] site." [42]

COMPANY B, 307TH AIRBORNE ENGINEER BATTALION, less the 3rd Platoon, attached to the 508th PIR, arrived minutes later, as part of the 508th Regimental Headquarters serial. The 1st Platoon, under the command of Lieutenant James A. Rightley, was dropped far to the west of their drop zone, coming down near St.-Sauveur-le-Vicomte. After landing, Rightley moved out to find his platoon. "We were scattered all over. I only found one engineer after landing, but many from the 508. We were to blow a bridge at Pont l' Abbé, but couldn't get there. For the rest of the night and D-Day, we kept losing men—lost and killed." [43]

Technician Fifth Grade Tom Goins, with the 1st Platoon, also landed near St.-Sauveur-le-Vicomte, about a hundred fifty feet away from a German command post and the middle of a nightmare. "My platoon sergeant, Sergeant [Everette H.] Langford's throat was cut while [hanging in his chute] in a tree. We did not have any chance. I moved around and picked up Lieutenant James L. Durham, who had a broken leg. We were surrounded by Germans—five of us ran into a German officer and we surrendered. The officer kept us from being shot." [44]

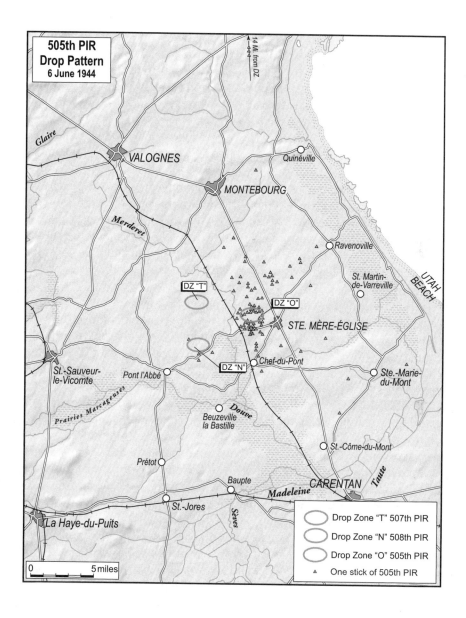

THE 505TH WAS THE ONLY REGIMENT in either the 101st or 82nd to have an accurate drop, thanks in large part to their pathfinder team and the experienced aircrews that had flown them into Sicily and Italy. The 1st Battalion assembled and moved west to secure the eastern end of the La Fière Causeway, while the 2nd Battalion moved northeast to block the main road from Cherbourg, and the 3rd Battalion moved toward its objective—Ste.-Mère-Église.

THE 3RD BATTALION ASSEMBLED QUICKLY after landing and prepared to move out. Private First Class Leslie P. "Les" Cruise and his Company H stick had landed almost entirely on the drop zone, and he quickly made his way to the Company H assembly point. "Within a short time our platoon was intact, along with many from other 3rd Battalion companies. Many troopers arrived with the much needed equipment from the bundles dropped from each of the aircraft. These supplies were distributed to all to help get them to our objectives, where they would give us the additional firepower that we required. I carried two containers of machine gun ammo in addition to my already heavy load.

"Along the road below I could see a group of officers talking to a Frenchman who had arrived on the scene, and he was pointing out some directions, at least he was waving his arms in several directions. Perhaps no one spoke French." [45]

Sergeant William Blank, with Company G, was close enough to overhear the conversation. "[Lieutenant] Colonel Krause questioned him about the town [Ste.-Mère-Église] and the degree of troop strength. We went into the town expecting a fight." [46]

Cruise was waiting for orders when the word was passed down the column that the company commander wanted to see the platoon leaders up front. "Captain [Walter C.] DeLong gathered H Company platoon officers together to pass along the orders given by [Lieutenant] Colonel Krause. The battalion, numbering over several hundred men, plus some troopers who had missed their drop zone, would move on Ste.-Mère-Église, where the glow in the sky was showing, and take the town and defend it. We could hear sounds of machine gun and rifle fire all around, but nothing was from our immediate location. We had secured our area and were waiting orders to move, which came after the confrontation with the civilian who had been convinced to join our group. With the assistance of our newfound friend, we moved out towards Ste.-Mère-Église with G Company in the lead followed by H and I Company groups. Some groups were missing by the planeload, and we had no idea where they were, but we could not wait for them because time was very important to our mission's success.

"It was quite difficult to see where we were going in the dark surroundings as we stumbled down the embankment to the roadway and moved down the road in single file. We had trouble staying in line and following the man in front. I assumed we were heading for Ste.-Mère-Église and I hoped that the colonel knew our route. The trees and hedges screened the silhouettes of the men to my front. I was taken by surprise when [the man ahead of me] suddenly seemed to vanish, when I realized that he had turned right off the road into what appeared to be a cattle trail through the hedgerow and about three feet below the surface of the road. I damn near fell flat as I stumbled onto the trail fresh with cow manure. 'Where the hell are we going?' I murmured to myself. This path was almost like a tunnel through the brush, which was hanging low over our heads as we meandered along, staggering in the soft turf. I heard low muttering from others, but loud noises would give us away to the enemy, who must know we are in the vicinity. Just as suddenly as we had entered this path, we now began to exit onto what looked like a main road, where we paused momentarily to reconnoiter and check locations." [47]

After Company G Platoon Sergeant Ron Snyder landed near Ste.-Mère-Église, he worked to get the platoon assembled. "It was very dark. Bewildered cows were everywhere, and confusion reigned. There were whistles and Very pistol signals and lots of hollering as we worked to sort out the thoroughly mixed up companies.

"Obviously, considerable time would be spent assembling. So Lieutenant [Travis] Orman suggested that I should take a few men and complete a secondary platoon assignment, which was to investigate a group of Quonset hut–like buildings at the west edge of town and clear them of enemy soldiers. Off I went in the black night with a couple of riflemen, and as we crawled through the fence to enter onto the highway, we froze in place at the sound of rapidly marching troops.

"Who were they? It sounded like German boots, but—maybe it could be English. We held our fire and let them pass. Later, I learned it was a company of the German 1058th Infantry bivouacked southwest of town.

"Just as we finished checking the building area for Germans, a huge flight of C-47s roared overhead, and the enemy antiaircraft firing from the town resumed, and we watched, sickened and enraged, as volumes of silver tracers ripped through the fuselages. I decided right then to go into town and silence those guns. By this time, I had picked up several stragglers and had a force of about ten men.

"We moved quickly, filing past the darkened houses that lined the street named Rue Chef-du-Pont. Enemy vehicles were roaring by on the main road ahead, and suddenly one truck braked to a stop, and troops from the back began firing wildly down the street. We sought refuge in doorways, and I ordered my men to withdraw. I feared the truck may drive down the street and shoot us like fish in a barrel. I left two riflemen to fire on the truck, to hold their attention, and with the rest of the men, I ran down a connecting street and then up a street paralleling the first street, hoping to outflank the enemy. This was always a main principle of our tactics. Never attack the strongpoint head on, but circle around and hit it from the flank. As we approached the main road, many German vehicles were still whizzing by, some with the headlights on, and the truck I was trying to outflank was gone. But through the trees on the town square, and illuminated by the dancing light and shadows from a burning house or a barn, I could see enemy soldiers loading several trucks, and against these, we directed all of our fire and drove them out of town in a hail of bullets." [48]

As some of the Germans pulled out of Ste.-Mère-Église, they took with them Company F trooper Private John Steele, whose parachute had caught on the church steeple, and who had been taken down and made a prisoner. "I was wounded in the foot and hobbling along on a stick under German guard with six or eight other GIs—being moved from a German battalion headquarters to their regimental headquarters. A small unit of German riflemen headed by a first lieutenant slipped out of the woods, stopping us. We were asked a lot of questions, which we didn't answer.

"The lieutenant cut my belt and flipped the buttons from the fly of my trousers with a hunting knife—tapping me on the chest with the point of the knife and said, 'So you won't run too fast,' in perfect English.'" [49]

JUST AS SNYDER AND HIS SMALL GROUP CEASED FIRING, veteran 3rd Battalion troopers who hadn't hit the drop zone converged on Ste.-Mère-Église from all directions. Corporal Chris Christensen was leading one such group of Company G troopers. "I had seen this red glow in the sky and heard small arms from the same area, so assuming this was where the action was, and not sure at all where we were, this direction seemed the most logical. I also felt we had missed the DZ, as all the planes I heard after landing were well off to my left. We hadn't gone very far when I picked up four more men from the 2nd Platoon. I now knew mine wasn't the only planeload to be dropped here.

"Moving out, the going was slow, much like running an obstacle course with all those damn hedgerows. After all the training and preparations we had made back in England, not one word had been mentioned about them. After a short distance, I could see we were approaching a small village, but I am still not sure what town it was. I had the men spread out on both sides of the road, and we started moving through the town.

"Up until now, I hadn't seen a soul, but had this eerie feeling of being watched, so I proceeded very cautiously along. The farther we moved in, the smell of smoke was much stronger and visibility much poorer. About now, there was a break in the houses, and we were approaching what looked like a village square. I halted the column and moved ahead to inspect what turned out to be a dead paratrooper hanging from a tree. Also, there were a couple more bodies lying close by." [50]

As this occurred, Krause and the 3rd Battalion troopers who assembled on the drop zone were arriving on the outskirts of Ste.-Mère-Église. Because the Frenchman had told him that the town was lightly held, Krause ordered elements of Company G and Company H to move quietly through the town and set up roadblocks on all roads leading into town before clearing it with Company I and Headquarters Company troopers.

As they cautiously moved down the main street, the paratroopers saw something that would shock, sadden, and enrage them. For Sergeant Bill Blank with Company G, the images would live with him forever. "We saw a number of troopers who had landed in trees and on light wires, all of [whom] were dead. They had not had a chance to get out of their chutes." [51]

As Corporal Christensen was checking out the dead bodies in front of his column, Lieutenant Colonel Krause walked up to him seemingly from nowhere, startling him. He ordered Christensen "to take my group back down the road I had just come in on and set up a defensive position facing out, behind the last house on the right. We were about to move out when [Krause] heard a couple of my men laugh. He immediately stopped me and started to chew me out. He complained that the men weren't serious enough. When he had finished, I snapped to attention and gave him a parade ground salute, all the time, hoping there was an enemy sniper in the vicinity who would see and realize he was an officer and plug him between the eyes. No such luck!" [52]

Company H set up roadblocks on the N-13 highway just north of town, the Chef-du-Pont road southwest, and the La Fière road west of Ste.-Mère-Église. Sergeant Norbert Beach's Company H squad set up a roadblock on the N-13 highway "on the northern edge of Ste.-Mère-Église and put out antitank mines." [53]

Private First Class Cruise was part of a two-squad group of Company H troopers assigned to the roadblock on the Chef-du-Pont road. "We deployed our landmines—glad to unload them from our musette bags, where we had stashed them in England about three hours ago. Three rows of mines were placed in front of our defense line, and we hoped they would stop any German tanks that might try to dislodge us. We were assigned positions to the right and left of the road as well as on either side of it in the ditches, and some troopers were given the areas in the fields [from which] to cover our flanks.

"Some troopers were assigned to dig in on each side of the roadblock about fifty feet behind the mines we had deployed across the road. [Norman J.] Vance, [Marshall A.] Ellis, [Francis B.] Gawan, and several others from the 1st Squad of the 1st Platoon were located there, and some troopers were assigned to the left flank along the hedgerows facing away from Ste.-Mère-Église. [Doyle T.] Jones, [Robert E.] Coddington, [Glenn J.] Carpenter, [Alan D.] Beckwith, and [Gilbert L.] Gamelcy were among these. [Richard A.] Vargas, Larry Kilroy, and I were on the right flank above an embankment at the roadside and about fifty feet from the road. Slightly off to the left were men of the 2nd Squad, commanded by Sergeant Edward White, with [Frederick C.] Neilsen, [Bernard A.] Cusmano, [Allen H.] Horn, [Boniface F.] Zalenski, and Davis, plus others spread out towards the next roadway where they linked with other H Company squads.

"In the predawn darkness Vargas, Kilroy, and I started our foxhole, with one of us watching while two dug, and then we exchanged diggers until completed. We were located in front of a three-foot–high hedgerow that ran perpendicular to the road, and we positioned ourselves so that we could cover effectively the field to our front. The hedgerow would provide some cover when we communicated with those on the road. In scanning the area, I realized that we were very close to the hidden trail we had taken to arrive in our present spot. I had gotten used to the darkness, and though it was cloudy, we could see shapes and outlines of things near us, but the high bank near the road obscured the men there." [54]

Company G set up roadblocks on the N-13 highway and Éconquenaèuville road south and southeast of Ste.-Mère-Église. Headquarters Company, 3rd Battalion set up roadblocks on the Beuzeville-au-Plain road east of town and the Bandienville road northeast of town.

Sergeant Bill Blank, with Company G, was defending a roadblock on the Éconquenaèuville road. "The Germans had dug some nice foxholes and trenches—this saved us much work. When daylight came, we went out to locate equipment bundles and retrieve whatever equipment that could be found." [55]

AFTER WAITING FOR G AND H COMPANIES to establish roadblocks, Krause sent Company I through the town, going house-to-house and building-to-building to clean out the Germans. They took about thirty prisoners and killed the few who attempted to resist.

A short time later, another group of Company I troopers who had overshot the drop zone entered the town from the east. Carrying his .30-caliber machine gun, Private First Class Bill Tucker moved cautiously into Ste.-Mère-Église with his assistant gunner, Private Larry Leonard. Tucker could see signs of fighting that had occurred earlier as he neared the church in the town square. "I stopped under a large tree inside a five-foot wall near the church. It was suddenly very quiet, and I felt very strange. It seemed as if something was moving close to me, and I swung the machine gun around. I didn't see anything until I looked up.

"There was a dead parachutist—caught in the tree and shot by the enemy— hanging from a tree right over my head. The soldier swayed back and forth. He had very big hands. His helmet covered most of his face. I felt shattered.

"As it began to get light, I began to look around carefully. The first thing I noticed was the body of another jumper about ten yards away in the tall grass near the gate. All he had on was his jump suit and harness. His boots were gone—who knows why? I guess he cut himself loose from his chute and equipment after being caught in the tree. He had apparently been shot down trying to get away. I got a good look at the trees that bordered the park. There were bodies or chutes of six or eight other paratroopers who had been caught in the trees and also shot by the Germans as they hung there.

"We ran from the park and across the square, in front of the church in the center of town. As I ran by a door of the church, I almost stopped when I saw an empty chute on the ground. Ten yards away, I saw the body of a German soldier. It was the first dead German I had seen in daylight in France. I would always remember his face. His skin was a little blue, and blood ran out of the corner of his mouth. His uniform looked immaculate. His rifle lay nearby with a fixed bayonet." [56]

This was undoubtedly the soldier Private Ken Russell had encountered a couple of hours earlier while hanging from the church roof, and who was shot and killed by his Company F mortar squad leader, Sergeant John Ray. The empty parachute most likely belonged to Private Russell.

AFTER THE REGIMENT JUMPED, Company E pathfinder, Private First Class Tony DeMayo moved out into the fields with the other pathfinders responsible for the lights and turned them off. "The radar men had to keep tapping out the code for the gliders, which were to come in next. We had to follow the same procedure." [57]

On the ground, Sergeant James Elmo Jones operated his ADF as the pathfinder teams guided the tow planes to the landing zone, which were the three fields the regiment had dropped on earlier. "We could hear additional planes coming in and could see by moonlight that they were pulling gliders. So, we gave instructions to turn on the lights again." [58]

Suddenly, Jones and the other pathfinders saw gliders cutting loose and gliding toward them to land on their field. "We were right in the middle of the field where the gliders were supposed to land. One of the problems was that we still had to continue transmitting on our equipment to bring in additional planes after the gliders came in. But, we had to try to get out of the way of the gliders landing. They were supposed to fly directly over and in line with the lights, make a one hundred eighty degree turn to the left, and come in and land at the far end of the field, so that they wouldn't inhibit the other gliders coming in behind them.

"There's never been a greater slaughter in the world than took place that night. If they came in low, they would fly into the hedgerows with trees on top. When they would try to pull up and go over, they would stall out. With equipment and [up to] sixteen men in each one, it was the most horrible thing that a person could see. Some of the gliders landed on top of each other, soldiers that were trapped or wounded would cry and call for help all night. And the gliders just simply kept coming." [59]

Private First Class DeMayo made it to the edge of the field as the speeding gliders began landing. "This is something I wish would never have to happen, because when the gliders started to come in, it was murder. There was just one crash after another, as they hit the so-called hedgerows. It was just like crumbling wooden matchboxes in your hand. We spent a lot of time helping the poor guys who could be helped, get out of the wreckage. You can take it from me, those glider boys really had it rough." [60]

Northwest of Ste.-Mère-Église, Lieutenant Jack Isaacs, with Company G, was still in the field where he had landed, having gathered about thirty-five men, most of whom he didn't know. "About this time, the gliders started coming into Normandy, and one of them chose this field that I had landed in to make his landing. He, with unerring accuracy, managed to hit one of those anti-glider poles, demolishing the glider, of course, demolishing his load, which was a jeep and some other equipment, and injuring every member of the crew of that glider. So these people, instead of serving as reinforcements to our little group of thirty-five, in effect became a liability to us. Shortly after this, we managed to get these wounded glider men to our little French house [in the corner of the field]. We noticed a German soldier step out into the field over to the east side and approach the injured man that we had left there. He came over to him, looked him over, and then shot him. Of course, this infuriated all of our jumpers, and he didn't survive his trip back to the hedgerow for having shot this man." [61]

Captain Alfred W. "Irish" Ireland, the regimental S-1, had been given the special assignment to make sure that the division received their antitank guns. The 82nd would need to defend the road network north and west of Utah Beach and would undoubtedly face German armor moving from the vicinity of Valognes and from the St.-Sauveur-le-Vicomte area toward Ste.-Mère-Église. The glider landing under fire was undoubtedly a harrowing experience for Ireland, who no doubt would have preferred to enter Normandy by parachute. He gained a new appreciation for what the "glider riders" endured. Upon reaching the division command post later that morning, he was asked about his trip in a glider. Captain Ireland replied only, "Those guys don't get paid enough." [62]

The gliders that brought in Batteries A and B of Lieutenant Colonel Raymond E. "Tex" Singleton's 80th Airborne Antiaircraft (Antitank) Battalion carried sixteen precious 57mm antitank guns, twenty-two jeeps, five trailers, ammunition, water, and medical supplies. However, Singleton wasn't able to assemble his battalion. "Antitank guns were scattered all over the area. It seems that we landed when all the Germans were awake." [63]

From his foxhole near the mined roadblock on the Chef-du-Pont road just outside of Ste.-Mère-Église, Private First Class Les Cruise heard some noises in front of the Company H position. "One of those gliders had landed about three hundred yards from our roadblock. We could hear the noise as they were getting out and removing equipment. Over their shouting we heard the noise of a jeep motor starting, and several troopers left the confines of our position to help.

"Before they reached the landing spot, a jeep rushed down the road passing them even as they shouted a warning about our mines ahead. The occupants of the jeep were in a big hurry as we at the roadblock heard their running motor coming in our direction. Above all the noise, the distinct yells at the block of 'hit the ground' were heard clearly, and we all buried ourselves in the dirt of our foxholes. The driver must have thought our men were Germans and was not about to stop. Down the road they came full throttle.

"[There was] a deafening crescendo of explosive sounds as a number of our mines blew the jeep and its troopers into the air. All hell broke loose . . . flashing lights . . . with pieces of jeep and mine fragments raining down around us. Directly across the middle of our minefield they drove, and immediately their direction became vertical, and in an arching skyward path they landed in the hedgerow beyond. We could hear the thump and bangs of falling parts all around us.

"The men had left the jeep on first impact, and they had become the first casualties in our area, but they would not be the last. We had lost about three quarters of our mines, which we had so carefully delivered, and they would be sorely needed in case the Krauts should attack." [64]

Despite the casualties, the 4:00 a.m. landings by the gliders were successful in bringing in the critically needed antitank guns. Gavin knew they would be needed soon to defend against German armor, which was sure to attack after daylight. "Despite the difficulties, quite a few of them got in. We got six antitank guns in around Ste.-Mère-Église for the heavy fighting against armor the following morning." [65]

As dawn broke at about 6:30 a.m., Lieutenant Colonel Krause walked to the town hall in Ste.-Mère-Église, where he took out his old, worn flag and raised the Stars and Stripes over the first town liberated in France. At 6:50 a.m., Krause sent a runner to the regimental command post west of the town to deliver a message to Lieutenant Colonel William E. Ekman that the 3rd Battalion had secured Ste.-Mère-Église.

CHAPTER 9

"A Small Unit Performance That Has Seldom Been Equaled"

Northof Ste.-Mère-Église, Lieutenant Colonel Ekman came upon Major Jack Norton, the regimental S-3, and together they moved south to find the regimental command post. On their way, they made contact with Vandervoort's 2nd Battalion moving north toward its objective, Neuville-au-Plain. Ekman used one of their radios to attempt to contact the 3rd Battalion, but was unsuccessful. Fearing that the 3rd Battalion had been misdropped or unable to capture Ste.-Mère-Église, Ekman ordered Vandervoort to move the 2nd Battalion south to assist the 3rd Battalion in capturing the town or reinforce them if they controlled it.

Vandervoort made a decision that would prove critical to the success of the invasion. "I sent the 3rd Platoon of Company D to Neuville-au-Plain to outpost the area that originally was to have been held by our entire battalion." [1]

Shortly after daylight, Lieutenant Colonel Alexander, the regimental executive officer, and his group found the N-13 highway, a couple of miles north of Neuville-au-Plain. "We ambushed a German patrol and a communications bus headed south—I would estimate about fifteen Germans, the communications bus, and some motorcycles. Thereafter, I and the regimental headquarters men headed for and found our intended DZ and the regimental headquarters CP." [2]

At Neuville-au-Plain, Lieutenant Turner B. Turnbull, platoon leader of the 3rd Platoon, Company D, deployed most of his strength on the east side of the N-13 highway on a slight rise in elevation about forty yards north of the hamlet. His men were positioned along a hedgerow running slightly northeast to southwest, facing north with a good field of fire for six hundred yards. Turnbull positioned his bazooka team near a house next to the east side of the road to give them some concealment.

One of Turnbull's assistant squad leaders was Corporal Milton E. Schlesener. "We dug in along both sides of Route 13. Our mortar squad could not find their mortar, but they did find some machine guns and lots of ammo in supply bundles that were lying in the area. We had no idea to whom they belonged, but these were gathered and used. Lieutenant [Isaac] Michelman [assistant platoon leader] took charge of that squad since it was off to the left and part of it in an orchard." [3]

Michelman's men, including squad leader Sergeant Robert J. "the Beast" Niland, Private First Class Horace H. Brown, Private John P. Slaverio, and Private Harold V. Dunnegan, covered the field west of the highway with their machine gun.

Corporal Schlesener noticed how peaceful everything seemed that morning. "It certainly did not seem like we were at war. Farmers were starting to gather their cows. People were walking along the road. There were no planes flying around. The fields were real lush with grass. Our boots made a sucking sound as we were walking through it. There were small drainage ditches along the edges of the fields, the dirt had been thrown into the hedgerows. Do this for a number of years—you get a deep bank to dig into." [4]

Private Gerald R. Weed was Turnbull's communications NCO. He had been a sergeant back in England, but had been busted. Weed was carrying a heavy SCR-300 radio, a roll of wire, and field telephone. "Lieutenant Turnbull said, 'Get a telephone.' So I strung a wire for a field telephone out there and I hooked it up." [5]

VANDERVOORT CONCEALED THE CONSIDERABLE PAIN caused by his broken ankle. "When I got into Ste.-Mère-Église, an elderly French woman, noticing I was using a rifle to hobble about, went into her house and came out with an old fashioned pair of wooden crutches and gave them to me. With these I was able to get about much better." [6]

When the 2nd Battalion entered Ste.-Mère-Église, they found it occupied by the 3rd Battalion. Krause and Vandervoort met and decided to divide the defense of the town—the 2nd Battalion taking responsibility for the northern and eastern portions, with the 3rd Battalion defending the western and southern approaches. Upon reaching the town, the 2nd Battalion surgeon, Captain Lyle Putnam, prepared for the inevitable flood of casualties who would soon need treatment. "We established an aid station in a large, two-story brick edifice on the [northern] edge of the town on the main road leading to Cherbourg, and began to collect our own casualties and some German [casualties]. We got all of the supplies we could find, beg, or steal." [7]

Captain Robert Franco, the assistant regimental surgeon, set up a second aid station just west of Ste.-Mère-Église, near the division command post. One of the seriously jump injured was Captain Matthew J. Connelly, the regiment's Catholic chaplain. Doc McIlvoy would later learn that Connelly had "sustained an anterior vertebral fracture of the spine and was in pain throughout the next thirty days that we were in combat, but would not let us evacuate him. Only when we were back in England would he be X-rayed and, of course, he was sent back to the States, He lived in pain for the next several years, eventually having to have both legs amputated." [8]

Private W. A. "Arnold" Jones, with Company F, was assigned to the eastern part of the Ste.-Mère-Église defensive perimeter. "My machine gun was set up in the cemetery. Now, the most horrible thing I saw during the war—to the right of where we were was a grove of trees. We looked over in the trees and Charlie Blankenship, [H. T.] Bryant, and somebody else were hanging in the trees dead." [9]

Captain George B. "Chappie" Wood was the regiment's protestant chaplain. "Colonel Vandervoort asked me to do something about the men hanging dead in the trees down in the village square. There were six of them. It was affecting the morale of the men to see their buddies' lifeless bodies hanging there. I had no burial detail, so I got a detail of six men with an officer from off the front line, which was just the other side of the wall of the cemetery where we were burying the men." 10

The men Chaplain Wood found in the cemetery were from Company F. It had been their buddies who had overshot the drop zone and landed in the square the previous night. One of the Company F troopers chosen for the detail to cut the men down was W. A. Jones. "[Sergeant] Spencer Wurst, myself, and somebody else went over and cut them down. That was the hardest thing. Bryant was a good buddy of mine, even though he joined the regiment after we got to Quorn. He was from Fort Worth.

"Two of us would hold them while the third would cut them down. We cut them down, got their chutes down, and rolled them up in their chutes for Graves Registration. That has stuck with me more than anything else." 11

Chaplain Wood and the men were finishing up when they began to receive an artillery barrage. "We got five men down and into the ground when all hell broke loose, and the men were ordered back to fighting. There was much anger among the men over the killing of their buddies hanging in trees, but I explained that this was what we could expect in our kind of an outfit." 12

Lieutenant Charles E. "Pinky" Sammon commanded the Light Machine Gun Platoon, Headquarters Company, 2nd Battalion. "[Lieutenant] Colonel Vandervoort instructed me to set my platoon up in a defensive position one mile north and east of the town of Ste.-Mère-Église. There was no enemy activity in our area at this time, although I could hear some firing in the distance. We found the area assigned to us by the battalion commander, and I established three machine gun positions, which I felt would give us good protection. I then set up a platoon command post and together with my runner took turns wrapping up in a parachute in order to get a little sleep.

"Dawn of June 6th was just breaking as I started out to check the three positions to make sure everything was in order and find out if the men needed anything in the way of equipment or food. There was at the time sporadic firing in the distance, but we had not seen or heard anything of the Germans in our area up to that point.

"As I approached the first position, I called out to the corporal who was in charge—the answer came back in the form of a long burst from what was unmistakably a German machine gun and one or two machine pistols. The bullets hit the dirt at our feet, and the two of us hit the ditch beside the road.

"What had happened became very clear to me at this point. The Germans had infiltrated our positions during the night and had either killed or captured the men I had placed in this position. As I lay there in the ditch with bullets whizzing over my head, I was not only scared, I was thoroughly disgusted with myself for being outsmarted by the enemy. I was worried and concerned about my men, and at the moment felt helpless to do anything about the situation. We couldn't get up without exposing ourselves to their fire, but soon discovered that as long as we stayed flat on our stomachs in the ditch, we were protected from their fire. They were set up at the junction of two irrigation ditches and were unable to depress the muzzles of their guns any further and couldn't see us due to the relative height of their position.

"I then decided that we should turn around in the ditch and attempt to crawl back to our own positions. We had gone about half way with the bullets clipping the tall grass over our head, when my runner who was now ahead of me panicked and got up to run. I tackled him just as a long burst of German fire hit all round us. From then on, I kept one hand on his foot as we continued to crawl up the ditch. We were making fairly good progress when an American machine gun began firing at us from our own positions. Since we were approaching from the direction of the enemy and were unable to stand up to identify ourselves, I could see no way out of our predicament.

"This time, however, the Germans came to our rescue. The first barrage of German artillery fire came into the position and forced the American machine gunner to abandon his position just long enough for us to jump up and make a run for it. We arrived at the machine gun just as the gunner did, who by the way, turned out to be one of my own men. Just for a moment I considered the irony of being killed by a machine gunner I had spent hours trying to train.

"All was confusion back in our own position. The Germans had infiltrated so well and struck so suddenly that no one knew what was going on. I managed to round up the remnants of my platoon and set up one machine gun to keep firing at the German position so they wouldn't attempt to advance further. I then had one of my men, who was armed with a carbine and rifle grenades, start firing grenades into their protected position.

"The best discovery of all, however, was a mortar man from one of the rifle companies with a complete mortar and a supply of ammunition. In parachute drops, this is a rare find, as often some vital part will be missing as a result of the drop. With the grenades and mortar shells falling into their position, the Germans had no choice but to move out. They couldn't go back up the same ditch they had used to get into the position, as we had set up a machine gun to cover their return. And besides, no doubt their orders were to go forward and wipe us out.

"One by one they attempted to go over the top of their protective embankment and into the ditch I had used to retreat only an hour earlier. There were about twenty men in the position, and about half of them made it into the ditch—the others were killed or wounded as they came out.

"Having become so familiar with that ditch earlier, I knew we couldn't reach them with our rifles and machine guns due to the difference in elevation of our positions. I decided the only way of reaching them was to go around on the flank and get above them and throw hand grenades into the ditch at the places I could observe the tall grass moving. We were so pinned down by artillery fire that I was unable to find anyone to go with me, and I hadn't seen hide nor hair of my runner since our narrow escape earlier. Equipment was scattered all over, and I found about ten ordinary fragmentation grenades and one Gammon grenade.

"From my position on the flank, I waited until I saw the grass move. I scrambled up the side of an embankment, ran across about fifty yards of open ground, which brought me to a position right over the ditch in which the Germans were working their way into our main defenses. I got rid of the Gammon grenade and headed back to the protection of my ditch. I disappeared over the side just as a German rose up out of the ditch and fired at me with a machine pistol. I waited for a loud explosion that never came—my Gammon grenade had misfired.

"Since they now knew where I was, I was hesitant about going back.

About this time a lieutenant [Alexander F. Sweeney] from the airborne engineers came running up the road in a crouched position. He said he had three or four men with him and would like to help. We crawled up the embankment so I could show him what I was trying to do. As we cautiously poked our heads up over the top, a machine gun cut loose from the German ditch. We both slid back down the embankment. When the firing stopped I got up, but he didn't, so I rolled him over. He was shot right through the head.

"I decided to give it another try, as the Germans were getting in closer all the time, which I could tell by the movement of the tall grass in the ditch that they occupied. I pulled the pins on two grenades and started across the open area. This time they went off just as I got back to the protection of my own position.

"The firing from their position stopped, and I carefully looked over the top of the embankment. Believe it or not, a white flag was waving back and forth on the end of a tree limb. Soon a German soldier climbed up over the top carrying the white flag and started in our direction. Two or three of the dead lieutenant's men were with me, and they were all for shooting him. I pointed out that he didn't have any arms and that we had to honor any attempt to surrender. He turned out to be a German doctor about thirty-five [years old] who spoke fluent English. He explained that many of their men were dead and wounded and that they would like to give up. He looked all around and seemed surprised that there were only two or three men in the position.

"I told him that we would not stop firing unless he returned and got all of the Germans to throw down their arms and to come out with their hands over their heads. He agreed to do this and after he returned, we sat there waiting for something to happen. We did not have to wait long, however, as shortly after he disappeared into their position we were the recipients of the heaviest barrage of artillery and mortar fire I had experienced in the war up to that point. It was obvious that the doctor's surrender was all part of a very clever German plot. As a result, we had to abandon this position, and I returned to the area where the rest of my men were entrenched. The German firing was very light now, and with ten or fifteen men we started a counterattack toward the very positions my men had been driven from at dawn. We reached the position alongside the ditch where the Germans had been holed up, and I saw that my grenades had done the job. Those that were not killed by the grenades got up to run and were cut down by machine gun fire from our main positions. There were about fifteen dead and wounded Germans lying about the position." [13]

Lieutenant Sammon and his men had just repulsed the first German attack against the defensive perimeter around Ste.-Mère-Église.

AT ABOUT 8:30 A.M., LIEUTENANT RAY GROSSMAN and about thirty men of Battery C, 456th Parachute Field Artillery Battalion, arrived in Ste.-Mère-Église with a 75mm pack howitzer. The gun was missing the breech block and the sight, which had been the contents of a door bundle on the plane, which had fallen out when the pilot took evasive action, rolling the plane to the left. Despite an intensive search by the gun crew after landing, the door bundle was not found. Grossman knew the gun was useless without those items. "I borrowed a jeep and retraced our steps and found the missing load, hauled it into town, and we finally had a complete gun." [14] Until the glider artillery battalions arrived that evening, Grossman's howitzer was the lone artillery support for the 505th PIR and the division.

AFTER CLEARING STE.-MÈRE-ÉGLISE BEFORE DAWN, Krause had placed Company I in reserve, positioned in the town in order to respond to an attack from any direction. The other rifle companies were dug in and manning roadblocks and the perimeter. The Germans shelling of Ste.-Mère-Église, which began shortly after sunrise, fell primarily in the town and on Company I.

Sergeant Bill Dunfee had come into Normandy with Company I as an extra NCO after attending a chemical warfare school in Northern Ireland. "The enemy really socked it to us, with 88s and Screaming Meemies. The 88s were using either timed or proximity fuses, because we were receiving air bursts. The Nebelwerfers [six-barreled, towed rocket launchers] were so erratic you couldn't tell where their rockets would land. We learned in a hurry the safest place to relieve one's bladder was in the bottom of your foxhole. If Mother Nature required further relief, you were in very serious trouble. We suffered a number of casualties during this bombardment, the most gruesome being when a rocket landed amid three men in a mortar squad. They were all killed; the explosion must have detonated a Gammon grenade in one of the men's leg pocket. The secondary explosion literally blew him to bits. His head, chest, and right arm were all that remained. We learned in a hurry to cut laterally into the side of your foxhole, for a place to hide the family jewels. My musette bag received shrapnel, destroying a Gammon grenade, but not setting off the Composition 'C' contained therein." [15]

The 3rd Battalion, German 1058th Regiment was located in wooded high ground (Hill 20) about a mile south of Ste.-Mère-Église near Fauville. At around 10:00 a.m., two companies of infantry and several self-propelled guns launched an attack north along the N-13 highway toward Ste.-Mère-Église. Effective fire from a 57mm antitank gun of the 80th Airborne Antiaircraft (Antitank) Battalion positioned at the roadblock on the south end of town stopped the self-propelled guns. The German infantry continued to advance along the hedgerows on both sides of the N-13. Private First Class Dominick DiTullio, manning a Company G outpost, almost single-handedly stopped the German infantry by ambushing the leaders. DiTullio would be killed the following day—never knowing that he would later be awarded the Distinguished Service Cross for his valor.

The German infantry withdrew a short distance to reorganize, while artillery and mortars positioned on Hill 20 pummeled the Company G positions—one shell hit four troopers with the 1st Platoon mortar squad. Private Marty Cuccio, the platoon's medic, was summoned to their aid. What awaited Cuccio was a scene of horrible carnage, made worse by the fact that he had shared a tent with all of them back at Quorn. "When I got there, [Private First Class William C.] Walter had got one leg shot off—[Private Robert E.] Holtzmann had both legs shot off—Smitty [Sergeant Stanley S. Smith], concussion had killed him—and the other guy [Private Robert L. Herrin] got killed with the concussion.

"Holtzmann, I gave him morphine, and I gave Walter morphine. [Captain Robert "Doc"] Franco came along. I had told Holtzmann when we were in England, 'If you get an injury to your head, I cannot give you a second morphine because that would kill you.'

"I had given him the morphine. He was telling me as Franco was there, 'Give me the morphine—I want to die.' He didn't want to live.

"I said to Franco, 'I just gave him morphine.'

"Franco said, 'Give him another one,' so I gave him another one. [Holtzmann] made a cross, the stretchers came, and they took him away. Holtzmann was only eighteen years old." [16] Holtzmann and Walter both died a short time later.

Krause ordered Company I to counterattack and throw the enemy back. The company moved south along a hedgerow-lined dirt road that paralleled the highway west of the N-13. Sergeant Bill Dunfee was carrying a BAR that he'd picked up during a lull in the shelling that morning. "We didn't know where we were going or why, just, 'Move out.' We hadn't gone too far before the point came under fire, killing three of the four men. Edwin Jones, the lone survivor, crawled back under our covering fire. He reported Captain [Harold H.] Swingler, [Private First Class Sam] Vanich, and [Private First Class George R.] Irving were dead. We had left our company executive officer in England in charge of the rear echelon, so we were leaderless." [17]

The front of the company column had turned east too soon and had entered the N-13 just in front of where the German infantry was reorganizing. The point knocked out several trucks with Gammon grenades, but was itself hit in the flank.

Company I took cover in the ditch along the road, as the Germans opened fire from the other side of the road, and the Germans set up a machine gun near where the road intersected the N-13, firing it straight down the road. The Company I noncoms took over as Private Jack Hillman saw Staff Sergeant Clarence Prager standing up in the middle of the road, "screaming at us to get our asses down! He said, 'I don't want any of you to get killed, I need you all.' Sergeant Prager was a soldier's soldier, a true leader of men." [18]

Private First Class Bill Tucker and the other troopers waited for orders while lying in the ditch, trying to return the enemy fire. "We were pinned down in that ditch and couldn't even lift our heads up. No one seemed to move. We didn't know what was happening up ahead, and it was awful lying there in the ditch. The Germans were in a ditch on the other side of the road only about ten yards away to our right for a time. They threw grenades over at us. We got some firing in, but the Germans fired at us from the fields to our left. We found that [First] Sergeant [Howard] Melvin alone had saved us from the left by covering our flank. With Captain Swingler gone, Lieutenant [Joseph W.] Vandevegt was in command of the company. Enemy firing didn't let up, and there was no choice but to move backwards in the ditch and find some place to get across the road. Just at the edge of town, we all made a dash across the road and into a sunken orchard near a house or farm.

"Larry [W. Leonard] and I ran into Sergeant [Charles C.] Matash, who had a bullet through his shoulder. Matash had been at the head of guys crawling in the ditch and had actually stood up in the open to draw fire so that others could get across the road. It was a dangerous move. Matash had real guts, and he later got the Silver Star for the bravery he showed." [19]

The counterattack by Company I evidently convinced the German battalion commander that Ste.-Mère-Église was strongly held, and no more infantry assaults were launched from the south. They continued to shell the town with mortars, Nebelwerfers, and 88mm antiaircraft guns.

The German battalion at Fauville blocked the beach-landed forces from linking up with the 505th. Lieutenant Roper R. Peddicord had landed with two planeloads of his 3rd Platoon, Company E, near Les Forges, south of Ste.-Mère-Église. One of his NCOs, Sergeant Cullen E. Clark, Jr., helped set up a roadblock east of the village, where they stopped an armored reconnaissance unit of light tanks with the U.S. 4th Infantry Division moving west from Utah Beach. "Lieutenant Peddicord reported to the commander, and the commander asked us to join his outfit as scouts. Lieutenant Peddicord replied that we would join him and go as far as Ste.-Mère-Église, where we would join our own unit.

"Together, we all moved [west] down the road about two miles and turned right. About five hundred yards down the road, we could see men moving all around and thought they were Americans. After we had gone about [another] two hundred yards, someone called us. We looked to our right and about fifty yards away was an American major. The major had broken his leg on the jump and had dug a hole to hide in. The major informed us that about three hundred yards in front of us were thousands of Germans, and that there were no American troops in that direction. The major said that he had been watching the Germans since dawn and that they were preparing for the seaborne troops.

"Lieutenant Peddicord asked the commander for three light tanks to make a reconnaissance. We put three men on the back of each tank and slowly proceeded down the road. Lieutenant Peddicord, a man named [Fred J.] Hebein, and myself were on the first tank.

"Two German machine guns started firing at us, one from each side of the road. Lieutenant Peddicord and I pulled the pins from hand grenades, and were going to throw them at the machine guns as we went past. The gunner in the tank was also supposed to fire his machine gun at the Germans while we were attacking. He fired a few rounds, then ducked his head back into the tank and held his hands up trying to fire the machine gun. I took over his machine gun and fired about half of the rounds [of the belt] back at the German machine guns. The machine guns were firing at the tank and bullets were ricocheting in all directions. While we were approaching the machine guns, Lieutenant Peddicord had unscrewed the cap off a Gammon grenade and laid it on top of the tank.

"We were about fifty yards from the machine guns when the Germans fired an 88mm. The tank commander got all shook up and started to back up, right into the tank behind us, which was still coming forward. When the two tanks hit, the [Gammon] grenade was rolling all around and the safety was almost out—one more bump and it would have exploded. I scooped the Gammon grenade off [the tank], beside the road, as the other tank hit us again, and as it landed, it exploded.

"It blew me up against the tank and off of the tank, fracturing a couple of vertebrae, cracking my pelvis bone, and causing internal injuries. I fell in a ditch beside the road, but could not move from the waist down. I remember looking up and seeing one man named [George R.] McCarthy hanging upside down by his leg from one of the tanks. I learned later that he broke his leg. Temporarily paralyzed and with no weapon, I grabbed handfuls of grass and pulled myself to what I thought was the rear.

"While doing this, I heard a shout and looked up ahead. . . . A German soldier had run up in front of me; he fired a machine pistol at me, and kept running across the road. I had my gas mask strapped to my leg, and he shot it completely off of my leg. Also, in my jump pocket of my trousers were some K-rations, which were all shot up.

"I got turned around and pulled myself to the rear. A German machine gun was firing at me, but the fire was a few inches above my head. Soon, I could hear American voices. I called out and an E Company man named [Jack S.] Flynn and another man, who I do not remember, picked me up and turned me over to the 4th Division medics. I learned later that Lieutenant Peddicord was killed the next day while on a patrol and never got to join E Company at Ste.-Mère-Église." [20]

Sergeant Bill Blank was at the Company G roadblock on Gambosville road, southwest of Ste.-Mère-Église, when the Germans hit their position. "By mid-afternoon, the Germans started to try to retake the town. They came at us from all directions. They made an attempt to drive a truck through our mines that we had spread across the road. We opened up with small arms, and the truck burned in the road." [21]

SHORTLY BEFORE NOON, PRIVATE GERALD WEED, with the 3rd Platoon of Company D, finished laying a field telephone connection from the Company D command post on the north end of Ste.-Mère-Église to Neuville-au-Plain. "I was up on the road with Lieutenant Turnbull and I also had a radio, besides pulling that damned telephone wire. So I had to stay right with Turnbull. We looked down the road and here came a Frenchman riding up on a bicycle. We stopped him—he could speak just enough English that we could understand him. We [could] see some guys coming up the road. We asked him and he said, 'Paratroopers with some German prisoners.' They were so far away we couldn't tell. We thought this was great." [22]

At that time Vandervoort arrived, bringing antitank support for Turnbull's blocking position. "About noon I went north to Neuville-au-Plain in a jeep with a 57mm antitank gun and gun crew. I told our 57mm antitank gun crew to go into position on the right of the road where a house offered some concealment. As we drove into Neuville-au-Plain, a French civilian passed us moving south on a bicycle. Lieutenant Turner Turnbull, the platoon leader, told me the Frenchman had just come from the north and had told them that a group of paratroopers had taken a large number of German prisoners and vehicles and were moving south on the highway and would arrive at Neuville-au-Plain shortly. As Turnbull and I walked over his position and talked, we kept watching the highway leading from the north. Shortly, a long column of foot troops appeared in the distance with vehicles scattered at intervals through their ranks. If these were prisoners, there was more than a battalion of them. We could make out the field gray of the German uniforms. On their flanks were individuals in paratrooper uniforms waving orange panels that were the recognition signal we were to have used to identify ourselves to friendly aircraft. Somehow, it looked just too good to be true. When the advancing column had closed to within about one thousand yards, I told Turnbull to have his light machine gun fire a burst into the field on the left flank of the column.

"That did it. The alleged German prisoners deployed instantly on both sides of the road and the leading vehicle, a self-propelled gun, instead of acting like the spoils of war the Frenchman said they were, opened fire on our position. Our 57mm antitank gun crew returned the fire and set fire to the leading SP [self-propelled] gun and one more that moved up behind it. A third German SP gun fired smoke shells into the road to its front to screen their position. The German infantry began to move forward on both sides of the road as their 81mm mortars started to range in on the 3rd Platoon position. I told Turnbull to delay the Germans as long as he could, then withdraw to Ste.-Mère-Église. With that, I returned to Ste.-Mère-Église to alert my troops as to what was on the way and to check our positions to meet it." [23]

Turnbull's men opened up as the Germans deployed into the fields on both sides of the road. With the slight high ground and six hundred yards of open ground east of the highway and a couple of two-story buildings on the west side, Turnbull had picked a great position from which to delay the Germans. However, the Germans sent troops from the rear of their column east and west, out of range and out of sight of the D Company platoon and their weapons, attempting to envelop Turnbull's platoon. As the afternoon progressed, casualties in Turnbull's platoon slowly mounted as enemy mortar and long-range machine gun fire took its toll. By about 5:00 p.m., the Germans were closing in on the flanks, threatening to get in behind the platoon.

Turnbull contacted Vandervoort on the field telephone to give him a situation report. After listening to the report, Vandervoort decided to withdraw the platoon, if possible. "The word came from Turnbull that the Germans were enveloping both flanks of his position and he couldn't hold on much longer. I sent one platoon of

Company E, then in reserve, north on the left side of the highway to attack the enveloping German infantry by fire, then withdraw to their reserve position. We hoped it would help Turnbull to withdraw under the cover of this diversion." 24

The 1st Platoon of Company E was led by Lieutenant "Pete" Peterson. "We moved quickly but cautiously north on the west side of the highway to Neuville-au-Plain. We saw groups of the enemy on the way, who apparently did not see us, so we did not engage them. Our primary objective was to assist Lieutenant Turnbull. As we approached his approximate position, my runner and [I] crossed the road, leaving our platoon in a concealed position in a hedgerow." 25

As Turnbull attempted to contact Vandervoort again, Private Weed heard him shouting over the noise of the firing and explosions. "He hollered at me and said the phone wasn't working. I traced that wire . . . I just grabbed the wire and started running with it." 26

As Weed ran down the ditch on the east side of the highway toward Ste.-Mère-Église, almost a mile away, he kept an eye out for the enemy, who had probably cut the line. Suddenly, off to his right, Weed saw Germans moving east toward him and the highway, to Turnbull's left rear. "I saw these Germans, and I don't think they saw me. When I ran out of the wire, the other piece was lying on the ground; I just kept going, because I knew the Germans had cut it. The only thing I could do was run to battalion headquarters and report what was going on." 27

While Lieutenant Peterson and his runner crossed the road to find Turnbull, Sergeant Otis Sampson set up his 60mm mortar on the left flank of the platoon, concealing it in some high grass. "A dirt road ran across the front of us. There was little foliage to obstruct our firing across it. Our CP was set up under a tree to our right. A lane ran directly from the position I was in up over a crest of a hill less than a hundred yards away. Here, a paratrooper lay as he had fallen, crosswise in the lane's center." 28

After running across the highway with his runner, Lieutenant Peterson crept carefully toward Turnbull's position, not sure whether they were expected. "Lieutenant Turnbull had a guard posted at the position we entered, who seemed to be expecting us. This would confirm that [Lieutenant] Colonel Vandervoort had communications with Lieutenant Turnbull, and we were expected. Lieutenant Turnbull was very calm, and he had the situation well in hand, for the rough position he was in. He had about six men killed and eight or ten wounded, plus he was running low on ammunition. They were getting heavy large [caliber] mortar fire, plus machine gun and small-arms fire. One particular machine gun was causing him the most trouble, and he asked us to try to knock it out. This gun was to his left front behind a farmhouse. Also, he asked us to draw fire upon ourselves, which might relieve his platoon enough to withdraw with their wounded. He said as soon as he had withdrawn, he would send a runner to give us the word.

"We moved back to our platoon and set up a line of fire on Lieutenant Turnbull's immediate left, the farmhouse with the enemy gun to our immediate front. We formed a perimeter defense with our power to the front. We commenced firing on order, firing BARs, mortar, bazooka, and small arms fire, making quite a racket. This was to reveal our position to the enemy and to try to knock out the machine gun at the farmhouse. We ceased fire shortly, and waited. All was as quiet as a church. Two scouts and I crawled and ran to the farmhouse with our platoon covering us. There was no sign of the enemy, so we fired a few bursts from our Tommy guns into the barn and house, and moved quickly back to our platoon position.

"After possibly five or ten minutes—all hell broke loose. The enemy, moving west down the road near the farmhouse and to our immediate front, walked right into our hidden left flank, who were stretched out along the hedgerow so that they were practically facing east. Corporal [Thomas J.] Burke, who had already won a Silver Star for bravery, with his Tommy gun; a [trooper with a] BAR; and three or four riflemen held their fire until the enemy was within a few feet of them. Then they opened fire. The surprised enemy took off in every direction, losing a good number of men. With that, the whole platoon opened fire with everything they had at the enemy. This included Sergeant Sampson, the greatest and most accurate mortar sergeant in the business. He fired at this close range and laid the shells down in a line right on their heads." 29

As soon as Peterson's platoon opened fire, Turnbull ordered his platoon to withdraw. The medic, Corporal James I. Kelly, volunteered to stay behind with the wounded. Sergeant Robert J. Niland with his Thompson, Private First Class Julius A. Sebastion with his BAR, and Corporal Raymond D. Smithson volunteered to cover the withdrawal.

Company D trooper, Private First Class Stanley W. Kotlarz was in position behind a hedgerow on the west side of the highway. "The word got around that we should pull back because we were being surrounded. Shortly after that, we started pulling back. We lost a guy named [Private William H.] Neuberger; he got hit in the stomach. We walked him across the road; we had to move back, and we didn't have too much time, so we put him over to one side, and I took some branches that were lying there and covered him up. Kelly stayed back with Neuberger, but he [later] died.

"In the meantime, my squad leader, Bob ["the Beast"] Niland, was going across the road to set up a defense on the other side of the road. He was just stepping over a hedgerow and they nailed him. It was a machine gun . . . an MG-42 . . . we heard the doggone thing. We could see the way he was hit . . . he was lifeless, he was bleeding, and wasn't moving. There wasn't any sense in trying to save him—because he'd had it." 30

As Turnbull's platoon pulled out, the fire from Sergeant Sampson's lone 60mm mortar devastated the German infantry west of the highway. "I used the mortar with direct firing from an open, high grass area, with just [Private First Class Harry G.] Pickels [the gunner] up there with me to feed the tube. We changed positions often, using various objects as sighting stakes. Our firing, along with the rifles and machine gunners, finally started to tell on the Krauts and their firing began to slack off. Just over the hill, the Jerries were crossing the lane one man at a time on the run. I timed the interval, and when I thought another would cross over, the tube was fed a round. And as planned, when Jerry was in the center of the lane, the shell hit, right to the fraction of a second. On the easing off of the firing, I gave a couple of the squad men a chance to use the weapon as I did, to get the feeling of what it was like under fire. I kept a close watch with my Tommy [gun].

"We had come in a little to the left of town and had met a strong force, much greater than ours. They were going to cut off Lieutenant Turnbull's platoon. As soon as the Krauts quit firing, Lieutenant Peterson, with Lieutenant [James J.] Coyle, took the rifle squads and went out to find Lieutenant Turnbull and his men. We knew the Jerries had suffered in our encounter with them, but had no way of telling how bad. So far, we had not lost a man. The fight had been short and heavy." [31]

As he and his men moved out to find Turnbull's men, Peterson saw a trooper approaching. "A runner from Lieutenant Turnbull reported to me that they had successfully withdrawn their platoon. We had firepower over the enemy, and having accomplished our mission, we made a tactical withdrawal, firing as we left, and continuing part way to our lines." [32]

With the help of Peterson's platoon, Turnbull's men had shot their way out of the German trap, then conducted a fighting withdrawal. Private First Class Kotlarz was one of just sixteen from Turnbull's platoon to make it out. "We were moving pretty fast. As we were going back, we'd stop and fire a few shots and then pull back." [33]

Private Weed arrived at Vandervoort's command post after running the mile or so from Neuville-au-Plain. "I told them what was going on. Vandervoort was propped up against a tree, and there was a naval officer that jumped in with us. They were talking and they gave me a couple of more men to go back. [Vandervoort] said, 'Go back and tell the platoon that we're going to shoot up a white flare. When they see that white flare, withdraw. They've got five minutes to withdraw before the USS *Nevada* is to lay down a barrage.'" [34]

Weed immediately took off on a run back toward Neuville-au-Plain. "Me and these two others guys [headed] down the edge of this field because we didn't want to be right on the road. So we got close enough to where we could see where the platoon was. I could see where the platoon was supposed to be, and I saw a couple of German trucks driving through there, so I knew the 3rd Platoon wasn't there anymore. About that time I saw the white flare go up." [35]

Five minutes later, Weed heard a low roar, as a salvo of massive fourteen-inch shells, fired by the *Nevada* from twelve miles away, arced overhead and impacted along the road in front of him. "We wanted to watch what was happening, because we could see those German trucks out there. So we just lay there and watched the whole thing. I had never heard anything like that before. Every one of those things landed within a radius of a couple of hundred yards. They were right on target. It was real effective. The Germans took off; they got the hell out of there." [36]

Lieutenant Turner Turnbull and his fifteen troopers walked into Ste.-Mère-Église at dusk. His platoon had delayed the reinforced 1058th Regiment, 91st Air Landing Division, for almost the entire afternoon, preventing an attack on Ste.-Mère-Église, buying time for more paratroopers to filter in to strengthen the defenses, and most importantly, preventing an armored counterattack on Utah Beach. Vandervoort called it "a small unit performance that has seldom been equaled." [37]

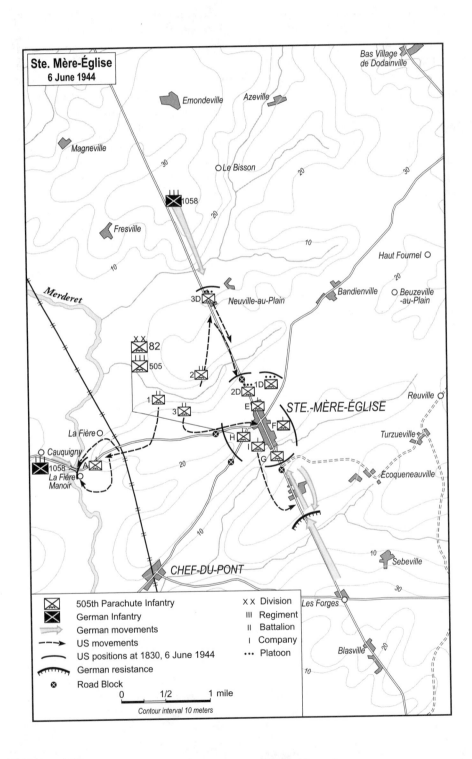

Ste. Mère-Église
6 June 1944

Bas Village
de Dodainville

Emondeville   Azeville

Magneville

30

Le Bisson   20   30

1058

Fresville   20

10

Haut Fournel O

10   20

Merderet   3D   Neuville-au-Plain   Bandienville   O Beuzeville
-au-Plain

X X 82

505   2

Reuville O

1   1D
2D

E   STE.-MÈRE-ÉGLISE

3   F

La Fière O   H   Turzueville

I

O Cauquigny   G   Ecoqueneauville

1058   A   20
La Fière O
Manoir

10

Sebeville

CHEF-DU-PONT   10

30

	505th Parachute Infantry	X X	Division	Les Forges
	German Infantry	III	Regiment	
	German movements	II	Battalion	
	US movements	I	Company	
	US positions at 1830, 6 June 1944	•••	Platoon	Blasville
	German resistance			10
⊗	Road Block			20

0   1/2   1 mile

Contour interval 10 meters

WHEN LIEUTENANT COLONEL ALEXANDER, the regimental executive officer, arrived at the 505th command post, he "found that Major Norton (regimental S-3) was set up and operating with a limited staff. They had contact with the 2nd and 3rd Battalions, but only sketchy reports as to the 1st Battalion and their situation at La Fière." [38]

The D-Day objectives of the 1st Battalion were to seize and defend the eastern ends of the Chef-du-Pont and La Fière Causeways. Companies B and C and Headquarters Company were mostly dropped north and northeast of the drop zone.

After landing, Private Dutch Schultz, with Company C, was alone until shortly after dawn. "During that time alone, I can't begin to remember what I was feeling—what I was thinking. I can only surmise that what I was feeling and what I was thinking was so deeply repressed because of my terrible fear—frightened—frightened that I was.

"It wasn't until 6:30 or 7:00 that I ran into my platoon leader and jumpmaster, Lieutenant Jack Tallerday. I was never so happy to see anybody as I was to see Jack Tallerday come around a hedgerow." [39]

Staff Sergeant Joe O'Jibway, a platoon sergeant with the 2nd Platoon, Company B, landed between Montebourg Station and Ste.-Mère-Église, badly injuring his left leg upon landing. "I never saw anyone until daylight and heard no reply to my clicker. I kept picking up people from 1st Platoon; all I had from 2nd Platoon was Medic Smith. I was with Lieutenant [James M.] Irvin [the company commander] and the 1st Platoon. We were six miles from the [La Fière] bridge.

"We started walking to our position [at the La Fière Causeway]. We were in the hedgerows and in the middle of a German division. Truckloads of Germans came down the road. We shot the trucks with bazookas, then moved on.

"We got to a hedgerow, and Lieutenant Irvin sent a young man up a tree to see what he could. A sniper shot him in the gut. Lieutenant Irvin took 1st Platoon over to a ditch—we had Germans all around us. Medic Smith took another guy who was shot in the head by the sniper on down the road.

"The Germans were firing at us. I couldn't run, due to my leg. I fell trying to get to Lieutenant Irvin's position." [40]

However, O'Jibway was able to find a haystack in which to hide. "They threw a couple of potato mashers at me. I put my hands up in front of my face—my hands were injured by the blast. I then rolled across the field to Irvin's position.

"The other sergeants and I suggested to Irvin we wait until dark and then escape our position. The [German] mortar fire was zeroed in and we lost four or five guys.

"Lieutenant Irvin then went out and held up a white flag. There were thirteen of us. I spent the next fourteen months as a POW." [41]

FORTUNATELY, COMPANY A HAD AN ALMOST PERFECT DROP and assembled on the drop zone, ready to move out to the company's objective, the eastern end of the La Fière Causeway, including the bridge over the Merderet River. Company A was under the command of Lieutenant John J. "Red" Dolan. "We hit our drop zone right on the nose, because within twenty minutes to one-half hour, I knew our exact location. I was able to identify a 'T' intersection, dirt roads eight to ten feet wide, near our drop zone—the upper arm of which ran generally east to west, the vertical arm running north to south, to meet the road running from Ste.-Mère-Église to our objective, the bridge at the Merderet River.

"We had the usual problems of reorganization in the dark; however, about an hour before dawn, Company A moved out from the drop zone with about ninety percent of the men accounted for.

"We moved along this dirt road, the north-south arm of the 'T' intersection. Just around here, I ran into Major [James E.] McGinity [1st Battalion executive officer]. He moved out with us. Order of march was 1st [Platoon], Company Headquarters, 3rd, and 2nd Platoons in that order. When we reached the road running east-west from Ste.-Mère-Église, a German motorcycle passed us going toward Ste.-Mère-Église. At this time, it was still dark, but daylight was starting to break. We crossed the road and started west toward the bridge, with a hedgerow to our right, between us and the road. Just about this time, contact was lost with the 1st Platoon, so the 3rd Platoon took the lead.

"About seven to eight hundred yards from the bridge, we came upon a dirt road running southeasterly from the road to the bridge. Hedgerows were on either side of this road; and beyond it in the direction of the bridge, was an open, flat field, about one hundred yards deep and about seventy-five yards wide. It was here that I figured the Germans would defend if they intended a defense of the bridge. I directed Lieutenant Donald Coxon to send his scouts out." [42]

Lieutenant Coxon responded by saying, "Well sir, if I have to send someone out into that I'll go myself." [43]

Dolan told him he didn't have to accompany the scouts. "[Coxon] had personal courage, but he didn't have the heart to order them out without going with them." [44]

There was no other way to find out if the enemy was waiting behind the hedgerow across the field. Dolan waited with the rest of his men, looking over the top of the hedgerow as the scouts moved out into the open field. "They got about one hundred yards. A few moments later, a German machine gun opened up, killing Lieutenant Coxon and one of his scouts, [Private First Class Robert G.] Ferguson. [Coxon] was hit badly and started to come back. While he was moving along another bullet hit him in the stomach. After that, he bled to death. Second Lieutenant Robert E. McLaughlin took over the platoon." [45]

Sergeant William D. Owens took Coxon's death hard. "He had been with us since our days in the Frying Pan at Fort Benning, Georgia. He [had] said to Sergeant [Palmer F.] Schuetzle and me a couple of days before the jump that he had a feeling that he wouldn't come back from this." [46]

The 3rd Platoon returned fire on the hidden German positions as Dolan decided to flank the Germans by slipping the 3rd Platoon to the south. "At the same time, I directed Lieutenant [George W.] Presnell to re-cross the road and attack along the northern side down to the bridge. This was done, and the 2nd Platoon didn't meet with any fire until they arrived at the bridge.

"With Major McGinity and [me] leading, a few men holding and returning frontal fire, the platoon flanked to the left. Because of the fire, we calculated that there was just one machine gun crew in our way. We cut back toward the road, traveling in a northerly direction. Major McGinity was leading and I was about three or four paces behind, and slightly to the right. There was a high, thick hedgerow to our left, and it was in here that I figured the machine gun was located. When we had traveled about two-thirds of the way up the hedgerow, they opened up on us with rifles, and at least two machine pistols. I returned the fire with my Thompson submachine gun at a point where I could see leaves in the hedgerow fluttering. Major McGinity was killed instantly. As luck would have it, there was a German foxhole to my left, which I jumped into and from where I continued to fire. I could only guess where to shoot, but I had to, as part of the 3rd Platoon was exposed to their fire." [47]

As Dolan was firing, his "radio operator, Corporal Frank Busa, moved forward and was hit by a sniper's bullet. McLaughlin thought Busa was alive and went out to get him. But, before he could make it, he himself was hit in the upper leg. The one bullet went up through the lower part of his stomach and came out of his buttocks.

"I spotted the sniper and killed him. I then crawled to McLaughlin to give him first aid and carry him out. The lieutenant was in such excruciating pain, he pleaded not to be moved.

"The platoon by now was under fire from two directions; from the point where I was pinned down, and also from the direction of the bridge. I can't estimate how long we were pinned down in this fashion, but it was at least an hour." [48]

In the thick bocage country, each field would become a self-contained and isolated area of action, where different units from the opposing forces could operate without the knowledge of one another until chance meetings would put them in contact, often with deadly consequences. Unknown to Dolan, groups of paratroopers from all three regiments were converging on the La Fière area.

PRIVATE CECIL PRINE, FORMERLY WITH COMPANY B, but now a wireman with Headquarters Company, 1st Battalion, got together with a replacement with Company B, Private First Class Floyd M. Baldry. "It was his first combat jump. Together, we spotted a line of troopers heading towards the La Fière bridge—we joined them. Later, we found out they were mostly A Company.

"On the way, Baldry and I found canisters. We opened them and found a .30-caliber machine gun, three barrels, gloves [to use to change hot barrels during firing], head spacer, and fifteen canisters of ammo. We moved them to the bridge and took up a commanding position over the bridge and prepared for action." [49]

Gavin was leading his group of about three hundred troopers, mostly with the 507th PIR, south on the railroad tracks. "I came upon the rear of the 1st Battalion of the 505th scattered along the edges of a small trail next to the railroad. I found out the battalion commander, Major [Frederick] Kellam, was up forward engaging a small force at the bridge. I put a temporary command post in there, and I tried to get in touch with General Ridgway. I had reports that he was then up at Ste.-Mère-Église." [50]

Gavin then decided to send about seventy-five men from his group on a wide flanking move to attack and capture Chef-du-Pont and the causeway from the east. A short time later, hearing that Chef-du-Pont was undefended, Gavin led another seventy-five directly south to attack the village.

While Dolan's men were pinned down, two other groups, unaware of Company A and one another, moved west toward the river, with the intent of turning north and approaching the causeway from the south. A group of mostly Company G, 507th troopers, under the command of Captain Ben Schwartzwalder, advanced west, south of Dolan's position, then turned north toward the Manoir, a large farmhouse and outbuildings on the south side of the main road just above the eastern end of the La Fière Causeway. This movement forced the machine gun crew that had held up Dolan to displace in order to stop the 507th group. The 507th troopers, with Lieutenant John Marr at the point, knocked out this machine gun crew, then continued north. The group passed the west side of the Manoir and started across the causeway, where Marr's men knocked out two more machine guns.

Somewhat behind the 507th group, another group of mostly 508th PIR troopers, commanded by Lieutenant Colonel Roy Lindquist, followed a similar route as the 507th group, entering the Manoir from the south and clearing light enemy opposition around the outbuildings. However, unknown to them, a number of Germans remained on the upper floors of the Manoir farmhouse.

Simultaneously, Lieutenant Dolan "made several attempts to move, but drew their fire. On my last attempt, I drew no fire. They obviously had pulled out. During all of this time, I could hear rifle and machine gunfire down by the bridge on the north side. This ceased about the time I returned to the rest of the 3rd Platoon, instructed the noncoms to reorganize, and to maintain their present position. I then crossed the road and located the 1st Platoon, commanded by Lieutenant [William A.] Oakley, on the north side. They were moving toward the bridge, so I instructed them to continue and dig in. I went down to the bridge and found that we had received an assist from some of the 508th Parachute Infantry. About this time, I ran into Colonel Ekman, and sent for my 3rd Platoon to dig in on the left or south side of the bridge. The 1st was already digging in on the north side." [51]

Lieutenant Dolan was under the impression that the 508th group had completely cleared the Manoir buildings and farmhouse of enemy troops. "But, unknown to us, there were about ten or twelve Germans holed up on the second floor of the stucco-type farmhouse. At the time they started firing, Colonel Ekman and I were casually looking the situation over." [52]

Dolan sent Lieutenant Oakley's 1st Platoon to clean out the enemy. Oakley's men circled west and approached from the southwest, where they engaged in a firefight with a couple of German snipers and enemy troops firing from the farmhouse. The firing Dolan and the others heard had been directed at a group of Company B, 508th, troopers to the east of the main building. The 508th troopers pulled back and approached through the outbuildings to the southeast, where they entered the garage of the farmhouse below the first floor and fired up through the floor, while Oakley's platoon opened up with a machine gun on the Germans in the farmhouse. Minutes later, the Germans waved a white flag from a window and came out with their hands up.

By approximately 2:30 p.m., the Manoir and eastern end of the causeway were secure. Lieutenant Homer Jones led Company B, 508th, across the causeway to link up with their regiment.

Lieutenant Dolan quickly organized Company A for a possible German counterattack. "We dug in, [with] the disposition of my company as follows: 1st Platoon on the north side of the road, the 3rd on the south, and the 2nd in reserve, about four hundred yards back, so that it could also protect the rear.

"On the bridge I had three bazooka teams. Two of them were from Company A and the third was either from B or C Company. The two Company A bazookas were dug in to the left and right of the bridge. Because the road itself was the causeway type, they dug in below the level of the road. The third bazooka was over more to the south where better cover was available." [53]

One Company A bazooka team of Private First Class John Bolderson and Private Gordon Pryne was positioned on the northern shoulder of the causeway. Pryne had been a rifleman with Company A when he jumped into Normandy. "But, on the jump, one of the guys on the bazooka team broke his ankle. They gave that job to me. I didn't want it, really, but they said, 'You got it.' I said, 'O.K.'" [54]

The other Company A bazooka team of Private Marcus Heim, Jr., the assistant gunner, and Private First Class Lenold Peterson were assigned to the southern shoulder of the causeway. Private Heim, a new replacement, had also recently been assigned as the loader. "There was a concrete telephone pole just in front of us, and we dug in behind it. I do not remember how many paratroopers were around; all I saw was a machine gun set up in the Manoir house yard. On the right side down the pathway a few riflemen were placed. We carried antitank mines and bazooka rockets from the landing area. These mines were placed across the causeway about fifty feet on the other side of the bridge. There was a broken-down German truck by the Manoir house, which we pushed and dragged across the bridge and placed it across the causeway." [55]

As Dolan was getting his company positioned and dug in, "Major Kellam arrived at the bridge with Captain [Dale A.] Roysdon, his S-3. He had most of his CP unit with him. I don't know whether or not a battalion CP had ever been set up as planned; at least, I don't recall having had any communication with it. Down at the bridge now was most of Company A, about one platoon of Company B, a platoon of the division engineers (mission to blow the bridge if necessary), about half of battalion headquarters company with mortars and machine gun sections, and several stray men from other regiments.

"The company dug in well and quickly. West of the Merderet River was a marsh at least one thousand yards wide at its narrowest point. The road running west from the bridge could better be described as a causeway." [56]

Shortly after his company had dug in, Lieutenant Dolan heard heavy German firing directed at the 508th troopers who had crossed the causeway earlier, caught near the west side of the flooded Merderet River when the Germans struck. "They were gone at least an hour when we saw several of them retreating back across the marsh. I remember that we helped several of them out of the river, which was quite shallow.

"Just about a half-hour before this attack, a 57mm antitank gun was assigned to Company A. I located this gun about one hundred fifty yards from the bridge on the road where it curves to the right as you approach the bridge. Incidentally, this was my CP and later the battalion CP. This gave the gun excellent cover and a good field of fire.

"The machine gun fire from the Germans was very heavy by now. We didn't return their fire, as there were no visible targets and our ammunition supply was limited." [57]

At approximately 4:00 p.m., Sergeant Elmo Bell, with Company C, saw German forces coming across the causeway. "This attack was led by three light tanks. These were French tanks. And ahead of these tanks, there were about twelve or fifteen paratroopers who had landed on the other side of the river and been captured before they got out of their chutes. They were marching ahead of the tanks. And the tank commander in the lead tank was standing up in the cupola directing these paratroopers to remove mines that were lying above ground, on the surface of that road, and throw them [into the water].

"As they came across and came nearer and nearer to the nearest shore, I was wondering when and who were going to give the command to open fire. I knew that we had to open fire, sooner or later, and everyone was hesitant to fire because there were twelve or fifteen paratroopers ahead of the lead tank, and they were very much in harm's way. But we all knew that before the tank reached shore, we had to take them under fire." [58]

Lieutenant Dolan was about forty yards from the bridge as the Germans came on. "The tanks were firing on us with machine guns and cannons. When the lead tank was about forty or fifty yards away from the bridge, the two Company A bazooka teams got up just like clockwork to the edge of the road. They were under the heaviest small-arms fire from the other side of the causeway, and from the cannon and machine gun fire from the tanks." [59]

Getting out of their foxhole, Private Heim and Private First Class Peterson stood behind the telephone pole in front of their foxhole in order to get a better field of fire. Heim then loaded the bazooka. "We had to hold our fire until the last minute because some of the tree branches along the causeway were blocking our view. As the lead tank started around the curve in the road, the tank commander stood up in the turret to take a look, and from our left the machine gun let loose a burst and killed the commander. At the same time, [we fired] the bazookas, 57 millimeter gun, and anything else we had at the Germans, and they in turn were shooting at us with cannons, mortars, machine gun and rifle fire." [60]

Sergeant Bell watched the tanks continue moving closer to the bridge. "When the lead tank was no more than twenty yards from the end of the bridge, the little [57mm] antitank gun fired. And whether it was by design or by accident, I don't know, but he knocked the track off the tank. The little 57[mm] was popping rounds on the front of that lead tank just as fast as they could load, but had no effect on the front armor. The lead tank was still operational except [for] its mobility; it couldn't move. And the main gun took this little 57 under fire and killed the crew, and the machine guns were raking our defenses up and down the river." [61]

At that very moment, Company A trooper Private First Class Dave Bullington was just about to open up with his BAR from his position in front of the hedgerow next to the river, north of the bridge. "[Sergeant Oscar L. "Stonewall"] Queen was the first one that fired. He had the machine gun off to my right. His tracers went right in front of me. He was firing at the infantry—his tracers went right over their heads in the center of their column. He was a little high, and I got him on the target, and then we let 'em have it. I don't know how many infantrymen there were; there might have been a couple hundred of them. They were all bunched up real close and made a real nice target. They were right up close to the tanks. All I remember was my BAR and Queen's machine gun. I don't know how many magazines I fired at them." [62]

Private Cecil Prine, with Headquarters Company, 1st Battalion, positioned across the main road from the 57mm antitank gun, fired the .30-caliber machine gun that he and Private First Class Floyd Baldry had found in an equipment bundle. "The infantry were moving on both sides of the road and firing constantly. Our machine gun was playing havoc on the side that we were on. Baldry and I were under very heavy mortar and rifle fire, since we had such a great position and were firing so many rounds." [63]

Private Heim fed another rocket into the bazooka as both teams concentrated on knocking out the lead tank. "The first tank was hit and started to turn sideways, at the same time was swinging its turret around and firing at us. We had just moved forward around the cement telephone pole when a German round hit it, and we had to jump out of the way to avoid being hit as it was falling. I was hoping that Bolderson and Prine were also firing at the tanks, for with all that was happening in front of us, there was no time to look around to see what others were doing. We kept firing at the first tank until it was put out of action and on fire." [64]

Dolan was in awe of the courage of his two bazooka teams. "They fired and reloaded with the precision of well-oiled machinery. Watching them made it hard to believe that this was nothing but a routine drill. I don't think that either crew wasted a shot. The first tank received several direct hits. The treads were knocked off, and within a matter of minutes it was on fire." [65]

Suddenly, Sergeant Bell heard the 57mm antitank gun begin firing once again, this time at the two remaining tanks as they returned fire with their 37mm main guns. "And they were firing as fast as they could load, but the troopers kept replacing the dead members of this little antitank gun crew. And as they were killed, they kept coming. As I recall, at least seven people were killed behind that little 57 millimeter gun." [66]

Heim continued to push rocket after rocket into the bazooka. "The second tank came up and pushed the first tank out of the way. We moved forward toward the second tank and fired at it as fast as I could load the rockets into the bazooka. We kept firing at the second tank, and we hit it in the turret where the body joins it, also in the tracks, and with another hit it also went up in flames. We were almost out of rockets, and the third tank was still moving. Peterson asked me to go across the road to see if Bolderson had any extra rockets. I ran across the road and with all the crossfire I still find it hard to believe I made it across in one piece. When I got to the other side I found one dead soldier, but Bolderson and Prine were gone. Their bazooka was lying on the ground and it was damaged by what I thought were bullet holes. Not finding Bolderson or Prine, I presumed that either one or both of them were injured. I found the rockets they left and then had to return across the road to where I left Peterson. The Germans were still firing at us, and I was lucky again. I returned without being hit. Peterson and myself, with the new rockets, put these to use against the third tank. This was one of the toughest days of my life. Why we were not injured or killed only the good Lord knows." [67]

Dolan couldn't believe the luck of his two bazooka teams. "To this day, I'll never be able to explain why all four of them were not killed. The 57mm [antitank gun] during this time was firing and eventually knocked out the last tank. The gun crew did an excellent job." [68]

Bell unexpectedly saw one of the Company C troopers leave his position. "[Private] Joseph C. Fitt ran out on to the bridge and dropped a grenade in that lead tank, and that silenced the guns on that tank. But until then, both the main gun and the machine guns had been firing constantly." [69]

The Germans fled across the causeway as .30-caliber bullets cut them down. Dolan quickly got his men resupplied in case of another attack. "My two bazooka crews called for more ammunition. Major Kellam ran up toward the bridge with a bag of rockets followed by Captain Roysdon. When they were within fifteen or twenty yards of the bridge, the Germans opened up with mortar fire on the bridge. Major Kellam was killed and Captain Roysdon was rendered unconscious from the concussion. He died later that day. Both of the bazookas were destroyed by the mortar fire. Lieutenant [Brock M.] Weir (Regimental Headquarters Company) and I carried Captain Roysdon back. I then took over command of the battalion, being the senior officer present." [70]

The regimental executive officer, Lieutenant Colonel Mark Alexander, was at the 505th command post when he learned of the deaths of Major McGinity, Major Kellam, and Captain Roysdon. "We had been unable to make contact with Lieutenant Colonel Ekman. I talked it over with Major Norton, our S-3 at the command post, and decided I should head for La Fière and the 1st Battalion defending the bridge at La Fière. I took my orderly Corporal Chick Eitelman with me. On the way, we had a scrimmage with several Germans, and Chick got one through his kneecap. Chick strongly objected, but I ordered him back to headquarters, where he could receive medical treatment. I proceeded to La Fière. On the way, I found a group of about forty 101st and 508th men lying in a ditch along the road. Supposedly, someone had held them in reserve. I did not know who, so I rounded them up and took them with me to La Fière.

"I found that most of A Company with Lieutenant Red Dolan were well organized and in a good situation on the right side of the road facing the Merderet River and bridge. I approved Lieutenant Dolan having moved his company back 150 yards from the intense mortar and machine gun fire along the riverbank. On the left side of the road was a mixed group of C Company, 505th, men occupying a house (called the Manoir) and some 507th men under the command of a Captain [Robert D.] Rae on the ridge above the Manoir. The whole position was receiving heavy fire from the west bank around Cauquigny—mortar, machine gun, and occasionally 88mm. Through my binoculars, I spotted two German tanks screened behind the buildings in the village of Cauquigny, across the river.

"I had located one of our 57mm antitank guns, abandoned in a defilade position about seventy-five yards above the bridge and on the left side of the road. There were two holes through the shield, apparently from an earlier duel with the Renault tanks, and there was no gun sight. There were six rounds of armor-piercing ammunition. I put Elmo Bell and two other men on the gun. I told them that if there was another tank attack to bore-sight the gun and when they were out of ammunition, to abandon it.

"We were shelled with mortar, machine gun fire, and occasional 88mm for the rest of the day. At one time in checking out our position and looking for wounded along the riverbank with medic Kelly Byars, we were caught in an exposed position and we had to [lie] in a foxhole for about twenty-five minutes while the Germans saturated the area with mortar fire. We had located an A Company man with a dollar-sized piece of his skull blown off and still alive. We gave him a shot of morphine, but judged it would be better to come back for him after dark with a stretcher. That medic, Kelly, was a real good man."[71]

Alexander's leadership instilled confidence in the troopers, and Dolan was certainly glad to have him on the scene. "Without exception, he was the finest battalion commander I ever served under."[72]

After getting the defenses reorganized, Alexander decided to return to the regimental command post to inform Ekman and the division staff of the situation. "I headed back to the railroad junction with the dirt road just as Gavin came in from Chef-du-Pont. Seeing that we were OK at La Fière, he instructed me to take command of the position. I asked him if he wanted me on this side of the river, both sides, or the other side. He instructed me to stay where we were on the east side and to hold fast, not allowing passage to the Germans."[73]

On June 6, two German regiments supported by armor had assaulted the 505th. One platoon had delayed the northern thrust for most of the day, and one rifle company had stopped the attack from the west.

CHAPTER 10

"The 82nd Airborne Division's Undiscovered World War II Equivalent of Sergeant Alvin C. York"

Duinch the night of June 6–7 at the La Fière Causeway, Sergeant Bill Owens, with Company A, stayed awake, alert for signs of German infiltration. "About 2:00 in the morning I heard a tank on the causeway and thought, 'Here we go again.' Then I heard them trying to push the disabled tank out of the way, and I knew if they succeeded, we would be through. So, I took a couple of Gammon grenades and crawled to approximately thirty to forty yards from them, as it was quite dark. The first one I threw missed and hit the disabled tank instead of the one that was trying to move it. But, the Germans didn't take any more chances; they put the tank in reverse and moved back. I threw the other grenade, but missed again." [1]

Shortly after dawn, the Company A commander, Lieutenant "Red" Dolan, was checking on the 1st Platoon positions on the north side of the road. "For about an hour before the attack, [the Germans] increased their mortar fire to the extent that the 3rd Platoon was just about knocked out, but not quite. I was not aware of this at the time. In addition to already heavy casualties, Sergeant [Lawrence F.] Monahan, the platoon sergeant, was fatally wounded. The 1st Platoon was under heavy fire also." [2]

At approximately 8:00 a.m., Owens "heard armored vehicles coming from across the river. We let them come on." [3]

As the German tanks and infantry approached, pathfinder Private Robert M. "Bob" Murphy waited in his hole. "Unless one has faced the grim reaper in the form of an oncoming enemy, one can hardly understand the fear and dread that runs through the mind of a frontline infantryman. You pray—you have the fear of death on your mind. You are watching armed men and tanks coming at you, as well as artillery and mortar explosions and shrapnel flying through the air around you. There is no thought in your mind to get out of your hole and run, because you would be cut down by rifle or shrapnel." [4]

As the German tanks and infantry came on, Private Cecil Prine, with Headquarters Company, 1st Battalion, opened up with a .30-caliber machine gun. "I saw the Germans trying to push the tanks that were knocked out [the previous day] and blocking the road, out of the way." [5]

Dolan could see two tanks and infantry coming across the causeway. "The tanks stayed out of effective bazooka range. (We had one bazooka left.) Not hearing any fire from the 57mm, I went over to it and found it unmanned. I tried to fire it, but the crew had taken the firing mechanism. I organized five or six men behind the hedge on the southerly side of the road with Gammon grenades, and just about this time, two of the gun crew returned with the firing mechanism. They knocked out the two tanks. They were two youngsters not more than seventeen or eighteen years old, who returned on their own initiative. I recommended them for Silver Stars." [6]

Owens, although relieved to see the German tanks destroyed, knew all too well what was coming next. "They tried to get the infantry through to knock us out. All we had was small arms and 60mm mortars, but we succeeded in driving them back. The Germans pulled back on the other side, and in about a half hour or so, they began throwing 88s and 4.2 [-inch] mortars at us. They really clobbered us. All our communications were knocked out. Private [William A.] Ross, with our walkie-talkie, took a direct hit with an 88.

"Then they sent the infantry again, and again we drove them back. After a little lull, they started all over again. This time Lieutenant Oakley was hit. I crawled over to him and gave him a shot of morphine and tried to bandage him, but he had a hole in his back near his kidney the size of a man's fist. I offered to send a man back to try and find a medic and take him back, but he said he could make it alone.

"Sergeant [Jim] Ricci and Sergeant [William] McMurchy had already been wounded and were out of action. All this time we were under heavy artillery fire. Right after Lieutenant Oakley left, I began crawling around, getting all the ammo and grenades from the dead and wounded, for I knew then we would need every round we could get our hands on. I took stock of what weapons, ammo and men we had left. It turned out to be a good thing, for right after that the Germans hit us again. They must have received reinforcements, for the artillery shells and mortars were coming in like machine gun fire. I don't know how it was possible to live through it.

"Then their infantry came again, and we gave them everything we had. The machine gun I had was so hot it quit firing. I took Private [Wesley H.] McClatchy's BAR (he had been wounded earlier) and I fired it until I ran out of ammo. I then took a machine gun that belonged to a couple of men who took a very near hit. They were killed. The gun had no tripod, so I rested it across a pile of dirt and used it. With this and one other machine gun and a 60mm mortar, we stopped them, but they had gotten to within twenty-five yards of us." [7]

Out of the corner of his eye, Company A trooper Private First Class Dave Bullington noticed that Sergeant Oscar Queen was having trouble with his machine gun. "He'd shake that thing and say, 'That thing is going out.'

"I said, 'Oscar, that thing is just getting broken in.' I wasn't going to tell him it was going out. He said he [had] fired about ten thousand rounds through it." [8]

As the fighting raged, Private Murphy noticed one of the company medics moving under fire from one wounded man to another. "Kelly 'Moose' Byers was a fantastic, brave hero, who spent two days out in the open, under heavy fire, giving medical aid to our A Company men." [9]

Sergeant Owens sent Corporal Darrell J. Franks to find Colonel Ekman, to request reinforcements and more ammunition. Minutes later, as the fighting raged, Private Murphy saw Sergeant Owens "running from one point to the other, grabbing all kinds of guns and firing them, because a lot of the fellows were wounded and not able to defend. Owens called over to me and said, 'Go and find Lieutenant Dolan and tell him we're out of ammunition and we can't stand another tank or infantry attack, and we need to move back.'

"So I got out of my hole and I ran back up the incline and across the road to where Dolan was looking down at the bridge, at the bend in the road, where we kept our wounded men. I told Dolan what Owens had said and asked him if we could move back.

"Dolan said to me, 'No,' and took a piece of paper from a little notepad and wrote something on it. He said, 'Here, give this to Owens.'

"I ran across the road, ducking the incoming rounds, back to Owens, and I gave him the note. I told him what Dolan said as he was reading the message, and I asked Owens what it said. Owens said to me, 'We stay—there's no better place to die.'

"Owens then said to me, 'O.K. nobody moves—let's get ready when they come over the bridge.'" [10]

Sergeant Owens expected the 1st Platoon would be overrun shortly. "I really thought we'd had it, but then they threw up a Red Cross flag and stopped firing. I quickly stood up and stopped my men. Then I sat down and cried. I had sent Corporal D. J. Franks back to find some help for us, but before he found Colonel Ekman we had fought them off. I was so glad to see him come back a little later, for I didn't really think he could get out. When they had the Red Cross flag up, I moved to where I could get a good view of the causeway. I estimated that I could see at least two hundred dead or wounded Germans scattered about. I don't know how many were in the river. It took them about two hours to get their wounded out, then they started shelling us, but not too badly, just enough to keep us on edge. They continued shelling us all day long, but it was only sporadic. They never tried to get the infantry across again after they raised the Red Cross flag." [11]

When Prine saw the Red Cross flag waved, he ceased firing the machine gun. "I remember the truce lasted half an hour. Baldry and I counted about 275 bodies moved by the enemy in those thirty minutes." [12]

Prine estimated that during the German attacks on June 6 and 7, they had "used about three thousand rounds and caused huge problems for the enemy. About every thirty minutes, we changed barrels, since they became white hot." [13]

Dolan told his men to prepare for another attack, but it never came. "The rest of our stay at the bridge was uneventful, except for the continued mortar fire, and at the end, artillery fire which damaged the 57mm. In conclusion, we held the bridge until relieved. In Company A alone in those days (three in all), we had seventeen known dead and about three times that number wounded. The rest of the battalion also had heavy casualties. I recommended Sergeant Owens and my four bazooka men for the DSC. The bazooka men were awarded the DSC, but Sergeant Owens was not. This is a story in itself." [14]

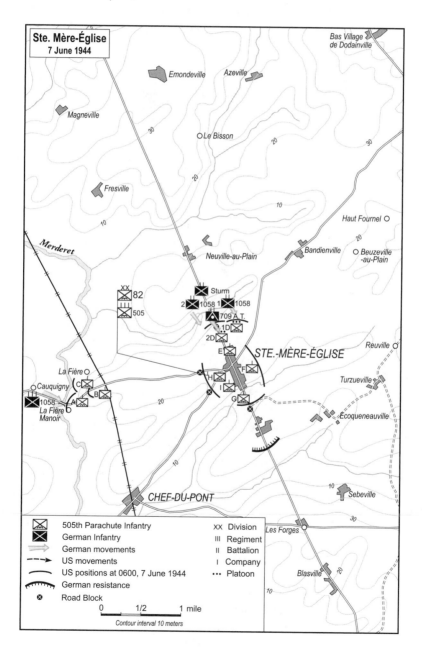

At dawn on June 7, Lieutenant Colonel Vandervoort was at his command post on the north side of Ste.-Mère-Église monitoring the situation just north of the town. "Shortly after first light 7 June, the 1st Battalion, 1058th Grenadier Regiment reinforced by elements of the Seventh Army Sturm Battalion, a specially trained counterattack unit, succeeded in driving the D Company platoon defending along the east side of the highway, back and away from the road on the north edge of the town. From the north, three battalions of German infantry supported by three artillery regiments and a number of 75mm and 7.62cm self-propelled guns marched south to clear a battalion and a half of American paratroopers off Highway N-13, the main road to the landing beaches. A fourth German infantry battalion south of Ste.-Mère-Église put the paratroopers in a vise. The German kampfgruppe operating with the usual German efficiency and ferocity powered methodically into the northern environs of Ste.-Mère-Église. A German breakthrough into the town appeared imminent." [15]

The 1st Battalion, 1058th Regiment, moved toward Ste.-Mère-Église east of the N-13 highway, while the Seventh Army Sturm Battalion and seven self-propelled guns of the 709th Antitank Battalion moved south on the highway, and the 2nd Battalion, 1058th, advanced south, west of the highway.

Defending the north side of the town east of the N-13 highway was the 1st Platoon of Company D, led by Lieutenant Thomas J. "Tom" McClean. The 2nd Platoon of Company D, commanded by Lieutenant Oliver B. "O. B." Carr, Jr., defended a roadblock on the N-13 highway.

The fighting was ferocious as the two platoons held off attacking hordes of German infantry supported by self-propelled guns, giving ground grudgingly. The Sturm Battalion and the self-propelled assault guns pressed the attack to the very outskirts of Ste.-Mère-Église. A 57mm antitank gun, commanded by Lieutenant John C. Cliff, Battery A, 80th Airborne Antiaircraft (Antitank) Battalion, engaged a convoy of trucks at long range, moving south on the highway toward the north end of town, carrying infantry from the Sturm Battalion. The gun crew knocked out the lead truck, disrupting the convoy. A German armored car then engaged Lieutenant Cliff 's antitank gun, but his crew knocked that out as well. Next, a German self-propelled gun drove forward along the highway, projecting smoke canisters ahead to shroud its advance—then suddenly appeared out of the smoke, moving rapidly. Lieutenant Cliff maintained observation on the gun and gave verbal adjustments to the crew as they loaded and fired.

When Private First Class Turk Seelye and several members of his Company E squad saw German infantry moving along the ditches of the highway, they "provided cover fire as the 57mm gun fired at the German [self-propelled] gun." [16]

The self-propelled gun got to within fifty yards of Vandervoort's command post before it was disabled with two rounds. However, the vehicle's 75mm main gun continued to fire at Cliff's gun at almost point-blank range. The antitank gun crew fired two more rounds through the front of the vehicle, finishing off the enemy crew, then moved their gun forward to the side of the knocked-out assault gun in order to have a clear field of fire. As they were getting the gun loaded, a second self-propelled gun up the highway fired, wounding the crew. With the antitank gun out of action, the self-propelled assault gun began moving toward the north end of town, projecting smoke canisters ahead to conceal its advance.

Private John E. Atchley, with Company H, courageously left his foxhole and single-handedly manned the antitank gun. Although Atchley had never fired an antitank gun, he loaded and fired, missing the oncoming self-propelled gun. He single-handedly reloaded the gun and adjusted the aim as the assault gun came on. At a range of about one hundred yards, he fired the second round, knocking out the vehicle. The other five German assault guns retreated, stopping the armored thrust at the very edge of Ste.-Mère-Église.

However, Vandervoort didn't have much in reserve to counter the German infantry. "D Company's reserve platoon consisted of Lieutenant Turner Turnbull (half Choctaw Indian) and sixteen survivors from Neuville-au-Plain. His platoon, first to meet the juggernaut from the north, had delayed the Germans bravely, but at a terrible sixty-percent cost in casualties. Dug in behind D Company was Company E, the battalion reserve. They had only company headquarters and two platoons. One was Lieutenant Peterson's platoon of two lieutenants and about thirty-nine troopers. The other was an improvisation of glider pilots and 101st stragglers totaling about thirty-five men and officers armed only with individual shoulder weapons.

"The situation brought 1st Lieutenant Waverly W. Wray, executive officer of D Company, to the 2nd Battalion, 505 command post early in the morning to get help. Waverly was from Batesville, Mississippi. He had acquired all of the woodsman skills as a boy. In his hands, a rifle was a precision instrument. He claimed he had 'never missed a shot in mah life that ah didn't mean to.' In his early twenties, at the peak of physical fitness and mental quickness, he had the combat 'sixth sense' of the true warrior—an indefinable intuition, which warns of danger before it appears. A veteran of Sicily and Italy, he was as experienced and skilled as an infantry soldier can get and still be alive. Personally, he walked with the Lord. Some of the troopers called him 'The Deacon' because of his deep-South religious convictions—but never to his face. He didn't drink, smoke, curse, nor chase girls. When angered, he would resort to 'John Brown.'

"He was one of a few men in the regiment whom the chaplain could count on being present at services every Sunday. A God-fearing young man of uncompromising courage, character, and professional competence, combat leadership naturally gravitated to Waverly." [17]

Private First Class Dave Bowman, a veteran trooper of Company D, described Lieutenant Wray as "fearless in his pursuit of killing Germans. Many accounts of his feats attest to that. He would go where no man would dare tread, unless he was leading them." [18]

Vandervoort listened as "Waverly explained the situation on the D Company front. The platoon, driven off the road, had suffered casualties, but was still intact and available for action. I told him to return to his company and counterattack the flank of the encroaching Germans. In his Mississippi drawl, he said, 'Yes, Suh,' saluted, about faced, and moved out like a parade ground sergeant major.

"Back in the company area he told his injured company commander, Captain T. G. [Taylor] Smith, what they had to do. He collected all of the grenades he could carry from the company headquarters personnel. Then, armed with his M1 rifle, an Army .45, and a silver .38 revolver stuck in his jump boot, he went on a reconnaissance to better formulate his plan of attack.

"The terrain was mixed agricultural farm fields, orchards, and pasturage bound by man-high field stone and earthen embankments. These were the renowned hedgerows of Normandy, bordered by sunken cow lanes worn by centuries of traverse. Enemies could be a few feet apart and not be aware of each other. The fields were small—few running more than 150 by 300 yards. Infantry could cross only at great peril. The checkerboard layout of the land forced the combatants into close alignment at ideal ambush and small arms killing range. In that maze of natural fortifications, troopers and Germans exchanged fire and jockeyed for positions all along the northern environs of the town. It took real courage just to move about, much less voluntarily go alone to find the foe. Waverly knew the terrain because D Company had occupied the ground earlier.

"With utmost stealth and courage, he moved up the sunken lanes, across the orchards, through the hedgerows and ditches sprinkled with German units moving forward for their next drive to take the town. He went north about three hundred yards along the enemy left flank, then moved west a couple of hundred yards at right angles to the German axis of attack. That brought him a hedgerow or two away from the N-13." [19]

Wray, acting as scout, led Lieutenant Tom McClean's 1st Platoon around the left flank of the 1st Battalion, 1058th Regiment—approaching it from the rear. Vandervoort described what happened next: "Then, moving like the deerstalker he was, he went south along a ditch until he heard guttural voices on the other side of the hedgerow. Stepping up and looking over the earthen embankment, he saw eight Germans in a sunken lane gathered around a radio. Covering them with his M1 rifle, he barked in his best command voice, 'Hande Hoch!' Most instinctively raised their hands, except one who tried to pull a P-38 pistol from the holster on his belt. Wray shot the man instantly.

"At the same time, two Germans stood up in a slit trench about one hundred yards to his left rear. With bursts from Schmeisser machine pistols, they tried to take his head off—clipping two 9mm pieces out of his right ear. Momentarily disregarding the hail of bullets from behind, Wray shot the other seven men in the lane dead.

"Whirling around, he jumped back down into the ditch, loaded another eight-round clip into his M1 and dropped the other two Germans across the field with a shot apiece. The eight dead Germans in the lane were the commanding officer and headquarters staff of the 1st Battalion, 1058th Grenadier Regiment." [20]

Lieutenant McClean arrived at the hedgerow across the field just in time to witness Wray's action. "My platoon was deployed along a hedgerow. I first saw Lieutenant Wray when he was approximately thirty to fifty yards to my left front. I saw him in a standing position firing down. I couldn't see who he was shooting at, as he was standing on a small rise from my position.

"I started to go to his assistance when I saw German troops approximately fifty yards to my right front. They were to Lieutenant Wray's left rear. Realizing that he did not see them as he was engaged in firing his rifle, I directed my platoon fire on the Germans." [21]

Private Frank Silanskis watched Wray disappear from view as he continued his one-man reconnaissance. "The next time I saw Lieutenant Wray is when he came out of the hedgerow kicking two German prisoners. Lieutenant Wray had part of his ear and his helmet strap shot away. He was mad. He kept saying, 'John Brown Germans.'" [22]

Platoon Sergeant Paul Nunan was amazed that Wray was even alive. "The bullet had struck his steel helmet almost dead center at the front rim. A quarter of an inch lower and it would certainly have gone into his forehead. Instead, the bullet was deflected and struck the hinge of his chin strap and clipped a piece of Lieutenant Wray's ear, leaving his face, neck, shoulder, and part of his uniform covered with blood." [23]

Wray positioned the platoon's 60mm mortar and a .30-caliber machine gun on the left flank of the German battalion, which was positioned in a sunken lane between two hedgerows. Lieutenant McClean's platoon spread out along a hedgerow perpendicular to the lane. Wray placed mortar fire at the far end of the lane, then gave adjustments to walk the shells up the lane toward his position. At the same time, the .30-caliber machine gun opened up, enfilading the German infantry packed into the lane.

The mortar rounds exploded as they struck overhanging tree limbs, raining shrapnel and large splinters of wood down on the Germans as machine gun bullets ripped into their flank. Germans spilled out of the hedgerows into the open fields, where McClean's platoon took them under small arms and machine gun fire. It was a slaughter.

After a few minutes, Sergeant Nunan saw a German major carrying a white flag move out into the field in front of the platoon's positions. Nunan, Captain Taylor G. Smith, Lieutenant McClean, and an enlisted man, acting as a translator, moved into the field to speak with the German.

Nunan noticed the Red Cross brassard on the German major's sleeve, signifying he was a doctor. "He spoke English well, and at the request of our captain, T. G. Smith, we agreed to a one-hour truce so that the Germans be allowed to leave their medics and wounded with us, and that a wounded American glider pilot be turned over to us.

"Suddenly our men on the right flank opened fire. Captain Smith, the major, myself, and two others were still exposed in the open field. Only later did we learn the Germans on the right flank had started to withdraw as soon as the negotiations started, which caused our men on the right to open fire again. Captain Smith refused the German terms and shortly after, a green flare was fired by the Germans, and we began receiving fire from German 88's." [24]

Company D trooper Private First Class Charles Miller hit the ground as aerial bursts sprayed the field and hedgerow. "They told us, 'Get the hell out of here!'—and we did. But, on the way out there was a good friend of mine, Red . . . Big Red [Corporal Kenneth W. Auther]. I thought he was taking a leak. Instead of that, his blood was coming out of his stomach, just like urine, just pouring out of him. What had happened, a medic told me later, a shell or bullet had hit the artery, that main artery, and it just burst open and he was dead in three or four minutes.

"There was nothing we could do—we're not doctors. It was awful to stand there and watch him die, but there was nothing we could do, except hold his hand, and try to make it a little bit easier for him." [25]

Meanwhile, demoralized survivors of the German battalion fled north, exposing the left flank of the Sturm Battalion, causing it to withdraw, and effectively halting the German attack. Shortly afterward, Vandervoort learned that the German battalion east of the highway had been destroyed. "D Company moved back into their original defensive positions. Midmorning, Waverly returned to tell me the D Company area was secure. There he was—minus part of his ear. Blood had dried down his neck and the right shoulder of his jump jacket, fore and aft. I said, 'They've been getting kind of close to you haven't they, Waverly?'

"With just a grin, Waverly replied, 'Not as close as ah've been gettin' to them, Suh.' Waverly led Company D in throwing back the deepest penetration the Germans ever made into Ste.-Mère-Église, and in the process shattered the 1st/1058th." [26]

After Company D's devastating counterattack, German artillery and mortars shelled Ste.-Mère-Église for the remainder of the day and night.

BY THE MORNING OF JUNE 7, no beach-landed forces had made contact with the division. General Ridgway had expected an armored task force commanded by Colonel Edson Raff to break through to Ste.-Mère-Église on D-Day. Raff's company of Sherman tanks would give the 82nd Airborne Division a heavier anti-tank defense.

About 10:00 a.m., Ridgway ordered the 2nd Battalion pathfinder team leader, Lieutenant J. J. Smith, to take a patrol to contact General Raymond O. Barton, commander of the 4th Infantry Division, requesting tanks to support Ridgway's hard-pressed troopers. For the patrol, Lieutenant Smith chose pathfinders Corporal Lewis D. Allen, Headquarters Company, 1st Battalion; Corporal Howard W. Hicks, Jr., Company G; Corporal George H. Purcell, Company A; and Private Julius A. Wyngaert and Sergeant James Elmo Jones, both with Company B.

Sergeant Jones was told "before we left, we had to take all personal items such as billfolds, pictures, everything but our dog-tags off our uniforms. We could not take any prisoners because we needed to get to the beach, which was approximately four miles away, as quickly as possible.

"We started and it seemed everywhere we went we either had to evade or kill German soldiers that were either trying to fight or trying to get away. Many of them were in our way, and we simply could not take prisoners. We finally made it to the beach. When we got there, we saw the American tanks parked under trees with canopies from some American parachutes spread out for sunscreen. They were listening to the radios on the tanks as to how the invasion was coming.

"As we literally ran up, we bumped into a lieutenant colonel, and Lieutenant Smith said, 'Take me to your commanding officer.'

"The lieutenant colonel said, 'I'm the commanding officer.'

"Smith said, 'Hell, I don't mean you, I mean General Barton.'

"So, [the lieutenant colonel] put us in a jeep. He went along, and we took off to see General Barton, who was in his headquarters vehicle. We burst into his room, and he heard our story. We had not shaved, we were dirty, we probably looked terrible. But, he was very reluctant to send tanks that far away, because they had not penetrated in any way up toward the center of the peninsula. We didn't know it, but there were two or three men in the command vehicle.

One of them spoke up and said, 'I think you should do it. I think you should send the tanks up.' We turned around, and there was General Lawton Collins [the VII Corps commander], who happened to be there at the time. Within fifteen minutes, we had five tanks and we were riding on the back of them to show them the best way to get back. Five tanks on the way toward Ste.-Mère-Église." 27

Early that afternoon, Krause, unaware of Smith's patrol, took some of his 3rd Battalion troopers to relieve Lieutenant McClean's Company D platoon from their roadblock northeast of town. Krause ordered McClean and his platoon to double-time to the command post of the 12th Infantry, 4th Division, at St.-Martin-de-Varreville, over four miles away, to determine the location and status of the 8th Infantry, which should have already pushed into Ste.-Mère-Église from the south.

As Lieutenant McClean and his men double-timed to St.-Martin-de-Varreville, they passed through area occupied by the 1st Battalion, 8th Infantry, but somehow, the two units missed each other. When Lieutenant McClean and his platoon arrived at the CP of the 12th Infantry, he was informed that the 2nd Battalion, 8th Infantry, had been held up by the 795th Georgian Battalion defending Hill 20, then by artillery fire interdicting their approach from the south, along the N-13 highway. McClean and his platoon then double-timed back the four miles to Ste.-Mère-Église with the information.

At about the same time, Company E platoon leader Lieutenant James J. Coyle received an order to report to the company command post. "I received an order from our company commander, Captain Clyde Russell, to go to the beach by jeep with two men from D Company, and try to contact the 4th Infantry Division to get one of their artillery observers to Ste.-Mère-Église to give us fire support.

"I was able to reach the 4th Division as they were moving from the beach. But they had only one observer left alive and could not release him to aid us. I noticed a tank unit along the road and explained our needs to the lieutenant colonel in command. But he could not release any tanks to me without orders from his command. It was frustrating to see all those tanks not engaged while we were fighting so hard a few miles away. But there was nothing a lieutenant could do, so I returned to Ste.-Mère-Église with nothing but a bit of helpful information: The tank commander was in radio contact with tanks which were assigned to us. He told me they were on their way to Ste.-Mère-Église from a roundabout route through Chef-du-Pont.

"As soon as I reported to battalion headquarters upon my return, we were given an order to move into position north of Ste.-Mère-Église to prepare to attack the enemy who were closing in on the town." [28]

Early that afternoon, Raff's armor arrived at Ridgway's command post, by taking the road west from the N-13 to Chef-du-Pont, then the road from Chef-du-Pont northeast to Ste.-Mère-Église, bypassing the Germans on Hill 20. Colonel James Van Fleet, commander of the 8th Infantry Regiment, 4th Division, arrived at Ridgway's command post a short time later. He told Ridgway that his 8th Infantry was fighting its way north up the N-13 highway and would reach Ste.-Mère-Église in about an hour. They decided to conduct a joint attack north from Ste.-Mère-Église at 5:15 p.m. The 2nd Battalion, 8th Infantry, would attack on the left flank of Vandervoort's 2nd Battalion, which would attack north along the N-13 highway.

Around 3:30 p.m., Lieutenant Eugene Doerfler, the 2nd Battalion S-2, arrived at Ridgway's CP and guided two Sherman tanks from Raff's force to the battalion positions just north of Ste.-Mère-Église.

The situation north of Ste.-Mère-Église was still critical. The almost complete destruction of the 1st Battalion, 1058th Grenadier Regiment, had temporarily relieved German pressure. However, five enemy self-propelled guns of the 709th Antitank Battalion and the Seventh Army Sturm Battalion remained north of the town astride the N-13 highway, while the 2nd Battalion, 1058th Regiment, was a few hundred yards from the town, positioned west of the highway.

The Germans shelled Ste.-Mère-Église while reorganizing for a renewed attack to capture the town. Private First Class Joseph L. Comer, at one of the Company H roadblocks, saw one of his good friends hit by a German shell. "Corporal Glenn 'Red' Carpenter, a BAR man, got his legs blown off and died of a loss of blood and from shock. It really hurts you when you lose a good friend but you couldn't dwell on it. You kind of had to put it in the back of your mind at the time." [29]

LIEUTENANT FRANK WOOSLEY WAS the acting commander of Company E, because Captain Clyde Russell had suffered a recurrence of malaria. Lieutenant Woosley rounded up about twenty to twenty-five misdropped troopers of the 101st Airborne and about ten men from Company E Headquarters and formed them into a provisional platoon designated as 2nd Platoon, Company E, and assigned them to Lieutenant Coyle.

Lieutenant Coyle's platoon would attack north out of Ste.-Mère-Église, west of the N-13 highway, with the 1st Platoon, Company E, led by Lieutenant "Pete"

Peterson, attacking astride the highway. Lieutenant McClean's Company D platoon would attack north, east of the highway—if it arrived in time after double-timing back from the 12th Infantry Regiment's command post. The 2nd Battalion, 8th Infantry Regiment, 4th Division, would attack north on the left flank of Coyle's provisional 2nd Platoon. The attack would commence at 5:15 p.m.

Private Earl Boling was a rifleman in Lieutenant Peterson's platoon. "As we were hearing rumors that the beach troops would be arriving soon, we were ordered to prepare to attack. Of course, this was good airborne strategy—when one is surrounded, tired, hungry, and low on ammunition, the best possible thing to do is attack." [30]

Near the Company D command post, Private First Class Stanley W. Kotlarz, with Lieutenant Turner Turnbull's 3rd Platoon, one of the sixteen survivors of the previous day's fighting at Neuville-au-Plain, moved out with the platoon just as a German artillery shell exploded in their midst. "I got hit in the wrist and in the arm, a guy by the name of Brown got hit in the head, and Lieutenant Turnbull . . . it sheered the top of his head right off. When it hit, all of us seemed to go up in the air. When I got up, I saw Brown crawling away, staggering. Turnbull was lying there with his brains peeling out of his head." [31]

The death of Turnbull, just a day after his heroic action, was a tremendous blow to D Company and the 2nd Battalion. Lieutenant Turnbull was one of those great young officers who led from the front. Sergeant Floyd West described him as "more than a damn good officer, he was my friend." [32] Vandervoort recommended Lieutenant Turnbull for a Distinguished Service Cross for his actions at Neuville-au-Plain, but he was later posthumously awarded the Silver Star.

Lieutenant Coyle organized his provisional platoon and moved them into position just north of town. "We took up positions along a road which runs west from the main highway. It is the road which has the last house on the north edge of the town.

"Two tanks which had been attached to us arrived, and they would cover our open flank as we attacked. There was heavy machine gun fire coming across the field from our front. My original order was to take my platoon across this field, but in the interval before our jump off time, 1715 hours, I got permission [from Lieutenant Woosley] to take them north up a dirt road on the left of the field, which provided better cover and concealment." [33]

It was a daring plan, which if successful would put Coyle's platoon on top of the Germans before they knew what hit them, if they weren't spotted coming up the road and cut to pieces with mortar, artillery, or machine gun fire.

Sergeant Otis Sampson was ordered to move forward to set up his squad's 60mm mortar to support the Company E attack. "I grabbed the mortar and with the rest of the squad, I followed the runner to the front where the forward squads had sought protection in a ditch on the near side of a sparsely planted tree hedgerow.

"Here, I was told by either Sergeant Smith or Lieutenant Peterson, 'Give us mortar fire in that next hedgerow. They are there in force.' The hedgerow ran west from the Montebourg road [N-13]." [34]

Shortly before 5:00 p.m., the 8th Infantry Regiment hadn't arrived and wouldn't be available to attack on the left flank of Company E. They would have to cover it themselves. Lieutenants Woosley, Doerfler, and Coyle met with the commanders of the two Sherman tanks supporting them and decided to use one tank and the provisional platoon to cover the left flank. Coyle, Woosley, Doerfler, and ten men from Company E headquarters would accompany the lead tank and cover the front and right when they reached the intersection with the hedgerow-lined lane, from which the German infantry was firing.

As the assault was about to commence, the 746th Tank Battalion task force that Lieutenant J. J. Smith had acquired from the 4th Infantry Division approached Ste.-Mère-Église from the east. Smith's pathfinders were riding on top of the lead tanks. Company B pathfinder, Sergeant James Elmo Jones, had to jump off from the rear deck of the tank he was riding as it rolled through Ste.-Mère-Église. "The tanks never really stopped long enough to let us off, but kept attacking north [out] of Ste.-Mère-Église." [35]

The tankers, knowing nothing of the planned attack, just barreled right up the N-13 highway around 5:00 p.m., running head on into the remaining five German self-propelled assault guns and German infantry on the highway.

Lieutenant Houston Payne, commanding the lead tank, knocked out two self-propelled assault guns and a towed antitank gun before his tank was hit and he was wounded. He managed to get his tank pulled to the side of the road. Another Sherman moved past Payne's tank and continued the attack.

Just before the attack, Vandervoort received a welcome hand from a newly arrived forward artillery observer. "The 8th Infantry field artillery observer placed a 155mm barrage two hedgerows in back of the German front line position."

Sergeant Sampson's squad, working like a finely tuned engine, opened up on the German frontline positions with their single 60mm mortar. "We were in plain sight of the enemy and bullets were flying by. My men didn't hesitate—they tried to give us mortar gunners the protection we needed with their rifle fire. The teamwork paid off. My first rounds overshot the hedgerow. Once the range was found, we laid them in, one round landing in a machine gun nest, killing them all." [36]

Sampson's gunner, Private First Class Harry G. Pickels, fed the mortar while Sampson adjusted the aim, as rounds exploded behind the entire length of the German-held lane. Simultaneously, Peterson's platoon unleashed a torrent of small arms and .30-caliber machine gun fire into points in the hedgerow across the field where Germans were spotted or suspected to be.

At 5:15 p.m., Coyle's platoon and the two Sherman tanks moved north up the lane, with Woosley, Doerfler, and Coyle walking on both sides of and just behind the lead tank. As they moved forward, the tank commander stopped the tank. Woosley moved around the tank to investigate. "We came to a dead American soldier lying in the tank's path just short of the enemy's position. The tank commander didn't want to run over the body. I had what I consider a combat lapse and walked right in front of that tank. I lifted the body, even looked at his dog-tags, with sorrow for his family. I laid him in a ditch so the tank could move forward. I returned to the rear of the tank. Lieutenant Coyle told me he was amazed that I was not killed." [37]

The column continued forward cautiously, as Coyle watched for any signs the Germans had the lane covered by a machine gun or worse, a self-propelled or anti-tank gun. "When we reached the intersection of another dirt road running east to the highway, we found the enemy behind the hedgerow bordering this road. We had come up on his flank, and by pure chance he had left it unprotected." [38]

Woosley couldn't believe their luck, and immediately got the lead tank into action. "When we reached the lane that was the enemy's position, I had the tank make a ninety-degree turn and fire down the sunken lane." [39]

The tank fired the .50-caliber machine gun, the 75mm main gun, and the .30-caliber coaxial machine gun, devastating the Germans packed into the narrow lane. Sampson's mortar rounds bursting overhead rained down on the helpless German infantry. Coyle deployed his ten Company E troopers into perfect enfilade positions. "We poured fire up the ditch from our positions. After about fifteen minutes of firing, a white flag appeared in the ditch. I called for a cease fire, and it was with some difficulty in all the noise of battle that I was able to get our firing stopped." [40]

Sergeant Sampson began to see some Germans emerge from the hedgerow to his front. "The rifle and machine gun fire along with the mortar shelling had many of the Jerries willing to come out with white flags. To stop those men from getting killed, I stood up and yelled, 'Cease fire! Cease fire!' But the tension was too high—the Germans ran back to the protection of the hedgerow." [41]

The Germans' intentions were not clear to Private Earl Boling. "The Germans started to surrender, then seemed to change their minds and started firing again. However, some had run into the open, and at this time Lieutenant McClean's D Company platoon opened up on their flank." [42]

The fire routed the Germans out of the lane, where Lieutenant Peterson's platoon decimated them. One of those troopers was Private First Class John Keller, rifle grenadier with the company. "Burke was to my right, and I noticed how close he was to the main road, which was also to our right. Next, I noticed he was standing up in the middle of the main road, blasting away with his Tommy gun. I ran up to him and saw a German running like hell down the road. I had a [high-explosive] grenade on my rifle and let the bastard have it. It landed in front of him by some yardage, but failed to explode. I don't know if I forgot to pull the pin, or if it just landed on the fin end and skidded. At that, he threw up his hands, turned and was walking back to us." [43]

The white flag convinced Coyle that the Germans had had enough. "Frank Woosley and I went up the road to accept the surrender. But before we got very far, two hand grenades came over the hedgerow. He went into the ditch on one side of the road and I on the other. We thought at the time that we had stepped into a trap.

"We returned to our position and resumed fire. This time we did not cease until the enemy ran out of the ditch into the large field next to it with their hands raised. When I saw that there were over one hundred of the enemy running into the field,

I went through the hedgerow with the intention of stopping them and rounding them up. But as soon as I got through the hedgerow into the ditch on their side, I was hit by machine pistol fire coming down the ditch. The Germans had not quit yet. One of my men followed me through the hedgerow and fired an unmanned German machine gun up the ditch, ending any further fire from the enemy." [44]

Sampson suddenly saw some Germans attempting to escape up the ditch bordering the highway. "I was set up on the extreme right flank of the field and when some tried to escape in the mouth of a ditch to the right front of me, I quickly brought my mortar into play there. It paid off.

"Mortar ammunition gone, I used my Tommy gun on the escaping Jerries. The ditch was their death trap. . . .

"I saw the backs of four still going. As long as the enemy had a gun in his hands, even though he was running the other way, to me it was open season on them. . . .

"It was Lieutenant Packard's Tommy gun I was using. It had more than paid for his death that occurred back there on the Volturno railroad yard in Italy. It was so easy, I felt ashamed of myself and quit firing. That was the one time I felt I had bagged my quota." [45]

The Germans, realizing there was little chance of escape, emerged into the field in front of their hedgerow. The number of Germans coming out of the lane worried Woosley. "The enemy seemed to come from everywhere with raised hands until it looked like an army. I had difficulty locating enough soldiers for the guard detail. I wondered what would have happened if they knew how small a unit I had left at this point.

"Corporal Sam Appleby, in helping to round up the prisoners, came across one officer who refused to move for him. With Appleby's own words, 'I took a bayonet and shoved it into his ass and then he moved.'

"You should have seen the happy smiles and giggles that escaped the faces of the prisoners to see their lord and master made to obey, especially from an enlisted man." [46]

Sampson, for the first time, became aware of the ghastly scene he had been too busy to notice during the fighting. "I remember very vividly looking over the dead and wounded in the ditch and the surrounding area. One mortar shell had landed on top of the bank near the deep ditch and partly covered some of the dead and wounded with a heavy layer of dirt. Every time a wounded man breathed, the soil would rise and lower. I could partly see the eyes of one man who was lying on his back. An awful scared look was in his eyes as I looked down on him. Fearing, I guessed, that I would put a bayonet into him. I made no attempt at helping them.

"I looked up. No more than fifty feet from me in the open field next to the hedgerow were about fifty to sixty Germans with their hands up, standing in a group. I saw the tall form of Lieutenant McClean from D Company. He was on the other side of the road with some of his men, where more of the enemy had surrendered. . . .

PHOTO GALLERY

Paratroopers with the 505th RCT putting on their parachutes, weapons, and equipment before loading their aircrafts for Sicily, July 9, 1943. *Photograph courtesy of Jan Bos*

The 505th RCT objective, code-named "Y," a crossroads and surrounding high ground where the highways from Niscemi to the north and Vittoria to the east met northeast of Gela. This objective was a chokepoint for the likely route of an enemy armored counterattack on the beach landings by the U.S. 1st Infantry Division. Note the pillboxes just below the ridgeline in the upper right of the photograph. *U.S. Army photograph*

Paratroopers with the 3rd Battalion advance to top of Biazzo Ridge, July 11, 1943. *U.S. Army photograph, courtesy of the 82nd Airborne Division War Memorial Museum*

The first Tiger tank captured by the 82nd Airborne Division on the Vittoria-Gela highway on the west slope of Biazzo Ridge. Lieutenant Harold H. "Swede" Swingler, with Regimental Headquarters Company, single-handedly killed the crew with a hand grenade.
U.S. Army photograph, courtesy of the 82nd Airborne Division War Memorial Museum

A 505th PIR pathfinder, a graduate of the first pathfinder school at Comiso, Sicily. He is holding a leg bag containing a Eureka homing device, used by pathfinders to guide aircraft to the drop zone at Paestum, Italy. *Photograph courtesy of Jerome V. Huth*

Heavily laden paratroopers with Headquarters Company, 2nd Battalion enter Naples, October 2, 1943. *U.S. Army photograph, courtesy of the National Archives*

The 505th Parachute Infantry Regiment encampment located the grounds of the Quorn House on Wood Lane in Quorndon, England. *Photograph courtesy of Jerome V. Huth*

The 1st Battalion PIR Pathfinder Team, June 5, 1944. *U.S. Army photograph, courtesy of Bob Murphy*

The 2nd Battalion Pathfinder Team, June 5, 1944. *U.S. Army photograph, courtesy of Julius Eisner*

The 3rd Battalion Pathfinder Team, June 5, 1944. *U.S. Army photograph, courtesy of the 82nd Airborne Division War Memorial Museum*

The vast sky train of aircraft of the 82nd Airborne Division pass overhead in the growing darkness on the way to Normandy, June 5, 1944. Aircraft flying in the nine plane V-of-V formation that carried one rifle company. A serial of thirty-six or forty-five planes made up a battalion. *Photographic still of U.S. Army combat camera film, courtesy of Tyler Alberts and http://www.combatreels.com*

Troopers run for the door of the church at Ste.-Mère-Église as enemy artillery pounds the town, June 6, 1944. *U.S. Army photograph, courtesy of the 82nd Airborne Division War Memorial Museum*

The three French tanks of the German 100th Panzer Training and Replacement Battalion destroyed by Company A and a 57mm antitank gun at the east end of the La Fière Causeway. *Photographic still from U.S. Army motion picture, courtesy of the Martin K. A. Morgan and the National Archives*

An 81mm mortar is fired by a crew with Headquarters Company, 2nd Battalion in defense of Ste.-Mère-Église, June 7, 1944. *Photographic still of U.S. Army combat camera film, courtesy of Tyler Alberts and http://www.combatreels.com*

A German self-propelled gun, single-handedly destroyed by Private John E. Atchley, just north Ste.-Mère-Église (foreground). A second self-propelled gun, knocked out by Battery A, 80th Airborne Antiaircraft (Antitank) Battalion, and the 57mm antitank gun used to destroy both vehicles can be seen in the background. *U.S. Army photograph courtesy of the 82nd Airborne Division War Memorial Museum*

Medics and Service Company troopers evacuate the wounded from the 505th PIR regimental aid station at Ste.-Mère-Église, while German prisoners are held in the same compound. *U.S. Army photograph, courtesy of the National Archives*

Paratroopers move cautiously through the dense vegetation of the Norman bocage. *Photographic still of U.S. Army combat camera film, courtesy of Tyler Alberts and http://www.combatreels.com*

Wounded German prisoners await treatment, while their dead comrades lie in the ditch on the right side of the photo. *Photograph courtesy of the 82nd Airborne Division War Memorial Museum*

The 505th PIR lands on DZ "N," September 17, 1944. *Photographic still of U.S. Army combat film, courtesy of the National Archives*

A Sherman tank of the British Grenadier Guards, attacking with the 2nd Battalion, is photographed moments after being hit by German antitank fire, as it moved into the open area near the traffic circle, south of the highway bridge. The tank "brewed up" as gasoline and ammunition exploded, killing the tank commander, September 19, 1944. *U.S. Army photograph courtesy of the Cornelius Ryan Collection, Alden Library, Ohio University*

Aerial photo of the Nijmegen bridge areas, taken by British RAF Number 541 Squadron on September 19, 1944. The view is facing north, with the railroad bridge on the left and the highway bridge on the right. The 2nd Battalion fought to capture these bridges and the southern approaches on September 19-20. *Photograph courtesy of Frits Janssen*

Opposite, bottom: The carnage and debris of war in Hunner Park, after its capture by Company F during savage fighting against an SS reconnaissance battalion, September 20, 1944. *Photograph courtesy of the 82nd Airborne Division War Memorial Museum*

The 88mm antiaircraft gun at the traffic circle which did so much damage to British armor the previous day is knocked out during the attack on September 20, 1944. *Photograph courtesy of the Cornelius Ryan Collection, Alden Library, Ohio University*

Top: A German self-propelled gun, knocked out during the heavy German attacks of October 1-2, 1944. *U.S. Army photograph courtesy of the Cornelius Ryan Collection, Alden Library, Ohio University*

Above: Company I paratroopers, dug in along the railroad embankment at Rochelinval, Belgium, fire across the Salm River at elements of the 1st SS panzer Division. *Photographic still of U.S. Army combat film*

Above: A 57mm antitank gun and crew with the 80th Airborne Antiaircraft (Antitank) Battalion defend one of the roads along the division's perimeter in Belgium. *U.S. Army photograph courtesy of the 82nd Airborne Division War Memorial Museum*

Right: A very young German prisoner captured at Fosse, Belgium during the bloody attack by Companies H and I on January 3, 1945. *U.S. Army photograph courtesy of the 82nd Airborne Division War Memorial Museum*

Above: These well concealed log topped bunkers were cleared during the costly attacks of January 3, 1945. *U.S. Army photograph courtesy of the 82nd Airborne Division War Memorial Museum*

Left: The 75mm pack howitzers of the 456th Parachute Field Artillery Battalion were manhandled forward in deep snow to support the rifle companies during the attacks of January 3-6, thanks to Herculean efforts by the artillery crews. *U.S. Army photograph courtesy of the 82nd Airborne Division War Memorial Museum*

Medics struggle to move their jeeps forward to support the 1st Battalion as it moves toward Weneck, Belgium, January 29, 1945. *U.S. Army photograph courtesy of the National Archives*

Above: The 3rd Battalion crosses the Elbe River in British Buffalos on the morning of April 30, 1945. *U.S. Army photograph courtesy of the 82nd Airborne Division War Memorial Museum*

Right: Paratroopers with the 3rd Battalion rest against the dike, while others dig in, after crossing the Elbe River in amphibious vehicles, April 30, 1945. *U.S. Army photograph courtesy of the National Archives*

"I started from the Montebourg road and walked west on the north of the hedgerow with my men trailing. It was a double hedgerow with a sunken lane in between. Here was where Jerry had made his stand.

"One wounded German looked at my canteen and asked what sounded to me like, 'coffee.' I gave him my canteen and moved on, forgetting the incident. . . .

"At the end of the field, I ran into Lieutenant Coyle. He had a large group of prisoners guarded by our company headquarters men.

"He told me part of the story of his attack. 'We caught them unaware. It took twice to make them surrender and then I got hit in the rear,' he said, laying his hand on his rear cheeks.

"'Let me take a look and see how bad it is,' I said as he lay on the ground. A bullet had almost completed its journey through both cheeks. I applied a bandage, saying, 'Lieutenant, just remember, I put your first granny rag on.' Completing the job, I said, 'Just lie here and I'll see someone picks you up.'" [47]

Coyle replied that he'd been all right before Sampson came along. "I was given first aid after the prisoners were collected, and rode back on a tank to the battalion aid station in the old school in Ste.-Mère-Église. The next day I left Ste.-Mère-Église in an ambulance to return to England and the hospital." [48]

After leaving Coyle, Sampson returned to the highway. "I was hailed by the wounded Jerry I had given my canteen to. I had forgotten all about him. He passed it back empty, but the look he gave me was one of thanks. . . .

"I met Jack Hill, roaming around the area on my return to the Montebourg road. He showed me a beautiful watch, saying, 'A German officer lost his arm and I bandaged it up for him. He could speak English well. He offered me the watch and I refused it. I didn't want him to think he had to pay me. The officer said, 'You might as well have it, for it will be taken from me later.' He seemed to be a very pleasant man and showed little sign of the pain he must have been in. . . .

"Our partial company, still minus two platoons, returned to our area in Ste.-Mère-Église without getting a man killed. The price the Germans paid for that short encounter in dead and wounded was terrific, not counting the men captured. We hit fast and hard, each man doing his part. The sight that met our eyes after that encounter was a gruesome one." [49]

As Private First Class Keller was escorting prisoners to the POW area, he noticed a high-ranking German officer, "A colonel, I believe—a man slightly grey at the temples, with a serious leg wound, who was being carried by two of his men. We hadn't gone too far when he asked me for a drink of water. I hesitated to give him one, as I didn't trust him—but I did and I couldn't help but notice, in spite of his defeat and pain, a look of relief or gratitude in his eyes.

"I relieved him of his Iron Cross, and we proceeded on our way. We came to a cluster of buildings, where I had his men place him on a door. Here, I searched him and took a Mauser pistol he had in his pocket, and rejoined my outfit at the front." [50]

The battle was an overwhelming victory. Before he was evacuated, Coyle received a preliminary prisoner count. "In this battle E Company, with two platoons, captured 168 prisoners. I do not know the number of dead left in the ditches. Lieutenant Peterson's platoon on my right flank captured the German commander. Corporal Sam Appleby shot one German captain as he tried to escape the trap. A platoon of D Company, commanded by Lieutenant Thomas J. McClean, captured a great number who tried to escape across the main highway [N-13] and ran into his position." [51]

While the paratroopers destroyed the German infantry, Lieutenant Colonel C. G. Hupfer and Major George Yeatts, with the 746th Tank Battalion, reconnoitered a route around the German flank by taking the road northeast toward Bandienville, then turning north. They skirted the open flank created by the destruction of the 1st Battalion, 1058th, that morning, via a secondary road to Neuville-au-Plain, in time to destroy two more German self-propelled assault guns, while losing two of their own tanks. They liberated nineteen American prisoners and took about sixty German prisoners.

Lieutenant Colonel Vandervoort was justifiably proud of his battalion's overwhelming victories that day. "We had annihilated the 2nd Battalion, 1058th German Infantry Regiment. The 1st Battalion, same unit was completely routed. Four hundred eight prisoners were captured and counted. Thirty-six enemy vehicles and guns destroyed. Four hundred fourteen enemy dead were counted within and in front of our positions." [52]

Later, when General Gavin saw the fields just north of Ste.-Mère-Église littered with German dead from the pervious day's fighting, he commented to Vandervoort, "Van, don't kill them all. Save a few for interrogation." [53]

LIEUTENANT JOHN CLIFF, WITH BATTERY A, 80th Airborne Antiaircraft (Antitank) Battalion, would later be awarded the Silver Star for his part with his antitank gun crew in knocking out the three German vehicles that morning. Private John Atchley, with Company H, was awarded the Distinguished Service Cross for single-handedly knocking out a German self-propelled assault gun. Lieutenant Eugene Doerfler, 2nd Battalion S-2, was awarded the Distinguished Service Cross for his actions in the attack of Company E that afternoon.

BY THE LATE AFTERNOON OF JUNE 7, Private Arthur B. "Dutch" Schultz, with Company C, at the La Fière bridge area, had endured almost continuous German shelling all day. "I was walking to the rear for some reason when I crossed paths with Lieutenant Colonel Mark Alexander, who had assumed command of the 1st Battalion, when a young trooper approached us and said that he had been hit. Both of us looked and couldn't see anything until he turned his back, exposing a gaping shrapnel wound. I was partially immobilized, while the colonel called for a medic and started telling this scared kid that he was going to be all right, while gently helping him sit down on the ground. What was so incongruous to me at that moment was the fact that this wounded trooper was able to walk, and the other was that this battle-tough commander showed so much tender care in the middle of all the death and destruction that was everywhere." [54]

Early the next morning, Lieutenant Waverly Wray took Vandervoort to the site of his remarkable feat the previous day. Vandervoort saw firsthand evidence of the action. "Waverly and I went over the ground he covered the preceding morning. The dead battalion commander and seven staff corpses were still there. It had to be an eerie shock to any German visiting the place. Across the field were two dead Schmeisser-armed grenadiers—both shot in the head.

"John Rabig, Waverly's first sergeant, summed up Wray's performance the next day with the comment, 'Colonel, aren't you glad Waverly's on our side?' Waverly's unique performance set him apart as an authentic hero, but he never showed it in his demeanor. He was nominated for the Congressional Medal of Honor. The recommendation was downgraded and awarded as a DSC. Those who knew him best think of Waverly W. Wray as the 82nd Airborne Division's undiscovered World War II equivalent of Sergeant Alvin C. York. He stands tall among those who made the great invasion succeed." [55]

CHAPTER 11

"I Would Rather Have A Platoon Of Those Men Than A Battalion Of Regular Infantry"

During the evening and night of June 7, the Germans pounded the 2nd Battalion with several large-caliber artillery barrages. Sergeant Eldon M. Clark, with Company D, hugged the bottom of his slit trench as explosions rocked the ground. "They had zeroed in on us. I was literally bouncing up and down.

"[Private First Class Allen B.] Davis was dug in about thirty feet behind me. Davis was in a slit trench and he got a direct hit—blew him to pieces. I got up to check on the guys [in my mortar squad]. The guys wouldn't let me look at him. They knew we were good friends." [1]

At the aid station in the schoolhouse in Ste.-Mère-Église, Captain George Wood, the regimental chaplain, witnessed the heroic efforts of the medical personnel. "Captain Putnam, [2nd Battalion] medical officer, performed major surgery, even to amputations, all night long with the few instruments he jumped in with on his person, in a blacked-out room of the schoolhouse, to the music of a rain of shells which never ceased." [2]

THAT EVENING, TO THE WEST near St.-Sauveur-le-Vicomte, Lieutenant James Rightley and remnants of his 1st Platoon, Company B, 307th Airborne Engineer Battalion, were being hunted by the Germans. "We were down to a few men—ten or twelve, I think. As we prepared to dig in and spend the night, we were attacked by a group of Germans. I was wounded three times and taken prisoner.

"On D+3, I think, while being transported in German trucks we, the prisoners, were strafed by American P-47s, and I think this is where a lot of the 1st Platoon was killed." [3]

COLONEL EKMAN EXPLOITED THE DESTRUCTION of two battalions of the 1058th Regiment, ordering an attack north out of Ste.-Mère-Église driving north to Montebourg Station, commencing shortly after midnight, the morning of June 8. The 505th PIR moved up to their line of departure, Neuville-au-Plain westward to the Merderet River, with the 2nd Battalion on the right and the 3rd Battalion on the left.

In the moonlight, while moving up the highway toward Neuville-au-Plain, Sergeant Russ Brown, with Company F, saw a gruesome sight along the road. "A tank had gone down a ditch with its track and ran over some Germans in the ditch. I heard some Germans call, 'Hilfe! Hilfe! (Help).'" [4]

By 4:30 a.m., the 2nd Battalion reached Neuville-au-Plain, where they found nineteen wounded troopers, including some from Lieutenant Turnbull's Company D platoon, holding the town. Hupfer's tanks had liberated them the previous evening. [5]

As Company I moved forward from the line of departure, Sergeant Bill Dunfee took his turn as a scout. "Attacking at night to avoid exposure in the fields between hedgerows is great, if you're not a scout. This puts horrible pressure on the scouts. We would send two scouts forward from one hedgerow to the next, [and] if all was clear, they would return and move the company forward. To be fair, we took turns; going in pairs we would rotate after two or three exposures. [Albert A.] Dusseault and I were taking our turn, when the plan misfired. We had gone to the next hedgerow and peered through; there was no sign of the enemy, so we returned and moved the platoon forward. We made it back to within a few feet of the hedgerow when the Germans opened up on us from their side with machine pistols and rifles. We hit the deck firing and started lobbing grenades over the hedgerow. They answered in kind with potato mashers. Our fragmentation grenades being superior, our side prevailed.

"We had one casualty, Lieutenant [Walter B.] Kroener, our acting CO; a potato masher had landed near him, blowing dirt and gravel into his face. He wasn't pretty, but wasn't seriously hurt.

"Continuing this night attack, [Richard L.] Almeida was shot through the armpit. A large artery was severed and the medics couldn't stop the flow. [He was] evacuated to the States with a useless right arm.

"Another casualty of this action was one of the new men. He was shot through the forehead, giving him an instant frontal lobotomy. What amazed me was that he remained lucid, he was able to walk with help, and his mental attitude could best be described as euphoric; he was, however, blind. I had the eerie feeling I was talking to a dying man. I assured him he would be evacuated, and all would be well. I'm afraid my voice betrayed my concern, because he told me, 'Don't worry about me Sarge. I'm going to live, you guys may not.' I admired his guts, but had no desire to trade places." [6]

ON THE MORNING OF D+2, when the division's 307th Airborne Medical Company arrived in Ste.-Mère-Église, the regimental surgeon, Major Daniel "Doc" McIlvoy, worked with them to improve the speed of treatment and evacuation. "By this time, all officers, from platoon leaders to division heads, had come to realize the importance of quick help for the injured and wounded.

"It was here that we began to change the rules of evacuation of wounded at the regimental/battalion level. We needed another step in our evacuation setup, rather than that outlined in the field manuals. So often were the battalion aid stations the center of activity that carrying [casualties] out, it was most important that they have jeeps driven by battalion aid men who knew the situation there. The medical company drivers, many of whom were older and less knowledgeable of the intense situation in which they found themselves, agreed. All vehicles in the medical company were placed under regimental surgeon control, who in turn put two medical jeeps with each battalion surgeon. One was used forward, while the second carried the wounded back to the regimental aid station. The regiment, in turn, had the medical company ambulances for clearing out men either to the medical clearing station or to any evac hospital that was placed near our units.

"The regiment medics operated by what would be synonymous to a clearing station, receiving wounded often who were held at battalion aid stations only long enough to stop bleeding, and because of the intense atmosphere, might be treated further for shock at the regimental aid station where, at least, it was a little safer. We officially adopted this plan and used it at all future airborne or ground operations, with considerable success." [7]

AFTER BEING ORDERED BY VII CORPS HEADQUARTERS to wait for the 4th Infantry Division to close up on their right flank, Ekman's troopers continued to drive north that afternoon, with the 3rd Battalion moving toward the town of Grainville and the 2nd Battalion attacking on their right toward Fresville. In this hedgerow country, a few Germans properly positioned behind hedgerows, taking advantage of every terrain feature, and using manmade objects to maximum effect, could inflict heavy casualties and stop the advance of forces many times their size, as D Company had demonstrated the previous two days.

An understrength platoon of Company I moved forward from a small crossroad hamlet astride the dirt road leading to Grainville, with one squad in the fields to the left of the road, another to the right, and a third squad, led by Sergeant Felix C. Sandefur, directly down the road. In the field to the left, walking about ten yards behind Private Arthur S. Hile, Private First Class Bill Tucker lugged his .30-caliber machine gun—a couple of strays from the 508th PIR acting as the assistant gunner and ammo bearer. "We started to attack through fields and two- or three-foot-deep hedgerows covered with thorns. There were also a couple of pig troughs that we went through or around.

"As we got up near the curve of the road, we heard Germans firing from the right with MG-42 machine guns. We figured Sandefur had run into it. Suddenly, they started firing in the field almost directly from our flank. That field was covered with ditches and grass between three and four feet high, so it was impossible to see anyone. Before we knew what happened, Hile had been hit through the chest and lay dead against a small hedgerow ten yards in front of us.

"My team was pinned down in tall grass by a line of Germans to our left and by a machine gun in front of us. Snipers in trees fired down on us from the hill at the right of the road." [8]

As Tucker was lying in the tall grass trying to figure out what to do, another German opened up, "firing a Schmeisser submachine gun at us, from less than thirty yards away in the grass. He had us pinned down so badly that we couldn't set up our gun. The only thing to do was to try to get back with the others. Since we couldn't

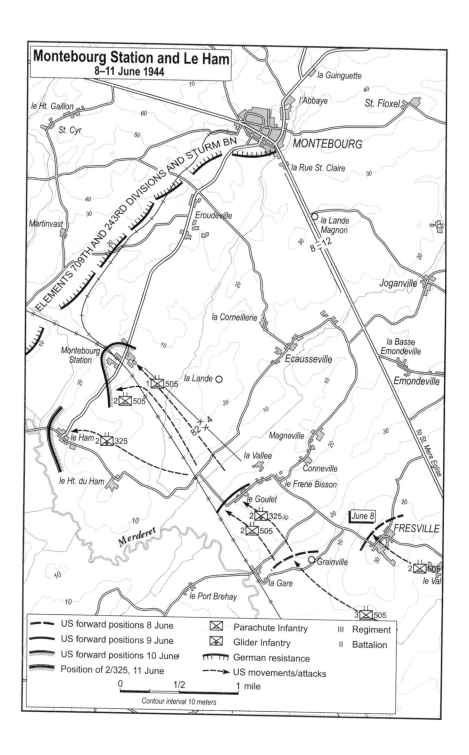

Montebourg Station and Le Ham
8–11 June 1944

le Ht. Gaillon
St. Cyr
Martinvast
ELEMENTS 709TH AND 243RD DIVISIONS AND STURM BN
Eroudeville
Montebourg Station
la Lande
le Ham 2⊠325
le Ht. du Ham
Merderet
la Guinguette
l'Abbaye
St. Floxel
MONTEBOURG
la Rue St. Claire
la Lande Magnon
8=12
Joganville
la Corneillerie
la Basse Emondeville
Ecausseville
Emondeville
1⊠505
2⊠505
la Lande
82×4
la Vallee
Magneville
Conneville
le Frene Bisson
le Goulet
2⊠325
2⊠505
June 8
FRESVILLE
Grainville
la Gare
le Port Brehay
2⊠505
le Val
3⊠505
to St. Mere Eglise

– – – US forward positions 8 June	⊠ Parachute Infantry III Regiment
——— US forward positions 9 June	⊠ Glider Infantry II Battalion
US forward positions 10 June	German resistance
Position of 2/325, 11 June	– –▸ US movements/attacks

0   1/2   1 mile

Contour interval 10 meters

go around the hedgerows, we had to rip our way through. I took the lead, and the two 508th men were right on my tail. I tore the hedgerow branches apart as thorns and heavy brush ripped my wrists. My hands were bleeding in no time at all." [9]

Pulling back to the crossroad, Company I reorganized and attempted to move around the German flank, to the right of the road. Tucker, heavily laden with his .30-caliber machine gun, followed Private First Class Ray Krupinski, the squad's BAR man, who had laid down a withering fire to cover the withdrawal of Tucker and his two men earlier.

Looking across the field they would have to cross, Tucker knew he would be at a distinct disadvantage carrying his machine gun. "[Frederick G.] Synold was on the right of the hedgerow covering us with his machine gun. Krupinski led the way across the field. Following him, came another combat engineer we liked. He had been with us before, and he liked to be with us. I followed the combat engineer by about ten yards, and Larry [Leonard] was behind me. We had all climbed over a three-board fence about four and a half feet high. Larry had just made it over when shots rang out. Our combat engineer was hit, right through the head. That left the three of us prone in the open field. There was nothing we could do except pull back over the fence. We had no cover, and the Germans were on high ground above us." [10]

As Tucker ran back and began climbing over the fence, a bullet pierced his jumpsuit jacket, hitting a Bible his grandmother had given him—another close call.

That evening, G and H Companies moved up on the right flank of I Company, and the entire 3rd Battalion, supported by tanks, jumped off in an attack toward Grainville. Troopers with fixed bayonets advanced in skirmish lines, as tanks knocked out most of the German frontline positions. The battalion pushed over a mile, capturing Grainville by 11:00 p.m.

That night, the 1st Battalion relieved the 3rd, which was placed in reserve south of Grainville. By the end of the fighting, Bill Tucker was bone tired after an advance that had lasted for twenty-three hours. When Company I went into reserve, Tucker's platoon was positioned where it had been "earlier that day, on the curve in the road, where Sandefur's squad had been. Larry [Leonard] and I settled in for the night in a six-foot-square former German foxhole with straw in the bottom. The Germans had used it for a machine gun to cover the road we had tried to move down earlier. The hole was a classic machine gun nest, and the gunners must have been really experienced. They had dug firing shelves on three sides, and the fourth was blocked by an immense hedgerow corner. They had a clear field of fire for at least seventy-five yards down the road where Sandefur had come from.

"As we moved around in the dark, someone found some bodies in a ditch about twenty yards from our hole. The bodies were Sandy and all his men, lying along the ditch about five to ten yards apart. Apparently, when Sandy's squad went down the road, the German machine gunner had fired at Sandy twenty yards away in the lead." [11]

The next morning, Corporal Harry Buffone walked over to the area where the bodies of Sandefur's squad lay. "[Private First Class Sam] Vanich and [Private First

Class George R.] Irving were dead along the side of the road. Sam, being my best buddy, was hard to take. He froze in the process of trying to get a package of sulfa to spread on his wounds." [12]

At 5:30 a.m. on June 9, the 505th pressed the attack north toward Montebourg Station, with the attached 2nd Battalion, 325th Glider Infantry Regiment (GIR), the division's organic glider infantry regiment, attacking on the right flank of the 2nd Battalion. The 1st Battalion followed behind in reserve, while the 3rd Battalion guarded crossings over the Merderet River.

That day, Company G medic Private Marty Cuccio was lying in a slit trench behind a hedgerow to avoid enemy sniper fire. "Somebody told a bazooka team that there was a sniper in this building. There was an opening through this hedgerow, and the team went that way through the hedge. When they came back through the hedges, there came these 88s coming in. An 88 shell hit the tree, came down, hit me on the inside of my leg—knocked off one of my testicles and my pelvis bone was shattered. I had small pieces in my shoulder and my knee.

"I took off and I went to another trench. After that, I couldn't move anymore and I had no voice. [Company G medic] Chris Perry came looking for me. I said, 'I'm here,' just loud enough that he heard me.

"He went back, I guess, to the aid station and he got a jeep. He took the jeep with a stretcher on it, put me on the stretcher, and took me back to the aid station. They were taking care of me, giving me plasma when I was at the aid station, and Chaplain [George B.] Wood gave me the sign of the cross on my head. I asked, 'Am I going to die?'

"He said, 'No, we always do that—you're not going to die.'" [13]

THAT MORNING IN CHERBOURG, Sergeant Harvill Lazenby, along with a group of Company B troopers who had been captured north of Ste.-Mère-Église on June 6, were moved south by train out of the Cotentin Peninsula. Lazenby and the other POWs were unloaded from the train when it reached a point where the rails had been cut by Allied bombing. "We were formed up in a column of threes, with guards on all sides, for the march to Germany. There were about one hundred fifty in the column—all units—4th Division, airborne, you name it.

"That afternoon, American P-47s strafed the column and killed about seventy or eighty guys. We buried them in a mass grave and [the Germans] decided to move only at night, because of the planes. Sergeant Bob Henderson [with Company B] and I escaped on the night of 11–12 of June, while being moved. We ducked and dodged enemy troops and returned to U.S. troops thirty-seven days after escaping. We were MIA for forty-two days. Lieutenant Jim Irvin also escaped and returned to Company B." [14]

ON THE EVENING OF JUNE 9, Lieutenant Colonel Mark Alexander, still in command of the 1st Battalion, reported to the regimental command post to discuss plans for an attack the following morning. "Lieutenant Colonel Bill Ekman had requested that I give the attack order. My order was for the 1st Battalion to lead, followed closely by the 2nd Battalion. After the 1st Battalion had taken Montebourg Station, the 2nd Battalion was to take the lead, turning to the left forty-five degrees and take Le Ham." [15]

That night, Lieutenant Frank Woosley, acting commander of Company E, reported to the 2nd Battalion command post to receive the attack order. "We were to move northwest towards Le Ham, with E Company on the left, D Company on the right, and F Company in reserve. A railroad track was our line of departure." [16]

The attack jumped off late, at 2:00 p.m. the following day. Following behind a rolling artillery barrage by the 456th Parachute Field Artillery Battalion, the 1st Battalion broke through the German frontline, along a canal, then advanced another one thousand yards to a creek. As it did, Private First Class Arthur B. "Dutch" Schultz, with Company C, noticed one of his buddies, Private First Class Raymond S. Gonzales, who had seen two of his closest friends killed during the first couple of days of the invasion. "He cried over their deaths and swore that he would avenge their deaths by not taking any prisoners.

"I ran by a wounded German soldier lying alongside a hedgerow. He was crying in a loud voice. I passed by him and stopped, for some unknown reason, and turned around. I saw Gonzales had put the muzzle of his rifle between the eyes of this German, while asking if he had a pistol. A moment later, Gonzales pulled the trigger. There wasn't the slightest change in his facial expression.

"I was both awed and appalled by what I saw. Most of me wanted to do what Gonzales had done. Along the way, I had been taught that a 'good German is a dead German.'" [17]

After crossing the creek, the 1st Battalion held up, while Alexander got an artillery smokescreen laid on nine hundred yards of open ground to the front. Companies B and C then pushed forward, with Company A following behind in reserve. Everything was going as Alexander planned. "The first part of the attack worked fine, and the 1st Battalion with a beautiful smoke screen got into and cleared Montebourg Station with minimum losses. While we were still clearing the village, Colonel Ekman, the 505th CO, came up and wanted to know what I was doing waiting on the east side of the bridge. I told him I was waiting until the battalion had cleared the village. We were standing at the northeast corner of the arching bridge over the railroad. In spite of my telling him that a German machine gun located on the road to Le Ham was firing on the bridge, he started to cross it. The Germans opened fire on him and he had to make a running jump off the rear end of the bridge. Colonel Ekman left to check on the 2nd Battalion. After we had cleared the village and the 2nd Battalion had passed through, I set up a CP about seventy-five yards east of the railroad overpass.

"The 2nd Battalion was one-half hour late in following, giving the Germans time to get set on the other side of the village, and they stopped the 2nd Battalion cold just beyond the village." [18]

Private First Class Irvin W. "Turk" Seelye was advancing across open ground just north of Montebourg Station with Company E, as the 2nd Battalion took over the attack. "Our skirmish line was spotted by the enemy as we crossed a railroad grade. Artillery—air bursts, were directed toward us. We passed through a lightly forested area. Corporal Ralph H. McGrew, Jr. was killed by a sniper. At about 1700 hours, Germans were spotted up ahead. Shortly thereafter, a mortar shell exploded at my side. I was blinded, [had] broken bones, and [was] bleeding. I spent the next twelve months in an Army hospital." [19]

Lieutenant Woosley tried to get his company moving again. "I was suddenly appalled at the confusion. I had temporarily lost contact with battalion head-quarters and with D and F Companies. I didn't know what was in front of me, or on either flank. I followed my original orders and moved into the attack until my company was pinned down by enemy small-arms fire and by artillery shelling that grew more intense through the evening and night. Three men were killed that night—they were all 101[st Airborne] men who were in their fourth day of combat." [20]

Alexander decided to go forward to see if he could give the 2nd Battalion a hand. "In a reconnaissance with my artillery observer, I had spotted a German multiple-firing railroad gun, I think a 40mm 'pom-pom,' north of the village. We brought in artillery fire on the gun and silenced it. The 1st Battalion was receiving a great deal of fire, including a lot of 'Screaming Meemies' from the north on our right flank." [21]

The 2nd Battalion, kept attacking until Company F reached the edge of Le Ham that night, but Ekman ordered a withdrawal about 11:00 p.m. after savage fighting. Several German platoon-sized counterattacks during the night were repulsed.

After the 1st Battalion dug in north of Montebourg Station, Private Dutch Schultz, with Company C, noticed "one of our platoon leaders, Lieutenant Gerald 'Johnny' Johnson (one of the best and bravest combat officers in any man's army) sitting by himself, deeply engrossed in his Bible. It was as if he was sitting all alone in church. At the time, I couldn't fathom anybody showing this kind of devotion to God, under such adverse conditions, especially a Protestant. I thought only Catholics had this kind of spiritual piety." [22]

By that night, the strength of 1st Battalion was down to approximately two hundred fifty men and officers.

On the morning of June 11, following a fifteen-minute barrage by the 456th Parachute Field Artillery Battalion, the 2nd Battalion made a limited attack on Le Ham. As Lieutenant Woosley led Company E forward, "enemy fire and shelling continued, and we were temporarily pinned down. An artillery shell hit close by—a dud. A messenger came, and hit the ground beside me. He told me that a flank of E Company was not holding. As I started to the area to assess the situation, a shell hit close by me—the blast caught me mostly in the face—one eye was blinded, and I received a small wound in my back. I was taken to an aid station, and then by truck to the coast." [23] Captain Clyde Russell, even though still affected by malaria, took command of Company E.

The 2nd Battalion's attack halted, and a base of fire was laid down on the defenders of Le Ham, while the 2nd Battalion, 325th GIR, assaulted the town. A storm of enemy machine gun and rifle fire stopped the glider troopers, who withdrew to reorganize. At 6:00 p.m., they renewed their assault, behind a ten-minute artillery concentration on the town, fired by the artillery of the 456th. By about 8:00 p.m. on June 11, the 2nd Battalion, 325th, had secured Le Ham at a tremendous cost. The 505th remained along the eastern side of the Merderet River, patrolling across the river until relieved by the 90th Infantry Division on the evening of June 12–13.

ON JUNE 13, THE 2ND BATTALION, 325TH, was released from attachment, and the 505th was trucked to an assembly area east of Picauville to rest and reorganize. Company I was detached to guard the causeway just south of Ètienville. The duty was easy, except for an occasional round of incoming enemy artillery. One of those rounds caught Company I trooper Private Jack Hillman sitting on a rock, driving white-hot shrapnel into his back. "I remember someone shouting, 'Medic!' for I was bleeding profusely, and could not move.

"Our company medic, Joe Piacenti, came on the double, cut off my jump jacket, and said, 'This is a bad one, don't move him.' The last thing I remember was being face down on a stretcher, and awakening in a hospital in England, when the surgeon said, 'You're a lucky chap, yank,' stating, 'another two millimeters, and you would have been a vegetable.' He then dropped a sliver of steel shaped like a miniature horseshoe nail into a metal receptacle. He also said, 'You can thank those who took care of you with quick thinking knowledge in not moving you about.'

"I am forever grateful to Joseph Piacenti, Company I medic, for his quick action and knowledge that had saved me from a disabling condition. The medics were our 'Guardian Angels.'" 24

On June 14, the division attacked from west of Ètienville westward toward St.-Sauveur-le-Vicomte. The severely depleted 507th PIR ran into strong enemy resistance, but captured La Bonneville that night and repulsed several enemy counterattacks. The understrength 325th GIR attacking west along the highway on the left flank of the 507th, engaged in savage fighting with exceptionally strong enemy opposition, but that night pulled up even with the 507th.

At 5:00 a.m. next morning, the 507th advanced about six hundred yards against light opposition before an enemy counterattack, supported by tanks and intense artillery and mortar barrages, struck their open right flank, halting the advance. The 505th, following in reserve behind the 507th, took over the attack.

At 11:00 a.m., Lieutenant Colonel Ekman issued an attack order. Lieutenant Colonel Mark Alexander's 1st Battalion jumped off at 3:00 p.m. "The 1st and 2nd Battalions launched an attack to the west—objective St.-Sauveur-le-Vicomte—to speed up cutting off the peninsula and isolating Cherbourg—1st Battalion on the right, 2nd Battalion on the left. To our left was the [325th GIR] and on our right the 9th [Infantry] Division.

"In leading off, the 1st Battalion had to pass through elements of the 9th Division on our right. It was a green regiment that was bogged down in a hedgerow and was getting shot to pieces by German mortar fire. Our experienced battalion drove the Germans back, and as I once said, we passed through the 9th like a dose of salts, and at the end of the day we had progressed about halfway to the Douve River north of Crosville, where we sat down for the night.

"We had experienced only sporadic resistance, mainly from a stone walled farmhouse and buildings. We had a few casualties, including Lieutenant Gerald Johnson [Company C] who had suffered a round through his shoulder, and a new first lieutenant replacement shot through the knee.

"We were again ahead of the 2nd Battalion, even though I had given Lieutenant Colonel Vandervoort my two tanks when he was held up by a rock walled farmhouse complex. We were again open on our right flank." 25

Advancing astride the highway to St.-Sauveur-le-Vicomte, Company D ran into a hornet's nest of German resistance at the hamlet of Les Rosiers, including two 75mm antitank guns and two 37mm antiaircraft guns used in a direct-fire, antipersonnel role. Private First Class David Bowman, a machine gunner with Company D, advanced through the extremely heavy enemy fire during this "combined infantry-tank attack, which developed into the most heated battle in which I participated in Normandy. We were moving forward under constant artillery and small-arms fire. The resistance was so heavy that we could move forward only in spurts. We'd hit the ground, open fire, get up, rush forward a short distance, and hit the ground again. A few men were hit during these movements. Some just lay there; others limped to the rear. Tanks were on our left flank, and I heard the rumble of some to our right.

"After moving forward some distance, our unit was halted and [William R. "Rebel"] Haynes and I were instructed to direct fire so it would complement that from the machine gunners to our right, Private Donald MacPhee and Private First Class Thomas Byrd.

"The enemy fire from small arms, tanks, and artillery was heavy. After an indeterminable passage of time, I heard Byrd shouting, 'MacPhee!' 'MacPhee!' (I later learned that both had been killed around that time.) Shortly after this unfortunate incident, Haynes was hit and went to the rear.

"We continued our advance . . . but for some distance we endured the sight of burning tanks and their hapless crews. One would see tankers, mostly German, I believe, but also many Americans, draped over the turrets, burning atop their burning tanks. Evidently, no quarter was given by either side, as would be expected under these conditions. When the tanks were disabled and the surviving crew attempted to abandon them, the enemy would mercilessly cut the men down." 26

Fire from German high-velocity guns was terrible. Corporal Wilton Johnson with Headquarters Company, 2nd Battalion, was working his way up the highway looking for a place to set up his machine gun, when he was wounded in the back by shrapnel from an aerial burst. "Private Elmer Pack, who was in my squad, pushed a rag in my back to stop the bleeding and probably saved my life." 27

Vandervoort took the two tanks from Company A, 746th Tank Battalion, and with the 1st Platoon of D Company, worked around to the right flank of the German position as fire from the 2nd Battalion 81mm mortars kept the Germans' heads down. As the 1st Platoon advanced north in a skirmish line across an open field toward a hedgerow running east and west, Sergeant Roy King was deployed on the extreme left flank of his squad. "I was hit by a very small piece of shrapnel in the calf of my right leg. It felt like when you get popped with a towel in the shower room. I did not even know that I was hit until later.

"We reached the next hedgerow when Lieutenant McClean called for squad leaders to meet in his location, which was a gun pit for a large gun, about five feet by ten feet by eight inches [deep]. We had been assembled for a short time when the enemy fired a burst from an antiaircraft gun, hitting the hedgerow and bursting into flak—a piece of which hit me in the neck at the level of my Adam's apple and about an inch and a half to the right. My mouth and throat filled with fluid.

"I thought, 'Blood.' *I knew fear.*

"Because I did not recover from hitting the dirt, the lieutenant asked, 'King, are you hit?' I did not answer, fearing that I'd pour blood forth. The lieutenant asked, 'King, are you all right?'

"My answer was, 'Hell no, where's the medic?'

"He said, 'Right up the hedgerow to the east.' I leaped from the pit to the border and over the hedge, and ran to the medic. When I arrived, he was holding one of us [troopers] in his lap, with blood pumping from his back. I immediately sat down and recovered normality. When he looked up at me, he turned pale, and I was frightened again. After a sulfa powder application, he bandaged my neck. Then he put me on a stretcher and said, 'Lie still until they come for you.'" 28

Lieutenant McClean's platoon hit the German flank and overran it, as Company E moved up to carry the attack through the enemy positions.

Private Earl W. Boling, an assistant BAR gunner, was carrying a heavy load of ammunition for the BAR as well as his own rifle as Company E moved up to assist the Company D platoon's flank attack. "It was in this area that Private First Class Julius Eisner was wounded in the calf of the leg by a 37mm projectile, and as an aid man attended to him, we passed through D Company and took up positions along a hedgerow to gain a field of fire, since we had by this time many casualties.

"As we placed the BAR in firing position, an enemy machine gun fired. John [W. Burdge], Private [William H.] Nealy, and I were about a foot apart, John being in the center. A burst of machine gun fire started—neither Private Nealy nor I were touched, but Burdge was struck in the left thigh—the bullet going through the left leg and entering, but not exiting, the right leg." 29

Boling quickly got a medic for Burdge. "As the aid man was treating the wound, Private Nealy and I found a position to return the enemy fire, and as the company started to advance and broke the enemy line, we were advancing up a long grassy field.

"We had gotten a couple of tanks in support for a change—as we neared the crest of the hill, one of the tanks seemed to be slow a bit, and Nealy and I saw a beautiful sight. There was Colonel Vandervoort with the cast still on the leg [of the ankle] he had broken on the jump—hopping on one crutch and pounding the back of the tank with the other one. I don't remember his exact words, but they were something to the effect that if the driver couldn't drive the tank up the hill, that he would put one of his men in to drive.

"Needless to say, the tank moved and Private Nealy, who was on his first campaign and had been a little nervous to that point, smiled and said, 'If that so and so can make it on one leg and a crutch, I can make it on two good legs.'" 30

By 7:00 p.m., the 2nd Battalion pulled up on the left flank of the 1st Battalion, and the regiment reorganized. The 3rd Battalion moved up to screen the regiment's right flank, because it was so far in front of the 9th Infantry Division, on its right. Before sunrise, Lieutenant Colonel Alexander ordered the 1st Battalion to attack again with the objective of reaching the Douve River across from St.-Sauveur-le-Vicomte. "We launched our attack at dawn, had stiff resistance from an 88 gun position, but by 1400 hours, we had reached the road paralleling the Douve River and were again ahead of the 2nd Battalion on our left. I could hear fighting on the main road to the southeast. The 9th [Division] on our right was far behind.

"I set up a defensive position on the river road, defending from the northeast and southwest. We had no more than taken up our defense than a German command car with four occupants drove right into us from the north along the river road. Our men shot them to pieces. I don't know how it happened, but a German artillery major survived the incident.

"Some Frenchman on a bicycle saw the action, turned around and pedaled madly back northeast on the river road. I'm sure he informed the Germans of our position. Shortly thereafter, I spotted German tanks on a road junction about three-quarters of a mile to the northeast on the river road. I had my artillery observer bring down a concentration of fire. When the smoke cleared, the tanks had gone and I saw no further German action in that area." 31

Lieutenant Clarence McKelvey, a forward observer with Battery A, 456th Parachute Field Artillery Battalion, decided to take a patrol to find "a couple of 88mm artillery pieces that they were intermittently dropping shells around where our troops were, and this kind of got on our nerves a bit."

The patrol moved near the suspected location of the enemy guns, stringing a line for a field telephone with them as they advanced. As McKelvey and his patrol neared a barn with a thatched roof, suddenly there was an explosion. One of his men was hit and the phone line was cut. After tending to the wounded trooper, McKelvey "hollered back to [Lieutenant] Henry [Aust], 'Tell [Lieutenant Robert N.] Edmondson to throw a round out here, so we can see where we are!'

"So he and [Sergeant Evan W.] Prosser went back and picked up a piece of the wire that was not cut and hooked the telephone on it, and had Edmondson shoot one out there. It came out and landed behind us, actually over to the right, and behind us. So I hollered back to Aust, 'Tell him it landed behind us. Call it four hundred short and fire another one.'

"This round comes out and it lands—we could see the smoke come out of it. Where we thought these guns were, was on the other side of this barn—we saw smoke come up there, so I hollered back, 'Call it two hundred over.' So the next round came out and it landed where I thought was right—behind the barn—and the [enemy] gun didn't fire anymore. We heard a little small-arms fire, but the guns had stopped firing. So I said, 'Let 'em have it.' They threw a bunch of other rounds out there and we had no more noise from there." 32 McKelvey received the Silver Star for his actions.

At midday, the 2nd Battalion, reached the high ground on the Douve River northeast of St.-Sauveur-le-Vicomte. From an upper story window of a chateau overlooking the town, Vandervoort saw thousands of German troops and horse-drawn heavy equipment moving south on the main north-south highway running through St.-Sauveur-le-Vicomte, attempting to escape before the peninsula was cut. Vandervoort immediately radioed Major Jack Norton, the S-3, telling him what he saw, but terminated the conversation before providing the coordinates. Norton deduced the location and quickly got word to Lieutenant Colonel Ekman, who in turn contacted General Ridgway, to arrange bringing artillery fire to bear upon the enemy concentration. As it happened, Ridgway had General Omar Bradley with him when he received word and decided to take Bradley with him to watch the impending fireworks.

Using a forward observer, every available artillery piece in the VII Corps within range, not engaged in support of another unit, fired a massive TOT (time-on-target) barrage. Artillery batteries fired at slightly different times depending upon the distance to the target and velocity of the shells fired so that all of the rounds fired would arrive on the target simultaneously. As the precise moment approached, the air filled with a low roar, which reached a crescendo as the shells converged on the target. A couple of seconds later, virtually the entire town and highway erupted in simultaneous explosions. After a slight adjustment to the fire, a second TOT barrage destroyed those German troops, vehicles, and horses not hit in the first barrage.

Private First Class James V. Rodier, an ammo bearer with the 81mm Mortar Platoon of Headquarters Company, 2nd Battalion, positioned on the high ground above the town "could see a self-propelled gun being knocked out in the town. There was other artillery coming from the same direction our mortars were firing. I do not know what kind of guns the enemy was using, but they were getting the worst of the deal." 33

As the second barrage lifted, Vandervoort ordered his battalion to cross the bomb-damaged bridge over the Douve River and capture St.-Sauveur-le-Vicomte. Company F would lead the assault and, upon crossing the bridge, circle the town to the north and block the road running west from the town. Company D following them would circle the town and cut the road leading south, and Company E would move straight through the town.

With his squad leading, Sergeant Spencer Wurst, with Company F, moved through a ditch beside the main road leading into town, waiting for the inevitable

German fire to hit them. "The Germans had taken position on the other side of the river to our left and right front, on slightly higher ground. They let us get almost fully deployed along that open road before they opened up. We hit the dirt as the shells skimmed the top of the roadbed, passing over our heads by two or three feet." 34

Wurst knew they had to move—and move now, because staying in the ditch would only result in more casualties. "The best we could do was get the hell out of there as fast as possible. We had to jump up and run across the bridge. The instant before we made our dash, [John P.] Corti, a BAR man in my squad, was severely wounded. He had been in a prone position close to a cement power pole, which was hit by one of the shells. As we made our rush, we couldn't stop, but the medic did." 35

Wurst and his men ran toward the bridge as German fire intensified. "We were taking considerable small-arms fire, which was particularly deadly in our situation. The Germans had us in sight and were firing rifles and machine guns directly on us.

"About a hundred fifty yards from the bridge, we were also taken under very heavy direct artillery fire. This was a minimum of 75mm, and probably larger, likely from self-propelled guns. These were HE—high explosive shells, not antitank." 36

Watching Vandervoort's men cross the bridge under tremendous enemy fire, General Bradley turned to Ridgway and said, "My God, Matt, can't anything stop these men?" 37

Ridgway replied, "I would rather have a platoon of those men than a battalion of regular infantry." 38

Sergeant Paul Nunan, with Company D, got his men across the river, where they turned left and began working around the town. "They sent my platoon around to the left and we were going back into hedgerows. I had a man out in front of the platoon and he was down in the roadway. All of a sudden, he jumped back into the corner of this hedgerow and he said, 'There's a German out there, and he jumped into the hedgerow.'

"I told the people right up front against the hedgerow, 'OK everybody stay down until I give the word, and then everybody stand up and open up against that hedgerow that's along the road.' I had a guy named [Private First Class] Norman Pritchard, who either didn't hear what I said or didn't care, so he stood up all by himself. A shot rang out and he had been drilled right through the heart. I told our guys to fire into the other hedgerow that was parallel to the road. Pritchard keeled over and after we had doused the area with small arms fire, I went up to him and saw he had taken one bullet. I thought of shooting him with the morphine syrette. I put it in his arm, and it stayed in a lump. And I realized he was dead. I've reviewed that in my mind I don't know how many times." 39

From high ground east of the Douve, Staff Sergeant Russ Brown, a 60mm mortar squad leader with Company F, was firing in support of the crossing when he heard the sound of planes and looked up. "Some P-47s tried to skip bomb the bridge while our men were still crossing. They missed, turned around, and tried again, but missed again." 40

The 505th PIR had moved past the bomb line that ran along the Douve River for that day. None of the planners believed the regiment would be able to cross the Douve until the following day. After crossing the river, Sergeant Wurst looked back, seeing orange smoke rising, a signal to the air corps that friendly forces were present. "From a distance, I could see Colonel Vandervoort, who had crossed shortly after we did, standing out in an opening with a huge orange blanket or panel. He was waving it like mad, standing there with orange smoke everywhere, trying to deter the planes. The bombs missed the bridge, but the planes also made some strafing runs." [41]

Lieutenant Colonel Alexander left a platoon to block the road running parallel to the eastern side of the river, and the 1st Battalion moved out on that road toward

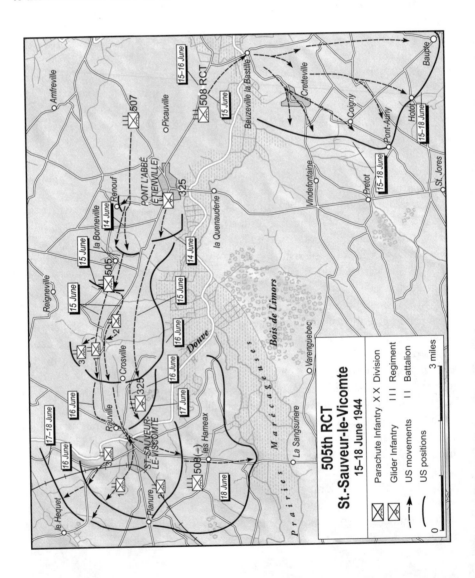

the bridge. Alexander, his radioman, and his orderly were ahead of the battalion, arriving at the bridge just as the last of the 2nd Battalion troopers crossed. There, Alexander met Colonel Ekman and General Ridgway. "Ekman ordered me to bring up the 1st Battalion. I told him they were already on their way, and the lead elements began arriving as I spoke. I directed them to speed up the crossing behind the 2nd Battalion." [42]

Private Earl Boling was acting as a scout for the 1st Platoon of Company E as it moved through the streets into the heart of St.-Sauveur-le-Vicomte. "As I turned the corner and moved a few feet down the street, a machine gun opened fire. I jumped over a nearby stone wall, about three feet high, and raised my head to try and ascertain where the fire was coming from.

"The German immediately tried to write his name on the wall with the weapon." [43]

Boling moved back along the wall to find his platoon. "At this time, [Battery C, 80th AA Battalion] brought forward a 57mm antitank gun and attempted to fire on the enemy guns, but immediately received a round of enemy fire, which killed one and wounded two of the crew.

"Some of the platoon members decided to use the gun for our protection, and as I recall, Private Clyde Rickerd went to a second story window with binoculars to direct and correct fire.

"As he was looking at the enemy position, he received a sniper shot which hit him in the second joint of the small finger of the right hand, and he had to vacate the window view. As Clyde later explained, 'I was looking at their positions and suddenly spotted this German looking back through a sniper scope, and before I could duck, I was shot in the hand. It was like looking through a keyhole and seeing an eye looking back.'" [44]

Company F kept out of the built-up areas as they skirted the north side of town, with Sergeant Wurst and his squad still leading. Wurst and Corporal Bill Hodge, acting as scouts, spotted three Germans walking, one right behind the other, along a hedgerow perpendicular to their advance, unaware of their presence. Wurst aimed and fired, hitting one of them, then drew a bead on a second. "Just as I was about to shoot, Bill opened up with his .45-caliber Tommy gun. One instant the German was in my sights, and the next he was flat on the ground. He must have been hit by a number of the .45 slugs, because he went down very fast. The other German threw his hands up in surrender, and we approached him after an intense visual search of the surrounding area. Bill and I moved up to where the bodies were lying, and Lieutenant [Jack P.] Carroll came up with a few others from the platoon. One of the Germans was dead, and three or four of our men gathered around to watch the other one die.

"This is one of the few times I actually saw at close range the result of my own fire, or that of my squad. I thought the German was suffering terribly, and without thinking, I asked the lieutenant whether I should finish him off. Much to his credit, he absolutely refused. The sight of that man lying there slowly dying lingers in my mind to this day. He has been the subject of many nightmares over the years. I hesitate to think what kind of dreams I'd have now if I'd put the man out of his misery." [45]

Company F advanced to the main north-south highway, where it ambushed German traffic moving south, scattering them, then pushed on until reaching the road that ran west from town. There, it set up a roadblock, preventing the Germans from using it as an avenue of retreat. Company D, likewise, cut the road leading south from St.-Sauveur-le-Vicomte.

The 1st Battalion crossed the bridge and helped Company E clear the town, which was heavily damaged by U.S. artillery fire. Late that afternoon, the 3rd Battalion arrived at St.-Sauveur-le-Vicomte, after being relieved by the 3rd Battalion, 508th.

Lieutenant Jack Isaacs was the fourth Company G commander thus far in the Normandy campaign. "We were directed to attack through the town, secure the high ground to the west of town, and the battalion lined up to do this with I Company on the right and G Company on the left. We launched our attack without any reconnaissance, very little information about what we might encounter. We were fiercely opposed by several German machine gun positions." [46]

Both companies advanced under this heavy fire from Germans dug in along the top of the reverse slope of a railroad embankment. Company G guided on the road to their right, which crossed the railroad embankment via an underpass. Company I moved forward toward the railroad embankment with their left on the road.

Sergeant Bill Dunfee, with Company I, could see a German tank, sitting hull-down in the underpass waiting for them. "There was a woods on my right across the tracks. I knew if we got into the woods the tank couldn't get at us. There were some P-51s flying above us, so we signaled to them and pointed out the tank. Two P-51s came down for a look-see; the dirty birds bombed and strafed us. 'Murphy's Law' continued to prevail." [47]

Despite German machine gun, small arms, and mortar fire, both companies reached the embankment, with Germans dug in on the other side, just yards away. Sergeant Bill Blank, with Company G, took a quick look to see if the Germans were pulling out. "I raised my head to look across and as I did, a German directly opposite rose up, and we looked each other in the eye and ducked down. The German threw several of those blue grenades at me, but they rolled to the bottom of the embankment and exploded without harm. When I rose up again, I caught him coming up with my Tommy gun. They had a small tank just up the road aimed at the underpass. He was firing down the road at anything that moved. Fortunately, he only had armor piercing shells and they didn't cause any damage until Colonel Krause tried to roll out a 75mm pack howitzer to fire back, which resulted in the loss of the gun and the crew. The tank made an attempt to drive through the underpass." [48]

As it did, a G Company bazooka team waited in ambush on the other side of the underpass, with only three rockets. As the tank came through, Private First Class Billy G. Hahnen fired two rockets, damaging the tank, which backed out of the underpass. Hahnen's team repulsed a counterattack by four other tanks, knocking out one with his last rocket.

As Company G continued the attack, both of Lieutenant Isaacs' remaining platoon leaders were hit. "Lieutenant [William F.] Mastrangelo was wounded while we were trying to cross the railroad embankment during the day at St.-Saveur-le-Vicomte. Night fell, and we continued to attack in the dark. And while [I was] talking to Lieutenant [Travis] Orman, he was killed. All other officers had been wounded, captured, or missing. So, I found myself as the sole officer left in Company G. We had started with eight. We were now down to one." 49

Around 10:00 p.m., the 1st and 2nd Battalions of the 508th PIR arrived in St.-Saveur-le-Vicomte, expanding the bridgehead south, moving down both sides of the highway leading south to La Haye-du-Puits.

During the night, Isaacs kept Company G moving forward with the help of his NCOs, who were now leading the remnants of the company's platoons. "My non-commissioned officers were quite equal to the task and we continued to attack. The attack continued all night long, dawn finding us actually having worked our way behind the enemy positions. I had only seventeen men left, the others having been lost or strayed or casualties. But we were in a strategic position alongside the road running west of St.-Saveur-le-Vicomte. We were actually two hundred or three hundred yards ahead of Company I, and when our position became known to the Germans, they started to withdraw from in front of Company I. Company I was delivering frontal fire, and we caused a great many casualties among the retreating Germans.

"Also, at point-blank range, in this position, we observed an 88mm gun being towed down the road toward us; it was accompanied by two or three other vehicles, and approximately twenty to twenty-five men. With my seventeen men lying just alongside the road in the hedgerow, when this group approached, the rapid fire that we were able to deliver as a complete surprise to them, wiped out everybody on the German side in this. We knocked out the tow vehicle, the 88, the two or three vehicles accompanying it, and this further dislodged the Germans who were still attempting to defend themselves against Company I, and it became a rather serious rout.

"I entered Normandy as a twenty-one year old platoon leader and in ten days was a forty-two year old company commander." 50

The following day, Private First Class Joe Comer, with Company H, looked around at the devastation that he had been too busy to notice the previous day. "There were bloated bodies of German soldiers, as well as cows and horses, around where the fighting was the most fierce. . . . The smell of death was always near. . . . How can you forget war?" 51

THE 505TH CONSOLIDATED AND EXPANDED the bridgehead west and north, while the 508th did the same, south and west. The next day, the 47th Infantry, 9th Infantry Division, passed through the bridgehead and attacked west to the coast, cutting the peninsula.

From June 17 to 19, the troopers' barracks bags caught up with them, and they were able to clean up, shave, and change clothes. The troopers now had bedrolls and blankets—and ate five-in-one and ten-in-one rations, much better than the C- and K-rations they had been eating.

A large number of shifts of officers took place. At regiment, Lieutenant Colonel Alexander temporarily transferred to the 508th PIR as executive officer; Lieutenant Colonel Walter Winton temporarily transferred from division as 505th executive officer; and several regimental staff changes were made. The 1st Battalion reorganization included Major Bill Hagan, executive officer of the 3rd Battalion, taking command of the battalion, and Captain Woody Long, commander of Regimental Headquarters Company, transferring as executive officer. Captain James K. Cockrell, Jr., took command of Regimental Headquarters Company. Captain Walter DeLong, the commander of Company H, replaced Hagan as 3rd Battalion executive officer, and the 2nd Battalion executive officer, Captain James T. Maness, took command of Company H.

Captain Hubert Bass, who had commanded Company F on D-Day and taken command of Headquarters Company, 2nd Battalion, on June 7, replaced as Company F commander by Lieutenant Joseph W. Holcomb. Bass was promoted to 2nd Battalion executive officer, replacing Captain Maness. Captain William E. Schmees, who had commanded Headquarters Company, 2nd Battalion, on D-Day, returned to command it again.

Numerous changes in command were made at the battalion staff and platoon levels. Most of the rifle companies reorganized into one or two provisional platoons.

One of the worst storms in fifty years struck the English Channel, lasting from June 19 to 21, damaging and sinking many Allied small ships and destroying the Mulberry harbor at Omaha Beach that brought much of the ammunition, rations, equipment, vehicles, guns, and men to Normandy. The supply tonnage at the onset of the storm, only seventy-three percent of plan, was reduced to fifty-seven percent. This forced Allied commanders to accelerate the capture of the Cherbourg port to replace the destroyed Mulberry harbor. Priority for supplies was given to the VII Corps' drive to seize Cherbourg.

On June 20, the 3rd Battalion attacked through the Bois de Limors against light opposition, digging in along the western edge of the forest. The regiment carried out aggressive patrolling while it reorganized and prepared for the next attack. The regiment didn't receive replacements in Normandy, even though severely depleted by almost two weeks of continuous combat.

From June 19 through July 2, overcast skies and rain made living miserable—wet clothing, waterlogged foxholes, and mud, on top of a shortage of rations. Both Allied and enemy aircraft strafed them while in the Bois de Limors. After one such incident of strafing by enemy aircraft, Lieutenant Bob Fielder, with Regimental Headquarters Company, overheard "Lieutenant Tom McKeage crouching in his foxhole quoting a *Stars and Stripes* paper, shouting, 'It says here, that we have air superiority.'" [52]

Sergeant Eldon Clark and his Company D mortar squad, now down to four men, occupied a single hole, which they had covered with branches and earth piled about two feet high. On the night of June 24, Clark received an order to fire a flare shell from his squad's 60mm mortar, because of enemy activity in front of the company's line. "We knew that firing that flare would mark right where we were. Right after we fired it, those 88s were coming in. We crawled in the tunnel of our hole—during the night the ground was just shaking. We had about two feet of soil above us and we were kind of worried that it might cave in on us.

"When the morning came, everything was quiet and we crawled out of there. [Private John O.] Haggard told me, 'You know Clark, I didn't go to church, but I did learn the Lord's Prayer in school. I just said the Lord's Prayer over and over all night long.'

"I said, 'That's what the Lord said, "When you pray, pray our Father Who art in heaven."'

"We were all standing out of the hole and we had this lemon concentrate that you put water in to make this lemon drink. All of the sudden—[an explosion]—and all of us just jumped back in the hole, except Haggard. He just bent down to be behind that ledge [of earth piled on top of the hole]. Then another explosion and he hit the ground. There was a hole above his right eye about the size of a silver dollar—you could see his brain. It had just killed him right then and there." [53]

The Germans took advantage of the bad weather to fortify their positions, lay minefields and booby traps, dig alternate fighting positions, zero in their artillery and mortars on likely routes of approach, and reorganize their forces.

From June 26 to 29, Company B platoon leader Lieutenant Stanley Weinberg was temporarily transferred to Company C and voluntarily led three different patrols deep into the German positions to gather intelligence. Weinberg was accompanied on these patrols by Staff Sergeant Herman R. "Zeke" Zeitner (Company C) and Sergeant Charles L. Burghduff (Company A), both of whom spoke fluent German; Sergeant Clyde E. Hein; Privates First Class Stanley Gurski, Wilbert Ward, and Fred C. Cunningham, all from Company C; and Private Luis Mendieta, with the regimental S-2 section.

During one of Weinberg's patrols, they were caught in an open field and pinned down by intense enemy fire. From the edge of the Bois de Limors, Lieutenant Gus Sanders, with Company C, could see Weinberg's patrol in the distance. "The Germans tried to blast them out. Stanley would not let his men surrender. We had no available artillery to help him. They dug in and fought in sight of the battalion, and did not give up for over twenty-four hours, before we could get help to them. This man, Stanley Weinberg, came back as one of the best liked officers in the battalion. He lost some men, but prevented his men from giving up by guts. For by that time, the Germans were hunting for the 'men with baggy pants' and were killing a lot of our boys who happened to be captured. We had very few Jews in our outfit, but those we did have were very much soldiers, and very tough and salty, showing lots of ingenuity, and loads of guts. I have great admiration for those Jews who served with us in the 82nd. They were real 'he' men and very tough." [54]

The Weinberg patrols reconnoitered routes into rear areas behind the German frontline, capturing several prisoners who provided valuable intelligence, which would pay huge dividends in the coming attack.

ON JULY 2, THE DIVISION ISSUED ORDERS for an attack commencing at 6:30 a.m. the following day, with the objective of capturing the high ground northeast of the town of La Haye-du-Puits. On the division's right flank, the 505th PIR would attack with

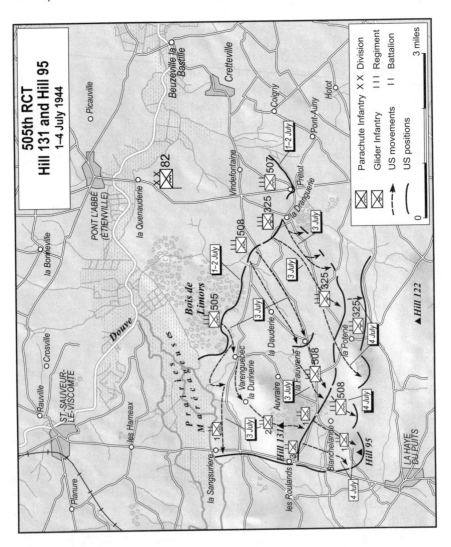

the 2nd Battalion leading, followed by the 1st and 3rd Battalions in a column of battalions. The regiment would move out of the Bois de Limors at 3:00 a.m. to the line of departure, a crossing over a creek that ran south through the village of Varenquebec. At that point, the 1st Battalion would move up and attack on the right of the 2nd Battalion, with the 3rd Battalion mopping up. The regimental objectives were to seize the northern slope and crest of Hill 131 and cut the highway from St.-Sauveur-le-Vicomte to La Haye-du-Puits. The U.S. 79th Infantry Division would be on the right flank of the 505th.

Lieutenant Colonel Ekman told Gavin of an opportunity to capitalize on the information gained by the Weinberg patrols. Ekman told Gavin, "One of the battalion commanders [Major William J. Hagan] reported that one of his patrols had found a flank route to the enemy rear, and that he could move his entire battalion to the enemy rear and roll up the enemy with little risk and small casualties."

Gavin replied, "No, too risky. If the battalion gets caught en route stretched out on the flank, it could be disastrous."

After a few moments, Ekman asked Gavin, "'How about if I send a reinforced platoon to see if we could turn the enemy flank?'

"Gavin looked at me very closely for a few seconds, nodded his head, and said, 'Okay!' then walked away." 55

Moving forward with the regiment at 3:00 a.m., Lieutenant Bob Fielder, with Regimental Headquarters Company, helped get the command post set up on the line of departure. "Lieutenant [Robert J.] Dwyer and I got down in a large shell crater that had been further excavated and waited for the incoming enemy fire as the attack started, and in it came!

"The Germans had an 88mm (3.52-inch bore) antiaircraft gun that they depressed and used to snipe against ground troops like a rifle. It had been raining and the ground was muddy. So there were Bob Dwyer and I grabbing mud, silently praying and telling each other that we would never complain about anything the rest of our lives. Those 88s absolutely tore the place up, and it seemed like the shells were close enough to crease our scalps. There was a crack, explosion, and boom (the boom in the distance was the 88mm firing and heard after the overhead noise of the crack and explosion of the shell). It certainly instilled foxhole religion.

"Lieutenant Bob 'Guinness' Dwyer was something else and a good friend, with a nickname given him for his love of ale. A blue-eyed Irishman with ice for nerves and a demolition expert, he was a quiet and likeable guy; always out front leading his men, emplacing or defusing mines. His men absolutely revered him." 56

The regiment's decimated rifle companies moved forward from the line of departure at 6:30 a.m. to assault prepared German positions. On the right, Ekman's one platoon, *reinforced with the rest of the battalion,* moved around the German left flank. The 1st Battalion followed the route scouted by the Weinberg patrols to the rear of the German main line of resistance, where they struck it from behind.

Private First Class Frank Bilich, with Company D, moved out, carrying the heavy SCR-300 radio on his back. "E Company was on the left, D Company up the middle, and F Company on the right. There was a little winding road that went back and forth up to that hill, and went around and disappeared. Our job was to come up from the front. At that time, we thought that was a real strong position." [57]

Captain Hubert S. Bass, 2nd Battalion executive officer, watched the battalion's troopers drive forward. "A heavy English fog had settled over the countryside. Enemy heavy artillery pounded our positions. Their infantry continued to withdraw in great haste." [58]

As the division attack got underway, Company B, 307th Airborne Engineer Battalion, swept mines and booby traps along the roads for tanks to advance, a very dangerous job. The Germans had concentrated their strong points on the roads to deny their use. While clearing the roads, engineers like Private Neil Droogan had to endure fire from machine guns, snipers, mortars, artillery, and antitank guns sited to cover the mined roadblocks. "[Private First Class] Danny O'Neill was killed—literally blown to bits—by a German antitank mine. I was hit by German mortar fire in my calf. My boot was blown off and my heel was cut to the bone. My buddy, Al Mayer, [was] hit—down across his eye." [59]

The primary obstacles for both the 1st and 2nd Battalions were mines, booby traps, and mortar and artillery fire. Shortly before 10:00 a.m., both battalions reached Phase Line "B," where the 2nd Battalion wheeled to the left and attacked the northern slope and crest of Hill 131, while the 1st Battalion pushed west to cut the highway from St.-Sauveur-le-Vicomte to La Haye-du-Puits.

Sporadic artillery shells landed in the area as Private First Class Bilich moved up the hill with company headquarters. "There was a little stone wall about two feet tall that separated the fields. There was a piece torn out of it, like a shell had hit it. We were crawling along that wall as we were going up the hill. We got about three-quarters of the way up and an artillery barrage came from a different direction. [Private First Class George] Rajner was up about two guys. There was Captain [Taylor G.] Smith, Sergeant [John H.] Rabig, a couple of other guys, and me. All of the sudden an SP [self-propelled gun] or something fired a direct round right through that opening, right where Rajner was—shrapnel just hit him all over. He moaned for a couple of minutes and told John Rabig, 'I'm in bad shape.' Orders were to keep moving—you can't do anything. They threw a couple more rounds in, but nobody got wounded.

"We made it to the top of the hill, and there was a dug in communications center, and the phones were still ringing." [60]

NEAR THE BOTTOM OF HILL 131, a private with the 2nd Battalion found a German field telephone wire that ran from the top of the hill to frontline German positions to coordinate artillery fire. The ingenious private suggested they follow the line, because no mines or booby traps would be planted along its path. Part of the 2nd Battalion advanced up this path and surprised the Germans occupying the observation post on the crest.

A brief firefight resulted when the surprised Germans at the observation post tried to fight back. Private First Class Robert M. Robinson, with Headquarters

Company, 2nd Battalion, was shot by a German officer with a pistol at a range of about four feet. "The shot knocked me to my knees—it felt like a heavy blow. I disarmed the officer and took the pistol. It wasn't until several minutes later that I realized that there was a hole in the front and back of the shoulder of my raincoat. It was then I realized that I had been shot clean through the shoulder." [61]

The observation post was quickly overrun, and eighteen Germans captured. By 12:30 p.m., the regiment had captured both of its objectives. Cleaning out pockets of bypassed Germans, the 3rd Battalion encountered more resistance than the two assaulting battalions, but joined the 2nd Battalion on Hill 131 that afternoon.

The following morning, the 1st and 3rd Battalions were ordered to capture the northern slope of Hill 95 to assist the badly depleted 508th PIR. As Sergeant Bill Blank and his squad of Company G troopers approached the foot of the slope, they began taking fire from the Germans on the hill. "One machine gun crew set up in the corner of a hedgerow and was quickly knocked out by a German machine gun on the hill. [Private Merrill M.] Marty Scherzer, our medic, went out to take care of them and was killed by the same gun. The killing of our medic made us pretty mad, and three of us decided to find the machine gun and put it out of action. [James C. "Fritz"] Fritts, [Roy L.] Pynson, and I started crawling up a hedgerow where we thought the gun might be. Fritz decided not to go any further, so Pynson and I continued on. After a short way, we heard some noises from the other side of the hedgerow. Not knowing for sure whether they were Germans, we decided to fire a shot over their heads to see if we could draw some fire. They responded with a couple of egg-shaped grenades, which rolled down the hill and exploded. We knew we had found them. I tried to unload a clip of Tommy gun ammo into their position, but the gun jammed. Pynson and I made a hasty withdrawal to our mortar position, where we proceeded to lay in a heavy concentration of mortar fire." [62]

By noon, the 1st and 3rd Battalions had driven the Germans from the northern slope of Hill 95. The 2nd Battalion, 508th, attacked through the 505th positions and captured the crest of Hill 95 about twenty minutes later, and in the process captured a number of enemy prisoners. Private Dwayne Burns, with Company F, 508th, took one of these groups to the POW cage. "F Company had captured a machine gun emplacement, and Woody and I were given the job of taking the prisoners to the rear. We marched the four of them down the road until we found the regiment that was in reserve and they said they would take them off our hands. We were glad to get rid of the Germans and get back to our own company.

"Later that afternoon I had to go back to the rear area and took the same road. There in the ditch were the same four Germans that we had turned over that morning. They were dead. I thought I was going to be sick. Someone had used a machete on their heads. Why! Why like this? Why them? These poor slobs were just pawns in the game of war, the low man on the totem pole. Just like me they had dreams, desires, ambitions, and maybe a wife or a sweetheart back home. Now they lay in the ditch with their brains oozing out into the mud. I wondered how long it would be before it was my turn to be lying in some dirty weed-choked ditch as my life slipped away. 'Oh Lord,' I thought, 'I'm going to be sick! How do you get used to looking at things like that? What is this war doing to us when we can do this to another human being?'

"I asked some of the men why they had killed the prisoners. They explained that it was the same machine gun crew who shot down their medic while he was trying to help our wounded. They demanded an eye for an eye." [63]

The action on July 4 ended the combat for the 2nd and 3rd Battalions in Normandy. When a German counterattack on July 6 pushed the 508th PIR off of Hill 95, the 1st Battalion assisted it in recapturing the hill by attacking around the eastern slope as the 508th attacked the upper slope and crest.

The regiment remained in place until July 8, when it was placed in VIII Corps reserve and sent to a rear area to clean up. That day, Lieutenant Colonel Ekman distributed a letter to the regiment that read:

To: The Men of the 505,

In the near future we will be released from our present positions and assembled in a rear bivouac area preparatory to our return to the base camp. I wish it were possible to get you all together at this time to tell you personally how proud I am of the record you have made in this campaign—which so far as I know, no other regiment can equal to date—with reduced personnel, limited transportation, and reduced armament. You have advanced rapidly, aggressively, and always with decisive results, to win all objectives: first Ste.-Mère-Église; then Le Ham, and Montebourg Station; then St.-Sauveur-le-Vicomte and finally Hills 131 and 95 and the area north and south of them. In addition, you have shown that you are most capable in a defensive position. I refer to Bois de Limors.

All commanders, whether of higher headquarters or adjacent units, have been impressed with your ability to accomplish your assigned missions in a superior manner and have asked what tactics we used. Your battalion commanders have passed on to them this information. We all know the secret—aggressiveness mixed with the proper amount of caution, a willingness to close with the enemy and keep him running once he starts, and the proper use of weapons at our disposal. You were quick to learn and beat the enemy at his own game.

I told you just before we took off for this mission that I knew that you would add to the laurels gained by the regiment in Sicily and Italy—you did, and I'm proud to say I know that I command the best regiment in the army today.

Be proud and wear your decorations accordingly.

William E. Ekman

Lt. Colonel, Infantry,

Commanding

The above will be read to all members of this command at the first formation after receipt.

On July 11, THE ENTIRE 82ND AIRBORNE DIVISION moved down to Utah Beach, where it waited to load onto seventeen LSTs for the trip to England. It was at this point that, when many of the troopers saw just how few of them were left from their units, they realized the extent of the losses. The casualties suffered in Normandy, particularly in the rifle companies, were horrendous. Private First Class Henry Matzelle, the company clerk, recounted those casualties suffered by Company D. "Of the 162 [officers and] men who went into Normandy, 23 were killed outright, 94 were wounded and evacuated, and 45 of us returned to England.

"Joe Ketz was the platoon sergeant of the 3rd Platoon. When Lieutenant Turnbull was killed, he was recommended for a battlefield commission. However, on June 26th, he was severely wounded and spent two years in army hospitals in the States. Needless to say, they withdrew the commission.

"Bill Neuberger was shot in the stomach at Neuville-au-Plain. He died as the Germans were taking him to Cherbourg.

"Tony Karmazin was shot in the spine and crippled at Neuville-au-Plain. He was taken to Cherbourg, but was freed when the Allies captured the port on June 25th. He has been in a wheelchair ever since." [64]

Platoon leader Lieutenant Gus L. Sanders was the only officer still on duty with Company C at the end of the campaign. "I took thirty-seven men and two other officers in my platoon and came out with no officers and seven men." [65]

Private First Class Frank Bilich, a replacement with Company D, had survived his first combat. As he stepped on the LST, he thought to himself, "I'm a lucky son of a bitch." [66]

The regiment's casualties in Normandy were 186 killed in action, 492 wounded in action (of which 353 returned to duty), 60 missing in action, and 164 injured in action (of which 129 returned to duty).

All three battalion commanders who jumped in Normandy were casualties. Major Frederick Kellam was killed, Lieutenant Colonel Ben Vandervoort was jump injured, and Lieutenant Colonel Ed Krause was wounded.

Of the nine officers commanding rifle companies when the regiment dropped in Normandy, five were still in command at the end of the campaign. Lieutenant Jim Irvin, Company B, had been captured, but escaped and eventually rejoined the regiment. Captain Anthony Stefanich, Company C, had been seriously wounded. Captain Bill Follmer, Company G, had been seriously injured on the jump. And, Captain Harold Swingler, Company I, had been killed leading an attack on June 6. The casualty rate among the platoon leaders was even higher.

The regiment had inflicted far more casualties on the enemy than it suffered, but an accurate count was not made. For its defense of Ste.-Mère-Église, the 505th was awarded the Presidential Unit Citation.

CHAPTER 12

"The Sky Is Full of Silk"

Returning to England, most officers and men found empty cots in their tents. Most of those missing had been injured or wounded—and most would return. Others, too severely wounded or injured, would carry painful scars, limps, disfigurements, and paralysis with them as constant reminders of their sacrifice and service with the 505th RCT. Still others were buried in Normandy, never to return to their loved ones and buddies.

Company D trooper, Charlie Miller's best buddy, Private First Class George Rajner, was killed on Hill 131. "Rajner had refused to buy GI insurance because of his ongoing war with his mother-in-law. He always said, 'If I die, she'll get it.' Well, he died, and she didn't get it." [1]

The regiment assigned replacements like Private Abraham Albert "Abie" Mallis to fill the ranks. His first impression upon meeting the veterans of Company B was, "These were a bunch of very tough customers." [2]

Privates Dennis Force, John Siam, Calvin Gilbert, William Martin, Frank Frederico, and John Lebednick were among those assigned to Company I. When Dennis Force "started hearing the war stories and the combat record of the 505, I was in awe. I wasn't sure a rookie like me was in the right outfit." [3]

Lieutenant James J. Meyers arrived with a group of replacement officers at Camp Quorn on July 18, 1944, and was assigned to Company D. "Upon entering the pyramidal tent that served as the D Company orderly room, the XO, 1st Lieutenant Waverly Wray, greeted me. Wray introduced me to the First Sergeant, John Rabig, and he informed me the company commander would return shortly. In the meantime, he assembled the other company officers.

"I stood a quarter inch short of six feet, which made me the runt of the litter of platoon leaders. They were: 1st Platoon, 2nd Lieutenant Thomas J. McClean, three combat jumps, a big Irishman and a former New York City policeman; 2nd Platoon, 1st Lieutenant Oliver B. Carr, three combat jumps, a son of the old South from Palm Beach, Florida; 3rd Platoon, 2nd Lieutenant Charles K. Qualls, two combat jumps, a giant of a man.

"Assistant platoon leaders were Lieutenant [Isaac] Michelman, hospitalized and recovering from wounds; and 2nd Lieutenant Russell E. Parker, a former 1st sergeant, three combat jump veteran, and the recipient of a recent battlefield commission. I was a replacement for 1st Lieutenant Turner B. Turnbull, killed in action in Normandy.

"Following the introductions, McClean asked me, 'What do we call you?'

"I replied, 'Jim.'

"He paused, looked at me and said, 'We have too many Jims in this outfit. From now on your name is Joe.' I thought he was joking. He was not and to this day my airborne colleagues know me as 'Joe.'

"When the CO, Captain Taylor G. Smith, returned, he met 'Joe'Meyers. He assigned me as Tom McClean's assistant. I had much to learn and Tom had extensive combat experience. He could teach me the ropes." 4

Lieutenant Meyers was briefed on the unofficial table of organization and equipment that had been adopted before Normandy, with the addition of a squad to each platoon in a parachute infantry company. "Company headquarters had a CO, XO, first sergeant, operations sergeant, company clerk, supply sergeant, supply clerk, and armorer. Each of the three rifle platoons had three twelve-man rifle squads, a 60mm mortar section, a rocket launcher (bazooka) team, and a platoon headquarters with a platoon leader, assistant platoon leader, platoon sergeant, and a radio/telephone operator (RTO). Each rifle squad had a light machine gun (LMG) and a Browning Automatic Rifle (BAR). One squad member was the assistant LMG gunner and the rest of the squad's riflemen had the additional duty of carrying added ammunition for the LMG. In our company, the only true rifleman was the squad leader. As long as the ammunition held out, the airborne platoon had roughly two to three times the firepower of a straight infantry rifle platoon.

"I soon met the men of the 1st Platoon and I noted this unit was different. Although I was only twenty-one, I was slightly older than most of the men and about the same age as the NCOs. Although I was one of the youngest officers in the regiment, the age spread was smaller. The captains were in their mid-twenties; the battalion commanders in their early thirties; Bill Ekman, the regimental commander was about thirty-four; and General Gavin was thirty-six or thirty-seven. Ridgway was the old man at fifty-one. Age wasn't a problem, but the men took note of my lack of combat experience. In various ways, they let me know I was the new kid on the block. D Company officers were close knit. They made it crystal clear: 'Make your friends within the company.'

"Enlisted replacements also joined the company, some from the packet I brought overseas. D Company set about integrating us into the organization.

"Our diet in England consisted of endless meals of Brussels sprouts and Spam. The troops could do nothing about the Spam, but during training, they never missed an opportunity to step on Brussels sprouts growing in the fields.

"Wartime England was a heavily populated country and space was at a premium. Tactical training took place on pastureland or uncultivated fields. This presented a problem to our troops. The English farmers used human feces for fertilizer. Although the feces was usually hard and dry, crawling through turds was not a popular pastime.

"Corporal Edward J. 'Ozzie' Olszewski shared some of his knowledge with me. While undergoing training in daylight scouting and patrolling, Ozzie and I sat on a high hill overlooking the training area. Ozzie quizzed me on the location of the patrols as they moved along fence lines and hedgerows below. My efforts to detect the movement of members of the patrols failed. But Ozzie knew the exact location of the patrols and the direction of their movement.

"He let me in on the tricks of the trade. As a patrol moved along a hedgerow, nesting birds took flight. Although I was familiar with livestock, I had not previously noted, or taken advantage of the curiosity of cows and horses. They almost always turn and stare at nearby humans. In combat, this type of information is life insurance." 5

In early August, General Eisenhower promoted Major General Ridgway to command the newly formed XVIII Airborne Corps, consisting of the 82nd, 101st, and 17th Airborne Divisions. Ridgway recommended Brigadier General Gavin for promotion to major general and command of the 82nd Airborne Division. In his recommendation he wrote, "Brigadier General Gavin possesses to a superior degree self-possession regardless of the pressure in and out of battle, loyalty, initiative, zeal, sound judgment, and common sense. His personal appearance and dignity of demeanor are in keeping with these high qualities, and to them he adds great charm of manner. He is a proved battle leader of the highest type, and in my opinion will make a superior airborne division commander.

"The relative rank of this officer has been considered, and to the best of my knowledge and belief he is the best fitted officer available in this command for the grade and position for which promotion is recommended." 6

General Eisenhower approved without reservations General Gavin's promotion and assignment to command the 82nd Airborne Division. At age thirty-seven, he became the youngest major general since George Armstrong Custer.

On August 16, 1944, General Gavin assumed formal command of the division. He assembled a staff, because many members of Ridgway's staff moved to XVIII Airborne Corps headquarters. Gavin retained Colonel Robert Wienecke, who had served as Ridgway's G-3, as the new chief of staff. He chose 505th veterans, Major Al Ireland, G-1 (personnel); Lieutenant Colonel Walter Winton, G-2 (intelligence); Lieutenant Colonel John ("Jack") Norton G-3 (operations); and Major Albert Marin, G-4 (logistics).

The 505th made a number of changes in command and staff positions as the regiment reorganized and trained for new operations. Lieutenant Colonel Ekman was promoted to full colonel. He filled the losses on his staff with Captain Charles Abrams, S-2; Captain William J. Harris, S-3; and Captain Jacob F. Wagner, S-4. Krause replaced Walter Winton as regimental executive officer, and Captain Bob Piper remained as the S-1. Major James L. Kaiser replaced Krause as 3rd Battalion commander. Major Woody Long replaced Major Bill Hagan as 1st Battalion commander, after Hagan broke a foot in an automotive accident.

In the 1st Battalion, Lieutenant John Dolan was promoted to captain and remained the commander of Company A. Lieutenant Jim Irvin, after escaping from

German captivity, was again the commander of Company B. Captain Anthony Stefanich returned from the hospital as commander of Company C.

In the 2nd Battalion, Captain Taylor G. Smith remained as the commander of Company D. The 2nd Battalion pathfinder team leader, Lieutenant James J. Smith, was assigned to command Company E. Captain Robert H. Rosen was assigned to command Company F.

Among the changes in the 3rd Battalion, Lieutenant Jack Isaacs was promoted to captain and remained as the Company G commander. Captain Jim Maness remained as Company H commander. Captain Archibald A. McPheeters took command of Company I.

Many additional changes and shifts in officers and men were made in battalion staffs and companies.

By mid-August, the Allied armies on the continent had broken out of the Normandy lodgment, encircled and destroyed most of the German forces west of the Seine River, and were driving rapidly toward the German border. The major obstacle to the drive was a shortage of gasoline. General Bradley utilized troop carrier aircraft to ferry gasoline to keep the armies rolling east.

On Tuesday, August 29, 1944, Gavin attended a conference at British General Frederick Browning's British I Airborne Corps headquarters and briefed on an airborne operation planned for September 3, to capture the bridges over the Escaut River, north of Tournai, Belgium. The division made preparations and was at the airfields when the operation was cancelled because of rain and Allied armor overrunning the area of the planned operation.

General Browning then developed an airborne plan to jump near Liège, Belgium, to block the retreat of the German army through that area.

On September 10, Gavin attended another meeting at Browning's headquarters. "It was conducted generally by Browning and had to do with a new plan envisioning a drop for the 82nd to seize bridges at Grave and Nijmegen and the high ground between Nijmegen and Groesbeek. That the plan would go through was all agreed to; Browning was to command it and had it all set up. The troop carrier lift was not set, however." [7]

The plan was part of British Field Marshall Bernard Montgomery's Operation Market-Garden. General Lewis H. Brereton, commanding the First Allied Airborne Army, wanted the operation to commence on September 14, but because troop carrier aircraft would not be available, the date was delayed until Sunday, September 17, less than seven days away.

The operation entailed dropping three airborne divisions behind German lines in southern Holland. They would seize and hold bridges over canals and rivers for a drive by the British Second Army north from the Dutch-Belgian border over the bridges to the Rhine, where it would turn east into the industrial center of Germany—the Ruhr valley.

The 101st Airborne Division would drop south of the 82nd, just north of the city of Eindhoven, seize two canal bridges at Son and Best and a small river bridge to the north at Veghel. Then, it would drive south through Eindhoven to link up with the British XXX Corps, spearheading the British ground force.

The British 1st Airborne Division, with the Polish 1st Independent Parachute Brigade attached, would drop north of the 82nd to capture and hold a single bridge over the Rhine River at Arnhem, sixty-four miles deep in enemy territory.

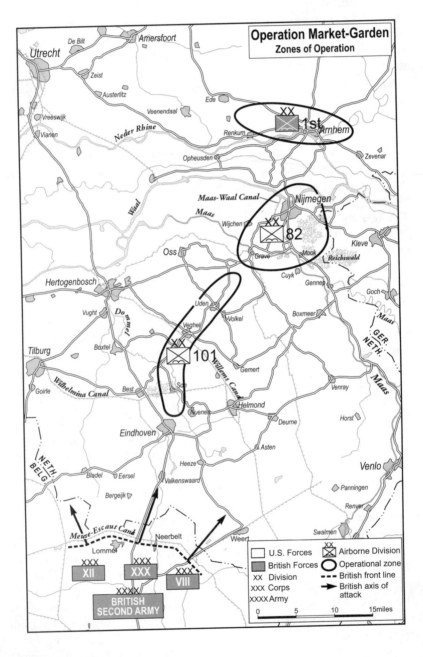

The 82nd Airborne Division's assignment would be extremely complex, requiring aggressive execution. The division would jump fifty-three miles behind German lines to seize four major river bridges and five canal bridges, including both the longest single-span bridge (the Nijmegen highway bridge) and the longest bridge (Grave bridge) in all of Europe at that time. To protect the route of the British Second Army, the division would also seize high ground southeast of Nijmegen and landing zones (LZs) southeast and northeast of Groesbeek for glider landings. The frontage of the division's area was enormous and the objectives ambitious. Only an elite veteran division could hope to accomplish the mission.

The work by Gavin's staff to put together the plan and pre-jump preparations in six days was nothing short of spectacular. Colonel Robert H. Wienecke, the chief of staff, learned of the operation on the evening of September 10. "I had gone up to visit the 505th Parachute Regiment on 10 September, and returned to find the Division Commander (Gavin) and the G-3 (Norton) had gone to Allied Airborne Headquarters for orders. By midnight we had our draft order ready." 8

The Order of Battle Summary report dated September 11 indicated the presence of significant enemy forces around Nijmegen, where the 82nd Airborne Division would jump: "It is definitely established that many of the SS training units which were near Amsterdam are now quartered in the excellent barracks in Nijmegen. It is estimated there are four thousand of these SS troops; moreover, troops are also reported in St. Canisius College and the Marienboom Girls' School. There is little doubt that our operational area will contain a fair quota of Germans, and an estimate of a divisional strength in this area may not be far wide of the mark." 9

Lieutenant Colonel Jack Norton, the G-3, had an incredible task to put together an operational plan in a very short timeframe. This would be the largest, most complex airborne operation ever attempted. The 82nd would have to seize enough of the four bridges over the Maas and Waal Rivers and five bridges over the Maas-Waal Canal to create a corridor for the British ground forces, while taking high ground south and east of Nijmegen, which dominated the bridges over the Maas-Waal Canal. The division had to be prepared to defend against armored attacks from the Reichswald to the east and southeast, and from the Arnhem area to the north. And the division had to be prepared to engage and destroy any German forces in the immediate area, including the SS troops reportedly around Nijmegen.

The final operational plan would be especially critical since there would be no opportunity to make modifications based upon lessons from rehearsals during the normal preparation phase. Working almost continuously day and night, Lieutenant Colonel Norton and his staff finished the planning for the operation and issued orders on September 13, a truly remarkable accomplishment in only three days.

All three of the division's parachute infantry regiments would drop south and southeast of Nijmegen on September 17. The veteran 504th PIR, again a part of the division after refitting after Anzio, would land south of Nijmegen and capture the bridge over the Maas River at Grave and bridges over the Maas-Waal Canal.

The 505th would jump south of Groesbeek, capture the town and the high ground to the west, and establish blocking positions south and east of Groesbeek to protect against attacks from the Reichswald and the Nijmegen-Gennep road. The 508th would land southeast of Nijmegen, seize the high ground, establish roadblocks south and east of the city, and upon the completion of these objectives, move to capture the bridges across the Waal River in Nijmegen. The 376th Parachute Field Artillery Battalion would land by parachute and support the division. Company C, 307th Airborne Engineer Battalion, would support the 504th, with Companies B and D assigned to provide security for the division command post. Battery A, 80th Airborne Antiaircraft (Antitank) Battalion, would land by glider with eight 57mm guns to provide the initial antitank defense. The remainder of the division's artillery (including the 456th Parachute Field Artillery Battalion), the rest of the 80th, and Company A, 307th Airborne Engineer Battalion, would arrive by glider on D+1.

The 325th GIR would land on D+2 and assemble in the division reserve area. The other elements of the division would move by sea, then over land to join the division.

The plan called for 7,250 paratroopers of the division to be flown to Holland by the 50th and 52nd Wings of the IX Troop Carrier Command in the first lift, September 17. The armada would consist of 480 planes carrying paratroopers flying in eleven serials, followed by one fifty-plane glider serial. Each nine-plane V-of-V wave in the parachute serials would fly at five-second intervals.

Gavin, concerned about the possibility of German armor hidden in the Reichswald, decided not to use pathfinders to mark the drop zones for the 505th and 508th prior to the jump. Leading the 82nd into Holland would be the 504th PIR pathfinders to mark DZ "O" scheduled for 12:30 p.m. Thirty minutes behind the pathfinders would be the 505th and division headquarters, jumping at DZ "N" south of Groesbeek. The 2nd Battalion was scheduled to arrive at 1:00 p.m., the 3rd Battalion at 1:04 p.m., and the 1st Battalion serial at 1:08 p.m. Elements of the 505th regimental headquarters would accompany the 2nd and 3rd Battalion serials, while division headquarters personnel would jump with the 1st Battalion.

The 504th would follow the 505th and was scheduled to jump at DZ "O" north of Over Asselt between 1:10 and 1:18 p.m. The 307th Airborne Engineer Battalion, less headquarters and Company A, was scheduled to jump on DZ "N" at 1:24 p.m. The 508th would follow the engineers, scheduled to jump at DZ "T" northeast of Groesbeek, dropping between 1:28 and 1:35 p.m. The 376th Parachute Field Artillery was scheduled to jump at DZ "N" at 1:40 p.m., giving the engineers just sixteen minutes to clear the drop zone before heavy equipment bundles containing the components of the 75mm howitzers and ammunition would drop.

The twelfth and last serial would be fifty C-47s towing gliders, twenty-two of which would transport eighty-six men, eight 57mm antitank guns, nine jeeps, and two ammunition trailers of Battery A, 80th Airborne Antiaircraft (Antitank) Battalion. The remaining twenty-eight gliders would land elements of division headquarters, division artillery headquarters, the 82nd Airborne Signal Company, the 82nd Airborne Reconnaissance Platoon, Forward Air Controller Team, and a British SAS Phantom detachment. The glider serial was scheduled to land on LZ "N" at 1:50 p.m.

The whole parachute and glider operation was planned to take one hour and twenty minutes from beginning to end, and only fifty minutes from the arrival of the first battalion-sized element.

Colonel Bill Ekman issued orders for the 1st Battalion to "establish road-block at Point 'A' [Mook], seize and hold railroad bridge at point 'B' [Maas River railroad bridge] and be prepared on regimental order to occupy high ground to the southeast." 10

Ekman ordered the 2nd Battalion to seize the high ground east of the Maas-Waal Canal and to "establish and maintain contact with 504th Parachute Infantry at canal crossings at points 'J' and 'K' [Bridges 7 and 8] and if necessary in order to gain contact, assist in the seizure of these crossings." 11 The 2nd Battalion would be the division reserve after capturing the high ground.

The 3rd Battalion was ordered by Colonel Ekman "to seize and hold Groesbeek. Send reconnaissance patrol at once to ridgeline to southwest of Groesbeek, clear and secure LZ 'N' for glider and resupply lifts, and secure roadblocks [east and southeast of Groesbeek] as indicated after seizing Groesbeek." 12

Somehow, word of the Holland jump reached Company G platoon leader Lieutenant Bill Mastrangelo in the hospital, where he had spent the previous nine weeks. He had been wounded in the right wrist and leg by a German grenade in Normandy, the leg wound requiring forty-four stitches. "After hearing of the new mission, I asked the doctor to discharge me and return me to my outfit. He told me he was intending to ZI me [transfer to the Zone of Interior, or the United States]. After bugging him for two days, he agreed, saying, 'O.K., if that is what you want.' He then discharged me.

"After arriving in Quorn, I reported to Colonel Ekman. He told me I could come in on the second wave. I told him I wanted to jump with my platoon, and he agreed, saying he needed all the officers he could get." 13

Another trooper, Private First Class John H. Allen, with Company C, had been wounded on June 7 and released from the hospital just as the regiment prepared to move to the airfields. "I was scared—after spending three months in a hospital and living like a human being—and here, I just got back in time to get a rifle and a pack and go again." 14

On September 16, Clifford W. Schrader, the Company A first sergeant, showed up at the airfield, surprising everyone in his company. Somehow, he had received word despite the tight security about the operation. "I broke my leg in the Normandy jump and was in the hospital on September 15th. I bribed a doctor to sign my release so I could get out in time for the jump." 15

A short time after the regiment had returned from Normandy, Sergeant Sylvester H. Meigs had secretly married one of the local English girls. Private First

Class Dutch Schultz and many of the officers and men were aware of this. "His squad constantly covered for him at midnight bed check. We lived in six-man tents, and they either put extra pillows in Meigs' bed or had somebody else sleep in Meigs' bed and put the extra pillows in someone else's bed. Some of the original company officers pulling OD [officer of the day], especially Lieutenant 'Johnny' Johnson knew about this arrangement. This almost backfired when the company was ordered to arise earlier than usual to prepare to depart for Cottesmore RAF field in preparation for the Holland jump. Not only were Meigs' squad members sweating bullets, but also Lieutenant Johnson, who had OD duty and had cleared Meigs as present for duty. As it turned out, Meigs returned to camp a little bit earlier than usual and managed to slip into camp through a back entrance that not too many troopers knew about. When told about Johnson's anxiety, Meigs quickly found him and saluted smartly, saying, 'Good morning, sir.'" 16

OFFICERS, MEN, AND AIRCREWS TAKING PART in the operation attended briefings at the airfields. Captain Arie Beste Breurtije, the Dutch liaison officer, conducted a briefing attended by Lieutenant Mastrangelo. "The Dutch Underground, having set up a perfect sand table of the DZ and the surrounding countryside, did a remarkable job of briefing us." 17

At the briefing he conducted, Major James Kaiser, the commander of the 3rd Battalion, felt the air of confidence his troopers seemed to exude. "My battalion was completely reequipped and shaken down. I was confident of their ability to fight. We were ready." 18

IN THE PREDAWN HOURS OF SUNDAY, SEPTEMBER 17, people awoke to the deafening, low roar of bomber engines shaking furniture and windows in homes and buildings all over southern England. From airfields all over southeastern England, 1,094 U.S. and British heavy and medium bombers began taking off to bomb German flak positions, airfields, and barracks in Holland in preparation for the airborne landings. The U.S. Eighth Air Force sent 872 B-17 Flying Fortress bombers, escorted by 147 P-51 Mustangs, to hit 117 German targets that lay along the troop carrier routes. The British dispatched 85 Lancaster, 65 Mosquito, 48 B-25, and 24 A-20 bombers accompanied by 53 Spitfire fighters to attack German defenses on the coast of Holland and barracks at Nijmegen, Arnhem, and Ede.

This would be the fourth combat jump for a good number of the men in the 505th. Many veterans, like Staff Sergeant Russell R. O'Neal, with Company A, shared the same feeling about the jump. "All of the old troopers who had come all the way from Africa with me felt the same as I. I felt that my time and luck was about to run out, in that I had three midnight jumps in combat, Sicily, Italy, and Normandy. I was anxious to get it over with, but was resigned to the fact that my Irish luck was about to run out." 19

Captain George Wood, the regiment's Protestant chaplain, making his fourth combat jump, held a well-attended church service early that morning. "Of the many thousands involved in this largest airborne invasion, there were only a few hundred for whom it was the fourth combat jump. We felt like fugitives from the law of averages. I shared the sense of apprehension with my men. On that Sunday morning I gathered as many men for a service as I could. I sought a spiritual motto to fit the occasion and finally decided on the last words from the Cross; 'Father, into Thy hands I commend my spirit.'" 20

Bill Tucker, with the 2nd Platoon of Company I, had been promoted from private first class to corporal and moved to the platoon's mortar squad just a few weeks earlier. Due to an injury to Sergeant Paul Hill in a practice jump and the illness of his replacement, Corporal Tucker was now acting squad leader, responsible for the lives of the troopers in his mortar squad. As a result, Tucker would be jumping last in his stick. "According to the briefing, we had to go at least forty-eight minutes over enemy territory. That was my greatest fear. I had always been afraid of going down with a plane, and as squad leader, I would have to jump at number twenty-two, the last man in the stick. Lieutenant Richard Degenhardt was our jumpmaster, and Staff Sergeant [James] Robinson was number two.

"While we loaded the plane, I did a lot of walking around and worrying. The worrying was new to me, but it had become my responsibility as squad leader to check the equipment bundle racks under the plane and make sure that the bomb release by the door would release them. As the last man, I had to pull the bomb switch as I jumped, a procedure that ran the risk of a jumper getting tangled up with the equipment bundles after they had been freed.

"About fifteen minutes before we loaded, I noticed a man in a leather jacket standing by the plane's tail. I got talking to him, and I thought he was part of the ground crew. I noticed his hands were shaking as he smoked a cigarette.

"I was pretty worried about the forty-eight minutes over enemy territory. I mentioned it to him, and he nearly had convulsions. Well, I thought, he must be the crew chief because he was going along with us. Finally, I asked him who he was. He said he was the pilot. The inside of my stomach turned." 21

As the paratroopers boarded their C-47s, they looked up and saw the sky beginning to fill with the more than 4,700 planes that would take part in the largest airborne operation in history. The first squadrons of the more than 1,500 fighter escort planes and fighter-bombers that would provide protection that day began to fly overhead. It was a comforting sight for the troopers.

At 10:19 a.m., C-47s from six airfields began lifting off the runways at five-second intervals, climbing to altitude, and vectoring to form up into formation. The 505th PIR flew in three serials. The 3rd Battalion and elements of Regimental Headquarters and Headquarters Company in serial A-3, and the 2nd Battalion and elements of Regimental Headquarters and Headquarters Company in serial A-5, took off from Folkingham airfield. The 1st Battalion serial, A-7, took off from Cottesmore airfield.

Lieutenant Bill Meddaugh, the Company E executive officer, was a veteran of three night combat jumps. "One of our company officers, Lieutenant Ted Peterson, had been wounded in the leg in Normandy, evacuated at that time, and returned to the company prior to our move to the airfields. He was limping badly, and it was obvious that his days in the airborne were numbered. His duties were limited to supply and administration, and he was very helpful during the few weeks prior to our departure.

"It became official, however, when we settled at the airfield that Pete was through as a paratrooper. It was a very poignant and painful time for all of us company officers who had served with Pete for the past eighteen months and had made three combat jumps with him. It was obvious that he wanted to go with us. I'm sure he felt like he was letting us down as he stayed behind. And we would have liked to have "old Pete" with us. He was dependable and we knew his capabilities.

"It was not in the cards, however, and as I strapped on my parachute and the rest of my gear, Pete was there to give me a hand. The word came down to board our aircraft, so I shook Pete's hand and he wished me good luck. He limped away to say goodbye to the rest of his good buddies as I climbed aboard my plane.

"In a few minutes our engines came to life and we were ready to roll. Planes began to move out of their parking positions and form a long line moving towards the active runway. I was standing in the open door in my customary place looking across the tarmac at what might be my last look at the English countryside.

"Suddenly, there was Pete, running alongside of my plane waving wildly in a frantic effort to get my attention. I waved back through the open door and Pete yelled at me. His words were drowned out by the roar of hundreds of engines, as more and more planes rolled out on the taxiways and began to take off. We picked up speed as we taxied and Pete was soon left behind. I had mixed emotions, which were impossible to sort out during this moment of intense excitement and anxious butterflies.

"But, I must have been thinking, 'You lucky son of a bitch, I wish it was me staying behind.' But, I knew I would have felt just like Pete—staying behind would have been unthinkable if there was any choice in the matter. As anxious and nervous as I was, I knew I couldn't be anywhere else at that moment. I had burned my bridges behind me when I volunteered for parachute duty so many months ago. This was where I wanted to be, even if some part of me rebelled somewhat. The die was cast!

"Our takeoff and movement into formation was routine but as always—exciting. We were to fly in a battalion serial, which consisted of three rifle companies and headquarters company—approximately forty aircraft. Each company was carried in nine or ten aircraft, depending on total number of personnel on the roster at that time. Each company flew in a V-of-Vs and the four companies flew in trail.

"After circling a few times to tighten up the formation, we headed towards the English Channel. What I saw in the next two hours prior to the jump was the most breathtaking and awesome experience I had ever been a part of. Aircraft formations, such as ours, were all over the sky. Three airborne divisions were involved in this operation—all of which were either airborne or close to it at this very moment.

"Takeoff points were scattered all over England from the Midlands to southern England—all converging on the drop areas which were about a sixty mile stretch from Eindhoven, through Nijmegen to Arnhem. In addition to all the troop carriers, squadron upon squadron of fighter aircraft were flying above us to provide protection from German fighters and to suppress flak installations. As we flew along our prescribed route and altitude, other formations, some carrying paratroopers, others towing gliders, would pass overhead or underneath on a different heading, giving the appearance of mass confusion.

"Standing up in the door of my plane I had a much better view of what was going on around us than the rest of my stick, who were reduced to watching through the small windows of the aircraft. I hooked up my static line in case I fell out, and stuck my head out of the open door as far as I could to enjoy the magnificent scene. It took my mind off the jump and upcoming fight." [22]

After his plane rendezvoused with the 1st Battalion serial, Company A first sergeant Clifford Schrader looked out the door at the armada in the sky. "I never saw so many planes in the air at one time. We saw bombers and fighters go over, and every way you looked you saw troop transports and gliders." [23]

Private First Class Dutch Schultz, with Company C, was sitting close enough to the door to have a good view of the ground below as the immense formation of troop carrier planes flew low over the English countryside. "It was exhilarating to see thousands of people on the ground waving to us as we flew over the British villages and towns. Later, it was reassuring to see the different fighter planes alongside of us." [24]

Sergeant Bill Dunfee, with Company I, looked out the door of his C-47, "and as far back as we could see, there were C-47s. There were P-51s flying cover for us, and about half way to our destination, we passed a group of B-24s returning from a bombing raid—we hoped in Holland. It is impossible for me to convey how impressed I was with this display of power." [25]

As jumpmaster, Lieutenant Meddaugh had a perfect view of the one-hundred-mile-long sky train of troop-carrier planes and gliders, moving in three columns, ten miles wide. Above and on both flanks of the sky train Meddaugh saw squadron upon squadron of fighter planes of all types—P-51 Mustangs, P-47 Thunderbolts, P-38 Lightnings, British Spitfires, Hurricanes, and Typhoons. "The sun continued to shine brightly, and as we passed over the channel it reflected off the water into a blaze of fire. It was a Sunday afternoon—in other times we all would have been off to the local swimming hole for a picnic. But today would be no picnic." [26]

Private Dennis O'Loughlin, with Company E, "could see some of the damn fools sitting in the open doors of the planes with their feet hanging out. There was some nose thumbing going on back and forth while flying along in formation—a few antitank grenades being tossed out. We didn't like the ack-ack setting those things off in the planes. They always sent us more grenades anyhow." [27]

As the 2nd Battalion serial crossed the flooded coastal areas of Holland, Lieutenant Meddaugh "watched the tempo of the mission start to pick up speed.

Sporadic small-arms fire rose to meet us, but in our immediate formation it was ineffective. I would estimate we were flying about 1,500 feet above the ground. And as I looked out the door I could see Dutch civilians running from their homes and waving to us. I was low enough to see their faces. I waved back. I could imagine their excitement, as it was obvious they recognized us as allied forces—and their liberators! It was a rare form of flattery.

"I was brought back to reality rather abruptly when flak began to burst intermittently around the formation—ugly black puffs of smoke. I began to see fighters diving toward unseen antiaircraft batteries, which added to the overall scene of pandemonium. I clearly remember at one point an air burst exploding straight out from the door of my plane, and I flinched—an involuntary but normal reaction I guess. No damage anywhere that I could see, and the formation drove on. It wasn't long before the crew chief came to my position at the door to warn me we were ten minutes from the DZ. I alerted my guys, and everyone made their individual last-minute preparations for the jump. At four minutes out, the red light over the door flashed bright and the show got underway." [28]

Lieutenant Jack Tallerday, the Company C executive officer, stood in the open door of his C-47 as the 1st Battalion serial approached the coast of Holland. "We were amazed at the flooding of the land by the Germans. Flying at approximately fifteen hundred feet, we could easily see the Dutch standing on the dikes or going to church. They were awe struck by this mass of airplanes. Many of them waved and we waved back." [29]

As the 3rd Battalion serial crossed Holland, Private John Siam, a replacement with Company I, was taking in the sights below. "While looking out of the window, I commented that it was becoming cloudy outside. The man next to me said, 'That's ack-ack you dumb bastard.'" [30]

Company C trooper Private Fred Caravelli watched war correspondent Edward R. Murrow conduct a recording for a radio broadcast to be aired later that evening, on board the plane as they flew over Holland. "During the flight, he came along asking everybody down the line who we were and if I had jumped in Italy. It was a beautiful recording." [31]

Captain Robert M. Piper, the S-1, and Colonel Ekman were aboard the C-47 leading the regiment into Holland. Piper "sat in the door looking at the beautiful countryside and the people coming out of churches along the way. Colonel Ekman and I talked about how the various participants had to be successful in order for the armored thrust to make the end run into Germany through the lowlands.

"Things went well for us until we were just a few miles from Groesbeek, where we were to jump. As we neared the Maas-Waal Canal the antiaircraft fire became intense. We could see gun crews, as we were only about one thousand feet above the ground. Several good-sized holes were put through the fuselage, but because some slow thinking Kraut wasn't taking a lead, they were all just aft of us in the tail section." [32]

Lieutenant Meddaugh, upon seeing the flash of the red light by the door, began getting his stick ready. "'Stand up and hook up!'

"I shouted the command over the noise of the engines and eighteen men struggled with the weight of the equipment they were carrying and got to their feet. Their static line was hooked to the anchor line cable running the length of the C-47 in the same motion.

"Sergeant Roy Joster, who was jumping number two right behind me, was carrying a large radio used for communications with battalion in addition to all his other equipment. He needed help to rise up and get steady on his feet. I had him jump right behind me, as I knew he could crowd the door and step out more easily when I exited.

"'Check your equipment!'

"My next command was hardly necessary, as these men were all pros with enough jumps under their belts to be counted on to be properly rigged up. Their safety was their own responsibility in these circumstances—hardly a school jump.

"'Stand in the door!'

"There was a visible rush as everyone crowded forward and closed up tight behind me and Sergeant Joster. Each man's reserve chute on his chest, pressed tightly against the backpack of the man in front of him. The slightest gap or interval between each man as he went out the door was multiplied many fold in the spacing between men as they landed on the ground below. Not as important in a daylight jump as it is at night, but good habits are not tossed aside easily." 33

Lieutenant William R. "Rusty" Hays, a replacement and assistant platoon leader with Company F, stood in the door as the 2nd Battalion serial approached the drop zone. "About five minutes out, we started running into flak. Since our altitude was only five hundred feet and we were slowing to one hundred miles per hour, preparing for the jump, we were pretty easy targets. As jumpmaster, I was standing in the door where I could get a clear view of all the black flak bursts. I could see every burst, I could hear the fragments as they zinged through the skin of the plane, and I sure wanted that green light to come on telling me it was time to jump." 34

As the 505th neared the drop zone south of Groesbeek, there was a sudden problem, because the 3rd Battalion serial and the 2nd Battalion serial were approaching DZ "N" at the same time almost side by side. With quick thinking on the part of Lieutenant Colonel Vandervoort, Colonel Ekman, and the pilot of the lead plane of the serial, the 2nd Battalion drop was changed to the open ground northeast of Groesbeek, near Kamp, on the edge of DZ "T," where the 508th would jump shortly.

Lieutenant James J. "Joe" Meyers, an assistant platoon leader with Company D, was making his first combat jump. "We passed over the Maas-Waal Canal, one of our checkpoints. I watched the lead aircraft in the formation for the silk of Vandervoort's parachute—our signal to jump. We had descended to drop altitude, six hundred feet above the ground. The green light went on, and I saw Vandervoort's silk appear beneath his plane. I hit the toggle switches that released the parapack bundles, gave the door bundle a shove, and followed it out the open door. My parachute opened, and I oscillated once or twice before I landed in a large, open field along with dozens of other jumpers." [35]

As he floated down, Captain Robert "Doc" Franco, the assistant regimental surgeon, looked over just as "a man near me, descending at the same speed, was hit. He screamed obscenities at his unknown assailant and promised to get him as soon as he reached the ground—he probably did." [36]

Private Michael A. Brilla, with Company F, was a veteran of the Sicily and Salerno combat jumps. "The lad next to me in the plane was making his first combat jump, and flak came through our plane and cut his leg. I asked him if he wanted to jump or go back in the plane, but he said he would rather jump. So he did, and we patched him up when we hit the ground." [37]

Lieutenant Meddaugh watched for the sight of his company commander jumping as his signal to go. "I waited for the green light to flash, the signal from the pilot to jump. But I watched the other planes in our company formation intently as well, because, green light or not, if I saw J. J. Smith jump from the lead plane, I would go immediately, to insure the company landed in as tight a formation as possible to facilitate our assembly on the DZ. This was standard operating procedure throughout the battalion.

"As I stuck my head farther out the door, I could see hundreds of parachutes in the air and on the ground out in front of the formation—Company D and Company F had led the battalion into the DZ and had already jumped. Adrenaline was flowing—I couldn't wait to get out of that airplane—my usual instinct seconds before a combat jump.

"Suddenly, I saw our six equipment bundles flash by underneath us. 'Shit, the pilot released the bundles too soon.' I knew this would make it more difficult to recover heavy equipment on the ground during the assembly phase. No time to worry—things are moving too fast. Let's get the hell out of here—flak bursts still in the vicinity of our formation. I see bodies coming out of the lead plane to my left front. J. J. has taken off!

"'Let's go!' I turned my head in the direction of the men behind me as I shouted the command and exploded from the door of the C-47. 'One thousand'—I'm floating, head tucked down on my chest. 'Two thousand'—my feet start to rise up and the weight of the chute rotates my body backwards as if I am sitting in a reclining chair. The roar of the engines begins to recede and the relative quiet is deafening. 'Three thousand.' I can see the silk deploying in front of me; come on baby, do your thing.

"The chute pops open with a bang. God, we must have been flying too fast. It feels like I hit a stone wall. The parachute harness bites in my flesh, and my body jerks violently as the brakes go on. The forward momentum slows dramatically, and the shock is absorbed in my leg and chest straps. I look up at the canopy and breathe a sigh of relief as I confirm a normal opening and no blown panels. Looks like number fifteen is going to be O.K. A quick look behind me and I can see that all the guys in my plane are out O.K. The sky is full of silk—what a sight. I turn my attention to the descent—we had jumped higher than planned—probably about 1,500 feet. There is a slight breeze, and the DZ is a huge open field with no trees or obstacles that I can see—a piece of cake. Five hundred feet—ah, ah! Do my eyes deceive me?

"A group of four German soldiers are running full speed across the DZ heading towards the spot where I expect to make contact with the ground. Are they after me personally? I frantically try to reach the .45-caliber pistol in the holster hooked to my pistol belt. My Thompson submachine gun is inaccessible, stowed underneath my reserve chute on my chest. The opening shock pulled my harness so tight across my entire body that I can't stretch my arm low enough to reach the pistol. I know I was the most vulnerable when I hit the ground and was still in my harness, and watch apprehensively as the group below me continues running like gangbusters.

"One hundred feet—to my relief I can see that my presumed executioners are not the least bit interested in me as an individual as they pass underneath me and continue to run towards the Motherland. One of them is unfastening his cartridge belt as he runs so he can increase his speed. I concentrate on my landing now and gather myself together for the impact. I land hard, as usual, but without further incident. I get out of my harness in record speed, throw my pack back over my shoulders, and ram a magazine of thirty rounds of .45-caliber ball into my Thompson. The adrenaline is still flowing, but all the butterflies are gone. Our parachutes and C-47s have done their job—transportation to the objective. Simply put, that is their function. We now revert to our primary role of combat infantry. Elite infantry in our own minds—but infantry, bottom line!" [38]

Private First Class Frank Bilich, a radio operator with Company D, landed and quickly got out of his chute. "[Private First Class George] Fotovich and I landed near Lieutenant [Tom] McClean. The DZ was drawing fire from German soldiers in a home across the road. Men were gathering up equipment bundles, and next to me was one with a bazooka and rounds.

"Lieutenant McClean said, 'Put a round into that house.' Fotovich loaded it—I took aim and fired. The shot went right through the window, but nothing happened. Lieutenant McClean said, 'Hit it again.' Again, we followed the same procedure and nothing happened.

"Lieutenant McClean's platoon moved out and we joined company headquarters. His platoon went to clean out the Germans from the farmhouse. Most of the Germans faded into the woods or left in vehicles. When he went inside, he saw a large group of women crouched and praying. Both bazooka rounds had hit the interior wall and didn't explode. In our haste to fire, I suppose we forgot to pull the arming pin [on the bazooka rounds]." [39]

A number of wooden flak towers mounting 20mm antiaircraft guns where the 2nd Battalion landed were put out of action in less than twenty minutes. Troopers climbed the towers and shot or grenaded those crews who didn't surrender.

Major Daniel McIlvoy, the regimental surgeon, was one of the few jump casualties, suffering a hairline crack in his left ankle. "I thought at the time that it was a severe sprain. It was quite swollen and painful, but fear or excitement seemed to modify or minimize my aches. I hobbled down the road and picked up several more aid men, and about one hundred yards from where we landed, we found a German ambulance—one of those ambulances that was being operated by a wooden gas generator. The wood burner generated gas, and the gas engine ran off of this gas that was produced. It was operated by a German driver, with whom we had little or no difficulty in persuading to join us." [40]

After landing, Lieutenant Meddaugh helped get Company E organized and ready to move out to their objective, the high ground overlooking Groesbeek. "The task of assembly, recovering heavy equipment from the equipment bundles, and moving towards our objective got underway with the usual confusion which always followed a mass drop. The SNAFUs were greatly reduced however, since it was broad daylight. We soon discovered we were not dropped exactly as planned, but the battalion was organized, oriented on the ground and moving off the drop zone in rapid order. The jump phase of Operation Market-Garden was over—and very successfully for E Company: no casualties and only a few minor jump injuries. What lay ahead of us for the next six weeks was to be much more painful and bloody." [41]

AT ABOUT THE SAME MOMENT that the 2nd Battalion jumped, the 3rd Battalion jumped at DZ "N" right on schedule. Major James Kaiser, the commanding officer, looked out the door as the serial approached. "Identification of the DZ was certain. I was the lead man in the first plane. The battalion waited until I jumped as the signal [for them to jump]. In my plane the boys were all laughing as I turned and said, 'Let's go!'" [42]

Staff Sergeant Bill Blank, with Company G, watched the action below. "I stood in the door all of the way after reaching the coast, watching the fighter escort attack ground targets and watching enemy antiaircraft fire.

"There was a rumor that one of the men wasn't going to jump. I put him at the end of the stick, just in case. About five minutes out, he came to me and said he had to go to the toilet in the rear of the C-47. I didn't think he had time and he probably hoped to be in there at the time of the jump. I am happy to say he went in, came out and jumped." [43]

Corporal Bill Tucker, with Company I, was the last man in his stick and responsible for releasing the equipment bundles underneath their C-47. "I was relieved when we got the order to jump, but as I started to go out the door the equipment release did not operate, which caused me to hesitate momentarily and give it a tremendous bang, so that it released. I then literally dove out the door (worrying about being too far off from the rest), the result of which was that my Thompson submachine gun smashed into my jaw and broke two teeth. The parachute risers were so corkscrewed that when they started to unwind I became dizzy.

"I landed just on the fringe of the woods. As soon as I got myself together, I ran about two hundred or three hundred yards across the field to where other members of my squad were gathering. It seems that we took a lot of time getting together, and I do remember seeing several aircraft go down. The first thing I did was switch my Thompson submachine gun for Private First Class [Jack C.] Wingfield's M1 rifle. In Normandy, a carbine jammed on me and I swore I'd never again use a magazine-fed gun in combat." 44

Company I trooper, Private First Class Jack Hillman, suffered one of the few jump injuries. "I hit the ground, landing on one of those sugar beets, breaking my left leg. The Dutch people assisted me on a wheel barrow to their home." 45

Lieutenant Bill Mastrangelo, who had left the hospital with forty-four stitches in his leg to jump with his Company G platoon, felt a searing pain upon landing. "My leg opened on the jump, and I had the platoon medic treat and dress it. This continued every day of the mission." 46

With shrapnel from enemy antiaircraft fire hitting his C-47, Private First Class Ernest R. Blanchard, with Regimental Headquarters Company, wanted to get out of the plane. "We began to descend on our drop zone; the ship came down lower and lower and slowed-up as we approached our destination. We knew it would only be a matter of seconds now until the green light was on and we would be out the door." 47

When his chute opened, Private First Class James E. McDavid, with Regimental Headquarters Company, looked down and saw he was over a group of farm buildings—"a farmhouse, barns, sheds, the works. My first thought was, 'This thing's bound to be full of Krauts.' On my way down, I saw what I thought were Germans running around and out of the farmhouse. I was [in addition to an M1] also carrying a .45 pistol, which I took out of the holster for use. Closer to the ground, I realized these people were Americans. Good thing—because when I hit the ground, I had to pull my pistol out of about two feet of plowed dirt where I jammed it on impact." 48

Lieutenant Bob Fielder, the assistant regimental communications officer, jumped with Lieutenant Edward A. Magdets, a member of a prisoner of war interrogation team attached to the regiment. "He spoke German fluently and had first-hand knowledge of the general area in which the drop zone was located. We landed adjacent to one of the Dutch farmhouses, and Lieutenant Magdets immediately knocked on the door and asked the occupants where the German soldiers were. The Dutch farmers told him that the Germans were not present in strength in the immediate area." 49

As he headed for the Company G assembly area, Private First Class John T. Diffin received machine gun fire from the edge of the woods. "First Sergeant [Tony] Castillo asked if I could see them from the flank. I told him yes, there were three men and an MG-34. I shot two and the third dropped the gun and ran.

"A Dutch captain and General Gavin came up at that time. First Sergeant Castillo said, 'Good job'—and our platoon assembled and Lieutenant [Jack

E.] Gavin [no relation] told me to move out as first scout. It was just like the sand table." [50]

THE NEXT UNIT TO APPROACH DZ "N" was the 1st Battalion, arriving about four minutes after the 3rd Battalion. Company B platoon leader Lieutenant Stanley Weinberg, from New Jersey, had a rather close call. "Just before I got up to stand in the door to look for familiar landmarks, a bullet came through the floor in the doorway." [51]

As Sergeant Zeke Zeitner's plane approached carrying a Company C stick, he leaned out the door looking for the drop zone and fell out, coming down just east of the Maas-Waal Canal. Zeitner walked the two miles or so and rejoined Company C near the drop zone.

Staff Sergeant Russell O'Neal, with Company A, and his stick made a soft landing right on the DZ. "Just as we hit the ground and were trying to get out of our parachutes and get our weapons together, I was watching a P-51 fighter plane dive and strafe some apparent German position near the field where we landed. After a couple of passes a German machine gun made a hit. The fighter plane caught fire and the pilot, not being injured by the direct hit on his plane, circled and slid into a safe belly landing.

"He jumped out and ran quickly up to me shouting, 'Give me a gun, quick. I know right where that Kraut S.O.B. is and I'm going to get him. Now, damn it, I'm going to miss that party I was going to go to tonight back in England.'

"We hated to see his nice pink pants and jacket get dirty. But he had to stay with us for a long time before he was finally sent back to jolly old England." [52]

Sergeant Harvill W. Lazenby, with Company B, made the jump without a hitch. "The most impressive thing that I recall was the troop carrier group that brought us in. They made a 180-degree turn after the drop—the flak guns were really hitting them. They held their formation while burning and never broke formation until they fell." [53]

Private Dutch Schultz, a BAR gunner with Company C, landed "on a recently plowed field—it was like landing on a soft mattress. As yet, we hadn't encountered any enemy resistance. So far, it was like a walk in the country on a sunny Sunday afternoon." [54]

THE 307TH AIRBORNE ENGINEER BATTALION began jumping nine minutes after the 1st Battalion. Staff Sergeant Frank Miale was a veteran of three combat jumps with Company B. "When we approached the drop zone, the flak was intense, then the word, 'Go,' and away we went in a rush of wind and jolting chutes. After landing, many gazed up at the awe-inspiring sight that was the mighty 82nd coming on in endless droves." [55]

THE LAST SERIAL TO LAND WERE THE GLIDERS carrying Battery A, 80th Airborne Antiaircraft (Antitank) Battalion, and various division and division artillery troops. The glider carrying Private Gordon A. Walberg, with Battery A, 80th Airborne

Antiaircraft (Antitank) Battalion, landed without incident. "We got the nose of the glider unlatched and proceeded to unload the glider—sending one person across the field to locate our jeep A-7. As the jeep backed up to hook up our 57mm gun, I signaled to Robert 'Moose' Hadden to search out the small farmhouse at the edge of the field. As we left the L.Z., I remember looking back to see if all was still going alright and just thankful to be down and safe, so far." [56]

Overall, the regiment's fourth combat jump in fourteen months had been a textbook operation, with the exception of the 2nd Battalion drop, a short distance away.

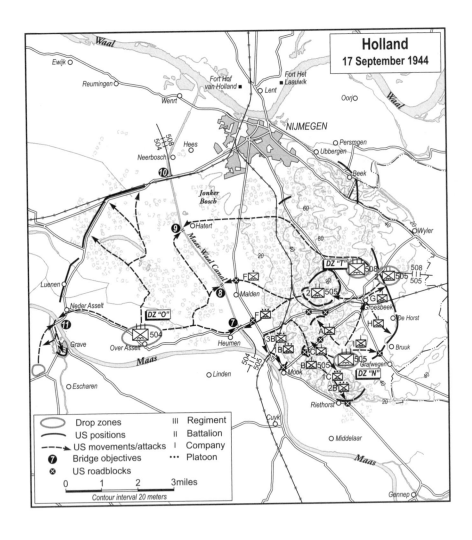

Holland
17 September 1944

Ewijk

Reumingen

Fort Hof
van Holland

Fort Het
Laauwik

Lent

Oorj

Wenrt

NIJMEGEN

508
504

Hees

Persmgen

Neerbosch

Ubbergen

Beek

Jonker
Bosch

60

Hatert

Wyler

Maas-Waal Canal

80

20

DZ "T"

508

508
505

Luenen

Malden

2   505

505

Neder Asselt

Groesbeek

De Horst

DZ "O"

F

H

Grave

Over Asselt

504

Heumen

3B

A

G

Bruuk

Maas

B

C

I

Linden

504
505
T

B   505

505

Grafwegen

DZ "N"

Escharen

Mook

1C

Riethorst

2B

Cuyk

Middelaar

Drop zones   III   Regiment
US positions   II   Battalion
US movements/attacks I   Company
Bridge objectives   ··· Platoon
US roadblocks

0   1   2   3miles
Contour interval 20 meters

Maas

Gennep

CHAPTER 13

"All Of The Men Worshipped Him"

The veteran 505th PIR quickly assembled and moved out to capture its objectives. Upon landing northeast of Groesbeek, near Kamp, Lieutenant Colonel Vandervoort radioed his company commanders, telling them the 2nd Battalion assembly point would be an observation tower to the west at Molenberg, on the northern edge of Groesbeek. After gathering weapons and supplies from equipment bundles, the battalion moved to the assembly point.

Doc McIlvoy, the regimental surgeon, who had found a German ambulance abandoned near where he landed, loaded his unit's medical equipment on it and joined the 2nd Battalion column. "On nearing the edge of the town, we saw a Volkswagen coming down the road, and after [it passed] several of us, we realized a Volkswagen wasn't GI issue. So finally, one of us decided to stop it. It turned out to be a German officer, who was driving down from Nijmegen and almost drove past a company or more of Americans without anyone knowing that this was anything unusual." [1]

After assembly, the 2nd Battalion moved west through the northern part of Groesbeek. Sergeant Paul Nunan was a platoon sergeant with Company D. "As we moved through Groesbeek against very light resistance, the Hollanders began appearing from their hiding places. They seemed overjoyed at our arrival and eager to help.

"A group of them approached me, dragging and pushing a man wearing civilian riding boots, breeches, shirt, and brown jacket. After several minutes of scrambled conversation and sign language, it developed that the man was a local official appointed by the Nazis. As my men led him away, he received several sound kicks in the rear end from the townspeople." [2]

The battalion cleared the northern part of Groesbeek against almost no resistance. Doc McIlvoy moved in and set up an aid station. "We set up our regimental aid station in a German PX, which was abundantly supplied with the usual delicacies of a PX, plus an unlimited supply of Bendectin, [an anti-nausea drug,] which we stored among our medical supplies to use at a later date, at such time when we had a little bit more to celebrate." [3]

The 2nd Battalion moved out toward its real objective, Hill 81.8, and the high ground west of the town. As platoon leader Lieutenant Jim Coyle, with the 1st Platoon, Company E, moved through the heavily wooded area, he had the fate of Sergeant Otis Sampson's squad weighing on his mind. "I was afraid that he and the 1st Platoon 60mm mortar squad might have been shot down.

"As we approached the high ridgeline that we were to attack, I realized that it could be a difficult assault. There was some low brush, but no cover from enemy fire, which might come down the hill. We moved up the hill rapidly, although it was a hard climb with all the equipment we carried. We reached the crest without being fired upon. At the top, we found many small barracks, all empty, although there were fires going and warm food on the stoves. I saw no weapons or combat equipment anywhere. It appeared to me that the troops who had occupied the barracks were from a Todt Battalion, a work group, which had simply fled as we came up the hill. I could not believe the Germans did not have machine guns or artillery on the ridge. It was the only high ground in the area and they did not defend it.

"We set up a company perimeter on the hill. In a little over an hour, Sergeant Sampson came climbing up the hill with the mortar squad and the men who had jumped in his plane. They had had engine trouble on his C-47 and had to turn back to England. He had transferred the bundles and his planeload of men to another plane, when they reached the airfield and had taken off immediately for Holland again. I was very relieved to see him and the mortar squad and was quite surprised that he was able to rejoin the company after only a delay of an hour or two." [4]

Sergeant Spencer Wurst, with Company F, ordered his men to dig in on ground overlooking a railroad track. "Our area ran northeast to southwest and was parallel to a railroad track, whose bed was 150 or 200 yards down the slope. Although the battalion was in reserve, not much over half of Company F was in the reserve defensive position. We dug in and passed the rest of the day uneventfully, awaiting orders. We sent some small patrols out to our front, and some contact patrols with the 1st Platoon roadblock out on one of the hardtop roads." [5]

Private First Class Robert R. Hughart was one of the troopers at the 1st Platoon roadblock on the main road that ran south from Nijmegen to Mook. "We were standing in and out of foxholes on both sides of the street. There were large two-storied homes and very large trees on both sides of the street. At dusk, two Germans came down the middle of the street on bikes. We waited until they got into the middle of us, then jumped out from behind trees and out of the holes, and tried to get them to surrender. One went for his pistol and was shot dead for his stupidity. The other got off his bike and we cut him down as he tried to run down the street." [6]

A short time later, Sergeant Russ Brown heard the sound of an approaching vehicle from the south, behind the roadblock. "A weapons carrier tried to run our roadblock, but the machine gun and everyone shot at it. The carrier hit a house and caught on fire. All night long the people in the house poured water on the fire from an upstairs window." [7]

Around dusk, Vandervoort's troopers heard a train approaching from the direction of Nijmegen. Everyone just stood dumbfounded as the train passed. Moving through Groesbeek, the train chugged past startled 3rd Battalion troopers on its way to Germany. An order was issued to stop all trains attempting to pass through the area. Sergeant Spencer Wurst, with Company F, who had attended demolition school, along with his squad, mined the tracks in the 2nd Battalion sector. All of the antitank mines had been allocated to the 1st and 3rd Battalions for roadblocks, so Wurst and his men very carefully molded the Composition C from Gammon grenades to the sides and tops of the rails. They did this in darkness, where one wrong move would result in the whole group being killed or wounded. The improvised mines were then armed, and Wurst and his men returned to their positions.

Just before dawn, Lieutenant Rusty Hays, a replacement with Company F, heard the sound of a freight train approaching from the direction of Nijmegen. "First the machine guns opened up; then it hit the Gammon grenades, which derailed the train. The engine came to a stop with steam hissing from the holes made by the machine guns. My guys went charging down the hill to shoot up the Germans on the train. I remember them bringing a German officer back who spoke English and was offended that even though he was wounded, they made him hold his hands up. He didn't get much sympathy; in fact, he was told that if he put his hands down, he would be shot." [8]

Also that morning, at the Company F roadblock on the road south of Nijmegen, Private First Class Hughart inspected the vehicle that the platoon had ambushed and set on fire during the night. "With daylight, we found two dead Germans in the cab all burned to a crisp, and found out the truck was carrying meat, bread, and jam. But this cargo was one big black mess. If only we had known at first, we might have been able to save something to eat." [9]

ON DZ "N" ON THE AFTERNOON OF SEPTEMBER 17, the 3rd Battalion assembled and moved to capture Groesbeek and establish a defensive line facing the German border to the east. Major Kaiser's veterans knew what to do immediately upon landing. "While my company COs, who were all combat and jump experienced, organized their companies for defense and attack, my German-speaking S-2 section moved into Groesbeek without shooting—took twenty-six prisoners by calling for a surrender from the second-rate German garrison troops." [10]

Lieutenant Walter B. Kroener was the logistics officer for the 3rd Battalion. "After jumping I instructed my S-4 section (assembled from all companies in the battalion) to clear ammo from the DZ. I then proceeded towards Groesbeek in search of vehicles." [11]

Shortly after landing, a farmer told Sergeant Bill Dunfee, with Company I, that a German soldier was hiding in his barn. "Taking a Thompson sub-machine gun, I entered the barn VERY cautiously. Within the barn there was a loft with a stairway leading up to a tack room. I figured, if he were still in there, that's where he would be. I went to the bottom of the stairway, and sprayed the door and sidewalls of the room with the Thompson—then called out to him in my best German, 'Deutsch soldaten, kommen sie hier, hände hoch.' There was no response, only the noise of harness and wooden shoes falling around me. I called out again, and punctuated it with another burst from the Thompson.

"Yelling at him again, I could see movement through the door I had shot away. My concern at this time was that he would roll a potato masher grenade down the stairs. He exposed an arm, waving a handkerchief. I told him to come on down, and took him outside. I turned him over to Jim Beaver [Company I] to take to regiment for interrogation. Jim told me when he returned, the poor bastard had shit himself. I had told Jim when he took the prisoner back, 'If he so much as blinks, blow his f—ing head off.' The German understood English." [12]

After assembling, Company I sent a combat patrol to the Reichswald to determine if enemy armor was located there. Private First Class Chris Zafiroff, a .30-caliber machine gunner with Headquarters Company, 3rd Battalion, was attached to the patrol. "We were fired on by the enemy, [but] we went to the [edge of the] Reichswald and then followed the road alongside the woods." [13] The patrol found no enemy tanks and that the woods were too dense for armor to operate.

About twenty minutes after landing, Lieutenant Bob Fielder, with Regimental Headquarters Company, found the site of the planned regimental command post— "a German storage area located in a wooded area nearby. I remember walking into a small wooden building, which had been very recently occupied by German soldiers. The fact that we had caught the Germans by surprise was apparent. On the table was a still warm cup of coffee, beside a German newspaper opened to a map depicting the current locations of the German and Allied forces." [14]

After assembling, Companies G and H moved to capture Groesbeek. Company G scout, Private First Class John Diffin, led his platoon into the town. "We went down the side street and the Dutch were yelling 'Oranje' (orange) and getting in our way. Lieutenant [Jack] Gavin told me to keep alert and move out." [15]

Sergeant Bill Blank, with Company G, went into Groesbeek expecting a fight. "We were met by cheering Dutch people with their orange armbands. They had quickly rounded up the few Germans and sympathizers.

"We started digging in on the edge of town facing the German border. The Germans were about one thousand yards to our front, and we could see them moving back and forth around some buildings. We laid some mortar rounds on a house, and it looked as if sparks were flying from it. I turned around and saw Captain [Jack] Isaacs and Lieutenant [Bill] Mastrangelo coming up from behind us in an orchard. I saw the limbs fall from the trees over their heads and told them to get down, as those sparks turned out to be a [37]mm gun firing at us, but a little too high." [16]

After mopping up Groesbeek, the 3rd Battalion established a line of roadblocks facing east from Kamp, where it tied in with the 508th PIR, south to the edge of Groesbeek, through Horst to west of Bruuk. At one of the Company H roadblocks, Private Charles E. Barnhart, an assistant bazooka gunner with Company H, began to dig a foxhole with his entrenching tool, when he saw a civilian approaching with a long-handled shovel. "He was also carrying two bottles of beer. He was a Hollander. They did not like to be called 'Dutch.' Dutch became Deutsch, which was German. He came over and handed me the two bottles of beer, motioned me over to a tree. That's what I did—I took the two bottles of beer, went over and sat under the tree, drank the beer and he dug me a foxhole. I would have liked to have spent a lot of time talking to him, but I couldn't speak the language. After he dug the foxhole, he took his shovel and went home.

"It's amazing how many people in the world speak English, but there are a lot of them. A bunch of kids came up and were talking to me, and asked questions. One kid asked me what was on my leg—because we had pockets built into our jump suits and carried rations in them. I tried two or three different words and could not get across to anybody. I finally remembered—chocolate bars! I said, 'Chocolate.' Everybody was still kind of blank there for a little bit.

"Then this one kid started jumping up and down, yelling, 'Chocolata! Chocolata!' I ended up giving away all of my chocolate that day, because I had a whole bunch of people around me. I never regretted it. I could always get more." [17]

Late that afternoon, Staff Sergeant Clarence Prager, with Company I, took an eight-man machine gun section from Headquarters Company, 3rd Battalion, in addition to a bazooka team and thirteen riflemen from Company I, to establish four outposts in front of the company's line.

As Prager's patrol moved toward the Reichswald, enemy machine gun nests opened fire on them. Prager personally destroyed two of these machine gun positions, then led his troopers in an assault on the remaining enemy, routing them after a fierce firefight. Prager then set up three outposts and took several men to establish a fourth, where they encountered a numerically superior German force. They attacked and drove off the Germans occupying the position and established the fourth outpost. Corporal Harry J. Buffone was with Prager at this outpost. "We could see Germans about a hundred yards down the road, waving to us to come down to them to surrender. Before we knew it, we were surrounded." [18]

German forces in overwhelming numbers counterattacked the small force manning the outpost. Prager ordered Buffone to get the BAR team moved back to the third outpost, while he personally held off the Germans with his Thompson submachine gun.

Buffone had just begun to pull the men back when he heard the sickening, unmistakable thud of a bullet impacting a human body. Buffone quickly looked back. "Sergeant Prager got shot in the face. I dragged him off of the road, leaving him, for I knew he was dead." [19]

Corporal Buffone covered the withdrawal of the patrol to the third roadblock, where he held it with the few men he had for four hours, even though overwhelming enemy forces made three assaults against the position, attacking from three sides. Buffone kept the company informed via a field telephone. He personally repaired the phone wire twice as enemy shrapnel cut it. Ordered to pull back, Buffone single-handedly covered the withdrawal of his men to the next roadblock, using his BAR. He then fell back to the roadblock, where he and his men held off all further enemy attacks.

Corporal Buffone was awarded the Silver Star and Staff Sergeant Prager was posthumously awarded the Distinguished Service Cross.

That night, Sergeant Blank took a reconnaissance patrol to the German border. "We moved out over the flat terrain, with no cover except the darkness. About a mile out, we found the Germans digging in, in large numbers. Each time we tried to go around them, we ran into more of them. We finally returned and reported the heavy concentration of buildup in that area." [20]

After checking his company's positions, Captain Isaacs returned to the G Company command post to get a little sleep when he heard a strange, low rumbling sound. "A railroad line runs from Nijmegen in a southerly direction to Groesbeek, whence it turns east and runs to Cleve, Germany. This line entered the division lines somewhere north of Groesbeek and left the division lines at Groesbeek.

"The railroad split the area allotted to G Company, of which I was the company commander. My company CP was located about fifty yards south of the railroad, where it crossed the main street of Groesbeek. My company lines were about seventy-five to one hundred yards east of this road.

"My first inkling of trouble came when I was awakened at my CP by a low, rumbling noise, which we at first attributed to enemy tanks. Taking what men and antitank weapons we had at the company CP, I set out for the source of the sound. As I arrived on the street and started toward the railroad crossing, I could see a train rolling past. It consisted of five or six assorted cars and had been coasting down a grade to our rear without making the usual noises of a steam train—hence, the low rumble.

"When the engineer realized he had cleared Groesbeek without being fired upon, he opened the steam valves and set sail for Germany—only about two miles away. We didn't get a shot of any kind at him, nor did anyone else in the division.

"It is ironic that we had the railroad bed mined with antitank mines, but on orders from above, had not removed the safety pins. It was also a quirk of fate that the bazooka man assigned to the railroad was not on guard at this time, it being his time to be off guard.

"Because so many units had been involved in letting the train get away and because our mines were ineffectual, we were spared a reprimand by General Gavin." [21]

THE 1ST BATTALION HAD TWO PRIMARY TERRAIN OBJECTIVES on September 17—the capture of a railroad bridge over the Maas River and the establishment of the southern portion of the division's perimeter, including the high ground overlooking the Gennep-Nijmegen highway and the high ground west and southwest of Groesbeek. Company C's orders were to clear DZ "N" of enemy resistance and then occupy the high ground southwest of Groesbeek overlooking the Mookschebaan, placing roadblocks on the highway, where it would become the regimental reserve. The Company A objective was Hill 77.8, south of the Heumenschebaan, placing roadblocks on the road and sending a patrol to contact the 504th PIR at the Heumen lock bridge.

Company B's initial objective was the high ground east of Bisselt, then the 1st and 3rd Platoons were assigned to capture the railroad bridge over the Maas River. The 2nd Platoon's secondary objective was to occupy the high ground northeast of

Riethorst, overlooking the Gennep-Nijmegen highway, and the establishment of roadblocks on the highway at Plasmolen and Riethorst.

After Company B occupied the high ground without resistance, Lieutenant Harold E. Miller, the Company B executive officer, set up the company command post. "The 1st and 3rd Platoons were at the CP at 1700 [hours] and the 1st Platoon set out for its objective at 1730. They saw Germans dug in on a line northwest to southeast about two hundred fifty yards. These enemy troops offered little resistance and thirty-three prisoners were taken. Having done this, the 1st Platoon with a battalion machine gun section and regimental demolition team attached, moved out to its objectives. It went to the railroad [tracks], got on the road leading southwest, turned, and headed for the bridge. They were then about four hundred yards from the bridge and were fired on by small arms." 22

When the Germans opened fire, Sergeant Harvill W. Lazenby took cover in a ditch to the side of the road. "I got a small-arms bullet in my left ankle and it almost took my foot off. We had taken some prisoners prior to that out of the little signal building up on the railroad by the track, and they were both killed in the attack. The Germans were holding the bridge, but at the same time they were setting demolitions." 23

Heavy German automatic weapons fire from houses along the road that ran under a railroad trestle near the bridge pinned down the 1st Platoon. Lieutenant Miller learned that "Private Donald E. Simonds and Private Isaac Cook were killed, and Sergeants Harvill W. Lazenby and Frank S. Kochanek, and Private First Class Santiago H. Esparza were wounded.

"One squad [led by Staff Sergeant James Elmo Jones] flanked to the right to overrun positions from which the fire was coming—in houses to that side—and then came on to the bridge. The remainder of the platoon got to the bridge, which was blown just as they reached the railroad tracks. The platoon had captured seventeen prisoners. The Germans blew three [37]mm flak guns [at the north end of the bridge]. The platoon then took up positions at the bridge and the road, laid minefields at the junction of the road and the railroad tracks, and put up roadblocks two hundred yards northwest and also southeast of the bridge along the main road. The roadblocks consisted of two BARs each. They blocked the southern road near the bridge with large concrete blocks which the Germans had intended for that purpose."

Meanwhile, Lieutenant Stanley Weinberg's 2nd Platoon and an attached fourteen-man machine gun section from Headquarters Company, 1st Battalion, moved out in route column across an open field, entered the northwest side of the Kiekberg Woods, then followed a trail, emerging just north of the hamlet of Plasmolen. As they did, the Germans blew up an ammunition dump. Weinberg's troopers individually charged forward, firing as they closed, overrunning several strong points as the Germans pulled out. After clearing Plasmolen, Weinberg left Sergeant Johnny F. Heggood, the 2nd Squad leader, with half of his squad and a machine gun to establish a roadblock on the Gennep-Nijmegen highway at Plasmolen facing east.

Weinberg and half of the remaining men crossed to the south side of the highway, and with Lieutenant Morris P. Guerrant, the assistant platoon leader, and the other half on the north side of the road, the platoon moved west out of Plasmolen toward Riethorst. Just minutes later, they ambushed a German staff car, killing a lieutenant colonel (Oberstleutnant Siegfried Harnisch) and capturing his driver and a major.

The platoon continued west toward Riethorst, fighting a heavy, close combat engagement as they advanced. Weinberg's platoon cleared Riethorst by about 3:30 p.m. Two machine guns from the attached headquarters company section were being set up on the highway east of Sergeant Heggood's roadblock at the bend in the Gennep-Nijmegen highway at about 4:30 p.m., when a German scout approached on a bicycle. The scout was killed, alerting a large group of Germans moving toward Riethorst from the east, who put mortar fire on the two machine gun crews and six riflemen supporting them. The Germans formed into a skirmish line and charged the position. One machine gun jammed when it became too hot. The German infantry got so close that the crew used their pistols to defend the position. The paratroopers repulsed the attack, but accurate German mortar fire forced some of the men from their positions.

Sergeant Fredrick W. Gougler, leading the headquarters company machine gun section, sent a runner to contact Lieutenant Weinberg, requesting help. Weinberg sent his mortar squad and half of a rifle squad to support Gougler's troopers.

At approximately 6:00 p.m., after clearing Riethorst, Lieutenant Weinberg sent Sergeant Heggood to the 1st Battalion CP to report his situation. Major Woody Long, commanding the 1st Battalion, responded by sending reinforcements to assist in the defense. "Much activity in the Reichswald area seemed to make imminent an attack. The 1st Platoon of Company C was detached and sent to reinforce the 2nd Platoon of Company B at Riethorst." [24]

Lieutenant Harold L. Gensemer was the platoon leader of the 1st Platoon, Company C. "I was instructed to take my platoon and a section of heavy machine guns from Headquarters Company, 1st Battalion, under Lieutenant [Guy R.] Anderson, capture the high ground around Riethorst and hold until relieved." [25]

Lieutenant Richard H. Brownlee, Gensemer's assistant platoon leader, woke the troopers sleeping in their parachute-lined holes and they moved out. When they arrived at Riethorst, Brownlee and the other officers discussed how to position their men to defend the area. "We decided to split the hill, with Weinberg and what was left of his group taking the south end and we would take the north end. The hill was about one hundred yards long and about fifty to seventy-five yards wide. It was topped with a residential type building in the shape of a Dutch windmill. It had quite a few trees on it and one other small building.

"Lieutenant Weinberg had set up a roadblock at the south end of the road fronting the hill, and at about 1:00 a.m., we decided to set up a roadblock in front of our [Company C] position. While Lieutenant Weinberg, the platoon sergeant, one or two automatic weapons men, and myself were discussing where we would place our weapons, we heard the sound of hobnailed boots coming down the road. We knew there could be no British in the area, so we dropped where we were to await developments. I was thinking [it would be wise] to let the Germans [go] on by and we could have them between Weinberg's roadblock down the road and ours behind them. Just as the head of the column of Germans—estimated at about twenty-four—reached even with us, one of my boys yelled, 'Hands up' in German— they didn't.

"In the ensuing skirmish I had my field glasses shot from around my neck and a bullet which glanced off of the stock of my tommy gun struck me in the right side at my belt line. One of my riflemen was shot in the right side at the same time and seriously wounded. After this fracas we moved our wounded back up on the hill." [26]

BY MIDNIGHT ON SEPTEMBER 17, the division had achieved almost all of its objectives, suffering few casualties. Tucker's 504th had captured the Grave bridge and Bridge Number 7 over the Maas-Waal Canal intact, providing a land route for British forces to link up with the division, and established a perimeter to the northwest across the Grave-Nijmegen road. The 505th had cleared Groesbeek and the high ground to the west; established a defensive perimeter from the Gennep-Nijmegen road near Riethorst to Kamp, to defend against attacks from the Reichswald; and had cleared Landing Zone "N" for the next day's glider landings. The 508th had captured the high ground at Berg-en-Dal, established a perimeter that ran northeast from Kamp to Wyler, cleared Landing Zone "T" for glider landings the following day, and had driven to within a few hundred yards of the Nijmegen highway bridge. The only major objective remaining was the capture of the Nijmegen bridges over the Waal River, and there was optimism that this objective too would fall in the morning.

EARLY ON SEPTEMBER 18, THE 3RD BATTALION was hit by extremely accurate artillery, Nebelwerfer, and mortar fire, which meant the Germans probably had an observer adjusting the fire. Each company sent out patrols to find the observer. Private John R. "Jack" Lyons was assigned to one of the Company I patrols. "House to house, our battalion was taking out several areas at a time. We found a Dutch girl was giving our location to Kraut artillery from a windmill. I think Malcolm Ternent took her out." [27]

Private First Class Cloid Wigle was sent on a similar Company H patrol. "We found two women in a three story house in the attic with a short wave radio." [28]

At 6:00 a.m. on September 18, Lieutenant Emil H. Schimpf, with Company B, led a patrol of twelve men from the area north of the railroad bridge into Mook, where it met little resistance, captured between sixty and seventy prisoners, and suffered no losses. The patrol left an outpost in the town and returned that afternoon.

From the high ground overlooking Riethorst, Lieutenant Richard H. Brownlee, an assistant platoon leader with Company C, moved down to the Gennep-Nijmegen road around 7:00 a.m. "After we reconnoitered the area we decided to set our road-block up consisting of a team of B.A.R. men with mines scattered on the road in front of them.

"Shortly after having placed our roadblock, a German Mark IV [tank] with the turret cut off and twin 40s mounted moved down the road from the north [from the direction of Nijmegen and Mook]. Our two BAR men engaged the tank and received for their efforts a direct hit from the tank, killing both men. We tried to hit the tank with bazookas, but could not damage it.

"When things quieted down a bit I returned to my foxhole, for I was still bleeding from where I had been shot in the side the night before. As I was dressing my wound, I felt a sharp protrusion in the wound and after digging around with my finger, finally found the copper casing from the lead bullet and removed it.

"Our FO [forward observer] was using the windmill as an observation post, and except for the fact we were continually taking a beating from heavy artillery, small arms fire, and mortars, he was laying in good, aimed fire. After some hours of this, the Dutch windmill was totally destroyed along with the FO, radio operator, and his runner.

"We had been receiving extremely heavy and accurate fire from mortars, and one burst caught four of my boys in a shell hole, destroying the bodies so badly we buried them in a common grave.

"We were ordered to retire from the hill. We left what prisoners we had and also our dead and started back to battalion. We were gone only a very short time when we were ordered to move back onto the hill and again take up our positions. After we were back in our positions, we again started to receive very heavy fire from the tank with twin guns mounted. He was really stripping trees—and men.

"Corporal [Dock W.] Allison took a bazooka to the forward south edge of the hill on a level with the tank to try to get it. But because it had sheets of steel [mounted on the sides] around its treads he couldn't damage it.

"Several of the men on top [of the hill] tried to throw Gammon grenades down into it without success. How Dock kept from getting killed by the tank when he was firing the bazooka, I can only guess. The fact that the tank could not depress his guns enough to reach sure helped.

"Lieutenant [Gensemer] was calling fire in on the concentration of infantry, forming one hundred yards to our front. But the artillery was rationed to five rounds per fire mission, which was not much good when you used three rounds to zero in on the target.

"I went to the forward edge of the hill at one time, and one of the riflemen was aiming very carefully and using all of the accepted techniques for prone rifle fire. After watching for a while, he pointed out to me where his field of fire was. There was a space in the dense trees ahead about twenty-four inches clear. If any German crossed this area, he was dead. He had accounted for eighteen that morning.

"At one time we could see a large group of infantry moving across our front to the west. I started running to the platoon CP to call battalion for help, and on the way was helped along very rapidly by an ME-109, which was strafing the hill, and as far as I was concerned had it in for me personally. I got to the platoon CP in a head-long plunge. I called Captain [Charles] Paterson at battalion yelling for help and received for my efforts, advice that we were to hold.

"We were finally given orders to fight our way off the hill and return to our company, which was on the front line in another sector. The enemy had us zeroed in real well along the route of egress that we had chosen, mostly with machine guns in enfilade. I told my boys that Lieutenant [Gensemer] would lead us out and I would bring up the rear. I told them under no circumstances were they to stop—even if one of their buddies was hit and knocked down, because if they stopped, there would be just that many more killed.

"About half way across, one of my boys stopped, stepped to the edge of our escape route and stated that he could see no Germans. He was killed instantly by German fire from a machine gun.

"I started out at the end of the group again. After we had reached comparative safety where we weren't under direct fire, I realized Sergeant [Sylvester] Meigs and his mortar squad weren't with us. I had to go back in and look for them, and one German machine gunner and I had a wonderful game of tag. Every time I would raise my head and yell for Meigs, he would answer me with a burst from his gun and I would dive for cover. Couldn't find Meigs, and I was afraid this boy with the machine gun might get lucky, so I went back to the group." 29

AT ABOUT 8:30 A.M., THREE COMPANIES of German infantry attacked from the Reichswald, hitting the Company I roadblock and outposts, driving them back about two hundred fifty yards. The fighting continued throughout the morning and into the afternoon.

IN ENGLAND, 454 GLIDERS AND THEIR TOW PLANES, carrying three of the division's four artillery battalions, including the 456th Parachute Field Artillery Battalion, and Batteries B and C, 80th Airborne Antiaircraft (Antitank) Battalion, took off for Holland, about an hour late, due to fog and low clouds. Lieutenant Ray Grossman, with Battery C, 456th Parachute Field Artillery Battalion, had great reason to worry about going into Holland by glider. "After what we had seen in France on the fate of the gliders, I was scared. You really don't know what fear is until you get in a glider for a daylight trip to Holland. No parachute—no control over your own fate." 30

Corporal John A. Price, with Battery A, 456th PFA Battalion, would at least have some control over his fate. "As a result of four and a half hours of solo in a Piper Cub civilian life, I was selected as co-pilot on our section. We flew in with our section and a 75mm howitzer." 31

SHORTLY AFTER NOON ON SEPTEMBER 18, Private First Class Arthur B. "Dutch" Schultz, with Company C, was manning an outpost position between "Tree Row," where his platoon was deployed, and the Reichswald, where the Germans were located. "Part of our company was ordered to clear the enemy off of our drop [zone]. Some Germans had slipped through the battalion perimeter during the night." [32]

Captain Anthony M. "Stef" Stefanich led two platoons of his Company C troopers forward to clear LZ "N." They swept across the flat, open ground of the landing zone, determined to kick the Germans out of the area before the gliders arrived.

Lieutenant Jack Tallerday was the executive officer of Company C, having made the Sicily, Salerno, and Normandy combat jumps with the company prior to Holland. "C Company was in the process of clearing the area of enemy forces between the Reichswald, near Grafwegen, south to the town of Riethorst. We had just flushed out about fifty to seventy-five Germans from a small ditch and wooded area and they were now running across a large open field. About a mile away was a large wooded area called the Reichswald. I had been coordinating the movement of the reserve platoon and fire of the weapons platoon.

"Our overall effort was first to protect and secure two gliders which had just landed in the area held by the Germans, and second to kill or capture as many Germans as possible. The C Company troopers were firing and the Germans were running away from us. It looked like a line of hunters in a rabbit drive and the Germans looked like rabbits running in no particular pattern." [33]

They successfully routed the Germans just before the first gliders began to land at approximately 3:00 p.m., coming down in fields behind the troopers.

Meanwhile, the fighting in the 3rd Battalion sector reached a climax at 2:15 p.m., about forty-five minutes before the gliders began landing on LZ "N." Eleven German tanks were spotted moving up to assist the German infantry. Company I called for artillery support, and a couple of minutes later, the 376th PFA Battalion's 75mm pack howitzers knocked out five tanks, forcing the remainder to withdraw to the Reichswald. Company I then counterattacked, drove the German infantry back into the forest, and reestablished the roadblock.

At 3:00 p.m., Captain Herman Alley, commanding Battery A, 456th PFA Battalion, riding in the lead glider in the serial, watched the tow rope fall away as his glider began descending over LZ "N." "My C-47 pilot banked, wagged his aircraft's wings, and headed back through the enemy flak. German artillery fire was working over the landing zone as we landed. The glider landed at about seventy miles per hour, plowing through a potato field. The landing tore up the nose of the glider, and the fabric ripped. I had a lap full of dirt and vegetables. The rough landing also caused the clamshell release mechanism on the glider to jam, and we couldn't get my jeep out. We got out of the glider quickly and took shelter until the artillery rounds moved away from us." [34]

The glider carrying Lieutenant Ray Grossman, with Battery C, 456th PFA Battalion, made a harrowing landing on the soft plowed fields of the landing zone. "The last 150 feet was complete blackness—the dirt shower blocked out everything. We got the gun out and headed for the assembly as quick as possible." [35]

As his glider neared the landing zone, Private First Class Darrell P. Willoughby, with Battery B, 80th Airborne Antiaircraft (Antitank) Battalion, readied himself for a quick exit. Willoughby loaded the large radio into his jeep and climbed into the driver's seat. "When we landed, the safety wire on the jeep pulled the nose up. We got the pilot out and had to cut holes in the glider to get to the ropes holding the jeep.

"[After driving the jeep out of the glider,] I had just put the thirteen-foot antenna up and I heard a noise and looked up. A glider took the antenna off. I didn't stay around too long, as the Krauts were mortaring the landing site." 36

As hundreds of gliders landed on LZ "N," one glider came in over the heads of Captain Stefanich's men, crash-landing near the German positions on the edge of the Reichswald. The Germans pummeled the glider with automatic weapons fire. Hoping to rescue the glider pilot and any passengers, Captain "Stef" yelled for his men to follow him.

As they neared the glider, Lieutenant Gus Sanders ran a few yards in front of the others, firing a BAR at the fleeing Germans. "Stef yelled for me to get down, and about that time he was hit." 37

One of the medics and others nearby immediately ran to the aid of their stricken captain. As the medic knelt down and administered first aid, Lieutenant Sanders, standing over Captain Stefanich, saw him look up. "He only said a few words, 'Gus, we've come a long way . . . tell the boys to do a good job.'" 38

The medic attending Stefanich stood up and walked toward a group of men gathered nearby, "crying and saying, 'He's gone, he's gone. I couldn't help him.'" 39

Lieutenant Sanders had lost his closet friend. "He was a top soldier, heavyweight champ of the 82nd, and all of the men worshiped him." 40

When the terrible news reached Dutch Schultz at his outpost position, he was stunned. "It was the only time in combat that I broke down and wept over somebody that I cared about. I felt like I lost an older brother. He was what I would have wanted to be. He was a born leader who led by example, not by virtue of rank. To the men of C Company, he was both our leader and our friend. None of us, to my knowledge, ever made the mistake of confusing the difference. It was not only a devastating loss for us, but the regiment as well.

"Lieutenant Jack Tallerday had the sad duty of taking over command of the company. As it turned out, he quickly became the commander in his own right." 41

When Sergeant Francis P. T. "Frank" Dwyer, with Headquarters Company, 1st Battalion, heard the news of Stefanich's death, he was deeply affected. "His death tore viciously at many of our hearts, because of the very great admiration so many had for him. Again, the Germans succeeded in forcing us to accept the hardly believable—that they could kill such a capable, energetic, devout company commander." 42

With German mortar and artillery shells pummeling the landing zone, Captain Alley began trying to get Battery A, 456th, assembled. "I could see some men on the back slope of a hill assembling and assumed they were Battery A men. Giving my driver, Private First Class Smith, orders to remove the jeep from the glider by chopping a hole in the side of the glider with the axe that was attached to it, I told him that I was going to go down and try to assemble the men that I had seen.

"Getting to the men took awhile, because the Germans kept firing artillery. I would run a little way, then fall flat to protect myself from shrapnel—get up and try it again—then repeat the process.

"In the meantime, the glider pilot and Private Smith had gotten the jeep out of the glider. I had only gotten half way to the assembled men when here comes the jeep—with these two men—going fast and bouncing over those rows of potatoes!

"We moved to the assembled men. It was confusing, and I knew that the Germans could see us. Therefore, I told the men to enter the woods onto a small trail. Turning right, we ran into Lieutenant [Bertram L.] O'Neill from headquarters, who directed me to Lieutenant Henry Aust, who was assembling the rest of our battery.

"One hour or so after our landing, Battery A was in position ready to fire, with half of our basic load of ammunition and all men accounted for. Our ammunition sergeant would go back later to bring in the rest of our ammunition." [43]

After retrieving his jeep from the glider, Captain Lester Stein, the surgeon for the 456th PFA Battalion, drove into Groesbeek, to the regimental aid station. As he drove slowly through town, a "covey of girls swarmed around, screaming, 'they'd qualified,' and displaying their parachute wings pinned on their dresses. That first wave certainly worked to jump them!" [44]

The glider carrying Captain Harold Thain, the commanding officer of Battery B, 456th PFA Battalion, landed some fifteen miles southeast of the landing zone, near the German border. "We retried our equipment, which included a jeep, howitzer, some ammo, and a radio, and assembled near a farmhouse. Soon after, we noted several German soldiers on bicycles who circled our position, and shortly thereafter, several cannon shells exploded near our position. Lieutenant [Wallace G.] Reid assembled a firing crew and directed several rounds of howitzer shells in that direction. We received no more enemy shelling.

"Since it was becoming night, we set out by jeep and foot over narrow roads, northeast to find the battalion. We captured one scared German soldier and took him with us. To prevent being fired on by our own 505th Infantry, when we neared their defensive lines, I kept trying to contact my brother Carl, the S-3, by radio to warn them. For security reasons, I used our childhood nicknames. He informed the 505, and we passed through their lines without incident and found the battalion." [45]

Thain was later awarded the Silver Star for his leadership and gallantry in safely guiding his men through enemy territory to the regimental combat team's perimeter.

TWENTY MINUTES AFTER THE GLIDER LANDINGS CONCLUDED, 131 B-24 Liberator bombers of the Eighth Air Force dropped 258 tons of supplies. The division recovered about 80 percent of the critically needed material.

ON THE EVENING OF SEPTEMBER 18, Lieutenant Gensemer received an order to move his platoon back to the hill at Plasmolen a second time. After reoccupying the hill, his platoon captured a German lieutenant colonel. Gensemer learned from an interrogation that the German "was in the area to look things over prior to bringing his unit into the area. Along with him, we also captured his briefcase in which were operation orders, overlays, etcetera. Prior to sending him to the battalion S-2, this individual informed me that his boys would soon kick me off the hill I was now on." [46]

That night, Private First Class John Diffin, a scout with Company G, accompanied his platoon leader, Lieutenant Jack E. Gavin, to check out locations for three listening posts in front of the company's observation post line. Diffin cautiously approached several farmhouses located along the road to their front. "At the first one, we noticed seven leather harnesses and gas masks lined up outside—a German patrol's equipment. [Lieutenant Gavin] told me to cover it and he would check the next house for a place for the listening post.

"The German patrol returned and were talking and laughing, while I took cover in a ditch. Lieutenant Gavin returned and was calling my name, and one of the Germans said, 'Americanische,' and they started pointing their rifles toward him, about twenty-five yards away.

"I opened fire on them and Lieutenant Gavin fired from the road—one got away—wounded. Lieutenant Gavin called for me—I told him I was alright. We took what papers we could find on the bodies and he gave me a Luger and told me, 'I owe you one, and a stripe.'

"On our return, he told me I would maintain the listening posts." [47]

Gavin decided to take a shortcut to the Company G outpost line by crossing the railroad embankment. Diffin asked him if he thought it would be safer to return the way they had come out, because those men would be expecting their return. He told Diffin not to worry. However, as Gavin stepped over the top of the railroad embankment, a Company G trooper shot him.

Diffin checked Gavin—he was already dead. "After the confusion of losing Lieutenant Gavin, Lieutenant [Thomas W.] Donovan took over and I took [Private Jack R.] Busch and [Private Callies] LaBlanc out to the listening posts, close to the German border." [48]

That night Sergeant Bill Blank reported to the Company G command post. "I was sent out to an outpost to take over after the death of one of our platoon leaders, Lieutenant Jack E. Gavin. He had been shot through the temple by one of his own men. It was an accident caused by his own instructions. He had told his men to shoot anyone crossing the [railroad] tracks. He crossed the tracks and was coming back, and was dropped in the middle of the tracks." [49]

In two days of fighting, the 505th had captured five hundred prisoners and had taken and held all of its objectives. However, after two attempts by the 508th PIR, the great Nijmegen bridges remained in enemy hands and would have to be seized before the British Second Army could relieve the embattled British 1st Airborne Division in the Arnhem area.

CHAPTER 14

"You Fired Fast And Straight Or You Were Dead"

By the morning of September 19, the 82nd Airborne Division was aware of the desperate situation of the British 1st Airborne Division to the north. The Dutch Underground had used the country's modern telephone system to put the British near Arnhem in touch with the 2nd Battalion, 505th PIR, commanded by Lieutenant Colonel Ben Vandervoort. "Sometime on September 18, 1944, the telephone rang in a little railroad substation in the Groesbeek woods. The caller was a British paratrooper at Arnhem. He said the British airborne had experienced stiff German resistance and needed the British armored column to link up and provide help as soon as possible. That information was passed to our regimental command post. Several follow-up calls in the same vein were received before we were ordered out of the area." [1]

By the early afternoon of September 19, German forces defending the two Nijmegen bridges were formidable. Kampfgruppe Euling, commanded by SS Captain Karl-Heinz Euling, who, along with his 9th SS Reconnaissance Battalion, had been attached to the 10th SS Panzer Division the previous week, defended the highway bridge. The force consisted of part of the attached 9th SS Reconnaissance Battalion, one company of 10th SS engineers, and an understrength battalion of panzer grenadiers of the 10th SS—another couple of hundred or so. Other units defending the highway bridge were the 4th Company, 572nd Heavy Flak Battalion (with four 88mm dual-purpose guns and eight 20mm antiaircraft guns), and a company of paratroopers of the Hermann Göring Training Regiment, defending the Villa Belvoir east of Hunner Park. A battalion of 10th SS tank crews without their tanks was dug in around Lent near the north end of the highway bridge. Defending the area between the two bridges were a group of reserve police companies and an assortment of other rear area units known as Kampfgruppe Melitz. Kampfgruppe Runge, consisting of an understrength NCO training school company of the Hermann Göring Training Regiment, three companies of a reserve battalion of the 406th Division, and some combat engineers, totaling some 500 to 750 men, defended the railroad bridge, the rail yard, and Kronenburger Park. In all, around two thousand Germans defended the two massive bridges.

Antitank guns covered all streets approaching the bridges, with strong points in key buildings leading to the open areas around the bridges. The SS grenadiers and engineers had dug deep trenches and gun pits in Hunner Park, the railroad embankment, and Kronenburger Park, fortified the ruins of the ancient Valkhof, and positioned 20mm antiaircraft guns at the approaches of the two bridges. The company of paratroopers defending the Villa Belvoir placed machine guns in windows on the upper floors, dug trenches around the building, and encircled it with barbed wire entanglements. Two Mark IV Panzerjäger self-propelled guns concealed in Hunner Park provided a mobile antitank defense. Two more were positioned to support the rail yard and bridge.

An SS artillery training regiment north of the river near Oosterhout and an artillery battalion of the 10th SS near the Pannerden ferry crossing provided indirect fire support. On the north side of the river, SS Major Leo Reinhold directed the overall defense.

General Gavin chose the 2nd Battalion to make the assault to capture the bridges. Vandervoort was justifiably proud of his battle-hardened battalion. "They were the fortunate survivors of three hard parachute night combat assaults—Sicily, Italy, and Normandy. Excepting a few handpicked replacements, yet to be bloodied in combat, they were aggressive, skilled warriors. Their marksmanship, battle reflexes, and survival instincts were finely tuned by being shot at—close and often. There were fraternal bonds between the battalion officers and men, especially the lieutenants. They were outstanding. They were raised to be last in the chow line and first out the door in the jump line. Their creed was, 'Take care of the men and they'll take care of you.' Based on mutual faith, it worked well. What the troopers had was esprit de corps. They thought of themselves as AMERICAN PARATROOPERS—the best damned soldiers in the war."

Vandervoort and his battalion were attached to the British Guards Armoured Division for this attack. "We were honored to be a momentary part of their distinguished company." 2

British infantry of No. 2 Company of the 1st Grenadier Guards Battalion and four troops of Sherman tanks of No. 3 Squadron of the 2nd Grenadier Guards Battalion were selected for the joint British/American operation. Some of the Guards' Sherman tanks were the Firefly version, which mounted a high-velocity 17-pounder main gun, which could take on any tank in the German arsenal.

This force was divided into two task forces. The Western Force consisted of Company D, 505th; one troop of tanks from No. 3 Squadron, 2nd Grenadier Guards; and one platoon of infantry from No. 2 Company, 1st Grenadier Guards, with the objective of the railroad bridge. The Eastern Force was composed of Companies E and F, and Headquarters Company, 2nd Battalion, 505th; three troops of tanks of the No. 3 Squadron, 2nd Grenadier Guards; and three platoons of No. 2 Company, 1st Grenadier Guards, assigned to capture the highway bridge.

The paratroopers and guards rendezvoused at the Sionshof Hotel just north of Groesbeek, then moved out at 1:45 p.m., northeasterly up the tree-lined Groesbeeksweg the four miles into Nijmegen. Company E was in the lead, followed by F Company, then D Company, headquarters company, and finally the No. 2 Company, 1st Grenadier Guards. Some of the paratroopers hitched a ride on the

Guards' Shermans, while others piled their musette bags and heavy weapons on the back decks of the tanks and marched ahead and alongside.

Twelve Dutch guides familiar with the maze of streets in Nijmegen rode on the tanks. Lieutenant James J. "J. J." Smith, commanding E Company, was very glad that the Dutch resistance was with them. "Dutch underground assistance was very valuable at this time, as they had intimate knowledge of the German disposition and their latest movements. We had been informed by the underground representative we had with us that there would be no resistance until we reached a point some six hundred yards south of the bridge. Their information stated that the Germans had extremely strong positions all around the bridge and that [they] had a number of antitank guns all around the position." 3

As the two forces moved into Nijmegen, the citizens came out to greet them. Company D's First Sergeant John Rabig, riding on one of the tanks, enjoyed the adoration. "Dutch people were crowded along the sides of the road. The nearer we got to Nijmegen, the fewer people there were. Soon the people just disappeared, and we were smart enough to know that the shooting would soon start—and it did." 4

As planned, at Wezenlaan the Western Force spilt from the column and moved west around the outskirts of the city via Groenestraat. Lieutenant Colonel Vandervoort remained with the Eastern Force. At approximately 3:15 p.m., Lieutenant J. J. Smith was advancing with the lead elements of Company E when Germans antitank guns opened fire on the Eastern Force. "The Sherman tanks that were leading the attack ran into enemy resistance and were receiving extremely heavy fire from 88s and other high-velocity antitank weapons. The enemy immediately placed [small arms and mortar] fire on the lead elements of the infantry, which was the 1st Platoon of Company E. All the mortar fire and artillery fire at this time came from this side of the bridge, and it seemed to be observed fire. We later determined this to be true, as we discovered snipers and enemy observers had radios and seemed to be in communication with the guns firing. The tanks, having been fired on, proceeded to place fire in the adjacent buildings and covered the area to our front with fire." 5

The Germans had positioned several strongpoints, consisting primarily of well hidden antitank guns covering key intersections, as well as snipers and machine gun positions in key houses, between the Eastern Force and the primary defensive area around the bridge. Lieutenant Colonel Vandervoort deployed his paratroopers into the buildings on both sides of the avenue. "Two rifle companies, E and F—abreast—began to clear a corridor two city blocks wide. There was no preoccupation with the security of our flanks. If anything jumped us, we would have a tank or two jump back. The two companies worked forward in the center of the blocks to avoid casualties inherent to city street fighting. We were in a residential neighborhood of tall, two-story, brick and stone row houses. Some were topped with attics and flat roofs. The troopers fought over the rooftops, in the attics, up alleys, out of bedroom windows, through a maze of back yards and buildings. Nijmegen wasn't all that neat and tidy. In the labyrinth of houses and brick walled gardens, the fighting deteriorated into confusing, face-to-face, kill-or-be-killed showdowns between small, momentarily isolated groups and individuals. Friend and foe mixed in deadly proximity. Germans would appear where you least expected them. You fired fast and straight or you were dead. A lot of gallantry took place unnoticed and unrewarded. The spontaneous nature of the combat required cool heads, courage, skill, and tremendous self-discipline.

"At times, the two rifle companies fought three platoons in line, which gave lateral width to the corridor. Eighty-eight-millimeter antitank guns were the main focal point of resistance. Some were well placed to stop armor, but not situated well to greet paratroopers coming over the rooftops. Among the heavy-caliber antitank guns, one had been disassembled and carried into a corner house to fire at street level from a cellar window. Where the troopers came at them from the middle of a block under cover of the houses, they were manageable.

"By far the most dangerous part of driving the Germans back fell to our rifle squads. They were thirteen-man squads organized and trained to split into three four-man assault teams. One team had a light machine gun; two had Browning Automatic Rifles. The squad leaders moved the assault teams around to support each other. Lieutenant platoon leaders controlled the show. With the self-assured instincts of veteran combat leaders, they kept all units moving forward more or less together. Eight to a company, they provided officer participation in all crucial actions." 6

To take a city block, squads of troopers from the same platoon occupied several of the row houses in the middle. The light machine gun teams set up on the top floors, while the second team from each squad climbed onto the roof to provide covering fire. Any Germans firing from windows or doorways in buildings across the street were exposed to fire from the paratroopers above. Guards tanks added suppressive fire with their .30- and .50-caliber machine guns. Under the cover of this fire, the third team from each squad moved quickly across the street, tossing grenades into windows, kicking in doors, and fighting room-to-room to clear each house in the building. As soon as the assaulting force entered the building across the street, the covering force moved up behind it to assist. Then the teams would do it again, but instead of crossing a street to the next row of houses, they would have to cross a brick-walled backyard, the alley, and then the brick-walled yard of the houses being assaulted. These squad-level teams worked side by side as a platoon to clear three or four connected houses in the middle of a city block, then blasted holes in the common walls to assault adjacent houses, working their way outward from the middle to the houses on the corners. Platoons sometimes worked forward behind one assaulting platoon and sometimes fought together in a line to clear a wide enough corridor, depending upon the nature of the opposition.

Private First Class James E. Keenan, with Company E, had not experienced street fighting, but he and the other paratroopers quickly adapted. "In fighting during the first day's assault on the city of Nijmegen, we were under heavy artillery and antitank fire in the street. Instead of advancing outside, we went from building to building by blowing holes in the walls and thus clearing street by street in this ingenious fashion." [7]

Vandervoort couldn't help but be impressed by how well his paratroopers and the British Guardsmen worked together. "For soldiers of different allied armies, it was amazing how beautifully the tankers and troopers teamed together. It was testimony to their combat acumen as seasoned veterans—both Yanks and Tommies. It required an intuitive sense of balance not to exploit the tanks as protection for the infantry, nor to preoccupy the infantry with screening the tanks. That depended on a lot of individual initiative. [Lieutenant] Colonel [Edward H.] Goulburn, a perceptive commander, more or less turned individual tanks loose and let them go up the alleys and through the yards with the infantry. The spearhead of the British column, which included the paratroopers, blasted its way up the avenue and into the side streets as required by the enemy dispositions." [8]

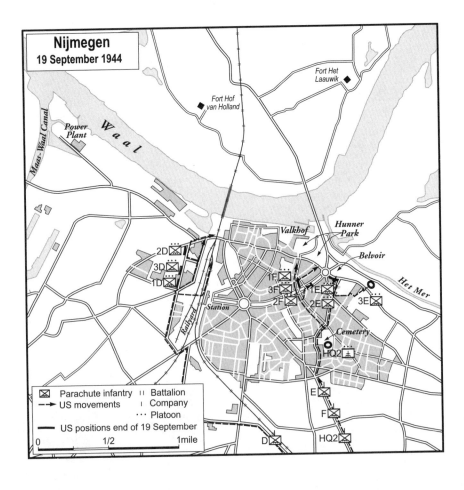

As the Eastern Force fought toward the highway bridge, the Western Force approached the rail yard about 4:15 p.m. Lieutenant Joe Meyers, the assistant platoon leader of 1st Platoon, was riding on a tank at the rear of the column as it turned from Nieuwe Nonnendaalseweg on to Koninginnelaan, just west of the railroad tracks, south of the train station. "As we approached the rail yard, the lead elements of our column came under both tank [from a self-propelled gun] and automatic weapons fire. All D Company troopers immediately dismounted from the exposed tank decks and took cover." 9

First Sergeant John Rabig could see tracers hitting the tank in front of him. "I kept behind one of the tanks which was shielding me. I felt safe enough. I began to see crazy Dutch boys, young kids about sixteen or seventeen, with an orange band on their arms, with guns, risking their lives. I tried to get them to go back, but they took no notice. All hell broke loose on the approach to the bridge. I learned later that six hundred Dutchmen had volunteered their services to General Gavin, using the weapons from our dead and wounded." 10

Platoon Sergeant Paul Nunan, with the 2nd Platoon, was riding on one of the tanks in the middle of the column. "We climbed off the tanks not far from a railroad yard and moved along the tracks leading to it. One platoon of the company was ahead of us. As we approached an underpass, we began receiving sporadic sniper fire. With a thousand places to hide, it was hard to tell where the fire was coming from." 11

With the 3rd Platoon in the lead, Company D and the five British tanks advanced up a street parallel and adjacent to the railroad tracks to the east, north to the railroad station and then north up Oude Heselaan. A section of light machine guns with Headquarters Company, 2nd Battalion, moved up onto the railroad embankment to cover the advance, but heavy enemy fire forced them to withdraw to the west. One machine gun squad rejoined the main force on Oude Heselaan, and the other, reinforced by a D Company bazooka team, moved to the next street west, Krayenhofflaan, and moved north to cover the left flank of the advance.

Captain Taylor G. Smith then told Lieutenant Waverly Wray, the executive officer, to take a few men, a bazooka team, and a machine gun squad to fire north up the tracks to keep the enemy on the east side of the tracks. Wray approached the company communications NCO, Sergeant Jerry Weed. "Wray said to me, 'Get a bazooka team, we're going up on the railroad tracks.'" 12

Lieutenant Meyers and the 1st Platoon were at the rear of the column, behind the 2nd Platoon. "As we advanced, we came to a building I took to be a railway station, or a freight depot. Wray came rushing to the rear of the column. He pointed to Lieutenant [Issac] Michelman, who had returned from the hospital a few days before the operation, and to me and beckoned us to join him. He had a rocket launcher team and a few men with him, and he instructed Michelman and me to take one rifle squad and come with him. We followed Wray around the station or depot and stopped briefly just short of the rail yard. Wray said a German tank was holding up the advance of the company. He would take his group and the rocket launcher and work his way down the west side of the rail yard and try to get in a position to take a clear shot at the German tank. Michelman and I were to take the squad and move through the rail yard to his right. Wray did not state precisely what he wanted us to do, nor did he indicate why his plan required a total of three officers. He was XO and an experienced combat veteran, while I was inexperienced. It is safe to assume he wanted us to cover his right flank and rear, and that's what we did. Wray moved to the left with his group, and he was quickly out of sight." [13]

Platoon Sergeant Roy King, with the 1st Platoon, was ordered to detach the machine gun team from one of his squads to support Lieutenant Wray, who would lead the advance along the railroad tracks toward the railroad bridge. "My machine gun crew went to the west of the railroad station, [but] I still had my BAR team. My remaining squad was assigned to guard the left flank of one of the tanks as we approached the bridge from our southwesterly position." [14]

Private First Class Dave Bowman was the machine gunner of the detached team that moved out with Wray, attacking north up the railroad tracks. "[Private First Class William R. "Rebel"] Haynes was again with me on the machine gun, to the right flank of the advance. A number of riflemen, including a BAR team, led by Corporal Julius Eisner, to the left, were supporting Lieutenant Wray and Corporal [Richard J.] Lord as they advanced up the tracks toward the bridge.

"We, on the machine guns, would fire a few bursts, then move forward with the bazooka team. Heavy fire—mortar, small arms, and maybe artillery—was coming from different directions at ground level."

Bowman concentrated intently as he fired the machine gun, when it suddenly jammed. "I glanced to my left and was shocked to note that Haynes was nowhere in sight, so I assumed he had been hit and left for the rear. (I later learned what happened. When I next saw him in France following the campaign, he chided me for ignoring him when he punched and yelled at me as he lay 'bleeding to death.' He was great for hyperboles. I guess because of the noise and distraction at the time, I was just oblivious to his efforts.) I worked with the gun for a while, trying to get it operating again." [15]

In the meantime, Meyers and the squad on the right moved up the tracks toward the bridge. "After advancing about fifty yards, we met a hail of automatic weapons fire coming straight down the tracks from the direction of the bridge. We hit the ground. But, there was almost no cover or concealment. Michelman crawled under a boxcar, and I was a few inches away to his left. A steel rail separated us.

"We couldn't locate the source of the automatic weapons fire, and we were discussing what to do. Michelman's body rose a few inches into the air, then settled back to earth. He was hit, and he commenced to check out his wound. The bullet entered his left breast, traversed his chest and abdomen, and exited at the waistline forward of his right hip. I glanced to my rear to check on the squad and saw Private Jacob T. Herman, Jr., kneeling directly behind me. I shouted an order for him to get down, but he did not move. I took a second look and saw a bullet hole in his forehead. He was dead." [16]

At the same time Wray and his group moved north on the railroad embankment, the 3rd Platoon moved into the houses on the left side of Oude Heselaan facing the railroad embankment, while the 2nd Platoon moved up to advance with the lead tanks along the street. Private First Class Donald E. Ellis, with company headquarters, was moving with the 3rd Platoon. "We got in the houses, and come to find out, they were in there, too. So, we were looking for a way to get up on top and shoot down." [17] Ellis and other troopers moved upstairs to the top floor, then found a door to the attic, and from there found a door up to the roof. Ellis and his group moved across the roof to the next house north and found the door that opened to the attic of that house. "When we got ready to go down, we lifted the door to make sure it was clear." [18]

Ellis and the group found Germans in the lower floors of some of the houses. "A couple of times, we were shooting at them going down the stairs. They would shoot at us and take off and go into the other houses [on Krayenhofflaan, west of Oude Heselaan] and we would get a shot at them." [19]

On the other side of the embankment, pathfinder Corporal Julius "Ike" Eisner, armed with a BAR, was working forward up the tracks with Wray's group when he was wounded in the leg by four or five machine gun rounds. "They split my leg wide open, from the knee to almost the crotch. Went right through, didn't hit the bone or nothing. I was lucky." [20]

One or more of the bullets hit a Gammon grenade he was carrying in the right leg pocket of his jumpsuit. "It took the whole top off the grenade, detonator and all. It was in two pieces." [21]

Private First Class Bowman, unable to get his machine gun working, picked up a carbine that was lying nearby and moved forward. "At this time, I was some distance behind and hastened to catch up. A couple of men who had been hit passed me, going in the opposite direction—one of whom I remember was Eisner, who had a large chunk of flesh torn from his right leg, just above the knee." [22]

Eisner, struggling, made his way back some distance, until he could go no further on the severely wounded leg. He was alone and bleeding profusely from multiple wounds. "There was nobody around there. And who comes along, but a Dutch guy with a bicycle stretcher. I was bleeding and he put a patch on me from the first aid kit I was carrying. He looked after me. Just patched me up, gave me the penicillin I was carrying, and put some sulfa powder on it. He put me on the bicycle stretcher and took me to a German hospital." [23]

Bowman continued to work his way forward up the tracks. "At one point in the advance, while lying on my stomach firing at the tower, movement of Germans slightly to my right caught my attention. They were running on a low, concrete platform, apparently heading to reinforce their comrades to our front. By the time I repositioned myself and began firing at them, only the characteristic German boots were visible between the platform and the bottom of a freight car, through which I was sighting. I emptied the carbine at them—but because of the small targets, the fact that I had, of course, never zeroed in the weapon, and the rapid pace at which they were moving, I am uncertain whether I had hit a single one of them." 24

Private Frank Aguerrebere, carrying an M1 with a grenade launcher attached, was following Lieutenant Wray north on the railroad embankment. "We were under heavy fire and we were looking for cover. There were a few sheds and box-cars in the area with troopers already using them. I lay on the ground by the rail-road tracks next to a trooper with a boxcar above us. The bazooka man [Private First Class Frank 'Barney' Silanskis] was standing alongside the boxcar and below him on the ground was his [assistant] gunner [Private First Class Joe Rajca]. As we were under heavy fire, a bullet ricocheted up and hit [Silanskis] in the face. He yelled and went to the rear. Another bullet, this time hit the [assistant] gunner on his buttocks, and he was carried back by four troopers. Other troopers were also hit and went back." 25

While hugging the ground, Private Aguerrebere heard Lieutenant Wray, who was well out in front of the rest of the troopers, shout for the bazooka team to move up. "I yelled to him that the bazooka man and some of his men had been hit and [had] gone back. I told him that I had a grenade launcher and some grenades. He said for me to come forward. I went and laid next to him, noticing that he was alone, risking his life, and appeared to be without fear.

"He pointed to a tower, way up in front, and said, 'See if you can hit it. I think someone is up there.' I got up on one knee, aimed, and fired. The grenade went short. He said, 'Let me try it,' grabbed my rifle, aimed and fired. Again it was short. The tower seemed to be very far [away].

"Suddenly, a trooper came up with a bazooka and ammunition for us to use. Lieutenant Wray loaded the bazooka, aimed, and fired. The tower was still too far, and the shot went short. He reloaded and said that he was going to move up closer and try again. He got up, went about fifteen feet forward. Suddenly, fire began and he was hit and fell down." 26

Farther back, Bowman also saw Wray get hit. "I glimpsed the sight of his helmet flying off and he hit the ground on his back." 27

Aguerrebere wasn't sure if Wray was still alive and decided to check on him. "We crawled to him, shook him, and asked if he was all right. He did not respond, so we figured that he was dead." 28

From where he was lying, Bowman watched Corporal Lord and Aguerrebere check on Wray. "The corporal then stood up, faced the rear, waved his arm, and shouted, 'Let's go!'

"We hastened to the rear with Corporal Lord in the lead. As I rushed on, I heard bullets zing by that spurred me on, while gravel to our front continued to be kicked up by shells and small-arms fire. After we reached the rear, a quick debriefing took place, primarily between Corporal Lord and the officers." 29

On the east side of the rail yard, Lieutenant Meyers saw a trooper moving back toward him through heavy automatic weapons fire. "[Sergeant] Gerald R. Weed, a member of Wray's group, hit the ground at my side and reported that Wray had been killed attempting to destroy a German tank with a bazooka and that the remainder of the group had withdrawn. There was no point in remaining in our exposed position and taking more casualties, so I decided to pull back. Michelman said he couldn't make it and to leave without him. I told him to remain, to play dead, and I would return for him in a few hours when it was dark.

"I issued the squad orders to withdraw in a single rush to the nearest cover, an earth berm used as a stop at the end of a rail siding. As we jumped to our feet and moved to the rear, streams of blue tracers enveloped us. Fortunately, no one else was hit." 30

Lieutenant Wray, D Company's executive officer, was always up front with the NCOs and enlisted men, wherever the action was the hottest. News of his loss was devastating to the D Company troopers. When Sergeant Nunan was told of Wray's death later that afternoon, he was shocked. "That really hurt. First Lieutenant Wray was one of the finest small-unit combat leaders I have ever known." 31

As word spread, it stunned the entire division. It had been Wray who had single-handedly killed the commander and entire staff of the 1st Battalion, 1058th Grenadier Regiment, in Normandy only three months earlier. Lieutenant Colonel Vandervoort described Wray as "one of our finest officers. Wray was a Congressional Medal of Honor nominee." 32

The machine gun squad and the bazooka team that moved north on Krayenhofflaan, got ahead of the main advance and received automatic weapons fire from a small park—Krayenhof Park, to the north. The machine gun squad moved into an upper floor of a building on the left side of the street and laid down a base of fire, while the bazooka team advanced and knocked out the automatic weapon firing from the park. The squad moved up to join the bazooka team, and they took the park after a brief but intense firefight. Realizing they were too far out in front, the machine gun squad and bazooka team withdrew south to buildings on Krayenhofflaan that overlooked the park.

With the 3rd Platoon moving through the houses and the 2nd Platoon moving behind the lead tanks moving on Oude Heselaan below, the force turned left and moved to Krayenhofflaan and then north again to Voorstadslaan, which ran east underneath the railroad overpass. As the first two British tanks turned onto Voorstadslaan and attempted to charge the overpass an antitank gun firing down the street from the other side of the overpass knocked out both tanks. Company D trooper Private First Class Frank Bilich saw one of the tanks catch fire, trapping its crew inside. "[Private First Class] Charlie Miller ran out under intense fire and pulled some of them out, then dragged them around the corner to a Dutch house. (We were later told that he was written up for a medal.)" 33

As the two tanks charged the overpass, Sergeant Nunan and some 2nd Platoon troopers ran across Voorstadslaan to Krayenhof Park. "Buildings faced the park on all three sides, and in one corner was a small air raid shelter. As we moved into the park, a sniper fired at us. I took cover in the entrance of the shelter behind a baffle, which protected the entrance. I had been carrying a white phosphorous grenade and a Gammon grenade in the pockets of my jumpsuit. After I took cover in the entrance of the air raid shelter, I took the grenade from my pocket and laid it on a parapet behind the baffle.

"On my left side was [Staff Sergeant] Herbert J. Buffalo Boy, a Sioux Indian from Fort Yates, North Dakota. We were also receiving sporadic machine gun fire from our right flank. The fire seemed to be coming from a railroad overpass, and the gun seemed to be well located.

"Lieutenant [Oliver B. "O. B."] Carr, the platoon leader, moved to the rear in an attempt to contact the company headquarters and ask that a tank be sent forward to assist.

"Lieutenant Russ Parker, his ever-present cigar clenched in his teeth, moved out into the open and sprayed the roofs across the street in order to discourage the sniper. There was a lull in the action for a few minutes as we stayed under cover, trying to locate the enemy positions.

"Buffalo Boy nudged me and pointed across the street to our left front. There, walking along the sidewalk, was a German soldier, obviously unaware of our presence. He was wearing an overcoat and had his rifle slung over his shoulder, and seemed intent on continuing down the street, which ran across our front. I told Buffalo Boy to shoot, and as he fired his M1, I opened up with my Thompson. I still don't know if we hit him, because at that instant, all hell broke loose.

"The entire park seemed filled with tracer slugs. There seemed to be three colors of tracer—red, orange, and light greenish color. The fire was coming from a fast-firing automatic weapon, just at the corner to our left and across the street. My first reaction was that a German tank had moved in on us. I remember thinking that if they had infantry with them, it was going to be a very tough day.

"The firing stopped as suddenly as it started. The Germans had either pulled back or were preparing for another attack. We had entered the park in the late afternoon and it was now getting dark. The word came up that we were to pull back about a block and consolidate our position for the night.

"As we began to pull back across the street to our rear, I was nearing the intersection when it started all over again. Another gun of the same caliber opened up. I was in the open and I could see that the gun was on wheels and was about a 20mm antiaircraft type. I saw the outline of a German lying behind a utility pole and cut loose with a burst from my Thompson. Three yards to my left, also caught in the open, a machine gunner from 2nd Battalion Headquarters Company fired his .30-caliber machine gun from the hip, Audie Murphy style.

"I felt a weight against my right thigh and realized it was my white phosphorous grenade. Grabbing it, I pulled the pin and threw it in the general direction of the enemy. It landed to the right rear of the position of the enemy gun and their fire ceased temporarily. Diagonally, across the street from me on the opposite corner, were some men from the platoon with a bazooka. I yelled at them to fire on the gun.

"As I recall, there was difficulty before they could get the first round to fire, but two rounds were finally fired. I couldn't tell if the enemy gun had been hit, but it quit firing. We crossed the street and began to retrace the route we had come. Only then did I realize that I had left the Gammon grenade in the entrance to the air raid shelter. I told someone I was going back for the grenade and to try to finish the gun before we pulled back. As a couple of men covered me, I hastily went back to the park and retrieved the grenade.

"As the rest of the platoon moved back, I moved as close to the gun as I dared. It seemed to be abandoned in the middle of the street, but I was certain some of the enemy were still nearby. I took cover behind a pole or a tree, unscrewed the fuse cap of the grenade, and pitched it. It exploded on the gun with a roar. I turned to rejoin my platoon and felt a blow at the back of my left knee, as though I had been struck with a club. I went down on the sidewalk and quickly got up. Although my leg wouldn't function properly, I hobbled back to the men covering me and they helped me back to the rest of the platoon. I was later awarded a Silver Star for this action.

"The platoon quickly set up defensive positions for the night and I joined the platoon headquarters in a yard near a wall of a house as German heavy artillery began to smash into the city. Our platoon medic, [Private] Lee Heller, cut open my pants leg and began patching my wound. I began to shake violently. A combination of shock, reaction from the fight, and the chill of the night air, I suppose.

"Lieutenant Carr ordered me back to the company command post, and Heller and another man helped me hobble a block or so to the house where our CP was located. The missile that struck me nicked a tendon just behind my knee, but by keeping my knee locked, I could navigate after a fashion. If I attempted to bend my leg, it would not support me.

"I entered the house where the CP was and found a spot on the living room floor and lay down. The house was spotless, and although there was an empty davenport in the room, I couldn't bring myself to climb on it in my dirty, bloody uniform." 34

As it grew dark, Company D and the three remaining British tanks pulled back to the west and occupied buildings on Krayenhofflaan. But, Private First Class Bilich and a couple of D Company headquarters troopers in a house on Oude Wertz weren't given the word to withdraw. "Captain Taylor Smith told us to stay there, nobody was pulling out. 'We are going to hold this position' were his last words. All of a sudden, the Germans were all over the nearby railroad track and we were cut off. What we didn't know was, the company had pulled back, leaving us to our fate." 35

In the house with Bilich were only two men, "[Private] Bill McMandon, and another guy. With us were three members of a Dutch family; the mother, who spoke English, and her two young daughters. Around my neck I had my dog-tags and a rosary my mother had given me. The Dutch lady asked if I was Catholic.

"The Germans were getting very close, so we went down into the basement from the kitchen. Those houses were built so there was another door and stairs from the basement that came up under the back porch, into a fenced backyard. All three of us were hiding under the stairs as a German officer brought his platoon into the building. Twice he came halfway down the stairs from the kitchen to give orders to the Dutch lady to fix coffee or something. By then the shooting had died down and it was all quiet. Every time he came down we thought about shooting him, but the rest would have got us. Her daughters were against a wall—she had only one small light on, and we had not been spotted in the darkness." [36]

Bilich and the other two men were trapped and could do nothing except hide and wait.

MEANWHILE, THE PARATROOPERS AND TANKERS of the Eastern Force fought their way through the city in more than three hours of continual house-to-house street fighting. As always, Lieutenant Colonel Vandervoort was right up with his troopers observing the action. "The Jerries fought hard and courageously, but the relentlessly closing tanks and troopers forced them to scramble to alternate positions and to fall back to continue the fight. To do so, they had to abandon some of their heavy weapons and bulky ammunition. The Guards Armoured Division gave us all the tank support we needed. Some Shermans and their crews were lost as we went along. Usually, it happened because the tank was employed too aggressively. There were street intersections a man could run across, but a tank would be hit by a high-velocity gun. In order not to lose tanks, the armor had to wait until the troopers moved ahead and solved the problem from the flanks. The formula was learned quickly, but unfortunately, the hard way. With the overwhelming preponderance of armored firepower, the foot soldiers and tanks moved methodically the last few blocks toward our objective." [37]

The 1st Platoon of Company E, at the point of the advance, came to a wide intersection with Mariaplein boulevard, which ran to the Keiser Lodwijkplein traffic circle. German fire from machine guns and an 88mm dual purpose antiaircraft gun began sweeping Mariaplein after the Lieutenant Jim Coyle, Vandervoort, and the 1st and 2nd Squads dashed across the intersection, accompanied by four British Sherman tanks. The 1st Platoon's platoon sergeant, Otis Sampson, waited at the corner of a building on the left side of the street to send the rest of the platoon across the intersection. "A shell fired from our left down the avenue caught the corner of the building and exploded. Lucky no one was hit. It had been close. Lieutenant Colonel Vandervoort crossed over from the other side and informed me to send a machine gun forward; then he took off back [across the street]. Clyde Rickerd volunteered, and with his machine gun across his shoulder, he hurried across the open area. The rest of the platoon followed: one at a time. I brought up the rear, and as I was about in the middle of the thoroughfare I sent a burst from my Tommy gun down its wide area as I continued to run to the safety of the buildings on the other side. The gun that fired the shell must have been moved so as not to give its position away or they would have used it against us." [38]

The point elements of the column moved down Dr. Claes Noorduynstraat, reaching the last houses before the traffic circle and the highway bridge. It was here that Lieutenant Coyle finally caught sight of the objective. "We cleared the last house and could see the bridge. I got quite a shock. I didn't expect it to be so large." [39]

Company E trooper Private First Class Earl Boling was advancing along the sidewalk as the lead platoon of four tanks slowly passed him. "As they passed, one of the drivers said the phrase used by kids all over England, 'Any gum, chum?' I gave him a pack of gum and he said, 'Thanks, mate,' closed the hatch of the tank, and turned the corner to his left." 40

As the tanks neared the open area around the Keiser Lodwijkplein traffic circle, Lieutenant Coyle saw the lead tank open fire with its main gun. "The roar was deafening, and I am sure they were not firing at any particular target, but to pin down the enemy." 41

As the first Sherman moved into the intersection with the cross street, Graadt van Roggenstraat, an 88mm dual-purpose gun positioned on the west side of the traffic circle opened fire. The first round hit the tank, which immediately caught fire. Private First Class Boling saw it happen. "He immediately tried to back around the corner. As we ran to the tank to try to help, it was engulfed in flames as the fuel burned and the ammunition exploded. We stood helplessly as the tank went up in flames; a second tank tried to locate the hidden gun and knock it out. It too was disabled, but the crew did manage to escape from this one and retreat back around the corner." 42

Lieutenant Coyle was moving up the street approaching the traffic circle with the third tank, when it suddenly "went into reverse and backed up about fifty feet to the houses we had just left. I went storming back to the third tank shouting at the commander to get back with us. He said he was hit. I told him he was not hit. (I could not see a mark on the tank.)

"A British sergeant jumped out of the tank and said, 'What's that then, mate?' pointing to a large hole on the other side of the turret which I had not seen.

"I felt about two feet tall. I didn't know how that tank took that hit without suffering any wounded or catching fire. I could see that the tanks were not going to make a move at that point and was trying to figure a way to get to a point where I could observe the position in front of me without being spotted.

"Just then, an elderly man and woman came out the back door of one of the houses facing the park and ran as fast as they could back the way we had come. I realized that if I could get the men on the second floor rooms in the front of the row of attached houses, we would be able to see and fire on the enemy in the park. I moved the platoon quickly into two of the buildings, cautioning them not to open fire before I gave the command. I knew that as soon as we opened fire we would receive heavy fire in return. I hoped that we would be able to spot the antitank guns and knock them out so the tanks and the rest of the battalion could advance on the bridge."43

Heavy fire from the traffic circle covering the intersection with the Mariaplein boulevard cut off the remainder of the column from the 1st Platoon of Company E. Lieutenant J. J. Smith, the Company E commander, was up front with Coyle's 1st Platoon. "The 2nd and 3rd Platoons were following up the 1st Platoon and had been stopped by enemy fire which covered the road intersection immediately in the rear of the 1st Platoon position. They were unable to move, and the situation at the time was looking rotten. Under cover of smoke from hand grenades which the British gave us, Lieutenant Meddaugh succeeded in bringing up the two remaining platoons." [44]

Meanwhile, Private First Class Boling moved with the 1st and 2nd squads, 1st Platoon, to clear the last row of houses in front of the traffic circle and Hunner Park. "We entered the back yards, which each had a block of brick wall about four feet in height around them. We crossed and checked the yards and houses—the first platoon moving forward through and past about four or five houses for the other platoons to use, then going into the next house to try to set up a field of fire over the park area from the second-floor windows.

"We could see the Germans milling around the park, bringing up more weapons and supplies. Carl Beck and Earl Hable set up a .30-caliber machine gun at a window on the left side of the room and I had the BAR at a window on the right side." [45]

Lieutenant Coyle got his men into the row of attached houses on Graadt van Roggenstraat, facing the Villa Belvoir, with the traffic circle to the left and Hunner Park beyond the traffic circle. "I kept the men back from the windows so they could not be seen by the enemy and set up our machine guns on tables near the front windows of two of the adjacent buildings. I could see German soldiers streaming across the bridge from the other side on foot and on bicycles. It was difficult to keep men from opening fire on them, but I wanted to get as many men in firing position as possible before we gave our position away.

"The Germans had no idea we were there. I knew this for certain when a crew manhandled a [50mm] antitank gun out of the park, and proceeded to set it up not thirty feet in front of us, pointing up the street to our right where the tanks had been knocked out.

"Suddenly, [Lieutenant] Colonel Vandervoort, the battalion commanding officer, and Captain Bill Harris, the S-3, came into the room where I was setting up our position." [46]

Staying back from the windows, Vandervoort looked down at the German positions around the approaches to the highway bridge. "Hunner Park was congested with Germans. Some were established in a small cluster of buildings, brick-walled gardens and walks leading to an ancient stone ruin on the river bluff—the castle of Charlemagne on the northwest corner of the park.

"Other enemy elements were concealed in air raid shelters and sandbagged small group trenches in the open park. The Germans had hastily converted an anti-aircraft position [of three 88mm dual-purpose guns] at the south end of the bridge to ground defense. Some self-propelled guns were visible, and one or two high velocity antitank guns fired from the left.

"We had to cross the park to reach the highway bridge. The Germans, in sizable numbers, had to be dislodged to give the tanks unmolested access to the bridge. From the second floor windows we looked down their throats. Time was running out for them unless they got help. Whatever their number, we had them outmaneuvered, outgunned and, in our bones outclassed. Why not? We had driven them back for blocks." [47]

Coyle explained his plan to Vandervoort. "I told him I knew we could knock out the gun as soon as we opened fire. I told the colonel I would hold our fire for five minutes. He told me he would try to move the British tanks forward when we opened fire. Then he left to see the British commander." 48

Platoon Sergeant Otis Sampson walked into the room about that time. "I saw a German soldier running across the street to the other side. I raised my Tommy gun to shoot him, but Coyle pushed it down. 'Not yet!' he whispered, 'It will give our position away.'

"It was such a perfect shot I hated to miss it. I had figured the Germans knew we were there. Coyle had quietly moved into this building with his men before I came up. He was right; if they didn't know we were there, the burst from the Tommy gun would have told them.

"I went into the cellar where some of our platoon men were waiting quietly in the dark, watching through the street windows. I had just left the building by the back door when . . . ." 49

Someone opened fire from the house next door to Coyle, who "immediately had the men in the house where I was open fire with the machine gun and BAR, and Private First Class John Keller knocked out the [50mm] antitank gun with a rifle grenade." 50

A number of Germans were cut down in the first few seconds, then they took cover in the trenches and gun pits and began methodically blasting each house on the block with small-arms and machine gun fire, while getting a fix on the paratroopers' locations. Private First Class Boling fired his BAR on full automatic, using clip after clip of ammunition, when suddenly he felt a stinging sensation. "I received flying brick chips to the right side of my neck. I reached up and got a handful of brick dust and traces of blood. In the dim light I thought I was wounded, but a check by others confirmed it was only a nick." 51

When the firing began prematurely, Lieutenant Smith signaled the Grenadier Guards to move their tanks up to the intersection on the right side of the 1st Platoon as planned. "Some high-velocity 75s opened up that had not done any firing as yet and made the positions of the tanks untenable. Two Shermans were knocked out in this bit of action, and the tanks retired to a cover position to wait for a new thrust." 52

Without warning, as Lieutenant Coyle and the men in the room were firing at the Germans below, "There was a terrific explosion in the room and it filled with plaster dust blinding everyone. When it cleared, I could see that an antitank gun shell had come through the wall from the room in the house next door on our left and continued through the wall to the house on our right. By some miracle, the only man wounded was Private Carl Beck. But he was seriously wounded in the left side of his head and face. We pulled him into the back of the house, and some men got him out to the back yard where the medics could pick him up." 53

Private Beck was barely hanging on. "A piece of shrapnel went into my mouth and came out the left side of my head, taking everything with it. I now know that it was my lieutenant, James Coyle, who saved my life by his prompt first aid." 54

As soon as Lieutenant Coyle had taken care of Beck, he returned to the front room. "Private First Class Clyde Rickerd and I then manned the machine gun and reopened fire, but we could not see exactly where the antitank gun firing to our left was located. Just as I realized that tracer rounds included in the ammunition were pinpointing our position for the enemy, another shell burst into the room from the left, hit the wall on our right, and fell to the floor in the room. We could not continue firing, and we moved back out of the front room.

"I went to the front room next door where the other squad of my men was, to check them out. No E Company men were hit, but a British [artillery] observer with a radio, who had moved into our position without my knowledge, had been killed by the concussion when the shell went through the room. He did not have a mark on him." [55]

When Coyle asked his men who had opened fire without orders, they told him that a British artillery observer "had walked into the room where our men were waiting, and seeing the Germans in the street in front of us, opened fire on his own." [56]

Sergeant Sampson watched Beck and Hable being carried out the back door of the building. "Beck was badly wounded. As Hable passed, I heard him tell his buddies, 'I'll be back as soon as I can.' It was a sincere statement." [57]

Between 6:00 and 6:30 p.m., the 2nd Platoon, Company E, moved into two houses on the southeastern corner of Graadt Van Roggenstraat and Barbarossastraat on the right flank of the 1st Platoon.

Because of the density of multistory buildings, Vandervoort's 81mm mortar platoon had found only one place with the vertical clearance from which to operate their weapons. "Our 81mm mortars were dug into deep gun pits between the headstones and monuments of an ancient cemetery a few blocks back. When firing, the troopers' torsos bobbed above and below ground. There was a ghoulish appearance to the scene—not for the superstitious or squeamish. It wasn't irreverence but necessity that placed them there. The old graveyard was the only open space in the neighborhood giving sufficient vertical clearance from the tall buildings to permit wide, full-range horizontal arcs of fire.

"The Tommies thought the layout was hilarious. Good natured banter about fornicating Yank grave robbers was run into the ground. It was well the Dutch residents had evacuated the area.

"Our 81mm mortar platoon was walking high-explosive shells up and down the roadbed of the massive stone-piered and steel-arched bridge. They hoped to get lucky and cut any exposed wires leading to demolition charges. Someone asked, 'What if they hit a charge causing the bridge to blow sky high?'

"'Then we'd know the bloody thing was booby trapped' was the reply. The 81mm shelling also sealed off access between enemy elements on the opposite sides of the Waal.

"One German tried to run north across the bridge. Our mortar observer fired one round that knocked him flat. He got up and began running away without his rifle. Then he stopped, turned around, came back, picked up his piece, and started away again at a full jog—weapon in hand. The mortar platoon leader ordered 'cease fire' and watched the good soldier run away." 58

Vandervoort ordered Company F to move around the left flank and approach the bridge area from the southwest. Lieutenant Rusty Hays was a new assistant platoon leader with Company F. "As we crossed streets perpendicular to our line of march, we would pause, gather into small groups, and run across to reduce exposure to enemy fire. The Germans were expected to be on our right, so as the tanks would cross a wide street, they would swing their big guns to the right, so if they received fire from down the street they'd be ready to return it.

"We came to a wide boulevard. We'd been told there was a German 88 antitank gun at a traffic circle two blocks down the boulevard to the right. My platoon ran across without drawing fire, and the tanks followed us, swinging their guns to the right as they crossed." 59

As one of the tanks crossed, its gun hit a small tree, causing the turret to spin around, accidentally firing a round from the 17-pounder main gun, hitting a group of troopers from Hays' platoon who were resting with their backs against the wall of a building. One of those in the group was Sergeant Spencer Wurst. "When the gun went off, the detonation was close enough to stun me. I was momentarily knocked out or lost my senses. I couldn't hear much for the next few hours, but I recall coming to and immediately remembering what had occurred. As for the tank, it just kept rolling down the street. Luckily, the round was armor piercing. If it had been high explosives, it could have been catastrophic, but it was already very bad.

"The second man to my right [Private Alfonso R. Aguirre] was killed instantly. The man next to me [Corporal George S. Ziemski] was seriously wounded but survived. As soon as I came to I grabbed my first-aid packet and started to bandage him as best I could. We had been taught to use the first-aid packet of the wounded man rather than our own, to insure we still had bandages if we were wounded ourselves. In the confusion, I wasn't thinking all that clearly, although my training did click in well enough for me to start working on him." 60

Company F mortar squad leader, Sergeant Russ Brown, and his troopers set up their 60mm mortar along the wide boulevard that ran southwest from the traffic circle. The median provided the overhead clearance needed for Brown's mortar. "Lieutenant [John] Dodd stopped and called me aside. He got out his map and showed me the targets he wanted me to fire on. We set up the mortar and set up aiming stakes that I plotted from the map. Lieutenant Dodd had a truck drop off a load of mortar shells. We had never had so much ammo to fire.

"[Private First Class] Douglas Trieber and [Private] Harry Peterman fired the mortar, switching from stake to stake—sometimes firing for effect. We must have been effective, because we were hit by a large gun, much bigger than an 88. They had us zeroed in, and Harry Peterman was killed." 61

After checking on his men, Lieutenant Hays moved out with his platoon. "About a block further on, just as it was getting dark, I was told that my platoon would be attached to the British tank company we were with. Our objective would be a wooded park area down the street about two blocks. Whenever the tanks stopped, the platoon's job was to 'nip up into the houses on both sides of the street and be sure there were no Germans with Panzerfausts in the houses.'" [62]

Sergeant Wurst and his squad moved out behind the tanks. "The British tanks were abreast of one another. We followed them as closely as we could, seeking maximum protection as we peered ahead into doors and windows. I don't know if I fired or saw any enemy soldiers, but they were there. As soon as we turned the corner, the tanks fired rapidly with their two .30-caliber MGs and 75mm cannon. The din was deafening.

"We got a lot of return fire from the head of the street, heavy small-arms fire. In addition to machine guns, rifles, and machine pistols, the Germans had dug in some 20mm antiaircraft weapons. I don't know if they were twins or quads, but when they're shooting at you, it hardly matters. They fired tracer rounds with a ratio of about one to four. It was late enough for the tracers to show up well in the dark.

"The fire became so heavy that the tanks momentarily stopped. They weren't damaged by the small arms and the 20mm fire, but it was a dangerous situation for the rifle squads. I got flatter than flat on the street, trying to get below a six-inch curb in a desperate search for cover. The fire immediately over my head cracked the air a foot or two above my body. I lay prone, hugging that curb for dear life, and I wasn't the only one. I don't think it gave us much protection except from our right front. If it hadn't been for the pavement, I'd have started digging." [63]

The tanks began moving again, and Lieutenant Hays and his men jumped up and moved down the street behind them. "The tanks moved slowly down the street towards the wooded park, and we followed. Just before we reached the park, the tanks encountered a roadblock, some trees that had been felled across the road. Fearing that there may be some antitank mines hidden in the trees, they stopped and my platoon tried to 'nip up into the houses on each side of the street.' On my side of the street, this wasn't possible; the house had been set on fire by artillery shells. Not only was this house on fire, silhouetting us against the flames, but there were houses on fire up the block behind us, also silhouetting us, including the tanks, against the flame. This was particularly scary to the tankers, since they knew somewhere in front of us the Germans had a big 88.

"By that time it was pitch dark. The troops of my platoon on my side of the street, unable to move into the house because of the fire, were milling around outside in front of the house, not knowing what to do." [64]

Meanwhile, Sergeant Wurst's squad moved around the tanks on the opposite side of the street. "I was reluctant because of the tank episode earlier in the day. At night, a buttoned up tank is practically blind. To advance around and move in front of those tanks would expose us to friendly fire as well as heavy fire from the enemy. We had almost gone forward enough for the traffic circle to come in view to our right front. It was a large area, and the Germans had dug in with at least one 88, as well as other heavy weapons. There were also most definitely mobile 20mm guns.

"We nevertheless moved around to the left of the tank to clear away the debris. At that very instant, a German antitank gun let loose. The German gunner was anxious and missed. The fire came from our right front and went across in front of the tanks. The gunner probably couldn't see them, but he had anticipated their movement into his field of fire.

"When an 88 fires on you at a distance of a hundred yards or less, you don't get much time to react. The tanks reversed, moving to the rear as quickly as their engines could get them there. One thing, and one thing only, saved us from being crushed—my squad had already started around to the left of the tanks." 65

Hays and his men were now exposed on the street without the protection of the tanks. "Just after the tanks left, someone called out, 'counterattack!' and a German hand grenade exploded in the front yard of the house where we were. One of the British soldiers was hit bad.

"Because of the fire behind us, we were reluctant to move from where we were. We didn't know how many Germans were in front of us and expected them to counterattack any minute. Then, suddenly, here came the tanks roaring back and [they] stopped in front of us. We carried the wounded man out and put him on the back of a tank, and keeping the tanks between us and the Germans we moved two blocks down the street to a school, where the rest of the company was and where we were to spend the night." 66

As the British tanks backed up, the platoon leader, Lieutenant Jack Carroll, along with Sergeant Wurst's squad took refuge in an outside cellar entrance off the street. After an exchange of hand grenades in the darkness with enemy troops, Lieutenant Carroll decided to break into a house down the street, get into the back yard, and then move back to find the remainder of the platoon. After a couple of Carroll's men found an unlocked house a short distance down the street, the remainder followed, moving through the house into the backyard. One of Carroll's troopers had pulled the pin on a grenade during the earlier exchange and was still holding it. Carroll "told him to throw it over the wall, and when he did this, it hit a wire and came back in the courtyard and went off not over ten feet away. We didn't even get a scratch. We had a real tough time getting back to our own lines that night, as we could hear them talking all around us." 67

Lieutenant Colonel Vandervoort had his men in position for an assault on the southern approaches of the highway bridge. "Companies E and F deployed in houses on the southern edge of the park waiting to be unleashed to finish the job. Our ammunition was plentiful with the exception of 60mm mortar rounds. All battalion communications—radio and telephone—were tied in 'five by five' [loud and clear]—better than 'Ma Bell.' A dozen or more Sherman tanks, motors idling, were ready to roll when ordered. Company D was downstream, fighting and dying for the railroad bridge. Except for Company D, our casualties, tanks and troopers, were negligible. In short, the battalion and the tanks were on the line of departure ready for a joint infantry/tank assault to put the armor over the river. There was time to establish a bridgehead north of the Waal before dark if the bridge wasn't demolished.

"So—I reported to the generals that 2nd Battalion was ready to take Hunner Park and put their tanks on the bridge. After consideration, they decided to consolidate our positions for the night and have their infantry, the Coldstream Guards, mop up the area to our left the next morning. The decision to pause was disappointing. The momentum was ours all afternoon. We wanted to continue while we had the upper hand.

"From dead and wounded enemy, our intelligence officer identified the reconnaissance battalion of the 9th SS Panzer Division. Were they the forerunners of the whole damn panzer division? That was what recon battalions usually did. The SS recon battalion T/O [table of organization] strength was six hundred, coincidentally about the same as 2nd Battalion's strength. The SS identification explained why few prisoners had been taken. The deaths-head skull and cross bones were the SS insignia. . . . In combat they were deceptive, prisoner-shooting bastards. Despite our mean opinion of them, they were tough S.O.B.s and could not be taken lightly." [68]

As darkness fell in Nijmegen, the paratroopers, Guardsmen, and SS grenadiers were exhausted from the fighting and needed sleep. But sleep was risky, as both sides used the night to conceal their movements. The Germans set fire to many of the buildings around their perimeter in order to prevent infiltration, and sent out night patrols to infiltrate the American positions.

The paratroopers used the darkness to get close enough to assault the German strongpoints around the approaches to the bridges. About 8:00 p.m., Lieutenant Smith ordered E Company's 3rd Platoon to move into position in the open area southeast of the highway bridge where it "found foxholes and trenches occupied by the enemy, and after several of the enemy were bayoneted in their holes, the remaining few attempted to retreat. They were attacked and wiped out in hand-to-hand battle in which trench knives were the only tools used." [69]

After taking over the German foxholes, Private First Class Don Lassen struck up a conversation with one of his buddies just before dawn. "Fred Hebein and I were talking and we heard some noise about halfway down the hill.

"Fred said to me, 'Let's go down and see what the hell that is.'

"I said, 'Just a minute, Fred, I gotta go back to my foxhole and tell [William A.] Muller'—he was my foxhole buddy—'where I'm going,'—because we always kept each other informed of what we were going to do. It took a couple of minutes to get back to my foxhole, and then I started back to join Fred in an exploration. Just as I got back to Fred, all hell broke loose from that area halfway down the hill. There was a whole squad of Krauts in there, and if I hadn't taken those couple of minutes delay, we'd have walked right straight into that squad of Krauts." [70]

AFTER DARK, LIEUTENANT MEYERS, with Company D, took a few men and went back to the rail yard to find and evacuate Lieutenant Michelman, who had been wounded during the earlier fighting. "I found [Private Jacob] Herman's body, but Michelman, who was only a few feet away, was gone. Apparently, he crawled out on his own. Later, we received word from the aid station of his evacuation.

"Fires from the burning buildings illuminated the streets, and the fighting continued as we advanced from one building to another. During lulls . . . we could hear sounds of heavy fighting coming from the direction of the highway bridge." [71]

As darkness fell, Lieutenant Jim Coyle and the 1st Platoon of Company E maintained their positions in several of the row houses overlooking the German positions south of the Nijmegen highway bridge. "We received the word that the attack was being held up for the night and that we were to hold our position. Enemy fire had stopped, and I placed men in the three houses on the ground floor to prevent enemy infiltrators from getting into position.

"I was in the upper front room shortly after dark observing the enemy area in front of us as best I could. Suddenly, a British tank opened fire across my front from the right, and a German tank replied from my left. I don't know how they could see each other in the dark, but a terrific crossfire of heavy-caliber tracers continued for almost five minutes. (The next day I saw the German tank, an old French model, knocked out near the traffic circle to the left of our position.) When the firing ceased, I saw that the tracer fire had set a public building on fire, and I could now observe the area to my front by its light.

"The company runner then gave me a message that I was to report to the E Company CP—about two blocks behind the 1st Platoon position. When I got there, the CO told me to plot my platoon's position in on the company's overlay. I had just completed the map when my platoon runner came in with the information that a patrol was moving in front of our area. The men thought the patrol was British and had not fired on it. But some thought it was an enemy patrol.

"I had returned to the platoon and went to the front of the house where Sergeant Ben Popilsky was observing from the doorway. He told me two men walked past on the sidewalk earlier, but he thought they were British tankers. Just then, the two returned and I could see in the light of the burning building that they wore the helmets and smocks of German paratroopers.

"Popilsky and I opened fire with our Thompson submachine guns. One of the Germans went down, but the other ran to our left and got behind a tree. He yelled at us in German, and Ben who understood it said he was asking to come back and help his comrade. I told Ben to tell him that we would take care of his comrade, who was groaning on the sidewalk. When Popilsky yelled back, I realized that Ben was speaking Yiddish to the German. The German then called us, 'Verdamdt Americanische Schweinhunds' and we called him a 'Kraut bastard.'

"I wanted the wounded German soldier as a prisoner, and I was not about to let the other man come back and pick us off in the doorway, now that he knew exactly where we were. He finally ran away, but when we crawled out to get the wounded German, we discovered that he had died." [72]

That night, a runner told Platoon Sergeant Otis Sampson, known as the "mortar artist" to the men in E Company, to report to Lieutenant Smith's command post. "Our company command post was in the cellar of a house [in] back of the one Lieutenant Coyle was holding. [Lieutenant] Smith told me to take two mortar squads and go to the east of where we were and shell the area across the street from Lieutenant Coyle. He showed me the position I was to set up in. I asked for a ruler to lay out my field of fire [on a map]. The spacious cellar room was dimly lit. I had entered the room during an interrogation of a large-built German soldier. The prisoner was using both hands to hold his pants up, for his belt had been removed and the buttons or zipper ripped open. I was given a table and a light to see by, and with the aid of a compass and a ruler, I oriented the map and measured the distance as 550 yards.

"Wesley Forsythe, our platoon runner, guided me to the chosen area by back alleys. I believe it was to the very end of the front street going east. A platoon of E Company men was already dug in across this front street in the open area that ran to the river.

"I set the two mortars up in the back yard of the corner house and distributed men in defensive positions. A telephone line from the company CP had been laid for the platoon across the street, but it seemed to be continuously out of order. The lieutenant of the platoon told me to hold my fire. I knew he was right, but that wasn't the reason I did it. The firing had quieted down. All I would have done is bring artillery down on us and the platoon in the open field. I could send one round over at a time, [but] between each round fired I would have to use a light to reset the delicate M4 sightings on the mortar. I wouldn't trust the weapon to hold its setting. I would be taking a chance of hitting my own platoon across the street. Taking one man with me, we went across the east side street in some shelled-out houses and picked up some couch covers and draperies for the mortarmen to keep warm. It was quite chilly. During the night, I heard cries for help, but not in our area. I had wondered if the cries were for real or someone trying to lure a victim in. Many parts of the city were burning. I didn't sleep that night, but kept guard." [73]

DURING THE NIGHT, AT THE CHAMPION CP, General Gavin struggled with how to capture the two Nijmegen bridges intact. The fate of the British paratroopers at Arnhem weighed heavily on his mind. "General [Brian G.] Horrocks, commanding British XXX Corps, General Browning, commanding the airborne corps, and General Allan Adair, commanding the Guards Armored Division, and I had a meeting near the sidewalk in front of the Malden schoolhouse late in the afternoon of September 19.

"Earlier Browning had warned me, 'The Nijmegen bridge must be taken today. At the latest, tomorrow.' The capture of the Nijmegen bridge was squarely on my shoulders. This I knew. But most important to me were the lives of General [Robert F.] Urquhart and the British First Airborne." [74]

Gavin knew that Vandervoort's battalion and the British Guards Armoured Division could seize the southern approaches to the bridges, but that the Germans would simply blow them up as they retreated. "I decided therefore, that I somehow had to get across the river with our infantry and attack the northern end of the bridge and cut off the Germans at the southern end. The question was how. There were no boats around Nijmegen. They had long ago been removed by the Germans." [75]

Gavin discussed his plan with General Horrocks and told him that if he could get boats brought up quickly, the 504th PIR would make an assault crossing of the Waal River as soon as possible. Horrocks agreed to the plan and instructed his staff to immediately have the boats brought forward. Gavin wanted to make the crossing in the predawn darkness, but Horrocks couldn't assure him that the boats would arrive by that time.

Later that evening, there was a large meeting at the Champion CP. Assembled were Gavin, British Generals Browning and Horrocks, officers of the Guards regiments and divisional staff, the 82nd divisional staff, and Colonel Tucker and his 504th regimental staff.

An observer at this meeting, Colonel George Chatterton, commander of the British Glider Pilot Regiment, noted that the British officers were wearing "corduroy trousers, chukka boots, and old school scarves. They seemed relaxed, as though they were discussing an exercise, and I couldn't help contrast them to the Americans present, especially Colonel Tucker, who was wearing a helmet that almost covered his face. His pistol was in a holster under his left arm, and he had a knife strapped to his thigh. Tucker occasionally removed his cigar long enough to spit, and every time he did, faint looks of surprise flickered over the faces of the Guards' officers." [76]

Gavin laid out a very bold plan. "Speed was essential. There was no time even for a reconnaissance. As I continued to talk, Tucker seemed to be the only man in the room who seemed unfazed. He had made the landing at Anzio and knew what to expect." [77]

Browning was "by now filled with admiration at the daring of the idea." [78] He immediately granted permission to Gavin to proceed with the assault crossing. Gavin planned to launch the boats in the Maas-Waal Canal close to where it empties into the Waal River, providing a covered position to load the boats and time for the men to become familiar with the boats before leaving the canal to cross the river. Gavin wanted to use every artillery piece the division and the British could employ to shell the opposite side of the river, together with direct fire from the British tanks and Tucker's 81mm mortars and machine guns as the 504th troopers crossed. Finally, Gavin wanted a heavy smoke screen laid on the far shore to conceal the crossing.

EVEN AS GAVIN AND HIS STAFF WERE PLANNING the crossing of the Waal, four German kampfgruppen were moving into position to carry out concentric sledgehammer attacks against the eastern and southern portions of the 82nd Airborne perimeter. They had built their forces over the last two days. The primary striking power would be paratroopers with the 3rd and 5th Fallschirmjäger Divisions, rushed from Cologne, Germany.

Kampfgruppe Becker, a battalion of approximately seven hundred paratroopers of the 3rd Fallschirmjäger Division, supported by five self-propelled guns from a fallshirm-sturmgeschütz brigade, would attack west through Wyler, Germany, pushing on to relieve the defenders in Nijmegen. Kampfgruppe von Fürstenberg, approximately five hundred men of a reserve reconnaissance battalion, supported by armored vehicles and light towed antitank guns, would strike at Beek and then drive west to Nijmegen. Attacking out of the Reichswald, Kampfgruppe Greschick, approximately nine hundred men of a Luftwaffe fortress battalion, plus an "ear" battalion of old men from the 406th Division, reinforced by several batteries of 88mm, 37mm, and 20mm antiaircraft guns of the 4th Flak Division, would attack west through Groesbeek to the heights beyond. And finally, Kampfgruppe Hermann—paratroopers of the 21st Fallschirmjäger Lehr Regiment, a battalion of artillery from a fallschirm-artillerie regiment, a few 88mm flak guns, and a company of Flemish Waffen SS—would strike from the south through Riethorst and Mook. This objective was the seizure of the Heumen lock bridge, the lone bridge carrying heavy traffic over the Maas-Waal Canal, severing the main Allied supply line.

THE NIGHT WAS RESTLESS, AND FOR VANDERVOORT, one more without sleep. "There were small patrol clashes. Outposts listened for vehicles on the bridge. A prisoner or two was taken. Illuminating flares burst over the front. Minor shellings were exchanged. Someone wounded cried in the park—or was it the SS baiting a trap? The Germans wanted a truce to take out wounded in the E Company sector. The troopers magnanimously stood by—weapons ready—while the evacuation took place. German patrols (some probable would-be looters) tried to enter houses we occupied. They were gunned down through the lace curtained front doors and windows. In the Nijmegen fighting the .45-caliber Thompson submachine gun didn't penetrate doors and walls as well as our .30-caliber weapons. Some innovative troopers switched to German Schmeisser machine pistols. To obtain more 9mm ammunition clips, they would shoot another Jerry. It was a self-sufficient if somewhat chancy supply system." [79]

During the night, Private First Class Earl Boling stood watch with two other E Company troopers in one of the houses overlooking the traffic circle. "A patrol with hobnailed boots was heard approaching. Because both the British and the Germans wore hobnailed boots, we were waiting to get a look at them to ascertain if it was friend or foe. As they passed from the back of a large tree and arrived almost in front of our positions, we could see their German uniforms and helmets in the light of the burning house, and it looked to be a five- or six-man patrol. At this time [Private First Class] John Keller, who was armed with a rifle grenade launcher, pulled the pin and threw a rifle grenade into their midst.

"I believe at least one was killed and one wounded in the blast. Another two or three ran toward the building where Private George [M.] Wood and I were at the first floor window. I opened fire with the BAR and one dropped near the sidewalk. I thought two more were outside the window ledge, so I tipped the BAR up and fired the last two shots of the clip over the window ledge; then tried to change a clip, when I saw the enemy soldier less than two feet away, holding to the window ledge with one hand and raising a Luger automatic with the other.

"I was so nervous that I dropped the clip and started to reach for my trench knife on my right boot when Private George Wood said, 'I'll get him,' and fired four times at point-blank range into the face of the German. With each shot I could see his head bounce, but he didn't fall until the fourth shot.

"Private Wood had used a Beretta automatic that he had been carrying into combat since his days in the Sicily invasion. I was certainly glad he had it along. I told George that I was sure that another German soldier was outside the room below the window level or behind some nearby bushes in the shadows.

"We 'sweat it out' until daylight was approaching. Meanwhile, one of the wounded near the curb of the street was moaning throughout the rest of the night. As dawn was breaking we could make out the figure of a German underneath the edge of some bushes with a grenade in his hand.

"Sergeant Popilsky, who had been raised in Chicago and spoke some of several languages, called out to the German to put down the grenade and come in the window, which he did. Sergeant Popilsky interrogated him and learned that he was a Polish soldier, conscripted into the German unit, and was not of the diehard SS troops that we were fighting." [80]

Private First Class Frank Bilich, along with the two other D Company troopers trapped under the stairway in the basement of the house near the railroad bridge, faced a dilemma. "By 2:30 in the morning all was quiet. We knew there was a guard on the back porch. If we stayed until daylight they would soon find us. The three of us had a whispered council of war. It was decided that we would make a run for it just before dawn. We talked about who was going first, second, and last. The way out would be up the stairs and out under the porch.

"Again, the officer came halfway down the stairs from the kitchen and asked for coffee. After he went back, we decided that this was our chance. We came up to the backyard and saw a wooden fence with a gate blocking our path.

"McMandon took off, hit the gate with such force that it burst open, and went through. I followed. There was a call to halt in German and somebody fired some shots. We were all through the gate and running down the backs of those houses, running until our lungs were ready to explode. We ran across a road and right over an E Company machine gun position and fell into a ditch. All the E Company boys could say was, 'Where the hell have you come from?' We didn't care. We had made it." [81]

CHAPTER 15

"We're Not Going To Pull Back . . .
If They Take Us Back,
They're Going To Have To Carry Us"

As dawn approached on September 20, there was an overcast sky with light rain. Around the railroad bridge, Lieutenant Joe Meyers, an assistant platoon leader with Company D, awoke from a couple of hours of fitful sleep. "D+3 found us facing a determined enemy in well prepared defensive positions guarding the approaches to the railroad bridge. The rail yards to the east, our right, were elevated about twenty feet above the street level. To reach them, you had to negotiate a steep embankment. Our attack followed a main street to an underpass of the main line. A German minefield, protected by fire, was sited in this underpass. In the distance, we were not far from our goal, the railroad bridge, but in time it was another matter. It was a temporary stalemate.

"Tom [McClean] and I set up platoon headquarters in the remains of the basement of a two- or three-story brick building. Except some rubble, the entire building was gone. Sound-powered phone lines connected us to the nearby rifle and mortar squads, and a telephone line linked us to company headquarters.

"Shortly after dawn on the morning of D+3, a jeep sped down the main street, through our lines, and into no man's land. The Germans greeted the vehicle and its occupants with bursts of automatic weapons fire. The sound of a German machine gun or machine pistol was very distinctive, since each had a higher cyclic rate of fire than similar U.S. weapons. The jeep carried an artillery forward observer (FO) and his team, who had come to join us. Instead of approaching with caution, the FO team raced straight through our position. The FO, a lieutenant, and his NCO died. The driver escaped and returned to our lines, where he joined Tom and me in the basement ruins. We gave him a cup of coffee and a cigarette to calm his nerves, before sending him to the rear." [1]

Lieutenant J. J. Smith, commanding Company E, had not slept the previous night. "At dawn heavy artillery began dropping in on us and did not cease all day long. During the night, snipers had succeeded in gaining positions within our company sectors, and sniping was carried out all day long. Details were formed to ferret out these men, but they were so well hidden that it was almost an impossible task." [2]

The 2nd Battalion attack was held up while the British Grenadier Guards cleared the built up area between the railroad and highway bridges. Things had settled down enough that troopers took advantage of the opportunity to eat.

Vandervoort knew that his men were very hungry, having exhausted the rations they had brought with them when they jumped. "Every back porch seemed to have a cage of Belgium hares and every house a garden. There was time to cook, so GI rabbit stew came on the menu. I don't recall that it qualified as gourmet." [3]

Corporal Charles Fergie and a few troopers with regimental headquarters company broke into a house near the railroad bridge. "There was a family there; mother, father, and a son and daughter. They were so scared, because they thought we were Germans. When they saw that we were American, they were so happy and [they] kissed and hugged us. We stayed there for about twenty-four hours. There was nothing there for them to eat except potatoes, but they cooked up a pot of them and shared them with us. It was the only solid food we had had in a long time." [4]

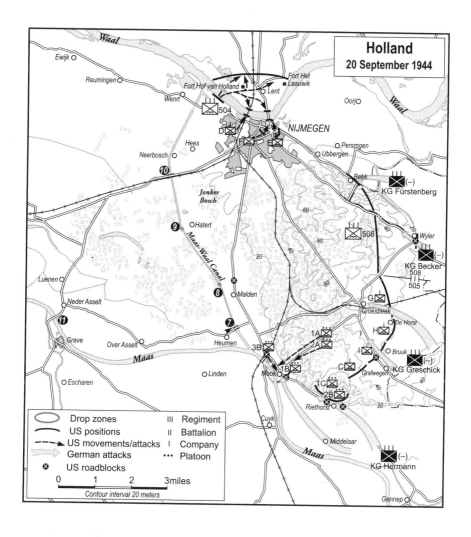

Lieutenant Robert J. Dwyer, with Regimental Headquarters Company, couldn't believe his eyes when "Corporal [Louis P.] Hogan of my demolitions platoon emerged from a basement with a cold bottle of Dutch beer. We were pinned down by small-arms fire. I drank the beer, thinking, 'If one must go, what better way.'" [5]

THAT MORNING, THE GERMANS LAUNCHED massive concentric attacks against the thinly held perimeter of the 82nd Airborne Division. The 4th Flak Division's 88mm, 37mm, and 20mm antiaircraft guns opened up with a massive barrage against the thinly spread 3rd Battalion, 505th PIR, troopers dug in facing east and southeast toward the Reichswald. Following the barrage, Kampfgruppe Greschick's assault drove the outposts back, pushing a half mile almost to the outskirts of Groesbeek before it was stopped. The German assault on Company G forced the withdrawal of the company's outpost at the location where the railroad tracks intersected the road east of Groesbeek. From his position on the main line of resistance, Captain Jack Isaacs could see the Germans occupy the outpost and set up a 20mm dual-purpose gun. "In preparing to retake the outpost position, we mortared it with our company 60mm mortars. We then launched a local counterattack and retook the position. While reconnoitering the ground between our position and the area to which the Germans had withdrawn, I was on hands and knees proceeding along a fence row, when I came face to face with an elderly Dutch woman of about seventy, crawling towards our lines. Her left arm was nearly severed above the elbow. I assume we had struck her, since the Germans had not shelled the area. She was in intense pain, but did not cry or show any emotion. I pointed towards our lines and she proceeded in that direction, while I continued my reconnaissance. I did not see her again.

"Later, in the next field and across the road south, we discovered the body of a small boy, of about four or five. A hog was trying to devour the child's body. We drove the hog away and to the best of my knowledge, the boy's body was taken away by Dutch civilians.

"I remember the honesty, honor, and integrity of the civilians, whose homes we destroyed and whose families we killed or maimed. They shared their shelter and food with us, and any veteran of the other drops will say that within a few hours in Sicily and Italy, our chutes were made into clothing, while in France, they just disappeared, but in Holland, they were gathered up by the civilians and turned over to us." [6]

During the German assault on Company I, several troopers were seriously wounded, including one of the medics. One the company's troopers, Private John R. "Jack" Lyons, had prior training in first aid. "We had several bad casualties that I knew how to treat. I had a senior Red Cross badge and an Eagle Scout first aid badge, and was made [an] I Company medic on the spot." [7]

IN NIJMEGEN, COMPANY E PLATOON LEADER Lieutenant James J. Coyle wanted to knock out the 88mm dual-purpose gun, which had fired the previous afternoon through the row houses that his platoon occupied. "I took five men through the back yards of the buildings on our left and worked our way to the end of the block, where I hoped to be able to spot the antitank gun which had fired. When we got into the attic of the corner building, I could see the gun with its crew in the street at the corner [across from the traffic circle]. We opened fire with M1s from the attic window. The crew could not spot our firing position. When one of their men was hit, they abandoned the gun and withdrew to a nearby trench where there were other enemy troops. We were firing down on them and hit some. The rest retreated into the park." 8

Corporal Thomas Burke and Private First Class Earl Boling decided to check the house next door for food. Boling was out of rations and very hungry. "As we started from the house we were in, we both heard a bullet snap over our heads, and as we ducked for protection near the wall of the house, I saw the body of Sergeant Popilsky. I checked him and he appeared to have been shot in the head as he had come over the garden wall, apparently to join us. I checked his pulse and found that he was dead." 9

Meanwhile, Coyle maintained his watch on the 88mm antiaircraft gun. "While waiting to see if they would re-man the gun, I sent Private [John L.] Gill back to the company CP to tell the CO where I was and what we were doing. When he didn't return as I had instructed, I sent another man. This man returned immediately and told me that Gill was lying wounded in the back yard next door. Gill told me that as he started back he had been shot from the back door of the adjacent house. We pulled him to cover. We threw grenades in the windows of the house, but the Germans kept firing out of the door. Corporal Burke tried to rush the door, but was hit with machine pistol fire and killed immediately." 10

He fell backward into Boling's arms. "As I tried to drag his body out, a grenade was thrown at me and I felt a numbing pain in my left leg near the knee. I fired a burst of BAR fire upon the stairs where the Germans had run. Some men attempted to throw grenades into the second floor windows at the Germans, but they were also throwing concussion grenades as well as potato masher grenades with a fragmentation sleeve on them." 11

While his men fired into the house, Coyle saw his medic signal him from over the wall at the next house. "He had heard us firing and had come by himself from the platoon CP to see if anyone was wounded. He shouted to me that Sergeant Popilsky was lying dead on the other side of the wall. Popilsky had apparently heard our fire from the attack [on the antitank gun crew], and had left the platoon on his own and had been killed as he started over the wall by the Germans in the house, who later wounded Gill.

"A grenade flew out of a window in the house and badly wounded Corporal [Richard] Crouse. I realized that we had to get out of the yard as we had no cover. And despite all our fire, the Germans were in a position in the house where we couldn't hit them, but they could hit us. I pulled the men out of the yard and blew the back of the house with a bazooka round. I then took the men back to our original position down the block. We had knocked out the antitank gun. The Germans abandoned it and did no more firing. But, we lost three men killed and one wounded." 12

AT ABOUT 9:00 A.M., German artillery intermittently shelled the two platoons holding the high ground north of Riethorst and Plasmolen, overlooking the Gennep-Nijmegen highway. Beginning at 11:00 a.m., artillery, 88mm, mortars, and Nebelwerfers plastered their positions. Sergeant Arnold G. "Dutch" Nagel, with Company C, heard the unmistakable screaming sound of German Nebelwerfers firing in the distance. "We all jumped in our foxholes, and when it exploded, it made the ground shake. Two replacements [Private J. D. Shelton and Corporal Roger F. Coffin] jumped in the same hole and a shell landed right in their hole. They never had a chance. My jump school buddy, [Private] Raymond Dionne, had his rifle lying crosswise in his hole, and when he jumped in the hole, he could not get all the way down fast enough and shrapnel killed him. He only had part of his shoulder and head sticking out—a very innocent and costly mistake." [13]

At about 2:30 p.m., coming up the highway from Gennep toward Mook, Kampfgruppe Hermann hit the eastern roadblock, manned by the 2nd Squad, 2nd Platoon, Company B, which included two machine guns (one from Headquarters Company, 1st Battalion), a bazooka team, and a rifle grenade launcher, with mines on the road to their front. The troopers were in foxholes covered with logs and dirt. A Mark V Panther tank moving along the highway, followed by infantry, hit the roadblock from the east. The tank fired machine gun and 75mm rounds at the positions, blasting the dirt off the tops of the foxholes, setting the ammunition on fire, and knocking out the machine gun positions on each side of the road. Private Abraham A. "Abie" Mallis was with the machine gun team on the south side of the road, when a shell hit the hole, splitting the barrel of the machine gun. "We had a direct hit on our emplacement." [14]

Mallis frantically tried to get the machine gun operating, then grabbed a carbine and fired a clip at the tank as it came to within fifty yards of his hole. The bazooka team fired four rounds at the side of the tank, with no effect.

The tank then withdrew three hundred yards, and together with two other Panthers and artillery, blasted the positions of the high ground just north of the road, forcing the troopers to the bottoms of their holes, and systematically leveling the five houses and windmill on the hill. This gave Mallis and others at the roadblock an opportunity to escape to the high ground north of the road.

The tank then knocked out the western roadblock six hundred yards away. Those troopers also withdrew up the hill. Lieutenant Weinberg's 2nd Platoon, Company B, and Lieutenant Gensemer's 1st Platoon, Company C, fought savagely against the reinforced battalion of German paratroopers, killing a large number of them. Riflemen behind a hedge south of the road engaged the German infantry following behind one of the Mark V tanks, then moved west, crossed the road, and moved up the hill to join their platoon. A machine gun and riflemen dug in on the hill north of the highway cut down many more enemy. Observers with division artillery and the 1st Battalion 81mm mortar platoon dropped concentrations of fire to the south and east. The 81mm mortar observer called in fire on the bottom of the hill when the German infantry began attacking up it. Weinberg's and Gensemer's troopers threw grenades down on the attacking enemy paratroopers as they came up the hill. The enemy infantry withdrew, and the hill was again hit with artillery and Nebelwerfers, which kept up a barrage on the hill until the following morning. That night, enemy infantry infiltrated to the bottom of the hill once again.

At 2:00 p.m., German paratroopers moved north across the flats toward Mook, following close behind a heavy barrage, which kept the defenders' heads down. Two squads, of Lieutenant William J. "Buck" Reardon's 1st Platoon, Company B, supported by two 57mm antitank guns at a roadblock just south of Mook, fought valiantly but were overrun. Troopers from both squads withdrew or hid out. Sergeant James Elmo Jones was able to withdraw most of his squad. "Four men of my squad were cut off and captured while we were trying to leave our position and re-group. [Private First Class] Raymond T. Mayers of Pennsylvania was killed by shrapnel. Mayers and I were very close—he was a replacement." 15

In all, the Germans captured six men, while Reardon and five others hid in cellars.

Lieutenant Harold E. Miller, who became the Company B commanding officer when Lieutenant Jim Irvin was wounded earlier, radioed the 1st Battalion requesting reinforcements. Company A's 1st Platoon, commanded by Lieutenant John Otto, and 2nd Platoon, commanded by Lieutenant George Presnell, moved out toward Mook via the Mookschebaan.

At 2:45 p.m., Miller committed the company reserve, Lieutenant Emil Schimpf's 3rd Platoon, and with the remaining 1st Platoon troopers fought a vicious house-to-house, room-to-room fight for the town. But overwhelming numbers of German paratroopers pushed Schimpf's platoon back and took the town by about 3:00 p.m.

THE 82ND AIRBORNE DIVISION WAS STRAINING to the breaking point by very heavy German attacks along the perimeter to the east and south of Nijmegen and by the battle to capture the bridges over the Waal River. Colonel Ekman took steps to stem the German penetration, which threatened to reach Bridge Number 7, the Heumen lock bridge, over the Mass-Waal Canal, which was critical to the supply route. Ekman called division headquarters and got a platoon of tanks of the British Coldstream Guards sent to Mook. Ekman immediately drove to the area northwest of Mook, where Lieutenant Schimpf's 3rd Platoon and the troopers from Lieutenant Reardon's 1st Platoon, who had been pushed out of town, reorganized for a counterattack.

One of the troopers in Schimpf's platoon was a young replacement, Private Northam H. Stolp, an assistant bazooka gunner. As Stolp was waiting for orders, B Company troopers Private Thomas F. Stoneking and Private William L. Mount took cover with Stolp behind a huge tree trunk that had fallen into the road. Stolp was surprised to see them. "Stoneking looked up at me and laughed as I said, 'I heard you were killed yesterday,' hardly masking my astonishment.

"He laughed and said, 'Nope, they didn't get me yet!' About that moment, we got sent up the street. We had been ordered by Colonel Ekman to 'get on up the street.'

"My partner [Martin Decker] and I, along with a shattered piece of our platoon, probably not over twenty men, were pushed up the main street of Mook at this time. We had not yet had any appreciable reinforcement and were spread out on a generally east/west line across the width of the town from the river on the west to the open fields on the east. The town was probably only two or three blocks wide in general. The 'lines' were only advanced one building at a time, and lost the same way, only to be regained by troopers shooting their way in and through them. The buildings on our side of the street were mainly two-story houses and combinations with little shops in the front of the lower floor areas. They were crawling with enemy troops. Generally, one could not see from whom or where the fire was coming.

"The boys on the other side of the road, which ran parallel to the river, were fighting their way through a huge 'monastery' or some such religious building, which was probably two blocks long. Its grounds were enclosed by a high brick wall on all sides except the riverbank side.

"The side which paralleled the street offered good cover for the men coming up that side, but left them entirely exposed to the fire coming from the houses on our side. They had a few large, elm-type trees like we did, similarly placed along the street. They offered cover from directly ahead, but nothing from our side.

"I recall six men working their way along that side of the street. One was coming along, from tree to tree, when he ran out of trees as he neared the point where the brick wall turned a right angle and went down one side of a sort of alley, which ran to the river. There was no cover left from there on. No one could cross the alley due to the intense machine gun fire coming up it from the riverbank area.

"The noise was intense and the confusion was total! I recall, in spite of the intensity of the situation and the immediacy of having to deal with someone who was firing down on us from a window directly over our heads, that the boy coming up the other side, about twenty yards back, was without a weapon! He would crawl a few yards then stop, and rise up on one knee and survey the road ahead. He seemed to be dressed in ODs [olive drabs] and looked for all the world like an Air Force member in his Class 'A' uniform!

"As I was trying to figure how to tell him not to cross the alley, I saw him jolted, once, twice, and yet a third time as if someone was kicking him in the chest. He fell forward, squirmed, and tried to crawl ahead toward the hidden enemy positions in the houses and hedges ahead. He died there, facing an enemy, without a weapon, doing his level best to force the Germans out of his world!

"He was untrained in infantry fighting . . . I knew nothing of what he was except that someone had told him to fight up the street! I have since identified him as the air force member who was found to have 'stowed away' on the gliders in the earlier lifts and made his way to our area. Another heroic American who wanted to be part of our fight for freedom!

"Along with this kid and a bit behind him was a long, tall Texan type. He was a glider pilot/warrant officer. He had a Thompson submachine gun and a lot of guts! He moved past the fallen airman and got behind the last tree before the alley. He and I exchanged some idiotic 'pleasantries' and returned to trying to become part of the concrete!" 16

From his prone position on the street, Private Stolp noticed something moving behind a pile of dirt, about two and a half feet high and fifteen feet long, on the opposite side of the street. "In those days the Germans had begun to run out of war materials. They had taken to making backpacks out of raw leather with the fur still on it. One frequently found brown and white, mottled cowhide packs thrown here and there.

"At that moment, I saw one of those cow colored backpacks going along sticking up just above the top of the dirt pile in the driveway. It was bouncing up and down as if a man was crouched over and sneaking toward the back of the property toward the river. I knew what it meant at once, and since I was unable to get a line on it, I called it to the attention of the long, tall Texan glider pilot across the street. He was in perfect alignment with the 'bandit,' with just sparse orchard trees between himself and the enemy. I asked him if he could see the window of the house straight ahead on the side facing him. He assured me he could. So I told him to sight on the first six inches of the dirt pile just below that window and tear it up from end to end.

"He complied beautifully. My mind said, 'Gotcha! You bastard!' the pack vanished. The height of the pile had been reduced measurably. The warrant officer glider pilot was smiling broadly across at me as he turned his Tommy gun clip pack end-for-end and reinserted it in his weapon.

"Score one for our side. Texas done good!

"About this moment, our medic, Jess Weaver, came up the middle of the street from behind us someplace, and moved to the body of a fallen trooper in the middle of the street. The man had been shot and fallen just about the same time the 'airman' kid on the other side had been hit. Jess came on 'all fours' creeping up the street. He kept checking ahead as he came. He would move a few feet, stop, and look up as if expecting to be hit. The look on his face was pure terror. Those of you who have experienced this sort of thing know what I mean. He had the red and white 'medic' cross on his helmet and by God's grace the enemy let him come on.

"His luck held, and he got to the alley level without any of the unseen bullets and shrapnel catching him up. He checked the guy in the street. He was obviously dead. Then Jess went back and over to the other side of the street to check several wounded there. [He] checked the airman (who was already dead and beyond help), and then went somewhere tending to the wounded along that side of the street. There were several. He should get the Congressional Medal [of Honor]. All this happened in a very few minutes. Time was stopped, and it was all in almost slow motion. It takes a long time to record each scene, but it was a long day!" 17

As Stolp lay pinned down, "Sergeant Floyd Baldry, Private Thomas Stoneking, and Private William Mount had come up from behind us, pounding up and past on a dead run. They went ahead of us into a small, sheet metal–covered sort of auto garage. It was set back about twenty to thirty feet as an alcove off the street. There was the usual apron driveway, much like any gas station would have. The far side was limited by a very high brick wall running at right angles to the sidewalk and the street. It was covered with heavy ivy vines. You could hardly see the bricks. It seemed [like] a good cover.

"They had a .30-caliber machine gun with a tripod/ground mount. Private Stoneking was the gunner, Private Mount the ammunition bearer and assistant gunner, and Sergeant Baldry the commander. They threw the gun down into place, [and] took their best targets of opportunity. They seemed in a quite safe place, having made it through the stream of machine gun fire coming down the alley across the street and every place else!" [18]

Private Stolp remained pinned down behind a large elm tree near the street curb by machine gun fire from the alley across the street and a position farther up the street. "It was almost at ground level, affording us only about eighteen inches of safe space over our prostrate bodies. The bits of tree were getting in our eyes and rendering seeing difficult. It was like being under a buzz saw in a sawmill!

"We did not dare to rise up and could hardly lift our heads to look ahead without being hit. During short breaks in the curtain of fire, we heard the shots of the guy in the house window above us. There was a continual 'whap-whap' right overhead." [19]

Stolp decided to try to throw a grenade through the second story window above him to knock out the unseen enemy. During a momentary lull in the machine gun fire, Stolp jumped to his feet and threw the grenade. "I remember feeling pretty good as I saw that the trajectory and alignment [of the grenade] was just right going in [the window]. At that very instant, Sergeant Baldry came staggering back toward us; he was standing straight up. His tongue was purple and sticking out about two feet it seemed. Blood was squirting out from under the collar of his jacket, which he was desperately trying to button up over the obviously gone neck! His eyes rolled back with only the whites showing and his head seemed to be falling off backwards. He lurched toward me. I screamed at him, 'Get down Baldry!' He was about to step into the line of bullets coming up the alley across the street.

"I was expecting a blast and anticipating a lot of junk coming out [of the window from the grenade's explosion] when, to my horror here came my grenade! Several seconds had already elapsed. It was timed to go off in three seconds, I believe. It was on its way back to me! I hollered 'Grenade!' to all and sundry around, and stared right at the damn thing, all the while expecting it to go off and take my life! My grenade had now landed near the house foundation.

"Sergeant Baldry fell at that moment, full length between the grenade and me. It went off.

"I don't remember much at that point, except I said to myself, 'If he wasn't dead already, that would surely have killed him.' I felt an intense relief it wasn't me. Then a great guilt assailed me. Another notch was cut into my already tattered nervous system.

"I didn't have time to think about it all. They were still shooting at us from the windows above. Why they couldn't seem to hit us, I cannot imagine. Just luck, I guess. We were surely a still and fixed target, not less than twenty feet away.

"I told my gunner to toss a grenade into the window. He stood up, rummaged around in his pockets like a man bemused and searching, peering slowly and rather 'lost like.' He found a grenade and still standing amongst the buzz saw, which was tearing up our tree, pulled the pin [and] the handle popped off. He held it out, looked at it as if expecting a message or something from it, and stepped back and lobbed it into the window.

"He watched it go. He had thrown it well and very hard. So, it must have cleared the shooters up there and hit the back wall of the small room. It had been held so long that it went off immediately. We got no more attention from that window! He dropped down again and resumed trying to become a part of the concrete beside me.

"Somewhere in this last sixty seconds or so, and right after Baldry died beside me, Mount came back staggering from the ill-fated machine gun position. He seemed to be 'out of it' entirely. His face was a lead mask of horror; his gait was almost a dream sequence. He walked past us, going to the rear. He was right on the sidewalk and walked right through the stream of fire that was barely passing over our prone bodies behind our tree. He did not seem to be hit, just shocked out of his mind." [20]

Staff Sergeant Michael Vuletich had seen Baldry's machine gun crew get shot. "The most heroic death witnessed by me in all of my war experience was Stoneking, killed behind his machine gun and set afire by a German machine pistol." [21]

As the remnants of the 1st and 3rd Platoons of Company B fought through town astride the highway running through Mook, two platoons from Company A launched an assault on Mook from the northeast. They attacked out of a wooded area across a wide-open field of about seventy-five yards, astride the Mookschebaan, a raised, causeway-like road that ran from northeast to southwest into Mook. The 2nd Platoon attacked to the left of the road, and the 1st Platoon guided on the right. Company A pathfinder Private Bob Murphy had been briefed that Company B was in a lot of trouble. "We were told we needed to go in there and overrun the Germans." [22]

Murphy, with the 2nd Platoon, was on the left side of the causeway-like road as the two platoons emerged from the wooded area and began their attack. "There was a lot of firing at us with machine guns and rifles. I was next to [Sergeant Charles L.] Chuck Burghduff, who was a pathfinder with me. [Lieutenant] Mike Chester said, 'OK guys, let's go.' And I turned to Burghduff and said, 'I'll . . .' and he got machine gunned up the side and killed." [23]

Private Murphy, an undefeated high school runner and hurdler "took off and ran across this open field, and when I went by this telephone pole I could hear the bullets whizzing by. I saw two Germans in the hole [behind the telephone pole]. I stopped, pulled a hand grenade out, threw it into the hole, and then ran like hell across straight ahead [toward Mook again]. When I got across the field, I saw about four guys inside a hedge up against a wall. These were American paratroopers. They identified themselves as B Company, 505.

"The rest of the guys from A Company came across [the field] and we really overwhelmed them. We went into Mook, through the houses to the left. My platoon went to the left; the other people went off to the right.

"There was no artillery or mortars. There was small-arms fire, rifle, and Schmeissers. It was all small-arms fire, hand-to-hand, man-to-man. Now, we took a lot of Germans [prisoner].

"I was loading my Thompson. I was putting another clip in, looking at my gun. A German came around the corner and belted me in the mouth with his rifle. I saw him and got hit at the same time. Apparently, he didn't have any rounds in his gun. [It] knocked part of my upper tooth out on the right hand side, chipped it. So, I disposed of him. I got the clip in and I fired." [24]

As the Company A attack reached the edge of Mook, Sergeant Bernard J. Tomardy, with the 1st Platoon, took cover at the corner of a house. "I remember a German lying on the ground about seventy-five yards in front of me shooting at an American on my right. I yelled for him to surrender. He didn't—there wasn't any other choice of what I had to do—so I shot him.

"I was wounded in the foot and stomach by a machine gun while climbing over an eight-foot anchor fence on the outskirts. I called one of the scouts from my squad and gave him my .45 automatic. I didn't feel any pain at this time, but knew I couldn't walk.

"A medic named Kelly Byars, from North Carolina, carried me over about six of those eight-foot anchor fences after I was wounded." [25]

The attack by the two Company A platoons relieved some of the pressure, but the situation was still critical. German paratroopers remained in the town in considerable strength. The 1st Platoon of Company A crossed the Mookschebaan and dug in on the slope overlooking Mook, while the 2nd Platoon, Company A, fought its way into town and linked up on the left flank of the 3rd Platoon, Company B.

The British tank platoon of the Coldstream Guards arrived, and at about 5:00 p.m., with the 3rd Platoon of Company B on the right side of the road, the 2nd Platoon of Company A on the left, and the British tanks moving down the road, attacked southeasterly through Mook in a furious hand-to-hand, house-to-house battle. The British tanks methodically blasted down houses containing enemy strongpoints.

Private Stolp was still pinned down at the same position in the street when he heard tanks coming down the road behind him. "A British tank came up our side of the street. It was blasting away with its .50-caliber and its cannon, and coming on quite fast. We were damned glad to hear and see it coming (for a couple of moments), as it would give us cover against the machine gun in the alley.

"We began to suffer from the counter fire directed from ahead of the tank. We were forced to squeeze, still behind our tree, by the fire coming down the sidewalk. This pushed me to have to crawl across the back of my partner. He seemed rooted to his spot. So, I crawled across and lay tucked up as far from the roadside as I could be, since he would not move a fraction of an inch!

"I was, in effect, lying rather out in the street. The tank seemed to feel its best path lay in skinning the bark off the street side of our tree. It came on steadily and [was] closing on our position. It would fire its cannon every few yards, apparently as fast as the gunner could reload. The .50 kept up an almost constant fire. It became more deafening with each second.

"Soon it was almost upon me where I lay at the street side. Each time it fired, the dirt and debris would lift, totally, cleanly off the street, and I with it. It made a clear space one could see through, moving the smoke and dust and all the debris that was in the air up and away for a second. Then it would slam all lifted objects back to earth with a tremendous force that knocked the wind out of me and dazed my eyeballs. The .50 kept hammering away. My ears were terribly painful, and I could only hear the guns.

"As the tank proceeded with this track and fire, it rolled so close to me that the extreme outer margin of its left track rolled onto the edge of the sleeve of my jacket. I felt nothing. My arm was spared somehow.

"The slamming effect of the cannon continued. The tank chose this spot to grind to a halt! My sleeve was still under the tread. I was about knocked out.

"It was at this point where the tank stopped with its tread pinning my sleeve to the pavement that I received the jolt of my life. A Panzerfaust impacted the right [other] side of the tank. It blew up the tank, and everything went with it." 26

The impact of the explosion blew Private Stolp into the building he was lying beside. "I found myself in the front, store portion of the house we had recently grenaded. I was erect as I recall and brushing glass shards off my jacket. I had my malfunctioning folding-stock carbine, a couple of bazooka rounds in their cases stuck in my belt somehow, and precious little else. I do not know to this day how I got there.

"Anyway, as long as I had somehow crossed the intersecting lines of fire and was in one piece in a house with the upper floor burning (and hopefully all dead enemies upstairs), I figured I had best continue and clean the house out. I charged stupidly but bravely through the doorway from the store part into the living quarters in the back. I recall there was something or someone just leaving. I felt, almost rather than saw, a jacket tail or something zip past the back door to the outside.

"At that moment my attention was drawn to a little can (like a tuna can) on the table, and some other clutter that looked as though someone had just hurriedly left off eating. I delayed my patrol to try the contents of the can. It was horrible stuff. I ate it. Probably, fortunately for me, there was only a very little left. I then went out the back door following the ghost that had zipped out as I came in. There was no one in sight." 27

The attack gained momentum, with the considerable help of the British tanks. Private Stolp and the other Company B troopers were finally able to move forward. "The rest of our attacking force to our west had reamed out the religious institution, crossed the damn alley, and silenced the endless fire that been keeping us pinned down at our side of town. The enemy force ahead of us had given some ground and pulled back a bit." 28

Stolp was about to uncover the mystery of how Sergeant Baldry's machine gun crew was shot. "I had cleaned out the house and gone around the back through the back door, then to the right and around the south side, which was where that insidious, ivy-covered brick wall started and continued out onto the street, which is just where (about four feet short of the street end) the wall window was. When Stoneking, Mount, and Baldry [had run] up and set the machine gun in the 'gas station' area, Stoneking was on the gun and was apparently 'sighting' with it.

"The Kraut behind the little vine covered brick wall window [had] waited until he [Stoneking] had his eye right up to the sight and poured a full burst of Schmeisser machine pistol right into his forehead. This totally hollowed out his skull, face, etc. and all, and his head dropped right down on and over the handle of the gun . . . it was totally inside his head. This guy had us all covered and could have stopped the whole drive right there. He wouldn't have been discovered till I had come around the house. It would have probably been the end of me right there . . . he had us cold. I believe he had killed all those who died there,

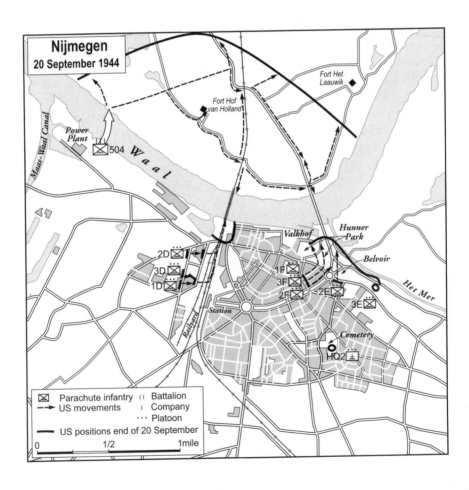

by himself. He then took Baldry next and then Mount. He couldn't hit me or my gunner because of the tree. He could, and did, hit everything else. We were totally unaware of his presence and therefore, could not have eliminated him. How I have always regretted that we did not detect him. What a target it would have made for our bazooka." [29]

As THE 504TH PIR WAS PREPARING for the Waal River crossing, Vandervoort's 2nd Battalion prepared for an assault to take the south ends of the highway and railroad bridges. The 3rd Platoon, Company E, reoccupied the buildings on Batavierenweg and the open ground facing the river that it had taken the previous evening, southeast of the highway bridge. The platoon was to stop a German counterattack from the east if it broke through the 508th PIR line. The plan called for the 1st Platoon, Company F, supported by two tanks, to attack Hunner Park from Walstraat on the left flank; the 3rd Platoon, Company F, to attack Hunner Park from Gerard Noodstraat in the center; and the 2nd Platoon, Company F, on the right would attack the traffic circle from Canisiustraat.

The 2nd Platoon, Company E, supported by two tanks, would attack from Graadt Van Roggenstraat due north toward the bridge approach. The 1st Platoon, Company E, from houses on Graadt Van Roggenstraat, as well the machine guns of Headquarters Company, 2nd Battalion, would provide cover fire.

However, Captain Robert Rosen, the commander of Company F, who had no combat experience prior to Holland, ordered a premature assault on Hunner Park without first informing or receiving permission from Lieutenant Colonel Vandervoort. Company F would make the attack without coordination with, nor help from, Company E and British armor.

With the 1st Platoon on Walstraat on the left, the 3rd Platoon on Gerard Noodtstraat in the center, and the 2nd Platoon on Canisiustraat on the right, Company F moved toward Hunner Park and the traffic circle. The 3rd Platoon passed through a section containing shops with large, plate glass windows, just as incoming heavy-caliber artillery could be heard. The troopers scrambled for cover in doorways of the shops as a shell exploded in the middle of the street. Deadly flying glass from shattered windows filled the air, and shrapnel wounded Lieutenant Jack Carroll, the 3rd Platoon leader. "I was wounded in the leg and taken out through the apartments by jeep and just escaped being captured." [30]

As Company F moved closer, 20mm fire whipped down the street, ricocheting off the wrought iron fences and hitting the brick fronts of the houses. It was just before 2:30 p.m., and Lieutenant Rusty Hays, the 2nd Platoon assistant platoon leader, was about to get his baptism of fire. "Soon we had the whole company in the front and back yards of the houses just across the street from the park, the company objective.

"About that time, the company commander comes up, swings his Tommy gun around his head, and shouts, 'Follow me!' and runs across the side street into the park. About twenty men—those that were nearby, and who heard him—followed him.

"As I started to follow him, I looked to my left and saw two Germans, carrying a machine gun, come out of the door from the stone wall about two hundred yards to my left. They put it down on the street and began to get in position to fire it. I stopped in the middle of the street and fired at them with my Tommy gun. Since a Tommy gun fires pistol ammunition, the Germans were a little too far away for accuracy, but they heard the slugs hitting around them and ducked back inside the stone door, leaving the machine gun sitting in the street.

"Since the machine gun was still a threat, I stopped in the middle of the street and looked around for a bazooka man who was nearby. I told him to fire into the door where the Germans had come from. When the bazooka round exploded in the door, I knew we had seen the last of those two Germans, even if we hadn't hit them. They wouldn't dare come out again." [31]

As this took place, Sergeant Spencer Wurst led his squad forward as the company poured out of the houses. "We got to the street and started into the park under direct small-arms, grenade, and machine gun fire at ranges of fifteen to seventy-five yards. We formed a crude line on the run and assaulted across the street. The enemy was well dug in, fighting from foxholes and trenches located between the sidewalk on back to a hundred yards into the park.

"Just as we got into the skirmish line, a crucial thing happened. A very big, scared German soldier—I only saw him flash in my mind—leaped up from a foxhole just inside the park. He lifted his hands up over his head as he ran across the sidewalk toward us. There was absolutely no doubt about his intentions. He had his hands up high over his head, very evidently wanting to surrender. But as he leaped up, many men fired on him. In combat you must react instinctively and quickly. This is what we did, and the man was practically a sieve before he hit the ground." [32]

This happened in plain sight of the SS grenadiers defending Hunner Park, who now believed the paratroopers were not going to take prisoners. Wurst and some of the troopers made it into the edge of the park. "I don't know how many men from either platoon made it across the street on the first assault, but we took many casualties. I got across and into the park. Just before I took cover, I saw Captain Rosen run back down the middle of the street. He passed me going full speed to the rear, holding both his hands over his mouth. He had evidently been shot through the face." [33]

With that, the attack fell apart—before Lieutenant Hays could follow them into the park. "The men who had gone into the park came running back, many of them wounded. The company commander was hit in the face and died just as he got back to my side of the street. A couple of more wounded came back, and then the man who asked me to get him out of the stockade so he could make the jump with us ran up to me and pointed to a wound in his chest and said, 'Quick, put a tourniquet on it.' Just as I grabbed him, he died.

"As we looked into the park, we could see one of our men on the ground, with a medic bandaging him. Finally, the medic came trotting back and said the man was still alive but would soon die from loss of blood if we didn't get him soon. Another officer and I dropped weapons and ran over to get him. I'm sure the Germans saw us, but didn't fire because we were there to pick up our wounded. The other officer grabbed his shoulders and I grabbed his feet. As I did, he opened his eyes. We carried him out of the park. I presumed he lived; I never heard from him again." 34

In fifteen minutes, F Company had lost five killed and two seriously wounded. The executive officer, Lieutenant Joseph W. "Little Joe" Holcomb, a veteran officer, highly respected among the men, assumed command of Company F. The troopers cleaned and reloaded their weapons, brought up more ammunition, and prepared for the next attack they knew would come very soon.

Shortly before 4:00 p.m., as the 3rd Battalion, 504th, was making its epic crossing of the Waal River, Lieutenant Colonel Vandervoort got the orders for which he and his battalion had been waiting. "Finally, it was decided to 'go for the bridge.' General Adair ordered a coordinated paratrooper/tank attack to put his armor over the Waal. Our company commanders and key officers gathered at the battalion observation post. Toward the north, from windows twenty feet above street level, we looked down into Hunner Park crowded with enemy emplacements. The park was the place the great bridge would be won or lost. We held the high ground, the good ground, from which to launch our attack. The smooth sloping area was, as I remember, a little less than one quarter of a mile deep and a little more than that wide. A 'bare-assed' prospect, somebody observed. There was no concealment, and firepower would be the only cover when we moved. E Company on the right and F Company on the left would assault the park. They would hit the park simultaneously with Goulburn's tanks, all moving together and try to finish it fast." 35

After receiving the attack order, Lieutenant Holcomb told his platoon leaders that the attack would commence at 4:20 p.m. Time seemed to stand still as Sergeant Wurst waited for the signal to begin the attack. "As we got ready to go for the second attempt, Lieutenant Holcomb calmly walked out on the street and gave the order to assault." 36

At 4:20 p.m. Company E's 1st Platoon and a section of the light machine gun platoon of Headquarters Company, 2nd Battalion, opened fire from the roofs and upper story windows of houses fronting the park and the traffic circle, into the trenches, gun pits, and buildings occupied by the enemy. Vandervoort's paratroopers moved out to assault Hunner Park, the traffic circle, and southern end of the bridge. Veteran Company F trooper Corporal W. A. Jones, Wurst's assistant squad leader, did not want a repeat of the earlier attack that had failed. "Everybody went in with the idea that we were not going to pull back. If they take us back, they're going to have to carry us back." 37

The Germans held their fire until everyone was exposed in the street, then the whole area exploded with the fire from almost six hundred trained infantrymen firing every available automatic weapon and rifle. The paratroopers fired from the hip as they ran forward. Tracers—waist high, chest high, head high, and a foot or so off the ground—crisscrossed the park and traffic circle. The firing was at almost point-blank range—25 to 150 yards. Plunging fire from enemy paratroopers firing machine guns from the upper-floor windows of the Villa Belvoir and SS gunners from the Valkhof filled the air. [38]

Corporal Jones had never experienced anything like the volume of fire in the park that day. "It was tremendously heavy . . . machine guns, 20mms, 88s, everything. The wall along the left, they had taken out bricks and put machine guns in the portholes." [39]

German snipers targeted anyone displaying signs of leadership. Lieutenant Hays ran forward into the park firing his Thompson submachine gun as he went. "Everywhere I looked men were falling. . . . I saw the new company commander [Lieutenant Holcomb] fall; a bullet had gone into the front of his helmet and had come out the back. 'He has to be dead,' I thought." [40]

Just minutes later, Lieutenant Bill Savell, commanding F Company's 2nd Platoon, was shot through both arms. The 3rd Platoon leader, Lieutenant Jack Carroll, had already been wounded seriously by artillery fire that morning. Company F was rapidly running out of officers.

Vandervoort watched from an observation post in a nearby building as the attack moved forward. "First Lieutenant John Dodd of [the 1st Platoon of] F Company was killed leading his platoon in the attack. A fine fighter, he was hit in the torso by an exploding 20mm cannon shell. It was a mortal wound that should have killed him instantly, but he was a hard dying young man.

"His platoon aid man, with tears in his eyes, gave his dying lieutenant an overdose of morphine to ease his pain. His platoon attacked the Kraut gun crew that killed their lieutenant. Furious, they gave no quarter, and the gun crew stood its ground." [41]

Private Wayne Galvin, with Company F, witnessed the attack on that gun crew. "Sergeant [Vernon L.] Francisco, being so upset about Lieutenant Dodd, stood right out in the open, throwing grenades at the Germans." [42]

Company F trooper Private First Class Robert R. Hughart was quickly pinned down by enemy machine gun and 20mm fire as he entered the park. "We lost our platoon medic [Private First Class Vernon D. Carnes]. He was lying on the ground beside me—a white tracer hit him in the left side of his chest." [43]

Sergeant James T. Steed, the Company F communications NCO, tried to help one of the badly wounded troopers, a "European kid who had served in the armies of four countries and spoke seven languages. He was very religious and so proud to be an American. He prayed and I yelled for a medic, but none came—there were too many wounded. He died with his head in my lap." [44]

Lieutenant J. J. Smith, commanding Company E, watched the 2nd Platoon, led by Lieutenant Nicholas J. Psaki, supported by two tanks, move out of the buildings toward the highway bridge approach. "Covered by automatic weapons fire from the 1st Platoon, the attacking echelon moved out with fixed bayonets. A hand-to-hand battle followed in which the 2nd Platoon men had to literally drive the Germans from their holes with grenades and cold steel." [45]

That afternoon, incredible courage was almost commonplace. Private Camille E. Gagne, a rifle grenadier with Company E, in position on the roof of a building overlooking the highway bridge approach, fired grenade after grenade at the

German mortar positions, preventing them from having direct observation of the attacking elements of the two companies. His fire was so devastating that an enemy Mark IV self-propelled gun fired at him from only four hundred yards away. Gagne courageously kept firing, helping to cut off the retreat of many of the Germans hoping to escape over the highway bridge.

Private First Class Clyde Knox, a Company E medic, saw German artillery zero in on the building that Gagne and three others occupied. "A German 88 gun crew spotted them—after the first round landed close by, they moved off the top of the building into a small shack. Corporal [Clifford W.] Putnam, who was the squad leader, said, 'The only way they will hit us now is by a direct hit.' A direct hit came in demolishing the building, killing Private [Robert E.] Nurse and Private Gagne, and wounding Private Paul C. Trotman and Corporal Putnam." [46]

Gagne posthumously received the Silver Star for his gallantry.

German artillery, direct fire from high-velocity antiaircraft and antitank guns across the river, and long-range machine gun fire hit the 3rd Platoon, Company E, troopers in the open ground southeast of the bridge, severely wounding Private First Class James E. Keenan. "I was hit in five places, including a nerve separation wound in my right ankle by a 240mm airburst. [Private First Class] Ed Arndt, at the risk of his life, came down the ravine into which I was blown, and carried me bodily up the steep incline into cover." [47]

Lieutenant Colonel Vandervoort was very thankful to have the tanks from the British Grenadier Guards supporting his troopers. "With those Shermans bearing down on them, the Germans aimed most of their fire at the tanks. Otherwise, more of the troopers would have been wiped out. Bullets bounced off Shermans like hailstones. Some were chipped, but none were holed. The Germans, stiffened by elements of the 9th SS Recon Battalion, kept firing full bore until overrun. Moving with the troopers, the tanks rolled over trenches and fired point blank into air raid shelters. It was 'walking fire' with tanks—the effect was devastating. The air in Hunner Park turned blue with hand grenade, cannon, rifle, and gun smoke generated by hundreds of combatants." [48]

In Hunner Park, Company F troopers were getting enfilade fire from the Valkhof ruins on their left flank as they moved forward. Lieutenant Hays was one of the few officers left in Company F by this time. "I realized something had to be done or all our men would be killed. To our left was a fifteen-foot stone wall; somehow it had to be coming from there. I looked behind me, and there in the street was a British tank. I ran back, banged on the tank with my Tommy gun, and climbed upon the tank. The tank commander stuck his head out. I told him my men were being slaughtered and we needed help. He was reluctant to leave his position. I begged him to come help, and finally he agreed.

"Before I jumped down from the tank, he handed me a bottle of brandy and said, 'Here, you need some of this.' I must have looked as shook up as I felt. I don't remember if I took his brandy or not, but I did direct him into the park.

"When he got there he said, 'What do I shoot at?'

"I said, 'I don't know. That wall must have something to do with this; shoot at that wall.' I thought at the time, it sounded pretty silly; but I didn't know what else to say.

"He may have fired his machine guns; I know he didn't fire his cannon; but suddenly the firing stopped. Later, I learned that the stone wall was a retaining wall for the ground in the old fort and the ground was flush with the top of the wall. The Germans had dug a trench along the top and were firing at us from point-blank range. The reason the firing stopped was that the British infantry had captured the fort." [49]

The fire coming straight at the paratroopers in the park did not subside, however. If anything, it increased as the troopers closed in on the SS grenadiers. The firing became so heavy that Sergeant Spencer Wurst took cover behind a tree. "From behind my tree, I observed [Howard R.] Krueger as he crawled fifteen or twenty feet to my right front. He actually reached down into a foxhole, grabbed a German, and pulled him out. He motioned the prisoner to the rear, and both of them crawled back to our skirmish line. The German didn't stop; he crawled another twenty feet and stopped to help our medic bandage one of our wounded. Very shortly thereafter, he was killed by German fire.

"I glanced to my right rear and saw Colonel Vandervoort, our battalion commander, approaching my position. Our dead and wounded were lying all around us, hit only moments earlier. We pleaded with the CO not to expose himself to the heavy fire, but he continued until he reached my position. He looked at me and calmly said, 'Sergeant, I think you better go see if you can get that tank moving.'" [50]

The tank that Hays used to suppress the fire from the Valkhof was still at the edge of the park, the commander justifiably concerned about 88mm guns and Panzerfausts.

Corporal W. A. Jones even witnessed 88s firing at individuals. "There was one 88 in the park and one down by the bridge. If you stuck your head up they would fire that thing at you." [51]

Sergeant Wurst asked Vandervoot to take cover, then jumped up and ran through a blizzard of fire to the tank. Wurst beat on the turret with his helmet and the tank commander once again raised the hatch. "I hollered to the tank commander, relating the colonel's order to move forward and continue firing. We talked a minute or two, and I pointed out targets. While I was showing him where he should shoot, I had to remain standing. Finally the tank lumbered forward, and I gave arm and hand signals to what was left of my squad to get up and start moving." [52]

Corporal Jones jumped to his feet and started forward, raking the holes and trenches with his Thompson as he advanced beside the tank. "We just kept going. Some of the Germans stayed in their holes, and some of them saw we weren't going to stop and left their guns and tried to run." [53] Jones and the others mercilessly cut them down as they ran.

Sergeant Wurst and his men came to a barbed-wire entanglement that ran through the middle of the park. "We wanted the tank to move through to make a path. Instead, it advanced a little to our left front. We went to the right and had a real time getting through the wire. [Larry] Niepling, with a shortened belt of ammo, was actually firing his light .30 caliber machine gun from the standing position as he moved through the wire." [54]

Sergeant Wurst's squad was the first to break through to the far side of Hunner Park. "When we got on the east side of the barbed wire, we dropped into a well constructed, World War I–type trench the Germans had dug. From here we had a good view that overlooked the approach road, the entrance to the bridge, and the bridge itself. I heard some shouted commands from my distant left rear that I later learned was British infantry moving up by the numbers." [55]

Vandervoort watched his paratroopers close with Germans fighting for their lives with the intensity of cornered animals. "'No-quarter' combat became the order of the day throughout that quarter-mile-square area. The fighting was so close, individual Germans were either too brave or too scared to surrender—probably both. The Germans seemed indifferent to death. The paratroopers retaliated with ice-cold ruthlessness. That gladiatorial test of wills gave a shocking crescendo to the battle. The British Shermans gave the troopers the cumulative edge. Position by position, the trooper/tank collaboration closed down Hunner Park. The enemy finally broke and ran east and west. Others were driven into the Waal." [56]

Sergeant Wurst and his men caught the Germans attempting to escape. "As we dropped down into the trench, groups of Germans started to withdraw across the bridge, taking cover behind the girders. This was a bad move. We had seized the high ground overlooking the bridge and had a perfect view. As soon as they dashed to the next girder, we had them. There were thirty or so to start, but I don't believe a single one got across.

"Right after, another group of Germans came from our left. This group was pretty smart. They rushed up the left side of the bank all together, went over the top, across the road, and down on the right side of the road that led to the bridge. There was a large drop-off on the east side of the road, so they gained the cover of the roadbed. They took us by surprise and got away with it." [57]

This group of about sixty Germans led by SS Captain Euling was the only one to escape. A few individuals were able to make it across the highway bridge. Of the six hundred or so, mostly SS grenadiers and German paratroopers, who defended the south side of the highway bridge, only about sixty were taken prisoner, and about sixty in Captain Euling's group escaped in the darkness east along the south bank of the Waal. Vandervoort's veteran troopers and the Grenadier Guards killed or mortally wounded the remainder.

As the fighting around the southern approach of the highway bridge wound down, Vandervoort's troopers and British Guards infantry mopped up small pockets of Germans. Private First Class Ken Russell and three Company F buddies were "standing, watching our last medic [Technician Fifth Grade Lloyd G. Ellingson] doctoring one of our guys, when an SS trooper near the rubble of the castle (that we thought a rabbit couldn't live in) dashed by us and shot the medic and killed him. It was such a surprise that we all opened up on him as he ran over the hill and killed him." [58]   Private Michael A. Brilla was one of the troopers who opened up on the German. "I have never seen so many tracers from our machine guns go through one man before he hit the ground." [59]

One of the SS prisoners taken at Hunner Park was a paymaster who Private First Class Bob Hughart said "had about twenty thousand dollars in German Marks in a briefcase. We could not use the money of course—but made it do for toilet paper." [60]

During the assault, a mortar shell had wounded Company F trooper Private Wayne W. Galvin. "My left wrist was shattered—I was also hit in the left thigh. I stayed for several more hours, then was helping to escort some prisoners back when my leg gave out." [61]

The scene in Hunner Park and the traffic circle was ghastly. German corpses and mortally wounded were lying half in their trenches and foxholes where they had been bayoneted or shot. Wounded and dead troopers littered the landscape, with weapons and the debris of war strewn everywhere. Despite German artillery fire falling just south of the bridge, the Grenadier Guards commander, Lieutenant Colonel Edward Goulburn, ordered a troop of four Sherman tanks led by Sergeant Peter Robinson to cross the great highway bridge. Everyone fully expected the bridge to be blown any moment. From his observation post in a building on the south side of the highway bridge, Vandervoort had a front row seat to watch Robinson's four tanks cross the bridge. "As Sergeant Robinson's lead Sherman approached the midpoint of the bridge, from dead ahead, an 88mm antitank gun opened fire. It should have been a mismatch. One or more tanks, knocked out, could block the bridge. Our tanks stopped and returned fire.

Vandervoort continued, "The lead Sherman fired its cannon as fast as it could load and sprayed the road ahead with its .30-caliber machine gun. The 88 fired half a dozen—more or less—near misses, ripping and screaming with an unforgettable sound—past the turret of the tank. In the gathering dusk they looked like great Roman candle balls of fire. Brightly glowing, 17-pounder cannon shots rocketed back along with flashing machine gun tracers. Suddenly, the 88 went silent. One of the tanks' .30-caliber armor-piercing rounds had penetrated the soft metallic end cap of the 88's recoil mechanism, causing the gun to jam. That improbable, long-odds happenstance of good marksmanship and good luck ended the shoot-out on the bridge." [62]

As Robinson's Shermans continued across, German General Heinz Harmel, commander of the 10th SS Panzer Division, looked through his binoculars from a concrete pillbox northeast of the bridge near Lent. Lieutenant General Wilhelm Bittrich, commanding the II SS Panzer Korps, had been ordered by Field Marshal Walter Model not to blow the bridge. Harmel was determined not to allow the bridge to fall into Allied hands. He didn't want to be brought to Berlin to be executed for allowing the British to cross the Waal River. When he saw Robinson's tank reach the center of the bridge, Harmel gave the order to the engineer waiting nearby to push the plunger on the detonator. "Get ready . . . Let it blow!" [63]

Nothing happened. "'Again!' I was waiting to see the bridge collapse and the tanks plunge into the river. Instead, they moved relentlessly, getting bigger and bigger, closer and closer." 64

Harmel turned to his staff and said, "My God, they'll be here in two minutes. Stolley, tell Bittrich. They're over the Waal." 65

Robinson's tanks linked up with 3rd Battalion, 504th PIR troopers, who held the northern end of the bridges. At around 7:15 p.m., the highway bridge was firmly in Allied hands. German artillery pummeled the southern approaches to the highway bridge in order to interdict troops crossing to reinforce the bridgehead. Heavy German shelling that evening effectively prevented British infantry from crossing the highway bridge.

The attack to capture the two bridges had been costly for the 2nd Battalion. Company F lost seventeen killed and twenty-three wounded in the two days of the attack on the bridges. Company E suffered nine killed and twenty-five wounded.

Company F trooper Private Donald W. McKeage was one of the extremely fortunate individuals who was not killed or wounded in the assault on Hunner Park. "The park was covered with dead and wounded Germans; the road was covered with our dead and wounded." 66

McKeage noticed that the citizens of Nijmegen began to appear from their cellars, even as German artillery fell just north at the bridge approach. "They had blankets and flowers for our dead troopers. They didn't show the same respect for the dead Krauts; they kicked the hell out of some of them." 67

The railroad bridge was also in Allied hands as the Germans defending the southern approaches to it stampeded across the bridge when the 3rd Battalion, 504th PIR, successfully crossed the Waal River, threatening to cut off their path of retreat. As they fled across the railroad bridge, nineteen troopers with the 3rd Battalion, 504th, opened up on them. The next morning, 267 dead Germans were counted on the bridge.

On the evening of September 20, Company D moved across the railroad bridge and moved into a nearby factory building. Captain Taylor G. Smith moved Lieutenant Charles Qualls to executive officer, replacing Lieutenant Wray, and gave Lieutenant Joe Meyers command of the 3rd Platoon. The responsibility of guarding the railroad bridge that night was assigned to Lieutenant Meyers and his platoon. "[Sergeant Edward F.] Murphy, my platoon sergeant, and I deployed one rifle squad under Sergeant Donald Olds to secure the south approach, Sergeant [Milton E.] Schlesener's squad to guard the north approach. In addition, we placed a guard in a sentry box located in the center of the bridge. The balance of the platoon remained at the factory, prepared to relieve the deployed squads if we remained in position for any length of time. Murphy and I took turns inspecting the positions at night." 68

THAT EVENING IN MOOK, THE 3RD PLATOON, Company B, and the 2nd Platoon, Company A, dug in for the night. The Germans pulled out during the night, moving south across the flats. A resupply of ammunition and three days of rations were sent in that night. Private Northam Stolp and some of his B Company squad dug in inside an apple orchard. "We seemed to be pinned down and [were] ordered to stay put. It had grown quite dark and now the entire town was ablaze. Virtually every house was afire! The orange glow was undulating and a nauseating smell, something like the fondly remembered smell of burning leaves in the fall, began to permeate the entire area. But, it wasn't pleasant like my memories of fall burnings had always been. There was something else in it and it subconsciously raised the hair on our necks." [69]

The troopers were exhausted and hungry, as the rations had not yet reached them. As Stolp and the others in his squad were reflecting on the loss of their friends earlier, a horrifying sound suddenly brought them back to an alert state of consciousness. "Whatever it was out there was coming. What in the hell was it? All at once we knew what we were sensing. It was a blood chilling sound. It was a sound the likes of which none of us has heard before or since (thank God). It was coming out of the wall of flames to our right front. From the little passageway on the unseen grassy trail to our right front, came a clot of humanity such as you've never seen! It was a formless mass, undulating, screaming, moaning in pure terror.

"People were staggering, falling, trying to run . . . their clothing was in some places afire, [and] they were carrying anything you can imagine. Many were men, many were little children, girls and boys of every age. Mothers carrying little babies and blankets . . . as smaller children clung to their dresses and were dragged, screaming and crying, along. All were screaming and hollering at the top of their lungs. Those with fire on them fell and rolled about in an agony and then got up to run toward us again.

"And now, we began to realize what the burning smell was! Many people had delayed trying to flee the battle and taken refuge in the holes they had dug in their basements. They were literally being cremated in their own homes! I still have trouble in the fall when the leaves are burned and the smoke pall hangs heavy in the light fog of a fall evening. You get no medals or Purple Heart for such wounds." [70]

THE 82ND AIRBORNE DIVISION, short one of its four infantry regiments, had, in the same day, withstood counterattacks along its thinly held, very long perimeter, while making an assault river crossing against superior numbers of the enemy and, with the support of the British armor and infantry, captured the two bridges over the Waal River intact. The 2nd Battalion was awarded the Presidential Unit Citation for its actions in the capture of the two Nijmegen bridges.

WORD SPREAD OF THE 82ND AIRBORNE DIVISION'S great feat of arms on September 20, 1944, as eyewitness accounts by Generals Browning, Adair, and Horrocks made their way to General Sir Miles Dempsey, commander of the British Second Army, who visited Gavin at the Champion CP on September 23. As Dempsey entered, Gavin saluted and Dempsey returned the salute, extending his hand and saying, "I'm proud to meet the commanding general of the finest division in the world today." [71]

CHAPTER 16

"Boy, I Feel Sorry For The First Germans Those Guys Get A Hold Of"

arly on the morning of September 21, Lieutenant Joe Meyers checked on his Company D platoon, which was responsible for security of the railroad bridge. "I took a stroll across the bridge, stopped to talk to the men on duty, and ended up at [Sergeant Donald H.] Olds' position on the south end. Olds had occupied the German flak crew's quarters in the stone bridge keep. He invited me to join the off-duty members of his squad for coffee and some abandoned German rations. After our meal, Olds and I walked outside the keep and stopped briefly to talk.

"Someone sounded the alarm when three German fighters suddenly appeared downstream, flying in our direction about fifteen or twenty feet above the water. As they neared the railroad bridge, the planes pulled up, dropped their bombs, and cleared the bridge by a few feet. Not one bomb hit the bridge. However, the upward force of the explosions blew away forty or fifty feet of train rail and decking from the bridge's center span. Although twisted and bent, the I-beams that supported the missing rails and decking remained intact.

"Olds and I ran to the edge of the decking and looked down about fifty or sixty feet to the water below. Although jumping out of an airplane did not bother men, walking on a twisted steel girder, sixty feet in the air, was a frightening experience. Olds and I negotiated the twisted beams and safely reached the far side. The sentry box was intact, but there was no sign of the guard. We ran to the box and found the sentry seated inside unharmed, but stunned by the explosions. Although badly shaken and hard of hearing, he was able to walk around after a few minutes.

"The German attempt to destroy the bridges indicated the importance they attached to the structures. I deployed the balance of my platoon to defend it." [1]

German infantry, supported by a flak-wagon and a tank, made an all-out attack on Riethorst and Mook at 1:00 p.m. later that day. Company A officers, Captain John Dolan, Lieutenant George Presnell, and Lieutenant Mike Chester, were at the battalion command post when the attack began. Borrowing a jeep, they took off for Mook. On their way, the jeep ran over a landmine and they were blown from the vehicle. All three were evacuated. Presnell and Chester would return after the Holland campaign, but Dolan was sent to the United States for treatment and wouldn't return to Company A. Captain James Cockrell, the commander of Regimental Headquarters Company, was transferred to take command of Company A.

The attack that afternoon was broken up by the 1st Battalion troopers and massive artillery support. The 456th PFA Battalion fired 566 rounds, reinforced by fire from the 376th PFA Battalion and a battery of British artillery.

The following day, the 2nd Battalion moved from Nijmegen to west of Groesbeek and went into reserve. Lieutenant Harold E. Case also took command of Company F. About 5:00 p.m., the Germans made another attack in the 1st Battalion sector and were repulsed.

On September 23, the 1st Battalion was relieved at Mook by the 2nd Battalion and consolidated its strength defending Riethorst. The 325th GIR landed that afternoon and moved up to relieve the 505th the next morning. The withdrawal by the 1st Battalion was made under heavy sniper and mortar fire. Several troopers with Company C were hit as it moved off of the hill. Lieutenant Richard Brownlee, with Company C, was waiting to receive orders when "one of my men by the name of [Private First Class Raymond] Gonzales asked permission to go back along the ridge we had just left to pick up the wounded we had left and remove them back to the hill. I told him I would not ask him to go, but if he wanted to at his own risk, and would join us later, 'All right.'" [2]

Gonzales returned to the hill where he found Private Walter Faranfontoff had died of his wound and Lyman L. "Lee" Baier, who had been hit in the back, but was still alive. Gonzales carried the badly wounded Baier on his back under fire to safety. While he was carrying Baier, Gonzales "met a Mexican boy who had lost his kneecap and begged me not to leave him there. I picked him up and carried him about a quarter of a mile." [3]

Gonzales then reported back to his squad. Brownlee was shocked when he saw him. "I thought he had been seriously wounded. He was covered with blood from top to bottom and physically beat. He told me he had not been hit, but it was blood from the men he had carried back from the hill. All of the time he was working with and carrying these men back for medical help, he was under fire. Both [Gensemer] and I tried to get him his country's highest honor for this action, but he had to settle for—I believe—the Bronze Star. We didn't have enough rank." [4]

LATER ON THE MORNING OF SEPTEMBER 24, the 505th moved to Nijmegen to guard the two bridges across the Waal River.

From September 21 to 24, the British could not force a crossing over the Rhine River and had to evacuate the remnants of the British 1st Airborne Division from the north side of the river. Of more than ten thousand officers and men who had jumped and landed by glider north of the Rhine, only about twenty-four hundred came back across the river.

Lieutenant Bill Mastrangelo, with Company G, watched "the British Red Devil Division (what was left of it) coming out of Arnhem, passing through my platoon, were very despondent, and would not respond to our greetings. Then I remembered thinking, 'Hell, they shouldn't be angry at us; we did our job.' I knew they were an excellent division, but after taking a beating and not actually accomplishing their mission, they were very disheartened. I remember feeling very badly about their condition." 5

Operation Market-Garden had failed, but not because of the fighting the three airborne divisions and the Polish brigade had done. The situation in Holland now settled into defensive static warfare, with the next month and a half marked by night patrol actions and sharp local attacks by both sides.

During the five days and nights in which the 505th guarded the Nijmegen bridges, the Germans shelled the highway bridge sporadically to interdict traffic. On the night of September 24–25, Lieutenant Gus Sanders, a platoon leader with Company C, heard firing from a listening post in front of his platoon's position. "Private [Sonnie J. "Rocky"] Rockford was killed protecting us from being overrun by some German paratroopers. They slipped up on us, and Rocky fought them until the last. We later found his body, with his knife stuck in his back, after being killed by German rifle fire. Many of our men gave their lives for their buddies in the 82nd, without a thought of their own safety." 6

On September 26, Private First Class Chet Harrington, one of the Company A medics, was called upon to come to the aid of a trooper, Private First Class Lee E. Shawver, who had been seriously wounded by shrapnel. "His right leg was off—his left leg was shattered below the knee. Sergeant [Fay C.] McIntyre and I pulled him back, carefully. We put tourniquets on him. But he went into shock, and we couldn't save him.

"I felt bad about losing him—I had known him since Sicily." 7

That same day, the 3rd Battalion moved to a sector southeast of Groesbeek and relieved the 2nd Battalion, 401st GIR.

At 8:00 p.m. on September 28, the British army relieved the regiment of responsibility for the bridges, and the 505th moved back to the Groesbeek area the following day. At 5:00 a.m. the next morning, September 29, after the regiment was relieved, German frogmen who had floated down the Waal River detonated explosive charges at both bridges. They dropped the southern span of the railroad bridge into the Waal River and blew a hole in part of the road surface of the highway bridge, but it remained usable and was repaired.

On September 29, a young lieutenant, Asa T. Hancock, recently assigned as a replacement with Lieutenant Bill Mastrangelo's platoon, Company G, approached Mastrangelo. Hancock insisted "on gaining experience, saying, 'How else will I become a combat officer, and besides, I want a German Luger.'" 8

Mastrangelo reluctantly let him lead a patrol going out that night. "On patrol, he and ten men were ambushed by German machine guns. Nine or ten men [were] killed or wounded. He was himself killed." 9

On October 1, the regiment was alerted to expect a heavy German attack that night. At midnight, heavy artillery, 88mm fire, and Nebelwerfers ("Screaming Meemies") began blasting the sector east of Groesbeek held by the 3rd Battalion. At 1:30 a.m., enemy tanks and paratroopers surged toward the roadblocks on the left flank of the sector at Kamp and the center east of Groesbeek. Private Charles

Barnhart, a bazooka gunner with Company H, was one of the troopers defending the H Company roadblock. "They started across a white gravel road. I thought it would be a good time to use the bazooka to see if it would do any good."[10] Barnhart fired the bazooka, hitting one of the Germans crossing the road and detonating. He and his assistant held off a group of German paratroopers, even though Barnhart was wounded by three rounds from a Schmeisser submachine gun and suffered a punctured lung. [11]

German tanks and infantry broke through the roadblock and moved toward the Companies G and H main line of resistance. Waiting on them were the veterans of four combat jumps. One of the Company H troopers, Sergeant Norbert Beach, got the word from one of the outposts that the Germans were approaching. "We had six [.30-caliber] machine guns, plus a .50-caliber machine gun in our company. We knew the Germans were coming, let them get within one hundred or so yards, fired flares to light up the area, and opened up with everything we had." [12]

The 456th fired fifty-six missions, targeting enemy artillery, Nebelwerfers, tanks, and infantry, while the 3rd Battalion committed its reserve and counterattacked the Germans at the Kamp roadblock. Colonel Ekman personally led this counterattack, which resulted in the capture of forty-one enemy paratroopers, who had taken shelter in houses and cellars. By dawn, Ekman's troopers had broken the back of the German assault.

The sunlight revealed bodies of German paratroopers strewn in front of Sergeant Beach's position. "The German medics raised the white flag and wanted permission to pick up their dead and wounded. This was granted." [13]

The next morning, Private Barnhart was still at the roadblock, where he saw the result of his bazooka round that had hit a German paratrooper and detonated the previous night. "It had hit down by his knee, and there were three of them there—the one in the middle had his leg torn up, and the men on each side of him must have had concussion, because they were dead and no holes in them." [14]

During the Sicily, Italy, and Normandy campaigns Major Doc McIlvoy, the regimental surgeon, had witnessed numerous acts of courage by his men. But he was particularly inspired by the bravery of Captain Alexander P. "Pete" Suer. McIlvoy watched Suer take one of the jeeps with a Red Cross flag on it and "swap German wounded for our own wounded boys picked up by the Germans." [15] Captain Suer was Jewish and, therefore, particularly at risk when he approached German lines with his jeep load of German wounded.

After the German attack of October 1–2, Private First Class Russell W. Fischer, with Company G, was catching some sleep in his foxhole after fighting all night. "I heard the word 'Soldaten—Soldaten,' and I looked up and a big German was looking down at me. I just about passed out. I looked at my rifle and at my knife, but either way, I figured I was a goner. Then he said, 'Kamerad,' and shoved a paper at me. I took it and read it. It was a safe conduct pass, which would guarantee him safety if he gave up. These leaflets had been dropped that [previous] night by bombers. I was really never so glad to read something in my life." [16]

On the 3rd of October Private First Class Dave Bowman and his assistant gunner, Private Frank Aguerrebere, were manning a .30-caliber machine gun along the edge of the Kiekberg Woods being shelled occasionally by German artillery and mortar fire. Around noon, Bowman saw a couple of troopers approaching their position. "Lieutenant [Tom] McClean and Private Ulysses [S.] Emerick came by carrying binoculars, clipboards, etcetera, and informed us they would be forward of our position. In other words, hold fire until they returned. Several minutes passed with no shelling, then a mortar shell exploded to the front, closer than usual. Less than a minute passed after that when Lieutenant McClean appeared, blood-splattered and visibly shaken, exclaiming that Emerick had been killed." [17] Lieutenant McClean had suffered severe wounds to his chest and arms, and was later evacuated to the United States.

On the night of October 5, Sergeant Bill Blank, with Company G, was at his platoon's command post. "Our ammunition started to get low and we had to fire only at sure targets. We had an outpost in a house in front of our lines. A call was received from them—they said the Germans were coming and asked if they should fire at them. They were asked how far away [the Germans] were. No answer came back, and the house was set afire." [18]

The outpost, manned by Privates Elmer J. Baker, Jack R. Busch, and Callies LaBlanc, was overrun. Private Baker was killed, and Privates Busch and LaBlanc were captured.

With the house still burning, Sergeant Blank was asked to take a patrol out to capture a prisoner. "With the burning building and the moonlight, it made movement very difficult. We spotted a great deal of German activity along our front, so we crawled down a small ditch about eight to ten inches deep toward the Germans. On the way down, we heard the sounds of the Germans moving the bolt back and forth on a machine gun off to our left.

"We moved down the road where we had seen the German movement, but all was quiet at this time. I was in the ditch on the side of the road, and my men were to the rear and right rear. After what seemed a long time, we spotted two Germans in the shadows off to our left, obviously on guard.

"One of my men began to cough, and the guards moved over to check. One of the guards got in the ditch with me up the road, and the other one came down the middle of the road directly in front of me. He was carrying a bolt-action rifle. I tried to get him to put his hands up. On my third try, he fired from the hip at me and started to run. He was hit at least thirty times by my Tommy gun and [Roy L.] Pynson's rifle. When the shooting stopped and I looked back, I saw all of my men running back toward our lines. They thought that I had been killed. I crawled out alone, with Germans taking pot shots at me without success.

"The next night, [Carl T.] Cantrell took another patrol out, and he followed the same route. Unfortunately, the machine gun that had not been working the night before was in action, and the patrol was stopped before they reached the road. One man was killed." [19]

Private First Class Earl Boling was manning a Company E outpost near the railroad tracks east of Groesbeek on the morning of October 9. "Since our outpost position was very vulnerable, a mortar observer from the headquarters company mortar platoon was sent up. I recall his name being [Sergeant Roy M.] Tuttle. He was in the position or foxhole next to mine, and we started to receive sniper fire.

"The sniper was using tracer ammunition—I told the men to keep low.

"Tuttle said, 'I will spot him and get a fire mission.' He raised his binoculars up for a look and was immediately shot. At this time, I ordered all men to fire at the enemy positions to our front, and under this covering fire, I crawled from the next hole to check on Sergeant Tuttle.

"When I slipped into the foxhole, I found that he had been shot in the left temple and was still alive, but unconscious, and was having difficulty breathing. As I picked up his phone to the mortar platoon, they were trying to contact him. I explained the circumstances, and the officer [Lieutenant John L. Cooper] on the line called one of our battalion doctors to the phone.

"[Captain Lyle Putnam] asked me to describe the appearance of the wound and the exact location. I then asked if there was anything I could do to help Tuttle. He answered, 'No—from the description of the wound and point of entry of the bullet, I don't believe you can do anything except try to make him comfortable, and if you know any prayers, say them.'

"About this time, there was a gasp from Tuttle and his breathing stopped. I could not get a pulse—I let the doctor know this, and he said, 'You have done all that you can,' and turned the phone over to the officer of the mortar platoon.

"The headquarters mortar platoon officer said, 'We are sorry to hear about Tuttle, but since he has been at your position (two days), he has plotted several targets, and we have the map coordinates. We are going to fire a saturation barrage. You stay on the phone to correct our fire if needed.'

"With that, the barrage started, and the German positions were smothered in mortar fire from the heavy mortar section. Within one hour or less, the Germans were waving a Red Cross flag, asking for a ceasefire. I notified the mortar section and the barrage stopped. The Germans came out under Red Cross flags to pick up dead and wounded, while one of their officers watched our position with binoculars.

"That night, as we were to go for rations, etcetera, we removed Tuttle's body. With three other men, I carried Tuttle on a litter, and without an audible word, the four of us removed our helmets and knelt for a moment's silent prayer. I was to think later that there were three different religious groups represented in this action of a prayer for a fallen comrade.

"It was quiet in our area for the next two days and nights, until we were relieved." [20]

The British 130th Brigade relieved the 505th PIR from this position on October 11, and the regiment moved to defensive positions along the flatlands south of the Waal River, where it relieved the 504th PIR. The 1st and 3rd Battalions held the frontline, while the 2nd Battalion was held in reserve.

On the night of October 17, the 2nd Battalion relieved the 3rd, occupying positions that ran south from the river to where it tied in with the 1st Battalion on its right. Company D occupied a brickyard adjacent to the southern bank of the Waal River. Lieutenant Joe Meyers was the platoon leader of D Company's 3rd Platoon. "First Lieutenant [Lawrence M.] Price joined the company and took over McClean's 1st Platoon. The [brick]yard consisted of three massive brick kilns, with smoke stacks that towered 150 feet skyward. These kilns were located atop a thirty-foot, east-west levee that paralleled the river. Behind the levee was a large, open area with a multitude of open-sided sheds used to store bricks. The surrounding area was level farmland, cut up into small plots by a series of drainage ditches and dikes.

"Captain Smith deployed the 1st and 3rd Platoons on line, and he held Carr's 2nd Platoon in reserve. Price's 1st Platoon extended from the river across the levee, south to the edge of the brickyard, where he tied in with me. I defended a three hundred yard sector extending south and tied into another company from our battalion." 21

One of the big problems during the stay in Holland was food. Meyers found that "the Dutch civilians were willing to share their meager rations with us, but they had so little food to spare, we were reluctant to accept their offerings." 22

Lieutenant Ray Grossman, with Battery C, 456th Parachute Field Artillery Battalion, thought he would never see the day when he would desire K-rations. "We had to draw British rations, and the staple item was Australian mutton stew—chunks of fat, grisly mutton, and big chunks of potatoes. You couldn't get the stuff hot enough that the tallow wouldn't congeal when it hit an aluminum mess kit." 23

Occasionally, Meyers and others picked fruit from trees, where it was available, but this did little to supplement their rations. "For the entire period of our stay in Holland, we were on cold rations: Ks and Ds initially, and later we switched to C-rations. Although no gourmet delight, C-rations were an improvement over Ks and Ds. Issued in a cardboard box, one ration consisted of three canned bread units (large round crackers and a can of jam), three canned food units, and an accessory package. As I recall, the food units were ham and eggs for breakfast, pork and beans for dinner, and meat and vegetable hash for supper. The accessory pack contained cigarettes, matches, toilet paper, a miniature can opener, and candy. The ration is fine for a few days. When you eat it seven days a week for two straight months, you are willing to face enemy fire to get a decent meal." 24

Sergeant Charles J. Kaiser, with Headquarters Company, 3rd Battalion, remembered one day when Major James L. Kaiser visited their front-line position in a Dutch farmhouse. Sergeant Kaiser was told that enough supplies weren't getting through. "We would have to live off the land. My answer was, if the major was hungry he could come back and have some chicken with us. We had fourteen chickens in the pot. He came back.

"One advantage of having a large number of farm boys in your outfit was that they were experts at slaughtering livestock and cutting up meat. We never went hungry." 25

One day, Sergeant Henry "Duke" Boswell, with Company G, went out with another trooper, Melvin Burnett, "to kill and butcher a cow. We found one, and

Burnett shot it in the ear with a .45, and it fell over. We were well on our way to butchering it, when we looked up and coming across the field were two persons.

"My heart sank, as we could recognize General Gavin and his orderly. I reported to General Gavin—he asked if I knew about the orders not to kill any more cattle, as we were ruining herds of the farmers. I replied that we knew of the policy, but I had seen this one hit by shellfire, and got help to butcher it, as we did not want the meat to go to waste. He agreed that was right, and after asking how we were getting along (food, clothing, mail, etcetera) he started off. After a few steps, he turned and asked, 'By the way, sergeant, where is the shell hole of the shell that killed the cow?'

"I looked around frantically, saw no hole, and said, 'It's under the cow, sir!'

"He smiled and walked off." [26]

In late October, the men had their first opportunity to clean up in more than a month when field showers were set up in Nijmegen. Also during that timeframe, the Company D commanding officer, Captain Taylor G. Smith, was promoted to 2nd Battalion executive officer. Captain George D. Carlson replaced Smith as CO of Company D.

Company F platoon leader Lieutenant Rusty Hays witnessed what would have been a humorous incident had it not been so serious to the parties involved. "The last two to three weeks in Holland were pretty calm. We got word that C-47s with coffee were being flown in. Up to this time, we had been on English rations, which meant tea instead of coffee. The only way to get coffee to us was by plane. Our guys were ready to revolt if they couldn't get coffee. It got bad enough that they loaded a C-47 with coffee and flew it in to us.

"Not being a coffee drinker, it made little difference to me, but the rest of the fellows could hardly wait. The 1st squad had found a cow that had gone dry because it hadn't been milked regularly. In anticipation of getting coffee, they worked with it until it started giving milk again.

"Finally, the coffee arrived. The next morning the 1st squad brewed up a big pot of coffee and went over to milk the cow. It was dry, and they were mightily disappointed.

"The next morning they found out what happened to their milk. They happened to go out to the cow a little earlier than the morning before, and found the 2nd Squad milking their cow. It looked for a while that a firefight would develop." [27]

Private First Class Gordon Pryne, with Company A, was staying in an upstairs bedroom of a two-story Dutch house on the evening of October 31 when he heard the unmistakable sound of Screaming Meemies in the distance. "I should have been in the basement. They hit the top of the house and the roof came down on top of me. My bed went down to the [first story] floor. It banged me up. I hurt my back. They sent me back to England for a month or more." [28]

Toward the end of the regiment's time in Holland, Private First Class Russell W. Fischer, with Company G, was sitting in his foxhole, trying to remember the officers and men who had been killed during the campaign. "So far, [Private Ernest L.] Ariasi, Lieutenant [Asa T.] Hancock, [Private First Class Charles] Zakrzewski,

[Private John P.] Corcoran, [Private Edward J.] Latek, Lieutenant [Jack E.] Gavin, [Private Elmer J.] Baker (one of my best friends), and [Private First Class Lawrence J.] Schehl—the most swell guy in the company. We had a company strength of 90 men left out of 142. I guess I was lucky so far." [29]

On November 10, Canadian forces relieved the 82nd Airborne Division. The men were happy to be leaving Holland, even though most had made friends with the Dutch citizenry. The fighting had once again been costly. The division suffered 535 killed in action, 622 missing in action, 1,796 wounded in action who didn't return to duty, and 821 wounded in action who eventually returned to duty. In addition, there were 327 troopers injured in action who didn't return and 196 injured in action who returned to duty.

AFTER ARRIVING AT SUIPPES, FRANCE, the regiment was billeted in stone French army barracks buildings. The men were given time to rest and relax, passes were generous, and many officers were on furlough. No one in the regiment could know that a catastrophe in Belgium would soon plunge them into the most costly campaign of the war.

A couple of days after getting settled, Colonel Ekman called the Company I first sergeant, Howard P. Melvin, into his office and told him that he was the new regimental sergeant major. Melvin responded, "'I was in Company I from the start and wanted to finish with them as first sergeant.' Colonel Ekman replied, 'Melvin, we are giving you fourteen companies instead of one. Fall in!'" [30]

In December, Captain James Maness, the commander of Company H, became the 3rd Battalion executive officer. Captain Maurice J. Fitzgerald replaced Maness as commanding officer of Company H.

The regiment soon began receiving replacements. One of those assigned to Company D was Private William E. Slawson, a veteran of the 1st Special Service Force, which had fought spectacularly in Italy and southern France before being disbanded on December 5 because it had sustained very high casualties. "I got assigned as an assistant machine gunner with a guy by the name of Julius Eisner. Eisner was a great man—he was a pathfinder in the Normandy drop. He would share anything he had—smokes, socks, etcetera." [31]

On the evening of December 17, Tech Sergeant Bob Gillette, with the Regimental Headquarters S-2 section, was enjoying a little French culture. "I was attending a ballet in the auditorium in the camp at Suippes. The performance was interrupted with the announcement that colonels 'so and so' report to headquarters. A little later, the announcement was repeated calling for all battalion commanders to report to HQ. Sometime later, the announcement called for all company commanders to report. Then came the announcement for all men to return to quarters, and the ballet was terminated.

"Returning to our companies we learned that we would move out as soon as possible by truck to assist with a problem in Belgium. That was about all we were told and was probably about all any of our leaders knew at the time." [32]

Lieutenant Dean McCandless, the 1st Battalion Communication Platoon leader, was playing craps on the second floor of the officers club when the officer of the day walked in and announced, "'The Germans have launched a major attack—this bar and club are closed. Sober up, alert your men, issue ammunition, and be ready to move out immediately.' That sobered us up in a hurry!" [33]

Sergeant Norbert Beach, with Company H, was assigned to nightly MP duty in Suippes. "While on patrol on December 17th at 10:00 p.m., we received word to get all personnel back to their respective bases." [34]

At 11:30 p.m., General Gavin "left with my G-1, Lieutenant Colonel Alfred W. Ireland, and my aide, Captain Hugo V. Olson, for the command post of the First United States Army at Spa[, Belgium]. The drive was very difficult due to the general conditions of the roads, rain and fog, and the absence of bridges on a number of important highways." [35]

Lieutenant Rusty Hays, with Company F, had turned in early and was asleep at the officer quarters in Suippes. "About 1:00 in the morning, there was pounding on the door. 'Officer's meeting in the battalion commander's room.' There, we were told that the Germans had broken through our lines in some place called the Ardennes in Belgium. We would leave for combat at 8:00 in the morning. 'Alert your men, then get yourself ready for winter combat and report back to your company in an hour. Dismissed!'

"With that, I broke and ran as fast as I could to the company area. There was one extra BAR in the company, and I wanted it for my platoon. After I got my platoon alerted and prepared for winter combat, I went back to my quarters to get myself prepared.

"Here's what I wore: regular cotton underwear, long underwear, wool pants, wool shirt, a field jacket (short, medium weight), combat pants, combat jacket, [and] wool overcoat. With the cotton underwear, I had four layers of clothes, and since we had buttons on our pants instead of zippers, I found it more convenient not to button any of the pants. Because jump boots fit snug and were not warm, I wore combat boots instead of jump boots. The only gloves we had were woolen with leather palms—not much help in the cold weather we would face. To keep our heads warm, we had a wool knit cap that we wore under our helmets.

"For a bedroll I had: a cocoon-type blanket sleeping bag, which is not very warm, but I could at least zip it up around my head. Two woolen blankets [and] a shelter half, which is a half-tent—not warm, but fairly waterproof and usually used as a ground sheet, and to roll my bedroll in to keep it dry. I was lucky. There were some men who, for one reason or another, did not have many of these items and had to leave for combat without them.

"All in all, our clothes and bedding would be far from adequate for the below-zero weather we would be in. The army had completely neglected to provide cold-weather gear for their troops.

"But there was another, even more critical shortage. We did not have a combat load of ammunition for our weapons and no magazines for our BARs, and BARs couldn't be fired without magazines to hold the cartridges." [36]

After completing his MP duty, Sergeant Beach returned to the barracks and went to bed. "It was a practical joke for the men in my platoon to wake me up when they went out on duty. They did so, and I ignored them as I usually did. Finally, they kept after me and I woke up to see that they were all packing and it was just 3:00 in the morning. They finally explained to me that we were moving out. Pack your gear and put on long johns, as wherever we are going, is going to be cold." 37

Sergeant Bill Dunfee, a squad leader with Company I, was asleep in his bunk at the barracks that night. "We were awakened out of a doze by Lieutenant Vandevegt, executive officer of Company I. We thought he was drunk or had lost his mind. He was sounding off about the Germans had broken through, and we were to move out before daylight. By the time we were fully awake, we realized he was neither drunk nor kidding.

"We were up and dressed within half an hour. Everyone got their combat gear together, including unauthorized ordnance—mine being a Colt .45 I kept near my heart in combat. While in Naples, Italy, I had a shoulder holster made, that worn under a jacket was practically undetectable. I slipped it under a blanket on my bunk. One of the new men saw me hide it and asked if he could see it. I nodded yes. Before I could stop him, he pulled the slide back, popping a round in the chamber and pulled the trigger. The bullet went through my combat pants, the woolen OD pants underneath, but not through my long-johns. No harm done—except, it got Vandevegt back in there. Someone told him it was a firecracker. I did tell the shooter that if he survived the operation, we had a date on our return. My initial reaction to being endangered in combat or otherwise was fear, followed by violent anger.

"We were issued K rations for two days, one fragmentation grenade, and a bandoleer of ammunition. We were assured we would get more before contacting the enemy. We had no mortar or machine gun ammo, and a bandoleer wouldn't last a rifleman very long in a good firefight." 38

Private John R. Jackson was a new replacement assigned to Headquarters Company, 2nd Battalion, as a battalion message center runner. "I went to the supply room for equipment, and there were no packs to carrying supplies. I wound up with a gas mask [and container, from] which I removed the mask and used the canvas bag as a pack for some socks and underwear. There were no overshoes available, so I went out with regular jump boots." 39

Private First Class Dutch Schultz didn't have an overcoat, "So I took a sleeping bag and made an outer garment of it. I put on some long johns, a GI sweater, a wool British Army garrison jacket, and my jump suit." 40

Private First Class James Rodier was the acting supply sergeant for the 2nd Battalion when the word came that the regiment was moving out. "I had weapons in the supply room to send to ordnance for repair and maintenance. Captain [William E.] Schmees said to give the weapons to the people, and they would have to use them." 41

COLONEL EKMAN WAS IN ENGLAND on the evening of December 17, and heard radio news broadcasts regarding the German offensive. He received a call at

11:00 p.m. from Colonel Robert Wienecke, who told him the division was moving out and that he was to report to the airport at 9:00 the next morning. Ekman knew the problems were immense in getting his regiment prepared for the move. "The equipment situation was critical. Many of the weapons were in Ordnance, [and] there were shortages in field rations and ammunition. All requests for such items had not been completely filled. Clothing was in the laundry, equipment was stored, [and] winter clothing had not been issued to the regiment. The personnel shortages were most serious in the case of specialists—particularly for crew-served weapons.

"The training program was not completely underway when the alert came; there had only been a week of very serious training during the month, and even this had been somewhat haphazard because the mortars had to be borrowed from the 508th Parachute Infantry. These mortars were returned at the time of the move, and as a result, the 505th went into battle with only three 81mm mortars and seven or eight 60mm mortars for the entire regiment.

"To complicate the personnel issue, at 0300 on 18 December, after the alert for movement had been received, but before the regiment left Suippes, two hundred replacements arrived. This left no time to get them oriented, classified, or properly distributed, and they were just thrown into the move." [42]

Many of the division's veterans who had been wounded in Holland were either still in hospitals in France or England or were just being released, like Staff Sergeant Wheatley "Chris" Christensen, with Company G. "I was in England, having recently been released from a hospital. Sunday afternoon on the 17th, I had gone into town and was in my favorite pub when a 505 officer came in and said all passes had been canceled. We were to report back to camp, as we were pulling out that night. That evening about fifty of us, plus about the same amount of rear-echelon service troops, were taken down to Southampton and loaded on a LCT—and from there over to France." [43]

Private First Class Jack Hillman, with Company I, who had been wounded in Normandy and then broken a leg on the jump into Holland, had been transferred from one hospital to another, ending up in a field hospital in Normandy. Hillman was fed up and wanted to rejoin his buddies in Company I. "I went AWOL from this hospital, winding my way back to Suippes. Just in the nick of time to enjoy a winter vacation in the Bulge." [44]

AFTER A DIFFICULT AND DANGEROUS DRIVE, General Gavin arrived in Spa, Belgium, the following morning. "I reported to General [Courtney] Hodges in person at about 0900 hours 18 December. At that time the situation appeared rather vague. The first reports of enemy contact at Stavelot were just coming in. It was reported that an enemy force at Stavelot had driven our troops across the river and had succeeded in capturing and destroying a large map supply. They apparently blew the bridge upon driving out our forces. The situation south and west of Stavelot was unknown, except that the enemy had evidently overrun our front positions. There appeared to be a large force of U.S. troops centered on St.-Vith. There also appeared to be a large pocket of the 106th Division surrounded in the Eifel.

"After some staff discussion, the commanding general, First U.S. Army, decided to attach the 82nd Airborne Division to V Corps. It was to close in an area in the vicinity of Werbomont. The 101st Airborne Division was to be attached to VIII Corps and would assemble in the vicinity of Bastogne. I placed a request with the First U.S. Army for tanks, TDs [tank destroyers], 4.2s [4.2-inch mortars], and medium artillery, and left the CP for Werbomont. At this time there was considerable movement west of service and command installations in and around Spa. It was apparently being evacuated.

"I arrived at Werbomont at approximately mid-afternoon and immediately made a reconnaissance of the entire area."[45]

BACK IN FRANCE, SERGEANT BEACH packed his gear and fell out with the rest of Company H, awaiting transportation. "We were to be ready at 8:00 a.m. and as usual, the trucks didn't get there until 10:00 a.m. They were eighteen-wheelers—open-air trucks. They loaded us on these trucks and we started moving to the front line." [46]

When the trucks arrived, Private First Class Malcolm Neel, with Battery A, 80th Airborne Antiaircraft (Antitank) Battalion, was one of the last to board his truck. "I was in a 2 1/2-ton, 6x6 truck sitting near the tailgate when I heard one of our guys, looking out at a group of cold, wet paratroopers standing packed into an open semi-trailer, say, 'Boy, I feel sorry for the first Germans those guys get a hold of.'" [47]

Private First Class Les Cruise was riding in a truck, packed with most of the 1st Platoon of Company H. "We rode north from Suippes towards Vouziers and Charleville-Mezieres, then east to Sedan of World War I fame. Much of the area that we crossed was famous battlefields of World War I, and some of the original trench works could still be discerned in the topography. Nevertheless, the champagne countryside was beautiful and green, even in December, as daylight revealed.

"We had trucks strung out for miles in one large convoy headed to the unknown. Daylight began to fade as we passed through Sedan, and our pit stops had made our progress slow, so that what would normally take several hours was taking all day. Bouillon was entered and passed. We passed one crossroad where a sign pointed to Bastogne, but we were on a road that passed through La Roche, as I read on another signpost. We then headed north to Aywaille and Werbomont, and some place called Spa. By this hour it was quite dark and I lost track of our location. We were bitching and moaning about the lack of information, but even though we griped, we had confidence that Gavin knew the situation and terrain." [48]

Private First Class Virgil Goodwin, a new replacement with Company B, was lucky enough to get a spot in the back of a tarp-covered 2 1/2-ton truck. "The road conditions were as rough as any we could ever imagine. When we got closer to the front we made several stops because the roads were jammed with civilians and soldiers coming from the way we were going. Some of the retreating soldiers wanted to know if we thought we could turn the tide. We told them that was what we intended to do." [49]

As the regimental convoy neared Werbomont, Private John Jackson, a new replacement assigned to Headquarters Company, 2nd Battalion, heard the sound of artillery in the distance. "I was nervous when I heard some loud reports. The older men said not to worry, because that was outgoing. I asked how they knew that, and was told that when you hear incoming, you will know." [50]

Upon reaching Werbomont with the lead elements, Regimental Sergeant Major Howard P. Melvin reported to General Gavin. "Gavin said, 'Take a patrol down the road (toward Basse-Bodeux) and don't stop until you run into the Germans!'

"Off we went! After two and a half miles, we observed a reconnaissance unit lined up in a field next to the road—no motors were running. Soon, the Germans began to get out of their vehicles carrying their individual equipment and small arms. It became apparent that they were out of gas and would set up a defense until they could be refueled. We ran back with the information." [51]

When Private John Gallo, with Regimental Headquarters Company, arrived in Werbomont with the lead elements of the 505th, he dug a foxhole and bought "some straw from a farmer to line the foxhole. The weather was so cold that John Moncak and I doubled up to stay warm." [52]

That night, Private John Siam and the other Company I troopers "got off the trucks to see flares in every direction. We said to the driver, 'Where are we?' He said he didn't know—didn't care, and drove off. We didn't even know what country we were in." [53]

When his truck arrived in Werbomont, Sergeant Norbert Beach, with Company H, wearily jumped off the tailgate and stretched his body to alleviate the cramped feeling in his muscles. Then Beach heard the order to move out. "You couldn't see anything. We were told to move out down this particular road, which nobody seemed to know where we were or what we were doing. It was muddy with light drizzle and we were slipping and sliding. You couldn't fall out because it was so dark you would have to stay in contact with the man in front of you. After several miles, carrying my full load, which included the forty-pound radio, I got extremely warm. So I opened my fly and got out my jump knife and cut out my long johns on the march. That was the last time I wore long johns." [54] That was a move Sergeant Beach would soon regret.

Colonel Ekman arrived in Werbomont at approximately midnight after landing at an airfield near Suippes at 3:00 p.m., driving for two hours to his now abandoned CP, and then through the night to catch up with the regiment.

Shortly after arriving at Werbomont, Staff Sergeant Joseph T. Jockel, with Company G, was assigned to the 3rd Battalion S-4 section, under the command of Lieutenant Walter B. Kroener. Jockel had previous experience in supply operations, and his experience would be critical in helping to get badly needed ammunition, food, ordnance, equipment, medical supplies, and warm clothing for the battalion. "We arrived in Belgium without any trucks of our own. They came one or two days later, relieving our fear of not being supplied with ammo and food. It was my job to go back to ordnance and quartermaster depots as often as possible to keep the front line equipped. Ammo boxes are heavy, and we handled an awful lot during this action." [55]

About noon on December 19, as the 505th marched east toward Basse-Bodeux, trucks belonging to the division arrived. As Lieutenant Bill Hays, with Company F, moved along the road, he saw them parked up ahead on the shoulder of the road. "Along the right side of the road was a line of trucks, their tailgates facing the road. As our men reached the trucks, someone would ask each one, 'What do you need?' As we passed the trucks, we were fully supplied with all that we needed." [56]

Hays would later learn the story of how those trucks got there from a captain with the transportation corps. "The officer in charge of the depot was told that when the trucks from the 82nd arrived, they could have anything in the depot without signing for it—something unheard of before in the army. This captain was put in charge of the convoy, and told to take it to wherever the 82nd was in Belgium.

"To get there in time, they had to drive all night with their lights on, rather than using the blackout lights. With their lights on, they would attract any German tank column in the area.

"These were 82nd trucks and 82nd drivers. From time to time, MPs would stop them and tell them they may be running into a German roadblock, and they better turn off their lights and stop there for the night.

"In every case, the drivers would say, 'No sir, we're 82nd Airborne and our men need this stuff up there in the morning.' And on they drove.

"We did need this stuff, and we got it just in time." [57]

Around noon on December 20, the 505th moved out of Basse-Bodeux toward the Salm River. The 1st Battalion marched southeast to hold the sector between Rencheux on the right, where it tied in with the 508th PIR to just south of Grand-Halleux. The 3rd Battalion moved southeast to defend a sector from Grand-Halleux on the right, north to La Tour. The 2nd Battalion moved eastward to occupy Trois Ponts, where key bridges across the Salm and Amblève Rivers were located, extending south to La Tour.

Companies E and F would defend Trois Ponts on the left flank of the regiment, while Company D would hold the section of the river across from La Tour. Company I would defend Rochelinval, with Company H defending the area south to Petit-Halleux, where it would tie with Company G, which would hold Petit-Halleux. Company A would defend the area south of Petit-Halleux, and Company C would defend a road bridge on the right flank, tying in with the 1st Battalion, 508th PIR. Company B would be the regimental reserve, positioned on the road leading northwest from Petit-Halleux. Trucks from division artillery would stand by, ready to transport Company B to the location of any enemy breakthrough.

Lieutenant Bill Meddaugh, the executive officer of Company E, was the acting company commander when Lieutenant J. J. Smith was evacuated to the United States with malaria shortly before the regiment left France. Meddaugh's troopers led the 2nd Battalion column as it moved out. "We pulled out of a bivouac area and began an approach march along a narrow mountain road leading to Trois Ponts. No maps were available and I wasn't sure where we were headed. I was asked to send one platoon forward by truck as an advance force to occupy the town and reconnoiter the immediate area around the town. I selected the 2nd Platoon under Lieutenant John Walas, who boarded the trucks and headed for Trois Ponts. The rest of the company (and battalion) continued the march." [58]

Lieutenant Colonel Ben Vandervoort, commanding the 2nd Battalion, didn't know much more than his men about what to expect. "There was no information about either enemy or any friendly forces in the area." [59]

Vandervoort and his command group moved out toward Trois Ponts in jeeps, at the head of the truck column carrying Lieutenant Walas' platoon. They didn't know whether they would run head-on into a German armored column or if they might be ambushed en route. But they needed to reach Trois Ponts if possible before the Germans.

The column entered the town without incident. Vandervoort made a reconnaissance in order to be able to deploy his battalion immediately upon arrival. "Trois Ponts was a small, rural village of two-story stone houses and shops. The town was in a narrow valley, overpowered by mountains, at the confluence of the Salm and Amblève Rivers. At Trois Ponts, the steep-banked Salm was a definitive barrier for vehicles. But its shallow headwaters were easily fordable by infantry willing to chance frostbitten feet. A few women and children were the only civilian occupants when we walked into the town. A handful of combat engineers (Company C, 51st Engineer Combat Battalion) were setting up a defensive position at the Salm River bridge in an attempt to prevent anyone's crossing. Those engineers were glad to see that parachute battalion.

"Holding Trois Ponts was the keystone of General Courtney Hodges' plan for the First U.S. Army to stop, drive back, and then destroy the German winter offensive. [Colonel] Ira P. Swift, assistant division commander of the 82nd Airborne Division, newly assigned to paratroops, took a personal interest in Trois Ponts. He ordered the 2nd Battalion to establish a bridgehead with just one company on the high ground to the east side of the Salm River. The remainder of the battalion was deployed on the west bank of the river in order to prevent the enemy from crossing.

"At the foot of the town the highway crossed the Salm River going east over a heavy timber bridge. Immediately across the bridge, the highway ended at the base of a bluff. It then split, turning north and south. The northern road led to two bridges crossing the nearby Amblève River. Hence the name 'Three Bridges.' The southern road climbed gently a few hundred yards, then turned left one hundred eighty degrees to the north over railroad tracks paralleling the river. The narrow two-lane road climbed steeply along the side of the one-hundred-foot-high bluff, cleft with a long, sheer highway and railroad cut. At a point opposite the bridge, now well below, the highway turned ninety degrees to the east then sloped gradually up to level ground. No vehicles could come into Trois Ponts from the east along this road without exposing themselves broadside to 2.36-inch bazooka fire from short range as they negotiated a hairpin turn for two-tenths of a mile." 60

Late in the afternoon of December 20, as the 2nd Battalion column approached Trois Ponts, Lieutenant Bill Meddaugh, the acting CO of Company E, took a jeep the short distance ahead into town. "I went forward to meet with Lieutenant Colonel Ben Vandervoort, 2nd Battalion commander. Lieutenant Walas had set up the platoon as a base of fire along the Salm River, on both sides of the damaged bridge, to cover the area across the river directly opposite the town. The terrain rose sharply across the river, giving the appearance of a cliff or bluff. A narrow road wound up the side of the cliff and disappeared in the woods to the left of the top of the mountain.

"A three-man patrol, under the command of Corporal Clifford Putnam, was working its way up the side of the mountain (not using the road) to determine the presence of any enemy troops in the woods over the crest of the bluff. The patrol disappeared over the crest and returned shortly, waving that all was clear." 61

Vandervoort deployed his battalion to defend against a river crossing. "On the west side of the Salm River, F Company and the Battalion Headquarters Company—particularly the light machine gun platoon and bazooka—set up a main line of resistance (MLR) among and in the houses on the river bank. Machine guns were sighted to provide flanking fires onto both sides of the bridge.

"A few more U.S. Army engineers drifted down from the hills into town. We were glad to take in those orphan engineers. They were scattered throughout the MLR so they could use their .50-caliber machine guns to provide an overlapping final protective line of fire.

"D Company was sent south on the riverbank road to defend the next nearest bridge, still intact, across the Salm. They were to destroy the bridge if attacked in force. Second Battalion habitually teamed with a platoon of Company B, 307th Airborne Engineers. They were sent with D Company to perform the demolition task. D Company and F Company maintained twenty-four hour contact with foot patrols on the west bank of the Salm.

"Our 81mm mortar platoon found a lovely observation post (OP) on the side of the mountain sloping to the north above Trois Ponts. From there they could see the road net to the east, the bottoms of both rivers, and the open field east of the E Company position." 62

Lieutenant Meddaugh was ordered to take E Company across the Salm River "to the high ground and to establish a defensive position denying enemy troops and vehicles the use of the road. I sent for the rest of the company and immediately ordered Lieutenant Walas to move the 2nd Platoon across quickly and set up a defensive position straddling the road, inside the woods, just over the crest of the mountain. When the balance of the company arrived, we moved across the bridge and up the winding road to get into position. I ordered Lieutenant Jack Bailey's 1st Platoon to move into the woods and dig in on the right flank of the 2nd Platoon. Lieutenant Howard Jensen's 3rd Platoon was kept in reserve and located in the immediate vicinity of the Company CP, which I established in a small home located on the road about one hundred yards from the 2nd Platoon positions." 63

Sergeant Julius D. Axman, with Company E, took two of his men on a reconnaissance patrol southeast along the woods lining the road. "We went into the woods along the road about twenty-five yards and stopped. It was dark by now—I was the rear man and didn't hear the other two men move out. About then, I heard a lot of troops moving up [from the south], so I headed in that direction. They were Krauts—they were setting up their radios and bringing up a lot of equipment.

"Well, I made the sign of the cross about a dozen times and said goodbye to my mom, when our [81mm] mortars started up across the river with three rounds. They didn't hit anything, but they fired again and hit the road the Krauts were on. All hell broke out—[the mortar fire] hit some trucks and started a fire. I could see shadows of Krauts running all over the place. I thought the whole German Army was after me.

"I put my hand on my helmet, my BAR under my arm and ran for the sound of the mortar blast. I got challenged by my squad—still not yet dug in. They sent me down to the CP. I told Lieutenant Meddaugh everything I saw, and then rejoined my platoon." [64]

Later that evening, Vandervoort crossed the river to check on the Company E positions. "The men dug in with their left flank slightly astride the road. Facing east, the bulk of the company selected positions in the edge of a dense wood at the top of the bluff. The wood ran off to the right, gradually expanding into a forest. To their front, the left side of the road was solid woods. The right side of the road was a wide-open field with little vegetation other than pasture-like stubble. From their positions inside the tree line, the paratroopers had ideal fields of fire on the road and across the open area.

"Antitank mines were sprinkled across their front. The E Company command post was located a short distance to the right of the road with the front line platoons. A 57mm antitank gun was dug into the right road shoulder, twenty or thirty yards behind the riflemen. First Lieutenant Meddaugh, the company commander, put a battery of six bazooka teams just ahead of the position in the woods on the left of the road. Behind the bazooka ambush, they placed antitank mines across the road. Before dark they settled down to wait in the bitter cold—no fires—no lights—no smoking.

"It was an excellent position for an ambush, but inherently a weak one to defend against armor accompanied by infantry. But up on the bluff, it was the best position available. The heavy woods left of the road provided the natural infantry approach, and the open area to the right of the road was good tank terrain. The Salm River separated the company from the rest of the battalion and prevented mutual support." [65]

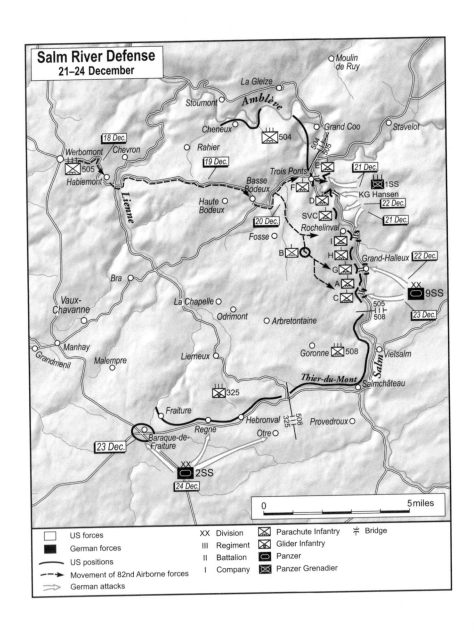

Salm River Defense
21–24 December

CHAPTER 17

"The Krauts Are All Around Us"

On the night of December 20–21, the 1st SS Panzer Division's Kampfgruppe Peiper, the armored spearhead for the entire Sixth SS Panzer Army, was trapped near La Gleize. Tucker's 504th paratroopers were attacking Obersturmbahnführer Joachim Peiper's bridgehead at Cheneux, and the 30th Infantry Division was squeezing the noose tighter. Peiper's men badly needed food, medical supplies, ammunition, and most of all gasoline. The 1st SS Panzer Division's Kampfgruppe Hansen, consisting of the 1st SS Panzer Grenadier Regiment, a heavy tank destroyer battalion (Panzerjäger Abteilung 1), and a battalion of self-propelled 105mm artillery (Abteilung 1, Panzer Artillerie Regiment 1), located at the town of Wanne, was ordered to break through to Peiper and open the way again to Antwerp, Belgium.

The closest road bridge spanning the Salm River in the vicinity of Peiper's kampfgruppe capable of carrying heavy armored vehicles and tanks was at Trois Ponts. If Kampfgruppe Hansen could seize this bridge intact or another to the south along the Salm, they could then drive northwest and attack toward the bridge at Cheneux and link up with Peiper's trapped men and armor.

Along the west side of the Salm River, a half mile south of Trois Ponts at La Tour, Company D defended a railroad bridge, a footbridge, and the bridge where a road following the Salm River crossed to the west side. Just after dark on December 20, the company's demolition man asked Lieutenant Virgil D. Gould to cover him while he set up booby traps on the footbridge. "Sergeant Jerry Weed chose me because I was armed with a Thompson submachine gun, and the other trooper that went with him was an Indian from North Dakota, Sergeant Herbert J. Buffalo Boy, who carried a BAR.

"We went with Jerry down to this swinging hand bridge and out on the bridge, and he set up booby traps in a series of three white phosphorous grenades connected to the rings to pull wires, with trips wires. We went up the hill and got behind this stone wall. Pretty soon there was a flash, when the first one blew up, then the second one blew up. By this time, there were two splashes in the water, because I suppose some people were burned pretty badly by this white phosphorous. We could hear a set of boots coming across that bridge and part way up the hill. Buffalo Boy and I poured fire on this bridge." [1]

Gould, Weed, and Buffalo Boy destroyed the German patrol.

A Sherman tank, positioned in the woods behind the company, covered the road and the railroad bridges. Just after dark, Lieutenant James J. "Joe" Meyers heard the tank start its engine and move out. "I tried to stop him, but he was gone before I reached his position.

"Our bedrolls were in Werbomont. We had nothing to keep us warm during the coming night. The temperature dropped below freezing and it snowed. There were two small farmhouses nearby, and we raided them for anything that would help us to survive the night. [Edward F.] Murphy and I ended up with a mattress over the top of the prone shelter we had dug. It did not help much." [2]

At about 3:00 a.m. on December 21, Lieutenant Bill Meddaugh, the acting commander of Company E, heard armored vehicles approaching. "Two armored half-tracks slowly approached the 2nd Platoon positions. The Germans were noisy, shouting back and forth and seemingly unaware of our presence. The first vehicle

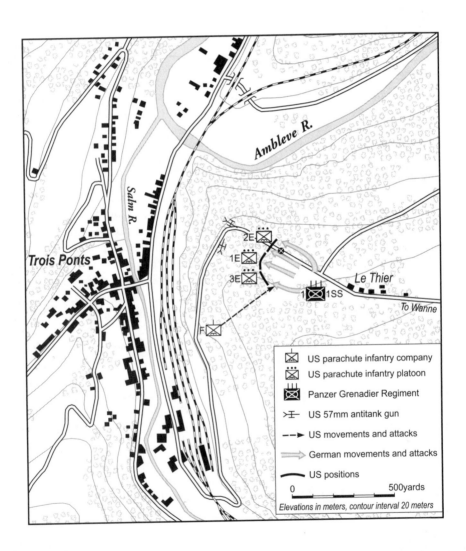

struck a mine and was disabled. Almost immediately, the second half-track was hit by bazooka fire and was destroyed. A brief firefight developed, and several enemy soldiers were killed. We had no casualties. The rest withdrew, and there was no further activity that night. We still had no firm information on enemy strength, but it was obvious that we were facing some sort of mechanized unit.

"At dawn or shortly thereafter, the Germans attacked straight down the road into the 2nd Platoon's positions—infantry was accompanied by armored vehicles. The enemy infantry must have worked their way in close to our positions before they opened fire, because Lieutenant Walas' call to me in the company CP was that 'the Krauts are all around us.'

"I was able to get immediate 81mm mortar support from battalion in front of the 2nd Platoon area, which was the most critical point. Lieutenant [John L.] Cooper of the 81mm Mortar Platoon came over to our position immediately and moved into the 2nd Platoon area, so he could direct mortar fire more effectively. Cooper did a tremendous job and was probably mainly responsible for slowing down the attack.

"I went forward to see what the 2nd Platoon's situation was at that time. They had suffered some casualties, but seemed to be organized and holding their own with the 81mm support. I then made a hasty visit to the 1st Platoon area. The attack was on a wider front than I thought, and the 1st Platoon was receiving a lot of pressure also, but not as concentrated as the 2nd [Platoon]. I returned to the company CP and committed the 3rd Platoon. I instructed Lieutenant [Howard E.] Jensen to move forward and reinforce the 1st Platoon and attempt to extend the right flank in a way which would allow enfilade fire to be brought down on the advancing enemy troops." [3]

Jensen's platoon moved up to a stone wall at the eastern edge of the woods facing the road. This position gave perfect enfilade fire into the left flank and rear of the attacking German infantry. Sergeant Julius Axman and his men spread out behind the wall just moments before they were hit. "A Kraut half-track sent four rounds of [77mm] heavy artillery at us. [Private First Class] Sam Durbin was hit and died later. Lieutenant [John J.] Fields was wounded.

"John Burdge, Jules Lankford, and I were sent up to the extreme right flank and started to shoot up a lot of Krauts. The half-track also came after us and was shooting his machine gun at us—I can't believe how lucky we were. I'll never know why that half-track didn't come over that rock wall." [4]

A 57mm antitank gun dug in near the bend in the road, just behind the 2nd Platoon, had a field of fire on the road and the open ground in front of the 1st Platoon. A second antitank gun positioned along the road farther down the hill could deliver a flank shot on any vehicle attempting to negotiate the bend in the road. The Battery A, 80th Airborne Antiaircraft (Antitank) Battalion gun section, was commanded by Lieutenant Jake L. Wertich.

The two half-tracks, destroyed earlier, blocked the road, and thick woods prevented armor from using the north side of the road. Any armored vehicle would have to use the field south of the road to go around the knocked-out half-tracks.

That ground was soggy, making maneuver by the twenty-eight-ton Jägdpanzer IV tank destroyers difficult. As enemy half-tracks moved through the field, Wertich's gun knocked out an SdKfz 250/8, mounting a 75mm gun with a flank shot.

At his command post in Trois Ponts, Vandervoort received the news that his battalion was facing the most powerful division in the German army. "First Lieutenant [Eugene A.] Doerfler, the battalion intelligence officer, confirmed the identification of the Germans killed during the night and early morning. The battalion reported to the division that E Company was engaged with elements of the 1st SS Panzer Division.

"In mid-morning a full-scale infantry attack, supported by four or five [tank destroyers], was launched against the company. The attack ended with German soldiers lying dead among the E Company foxholes and with other Germans taken as prisoners. The resistance probably surprised the German commander. The terrain dictated a tentatively held blocking position. The crazy American paratroopers didn't seem to know how to read a map and persisted in staying at the edge of the woods and covering the road with fire.

"From the mortar OP we could watch the panzer formations maneuvering and massing for another attack. The road was clogged with panzer grenadiers (in vehicles and afoot), self-propelled artillery, and mobile flak towers. It was an extremely well-equipped panzer kampfgruppe of great size—and an ominous sight for a unit that had one small 57mm antitank gun. The young German 'blackshirts' killed in the E Company foxholes were determined to power their way to the west. Some of the panzer artillery, mortars, and 20mm flak wagons began firing into the E Company area." [5]

Private First Class Edward W. Arndt was a machine gunner with the 3rd Platoon. "We were fighting Germans at close range all morning. I thought we were all ready to meet our Maker. [Private First Class] Charlie Varvarkis, a Greek trooper, 3rd Platoon, never got up from his prone position—mortars and 88s exploding in the treetops and waist high machine gun and rifle fire—ground fire—all you could do was lie down and take it.

"Fred Hebein knocked out a half-track full of Germans that a.m. with a bazooka. I got a squad of Germans with my machine gun—I always carried it with a belt of 285 .30-caliber bullets, ready to fire." [6]

Lieutenant William W. Reed, Jr., a forward observer with Battery C, 456th Parachute Field Artillery Battalion, directed fire from the entire battalion's 75mm howitzers, while the 2nd Battalion 81mm mortars and E Company 60mm mortars pounded enemy troops and vehicles. However, the fanatical attacks by German infantry, supported by fire from armored vehicles, continued, and Meddaugh had no reserve to counter a breakthrough. "As the morning wore on, the situation became more tenuous. 2nd Platoon was suffering heavy casualties, and it appeared they were not going to be able to hold on much longer. The 1st and 3rd Platoons were also being pressured badly, and casualties were mounting. The 2nd Platoon's situation particularly was getting desperate. The Germans had overrun part of the platoon area and were occupying some of the foxholes dug by our own men. They had captured two or three men in the process. They were last seen being moved to the rear of the enemy lines.

"Captain T. G. Smith, 2nd Battalion executive officer, joined me to get a first-hand assessment of my ability to hold on. It was my opinion that we should withdraw. I felt like we had our back to the wall and, although we had never retreated in our combat history, I was very concerned for the safety of my men, and I began to feel that I was losing control of the fight." 7

Lieutenant Colonel Vandervoort requested permission from Colonel Swift to withdraw Company E. "With this vastly superior force bearing down on them, and with their backs to the river, the bluff position was rapidly becoming a trap. Prudence dictated that we pull the company back to the more favorable defensive position on the west side of the river. The terrain would help us separate tanks from infantry and put the clambake on more equal footing. The assistant division commander did not concur.

"There was no better combat company commander than [Lieutenant] Bill Meddaugh. He and his company—about 140 men and officers—were proud, tough, battle-seasoned soldiers. His orders were to stay and try to hold the Germans east of Trois Ponts. Unless ordered off of the position—[and] confronted with being surrounded and captured—they probably would have gone down fighting under the treads of the tanks.

"Disaster seemed imminent. Facing the better part of a panzer division, not one man of E Company left his fighting position. They were superb.

"Determined not to lose E Company, I sent Company F across the river to the south to try to hit the next German tank attack in the flank. This would facilitate breaking off the engagement if we could get permission (or when I decided, to hell with permission) to pull E Company back." 8

Vandervoort ordered Company F to move up the hill through the wooded area to the east of Lieutenant Meddaugh's position. When they emerged from the woods, they would be on the right flank of Company E and would be able to deliver fire into the flank of German infantry attacking across the open field.

Lieutenant Rusty Hays' Company F platoon, on the right flank, moved just inside the eastern edge of the woods. Unknown to Hays, SS panzer grenadiers were moving to outflank Company E. "With our scouts out in front, we started through the woods. On our right was a foggy, open field, with a ditch running along the edge of the woods in the direction of our advance. The scout [Private First Class Paul V. Zahurance] with the BAR was walking down the ditch. Suddenly, he threw his BAR up and emptied his twenty-round magazine straight down the ditch, knocking out an entire German squad trotting along the ditch toward us. That BAR saved some lives in my platoon. He couldn't have knocked out the entire squad if he had been armed with a rifle.

"Right then, I knew we were facing a well trained enemy. Almost immediately, the rest of the Germans began moving through the fog to get around our right flank. With the fog, we couldn't see them. But we could hear them shouting commands as they ran. They may have been well trained, but our men could think for themselves. Without a word from me, the machine gunner ran a few steps into the open field, knelt, and put his machine gun across his knee, and ripped off a six-foot belt of grazing fire in the direction of the voices. We could actually hear the bullets hit home. His assistant gunner came up with a tripod and a box of ammo, and they hosed down the field pretty thoroughly. That stopped the attack, dead." [9]

Corporal Don McKeage and the rest of Company F emerged at the edge of the woods "just in time to save E Company's ass, as the Germans really hit them head on. We ended up on E Company's right flank, as the German column plowed on. We shot the hell out of them." [10]

Meanwhile, Colonel Ekman, alerted of the situation while coordinating the tie-in of the regiment's right flank with the 508th, drove to Trois Ponts. He received a briefing, and after conferring with Colonel Swift, they decided to order a with-drawal. Swift told Vandervoort, "Bring them back." Vandervoort immediately told his S-3, Lieutenant Pinky Sammon, to radio that order to Lieutenant Meddaugh and Lieutenant Harold Case, the Company F commander.

Vandervoort then jumped into his jeep and was driven to the E Company command post. "As we passed the 57mm gun, the crew was getting ready to move back into the town. We arrived at the company CP at the same time that a combined infantry and tank assault was culminating its attack on the company's foxholes. Four or more tanks, with infantry, were closing across the open area to the right front and spraying the edge of the woods with machine gun and cannon fire.

"The first wave of the German infantry assault was momentarily piled up on the left side of the highway by a deadly fusillade across the open road. I ran to Meddaugh and told him to get his men back into town to constitute the battalion reserve, and to DO IT NOW! Bill passed the word to his company to withdraw. They began moving back through the woods accompanied by a hailstorm of bullets pruning bark and leaves from the trees. A panzer grenadier company pushed across the road—some shouting in English, 'Halt, Americans! You are surrounded.'

"Meanwhile, Corporal Jerome Russell, my driver/radio operator, had whipped the jeep around. Taking 'T. G.' [Smith] with me, I jumped back in and we started down to Trois Ponts—urged on by swarms of 9mm slugs from Schmeisser machine pistols. Halfway down the road we passed the 57mm AT gun jackknifed into a ditch and abandoned by its crew.

"The left flank of E Company, hit by the full weight of the panzer infantry's flanking assault, maintained their composure and kept their weapons. But with the Germans flowing behind them on the other side of the road, they could only move into the concealment of the thick woods and towards the bluff. Farther to the right, tanks and their accompanying infantry were slower to close. The E Company troopers were making the panzer grenadiers with their [tank destroyers] pay a high price for progress across open ground. Ordered to withdraw, the troopers, with their previously learned lessons in close-quarter fighting at

Nijmegen, Holland, intuitively improvised 'walking fire' in reverse. Moving backward and using the trees for cover, they simply out-shot any pursuer who crowded them too closely." [11]

Private First Class Eddie Arndt, with a .30-caliber machine gun to carry, waited for the right moment to make his move. "Us old timers were yelling at the new replacements to lie down until a break in the fire came—but they got up and ran and got cut down." [12]

Lieutenant Jake Wertich and the crew of the 57mm gun near the curve assisted the withdrawal by maintaining fire on enemy infantry and vehicles. However, SS grenadiers had penetrated through the woods immediately north of the road, overrunning part of the 2nd Platoon and the six bazooka teams. The Germans suddenly opened fire on Wertich and the gun crew from the woods at close range, killing and wounding some of them. Corporal Stokes M. Taylor grabbed a BAR, ordering those who could, to withdraw, while he covered them with the BAR. Taylor fired clip after clip, pinning down the Germans in the woods, allowing the others to withdraw. Wertich remained with the gun, manning it by himself, keeping German armor from gaining the road, until both he and Taylor were shot and killed. Lieutenant Jake L. Wertich and Corporal Stokes M. Taylor were both later posthumously awarded the Distinguished Service Cross.

Around the bend in the road, Corporal Gordon Walberg hitched up the other 57mm gun to the jeep, but before they could pull away, Germans coming through the woods shot down the crew, killing and wounding almost everyone. Walberg and a couple of others managed to make it down the hill.

Lieutenant Meddaugh had not had time to direct an orderly withdrawal back to Trois Ponts. "The withdrawal was disorganized, and men formed small groups in the attempt to get out. I had the company headquarters group and a few men from 3rd Platoon who had become separated and drifted back. As we started to move down the road, we came under automatic weapons fire. The Germans had been able to break through at some point and put fire on the road.

"We considered dropping down the side of the cliff to the ground below, but it was about a twenty-foot drop. I rejected that move, and by moving in single file and staying close to the bank on the side of the road, we managed to work our way down the road to the bridge.

"This was not the bridge at the edge of town; this bridge went over railroad tracks. Due to the small-arms fire being directed at the bridge, we were forced to dash, one by one, across it. We crossed the river on a small foot bridge and moved through town to an assembly point. The rest of the company made their way back by similar means and drifted in over the next hour or two." [13]

Arndt pulled back through the woods behind him, but as he moved down the hill, he emerged into open ground. Fortunately, fog partially hid him from view. "All of a sudden, I was on the ground—it was like an electric shock to my leg. I couldn't believe it—my foot and boot were facing another direction and blood running like hell.

"[Private Gordon M.] 'Stinky' Stiner got it at the same time through the head.

"How I kept my cool, I don't know. I took off my belt as a tourniquet above my left knee, took my aid packet off my belt, injected myself with morphine in my left arm, took sulfa tablets with a gulp of water from my canteen, and I started doing pushups and crawling as fast as I could down the hill.

"Had I found my combat knife, I would have cut off my left foot—it was grotesque and hurting like hell. I cinched up my belt tighter and yelled for George McCarthy and [Richard L. 'Mickey'] Johnson to come back and help me. They, too, were crawling for cover and heading for the road above the railroad yard. They waited for me to catch up and helped me to the edge of a forty-foot precipice above the rail yard.

"How to get me down to the aid men with stretchers down below—funny how your mind works so clearly when in distress. I spotted a huge stack of [2x12] lumber planks [thirty-feet long], where the medics were below, and yelled to them, as did George and Johnson, to lay the planks against the cliff wall as a slide, which they did. Johnson—that beautiful, big nosed bastard—grabbed me by the collar and lowered me as far as he could, while bullets and shrapnel were flying everywhere. He let me go on the planks—I slid down to the waiting medics, who put me on a stretcher and carried me across what seemed like two hundred yards of bullets and railroad tracks to a Red Cross truck with stacked litters." [14]

Private First Class Dennis O'Loughlin was carrying his 60mm mortar down the hill. "We were rolling and tumbling down that steep hill, all trying to stay below the bullets. I soon left the mortar again, and picked up speed. I remember looking back up at the Germans on top of the hill and thought of movies I'd seen of Indians coming out on the hills and firing down. It was a hell of a time to be thinking about movies.

"We were pushed right down to the top of the bluff over the railroad at the foot of the hill, and some guys went tumbling right over the edge. Some were hit and some weren't. I had a slight draw spotted before I got there and went down it in a hurry, so I wouldn't have quite so far to fall. I ended up rolling, trying to break my fall and lay on the speed, too.

"At the bottom of the bluff on the railroad tracks, some of us got up and ran across the highway and over the river bank to cover, and some didn't. Some were shot up, so they weren't able to, I think." [15]

Lieutenant Colonel Vandervoort barely made it back in the jeep. Now, he watched his troopers appear at the top of the bluff created by the railroad cut. "When they reached the edge of the bluff, they jumped down the sheer cliff, picked themselves up, and ran the one-hundred-yard gauntlet across the two roads, railroad bed, and river, under the cover of friendly protective fire delivered by our troops on the other side of the river. The latter had been told to engage any Germans appearing on the bluff.

"A number of troopers injured their backs and limbs—sprains and breaks—leaping down the cliffs, but no one was left behind. Other members of the company would grab the injured and drag them along.

"It was an opportune time for the Germans to start pushing into the town of Trois Ponts. E Company was in momentary disarray. F Company was still on the other side of the Salm. D Company was downstream holding off another attempted German crossing. Battalion headquarters, the headquarters company, and those 'damned engineers' were all that stood in the way of a major breakthrough. Troopers and engineers, dug in along the riverbank and in the Trois Ponts houses, fought back with their .30-caliber and .50-caliber machine guns. We blew the highway bridge over the Salm as soon as the last E Company trooper cleared the area. More German infantry opened fire along the bluff. The Germans and Americans engaged in rapid-fire machine gun and rifle fire at ranges from 150 to 300 yards. The Germans began hosing the streets of Trois Ponts with their automatic weapons. But the exposed rim of the cliff was no place to duel with dug-in defenders. The paratroopers settled down to some old fashioned sharpshooting and spilled a lot of blood on the bluff." 16

Corporal Don McKeage and some of the Company F troopers helped troopers injured by jumping from the sheer cliff near the railroad depot. "Private First Class [Richard R.] Baldwin of E Company was coming down the road. He was an ammo bearer for a machine gunner by the name of [Private] George Sonnenburg. He told me that George was hit bad, and wouldn't make it. George was from California, We went through basic training in Texas in 1943 and jump training at Fort Benning, Georgia. I and a few others stayed by the depot until we had all the troopers back across the river." 17

Lieutenant Meddaugh assembled the Company E survivors behind a hill to the west of Trois Ponts. "The casualty figures—killed, wounded and/or captured—were high compared to previous combat situations. It was a particularly traumatic experience in that the company was for the most part overrun, or at least penetrated in some areas. Our relatively disorganized withdrawal added to the shock. As we regrouped, most of the men were in a high state of excitement. I remember one 2nd Platoon man specifically losing control of himself, and he had to be restrained and ultimately evacuated. We never saw him again.

"In spite of this, we were able to quickly reorganize and prepare to move back into Trois Ponts. That order came through shortly, and we moved into defensive positions in houses on the edge of the river, where we stayed for the next day or two." 18

The Germans now shifted their effort south to the Company D sector across from La Tour, where both a railroad and a highway crossed the river. At about 8:30 p.m., 1st SS grenadiers charged across an open area near the east bank of the river as automatic weapons fire from the wooded hill on the other side covered them. Lieutenant Joe Meyers, caught out of his foxhole, took cover behind the railroad embankment. "As the Germans advanced, we opened fire and slowed their progress. Suddenly, friendly artillery fire began to fall on the attacking force and they withdrew into the dense woods." 19

Later that night, Meyers was lying in his hole, trying to sleep for the first time in four days. "We heard screams for help in English coming from the German-held hill.

The Germans had captured several wounded E Company troopers. We assumed the 1st SS Panzer was torturing our comrades. I was one of many troopers who made a mental note to avenge this foul deed if the opportunity presented itself." [20]

A couple of miles south of Trois Ponts, at the tiny village of Rochelinval, lay the next road bridge capable of supporting heavy armor. In addition, a footbridge over the river was located about two hundred fifty yards north of the road bridge.

The Rochelinval sector was the responsibility of Company I, which dug in along the embankment of a railroad cut running parallel to the river, and on the steep hill behind it. Company I had established outposts and was patrolling east of the river at La Neuville.

After preparing the demolition charge on the bridge at Grand-Halleux, Private First Class Neil Droogan, with Company B, 307th Airborne Engineer Battalion, received an order to move to Rochelinval and wire that bridge for demolition as well. "[Private] Joe Parisi and I took two cases of TNT, and a jeep and driver drove us there and left us. I placed the wires and TNT on the far side bridge. The 505 decided not to blow the bridge at that time.

"I moved into a 505 foxhole—cold—no blankets or overcoat." [21]

Droogan drove up the hill to the house serving as the Company I command post to get blankets. "The windows were all camouflaged with blankets. They wouldn't give us any—they needed them for security." [22]

At about dusk on December 21, Sergeant Bill Tucker, with Company I, was checking on the outposts. "Private [Willis E.] Maglothin had a light machine gun set up at one outpost across the river with his assistant gunner, [Private] Gus Augustine. The outpost was about fifty yards from the river and seventy-five yards from a bend in the road ahead coming from the east. They had also placed antitank mines across the road on its surface. Suddenly, the rumble of tanks was heard and the noise of men yelling, and several black-clad Germans came around the bend in front of a huge tank. These were SS troops, who simply picked up the mines and threw them aside. At that point, to my surprise, Maglothin fired at the tank with his little light machine gun. The long tank turret swung around toward us and I dove into the nearest depression, somehow remaining unscathed as a shell exploded nearby.

"We had to drag a badly wounded Maglothin back across the river, which ended the outpost. Gus Augustine had been hit in the leg by [shrapnel from] the tank cannon and was to go back with the other outpost group, but he was in such pain that he could not be moved, and was captured by the Germans." [23]

Company I medic Private First Class Jack Lyons was also across the river at one of the outposts. "[Private Calvin C.] Gilbert opened up with a bazooka and knocked out a half-track and set it on fire. Then the tanks opened up on us, and the shells went over and hit the ground behind us. When the tanks continued to fire, we got the order from [Lieutenant Charles R.] Christian to pull back across the river." [24]

Just as the troopers from the outposts made it back across the river, Private First Class Neil Droogan heard armored vehicles approaching and prepared to detonate the charge rigged to the bridge, even though he couldn't see the approaching

Germans. "I could hear the Germans talking and directing the tanks to cross the bridge. That's when I blew it." [25]

Sergeant Tucker watched the road bridge go up, with a German armored vehicle on it. "Then, a heavy firefight took place from one side of the river to the other. It was pitch black, and the darkness became like daylight at times, lit by the tracer bullets and explosions. The Germans were unloading with 20 and 40mm automatic gunfire, as well as occasional tank cannons. They kept their tanks just inside the wood line along the roads running from the east. The 'Okite' [code name for Company I] main line replied with rifle and machine guns, and also well aimed bazooka shells." [26]

During the defense of the Salm River, Lieutenant Dean McCandless, recently promoted to regimental communications officer, was having problems with phone lines to the battalion command posts cut by enemy artillery fire, as well as tanks and tank destroyers attached to the division running over them, disrupting communications. "My wire parties were just totally exhausted. Colonel Ekman asked me why we were having this problem. I told him of the problem and suggested that if I had a vehicle for the wiremen, they could go to the center of the line, tap in and find out which half had the break; and then to the center of that half and tap in again, thereby quickly finding the break without endless walking the line. He immediately grasped the problem and said, 'Take Krause's jeep!' I did, with foreboding. My parties were grateful and kept our lines open much better." [27]

Between La Tour and Rochelinval, the 505th's regimental sergeant major, Howard Melvin, was in command of a makeshift force defending that sector of the river. "Colonel Ekman was disturbed by a long, open space between the 2nd and 3rd Battalions on the 505th's line west of the Salm River. He said he would send me troopers from headquarters and service companies, and I should place them on line to fill the breach. Two trucks brought forty troopers into the area. I briefed them on their mission, saw that they had ample ammo, [and] told them they were only to fire directly to their front. I then placed them along the open space with orders to dig in and set their weapon sights at three hundred yards.

"Then I tied in both ends. The 505th's Company I was on the right of my group and Company D was on the left. Each of these companies had set up two machine guns to fire an X-pattern to cover the open area. The machine guns had excellent fields of fire, and we told them not to change their X-pattern, if a few of the enemy got through—as we now had forty riflemen in the gap to take care of that problem." [28]

When a platoon from the 1st SS Panzer Grenadier Regiment began an assault crossing on December 22, Melvin's scratch force was ready. "When the Germans attacked, everyone fired! The headquarters and service troopers only had M1 rifles, but the enemy was being cut down right in front of them, with many floundering in the knee-high Salm River. When the attack was over, the cooks from the Service Company were ecstatic, yelling how many they had killed. Of course, it wasn't all [because of] their fire, as the crossfire of the machine guns did most of the damage.

"Major Kaiser took a group out to the river, looking for survivors to capture and interrogate. No second attack came." [29]

The previous day, December 21, Captain Jack Isaacs, the twenty-two-year-old commander of Company G, held the sector south of Rochelinval at Grand-Halleux and Petit-Halleux. "We established our defensive positions with one platoon (thirty to forty men) [led by Lieutenant George E. Clark, Jr.] east of the river in Grand-Halleux. We also had a three-man outpost on the high ground east of Grand-Halleux with communication thereto. We maintained patrol contact with our outpost to the east, and beyond, but made no contact with the enemy. My remaining two platoons were on the west bank of the river in Petit-Halleux. They occupied positions on the high ground immediately to the west.

"Because of the chaos created by the German breakthrough, there were scattered elements of other units in our general area. [Major] Kaiser had commandeered a wandering section of (two) 90mm tank destroyers, and my company had found an abandoned quad-mount (four barrels) .50-caliber AA gun, which my men could operate. The two tank destroyers were placed on the road leading to the west from Petit-Halleux, about half way up the hill and behind some houses for concealment. The quad-fifty was also in this area but across the road to the north from where it could fire onto the river and Grand-Halleux. I also had on call, if needed, the battalion 81mm mortars and a battery of artillery from division. I also had my own 60mm mortars (three). I established my company headquarters in the red brick building, just west of the railroad on the north side of the road." [30]

The following day, elements of the 9th SS Panzer Division moving west concentrated east of the Salm River, near Grand-Halleux. The 505th now faced elements of two SS panzer divisions, each with an official strength of 17,809.

That day, Staff Sergeant Chris Christensen, released a few days before from the hospital in England, caught up with his company. "I reported in to Company G, where I was a staff sergeant in charge of the 1st Squad, 3rd Platoon. There, I was told we were in Petit-Halleux, Belgium, on the Salm River.

"To the right of Petit-Halleux was the 2nd Platoon, and to the left of the town on the CP side was the 3rd Platoon in company reserve. The 2nd Squad of the platoon was across the Salm River with the 1st Platoon. On taking over my squad, I found them dug-in about a couple of hundred yards west of and running parallel to the railroad. Farther back up the hill was the mortar squad position, and just a little to the north was a machine gun section from 3rd Battalion Headquarters Company. I don't remember if this section was attached to us, but it was a welcome addition. Plenty of big guns [were] firing in the distance, but nothing close. One thing I did notice, which I thought strange, was the number of civilians that were still around. Usually when something was brewing they would be long gone. Looking back, what choice did they have? There were no safe places to go.

"That evening, shortly after dark everything was quiet, and then in came a few small-caliber mortar shells. These fell harmlessly in and did no damage, as everyone was dug in, but it told me two things: first, [the enemy] knew our position, and second, he has sent his calling card. About this time I left my hole to alert my men and remind them not to fire until I gave the signal. We had troops across the river." [31]

The G Company listening post was located in a blacked-out house on the eastern edge of town, on the slope of the hill above Grand-Halleux. Sergeant Willie B. Beaty's mortar squad, composed of Private First Class William Sanchez, Private First Class Raymond L. Daudt, Private First Class Wilson N. Whicker, and Private Roland M. Thomas, manned the outpost. The squad was positioned on the first floor of the house for security and would rotate one man on the second floor, maintaining observation. Shortly after dark, Private First Class Daudt heard the trooper maintaining observation coming down the stairs. "Whicker came down and said, 'Daudt, I think they're coming.'

"I went up there and geez, they were all over the slope. They were right down in front of the house by then." [32]

Daudt quickly ran down the darkened stairway and put on his gear. "There was no way of getting out of that house and running. They were all around. There was a vineyard in the back, and there was no way out the back.

"Just before I got to the front of the house, the firing started. There was one guy shooting at Beaty and I shot at him—I missed him I guess. I knocked out a window and shot out of it, then I shot out of the door. I shot a clip or two of ammunition, and I said, 'To hell with this.'

"I took off [out the front door] through the middle of the Germans. Sanchez got killed by a grenade at the door after I went out.

"All you could see were shadows. I ran like hell down the street. It was a pretty steep hill—I came down that thing just flying." [33]

Sergeant Beaty died at the listening post. However, Captain Isaacs received a message from him before he was killed. "From our company headquarters, I made contact with Sergeant Beaty, the commander of the post, and he informed me that there were many Germans attacking our main line with a tactic that I had not seen before, in spite of experience in Sicily, Italy, Normandy, and Holland. They came charging down that hill—screaming and shouting and trying to dislodge us. We thought then, and still do, that it was a battalion of SS troops, so we would have been outnumbered about seven to one." [34]

On the west side of the river, Sergeant Christensen expected an attack very shortly. "When you heard only the German weapons, you could surmise the outpost had been overrun. The firing then started to pick up as Jerry started down the hill and ran into the platoon, which was across the river." [35]

DAUDT MADE IT TO THE ROADBLOCK DEFENDED by a squad of the 1st Platoon, which then opened fire on the horde of Germans. "That's where my outfit was—I got down there and fired a few clips. That was one hell of a night. The Germans started coming down that hill, screaming, thinking we would run off—it didn't help them—a lot of them died." [36]

Lieutenant Clark and his platoon maintained its position, fighting an estimated battalion of German infantry. Overwhelming numbers of enemy troops, supported by self-propelled guns, soon moved around the flanks of Clark's platoon and almost surrounded it. Lieutenant Clark, exposed to heavy enemy fire, maintained control of his platoon. He withdrew the forward elements at the roadblock, covering them with the other squads, then conducted a fighting withdrawal to the west side of the river.

Christensen and his men "still hadn't opened up yet, as I still didn't know the location of the troops. The fighting about now was getting very intense." [37]

After receiving the message from Beaty at the outpost at about 7:45 p.m., Captain Isaacs grabbed his weapon and left his command post to check on his men. "I immediately went to the bridge site and found my platoon in Grand-Halleux being driven back across the river with Germans in hot pursuit. The bridge had been prepared for demolition by our engineer battalion and was manned by a detachment from that unit. The bridge was blown with Germans on it." [38]

Private First Class Daudt had just made it across the bridge and jumped behind a nearby low concrete and rock wall when it was blown. "I was right next to it—it about blew my head off." [39]

When he heard the bridge explode, Christensen knew that the 1st Platoon was now on the west side of the river. "The ones who hadn't made it back across the river by now, probably wouldn't. About this time, Jerry made his second and maybe third fatal mistake of the evening. They must have been all crowded together and were screaming at the top of their lungs while charging down the hill. By all this yelling, we knew their exact location. Darn near as good as seeing them. This was our cue to open up. When we opened up, I think everything started firing at the same time. I had never seen anything before or after that could equal such a concentrated wall of fire that we laid down on them that evening." [40]

Private First Class Chris Zafiroff, with Headquarters Company, 3rd Battalion, was manning a light machine gun supporting Company G. "I directed my .30-caliber machine gun fire from the muzzle flash of the machine pistol or MG-42 on the other side of the river. I know I got their attention by receiving a volley of return fire, which, thank the Lord, was short and wide." [41]

Hearing both platoons on the west side of the river open up, Captain Isaacs grabbed the handset of the company radio. "I called for our artillery and mortar support fire, which was delivered promptly. Also, at this time the quad-fifty came into action with devastating results. The Salm was no barrier to foot soldiers, and there were Germans attempting to cross the river by wading it.

"The quad-fifty and our other supporting fire brought the German advance to a halt at the river's edge. To my knowledge, not a single German soldier reached the west bank, nor was any further attempt made by them to do so while we were in these positions. We subsequently learned from prisoners that the screaming attack had worked on less experienced units, and some of them had broken. We had not." [42]

Christensen saw tracers from positions both upstream and downstream from the Company G positions. "There was fire coming from support groups I wasn't even aware we had. After awhile the firing stopped almost as quickly as it had started. At this time there was a hush that fell over the valley that was real eerie. There wasn't a sound from either side for a few moments. When the silence was broken you could hear them screaming in pain, begging for help, moaning, pleading, some I even remember cussing us in English. We must have massacred them. I can't believe Jerry would make such stupid mistakes as he made that night.

"Shortly after the fighting had stopped, I was given orders to move my squad out of my present position and set up a defensive line between the railroad track and the river, running parallel in between. I had the men dig in about fifty feet apart, and I stayed in the center with my assistant down on the far end. We hadn't much more than got dug in, when our artillery started shelling. Luckily, this didn't last too long, as I am not too sure we weren't getting as much as Jerry.

"Anyway, things quieted down for the rest of the night. You could still hear them on the other side of the river tending to their wounded and carting them out. A lot of vehicle traffic also.

"In this present position, it felt like you could darn near reach out and touch them. To make things more eerie, there was now a fog beginning to settle in. I couldn't see much, but sound sure travels. All night long I was thinking about this exposed position and the trouble we would be in come daylight, but I was sure we would be pulled out before then." [43]

Company G remained on alert the rest of the night, but the Germans didn't attempt another crossing. Just before sunrise the next morning, Isaacs heard shouting from the far side of the river. "Inadvertently, we had left one of our men on the east side of the river. During the night, he had made his way as close to the river as he could, and near dawn he shouted to our side that he was coming across. He made a mad dash for our side and surprisingly drew no fire from the Germans. He survived this ordeal only to die a few weeks later in another battle.

"From the top windows of my headquarters building I could see the whole area. Daylight of [23] December revealed five enemy tanks to our front, on the hill and at the edge of the woods. The section of tank destroyers was called into action." [44]

Private First Class Zafiroff watched one of the tank destroyers engage a Mark VI Tiger and a Mark IV. "The 7th Armored tank destroyer, with its 90mm [gun], hit the first tank, then shot the second tank, and then put another shell in the Mark VI. Two crewmen of the Mark VI exited their tank and were running back. At this point, the tanker opened up with the .50-caliber machine gun, killing both." [45]

The remaining German tanks opened fire on the tank destroyer, then withdrew into the woods. A short time later, Captain Isaacs watched the tank destroyer section withdraw. "I subsequently learned that it was customary for a TD section to withdraw if it lost a crewman; therefore we lost this heavy antitank defense. I thought this a strange practice, if true, because we manned our weapons until there was no one left to man them. Other than sniping, there was no further enemy action at this position." [46]

A low-hanging fog that was concealing the Company G positions from German view began to evaporate. Sergeant Christensen became concerned about his squad's exposed position. "The Jerries on the hill at Grand-Halleux were going to be looking right down our throats. If not picking us off, he could've at least kept us pinned down. The fog was beginning to lift and I realized it was now or never. I sent word, passing it down the line from man to man for them to stay down. I was going to try and break out and get help. My hope was Jerry would get caught napping. My luck ran out just about two-thirds of the way from where there was some cover. One guy opened up on me, but his aim was off, and I was able to jump in a hole with one of my men, who was dug in there. I stayed there in that position as long as I dared, and I tried to make it the rest of the way. Either luck was with me or he was a bad shot, because I made it to cover without getting hit.

"Alex Jones in the next hole saw me make it out, so he tried the same stunt. He didn't go ten steps before he was hit and was down. I crawled back as close as my cover allowed and called out to him. Getting no response, I did not know if he was alive or dead. About this time, I looked over to the railroad embankment, and I saw one of our medics, Chris Perry, standing on top holding a Red Cross flag. One man started firing at him, but his aim was off and the bullets kicked up dust at Chris' feet. He stood perfectly still and the guy quit firing.

"Chris then walked down off the embankment and over to Jonesie. He rolled him over and patched him up. He then proceeded to get Jonesie to his feet and helped him off the field into the house where the platoon CP was. I couldn't believe this. I had never seen a more heroic act. Incidentally, I doubt if Chris even got a pat on the back for this act. Another thing I couldn't believe was the Germans letting him get away with it. I suppose we let them get their wounded out the night before, so maybe they were returning the favor.

"About this time I made it up to the CP. Everything was in an uproar. Colonel Kaiser, the battalion commander, was on his way. He no more than came in when he saw and understood my predicament. He called in some smoke. I was told to go back and alert the men what to expect and to get ready.

"I hadn't much more than gotten back when I could hear the shells coming. It was a perfect drop. You couldn't have painted a better one. From the time the smoke shells landed and until the time it took the men to vacate their positions, I think it would have broken a record.

"After the last ordeal, we moved back to our original positions. Nobody slept last evening, so most of them were catching a few winks." [47]

South of Petit-Halleux, Company C defended the most southerly bridge in the regiment's sector. Two 57mm antitank guns from Battery A, 80th Airborne Antiaircraft (Antitank) Battalion, supported Company C. On the afternoon of December 23, Private First Class Malcolm Neel's gun crew dug in their gun in the yard of a farmhouse. "The other settled closer to the bridge. That night, we were attacked. The paratroopers who had crossed over to the east side of the Salm fell back to the high ground we were on. The attacking Germans were yelling, more like roaring, as they came down the other side of the river. This was the only time in the war I threw up, waiting for the Germans to come up our side of the hill." [48]

Company C veteran Sergeant Elmo Bell had watched engineers with Company B, 307th Airborne Engineer Battalion, rig the bridge for demolition a few days earlier. "The engineers didn't blow it until the lead tank was on the bridge. When they blew the bridge, the other tanks moved into position parallel to the river and started delivering intense fire on our side, but we were well dug in, camouflaged, and concealed. We were able to put down enough small-arms fire on the tanks to cause them to button up. When they were buttoned up, their visibility was so limited that they realized that they were vulnerable, and they started backing the tanks out of position. The infantry moved up and took their place. The infantry just kept coming, and we had all of the advantage. They were in the open—they had very little cover. It was just wholesale slaughter.

"Finally, they ordered the Germans to cross the river, to wade or swim the river and the Germans hit the river. It was just unbelievable slaughter there. One PFC machine gunner is believed to have killed between sixty and eighty Germans—one man. The irony is that his platoon sergeant ate him out because he shot almost four hundred rounds of ammunition.

"I don't remember any other time that our people felt downright sorry for the Germans. But that [attack was] so futile and so hopeless that our people really felt sorry for them, because it was obvious that no man was ever going to reach our bank—nobody was going to cross the river. It was uncharacteristic of the Germans to sacrifice people when there was nothing to be gained, and that's what they did." [49]

The 505th still held the Salm River line, despite attempts by the 1st and 9th SS Panzer Divisions to capture a bridge or establish a bridgehead. The fate of Kampfgruppe Peiper was sealed.

DURING THE EVENING OF DECEMBER 23, the 2nd SS Panzer Division overran the Baraque-de-Fraiture crossroads on the far right flank of the division. The road north to Werbomont was open as far as the village of Manhay. The U.S. 3rd Armored Division, responsible for the road, was unable to secure it. The division was threatened with an entire enemy armored division in its rear. Early on December 24, Gavin shifted his thinly spread forces to meet the threat to the division's right flank. "At about 0545, December 24, Colonel Tucker was ordered to leave the smallest possible force in the northern sector and to move [the 504th PIR] south to Bra by motor without delay. He had been given a warning order about twenty-four hours earlier. At about 0645 the 505th was ordered to regroup one battalion, the 2nd, and have it prepared to move [to] division reserve without delay; warning orders had been given to them to prepare for this prior to this time." [50]

However, British Field Marshal Bernard L. Montgomery, commanding all forces north of the German breakthrough, arrived at the XVIII Airborne Corps command post in Werbomont that morning and ordered Ridgway to withdraw the 82nd Airborne Division to shorten its line, saying the division "could now withdraw with honor to itself and its units." [51] Montgomery told Ridgway that it was time to "sort out the battlefield and tidy up the lines. After all, gentlemen, you can't win a big victory without a tidy show." [52]

Sergeant Bill Dunfee, with Company I, had served with the regiment since its formation. "There was great concern about troop morale. This division had never withdrawn in its combat history. My unit was on the Salm River, and we hated like hell to give up what we had fought so hard to keep. We knew the withdrawal wouldn't be easy either, especially at night. We were very much aware of German presence in our rear, and that they spoke English and had American uniforms and vehicles." [53]

That afternoon, Captain Jack Isaacs, commanding Company G, returned to his command post after checking his company's positions in Petit-Halleux. "We were advised by Colonel Kaiser that we would withdraw from these positions during the night of December 24–25. We were dismayed at this order because we had never given up a position before, and since we had stopped the Germans on December 22, we thought we could do so again. Nevertheless, the order was given and preparations made to withdraw. Standard procedure called for leaving a rear guard in position to protect the withdrawing force, and this was done. It was also customary for a senior officer to command this rear guard. In this case it was Captain James T. Maness." [54]

Sergeant Christensen had heard his men talking about it earlier. "All day, there had been a rumor circulating that we were pulling back that night. This I did not pay much attention to. Anyway, this one proved true. The company was to pull out very quietly at midnight so as not to alert Jerry, and move to a new position. In fact, the whole regiment was pulling back. It seemed the whole front in our area was overextended. A short time later, I got called down to the CP and was given some special instructions. After dark, I was to move my squad back to the position we had just gotten out of that a.m. Furthermore, when the company moved out at midnight, we were to stay until five o'clock the next morning, acting as the rear-guard for the company. I was also briefed on where we were to meet up the next day. On returning to my squad, I got them all together and explained everything I knew, putting special emphasis on where the company would be and how to get there in case we became separated." [55]

By the afternoon of December 24, Staff Sergeant Joseph T. Jockel and the 3rd Battalion S-4 section had relocated the battalion supply dump to the high ground west of Basse-Bodeux. "Frozen turkeys arrived by quartermaster trucks. They were refused and sent back to keep for another day. At the time, we had no cooks or stoves to handle the turkeys. We were eating C and K rations, or anything else available.

"Civilians were fleeing westward. Army trucks assisted as best they could. Some buses were shuttling them farther west. While waiting for a bus, a group of about twenty civilians entered a nearby barn to stay warm. I could hear them praying.

"Soon, a young woman came out crying, and told me that they had to leave the old grandpa at home, and feared for his life. Seeing I had a jeep standing by, she offered to supply a guide if I let the jeep go back down to the town. I told her story to the jeep driver, who quickly volunteered.

"I knowingly disobeyed orders and let the driver and guide go. I worried for a half hour before they returned with grandpa. I took him into the barn to reunite with his granddaughter, but there were no young women in the barn. I watched the group load on a bus, and no girls appeared—who could that have been?" 56

After dark on Christmas Eve, Sergeant Christensen moved his men into position to cover the G Company withdrawal. "That evening about eight o'clock or so, we resumed our positions down by the river for what we knew was going to be a long night." 57

By 9:00 p.m. at Rochelinval, Company I platoon Sergeant Bill Dunfee had his men packed up, ready for the order to move out. "Fortunately, our machine guns were still dug in, covering the shallows of the Salm to our immediate front. We were lying back on our packs dozing, when all hell broke loose. The Germans came from our rear, shooting and yelling like a bunch of Indians. I didn't have to see them to know who it was; the rapid rate of the German machine guns and the pink tracers told me. They wanted to go home for Christmas, too.

"We immediately hit our foxholes and started firing. I would estimate a company-strength group started through my area. Some made it to the river and some didn't. I would guess less than half made it to the far bank. Our machine guns being in place and sighted in really chewed them up, as they attempted to ford the river. When the smoke cleared away, we realized we were attempting to withdraw through an enemy force that was withdrawing through us.

"This may not be unique in military history, but it was a new experience for us. When we finally moved out around 22:30 hours, we moved as if attacking to our rear. It was a cold, moonlit night with good visibility. It was too light for us." 58

Sergeant Bill Tucker and his mortar squad were bringing up the rear of the column as Company I moved quietly through the woods. "Suddenly, we heard machine guns and rifles as the Germans attacked our point. We dropped to the ground, and in the blackness around us, there were flashes everywhere. I rested my rifle across the body of a supply orderly whom I assumed was dead—but later found was frozen with fear. The point up front kept calling back for machine gun fire on the flanks and for mortar fire ahead of the column. After a short while, we pushed on as enemy fire let up briefly.

"All kinds of firing suddenly split the night on all sides. We laid down lots of mortar shells beyond the head of the column. The 3rd Squad of 1st Platoon on the point pushed on, and even with all the firing, no one seemed to get hit." 59

After the firefight, Company I moved forward again, wary of an enemy ambush. Platoon Sergeant Bill Dunfee was up front near the point of the column. "Ray Maikowski was out with the point. He noticed movement alongside the road and eased the safety off his M1. The man hiding heard the click and made his presence known, claiming to be an American. Mike told him, 'Put your hands behind your head and get your ass out here in the middle of the road, where I can see you.'

"He was an American major (Hal D. McGown) of the 30th Infantry Division who had been captured in earlier fighting at La Gleize. He thought for sure, Maikowski was going to shoot him. Knowing Mike, his fright was justified. After he got over his fright, he told us he had been a prisoner of five to eight hundred Germans that had charged through our lines about an hour earlier." [60]

Those Germans were the remnants of Kampfgruppe Peiper, who had crossed the Amblève River, infiltrated south, and were making their way to the Salm River when they ran into Company I, both along the river at Rochelinval and in the woods during the I Company withdrawal.

At the rear of the Company I column, Private Millard W. Edgerley and two other members of his 60mm mortar squad were separated from the rest of the company—struggling with their heavy loads. "We heard a squad or more of Germans coming toward us. We lay in the snow as about a hundred Germans passed by—not more than thirty yards. It was a very bad night lying in the snow and cold." [61]

Company G pulled out of Petit-Halleux a little before midnight, later than the companies that had to move cross-country. They took the road leading west, then north through Bergeval to the main east-west road from Basse-Bodeux to Trois Ponts. However, Captain Isaacs was concerned because the road had iced over. "At some time during these events a freezing rain had fallen and the road west out of Petit-Halleux became a problem. As parachutists, we had no vehicles, so we were required to carry whatever we had or needed.

"As we were preparing to withdraw, we decided to use a local inhabitant's sled and horse to carry our heavy equipment. All went well until the horse went down on the ice and could not get up. Nor could we get it to its feet, so we had to abandon our idea, the horse, and the sled. We did manage to carry our own equipment, but had to disable the quad-fifty and leave it." [62]

Private First Class Chris Zafiroff, with Headquarters Company, 3rd Battalion, moved out with the G Company column through the falling snow, carrying his .30-caliber machine gun. "We were withdrawing single file in order to close up our lines, [when] one artillery shell hit our line of troopers. One man screamed in pain—others along with myself (in a low voice) yelled, 'Shut up you S.O.B. You will get us all killed.'" [63]

As soon as Company G left, Sergeant Christensen with the rear-guard platoon changed the positions of his men. "One man I pulled out of line and placed on the street in front of the house where the platoon CP was. I didn't want any surprises coming from that direction. I moved out in back of the CP. From here, I thought I could control things better. I knew in my mind if we got hit down here that I would pull them back to our old positions. There I thought we could hold them off, for a while at least. Down here we wouldn't last five minutes.

"The company had been gone only an hour or so when I started hearing heavy firing from the direction they would be traveling. From the sound of things, this did not sound like an isolated pocket of the enemy either. This went on for a while and then finally faded out. There were also big guns firing, which seemed to be coming from every direction.

"My position remained quiet though, until about 3:00 a.m., when one of my men came up and told me he had just heard Jerry crossing the river just below him. On further questioning, he said it was only a small group, so I knew it could only be a reconnaissance patrol.

"This, I knew, wouldn't give us any trouble unless they turned around and came back into the town from the other end and found it empty. I knew Jerry would then move in and occupy it. I hoped they would wait until after daylight, as we would be long gone. The rest of the night proved uneventful.

"Promptly at 5:00 a.m., we vacated our positions and started out. I had already briefed the men to stay well spread out and we would be moving at a brisk pace, also we would stay on the road. Up until now, I don't remember any snow, but the weather was getting colder. It must have rained or hailed sometime during the night, because the road in places was icy. Along this route I felt at anytime we would be ambushed, but we did not see one German. It was sure a welcome relief when I pulled into where the company was now dug in.

"I reported to my company commander, Captain Isaacs, and the first thing he said when he saw me was, 'I didn't expect to see you again.' He thought I would run into the Germans this morning [that] the battalion had encountered last night.

"'Pleasant thought.'

"In this new position, we were dug in on the forward slope of a high hill." [64]

At Rochelinval, Private First Class John Siam, with the Company I rear guard, was on watch in his hole at around 4:00 a.m. "Our 2nd Platoon minus the mortar squad was left on the river as rear guard. I was talking to [Private] John Lebednick. He came to relieve me on the machine gun. We were both from Worcester, Massachusetts, and had a discussion about what we thought was going on in Worcester. Before I left him to return to my hole to sleep, we agreed that we would meet next Christmas in a beer joint called Logan's and would tie one on. About fifteen minutes later we heard a BAR firing on our left. That was [Victor P.] Zoromski firing at a German patrol. [Frank G.] Federico ran to join Lebednick on the gun, and shortly after, the Jerry patrol ran into us. Lebednick halted them, and one of them jumped into the railroad tracks and opened up with a machine pistol. We were returning fire when Federico jumped into my hole and said he was hit." [65]

Company I medic Private First Class Jack Lyons was at the command post when the wounded Private First Class Federico came in. "He was shot through the side. I dressed his wound. By then, it was time to pull the unit out and go back to our lines." [66]

When Lieutenant Charles R. Christian ordered the 2nd Platoon to pull out, Private First Class Siam went to find Private Lebednick. "Lieutenant Christian and I checked the position and found out that Lebednick had been killed. He was either hit with a grenade on the side of his head or he caught a burst from a Schmeisser, and part of his head was gone." [67]

Meanwhile, Private First Class Lyons helped the wounded Federico make it to the road, where everyone was forming up. "We went over the railroad bridge and left our mines exposed on top of the bridge [over the railroad cut]. The engineers had blown a pretty good hole in it. Then we went up the hill toward the village, and Lieutenant Christian asked if anybody knew the way to go. I told him I knew the way up the road through Rochelinval and through the farmhouses. As we reached the edge of the village, we heard German voices all around us in the village and through the woods. They were probably lost, but there were a lot of them." [68]

As they moved silently through the village, Private First Class Siam heard German voices very close by. "[Lieutenant] Christian ordered us not to fire, but to keep moving. Christian's courage and leadership saved the lives of every man left in our group. He deserved a commendation and a medal, but never got one." [69]

The Company I rear guard continued on without further incident, with Private First Class Lyons leading the way. "We came in through F Company, 3rd Platoon, I believe. They challenged us—nobody knew the password. We yelled out a few obscenities and names, and they took us in." [70]

Sergeant Bill Dunfee and the other troopers in Company I had spent the entire night moving and fighting. "By daylight, we had reached our new positions. It was bitterly cold and windy. We were told to dig in and establish a line we could defend until the end of the war, if necessary. [Charles P.] Lupoli and I selected a spot that was just below the high ground to our rear. It jutted out far enough that we had a clear field of fire to our right and left, and across the valley—possibly a half mile to the woods on the other side. We were at the edge of a wooded area on our side of the valley.

"During the day of 25 December, we dug a cave and covered it with tree limbs and the dirt we had removed. We had three firing openings and felt we would be safe from anything but a direct hit from an 88. By that evening, the roof was beginning to sag, and we were outside cutting down a tree to reinforce it, when a mortar round came in and landed between us. Lupoli caught shrapnel in his foot and I was knocked down, but not injured. I carried Lupoli back to the company CP and he was evacuated. While at the CP, they had brought the mail forward, and I had a box of Christmas cookies. I tried to get Lupoli to take some of the cookies with him, but he refused. We shared everything and were inseparable. I sure missed him." [71]

CHAPTER 18

"The Company I Came To Know and Love No Longer Existed"

O n Christmas morning, Lieutenant James J. "Joe" Meyers, a platoon leader with Company D, and his men dug in on a hill overlooking Trois Ponts, in an open pasture on both sides of a haystack. "It was a beautiful, clear day and the Army Air Corps was out in force. A fear of disclosing their location and inviting air attack caused the Germans to refrain from firing at us. We moved freely about our position. There was no turkey dinner, but we received ten-in-one rations—a welcome change after a constant diet of C and K rations. The ten-in-one was a large box that contained ten rations, or thirty meals for ten men. Unfortunately, the food in the ration could not be broken down into individual servings and eaten in a foxhole. It was necessary to cook or heat portions of the ration before dividing and serving it to the men. At the time of issue, [Sergeant Donald H.] Olds asked me if he could bring a few men to the haystack to eat after he had cooked the meal. I made another mistake. I approved his request.

"Around noon several flights of P-47 fighters came over and attacked the German positions to our front and to the front of the 30th Division on our left flank. We sat on the edges of our foxholes like spectators at a sporting event and cheered as our planes carried out their bombing and strafing runs. Other flights of P-47s came in. Instead of attacking the Germans, several flights attacked the 30th Division. I saw three fighters circling to our front, and suddenly they peeled off and made strafing runs on our position near the haystack, about fifty yards away from my hole. I stood up and waved at the pilots as they came in, but they took no notice. Normally, we would have had signal panels to display or colored smoke to mark our position. Because of our hasty departure from Suippes, we had no means of signaling the aircraft.

"They circled and on the second pass the lead aircraft dropped a bomb that landed near the haystack. The bomb exploded and obviously killed or wounded some of my men." [1]

Luckily, Private V. P. Dewailly was in his foxhole when the three P-47s made their bombing and strafing runs. "Suddenly, they began diving toward us and dropping five-hundred-pound bombs. They would dive, strafing us, then drop their bomb. My foxhole was about 125 feet from where the bomb hit [the troopers near the haystack]." [2]

Seeing his men hit, Lieutenant Meyers immediately jumped out of his foxhole and "ran forward across the open field toward the haystack as the second plane made its strafing run. I hit the ground midway and I could hear and feel the .50-caliber machine gun rounds striking the earth around me. Unharmed, I jumped to my feet, ran to the vicinity of the haystack, and jumped into a prone shelter occupied by one of my men. He was kneeling and I landed across his legs. The third plane finished its strafing pass and I decided to look around. I first turned my attention to the man in the hole with me. His head was a mass of pulp spread out on the ground next to the hole. I could see some of his teeth amid the gore. It was the remains of Private [First Class Edwin G.] Davis. Sergeant Olds was also dead. Private [John L.] Grant, severely wounded, died later. I crammed a mess kit spoon down Grant's throat to keep him from swallowing his tongue and gave him a shot of morphine. Several others arrived and helped evacuate the wounded." 3

Company D lost five men killed and four wounded, one of whom, Private Grant, died the following day. Meyers was infuriated over the senseless loss of his men. "The P-47s had expended their ordnance and returned to base. I could only think of three pilots landing, going to the officer's club for dinner and a drink, and then spending the night between clean sheets in a warm, safe environment. I felt extreme guilt, anger, and frustration. I was guilty of allowing the men to gather together near the haystack. I was angry because the ten-in-one rations contributed to the loss. Most of all, I was furious at the pilots who attacked us.

"A simple check of a compass and the terrain would have told them we were friendly. If the god of war had delivered the three pilots into my hands that day, they would have been dead men. My frustration came from my inability to do anything about it. I have had many enjoyable Christmas seasons since that day, but not one Christmas has gone by without my recalling that fateful day in December of '44." 4

In addition to Olds, Evans, and Grant, Private Kenneth R. Craig, Private Bernard J. Schroeder, and Private First Class Edwin G. Davis were also killed. Private First Class Frank Bilich felt a deep personal loss as a result of the deaths. The "episode was tough for me to understand, especially since [Private Kenneth R.] Craig was the kindly soldier who gave me a lot of advice in that Quonset hut in Northern Ireland." 5

On December 26, Private First Class Les Cruise, with Company H, was sitting in his covered foxhole at a roadblock when someone said that mail had arrived. "At the call, I received a package from my mother, with a pen and pencil set enclosed, along with a box of candy, which would make the rounds and disappear quickly. With the new pen and pencil set, I could write letters on 'V-mail.'

"Mail call was always a happy time for most of the men. We appreciated mail call, and more particularly at the front. It was great to stand with the troops, all hungry for some attention and news from home, and to hear your name called for a letter, or a package from home areas, it's like a shot in the arm. It uplifted you from the current situation and reminded you of where you've come from and your ties with others." 6

On December 26 and 27, most of the troopers ate a Christmas dinner. Platoon Sergeant Bill Dunfee, with Company I, was very grateful to eat a warm meal, the first since leaving France more than a week earlier. "We went back a squad at a time after dark and chowed down. It was really appreciated. After all those K-rations, our bellies felt like our throats had been cut." [7]

Even though his dinner was almost cold when he received it, Private First Class Virgil M. Goodwin, with Company B, was just happy to get a meal. "When you haven't had much to eat for a few days, you don't complain—enjoy what you have." [8]

A second tragedy struck Company D on the evening of December 26, when Sergeant Henry Jakiela went out to check on the company's outposts. One of Jakiela's own men shot and killed him by mistake. That evening, Private First Class Dave Bowman, along with three other Company D troopers, loaded the bodies of Jakiela and the men killed the previous day by the errant bombing onto a trailer for transport to the graves registration unit. These dead troopers had been their buddies. "When we arrived where they had been stacked, a jeep with a trailer was idling nearby. As callous as it may sound, we simply picked each up by the shoulders and feet and tossed them into the trailer—much as one would so many gunnysacks full of feed. One touching moment in this whole episode came when Jakiela's body began to roll off. [Corporal William] Bennett, his close friend, grabbed and repositioned him, at the same time saying in a soothing and casually intimate way, 'Hold on there, Jake.' The jeep then pulled off without a second glance from any of us." [9]

The following night, Technician Fourth Grade Allan Barger, with Company D, finished digging a new slit trench and needed something to cover it. "I was walking across the frigid snow and wrestling with a bunch of old boards when I ran into Captain [George D.] Carlson with a couple of headquarters men, and since I didn't have the password, I just told him so and gave my name. That was O.K.—but for a second, I didn't know whether it would work.

"I was given instructions to pass a message to one of the BAR outposts, and since that soldier had just shot his own sergeant by mistake the night before, I advanced very cautiously to his position and didn't hesitate to holler to let him know I was approaching him. We knew each other fairly well.

"His sergeant was Henry Jakiela, who had just won a $1,000 savings bond in a raffle back at Suippes. He was well liked by all of us, too." [10]

DURING THE NEXT FEW DAYS, the regiment rested and readied itself for the inevitable counteroffensive to drive the German army back to its start line. During this period, Captain Taylor G. Smith, the 2nd Battalion executive officer, rotated to the United States on a thirty-day leave, replaced by Captain William R. Carpenter.

On January 2, 1945, Lieutenant Bill "Rusty" Hays transferred from Company F to D. It was also his birthday. That night, Hays prepared for the coming attack, scheduled to commence the following morning. "Each soldier took his overcoat and all his sleeping gear, rolled it in a bundle, and left it to be brought up at a later date after the attack. The idea was that we'd not be weighed down with this extra weight.

The snow was about two feet deep and, the temperature about ten to twenty degrees below zero. While we were moving, the cold was not too bad. We were acclimated to the cold by that time. But it was impossible to sleep at night. We were already too lightly equipped for the weather we faced, and to drop what warm things we had and have to lie down in the snow to sleep was miserable.

"The night before our attack, I was faced with spending a miserable night in the snow in well below zero weather. Then, I remembered something I had read about when I was a boy. When I was growing up, I enjoyed reading Indian lore. One of the things I read about was how Indians managed to sleep warm when they were caught in the woods and had to spend the night. They had a technique of making a warm bed from fir, spruce, or pine branches. I decided to see if it would work for me. It took me an hour to prepare my bed, but it was well worth it. That night I slept soundly and warmly, thanks to the Indians." [11]

At dawn on January 3, 1945, the American counteroffensive began in the midst of one-to-two-foot-deep snow, fog, and an overcast sky. The German 62nd Volksgrenadier Division was dug in opposite of the 82nd Airborne Division. Technician Fourth Grade Barger was weighed down in the deep snow by a heavy SCR-300 radio and other gear as Company D moved to the line of departure before dawn. "We started to walk and walk, endlessly through the night without having the least idea where we were going. We would get sore from walking and want to rest. We would get stiff from stopping because of the extreme cold, and want to move. Hour after hour.

"I kept repeating silently in my mind the Twenty-third Psalm . . .

"A little before eight o'clock in the morning of January the third of the new year, we finally worked our way down through some brush, and apparently we were facing east near a road and awaiting orders. I often thought this was a curious moment, as we stood around joking about this, even though we were uptight and fully aware that something big and dangerous was about to happen.

"I was reminded of a picture I used to study back in my school days with the title, 'Over the Top.' The soldiers were portrayed coming out of their trenches in World War I and heading into no man's land. As a mere boy, I used to wonder if I would have enough courage to do that. Well, now I would find out! I found there are times you do something whether you like it or not, even though fear is slicing through you, every minute vein in your body.

"We crossed a road to our front. I was staying close to Captain Carlson most of the time now, as I was his radioman to battalion. However, he ran across another road to our left flank near a 'Y' junction, telling me to stay where I was. He wasn't gone very long when he called me over. I ran over to where he was sitting—in a ditch—and slid over beside him.

"Then someone said, 'Hey! Barger, look what you just did!'

"I looked and a chill went up my spine, for I could see clearly in the light snow that my feet had slid right up against a small antipersonnel mine, and I had even left a layer of mushy snow up against it. I had been within a hair's breath of triggering it.

"Shortly after that, we moved eastward along this road, and it was easy to see there was a bloody battle going on just up to the front of us. Jeeps were hauling out one load after another of wounded and swiftly moving to our rear.

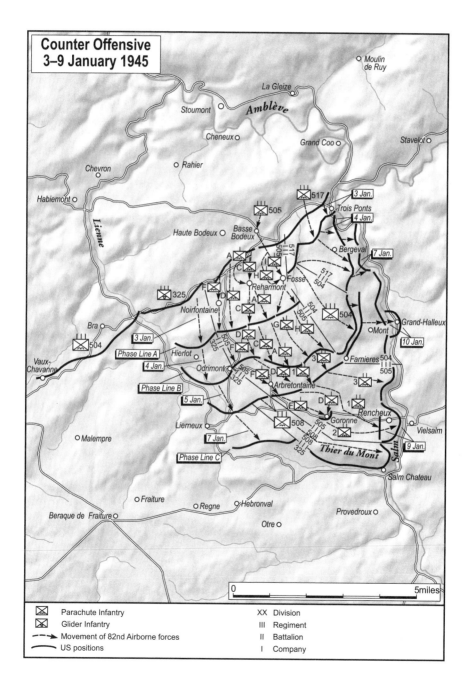

"We proceeded down a narrow road through a little boggy draw, and started up a gentle slope on a small lane running between two frozen meadows. Our battalion commander, Lieutenant Colonel Vandervoort, called Captain Carlson and our group over to his side and asked if we knew where F Company was. We didn't know and said so.

"So the colonel said he had sent them further up the lane into the edge of the woods to our west and asked if we would go check them out." [12]

THE 2ND BATTALION ADVANCED TOWARD the farmhouses of Noirfontaine with Company F on the right, west of the road running south to Arbrefontaine. Sergeant Russ Brown, a four-jump veteran with Company F, led a 60mm mortar squad. "[Private First Class] Victor Saragosa had been in the 3rd Platoon mortar squad, but he was placed in my squad, because he was about the only one left in his squad.

"At the start of the attack, we rode on the tanks, until we were fired on. We jumped off the tank and some of the men had trouble crossing a ditch—the snow was so deep. I had the mortar, and Saragosa took it from me as we walked away from the tank. An 88 fired at the tank. Saragosa and I hit the ground—Saragosa was riddled with shrapnel and killed. My ears were ringing and I thought I was O.K. Someone said, 'Brown, you are bleeding.' I had a piece of shrapnel go through my ear, but that was all. I was O.K.

"I went into the edge of the woods and a German came out with his hands up and he handed me a folding trigger .22 pistol. It was so small, I put it in my watch pocket.

"I saw Staff Sergeant Bonnie Wright lying on the side of the road with someone else. He was wounded [and later died]." [13]

Shortly after Company F dismounted, German tanks and self-propelled guns quickly knocked out two Sherman tanks and two M10 tank destroyers. Corporal Don McKeage was moving with the company headquarters group. "Company headquarters included a machine gun section from the 2nd Battalion, Headquarters Company; a total of nineteen men, led by Lieutenant [Harold E.] Case.

"Three platoons disappeared into the woods. We started up a fence row and figured we were behind one of our platoons. As we entered the woods, all hell broke loose. Two mortar shells hit with tree bursts right on our group. Sixteen of our men, including the complete machine gun section, went down—all wounded. Three of us were O.K.—Lieutenant Case, James Shuman, and myself. The Germans opened up with rifle fire. I had my rifle shot out of my hand. For some reason, the platoon was not where we figured."

Company D moved south on the left, east of the road, toward Noirfontaine, with Lieutenant Joe Meyers leading the 3rd Platoon. "Heavy mortar and artillery fire greeted us at the line of departure (LD). A short distance beyond the LD we forded a small stream and advanced into large, open, snow covered fields. The mortar and artillery fire was very heavy, and suddenly I felt a hot burning sensation in the fleshy part of my right upper arm. A medic cut away the layers of clothing [and] informed me I had a minor shrapnel wound.

"We continued to advance and arrived at a road junction where we halted briefly. Vandervoort joined [Captain George D.] Carlson and me. He wanted a patrol dispatched to contact the 3rd Battalion on our left. I volunteered to take the patrol, but Vandervoort wisely told me to send an NCO. After I dispatched the patrol, Carlson and I discussed the best route of advance. Directly to our front was a large, open field about one hundred fifty yards wide and three hundred yards long. A few yards inside the field, we saw a German antitank minefield hastily installed on top of the ground and covered by the new snow. It was not necessary to expose the entire company while crossing this open field. I recommended the 3rd Platoon cross the field, and that Carlson move the company along a covered route on the far side of the field. Carlson would have me in his sight all the way, and we could link up in the far woods. Carlson agreed. The 3rd Platoon crossed the field without losing a man.

"When we reached the woods at the far end of the field, we discovered several hastily installed booby traps and halted to disarm them. One of my BAR men, Private First Class James McKinney, flushed out and killed a couple of Germans. McKinney was a good soldier. His motto was, 'When it's too tough for everyone else, it's just right for me.' He lived up to it." 14

Meanwhile, the rest of the company moved up the narrow, tree-lined lane. Vandervoort had told Captain Carlson that when they made contact with Company F to radio him with the position. The SCR-300 radio operator for Company D was Technician Fourth Grade Allan Barger. "Just as we got to the position we expected to find F Company, we found them. But before we could even say a word on the radio, a shell struck right in our midst.

"I felt the left side of my face and my left shoulder go numb. And as I passed out, I remembered having been told in the case of such wounds, the portion damaged would turn numb. So of course, I thought the whole side of my face was removed along with a chunk of my shoulder. That meant I was finished. To myself I made the voiceless scream: 'I'm not ready to die!' It was as though I wanted to get my soul screwed on right before I left this planet.

"It was joyful surprise when I came to, and found all I had was a small, bloody hole in the top of my shoulder. A piece of shrapnel had gone through both my radio and musette bag shoulder straps and a thick layer of clothes. It lodged right next to my shoulder blade.

"As I looked around me I discovered a whole cluster of men wounded or dead on the floor of the forest. Captain Carlson was not only wounded in the leg, but Lieutenant Virgil Gould was lying on the ground with a hole in his knee. We were the lucky ones, for our operations sergeant, Freddie Freeland, was mortally wounded by the same burst. The medics were pretty busy dressing our wounds and, of course, giving us shots." 15

The D Company headquarters group was the second to be struck down, and the attack was just getting under way. Meanwhile, Lieutenant Meyers and his platoon were finishing disarming the booby traps. "A runner arrived and reported mortar fire had wounded both Carlson and [1st Sergeant John] Rabig, and had killed or wounded several other men. I assumed command and sent for [Lieutenant Lawrence M.] Price and [Lieutenant Marshall] Hughes. While they were coming, I contacted [Lieutenant] Harold Case, F Company commander, and informed him of our situation. When Price and Hughes arrived with the company radio, I notified battalion of our situation. I decided to continue the advance with three platoons in column, 3rd Platoon leading. Deployed platoons are difficult to control in dense woods, and, although mortar and artillery fire was extremely heavy, enemy resistance was spotty. The attack continued until shortly before dark, when we stopped and dug in for the night." [16]

The 1st Battalion was assigned the hamlet of Reharmont in the center of the 505th zone of attack. As Company C moved directly toward the village, artillery fire exploded around them, wounding Lieutenant Gus Sanders and a couple of his men as they approached a stream. After wading across the freezing stream, they moved up a wooded hill toward Reharmont. The woods concealed the Company C skirmish line until they were within a hundred yards of the town. Sergeant Elmo Bell had an uneasy feeling as Company C moved through the woods and began to emerge into open ground about one hundred yards in front of Reharmont. "This little village was separated from the woods by a wide expanse of open ground. There were a bunch of little stone houses in the village there that the Germans occupied, and these stone houses would provide good protection against small arms." [17]

Intense German fire from Reharmont cut down Lieutenants Walter Haupt and Wilbert H. Robbins, Jr., as they emerged from the woods, leading their platoons. Assistant platoon leader Lieutenant Edwin Barker took command of Haupt's platoon, only to be wounded so badly by machine gun fire that the medics didn't think he would live. Despite the grievous wounds, Barker held on and survived. Machine gun, small arms, and mortar fire decimated Company C as it emerged from the woods. Bell realized that the company couldn't advance across this killing field. "They had fields of fire—it became obvious to us early on that nobody was going to cross that open ground in daylight without tank or artillery support. So we fell back into the woods and started screaming for artillery fire and tank support, and neither were forthcoming.

"We started looking, trying to use our mortars, but there were no holes in the overhead canopy to shoot through. So we were just sitting there, taking the punishment." [18]

In the woods near Reharmont, Sergeant Frank Thompson, with the 1st Battalion 81mm mortar platoon, was up front with the rifle companies, acting as a forward observer as enemy artillery ranged-in not only the attacking elements but the rear elements as well. "The other section sergeant, Richard V. Williams, was killed by an artillery shell [that landed] in the support area, and Levi Horsechief, one of his gunners, was wounded." [19]

Company C trooper Private First Class Joseph V. "Joe" Tallett was told to take cover "on the side of the hill and wait for the tanks or until A Company flanked the enemy's positions. Looking down the hill, I could see the combat engineers working on the bridge. They were taking heavy casualties. Working along with them in water up to his chest was the commander of the 82nd Airborne Division, Major General James M. Gavin. This was typical of 'Slim Jim,' a warrior and an inspirational leader to his men." [20]

Sergeant Louis C. Scarborough, with Company C, took what little cover he could. "I was sitting behind a tree. German tanks [fired]—an 88 [round] hit the tree, took my pack, and I had a scrape in my back and neck. We took morphine from the dead guys." [21]

Sergeant Bell and others tried to help their wounded buddies, but it was difficult, without overcoats, blankets, or sleeping bags. "Our greatest concern was the inability to care for the wounded. Many of our members died from superficial wounds that normally would not have been life threatening. They died simply because we couldn't keep them warm. When a person is wounded, the loss of blood lowers the body temperature. The blood-soaked clothing freezes and reduces the temperature even more. The individual is then likely to die from shock or hypothermia." [22]

Company A moved to the right of Company C to flank Reharmont. Private First Class Dave Bullington had been with Company A since its inception, and had made all four combat jumps. "I was carrying a box of machine gun ammunition. They started shelling us with artillery and mortars. A lot of that stuff landed in the trees; it didn't do much good to get on the ground with all of that stuff going off over your head. We were attacking in one direction, and all at once we made a ninety-degree turn to the left. We moved up and I didn't get very far; a couple of men and I ran and got behind a mound of dirt. I no sooner got there than the Krauts opened up with a machine gun and hit me in the hand. I still had my hand on that box of ammunition. I guess if I hadn't had my hand on that box of ammunition I wouldn't have gotten hit. I couldn't hardly tell which hand I was hit in, because they were both hurting, it was so cold. I got evacuated that time. The war was over for me." [23]

With Company A now positioned west of Reharmont, and Company C north of it, Company B, the battalion reserve, was brought up but was hit by Germans on their right flank, inflicting several casualties. Sergeant Mike Vuletich, the company communications NCO, took command of fifteen troopers on the company's flank and led them in a bayonet charge, resulting in the capture of ninety-five enemy enlisted men and one officer. Vuletich's actions would later result in the award of a Silver Star for his leadership and heroism. A couple of Sherman tanks arrived shortly after the engineers repaired the bridge, ending the German resistance. Company B and the tanks moved forward to join the other two companies.

Private Cecil Prine, a wireman with Headquarters Company, 1st Battalion, was following Company B, laying communications wire as they moved forward. "I had to wade through a stream that was half ice and half water." [24]

For two hours, Company C suffered severe casualties from almost constant fire from four 88mm guns and mortars. Finally, Private First Class Tallett, with

Company C, was ordered to move up to the front of the woods. The company was ready to assault the town. "A combination of getting the tanks across the creek and A Company flanking the German position broke the stalemate. We rolled up their line and killed and captured about a battalion of Germans." [25]

The objective was taken by around 11:00 a.m., but the assault had cost Company C half of its strength. The battalion moved out and was on its phase line a couple of hours later.

ON THE LEFT FLANK, COMPANY I WAS ASSIGNED TO SEIZE FOSSE, with fire support from Company H on a hill to their right. Company G moved behind in reserve. One of the Company I medics, Private First Class Jack Lyons, was expecting an easy day. "We had been told that our objective was Fosse, and that there would not be a lot of resistance. There was supposed to be some sort of German 'Volksturm,' or old soldiers, or something." [26]

At 7:00 a.m., Private First Class Les Cruise moved out with the Company H column toward Basse-Bodeux. "When we arrived at the crossroads of the town, the companies fanned out into battle formations in preparation for the attack.

"At 8:30, we began our trek through the front lines back towards Fosse. As we labored through the heavy snow up the first hill outside Basse-Bodeux, we received some incoming artillery fire that went over our heads and landed well beyond us. This tended to sharpen our senses and make us wary of the possible dangers awaiting our advance.

"We passed over the crest of the second hill, where I could see how devastating artillery can be; for along my pathway lay a dead German soldier, with his head cleanly severed and nowhere to be seen. The red color of his bloody neck was mute testimony to the power of the shells. I almost puked at the sight, as I turned away." [27]

As Company I made its way through the deep snow to the initial point, Sergeant Bill Dunfee was near the front of the column. "As we moved down this road, there was a tree burst over my head that nobody heard coming. [Private Louis] DiGiralamo, who was directly behind me, was killed instantly, [and] Jessie Clark was across the road and caught shrapnel in his leg and foot. I was knocked down, and the butt of my BAR came down on my middle finger, putting a permanent kink in it. Shrapnel tore away my left breast pocket, mangling the hell out of my toothbrush and toothpaste. There was just this one round that came in, and we were up and on our way." [28]

Company I veteran Sergeant Bill Tucker moved through the deep snow with his mortar squad and their heavy loads. "We trudged uphill to Fosse, and our tails dragged. We went along in single file. For about half an hour, we had no trouble as we climbed the snowy hills." [29]

Near the bottom of the hill, Private First Class Dennis Force began the climb up the snow-covered slope to Fosse on the crest above. "It was quite heavily wooded until we got to the first hedge. Then we went into attack formation with [Sergeant Charles] Matash and the squad." [30]

Sergeant Dunfee struggled as he moved through the deep snow weighed down by his BAR and the heavy ammunition he carried. "When I got to within seventy-five yards of our objective, the Germans opened up with a vengeance. We were pinned down by rifle and machine gun fire from our front, as well as the woods on our left. I found a roll in the ground and bellied down." [31]

Just as Company H came over the wooded crest of the hill northwest of Fosse to give fire support to the Company I attack, enemy artillery and mortars opened up on them. The company halted, but Private First Class Cruise knew they couldn't stay there. "Trees were being shattered all around us, along with the ground shaking from the bursts. Off to my right, the machine gun crew of [Hans F.] Frey and [Leon W.] Vassar, both went down, along with our platoon leader, Lieutenant [William A.] Rowe, and several others.

"A medic raced forward to assist. We seemed bogged down for some reason, and I wanted to get out of this trap. I had planted myself behind a tree, with my rifle in my right hand, and in my left, a box of machine gun ammunition. Shells were landing all over the area, shattering trees above us. It was pandemonium!

"A shell exploded with terrific force directly overhead in the tree and set my ears to ringing and numbed my senses. 'Boy was that close,' I thought, as I began to feel a throbbing pain in my left hand. When I looked down, I saw the red of my blood oozing through the glove on my hand, and I realized that I had been stung by the shrapnel from the exploding shell. My whole arm seemed paralyzed with the searing of the flesh. I felt a burning sensation up my limb.

"I removed my glove to see the damage; then called back to [Private First Class John E.] Atchley that I had been hit. He rushed forward to lend a hand, carefully placing the sulfa powder on the hand and wrapping a bandage around the wound. My flesh looked like a piece of raw meat before he covered it, with my thumb just hanging loosely, almost severed. I could hardly move my arm. My nerves were deadened. He then gave me a morphine shot from his first aid kit. By this time, I was in a sitting position by the tree, and the command to continue the advance was given.

"The medic who had attended others in the squad came over and said to me and other wounded troopers to walk back to the aid station if we were able, and he would get litter bearers for those not able to walk. Private [Donald R.] Lewis and I started back to Basse-Bodeux, our line of departure several hours ago." [32]

Sergeant Tucker and his mortar squad worked their way around the right side of the hill, when Tucker heard bullets crack by him and the snow kick up as several bursts hit among his men. "Suddenly, we were fired on by machine gun posts at our left rear. We had passed them, but they were closer to the top of the hill than we were. Enemy firing seemed to be on both the left and right. Germans were dug in both inside and outside the town. They had set up strong machine gun posts at the actual crest of the hill and could look down into the valley. We were in between the machine gun outposts and the town, which also held German forces.

"I ordered my squad into action and ran up to the next level of the hill to get a line on the German machine guns. Part of 3rd Platoon was sheltered behind a ledge. I glanced up, but machine gun fire knocked snow into my eyes.

"Captain [Archibald] McPheeters was at the head of 1st Platoon and pinned down at the left about fifty yards from the top of the hill. [Corporal William A.] Hallahan started to get up and move that way. He was shot through the head." [33]

Sergeant Dunfee saw one of the original members of the company, Private First Class Richard W. Cutler, get hit. "Dick had made it to the hedgerow—he raised up with his BAR to fire on a sniper who was in a barn loft to our immediate front. His last words were, 'I'll get the son-of-a-bitch!' The sniper was waiting on him to raise up. Dick took a bullet through the chest, groaned, and died. Dick and I had been friends since basic training.

"It hurts to take any casualties, but as the original men are being taken out, you become more aware of your chances with the law of averages." [34]

Sergeant Tucker was shocked when "Cutler, a veteran of campaigns since Africa, was killed. He left a wife and two children. [Sergeant Arthur M. "Tommie"] Thompson ran over and held Cutler in his arms as he died. They were really close buddies." [35]

Near the crest of the hill, Sergeant Dunfee tried to move up to a hedgerow about twenty yards in front of him. "Every time I attempted to move from the trough I was in, I drew fire. In my mind's eye I could visualize the German just begging me to raise up just a little more, so he could blow my head off. I had done that very thing, when the shoe was on the other foot. I was very scared and frustrated. I eased over on my back and wondered where the hell was that company of the 551st [Parachute Infantry Battalion, attached to the division,] that was supposed to clear the woods on our left." [36]

Also pinned down near the town, Private First Class Howard C. Goodson hugged the ground as machine gun bullets kicked up snow in his face. "They had machine guns all along the top, on that road. It was the most scared I have ever been, and I was alone." [37]

Private First Class John Siam, carrying a .30-caliber machine gun, was down the hill somewhat. "[Lieutenant Charles R.] Christian ordered our machine gun and [Calvin C.] Gilbert and his bazooka to get to the top of the hill and return fire in the wooded area. As soon as we opened fire, Jerry mortars rained in on us. I stopped firing and asked Martin if he was O.K., because a mortar round landed close to his foot.

"Martin said he was O.K. and then said, 'Gilbert's hit.' I looked to my left and saw Gilbert on his hands and knees with blood pouring out of his mouth. He was shot through the nose, and the bullet took his teeth out and came out his ear. Christian ordered us back down the hill." [38]

Sergeant Tucker couldn't see any way out of the situation. "If we moved forward, machine gun posts would probably nail us. We couldn't move back either, or we would lose the attack. We could move only by crawling. We had to lie flat where we were in the snow. German artillery screamed into us and crunched all around. It was terrible. We wanted to dash forward at the town, but others had tried and were killed. The Operations Sergeant, William F. Reynolds, crawled ahead of us. He was killed." [39]

Lieutenant Christian ordered the 2nd Platoon to move back down the hill and then move around the right side again. Private First Class Siam, carrying his machine gun, finally caught up with the platoon on the right side of the hill. "That's when Christian said, 'Okay, get that machine gun up the hill here,' and we said, 'We don't have any ammo.' [Private First Class] Nick Cavallaro, being the kind of guy he was, immediately grabbed the cans of ammo and took off, and I ran up right behind [Christian]. As I ran, I saw guys were going along the top line of the hill toward the town and were silhouetted. I was along the right side just below.

"As we reached the top of the damn hill, all of a sudden Cavallaro caught a machine gun burst straight in his neck and his chest. He hit the ground as hard as anyone I ever saw hit the ground." [40]

The same burst hit Sergeant Tucker. "Three of us were hit. Bullets through the neck partially ripped Cavallaro's head off. A bullet hit my rifle and ricocheted into my left shoulder. Another bullet smashed into the rear of my helmet, ripped through the liner, and tore a big hole out in the front. The bullet had left just a little burn at the top of my head without breaking the skin. In a split second, it occurred to me that I knew the closeness of death." [41]

Just behind them when they were hit was Private First Class Dennis Force. "John Siam and I side-by-side hit the snow. Then I jumped up and ran to Nick, grabbing him by the shoulder straps. I guess he was dead; I rolled him over and hollered for a medic." [42]

Private Pat Passero heard the call for a medic. "I told a sergeant right alongside me, 'I'm going to go up and get him.'

"He said, 'No, no don't go. They got him pinned down.'

"I put both hands on each side of me, holding the medical packs down. I slipped through the fence and these bushes, and I ran across this field, more or less in the open. I was so naive that I figured that having this bright Red Cross brassard on my arm and kit, the Germans could see that I was a medic. I was going more or less right out in the open. I cut right across this field crouching down with my hands on my side, keeping the medical packs from slapping up against my legs. As I was crouching and running up this hill, I could see the tracers coming at me. I said to myself, 'You know, these guys are firing at me. They mean business.' But I didn't get hit while I was running, and I got to the top of this field." [43]

Seeing the medic approaching, Private First Class Force moved out of the way. "I jumped up and got about twenty feet away and hit the snow as machine gun fire came at me from the left." [44]

Passero got up to the wounded men and stopped. "There were four guys lying there. They looked up at me when I came, and I looked the situation over. I could see one guy lying there with a big wound in his neck—it was all blood. I could see he was the worst hit of all because he wasn't looking at me. The other guys were talking—yelling to me, saying things, but I couldn't comprehend because I was trying to concentrate on what I had to do. So I yanked the medical packs off over my head, and I knelt down alongside the guy I figured needed the most attention." [45]

As Passero knelt to work on Private First Class Cavallero, he suddenly went down. At first, Passero didn't realize he was hit. "Immediately, I felt my legs go from underneath me. I was kneeling and it felt like something plowed right into me and it knocked me flat on my face. I kind of thought I got hit, but it didn't hurt so much, as it was surprising. I went to raise myself up on my elbows and I felt I got hit again. I got hit in the back this time—got slammed down to the ground again. So I just lay there." [46]

Just a few yards away, Force asked Passero how badly he was hit. "Then, while I was talking to Passero, I was hit in the face and in the arm." [47]

Just minutes later, the other company medic, Private First Class Jack Lyons, was hit by mortar fire. "I believe it was Joe Novak who patched me up. I said I was okay to stay. I wasn't in any pain; the pain came later." [48]

When the firing started, Sergeant Harry Buffone had dropped behind a slight ridge on the right side of the hill, shielding him from the crossfire from the left, somewhat. "Lieutenant [Richard H.] Degenhardt yelled, '1st or 3rd Squad, follow me!' They all took off and managed to get out of sight. Then we heard a lot of machine gun fire. We heard later that every one of them got caught in a gully, and the machine gun fire got all of them." [49]

A machine gun burst ripped into Degenhardt's chest, mortally wounding him, and hit several of his men. The call for a medic sent Private First Class Lyons to the aid of Degenhardt and the other wounded men. "I got maybe thirty yards from him and I got hit again. Captain McPheeters had been hit not long after I had left him to go out to Degenhardt. When I came back down, they told me he had been shot through the head and killed instantly." [50]

Captain McPheeters had attempted to lead the 1st Platoon forward in a frontal assault on the town, but had been cut down before taking more than a half dozen steps.

Sergeant Tucker and the wounded men lying with him worked their way back down the hill. "We rolled ourselves and the wounded down the hillside away to where we were safer. The remainder of the platoon had failed in its attack on the main German machine gun outpost and rejoined us on the hill's lower ledge. We couldn't move. German artillery slowly [was wiping] us out. The noise was terrific. We had to do something. We had to try something new.

"The 1st and 3rd Platoons were still out in front about a hundred yards from the town. They were pinned down. We moved again toward them, staying along the side of the hill. A little cart path wound up to the town. To its right was a big haystack. Some guys were behind the haystack with their backs to us. Everyone was flattened out on the snow. German shelling got worse. I pressured Lieutenant Christian for an open assault on the town because of increasing losses from shelling. About the only moving around I could do was crawl over to the haystack and sit with [Pvt. Rudy] Tepsick for a few minutes. Then I would crawl back, all the time arguing with Lieutenant Christian about what we could do. Lieutenant Christian wanted to get some orders from somewhere. We had no company commander, and no [other] officer around us.

"From his place with 2nd Platoon, [Sergeant Paul] Hill appeared, holding a wound in his neck. 'So long boys,' he said. 'I finally made it.' We had lost at least fifty men dead and wounded on the hill." [51]

As Private Millard Edgerley and his mortar squad lay flat, pinned down in the snow, he saw "hot shrapnel sizzling around us," [52] as enemy mortar and artillery fire fell among the Company I troopers.

The 3rd Battalion commander, Lieutenant Colonel James Kaiser, ordered Company H to assist the Company I assault. Sergeant Bill Tucker and a couple of other Company I troopers were sitting behind a haystack, trying to decide what to do next. "Suddenly, as we sat there, we saw H Company in the valley three hundred yards away. They were moving in to give us a hand." [53]

German artillery and mortars began pounding H Company as it moved through the deep snow in the valley. Corporal Joe Comer, a four-combat-jump veteran, hit the ground as the first rounds impacted nearby. "All you can do is get down there and try to get your belt buckle to dig you a hole to get down in that snow. Of course, that wouldn't do any good, but it felt like you could just feel them come right over you, and they would hit down behind you just a little ways—that's frightening. They would catch you out there and they would drop them around you in a square, and you had to try to get out of there before the shells closed in on you." [54]

Staying where they were would only result in more casualties. As soon as there was a break in the incoming artillery, the Company H veterans got back up and started moving forward, so that German artillery observers would be less able to get a fix on their position. Heavy German machine gun and rifle fire hit Company H as it moved up the slope northwest of Fosse. The communications sergeant, Norbert Beach, knew they had to keep moving forward or they would be annihilated. "We attempted all morning and into the afternoon to try to take this town, but were always turned back because of heavy machine gun fire, and we had no cover. The approach was an open field, which the Germans covered with machine guns and rifle fire. We could not make a move with that kind of firepower." [55]

The diversion of German fire to pin down H Company gave some of the Company I troopers, including four-combat-jump veteran Private First Class Howard Goodson, the breathing space to work their way closer to the German positions. "I was crawling in that damned snow. I kept getting closer. Matash and his group were near the top of the hill pretty close to the road the Germans were on." [56]

Finally, Goodson and others worked in close enough to pick off some of the enemy machine gunners. Shortly after noon, as if receiving a gift from God, Sergeant Beach heard the sound of tanks approaching from the west along the road to Fosse. "We got behind the tanks and got into the edge of the town." [57]

Company H moved into the western edge and behind the town, while Company C, 551st, closed in from the east. When the Germans turned their attention to counter the threats on their flanks and rear, Company I began to advance into the town from the north.

Private First Class Siam put his machine gun over his shoulder and moved up the hill through an appalling and horrific scene. "I saw the bodies of our other machine gun team, both killed, McPheeters' body, parts of bodies all over the hill, and Lieutenant Christian bandaging his head." [58]

The veteran troopers of Companies H and Company I, and Company C, 551st, destroyed the German battalion holding Fosse after vicious house-to-house fighting. Out of the 600 or so defenders, only about 125 were captured, including the battalion commander. The scene was ghastly—dead troopers lay in the snow in front of Fosse, and German corpses littered the village. Most of the German wounded would die of exposure that night. Casualties were so high that the medics had their hands full evacuating all of the wounded troopers. Every officer in Company I had been killed or wounded. Two of every three troopers in Company I were casualties. That evening, Lieutenant Joseph Vandevegt arrived from regimental headquarters to take command of the remnants of Company I.

Company H suffered terribly as well—Private First Class John Atchley, a recipient of the Distinguished Service Cross for his action in Normandy, in which he single-handedly knocked out a German self-propelled gun, was killed. But, Company H was still a capable fighting force as darkness fell.

That afternoon, Sergeant Tucker was evacuated to the aid station at Basse-Bodeux, where the regimental command post was located. "At regimental headquarters, the ground and buildings were littered with dead and wounded men. The surgeon worked on me with sulfa and quick bandages. Men were dying. My wounds felt small as I looked around at the others. I told the surgeon I didn't want any help. He said to go back with the other wounded men in the truck. My wounds were still not fully dressed, so I hung around the yard. [Lieutenant] Colonel Krause, who had become the regimental executive officer, paced up and down. I said to him, 'Well Colonel, the old guys got it today.' Colonel Krause stopped. He gazed at me and beyond me. There were tears in his eyes." [59]

Staff Sergeant Walter L. Tuttle, assigned to a 155mm battery of the 592nd Field Artillery Battalion, entered Fosse the following day. "We had been called on to fire for the 82nd Airborne Division. They had just cleaned out Fosse, and when the 82nd cleans out a town, it is clean. German soldiers were lying everywhere, frozen stiff in the snow, some were lying in the road, and our trucks smashed them to pieces. The 82nd added an ironic touch by standing one up against a fence in the position of a route marker. He had fallen with an arm outstretched and had hair a foot long, frozen as if the wind were blowing it straight out." [60]

As the fighting died down, Colonel Ekman and some of his staff personally searched the snow-covered battlefield for wounded troopers not yet evacuated. After the fighting at Fosse ended, Sergeant Dunfee moved out with the survivors of Company I to set up a defensive perimeter around Fosse, while G and H Companies pushed eleven hundred yards farther south to Phase Line A. "The fighting had died down except for artillery exchanges. We then became aware of how cold we were, since we had dropped our packs and overcoats prior to the attack. I tried to get authorization from our platoon leader to send a detail to the rear to retrieve our equipment. He wouldn't O.K. it, but agreed to my going to the company CP and checking it out with the company exec. When I got to the CP, they had already retrieved their equipment, and most of them were sacked out. I tried to awaken the exec, but he had been running on amphetamines, and when they ran out, so did he. That was good enough for me; I went back and sent a detail from each squad to retrieve our equipment. They didn't return until almost daylight. We had been through a freezing rain prior to this attack, so our overcoats were frozen stiff. We did have a dry blanket wrapped in [each] shelter half, and wrapped [ourselves] up in those.

"I believe that was the coldest I've ever been. At dawn, we lit some small fires from K-ration boxes and had some warm coffee, and a couple of K-rations. We had not eaten in about twenty-four hours.

"During this campaign I learned there is a point where you get so fatigued, cold, and hungry that you almost lose the fear of death. You fight and scratch with all the energy you have to survive; you are animal-like in your will to live." [61]

That same night, Sergeant Beach sorely missed the long-john underwear that he had cut off a couple of weeks earlier. He was without his blanket, overcoat, and sleeping bag. They were still in the field where his company had left them early that morning. "We got orders to move out to a certain wooded area. It began to snow as we moved out about dusk. It got extremely cold. Our equipment did not catch up with us, and we had orders of no campfires.

"I had secured a blanket off of one of the Germans. One of my buddies and I got under it and tried to keep warm, but it got damp from the snow. There was no way of staying reasonably warm.

"So about 2:00 a.m. he and I decided to see if we couldn't start a fire of some kind, thinking it was better to be shot by the Germans than freeze to death. So we scraped up enough wood and cut it up into small shavings to get it started, as it was damp. After considerable effort, we got it going, and as the flames began to light up the area, more troopers came in with more wood. Consequently, by 4:00 a.m. we had a big fire going.

"We drew no enemy fire and were not reprimanded for the fire, as officers gathered around it just like we did. But this night we had quite a few men get frostbite on their fingers, ears, and hands. Luckily, I had a couple of changes of socks with me, which I changed to keep my feet dry." [62]

The night of January 3, men suffered terribly from the cold, as the regiment's S-4 supply sections weren't able to bring up coats, bedrolls, blankets, or food. The evacuation of the wounded, bringing up ammunition and water, and moving artillery forward took priority over bringing the other items forward to the troopers. Logistics were severely limited by the lack of roads—there was only one road leading south to the positions of each of the regiments.

Most troopers were wearing only long johns or an olive drab wool sweater under their jumpsuits and jump boots. Freezing to death was a real danger. The experience of Private First Class Virgil M. Goodwin, with Company B, was typical.

"I was miserable, cold, and hungry, with feet that had no feeling in them. It was one of the most miserable nights I have ever spent. I dug out the snow and put some pine boughs down. I tried to sleep on that, but it was so cold, you were afraid to go to sleep because you would never wake up. I spent most of the night leaning up against a tree standing on pine boughs. When you started to go to sleep you would start to fall and wake up; then jog in place to try to get the circulation going in your feet." [63]

Private First Class Chris Zafiroff, with Headquarters Company, 3rd Battalion, was wearing only his jumpsuit and long-handle underwear. "This was the coldest I had ever been. I had to jog in place and kick [tree] stumps in order to get feeling in my feet. I missed the overcoats and sleeping bags. We were told that these items would catch up to us. (They never did.) I, along with other troopers, lay down under pine trees. I never did get warm. . . .

"What I wouldn't have given for a drink of water. I tried eating snow—only getting my face and mouth wet. I could hear water rushing in the stream. During darkness, I came to the edge of the rushing water. I laid down on the bank and with my canteen cup, tried to reach the water without falling in. I could not reach the water, so I went back to eating snow. Later, I found an aid station and was evacuated with frostbitten feet, hospitalized, and later discharged." [64]

Troopers used just about every means at their disposal to get a little warmth. Private John Jackson, with Headquarters Company, 2nd Battalion, was a message center runner. "On one night, I spent most of the time standing behind a running tank so the exhaust would keep me warm. One night, I tore a sack into strips and lit them one by one in my foxhole to keep my feet from freezing." [65]

Staff Sergeant Joseph Jockel, with Headquarters Company, 3rd Battalion, noticed that some of the troopers improvised due to the lack of winter clothing, "cutting four holes in their sleeping bags for arms and legs, and walked around using their bags as overcoats." [66]

TRENCH FOOT AND FROSTBITE began to take a toll on the officers and men, and that toll would increase with each day spent without overshoes and overcoats. The attack on January 3 had been the most costly in the history of the 505th PIR and the 82nd Airborne division. The attack of January 3 had also severely crippled the 62nd Volksgrenadier Division, which lost almost two entire battalions, a third of its infantry strength, to the 505th.

Now, at dawn, men who had received little or nothing to eat and almost no sleep in order to keep from freezing to death prepared to carry the attack forward yet again. The coming light of the dreary, overcast day would make these men drowsy as they struggled to advance through deep snow.

The 2nd Battalion encountered significant resistance in its zone of attack. The Germans were determined to hold on to the road to deny its use to the 505th and to protect the primary route for supplying their own troops. Early on January 4, the battalion attacked toward Arbrefontaine. Corporal Don McKeage moved with the

Company F skirmish line through about forty feet of woods and "started across the open field towards the German line—a fence row—maybe three hundred yards in front. We all walked out of the woods in line, firing forward. One of our sergeants, Vernon L. Francisco, was killed when he mounted a tank destroyer to fire a .50-caliber machine gun at the Kraut line. When we reached the wooded fence row, many Krauts stood up with their hands in the air.

"As we moved on from this point, there was a curve in the road to the right. The tank destroyer, which had a 90mm gun, continued for another four hundred yards, where the road turned back to the left. Lieutenant [Harold E. 'Casey'] Case and I walked up behind the tank destroyer. Just as we arrived, a German tank from behind us let go with an 88, right over our heads, and just missed the turret of our tank destroyer. Without hesitation, that 90mm swung over our heads, placing Case and me directly below the muzzle. I immediately knocked Case and myself to the ground, and the tank destroyer fired.

"Our tank destroyer had knocked out the Kraut tank to our left rear. We kept moving and finally came to the top of a hill, where we could see the town of Arbrefontaine around a big curve in the road, to our right front.

"Within a couple of minutes, a German Tiger tank caught us in his sight and knocked out our tank destroyer." [67]

Lieutenant Joe Meyers, commanding Company D, deployed his men in the woods on the east side of the road, and the company moved south. "Enemy mortar and artillery fire was intense. We were advancing through fairly dense woods, and every round was a tree burst. Shortly after we jumped off, I received word that [Lieutenant Marshall] Hughes was dead. Wounded by mortar fire and placed on a stretcher to await evacuation, he died when another round landed next to his stretcher. In the three days he was with us, I hardly got to know him.

"Ground resistance stiffened. The attached platoon of tanks moved up to support the attacking rifle companies. [Lieutenant] Russ Parker, now with Company F, was shot off the deck of an M4 tank while manning the tank's .50-caliber machine gun.

"About noon, we briefly broke out of the woods at a turn in the road and came under direct fire of some distant 88s. Unlike indirect-fire weapons, the direct-fire 88 got your attention immediately. You knew the gunner had you in his sights. If he could see you, he could hit you. One of the casualties of the 88s was Private Alfredo R. López, one of the 3rd Platoon's finest soldiers. A citizen of Ecuador, López volunteered for service in the U.S. Army while attending college in the States." [68]

Gavin was almost continually up front with his troopers, returning to the division command post at night for updates on the situation. Private Edward P. Laughlin, a replacement with Regimental Headquarters Company, will never forget the first time he saw General Gavin. "My unit was groveling in icy roadside ditches, in snow and rain, with German artillery and mortar fire constantly dropping in on us. We were waiting for a pause in the firing so we could get to our feet and continue moving forward in our attack on German positions. General Gavin was almost jaunty in striding down the middle of the road with his two huge, tough, and mean bodyguards, each carrying a submachine gun. Gavin carried an M1 rifle slung over his shoulder.

"Sergeant [Robert M.] Tague, my squad leader, personally knew the general from combat jumps in Normandy and Holland. He yelled at him, 'You better get your ass off that road, general!'

"The general slowed and turned and looked. He smiled in recognition and said, 'How are you, Sergeant Tague?' and kept on walking." [69]

Lieutenant Meyers and his men kept moving forward despite the 88mm and artillery fire. "We pressed on and in the late afternoon we seized the high ground overlooking the town of Arbrefontaine. As we approached the town, we came under fire from a lovely villa. I had two tanks supporting me. They answered the fire of a machine gun positioned behind open French doors on the villa's ground floor. The machine gun fell silent. When we were fifty yards away, a German officer stepped to the door, pistol in hand, and began to fire at us. Within seconds he was dead. We killed several of the enemy as they tried to escape out a side door. I received orders to halt and dig in for the night." [70]

At the end of the day, Company D trooper, Private First Class Dave Bowman and his assistant gunner set up their gun and flopped down in the snow—exhausted. "I was beginning to get comfortable—well, as comfortable as possible in two or three feet of snow at zero degrees—when I received word to report to company headquarters. I always hated such orders. Usually nothing good came of them. As I slogged my way over, a shell exploded near the headquarters, and activity there increased. I quickened my pace, and upon arrival saw Corporal [Edward J. 'Ozzie'] Olszewski lying on the ground with blood pouring from the area around his heart. The company clerk, Henry Matzelle, who was standing nearby, told me the blood had been spurting out like a miniature geyser. A captured German officer who had been standing by observing the whole thing, coldly mumbled, 'Kaput' and walked away.

"Oszewski dead—that was hard to take. He was one of the old timers, both in age and in the time spent with the 505. He was in his early thirties and came into the '05 at the beginning, at the Frying Pan area, and remained with us throughout. He was a stout, strongly-built mesomorph, whose only weakness was that he found it difficult to keep up on our frequent sprees of double-timing. One of the rare times he dropped out, I heard him bitterly moan, 'They can't make a race horse out of a work horse.' I do not recall his ever missing any combat at all—from wounds or from illness. Now, near the end of the war, he was killed." [71]

In the center, the 1st Battalion reached the next phase line by 10:00 a.m., against almost no opposition, after destroying the German battalion the previous day. The advance was so rapid that the battalion surprised a number of Germans who believed they were in a rear area. Private First Class Joe Tallett, with Company C, witnessed one such incident. "Two 7th Armored tank destroyers caught two Tiger tanks refueling in a field. The TDs had 90mm guns. Each of the TDs fired one armor-piercing and one high-explosive round, destroying the Tigers.

"That same day, we received heavy mortar fire. Virtually all of the company headquarters was hit. Our company commander, Captain Jack Tallerday, although hit in the back, refused to be evacuated." [72]

About noon, a German major riding in an American jeep was ambushed and captured at one of the 1st Battalion outposts, along with a map indicating the route of the major's battalion, moving up to replace the battalion destroyed the previous day. Major Woody Long, the 1st Battalion commander, quickly rounded up some headquarters company personnel and a Sherman tank, and moved out to hit the German battalion. The attack died out when a Panzerfaust knocked out the tank, and the German battalion pulled back to high ground.

Major Long, determined to strike before the Germans got reorganized, scraped together two squads from Company B, led by Lieutenant Stanley Weinberg; one from Company C, led by Staff Sergeant Herman "Zeke" Zeitner; and two Sherman tanks. A firebreak afforded a route for the tanks to the high ground. With Weinberg's two squads in a skirmish line in the woods to the left of the tanks and Zeitner's squad in the woods to the right, the makeshift force moved forward. The men couldn't keep pace with the tanks in the deep snow, and the formation was changed to one man breaking a trail for two or three men. The lead tank was about fifty yards or so out ahead of the infantry as it moved up the slope of the high ground. As it neared the crest, a Panzerfaust damaged the tank. The tank crew opened up with its two machine guns, spraying everything around it. The second tank's machine guns opened fire to assist the first tank, while moving up the slope with the infantry, then moved around the damaged tank and over the crest of the hill.

Suddenly, Long's paratroopers, finding themselves in the midst of the enemy battalion, fired furiously at every suspected German position. After about a minute, Germans began coming out of their holes with their hands raised, yelling, "Kamerad" and "Nicht schiessen." The firing stopped as the paratroopers found themselves in the middle of two hundred or so Germans with their hands up. Sergeant Zeitner, speaking fluent German, ordered a German officer to get his men lined up in a column, which he accomplished with a few shouted commands. The German walking-wounded were placed between the other prisoners on the outsides of the column, who assisted them during the march through the deep snow. Long's men brought back the entire understrength battalion to add to the POW cage. Miraculously, the troopers hadn't suffered a casualty.

To their left, the 3rd Battalion moved south against little opposition, having annihilated the battalion in front of them at Fosse. The greatest obstacles, again, were the snow, the weather, and the terrain. The single road along the axis of the regiment's advance made supplying it tenuous, at best. Staff Sergeant Joseph Jockel, with Headquarters Company, 3rd Battalion, was the S-4 supply sergeant. "The snow was quite deep, and truck movements were more difficult. One night, a loaded ammo truck went off the road into a ditch. Standing in front of the truck, I noticed a reel on the front bumper with steel cable on it. The driver confirmed my belief that it was a winch, but he had never used one—he wasn't even sure how to operate it—but he quickly learned how to unroll it. We wrapped it around a tree and winched the truck back on the road. This scene was repeated time and time again, until we got out of that damned forest." 73

Late on the afternoon of January 4, the 62nd Volksgrenadier Division fell back to reestablish a main line of resistance on more favorable terrain. The following morning, the 2nd Battalion moved into Arbrefontaine, against only a rear guard, which pulled out after a short fight. Company F's last officer, Lieutenant Harold Case, was wounded during the advance. Don McKeage, who had entered the fighting as a corporal on December 18, was now the acting first sergeant and took temporary command of the company until Lieutenant John B. Phillips arrived from battalion.

In the 3rd Battalion sector on January 5, Sergeant Bill Dunfee, along with an understrength platoon of Company I, conducted a combat patrol to make contact with the enemy and capture a prisoner for interrogation purposes. "We hadn't gone too far until we found a wounded German. He had been shot through the left eye, the bullet exiting behind his ear. I was surprised at how little blood he had lost. He was quizzed by [Arnold W.] Bartsch, whose parents were born in Germany—he claimed to be Polish. Questioned by our Polish-speaking trooper, he claimed to be German. We tired of that game in a hurry, and left him. Moving on several hundred yards, we came upon a German battalion headquarters. Their defense was set up facing away from our approach. We were able to get very close before the firefight started. They were completely surprised. During this firefight was the first time I saw Germans shooting their own people. I observed several being shot as they attempted to surrender. We shot them up pretty good and got a prisoner. I told my squad to fall back and I would cover them with my BAR.

"There was a young German soldier crawling up to within a few feet of where I was firing, holding his hand out, pleading. He was bleeding in several places, and I motioned for him to stay away from me, and continued firing over his head. The thought did cross my mind to finish him off, but I hadn't sunk that low yet.

"I turned and ran back towards my patrol. Running in that deep snow was a slow process. I had a momentary thought that my guys had abandoned me and I would be shot in the back. They were covering me—I had become disoriented. When you are in a snow-covered pine forest, everything looks the same.

"We had sustained a casualty and had improvised a litter and ordered the prisoner, who was a German first sergeant who spoke English, to act as a litter bearer. He started quoting the Geneva Convention and refused. I came unglued and took a swing at the insolent bastard. My swing was so violent and the footing slick, I missed him and went down myself. I looked up and he was laughing at me. I started to pull the bolt back on my BAR. As I did, Oscar Mewborne blindsided the German with a right hand that decked him. To this day, I'm indebted to Oscar. Had Oscar not hit the German, I would have killed him. I am thankful that I don't have that on my conscience. When the German came around, he was very cooperative.

"Evacuating the wounded was a very serious problem. There were two incidents that were fresh in my mind at the time. One of our men had been shot through the chest and lung. Our medic radioed the battalion aid station—he was told there was no help available to bring the wounded out. Walk him out, or stay there and [he would] die. Another man had tangled with an artillery shell; his right hand and forearm were blown away, and left arm badly mangled. They walked out, so none of us were in any mood to discuss the Geneva or any other convention, especially with a German version of a guardhouse lawyer. I don't know if the German realized how close he came to death. It bothered me that I had become so callous—that I would have killed an unarmed man." [74]

On January 5, the 1st and 3rd Battalions advanced one thousand yards against virtually no resistance. Sergeant Elmo Bell found that sleep was impossible and talking was difficult during this period. "There was no sleep—granted, we got a little rest—but there was no sleep, because you never ever quit shaking or your jaw trembling, your teeth clattering. That was constant—around the clock.

"Everyone's lips chapped to the extent that it was painful to talk, and your teeth clattered all the time—it was embarrassing to try to talk. The conversations just came to a halt. Even commands and orders were given with gestures and nods of the head—there just wasn't any conversation going on.

"Frostbite was a constant problem. In fact, so many people had foot infections caused from either athlete's foot or frostbite or both. Many of the troopers had their feet wrapped in burlap rather than wearing boots.

"Our morale was rock bottom. Up until the Battle of the Bulge, the morale was sky-high, it never did waiver. But, during the Battle of the Bulge—and I think it was the unnecessary loss of so many people—it just seemed that there should be some way to prevent people from dying of superficial wounds, and we all really hit rock bottom.

"I think people were a little more ready to die during the Battle of the Bulge, because so many good people had concluded early on that they would be killed during the war—that they'd never go home. They had gotten accustomed to that approach—that conclusion. During the Battle of the Bulge the quality of life was so poor, it didn't matter if death occurred today or tomorrow or next week. If you lived another week, that was just going to be another week of pure, unadulterated misery. There was nothing to live for. People were more inclined to take chances during the Battle of the Bulge, because the quality of life was so poor, and life was so miserable.

"You value sleep above everything else. You reach a point that perpetual sleep begins to have an attraction—you reach the point where you're just ready to give it all up and go to sleep forever. It doesn't matter if it's today or tomorrow or next week—the sooner, the less misery." [75]

Engineers with the 307th Airborne Engineer Battalion bulldozed a road through the woods, and on January 6, the two battalions' bedrolls, sleeping bags, blankets, overcoats, and musette bags were brought up—very much appreciated by the cold, exhausted, hungry troopers.

That evening, Lieutenant Joe Meyers, commanding Company D, reported to the 2nd Battalion command post to receive attack orders for the next morning. "The battalion, reinforced by tanks and tank destroyers, would attack with E and F [Companies] along the Arbrefontaine-Goronne road that lay in a valley. D Company would make a secondary attack to seize the high ground north of Goronne. The success of the main attack, moving down the valley, depended upon the secondary attack seizing the high ground overlooking Goronne. Moreover, we were jumping off about two hours before dawn. In the initial phase, it was a night attack—a difficult operation to control over a distance of several thousand yards.

"I returned to the company, and I issued the attack order to my platoon leaders. We had a large, open area of about three hundred yards to negotiate before reaching the base of our objective, a very large, heavily wooded hill. I anticipated the Germans would defend along the wood line, but I could not be sure. We would advance in a column of platoons, with patrols to the front for security. I closed by instructing both platoon leaders to send runners to company headquarters." [76]

Before dawn the next morning, Meyers sent a runner to make sure that both of his platoon leaders were awake. "At the appointed time, company headquarters and the 1st Platoon saddled up and moved to the 2nd Platoon's position. I crossed the LD on time with the 1st Platoon. We advanced under cover of darkness over open, snow-covered fields for several hundred yards. Patrols checked out the edge of the wood line and reported the area was clear of enemy. We moved into a heavily wooded, cultivated pine forest with aligned trees tightly spaced in rows that ran at a tangent to our direction of advance. The darkness and the tree alignment made it extremely difficult to maintain an accurate compass heading through the dense woods. I abandoned the use of the compass in favor of moving uphill toward the high ground that was our objective. As we advanced uphill, we came upon a firebreak, where I found German communication wire, and I followed the wire uphill some five or six hundred yards. As we neared the top of the hill, we left the cultivated forest and entered a naturally wooded area. The point signaled a halt, and a messenger returned to tell me the point heard sounds of men snoring. I joined the point, only a few yards ahead, and listened. I could hear men snoring to our front, flanks and left rear.

"Using the men on the point, we organized two teams, one to work each side of the firebreak. The teams went from foxhole to foxhole awakening the sleeping German soldiers, disarming them and bringing them to the column where we passed them to the rear. It was a slow work, but all was going well. We had disarmed and captured about six or eight prisoners in this manner when a shot rang out at the rear of the column. One of our men was about half asleep on his feet. He looked up, saw a German POW, and in his confusion, shot him. All hell broke loose. We came under heavy small-arms fire from what appeared to me to be all directions. We managed to form what amounted to an elongated perimeter. The

Germans to our rear must have panicked, for they withdrew, permitting the 2nd Platoon under First Sergeant [Thomas J.] Rogers to join us as first light broke. With Rogers on the left and [Lieutenant Lawrence M.] Price on the right, we pressed forward, clearing the area of enemy until we reached a second firebreak that ran at right angles to our direction of attack.

"At this firebreak we came under heavy machine gun and rifle fire and the fires of supporting mortars and artillery. Both Rogers and Price reported they were pinned down at the edge of the firebreak, a few yards from the defenders. I was only ten or twenty yards to their rear. By inspection, I was able to determine I was on my objective. The topographical crest lay only a few yards beyond the German position to our front.

"A lieutenant [Henry G. Coustillac] from the division AA battalion crawled up to me and reported he had a 57mm AT gun and crew with him. He reported his crew had attacked and destroyed a German machine gun to our rear on the way to our position. I was unable to reach the battalion on my radio, so the AA officer filled me in on the situation. He reported the battalion was held up in the valley by German infantry supported by two Tiger tanks. If we could seize the crest of the hill, he might be able to get a shot into the rear of one or both of the tanks. While all this was going on, we continued to exchange fires with the defenders at very close range. The AT officer returned to his crew, and minutes later I saw the slim figure of my battalion commander, Ben Vandervoort, crawling up the firebreak to my position. I briefed him on the situation, and I informed him I could muster a reserve of about ten men from my company headquarters, a mortar squad, and the AT gun crew. He said he had about six men (I assumed his driver, staff, and security) with him.

"He said, 'Give me about five minutes to get in position, then make a frontal assault with your platoons and company headquarters. I'll flank them with the battalion staff.'

"We carried out the assault as ordered. As we overran the position we received a heavy concentration of mortar fire. The AT officer was advancing a foot or two to my left, and [Donald E.] Harris, my runner, was immediately behind me. I saw an orange flash about five yards to my front.

"[Lieutenant Coustillac] threw his hand to his forehead and said, 'Joe, I'm hit.' He was dead when he hit the ground. Harris was on the ground behind me, severely wounded in both legs; I stood there feeling my body to see if I still was in one piece. Except for a multitude of tiny, needle-like fragment that sprayed my exposed face and hands, I was unharmed. A messenger arrived within minutes to tell me Vandervoort was wounded. I assume the same volley of mortar fire that killed the AT officer hit him. By the time I reorganized the company to protect against a possible counterattack, Vandervoort was gone, and I later learned he lost an eye. During my thirty years of service, I hope I was able to instill in the young troopers who served under me some of the outstanding traits of character and leadership I observed in Colonel Vandervoort. He was a true warrior." [77]

IN THE VALLEY BELOW, COMPANY F MOVED DOWN THE ROAD toward Goronne as the main attack began. Sergeant Russ Brown was leading his 60mm mortar squad. "We advanced to a small church and some trees. We saw two Tiger tanks. They were shelling the troops on our left flank and then they shelled us. We fell back and cut across a field. That was when 2nd Platoon mortar squad sergeant Phil Lynch was KIA. [78] We went into a wooded area and stopped near the church." [79]

Brown and Lieutenant George Essex decided to continue the advance by using the woods that lay on the other side of an open area as concealment from the two German tanks. "Lieutenant Essex asked Sergeant E. D. [Edward D.] Jones to send one man across an open field to the woods. He was shot when he got to the woods.

"Lieutenant Essex and the mortar squad, plus [Private First Class] Frank Rojas walked to the corner of the [same] woods, and four Germans came out—hands up. Lieutenant Essex went back, but my squad, with Rojas, went into the woods." [80]

Brown led his squad through the woods, emerging on the far side. "In a field about two hundred yards ahead was a pile of straw, and up came a German—he shot [Private First Class] Lowell Schell. We all fired—Frank Rojas fired his bazooka. When we got to the pile of straw, the German was dead. He had a rifle with a scope. I took the rifle and gave it to someone. I had enough to carry with my Thompson.

"We went back to the woods and found Ken Olsen wounded and [Private First Class] Charles Krka, who DOW [died of wound]. On the way into Goronne, Frank Rojas was killed." [81]

Meanwhile, Company D reached the crest of the hill, and Lieutenant Meyers made contact with 2nd Battalion. "I reported the AT squad was moving the 57mm gun in position for a shot at one of the Tigers. I was instructed not to fire, a TD was en route to my position. The TD arrived about two hours later with a captain in command. I pointed out both Tigers. The nearest one was in a ditch at the side of the road. The tank's hull was in defilade, its turret exposed. We were above the tank and to its right rear. The captain moved the TD into position. He placed the 57mm nearby, and he ordered both guns to bore sight before firing at the target. This accomplished, he ordered both crews to take cover in foxholes while he and one 57mm crewmember prepared to fire the two guns.

"As soon as the guns fired, the captain and the crewmember would take cover in nearby holes. The Tiger tank with its 88mm gun was a formidable opponent. If you missed a shot at a Tiger, you were in for big trouble. Earlier in the day, the regiment had lost several tanks and TDs to the two Tigers in the valley. A few minutes before the TD was scheduled to fire, a platoon of M4 tanks rolled in and reported to me. If the TD successfully eliminated the Tiger, I was to attack down the hill and seize Goronne. After I issued the necessary orders, the two anti-tank guns fired. After a minute or two, the captain and I inched forward and took a look. [The TD and the 57mm gun had each] scored a clean hit and disabled the Tiger. We observed the other Tiger withdrawing into Goronne and heading up the Thier-du-Mont, a large hill mass across the valley in the 508's sector.

"With the tanks in support, we immediately launched an assault down the hill.

As we broke the military crest, we came upon a battery of horse-drawn artillery. The Germans were attempting to hitch up their teams to the howitzers and withdraw. At a range of about fifty yards, we engaged the battery with both tank and infantry weapons. It was a turkey shoot. The tanks engaged and disabled the howitzers, and we directed our fire at the men and the animals. It was a wild scene, horses rearing and plunging, tanks firing, and the men shouting as we overran the position, an aid station, and a nearby CP.

"During this assault, I saw my first and only enemy soldier killed with cold steel. One of my men jumped in a foxhole and landed on a German hiding in the bottom of the hole. The German probably wanted to surrender, but the trooper's blood was up. He pulled his trench knife and killed him with repeated blows. I estimated we took about fifty to seventy-five prisoners, including one German female nurse, plus horses, howitzers, individual weapons, etc. We didn't stop to count. We moved straight for Goronne. As we approached the town, the tank platoon leader got a report a Tiger was in town, and he refused to accompany us. We secured the town without meeting enemy resistance.

"The road into Goronne, a cobblestone street that branched off at right angles from the Arbrefontaine-Vielsalm road, climbed part way up the Thier-du-Mont. About a block off the main road, this street broadened to form a small plaza. Here a farmer and his two attractive young daughters greeted us and invited me to use their home as my CP. The house was a large, two-story structure with a barn attached. I accepted the invitation and we moved in after we set up our defensive position." 82

During the attack that day, Private Cecil Prine, with Headquarters Company, 1st Battalion, was repairing field telephone lines that had been severed by enemy artillery and mortar fire. "My feet hurt so badly that I could barely move.

"General Gavin came by and said, 'Did you wade through that stream on 3 January?'

"I said, 'Yes sir.'

"He said, 'Your feet are frozen; get to the aid station about two hundred yards up the road and have them look at your feet.'

"They cut my boots off, and I spent three months in a bed with my feet elevated and didn't know if they could be saved." 83

Later that day, Lieutenant Dean McCandless, the regimental communications officer, returned to the regimental command post. "Colonel Ekman told me that he wished to set up his next command post in the village of Goronne. By this time, I had a jeep assigned to me, and I drove to check the wire parties that I had following behind the battalions in attack. I found the party headed for Goronne, just where I'd left them a half hour earlier. I was displeased and told them of the need to get into Goronne and set up a switchboard for Colonel Ekman.

"They said, 'There are Germans there in those woods.' That is—by the trail we were following. At this point, the trail was too narrow for my jeep.

"I'm not too proud of what I said next—'Germans Schmermans—the 2nd Battalion has been through here already. Come on, let's go.' I and my jeep driver started up the trail, and as the wire party began to follow, I'd gone only forty or fifty paces when hit by a burst from a German machine pistol and knocked flat into the snow.

"My driver ran back around a curve and yelled, 'Lieutenant, are you hurt?'

"I yelled, 'Why do you think I'm lying here!' Then I shut up, fearing more fire— I remained very still and quiet. Some minutes passed when I heard footsteps in the snow, and I feared a German [was] about to finish me.

"Instead, a voice said, 'Lieutenant, can you move?' It was a battalion surgeon! (I think, 2nd Battalion.) What a relief!

"My wounded left shoulder did not limit me from arising and walking back to his aid station—even in the cold. He exposed my shoulder wounds and dressed them, front and back, and gave me a sling over my arm. I pleaded to stay with my men; with the sling, I was in little discomfort. I felt obligated to go on and get a switchboard set up for Colonel Ekman in Goronne. [The surgeon] insisted that I go back to the regimental aid station." [84]

The 2nd Battalion's capture of Goronne came at a terrible cost—the loss of their highly respected and much loved commander, Lieutenant Colonel Vandervoort, whom many in the battalion thought invincible. One of Vandervoort's radio operators was Technician Fourth Grade Donald L. Brown. "I spent many hours with Colonel Vandervoort—one of the most fearless people I have ever known. When shells were coming I would instinctively hit the ground, but he would be surveying the situation, standing." [85] Private John Jackson was one of the battalion runners. "I felt a deep loss when Lieutenant Colonel Vandervoort was hit." [86]

General Gavin was up front with the infantry when he received word that Vandervoort had been wounded and had been evacuated to an aid station at Arbrefontaine. "When I got there, he was on a stretcher in an ambulance. He had been hit in the eye by a shell fragment and apparently had lost one eye. I felt very bad about it, because just a day or two earlier we had been talking about bringing Vandervoort to division headquarters. He had been commanding a company and then a battalion since Sicily, and the veterans among us believed that the chances of his luck running out were quite high and that we should make a change." [87]

The battalion executive officer, William R. Carpenter, recently promoted to major, replaced Vandervoort as 2nd Battalion commander. The battalion also lost Lieutenant Bill Meddaugh, the Company E commander, evacuated with pneumonia, replaced by Captain Charles L. Barnett.

On January 8, the 505th moved east and captured the high ground north of Rencheux overlooking the Salm River and established a roadblock between Goronne and Rencheux. The following day the 2nd Battalion took Rencheux. Because of casualties taken earlier, Earl Boling, promoted from private first class to staff sergeant the previous day, led the 1st Platoon, Company E. "The morning of the 9th of January, we again moved out—this time to take the village of Rencheux. Although the resistance in this area was considered light, and mostly of the rear-guard type action of the Germans, I did lose another good man here.

"Private [William H.] Nealy was wounded just before we arrived at a row of houses, where we were to establish our defensive line. I secured an aid man for Private Nealy, who determined his wound was in the stomach and abdomen, passing into the body and apparently striking the spinal column.

"As he was unable to move his legs, or had no feeling in the lower body, the medic advised against moving him until the medical vehicle could arrive. I told Nealy I would return later, and proceeded to the line of houses where the platoon was placed in a defensive line, with a machine gun on the right flank and the BAR on the left flank. The rest of the few men left in the platoon were positioned in the houses facing the river, with orders that the men on the flanks were to be relieved periodically for a chance to [get] warm in the houses. While checking the houses, we found one lady still in the area. She spoke good English.

"I advised her to stay in the basement in case we received shellfire, and told her I was going to check on a wounded man. She gave me a quilt to cover him with, and I returned to Private Nealy's position. He was very cold, and apparently going into shock. I covered him with the quilt, and he asked me if I would mind praying with him. I took his hand and we said the Lord's Prayer together. At this time, a medical jeep arrived and he was placed on it. I wished him luck as he was taken away. The next day, I learned that he had died of wounds on the way to the clearing station." 88

That day, Private First Class Dutch Schultz reported to Company C, having been evacuated before Christmas with an upper respiratory infection, dysentery, and stomach cramps. "I reported for duty to a company that was virtually wiped out. The officers were all gone and we had about thirty men left. If I could have cried, I might have gotten some of the pain and guilt out. I lost some good friends who taught me how to survive in combat and often inspired me with their courage and sacrifice. In a larger sense, I realized that the company I came to know and love no longer existed." 89

On January 10, the U.S. 75th Infantry Division relieved the 82nd Airborne Division. The 505th's survivors of the prior week of combat loaded onto trucks and were driven to the town of Theux, Belgium, to rest and reorganize. Staff Sergeant Chris Christensen was one of the few old-timers still left in Company G. "At this time we were down to less than 50 percent strength. In the past, we had lost more men killed, but no other place took quite the toll as the Ardennes." 90

CHAPTER 19

"Is This Armageddon?"

The citizens of Theux welcomed the tired, dirty troopers of the 505th into their homes. When Staff Sergeant Joseph Jockel, with the 3rd Battalion S-4 section, arrived, he had gone "three weeks without washing or shaving. My hands and face were crusted and black, with multiples sores.

"Upon arriving in Theux, I was kept busy arranging resupply matters. The [headquarters] company's men were told to knock on doors and ask for warm shelter. Squad leaders kept records of who was where. After dark, I began my search for shelter. Off on a side street, I knocked on the door of a darkened house. A little old lady answered and invited me in. She was not the least afraid of an American. Over the next few days we developed a magnificent relationship. She called me 'mon fils' [my son] and I called her 'mama.' I never had it so good—every night she would preheat my bed with hot bricks. We shared quartermaster supply rations and an added coal supply, dumped at her front door.

"Luckily, a Christmas package was delivered with a large fruitcake, which I let mama eat most of—because she believed it was heaven sent. She truly was a wonderful Belgian lady." [1]

Sergeant Harry Buffone, with Company I, was extremely grateful for the kindness of the people of Theux. "I would give a million dollars to the town if I had it. My buddy, Roy McDaniel, and I were assigned to a house [where] an old man about seventy-five and old woman, about seventy-four [lived]. They took us in and the first thing, the woman insisted that she was going to give me a bath. The only way I got out of that was I let her wash my back. They gave us their bed and warmed bricks in the oven to put at our feet. The only way I could repay them was to carry to them used coffee grounds from the kitchen in five-gallon buckets. They spread the grounds on the flat roof of their back porch to dry in the sun, then when good and dry, they would put it in jars. We would join them for coffee at times and the coffee was pretty good." [2]

It was the first opportunity for most of the men to reflect on what they had experienced and grieve for those lost. Each company in the regiment had suffered horrendous casualties. When Company I was assembled in the street, Private First Class John Siam counted only "eight men left in the 2nd Platoon." [3]

So many of the old men who had survived Sicily, Salerno, Normandy, and Holland were killed, seriously wounded, or evacuated with severe frostbite or trench foot. Those left felt almost alone. Lieutenant Joe Meyers mentally checked off the names and status of the officers who were with Company D when it left France for

Belgium: Captain George D. Carlson and Lieutenant Virgil Gould, wounded in action; Lieutenants Charles Qualls and Marshall Hughes, killed in action; and Lieutenants Tom McClean and Lawrence M. Price, wounded in action. Meyers was the only officer of the eight still on duty; although Lieutenant O. B. Carr, an officer in the company, was on temporary duty with the pathfinders.

For the first time since leaving France on December 18, troopers took showers, were issued new clothes and jump boots, and received medical treatment for minor injuries and illnesses. After arriving, Meyers received his "B" (barracks) bag, as they finally caught up with the regiment. "I went upstairs where I had my first bath since leaving Suippes. A big copper bathtub, filled with hot water, was waiting. Soap and clean towels were nearby. It was heavenly. I dressed in clean clothes and, for the first time in weeks, I felt like a human being.

"Our battalion mess operated nearby, and we ate three hot meals every day. The day following our arrival in Theux, the regimental officers assembled in the local theater to hear an address by General Gavin. It was a small group; we had not yet received replacements. From the outset, it was obvious Gavin thought he was talking to the officers of the 2nd Battalion, not the officers of the entire regiment. His mistake was understandable. Our ranks were very thin.

"On our third day in Theux, I arose at 0630, dressed, and started downstairs, where I met General Gavin and Bill Ekman on the stairway. I reported to the general and he asked me what training I had scheduled for the day. I replied, 'None.' I was giving the men an opportunity to rest. He nodded and told me to report to Colonel Swift, the assistant division commander, at a nearby road junction at 0800 hours the following morning. Tanks would be at the site, and we would undergo tank-infantry training. I said nothing, but I boiled inside. What the hell was Gavin thinking? We had been fighting with tanks for the past three weeks. When I cooled off, I realized he was sending me a message: stop feeling sorry for yourself and your troops; get this show on the road; and there is still fighting to be done." 4

The regiment shifted its personnel to fill gaps, enlisted men were promoted to non-commissioned officers, and changes in command were made. Captain Taylor Smith returned as 2nd Battalion executive officer. Captain William C. Martin replaced Lieutenant Meyers as Company D commander. Lieutenant O. B. Carr, returning from pathfinder duty, became the Company D executive officer. Captain Charles Barnett remained as the Company E commander. Lieutenant Bill Hays returned from the hospital to command Company F.

As the regiment received replacements, new equipment, weapons, and winter clothing, it reorganized and conducted training in combined tank-infantry tactics and the use of the German Panzerfaust, of which many had been captured in Holland and Belgium. Gavin felt the Panzerfaust was the only effective antitank weapon against the German main battle tanks, the Mark V Panther and Mark VI Tiger II.

Private First Class Dutch Schultz was billeted with a Mrs. Mexher and two children, including her sixteen-year-old son, Jose, with whom Schultz developed a friendship. "On 26 January 1945 (my birthday), we were told to get ready to leave that night.

Before leaving, Jose gave me a snapshot of himself on a bicycle. His name and address were on the back of the photo. When we left that night to return to the battlefield, Mrs. Mexher and her two children were crying as if we were part of the family." 5

The division was trucked to the St.-Vith area, where it would move east through the lines of the U.S. 7th Armored Division to spearhead a drive eastward to pierce

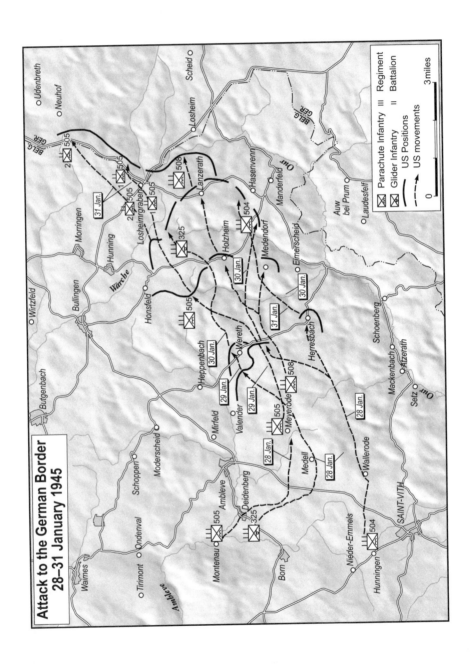

**Attack to the German Border
28–31 January 1945**

the fortifications of the Siegfried Line on the German border. The 505th PIR arrived at Born, Belgium, north of St.-Vith, from 4:00 a.m. to 7:10 a.m. on January 27, where it unloaded and marched to Montenau. The supporting units—the 456th Parachute Field Artillery Battalion; Battery A, 80th Airborne Antiaircraft (Antitank) Battalion; and Company B, 307th Airborne Engineer Battalion—arrived from 9:30 a.m. to 9:45 a.m.

Gavin's plan for the initial attack was two regiments abreast, the 325th GIR on the left and the 504th PIR on the right, with the 505th PIR following behind the 325th, and the 508th PIR following behind the 504th. When the attacking regiments' momentum slowed, the trailing regiments would pass through to continue the drive.

That night, the troopers left behind their musette bags, overcoats, blankets, bedrolls, and sleeping bags. The troopers were now outfitted with long-john underwear, wool sweaters, gloves, and shoe pacs. Most wore white snow capes, pullovers, and bed sheets or mattress covers to serve as camouflage. However, they were facing weather and snow depths much worse than before.

At 6:00 a.m. on January 28, the division attacked eastward in knee-deep snow, surprising the Germans and capturing the Belgian towns of Wereth and Herresbach. The following morning, the 505th passed through the 325th pushing two thousand yards northeast, capturing the high ground fifteen hundred yards southwest of Honsfeld, Belgium, where it established defensive positions and sent out reconnaissance patrols and contact patrols with the 1st Infantry Division on the left.

Private First Class Schultz was now the C Company scout. "Our company wasn't much bigger than a platoon. It was bitter cold and the snow was waist deep. Since I was the company scout, I was the one who broke the trail—the first to walk through the snow and establish a pathway for the rest of the men to follow. This was hard work, and after doing this for a couple of hours I was exhausted." [6]

After reaching the regiment's new phase line, Schultz dug through the deep snow and hacked out a shallow hole in the frozen ground. "I didn't spend too much time making a deep hole. I was too tired and, as quickly as I could, climbed into my sleeping bag and placed my .45 on my chest and proceeded to fall asleep. Getting into a sleeping bag was one of the few pleasures of battle in cold weather. My clothing was always wet and after a period of time in the sleeping bag, my body would produce steam, which produced additional warmth. (It was a bitch, though, getting out of that sleeping bag in the morning.)

"I was sound asleep when I was awakened by a firefight right over the top of me. One of the new men that joined us in Theux was on guard, sitting with his back to a tree. He spotted a patrol of Germans moving toward us and opened fire with an automatic weapon. After the shooting was over, I raised my head and saw several dead Germans no further than twenty feet. After commending my fellow trooper, I went back to sleep.

"It amazed me then and still does that this fellow trooper had the stamina to stay awake after the day we had." [7]

Over the succeeding days, Schultz and the other troopers of the regiment struggled as much against the deep snow and cold as against the enemy. "We were exhausted, both physically and mentally. About the only thing going for us was a spirit of determination and honor that had been passed down to us from the old timers. At times, I felt dead, but too stupid to fall over." [8]

On January 30, the 325th passed through the 505th and drove east to capture Buchholtz, Belgium, then advanced to a railroad line running from Losheim, Germany, to Honsfeld, Belgium. The 505th passed through the 325th positions on the morning of January 31, the 1st Battalion moving toward Losheimergraben, Germany, and the 2nd Battalion aiming for a key road junction northwest of the town.

At 4:30 a.m., the 1st Battalion moved toward Losheimergraben in a column of companies, with Company A leading. The tanks supporting the attack couldn't negotiate the high railroad embankment, so the battalion proceeded without them. Shortly after daybreak, Company A approached Losheimergraben, defended by a company-sized force. After Company A waited for Companies B and C to come up on its flanks, the battalion swept through the town, killing about fifty and taking about fifty prisoners, capturing it by 11:30 a.m.

At 5:30 a.m., the 2nd Battalion, with Company D leading, moved in column east along a road toward their objective. Lieutenant Joe Meyers was the platoon leader of the 3rd Platoon. "Three 105mm self-propelled howitzers joined D Company in lieu of tanks. The personnel manning these SPs were artillerymen, with no experience in tank-infantry operations. [Lieutenant John H.] Cobb's 1st Platoon and the attached SPs led off. [Lieutenant Albert W.] Short's 2nd Platoon followed, and I brought up the rear with the mortars. The XO normally moved at the rear of the column, so O. B. Carr and I walked together. It was pitch black as we advanced along a dirt road flanked by natural forests.

"Approximately fifteen minutes after we crossed the line of departure, an explosion occurred near the head of the column, and almost immediately a fire illuminated the area." [9]

Private Bill Slawson, a machine gunner, was riding on one of the self-propelled guns. "We hadn't gone very far when a sneaky Kraut tank up the road fired a round and hit the first [self-propelled gun] and it caught fire and lit up the whole woods. I jumped off the third [self-propelled gun]. The second [self-propelled gun] went past us after it turned around, like a bat out of hell. He missed us by inches, throwing snow all over and covering the boxes of machine gun ammo with snow.

"Captain [Bill] Martin, standing out in the middle of the road with his .45 in his hand, hollered, 'Slawson, get that machine gun in action.' We were probing in the snow for the machine gun ammo boxes. The Krauts were firing tracers at us from the woods. They were all around us. Finally, we located an ammo box, put the gun on a log, the tripod sunk in the snow. The cotton webbing belt was swollen with moisture and wouldn't feed in the gun, so we cut off [a] foot of webbing and finally got it loaded." [10]

The second self-propelled gun raced back through the D Company column, stopping ahead of Lieutenant Meyers. "Our troops had taken cover in the woods to either side of the road, but except for an occasional burst from a German machine gun, there was no sign of serious enemy opposition. After working his way forward and conferring with Martin, O. B. returned and informed me the attack had bogged down. He instructed me to go up the left side of the road and kick some tail, while he moved up the right side of the road. As I worked my way forward, the reason for our lack of progress became clear. The troops were taking advantage of this opportunity to get some rest. I located a squad leader who informed me a rocket launcher team was attempting to get into position to fire on the German gun that knocked out our SP. There was sporadic firing, and in a short time a messenger returned with the news the rocket launcher team had knocked out a Panther tank. The skirmish appeared to be over, and I headed for the Panther.

"When I arrived, I found [James A.] 'Baby' Donlon inside the tank, attempting to start the vehicle. Donlon, a rocket launcher gunner, had fired a round at the tank and hit the vehicle's armor-plated skirt. Apparently, the crew thought the round had disabled the vehicle, and they bailed out of a perfectly good tank. In a few minutes, Donlon had the tank running, and he drove it up and down the road before disabling both the gun and the engine. It was about first light when we moved out." [11]

At around 7:00 a.m., the 2nd Battalion ran into a strong enemy force near the crossroads, backed by four self-propelled guns, which knocked out the lead tank moving with Company F. The 2nd Battalion deployed as the other tanks and self-propelled guns were brought up, then attacked, overrunning the German force and capturing the road junction.

That afternoon, the 505th received an order to advance northeast to be in position to attack the Siegfried Line the next day. The 2nd Battalion advanced to the high ground opposite of the small hamlet of Neuhof. The 1st Battalion on their right flank extended the line southwesterly, maintaining contact with the 508th at Losheimergraben. The 3rd Battalion moved up in reserve, prepared to assault the fortifications the following morning.

Private Paul R. Brandt, a replacement, joined Company E on January 31. "I saw about twenty guys there—so I asked a stupid question—where are the other platoons? The company then had only thirty-four men." [12]

The regiment maintained its position the next day, February 1. It conducted reconnaissance patrols to the Siegfried Line and contact patrols with the 508th PIR on the right and the 1st Infantry Division on the left.

On February 2, the 325th passed through the 505th and assaulted the Siegfried Line at Neuhof and Udenbreth, Germany, on the left. The 504th passed through the 505th positions in the center, attacked east, and captured the Hertesrott Heights. The 505th attacked southeasterly on the right flank of the 504th, driving as much as four thousand yards against very light opposition, with the left flank reaching the Siegfried Line defenses. Only Company G on the left flank encountered the fortifications that day. Sergeant Bill Blank had served with the company since the Frying Pan. "We moved into the forest to attack the Siegfried Line. The German resistance was constant and often at close contact. We came to this clearing in the forest, and we began to receive some fire from the other side. The hillside on the opposite side of the clearing was lined with pillboxes, and through the center of the clearing was a small stream and barbed wire. We were ordered to advance across this clearing to attack the pillboxes. The creek was about chest deep, and the barbed wire slowed the crossing and made us perfect targets. We lost one man at the creek. In the immediate area where we crossed, there were two pillboxes. We could not hear any sounds from the boxes, so three of our men led by [Technical Sergeant Joseph W.] Krompasky attempted to enter the pillbox. They were immediately fired upon by a machine pistol, which killed Krompasky and wounded the other two. I crawled up on top of the pillbox where there was a chimney and dropped a Gammon grenade down the chimney. My grenade killed one and forced the surrender of fourteen. They had captured three 82nd men, who were held prisoner in the pillbox, [whom] we recovered. At approximately the same time, [William A.] MacDonald attempted to enter the other pillbox and was shot in the head by a machine pistol. He was seriously injured, but was still alive." [13]

Sergeant Chris Christensen, and what was left of his G Company platoon, attacked the pillboxes across the clearing. "These pillboxes we found to be heavily manned and had fire lanes cut where one pillbox supported the next. Before the day was out, our company was credited with knocking out four or five of these. This was not done without paying a price, as we were now down to one-third strength. At this time, you could see the German soldier was putting up a much weaker resistance than he had just a few weeks prior. There was no reason he should have surrendered even the first pillbox. There, we took about fifty prisoners who were well protected and armed. At this time, we were understrength and out of ammo. I had one clip left—eight rounds. The heaviest thing we were carrying was the bazooka, and this wouldn't even chip the paint. This was not the German soldier we had been fighting since we landed in Sicily, back in July '43. For the most part, we [had] found him to be a tough opponent." [14]

After dark, Sergeant Blank and his men advanced beyond the pillboxes to dig in for the night. "I was instructed to take a patrol to contact H Company and let them know where our position would be. I was cautioned by the battalion commander to be careful because the area was full of mines. This was amusing because it was dark and the snow was deep. That night we dug in and attempted to stay warm, even though we had been soaked from wading the creek. The next day, February 3, 1945, we were told we were being relieved. As we started marching single file down through the forest to cut down on our chances of stepping on mines, I was unlucky enough to step on one. The medic was just behind me and was knocked down. He started working on me immediately, and Chris Perry, our company medic, came back to where I was and took over my case. I was carried by litter until put on a Weasel [a tracked amphibious vehicle] and taken to a road,

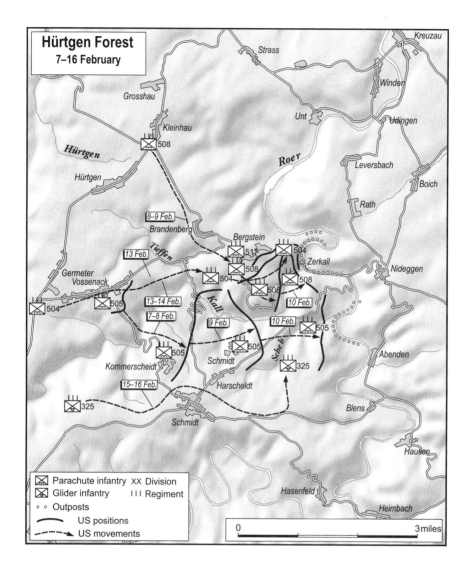

Hürtgen Forest
7–16 February

Kreuzau
Strass
Grosshau
Winden
Unt
Udingen
Kleinhau
508
Hürtgen
Roer
Leversbach
Hürtgen
Boich
Rath
8–9 Feb.
Brandenberg
Bergstein
513
504
Zerkall
13 Feb.
Treffen
Nideggen
Germeter
Vossenack
504
508
504
508
13–14 Feb.
Kall
508
7–8 Feb.
10 Feb.
504
505
9 Feb.
10 Feb.
Scheb
505
505
Abenden
505
Schmidt
325
Kommerscheidt
15–16 Feb.
Harscheldt
Blens
325
Schmidt
Hausen

Parachute infantry XX Division
Glider infantry   III Regiment
○ ○ Outposts
US positions
US movements

Hasenfeld
Heimbach

0   3 miles

where I was transferred to a jeep, which took me to an aid station. I was unconscious during much of the time and do not recall how far or how long was required to transport me to the field hospital in Spa, Belgium. There, my left leg was amputated below the knee." [15]

On the morning of February 3, the Germans mounted strong counterattacks to retake portions of the Siegfried Line lost the prior day. The Germans suffered high casualties and were thrown back. The 505th then continued the attack southeastwardly, at an oblique angle to the fortifications, and was relieved later that day and trucked to Vielsalm. There, the regimental combat team, now at about one-third strength, was billeted at Salmchâteau, Belgium, just south of Vielsalm. From

February 4 to 6, the remainder of the 82nd Airborne Division was relieved in place and trucked to the Vielsalm area.

On February 6, the 505th RCT, designated Task Force "A," commanded by Colonel Ira P. Swift, the assistant division commander, was trucked thirty miles north to the vicinity to Vossenack, Germany, in the Hürtgen Forest, about twenty miles south of Aachen, Germany, relieving elements of the 8th Infantry Division the following evening.

The Hürtgen Forest—the meat grinder that had crippled a number of U.S. Army divisions the previous fall, was by this time a scene of utter devastation. It was reminiscent of the battlefields of World War I—towns flattened, tree trunks splintered, and ground pocked with countless craters.

Company G platoon sergeant, Chris Christensen, was leading a platoon of mostly young replacements. "The move was painfully slow, and we did not arrive at our destination until late afternoon. After unloading, we started down the trail into the forest. We had only gone a short distance when we got the order to halt and dig in. As usual, we set up a defense for the night, and I started checking to make sure this was being done. All this was taking time, and when I finally got dug in it was dark. After I finished, I lay down in this shallow trench and stretched out. I could not have been in there but a few moments before I caught a whiff of this horrible odor. There was no mistaking this smell. I had dug in on a decaying corpse. Needless to say, I was the one to vacate the hole. The rest of this sleepless night I spent sitting on the ground leaning against a tree." [16]

On February 8, the 505th jumped off southeast of Vossenack, advancing twenty-five hundred yards southeast to Kommerscheidt, Germany, against almost no opposition, except sporadic artillery fire and minefields, causing few casualties. This took the regiment through the Kall River valley, nicknamed "Death Valley"—the site of the destruction the prior November of the 112th Infantry Regiment, 28th Infantry Division, a Pennsylvania National Guard unit before the war.

It was an unforgettable experience for Christensen. "As soon as it got light the next morning we moved out. Most of the snow had melted, and we were now plowing through a muddy mess. We were entering an area where some terrific fighting had taken place. The first indication of this was when we noticed the shell holes, plus the havoc the artillery had done to the trees. These, in places, looked as if someone had taken a giant scythe and mowed them down.

"Proceeding farther down the trail, things got progressively worse. The trees here had been destroyed with a vengeance—most had been blown to ribbons. Also, scattered among this debris were countless bodies or parts of [bodies]. By their shoulder patch, 'The Red Keystone,' you knew they were the remnants of the 28th Infantry Division. The sickening part was they had lain there all winter covered in a blanket of snow. Just a short distance farther in, we came to what had been an aid station. Hundreds of bodies [were] stacked like cordwood along with heaps of amputated arms and legs. Many of the bodies were still lying on litters. These were probably being attended to when Jerry unleashed this massive barrage wiping out this aid station. By the amount of shell holes and destruction centered in this one area, this was no accident. Jerry must have had direct observation. Some of these bodies were just beginning to appear through the melting snow, and a more gruesome sight you wouldn't believe.

"On the trail until now, we had been enclosed in the forest on both sides. All at once we approached a break in the trees on the left side. Here we had a good view of the valley floor below, which was loaded with wrecks of burned-out U.S. tanks. I would say there were well over a hundred in this small area. I couldn't say a tank battle had taken place there, as I did not see one destroyed Kraut tank. The Krauts were probably sitting back with their 88s and artillery, and annihilated them. Just about all of these tanks had burned, so it would be safe to assume the charred bodies of the crews were still inside." [17]

Seeing the remains of the 112th Infantry Regiment shocked Sergeant Bill Dunfee, who had served with Company I through each of its campaigns. "They were obviously withdrawing and were trapped. There were trucks, tanks, jeeps, trailers, and tank destroyers—bumper to bumper, and all shot to hell. Tanks had thrown their tracks; trucks, jeeps, and trailers had turned over; and some had burned.

"I had been exposed to the carnage of war in four airborne operations prior to this, but I had never seen anything that could compare to what we viewed in this area. Freshly killed troops in various stages of dismemberment are gruesome enough for the average stomach, but these men had been through a freeze and thaw. They had lain there since November, and their flesh had rotted and was peeling away from the skeletons. Some were on litters; hopefully they were killed outright, and not abandoned to freeze to death.

"There was complete silence in our column, each man handling this horror in his own way. For me, it was the most shocking single experience of the war. If anyone needed incentive to fight, this gave him ample reason." [18]

The devastation was particularly painful for Sergeant Russ Brown, with Company F. "I was from Pennsylvania, and it made me sick to see the 28th soldiers lying all around." [19]

Company I veteran Sergeant Harry Buffone was almost overcome by the smell. "By the time we reached the bottom of the valley, the stench was so bad, most of us lost our rations we ate that morning. And with the load we were carrying, it took all of our strength to climb out the other side of the valley." [20]

The following day, February 9, the 82nd Airborne Division attacked eastward with the objective of reaching the western shore of the Roer River upriver from the Schwammenauel Dam, then make an assault river crossing above site of the dam. The 505th moved out that morning, against only harassing artillery fire. Upon reaching the town of Schmidt, Sergeant Christensen found another scene almost as appalling as the previous day's. "What I really saw was just a pile of rubble. The town had been flattened. Here, a terrific battle must have taken place. There were bodies strewn everywhere—some of these, tanks had run over and flattened.

"Charred bodies were hanging out of turrets where the crews had tried to bail out of these burning hulls. You could see an arm or leg lying around, but no body [that] it had been attached to. Had some wild animal been dragging this off to feast on later? You shook your head and wondered, 'Is this Armageddon? Has the civilized world gone mad?'

"What I had witnessed in the Hürtgen would leave a lasting impression. This place must have been the closest to hell one could get without entering the gates." [21]

The 505th put out patrols that night, finding no enemy to its front. The following morning, February 10, the regiment took the high ground west of the river before first light. Outpost lines, established along the west bank to prevent enemy infiltration across the river, were relieved during darkness every night. The regiment remained in this position until the night of February 18, when it was relieved by elements of the 9th Infantry Division. The 505th marched back to a pickup point west of Schmidt, then trucked to Walheim, Germany, near Aachen, where it spent the night. The next morning, the regiment was trucked to the train station in Aachen, where it loaded onto 40 & 8 boxcars and traveled by rail to the Rheims, France, area. The Suippes base camp had been taken over by an army hospital, so the regimental combat team was billeted in tents nearby.

Even tent quarters were welcome to Sergeant Bill Dunfee, with Company I. "They had a pyramidal-tent city set up for us, mud and all. It sure beat the hell out of where we had been. We were allowed to use the showers in our former quarters—but not with the nurses. It was good to be home." [22]

The skeletal force that was the 505th RCT arrived in France in terrible need of rest, new equipment, and replacements. Staff Sergeant Earl Boling, released from the hospital at the end of February, was shocked when he rejoined the regiment. "There were few of the original men of the regiment left—and even the first replacements of the EGB units who had joined as replacements in Africa were mostly gone. With the number of killed in action, wounded, reclassified and not returned to duty, and missing in action, the ranks of the men with three and four combat jumps were growing ever thinner." [23]

Sergeant Paul Nunan, returning from a thirty-day furlough to the United States, found the Company D tents. "I walked around the company area for ten or fifteen minutes before I saw anybody I knew." [24]

Passes were issued to the officers and men, along with a few days to rest. Meanwhile, replacements were brought in, many directly from the United States, where most had just graduated from parachute school.

Those wounded in Holland and Belgium returning from hospitals brought unit cohesion back to their respective companies. However, the personnel rosters of most of the rifle companies was almost unrecognizable from those who had jumped in Holland less than six months earlier. Most companies were led by new officers, and many enlisted men were now non-coms. Over the next several weeks, numerous promotions and changes in command took place. Lieutenant Colonel Krause, the regiment's executive officer, was rotated home. Major Talton Long succeeded him as regimental exec, while Captain James T. Maness was promoted to major and took command of the 1st Battalion.

Parades and reviews were held, with decorations for individual and unit valor awarded. Private First Class Edward P. Laughlin, with Regimental Headquarters Company, was at an outdoor memorial service held for troopers killed since Normandy. "It was cold, rainy, with some snow flurries, and was generally a miserable day for all participants. It seemed as if we were standing in military formation on that field for an interminably long time. Although the crummy public address system prevented us from understanding much of his speech, it was apparent that Gavin was choked up. Then the bugler started playing 'Taps.' There wasn't a sound to be heard from several thousand men in that field. That bugler produced the most eerie, echoing, and bone chilling sounds that would tear out a person's heart. All I could see was sprawled and torn bodies in the snow, frozen blood, bodies contorted from dying violently or by freezing, and the setting in of rigor mortis. Tears flooded my eyes—and also the eyes of most of the troopers standing rigidly at attention." [25]

General Gavin addressed the assembled division, telling them they would be in on the fighting to finish the war in Europe. The regiment began training again to rebuild unit cohesion. The veterans, tired of the repetitive training they knew by heart, helped the young replacements learn the tricks and techniques that would keep them alive and insure success in combat.

On March 30, General Gavin received orders attaching the division to the U.S. Fifteenth Army, and to move the division to a location southwest of Bonn, Germany, to patrol the west bank of the Rhine River, across the river from trapped German forces in the Ruhr pocket. On the morning of April 2, eight trains and numerous motorized convoys carrying the division's artillery and antitank units began the journey by rail and truck to Germany. That evening and all of the following day, trains carrying the division unloaded at a single rail siding at Stolberg, Germany, with completion shortly before 12:00 a.m. on April 4.

The 82nd Airborne Division began relieving the U.S. 86th Infantry Division on the evening of April 3 and completed the task by 8:30 a.m. the following morning. By that time, the division's positions stretched from the town of Worringen, eight miles north of Cologne, extending south through Cologne, to Grau-Rheindorf, thirteen miles to the south—a total frontage of about thirty-two miles. The 504th's sector extended north from Cologne, while the 325th occupied Cologne, and the 505th sector spanned from just south of Cologne to just north of Bonn.

The 505th set up positions fronting the Rhine in factories, homes, and commercial buildings, with listening posts along the river, manned only at night. Any movement observed by the enemy brought artillery, mortar, and 20mm antiaircraft fire from across the river.

Company F occupied a row of houses several hundred yards from the river. Technician Fifth Grade William F. Borda was a replacement with F Company. "Sam Formicola, Bob Burdick, Ken Stillings, and I had a .30-caliber machine gun on the third floor, looking out on the river. We could see the Krauts in trenches on their side." 26

Sergeant Bill Dunfee and his Company I platoon occupied a factory overlooking the Rhine on the left flank of the regiment's sector, nearest to Cologne. "From my vantage point, I could see the church spires and buildings of the city some few miles distant.

"Since the river was swollen, due to the spring runoff, we had a clear view and field of fire. There was a floodplain to our front of about two hundred yards, then the river itself. We kept a listening post of one rifle squad at the river's edge, both day and night. My problem with this arrangement was that, there was no way we could evacuate this position if the enemy mounted a determined attack. We would surely get picked off in any attempt to withdraw to our MLR at the factory. Fortunately, no attack came, and it was fairly decent duty.

"While in this sector, each battalion was ordered to send a patrol across the river every night to satisfy the insatiable appetite of the XXII Corps for information. I've thought many times during and since the war, how easy it is to sit in corps or division headquarters and order out patrols—especially since it's not your ass that's on the line." 27

Aggressive patrolling across the Rhine River continued in order to capture prisoners for interrogation by the division G-2 section to determine enemy intentions. The patrols suffered some casualties, mostly from enemy minefields planted along the eastern shore and by drowning. Sergeant Earl Boling, with Company E, was told that patrols across the Rhine would begin on the night of April 5–6. "Our company sent a patrol out the first night, which upon landing ran into heavy enemy fire. In trying to find cover, they ran into a minefield, resulting in two deaths [Sergeant Frankie B. Ensley and Private First Class Francis H. Markwood]." 28

The two remaining members of the patrol, Lieutenant Howard E. Jensen and Private First Class James E. Keenan, tried to get back across the river the next morning. Lieutenant Jim Coyle, the Company E executive officer, away from company headquarters the night the patrol was conducted, found out the next evening what had occurred. "Jensen and Private First Class Jim Keenan were trying to get back to our lines, but it had turned light before they could get organized for the return. They were caught by enemy fire on the return trip. They had jumped out of the kayak to avoid the fire, but Jensen was shot in the head and Keenan had to swim the rest of the way to our side.

"The next night, Major Carpenter, the new battalion CO, had ordered another patrol to check for the body of the man who was killed. I don't know if they wanted the body recovered or if they thought the man might still be alive. They had observed the body with high-powered artillery binoculars during the day without any sign of life as far as I could see. The patrol was assigned to Lieutenant John O'Dea, an officer who had just joined the company.

"I was on the bank with several men when O'Dea and one other man left in a kayak. They had only been gone about fifteen minutes when a terrific explosion lit up the sky on the other side. It had to be a Teller mine. We waited to see if anyone would come back from the patrol. In another twenty minutes, the man who had gone over with O'Dea came running along the bank in a state of shock. He said O'Dea had stepped out of the kayak in the dark and had apparently tripped a mine. Without any discussion, Major Carpenter and Captain [Charles] Barnett got into a nearby kayak and started for the other side. I didn't understand this move—it was no place for a battalion and company commander.

"They had just about gotten out of sight on the river when I heard what I was sure was the kayak overturn. There was some splashing, but no other sound. I immediately stripped to my shorts and started to swim out to them. Carpenter's jeep driver came in after me. As I swam out, I heard their first cries for help and swam toward the sound. Before I got to them, the cries for help stopped. I called to them, but got no reply. When I got to about where I thought they might have overturned, I dove down a few times, but realized it was useless in the pitch dark.

"I also discovered that the current in the river was now much stronger that it had been nearer the shore, and that I was caught in it. I did not realize this at first, until I saw a large boat or barge go close by me in the dark at a fairly rapid clip. My first thought was, 'What is this boat doing going up the river in the dark?' I knew I was disoriented, but had enough sense to finally realize that the boat was sunk and stationary. It was I who was moving rapidly down the river!

"It was pitch black. I couldn't see the shore, but I knew if I kept the current coming from my left, I could swim to the bank on our side of the river. I finally reached the bank on our side and then thought of another problem. I did not know how far down the river I had been swept. I had no way of knowing what unit I might encounter. All I had on were my shorts and dog-tags. All I needed was to have some trigger-happy green guy see me some out of the river, think I was a German coming from the other side, and shoot without challenging me. I had barely climbed up on the river bank when I was challenged. I gave the countersign and my name and unit. I had been challenged by Staff Sergeant [Louis] Yarchak, one of the old veterans of F Company, who had gone back to the States [on furlough] in my group.

"Yarchak took me to the F Company CP, got me a blanket, and I got on the phone to Captain T. G. Smith, the battalion executive officer. I told him what had happened and that I knew Carpenter and Barnett had drowned. I told him that I would be willing to go across the river just before dawn to look for O'Dea when it got light—but I was not about to go stumbling around in a minefield in the dark. Captain Smith immediately told me that Colonel Ekman, the regimental commander, had already been told that Carpenter, Barnett, and I were missing, and that no one was going to go across the river until further orders.

"The next day, Colonel Ekman came to our company CP. He was furious over the loss of five men, including a battalion commander. He ordered me to write up a complete report and forward it to him at regimental headquarters. He then told me that I would take over as company commander. Then he broke my heart by telling me that it would only be temporary—that I didn't have enough seniority to keep it." [29]

THE U.S. 13TH ARMORED DIVISION, advancing north on the eastern side of the Rhine River, captured the territory across from the 505th, eliminating the need to man positions along the river. The 505th began assembling in battalion areas on April 14, preparatory to occupation duties. On April 17, the 505th moved to the vicinity of Bruhl, a rural town a short distance from Bonn.

Lieutenant Joe Meyers had replaced Lieutenant O. B. Carr as Company D executive officer while the regiment was at Salmchâteau, when Carr received orders to report for pathfinder training again. Meyers received a briefing before the move to Bruhl. "Rumors abounded of the formation of stay-behind groups of resistance, called 'Werewolves.' Our mission was to patrol a large assigned area and secure it against possible 'Werewolf' attacks. D Company used a village schoolhouse as its CP and billets. As executive officer, I planned and supervised the execution of the company patrol plan. At my request, [Captain] Bill Martin ordered the village mayor to requisition and deliver to us several serviceable bicycles for use by our patrols.

"The mayor selected the poorest machines for our use. The defective bikes broke down, making it difficult to cover all of our assigned patrol area. I repeatedly urged Martin to lay the law down to the mayor and insist on the delivery of better machines. For some reason, Bill was reluctant to follow this advice. On the other hand, he was quick to find fault with the patrolling. One afternoon, the matter came to a head. In response to a critical remark, I informed Bill that until he 'got off his ass and put some heat on the mayor,' I couldn't properly execute the patrol plan. Hot words ensued. Earlier in the day, Special Services had delivered recreational gear that included boxing gloves. Bill, a former Army boxer, invited me outside to put on the gloves, and I accepted his invitation.

"At the supply room, Bill and I learned the boxing gloves were [checked] out. We walked into the schoolyard where a large group watched two men spar. When the match ended, Bill asked if anyone objected to the two of us putting on the gloves. Delighted at the prospect of seeing their CO and XO square off in the ring, the men quickly designated seconds, appointed a referee, and named a timekeeper. We stripped to the waist, put on the gloves, and made ready for individual combat. Bill was stocky and thick-set. We were about the same weight; however, I was several years younger, three inches taller, and I had a reach advantage. The referee called time and the match started. Speck McKenna's boxing lessons stood me in good stead. I had a stiff, punishing left jab and I knew to follow it with a right cross. We fought two rounds before Bill suggested we quit. He did not lay a glove on me and he got a free boxing lesson. Bill showed no signs of holding a grudge. In fact, he treated me with more respect, and in later years, when he commanded a battalion, he asked me to join his staff.

"The following day, the 2nd Battalion moved to Bonn, the future capital of West Germany. Again, our mission was to neutralize a potential Werewolf threat. We were to conduct a house-to-house, building-to-building, search of the city for illegal weapons, explosives, etc. We carried out this search in a manner designed to convince the local population that we meant business. After dividing the city into sectors, the sectors to be searched were sealed off. The first day, I led a team that searched the Bonn City Hall and its adjoining air raid shelter. The shelter, which rose several stories above ground, was also a flak tower. There were four or five underground levels. The regional air defense CP occupied one of these underground floors. At the lower levels, we discovered room after room filled with oil paintings and other art objects. I reported this to the U.S. military government authorities.

"The following day we searched residences and business establishments near the center of town. We were to search everything and to break into locked rooms, cabinets, etc. Initially, almost every dwelling or shop had a locked door with a 'lost key.' After we shot a few locks, the owners got the message. Lost keys, they claimed not to have seen in years, suddenly appeared. While searching a basement under a shop, we came across the find of the operation—a cellar full of wine and other spirits. The owners were nervous, and I was certain they would move the liquor as soon as we departed. Two men were posted atop a nearby building where they could observe the shop. After dark, several civilians moved the booty to another cellar several blocks away. My lookouts noted the new location and reported it to me. I borrowed a 2 1/2-ton truck, and the next morning we backed up to the door where the cache was stored, loaded the spirits, and drove away." 30

On April 23, the division was alerted for possible movement, then received orders to move by train and rail to the Elbe River, northeast of Hanover, Germany. The division was relieved two days later.

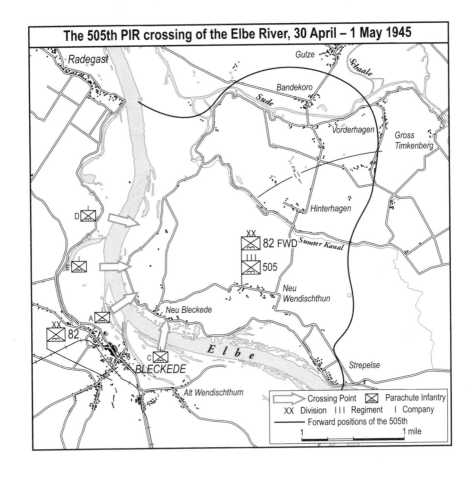

The 505th PIR crossing of the Elbe River, 30 April – 1 May 1945

CHAPTER 20

"Fugitives From The Laws Of Averages"

In April 1945, the advance of the Soviet army across northern Germany caused concern at Supreme Headquarters Allied Expeditionary Force (SHAEF) about possible Soviet occupation of Denmark. Eisenhower's staff ordered the British Second Army to cross the Elbe River and drive to the Baltic Sea, to make contact with Soviet forces before they could turn north into Denmark.

This operation required immediate execution, which was not Field Marshall Montgomery's strong suit. Therefore, Supreme Headquarters attached Ridgway's XVIII Airborne Corps to the British Second Army and assigned it to carry out the operation. For this operation, the corps would consist of the U.S. 8th Infantry Division, the U.S. 7th Armored Division, the 82nd Airborne Division, and the British 6th Airborne Division.

On April 26, the 505th moved northeast by rail to a staging area at the town of Bleckede, on the Elbe River. Lieutenant Joe Meyers, the Company D executive officer, was playing pinochle with several other troopers in one of the 40 & 8 boxcars as the train moved north. "The weather was warm and the right boxcar door was open. Some men slept in improvised shelter tent hammocks suspended between rings installed to tether horses. Other men slept on the floor. A few men cooked meals on small gasoline stoves, while still other troopers sat with their feet dangling out the door. We played cards on two C-ration boxes covered with a GI blanket. One of the men sitting in the door announced our train was approaching the new Franklin D. Roosevelt Memorial Bridge over the Rhine River. The bridge, a large wooden structure, was high above the stream, and its western approach was sixty or seventy feet above the surrounding terrain. Several men displayed an interest and moved to the door to get a better view. Our boxcar began to bounce around and someone remarked on the rough tracks. At this point, another man shouted out, 'Rough tracks, hell! We're off the tracks!'

"The boxcar began turning on its right side. No one had to tell these troopers it was time to bail out. With few exceptions, they cleared the boxcar in seconds. Seated at the rearmost of the car, I was one of the exceptions. Ammunition, mortars, machine guns, and rations stacked against the car's back wall came down on me when the engineer applied the emergency brakes. After the boxcar was on its side, I freed myself, discovered I was alone, and crawled to the door. The train was still moving and the ground flashed by a foot or two below the open door. After positioning my body parallel to the door, I rolled out of the boxcar and on to the ground.

"My timing was perfect. The only rail switch in sight struck me squarely in the back. The boxcars were speeding by a foot or two above my head and they provided me the incentive I needed to get clear of danger. I had no feeling in my legs, so I used my hands and arms to pull my body clear. Finally, I got sideways to the slope, let gravity take over, and rolled down the embankment until I reached the bottom some sixty or seventy feet below.

"One of the platoon medics gave me a shot of morphine and loaded me on a stretcher. That is the last I remember. I awoke in the enlisted men's ward of a field hospital near München-Gladbach, Germany." [1] The troopers on the derailed cars were loaded on other boxcars, the derailed cars unhooked, and the journey continued uneventfully.

On the night of April 28–29, the lead element, the division reconnaissance platoon, arrived at Bleckede and sent three patrols across the Elbe River to probe enemy defenses along the river. Only one patrol encountered stiff opposition, reporting it to division headquarters.

The trains carrying the 1st and 2nd Battalions began arriving in Bleckede in the predawn hours of April 29. Only a few officers and men in the regiment knew their mission—make an assault crossing of the Elbe River. Most troopers thought it would be more occupation duty.

When briefings were conducted after arrival, the officers and men couldn't believe it—why was this regiment selected to make an assault river crossing during the closing days of the war, after all of the combat it had seen? It was especially hard for the "old men" of the regiment, many of whom had made four combat jumps, fought five previous campaigns, and been wounded one or more times. Many felt their luck would run out—and they would be killed, seriously wounded, or drown during the closing days of the war.

Private First Class Dutch Schultz, with Company C, had served with the regiment in Normandy, Holland, the Ardennes, the Hürtgen Forest, and the Rhine River. "We soon learned the 505 would spearhead an assault across the Elbe River using small canvas and wooden boats, without any life jackets. This was to be our first river crossing. We knew nothing about these boats, much less crossing rivers in the middle of the night. The Elbe River was over 1,200 feet wide, which gave pause about how long we would be exposed to mortar and other fire. We knew the war was winding down. This raised our anxiety level about possible mishaps so close to the end. The longer we were exposed to combat, the more we felt like fugitives from the law of averages. In addition to all of the other combat risks of the past, we now faced the possibility of drowning." [2]

With 3rd Battalion still in route, the 1st and 2nd Battalions, and engineers from Company B, 307th Airborne Engineer Battalion, would make the initial crossing. Two companies from each battalion would cross in the first wave. Engineers were assigned to ferry the boats back for the second wave, consisting of the remaining rifle companies and headquarters companies of each battalion. In addition, other engineers were assigned to clear minefields. The attached regimental demolition platoon would deal with obstacles and pillboxes. Companies A and C from the 1st Battalion and Companies D and E from the 2nd Battalion were selected to cross in the first wave. Company D would cross on the left flank, with Company E on their right to the south. Company A would cross on the right of Company E, in the middle of a bend in the river, while Company C would cross on the far right, from south to north, due to the bend in the river. The operation would commence at 1:00 a.m. on the morning of April 30.

As darkness approached, Technician Fifth Grade Bill Borda, with Company F, waited anxiously for the boats to arrive. "It rained, snowed, and sleeted while we were waiting for the assault boats. Sergeant Steve Epps, a real leader—a 'follow me men' type—was about 'half in the bag,' having dug up a batch of Holland gin." [3]

The British army had hurriedly evacuated the townspeople of Bleckede, before they had a proper opportunity to hide items like their booze. The citizenry had buried most of it in their backyards, which the 505ers quickly found and consumed. That night, when the 3rd Battalion arrived, Sergeant Norbert Beach, a four-jump veteran with Company H, made one of those discoveries. "While waiting in this small town on this [west] side of the Elbe River, out in the cow lot, I happened to find two fifths of Canadian Club [whiskey], imported 1934. Consequently, six of us crossed the river flying high the next morning." [4]

Lieutenant Jim Coyle received orders that his 1st Platoon would lead Company E across. "My main concern was that with our inexperience in river crossings, could we keep the platoon and, for that matter, the company together? The Elbe was, with the spring flood, at least 150 yards across in our area, with a swift-running current. I was praying that we would all land together so we could organize on the other side. We were told that we would have a large concentration of artillery fire for support prior to our crossing at 2000 hours. We were to move our boats into the water under cover of the artillery. We were not informed of the kind of resistance we would receive from the enemy on the other side when we landed.

"Shortly after dark, we organized the company and moved down to the area chosen for embarking. We spread the men out in the area and waited for the trucks to arrive with the boats and the engineers who were to man them. When 2000 hours arrived, the artillery commenced firing. It was the greatest barrage that I had seen. Large-caliber guns fired for at least one-half hour, and 40mm antiaircraft Bofors placed direct fire like machine guns on the opposite bank. The problem was that our assault boats had not arrived by the time the artillery ceased!

"It became very quiet. Then a drizzle of rain began, which lasted for the next two hours, while the men stood around in the pitch dark, waiting for the boats. For the first time in the war, I had a feeling of dread about an operation. The element of surprise was gone with the artillery barrage. With that amount of artillery preparation, the enemy would know that an attack was coming. I had visions of the company stepping out of the boats and into a minefield as had happened to the patrols across the Rhine only a few weeks before. Waiting for those boats in the rain was very nerve wracking.

"The boats finally arrived. I can't remember how many hours behind schedule they were. I don't know what kinds of boats I expected, but I was unpleasantly surprised to see that each boat could carry about eight men at most with one engineer per boat. We were going to do the paddling. We unloaded the boats from the trucks, assigned the men per boat, and carried them down the bank to the water." [5]

Shortly before 1:00 a.m., on the left flank, Company D loaded into their boats and started across. The troopers in Technician Fourth Grade Allan Barger's boat initially had difficulty rowing together. "At first, since we had never practiced doing this, we started to zigzag clumsily for a bit. Then Captain Martin, who was kneeling just in front of me in the middle of the boat, started giving the paddlers a cadence. That did it. We began to move evenly across the silvery body of flowing water. And so did the rest of the company. We were in the lead.

"As we approached the shore, I saw the distant bank as a foreboding silhouette. I kept sucking in my guts anticipating machine gun fire opening up on us any minute. This could have been a disaster. But before we knew it, we were coming up to a small boat landing. and we stepped out onto some dry floats. Still, we kept expecting the enemy to open up on us, but nothing happened as we walked to shore. We didn't even get our feet wet! We walked up a pathway and worked ourselves over in the darkness to an empty old barn and went inside to wait for the others to catch up to us." [6]

To the right of D Company, Lieutenant Jim Coyle's Company E boats had similar difficulties. "We pushed off and I headed the lead boat to the outlet of the little bay toward the river. Just before we were about to leave the protection of the inlet and enter the river proper, I heard a lot of shouting behind me. I looked around to see that only a couple of boats were following me. I couldn't imagine how it had happened (we had briefed the men on the size of the river), but I could see that the rest of the company had paddled across the inlet and with the best of spirit, including rebel yells, was assaulting the opposite bank of the inlet.

"I put our boats ashore and went back along the bank to stop the premature landing. I started yelling as I approached them, because it occurred to me that if they thought they were on the other side of the Elbe, they might think I was the enemy coming at them. I told them that they hadn't crossed the river yet, and we finally got the company reorganized and headed out toward the river.

"By this time, the rain had stopped and a fairly bright moon had come out. This was a mixed blessing. We could see the other boats to stay organized during the crossing, but the Germans could see us coming, too.

"As we crossed the river, we were able to stay in a column despite the current. When we approached the enemy side, I was waiting for the enemy to open fire, but none came. Our boat pulled in near a small jetty and we landed. One of the men told me that he heard Germans talking in a building on a small dock. I told him to ignore it. If they were enemy soldiers, they were not going to fire on us, or they would have done it before we landed. They could be mopped up later.

"The 1st Platoon quickly spread out into a mini beachhead, and the rest of the company followed us ashore. I could hardly believe that after all of my fears and all that had gone wrong, there was no minefield, no enemy in sight, and we were ashore without losing a boat or a man. We quickly got the company organized and started moving inland." [7]

The lack of enemy resistance on the far shore surprised Company E trooper Sergeant Earl Boling. "I guess some of the Germans had figured it was too late in the war to die for a lost cause. However, a bit later, we were getting more action from machine guns and 20mm flak guns fired from the depressed position to cover the fields in a sweeping field of fire. But these were being knocked out, their crews captured, and started to the rear as prisoners, with a token guard to keep them moving." [8]

After Companies D and E landed, the engineers brought the boats back to the west bank, and Company F loaded into them and rowed across. Technician Fifth Grade Bill Borda's boat also struck the sandbar. Everyone jumped out, pulled it to the other side, and continued rowing. "Going across was a real chore. When we neared the far shore, Steve [Epps] stood up, said, 'Follow me, men,' stepped out and went under, but popped up almost immediately. I grabbed his pack and held him up until he could stand, and then we all moved forward. We were supposed to cross two phase lines, but we were beyond four of them by 10:00 a.m. and [encountered] little opposition." [9]

To E Company's right, Company A crossed at a bend in the river where it changed from flowing east to west, and turned north. The canvas boats worried Company A Private First Class Clarence M. Stoll, Jr., more than the German opposition. "I was somewhat nervous. I was in one of the last group of boats to cross and had no problems." [10]

The troopers caught many Germans asleep in their foxholes, where they had sought shelter from the drizzle and snow—and quickly rousted, disarmed, and moved them to the rear.

Crossing on the right flank, Company C moved north across the river. Somehow, Private First Class Dutch Schultz ended up in the same boat as Major Jim Maness, the 1st Battalion commander. "He sounded like a coxswain counting cadence for one of the Ivy League rowing teams. At mid-river, it started snowing and at the same time, we collided with another boat, which led to a shouting match about who had the right of way. At any moment, I expected the Germans to throw everything at us but the kitchen sink. I waited, but nothing happened. It had to be the grace of God that guided us to the other side.

"Once on shore, a lieutenant who had been sitting in front ordered me to follow him. We started running at full speed, until we came upon a lighted farmhouse. The lieutenant shouted in German for the occupants to come out. Two women came out of a doorway—and at the same time, I saw some shadows behind them and told the lieutenant, while running to the rear [of the house] where I found German soldiers and shouted, 'Hande hoch!' They obeyed. A few minutes later, the lieutenant marched in several more prisoners. We must have taken at least twenty prisoners.

After searching them for weapons, we ordered them to sit on the floor. About the same time, a military news reporter walked into the barn. He and the lieutenant greeted one another as friends. They talked for a moment and then decided to question the women, who were still in the house. I was ordered to stay and watch over the prisoners.

"After sitting down on the stairway leading into the house, I lit up a Lucky Strike cigarette and started puffing on it. Suddenly, I realized that the prisoners were intently watching every move I made smoking this cigarette. To rid myself of guilt and find some peace, I tossed them two packs and motioned for them to light up. We eventually produced a cloud of cigarette smoke that permeated the barn. Shortly, one of the men (a senior sergeant) indicated that he spoke English and that they were policemen from Hamburg, Germany, recently conscripted into military service. He then proceeded to ask me if I wanted a Luger pistol. Without hesitation, I said, 'Yes.' Rear echelon troops were paying $150 for these guns. He walked over to a corner and reached under something and pulled up not only a Luger, but also a P-38 pistol, both of which were in holsters. He gave them to me.

"I first tried putting them in the patch pockets of my combat pants, but couldn't do it because there were too many personal items, military gear, ammunition, rations, etc. Instead I put them onto my web belt, where I already was carrying a Colt .45 pistol. With three handguns on my belt, it appeared that I was 'slightly' overdressed.

"Soon, we heard a large contingent of troopers approaching the barn. I shouted, 'Don't shoot! Americans are in here.'

"One of them came in and asked, 'Where did the Krauts get the cigarettes?'

"I told him, 'I don't know.'

"He looked at me scornfully, knowing I was lying. He must have considered me a recent replacement who didn't know his elbow from third base. While I wasn't ashamed about lying, it was embarrassing to me that he caught me giving cigarettes to the enemy. It wasn't considered proper behavior by some of my fellow troopers (a sign of weakness)." [11]

The engineers returned to the west side of the Elbe and picked up Company B and Headquarters Company, 1st Battalion. Staff Sergeant James Elmo Jones, with Company B, was concerned about the combination of flimsy boats and new men. "We were given flat-bottom boats approximately fourteen feet long to cross the river in, and had many replacements who had not been in combat before. None of us had any experience in how to row. We were given six paddles to use, and everyone it seemed was rowing in the wrong direction—the boat started going round and around in midstream. The current was very swift, and finally I made everyone stop but two of us to get the boat across." [12]

Lieutenant Frank Herkness, the platoon leader of the 1st Battalion's 81mm mortar platoon, was concerned that "the boats were dangerously overloaded, both with men and equipment." [13]

Caught by surprise, German artillery pounded areas west of the river, particularly Bleckede and the crossing points. The Company B, 307th Engineers ferried the remainder of the 1st and 2nd Battalions across before dawn, and the 3rd Battalion crossed shortly after dawn in British amphibious vehicles known as Buffaloes. Sergeant Bill Dunfee, an original member of Company I, was surprised to learn that the 1st and 2nd Battalions had made a river crossing the previous evening— and that the 3rd Battalion would be crossing in daylight. "This did not do much for the morale of the 'old men' who had made four combat jumps and partici- pated in six campaigns. None of us cared for the dubious honor of being the last casualty in the ETO.

"While waiting to be ferried across in British Buffaloes, we suffered a number of casualties from incoming artillery. The primary target was the pontoon bridge that the engineers were erecting. The area was sprayed almost constantly with artillery. A personal loss at this time was [Staff Sergeant Robert E.] Wallace, who was one of the original members of the 505th. Wallace had been hit, and a medic, George Patrick, was working on him when another shell arrived, killing Wallace and wounding Patrick. This made you think about your chances of survival and I was damned glad when the Buffaloes showed up and took us across the river.

"After crossing the river, we spread out as skirmishers and attacked. Small arms fire was moderate, but the artillery continued to harass. What was especially fright- ening was the German use of 20mm antiaircraft guns. They had a lot of them—and what appeared to be an unlimited supply of high-explosive ammunition. They were using these 20mms like machine guns. We were well aware that getting hit would send you back to the States in a mattress cover. We also believed that the Germans must know that the war was over for them. They seemed to be determined to make us pay, or perhaps Hans wanted to brag to his grandchildren that he had held out until he was out of ammunition." [14]

As careful as the veterans of the regiment were this close to the end of the war, they were still being killed or wounded. Private Robert E. Erikson had been assigned to Company G after the 2nd Battalion, 509th PIR, had been disbanded. "All the pris- oners we were taking were older men and teenagers.

"I crawled under a fence and was holding the barbed wire for [Private First Class Paul M.] Lazar, the BAR man, when I was shot through the left chest. A medic put a compress on the wound, put my musette bag under my head, and gave me a shot of morphine." [15]

Staff Sergeant James Elmo Jones, with Company B, witnessed one tragedy as the result of an overly aggressive platoon leader. "We had a young lieutenant [Morris P. Guerrant] in his first combat, who got his platoon pinned down in an open field and got [four] of them [in addition to himself] killed. If he had waited thirty minutes more, it would have been unnecessary, as artillery knocked [the Germans] out." [16]

The regiment rapidly expanded the bridgehead, disposing of light resistance and pushing east, north, and northeast. As the 505ers closed, most German soldiers chose not to die for the Fatherland, and large numbers, hiding in houses and wooded areas, were captured.

After taking his prisoners to the rear, Dutch Schultz set off to find Company C, less than a mile to the south. "It was about 0900 hours when I found C Company. They were moving inland against sporadic small-arms fire and heavy 20mm high fire designed to explode over our heads. During one of these barrages, I got caught in the open and ran for cover to a nearby ditch. Upon jumping into it, I saw a German soldier, who wasn't more than sixteen years of age. We were about ten feet apart, with both of our weapons aimed at each other. In a few seconds, he dropped his rifle and raised his hands over his head. I never understood why I didn't shoot him the moment I saw him. I had been told many times to shoot first and ask questions later.

"In late afternoon, we were still mopping up when a German machine gun opened fire on us from a nearby wooded area. For the sake of glory, I decided to go after it with hand grenades. After running into the woods and crawling about fifty feet in the general direction of the machine gun, I suddenly thought, 'Why in the hell am I doing this?' Without so much as a second thought, I retraced my steps and rejoined my platoon." [17]

Despite heavy artillery falling around them, corps engineers built a pontoon bridge, completing it by 8:00 p.m. on April 30. The 504th PIR, British infantry, and elements of the U.S. 8th Infantry Division crossed the river and moved into the bridgehead that day. By day's end, the 505th had established a large bridgehead and dug in for the night.

At 5:52 a.m. the next morning, May 1, the 505th attacked eastward, with the 504th on their right flank and the attached 121st Infantry Regiment, 8th Infantry Division, on their left. The attack moved as far as nine miles against light resistance. The 505th reached its objective, the Correnzien forest, by mid-afternoon. That same morning, German radio in Berlin announced the news of Hitler's death, claiming he had died fighting Bolshevism.

The 325th Glider Infantry Regiment arrived on May 1 and passed through the 505th's lines to continue the attack the following morning. The following day, the division assigned the 505th control of two camps established near the towns of Dellien and Zeetze to handle displaced persons (DPs) and German POWs.

At 10:00 p.m. that night, General Gavin accepted the unconditional surrender of the German 21st Army. The following day, the 82nd Airborne Division began the overwhelming task of processing an estimated 144,000 prisoners, another 10,000 freed Allied prisoners of war, and uncounted displaced persons.

Sergeant Russ Brown, with Company F, watched the spectacle of masses of German soldiers moving along the road and gathered in fields on both sides. "The German army had very many horses to pull the guns and other equipment. They were hoping to cross the Elbe River and be in the American zone. They did not want to be in the Russian zone.

"I talked with a young German who said, 'If you go fight the Russians, my men will join you.'

"I said, 'The Russians are our allies.'" [18]

Troopers took German army vehicles for personal use, including motorcycles, convertible-topped Kubelwagens, and staff cars. Suddenly, the regiment was "mechanized." Company G confiscated horses from a Hungarian cavalry unit, later using them for organized horse races.

Also that day, the 325th GIR made the first contact with the Red Army. Gavin and his staff met with the commanding general of the Russian 8th Mechanized Corps and his staff to draw up lines of demarcation later that day.

Division headquarters issued an order on May 4 dividing the division's zone of operations into sectors, each of which was to be searched for weapons and explosives. In addition, all German personnel were to be screened, and infrastructure was to be guarded.

On May 5, a concentration camp was discovered a couple of miles north of Ludwigslust, outside the tiny village of Wöbbelin. Captain Philip M. Hannan, the Catholic chaplain of the 505th, and his assistant, James M. "Jack" Ospital, hurried to the camp to do what they could for the victims. "The camp was a repulsive, absolute horror. The grotesque, emaciated bodies were lying in clumps in the dormitories, many were still in the tiers of rough bunks, made of branches, and the survivors were barely able to walk. The stench was pervasive.

"I quickly walked through some of the dormitories to find if there was any semblance of authority with which to begin the necessary assistance to the living. I found a small group of prisoners sitting in one building, and as I approached them, the prisoners deferred to a small person sitting in their midst. He was a Belgian Catholic priest, so weak he could not stand, but still consoling and encouraging a group of fellow prisoners.

"He told me that he and another Catholic priest had been arrested and sent to a camp in Germany in the first weeks of the offensive against Belgium and France in 1940. The other priest had just died. He said, with that complete resignation of prisoners who had lived in hopeless situations, that no one had come to help them. A few curious Allied officers had taken a look and left in utter frustration.

"I hurried back to get permission, and perhaps some help, from Colonel Ekman, our CO. He was compassionate but firm: 'I can let you and your assistant give assistance to the prisoners, but I cannot allow anybody else to go with you. The camp is full of disease, and I can't let my men get diseases. We are combat troops and must keep in shape.'

"Back to the camp—we decided to bring the survivors to an empty space near the gate to facilitate their being taken to some hospital—still unknown. Sporadically, a couple of enlisted men from a nearby American division came to the camp to gawk, and we promptly tried to enlist their help, with no success. Finally, an officer brought a wheezing German truck, with a German driver who looked as worn out as the truck. Then he left.

"Jack and I began to load the survivors into the truck, amazed at the fact that so many had survived. The emaciated bodies weighed, I guessed, about sixty or seventy pounds. The few survivors who could walk tried to help, but the spirit only was willing.

"From my brief conversations with the survivors, I found that the majority were Catholics. When we had loaded the truck, I stood at the front of the cab and gave absolution to all, after leading them in an act of contrition. The driver pleaded that the truck was near a complete breakdown. I overruled his plea, ordering him to take the men to the hospital in Ludwigslust, not very far away.

"Not knowing whether the truck would return, Jack and I started to talk with the remaining survivors. The Belgian priest refused to be helped, saying that all the others must be helped. The Dutch prisoners refused to be moved unless all could be moved at the same time. 'That may mean that you must stay here tonight,' I warned. Agreed, they would stay together.

"A very curious character was among the survivors and he was in relatively good shape. He said he belonged to the French Intelligence and was of Greek descent. His good physical shape made me doubt his story. Finally, I found a Dutch naval captain who had been taken prisoner after his cruiser had been captured. I instantly made him the commanding officer of the camp.

"A Red Cross girl from the 82nd (Dorothy was her first name) came to the camp to volunteer. I gave her one glance at one of the dormitories and convinced her that the clean up was the work of the men. Many of the prisoners died in their bunks, suffering from lethal bouts of diarrhea. The effluent from the top tiers poured down on the lower tiers, creating a horrible mess, with an almost unbearable stench.

"At one point, I went back to see the Belgian priest to force him to accept some assistance. He was calmly adamant, and was perfectly resigned to die. He said that he had often celebrated Mass late at night. 'I always could bribe some guard to give me a few drops of wine and a small piece of bread to consecrate. It was great support for the prisoners.'

"He became the inspiration for all the prisoners, some of whom were Russians and Jews. Practically every nation in Europe was represented among the prisoners. According to their estimates, there were about four thousand men in the camp at the beginning, and about a third survived.

"We could not finish our rescue work in one day, so the next day we came back. Shortly after arriving, we saw a funeral procession. A halting line of prisoners, dressed in wretched and raggedy striped uniforms, were walking single file behind a body resting on a rough wooden coffin. The procession wended its way to the nearby woods. It was the funeral of the Belgian priest, who had died just before I arrived at the camp.

"I was not invited to participate in the funeral. I did not qualify. It was only for those who had suffered together for almost five years. That fraternity was not broken.

"We were able to transport the rest of the ill prisoners to the hospital and to settle a problem in the hospital. Some of the sick prisoners had begun to strike at or hit the nurses in their rage against the atrocious treatment in the camp. A firm order restored peace, at least for a time.

"Supplies from some Army commissariat came into the camp, and the Dutch captain, the commandant, regulated the distribution. Of course the men of the commissariat tried to make the prisoners take only soup and very soft food as their first nourishment, but the pangs of hunger were too strong. The result—a number of ghastly sick prisoners, including the commandant." [19]

Many of the 505th RCT's officers and men visited the Wöbbelin Concentration Camp, personally witnessing the atrocities of the Third Reich. General Gavin ordered the leading citizens of Ludwigslust to dig graves for two hundred of the inmates in the park in front of the Palace of the Grand Duke of Mecklenburg, which was a part of the town square. Gavin required all of the townspeople and a group of captured German army officers to attend the funeral on May 7. The nearby towns of Hagenow and Schwerin held similar funerals for two hundred at each location the following day.

During the early hours of May 7, at SHAEF headquarters in Rheims, France, the Germans signed documents agreeing to the unconditional surrender of all German forces to the Allied nations. General Eisenhower sent the following telegram to the Combined Allied Chiefs of Staffs: "The mission of this Allied Force was fulfilled at 0241 hours, local time, May 7, 1945. Eisenhower"

The surrender of all German forces took effect at 11:01 a.m. on May 8, 1945. It had been a long, costly struggle. The 505th PIR had lost 465 killed in action, 146 missing in action, 1,760 wounded in action and not returned to duty, 1,081 wounded and returned to duty, 357 injured and not returned to duty, and 263 injured and returned to duty.

The 80th Airborne Antiaircraft (Antitank) Battalion had suffered 42 killed in action, 17 missing in action, 91 wounded in action and not returned to duty, 57 wounded and returned to duty, 46 injured and not returned to duty, and 40 injured and returned to duty.

The 456th Parachute Field Artillery Battery had 44 killed in action, 1 missing in action, 104 wounded in action and not returned to duty, 65 wounded and returned to duty, 16 injured and not returned to duty, and 8 injured and returned to duty.

The 307th Airborne Engineer Battalion, of which Company B supported the 505th RCT, lost 94 killed in action, 34 missing in action, 235 wounded in action and not returned to duty, 140 wounded and returned to duty, 21 injured and not returned to duty, and 14 injured and returned to duty.

When Sergeant Earl Boling, with Company E, heard the war was over, he walked to a small German church across the street from his platoon's quarters. "I thought of the many brave and good men it had taken the lives of, to get us this far—and of the words of Lieutenant Charles Barnett on the *George Washington* troop ship over two years before: 'Many of us will not make it back, but the ones that do will have had an adventure to remember the rest of our lives.'

"And of [Corporal] Tommy Burke, who had said, 'If I die and you live, don't forget to tell my mother how it happened. I wouldn't want her to ever think I got it in the back, running away.' I vowed that when I got back, that I would see Mrs. Burke, and I said a silent prayer that I had made it this far. I thought of all the others who wouldn't make it home." [20]

Although the Allied victory in Europe was something to celebrate, General Gavin put that victory in the proper perspective. "We had come to the end of the war in Europe. It had been costly. More than 60,000 men had passed through the ranks of the 82nd Airborne Division alone. We had left in our wake thousands of white crosses from Africa to Berlin. And when it came to an end, there was not a man in the ranks of the 82nd Airborne Division who did not believe that it was a war that had to be fought." [21]

With the war in Europe over, most of the officers and men of the 505th RCT were anxious to return to the United States and civilian life. The U.S. military used a points system to determine who went home first. Points were accrued for the number of months in the service, the number of months served overseas, Purple Heart awards, awards for valor, and other factors. Those with the highest number of points would be sent home and discharged first, as soon as transport was available, because priority was given to units transferring to the Pacific Theater. Many of the old-timers had been with the regimental combat team for almost thirty-six months and overseas for twenty-four months. Most had a Purple Heart medal with one or two Oak Leaf Clusters and a Bronze or Silver Star medal. In May, the army sent men with the regiment with one hundred or more points home.

During the last three weeks of May and first week in June, the division spent time screening and guarding German prisoners. Returning from the hospital after injuring his back and nearly losing his life in the train derailment a couple of weeks earlier, Lieutenant Joe Meyers found the Company D command post at a farmhouse about a mile east of the Elbe River. "D Company was designated to receive and hold all SS prisoners captured by the 505th at the small village of Privelack on the east bank of the Elbe River. The village consisted of a dozen or so houses and assorted outbuildings situated along a levee that protected it and the surrounding farmland from the flood waters of the Elbe. Several farmhouses provided adequate billets for our troops, but there were no facilities to house or detain the 250 SS PWs we were to guard. [Captain] Bill Martin turned the job over to me.

"A pasture with a water well was close at hand, and after examining the area, I concluded this was a good location for the PW enclosure. Enclosed by a four-strand barbed wire cattle fence, there was nothing to prevent the PWs from escaping during the night. No barbed wire was immediately available to build a proper enclosure, and there was no way of lighting the enclosure at night. German soldiers wanted to escape and cross to the west bank of the Elbe River, because they believed that all PWs east of the Elbe eventually would be turned over to the Russians. We didn't know it at the time, but they were correct.

"By the time the SS PWs arrived at Privelack, I had a plan to keep them in custody. The senior lieutenant in command of the prisoners was an Estonian, and his troops were German, Estonian, and Latvian. Rank is a matter of importance in every army. I asked the lieutenant to give me a list of all of his officers and NCOs in order of rank. When he completed this list, I had each verify his position on the list. With the order of rank firmly established, I advised them we were unable to secure the

PW enclosures during the hours of darkness. Although guards would be on duty twenty-four hours a day, they were responsible for security. We would jointly make a count of the number of prisoners in custody and agree upon the exact number. Each morning we would repeat this joint count. If one, two, or three prisoners were missing, we would shoot the same number of officers or NCOs, starting with the senior officer and working down the list.

"We then held an inspection for weapons and ammunition. We found very little contraband, but I suspected the SS men still had weapons. I informed the SS lieutenant of my suspicion and ordered him to make his own inspection of his troops. No questions would be asked about any weapon turned in before a specified time. After that, we would shoot any PW found with contraband. When the period ended, a large table was loaded with weapons surrendered by the SS. These were harsh measures, but we were dealing with SS men, the elite of the German Army, not Boy Scouts or regular soldiers. The measures violated the Geneva Convention, but they got the job done. We didn't lose a single SS PW, and no SS man attacked our troopers. Unfortunately, we were not so fortunate where the Wehrmacht was concerned.

"While I was resting one afternoon, I heard several shots ring out nearby. I rushed outside and one trooper reported [that] the shooting came from the top of the levee and found our sentry on the ground with a bullet wound in the stomach. He [had] stopped two unarmed German soldiers who were attempting to cross the levee to the river below, and [had] decided to search the men before he escorted them to the PW enclosure. While emptying his rucksack, one German soldier fired a concealed pistol through the bottom of his pack. After falling to the ground, our man was able to get off a couple of rounds at the fleeing soldiers.

"I was furious! The war was over. These two men inflicted what probably was a fatal wound on one of our men. I told the troopers who had assembled at the spot that we were going to run both Germans to ground. We split into groups and set out on the run to capture them. After a short chase, we captured both men and I personally shot both of them. If I had it to do over, I'm not certain what I would do. I might shoot them again, and I might not—I just do not know.

"Killing does not bother me, and I've never lost any sleep over the incident. In any case, the war was over and those were the last two rounds I fired in anger. In 1989, a trooper from D Company informed me that after the war, he met the soldier who was wounded by the Germans at Privelack. The man had recovered from his wound. A 'gut shot' is a terrible wound. I was pleased to learn the man survived." [22]

One of the activities that the troopers used to pass the time was organized horse races, using horses confiscated at the time of the German surrender. The racetrack was known as "Sour Kraut Downs." Handicapping and betting was almost as professional as the racetracks in the United States.

Sergeant Russ Brown, with Company F, attended one of the horse races at Sour Kraut Downs, organized by the regiment. "F Company had a horse in the race and the jockey was a cowboy from Oklahoma. The horse broke his leg, so F Company was not lucky or happy." [23]

Private First Class Virgil Goodwin was a jockey during those horse races. "Sour Kraut Downs was the highlight of my time in the army. I was born and raised on a farm until I went into the army. A horse was my only mode of transportation. I was used to a western saddle, and the Germans had English type. The races were short lived, because we had to move on." [24]

ON JUNE 1, THE DIVISION WAS RELIEVED from their occupation duties. The 505th PIR and Company B, 307th Airborne Engineer Battalion, left the following morning by train for Camp Chicago near Laon, France, arriving on June 5. The 80th Airborne Antiaircraft (Antitank) Battalion and the 456th Parachute Field Artillery Battalion traveled to Camp Chicago by road.

Another group of high-point officers and men left for the United States a few days later. The division moved again, from June 12 to 15, to the town of Epinal, near Nancy, France.

The army made a decision to exchange the high-point men in the parachute units of the 82nd Airborne Division with the low-point men in the 507th Parachute Infantry Regiment, 17th Airborne Division, which was about to be deactivated.

On June 21, the 505th held a ceremony for about one thousand of the departing high-point men. Staff Sergeant Arnold "Dutch" Nagel had served with Company C since it was formed. "Company C had 112 members [plus eight officers] in 1943 at Fort Bragg. By the end of the war, we had been sent 252 replacements. At the end of the war, only three soldiers from my squad with four combat jumps were left. Each of us had been in the hospital at least once. I was the fourth squad leader." [25]

Sergeant Norbert Beach had served with Company H all the way from the Frying Pan to Berlin, making four combat jumps and fighting in six campaigns in the process. "I had eighty-six points. The departure ceremony was very emotional for me—to leave the troopers I had served with—but I was ready to go home." [26]

Sergeant Joseph Jockel, with Headquarters Company, 3rd Battalion, one of the high-point men, would never forget the ceremony. "It was like a formal retreat parade—band and all. On one side of the field were the 505 and on the other side facing us was a regiment recently arrived in the ETO. High pointers and low pointers marched off to separate sides of the field—very impressive proceedings.

"But the next announcement was devastating. Imagine—82nd patches were to be removed from our blouses and replaced with one indicating another division. No way were we going to satisfy that order. I remember one old timer of the 82nd saying, 'It will take four or five field-grade officers holding me down to take off my AA patch.'

"A day or two later a compromise was reached where we were allowed to wear both patches, one on each shoulder." [27]

Colonel Ekman and the troopers remaining with the regiment paraded in review for the departing troopers, who then passed in review for Colonel Ekman and the regiment. It was highly emotional for the troopers parting with buddies and friends with whom they had fought alongside and shared their food and foxholes. Allen L. Langdon had served with Company C since Italy. "Even the most callous could not help [but] feel a surge of emotion as the veterans marched by, as it was not goodbye, but the end of an epic." [28]

Despite combat in Holland, Belgium, and Germany, Lieutenant Joe Meyers, the Company D executive officer, didn't have enough points to go home. "A week or two after our arrival in Epinal, [Colonel] Bill Ekman assembled the regiment and announced the 82nd Airborne Division would occupy the U.S. sector in Berlin. Bill had just returned from Berlin, and he painted a glowing picture of the assignment and the city. We would be America's honor guard in the former German capital. He urged one and all to accompany the regiment to Berlin. I was a little short of the points needed to return home, so I decided to extend and go to Berlin. The Berlin assignment gave the 505 a new sense of purpose. Emphasis shifted from combat training to the skills of a spit and polish garrison soldier. The transition was relatively painless. Unlike many units in the immediate postwar ETO, the 82nd was a disciplined unit. The troops shaped up in good order, and there was time left over for recreation." [29]

At the end of July, the troopers of the division loaded on 40 & 8s for the five-day train ride to Berlin, inside the Soviet Zone of Occupation, arriving between August 1 and 8. When his train arrived in the town of Helmstedt, Lieutenant Meyers helped get the Company D troopers off the train. "After four days in boxcars, we looked more like tramps than soldiers. At Helmstedt, we marched a short distance to a large indoor swimming pool, where we showered, shaved, and swam before starting the final leg of our trip. There were several rail lines from Helmstedt to the Soviet Zone; however, once we crossed into Soviet territory the other lines had been removed, leaving a single line.

"We were to dress in Class A uniform and detrain at Tempelhof Station around 0900 hours in the morning—0900 hours came and went, without sign of Berlin. Around noon we arrived in the Berlin rail yards. The Soviets had removed all the automatic rail switching equipment, transported it to the Soviet Union, and replaced it with a manual system.

"We circled Berlin several times without reaching our destination, the Tempelhof Station. Around 1600 in the evening, General Gavin located our train and flagged it down. He abandoned the idea of getting the regiment to Tempelhof Station, and we detrained somewhere in the U.S. Zone. After a delay, trucks arrived and moved the 2nd Battalion to a camp located on Berliner Strasse, about a block from the Soviet T-34 Tank Monument.

"Governed by a Kommandantura made up of high-ranking members of the occupying powers, Berlin had four zones—American, British, French, and Soviet. In theory, we could move freely in and out of any of the city's occupied zones. This was true in the American, British, and French Zones, but the Soviets obstructed and otherwise discouraged any Allied entry into their zone. Of course, they continued to exercise their right to access zones of the other occupying powers.

"Our first order of business was to secure the outer perimeter of the U.S. Zone. Surrounded by the Soviet Zone of Germany, the outer perimeter of all Allied sectors of Berlin abutted occupied Soviet territory. Armed deserters from the Soviet Army roamed the streets of Berlin in gangs, murdering, raping, and looting. Other Soviet army personnel, officer and enlisted, were simply unruly, troublemaking drunks. No one was safe, including American army personnel. Roadblocks were established on main routes leading into the city in an effort to monitor and control military and civilian traffic.

"The Soviets tried to run over us roughshod. They ran roadblocks and fired their weapons indiscriminately. Our men were combat veterans, and this did not sit well. The division killed about twenty Soviets the first month in Berlin. Orders forbade the carrying of weapons while off duty. Conditions were so bad, common sense dictated otherwise. On duty I carried a loaded issue pistol and off duty a concealed weapon." [30]

The area of Berlin where Lieutenant Ray Grossman and Battery C, 456th Parachute Field Artillery Battalion, were quartered was not heavily damaged by war. "We lived in a comfortable house. Our duty was mostly guard duty, and the troops were not that interested. Morale was bad and discipline was hard to enforce. There were lots of girls and a big black market—a carton of cigarettes went for two hundred dollars." [31]

A few weeks after arriving in Berlin, Lieutenant Meyers reported to Colonel Ekman's headquarters for a special assignment. "The 505 would organize and train a company-sized-unit honor guard for visiting dignitaries. I was to select the personnel to man the company from units throughout the regiment. Ekman instructed me to set up a company tailor shop, barbershop, and other facilities in the unit's area. He wanted the company organized and trained immediately. I selected a cadre from the 2nd Battalion and set about cleaning up an empty barracks. I sent an NCO with a jeep and trailer to locate and confiscate sewing machines, barber chairs, and other essential equipment for the shops. A few hours later, the items were in use.

"The following day, two military government agents informed me I was under investigation for unauthorized acquisition of private German assets. This came as a surprise to me and, I assume, to my regimental commander. The matter must have been settled out of court, because I kept the equipment and I heard no more about it.

"When the unit billets were ready, I selected about four officers and one hundred fifty men, all five feet eleven inches or taller, from other regimental units. For several weeks these men underwent intensive training in the manual of arms, drill, and ceremonies. Uniforms were tailored, rifle stocks boned and oiled, pistol belts blanco'd, helmets enameled, etc. After completing our training we greeted U.S. senators and representatives, general officers, and other VIPs at Berlin District Headquarters and Tempelhof Airdrome.

"Each of the three regiments of the division had honor guard companies. The VIP traffic was lighter than anticipated. A single company could easily handle the duties; hence, we inactivated the escort company in the fall." [32]

On V-J Day, Generals Eisenhower and Patton, Soviet Marshal Georgi Zhukov, and British Field Marshal Montgomery arrived at Tempelhof, where they reviewed the 82nd Honor Guard Company. After the review, General Patton said, "In all of my years in the army and of all of the honor guards I've ever seen, the 82nd Berlin Honor Guard is the best." [33]

As summer ended in Berlin, General Gavin felt the division would remain a part of the future peacetime army. "Airborne warfare was entirely new in the U.S. Army, and we were certain that there would be an airborne division in the postwar Army. We were sure, too, that it would be the 82nd.

"Then came the blow. In early October we received a cable from Washington informing us that the division was to be disbanded in Europe, that it was through." [34]

This was devastating news to everyone in the division. The 101st Airborne Division was chosen to be the one airborne division in the peacetime army after the demobilization.

But Gavin knew that his troopers would always carry with them the pride of having served in the 82nd Airborne Division. In an anonymous letter sent to him from a lieutenant in the division, Gavin read, "We know that somewhere there will always be an 82nd Airborne Division, because it lives in the hearts of men. And somewhere, young men will dare the challenge to 'Stand up and hook up' and know that moment of pride and strength which is its reward." [35]

Gavin contacted influential people in Washington in the hopes of having the decision changed, but to no avail. Gavin then turned to Lieutenant Colonel Barney Oldfield, who had been in the newspaper business, a radio announcer, and a Hollywood press agent for Warner Brothers Studio. He had qualified as a paratrooper in the summer of 1942 and was the 505th's first S-2, when Gavin had commanded the regiment. Oldfield immediately organized a media blitz throughout the United States, sending stories of the division's officers and men to their hometown newspapers, with a subtle message. He assembled a team to write the stories and solicited the help of correspondents in Berlin. "There were a lot of correspondents hanging around the bars in Berlin and Paris press clubs with nothing to write about, so we encouraged any and everybody to send home to their newspapers 'why' stories—specifically, why not the 82nd as the surviving U.S. airborne division?

"If one of the correspondent's head was throbbing from the previous night's excesses, we had someone write his 'why not the 82nd Airborne?' story for him. As one of them, leaning against the bar, told me, 'Hell, I'll put my byline on any good writing!'" [36]

Oldfield's team sent out thirty-six bags of mail addressed to every newspaper with a circulation of more than ten thousand and to every radio station in the United States.

Citizens sent letters with the newspaper clippings attached to their representatives in congress and the secretary of war asking why the 82nd Airborne would be deactivated, when it had a longer and more distinguished combat record than the 101st. The grassroots campaign worked. Gavin received the news in late

November: "We were notified that the division would not be disbanded. Not only that—it would return to the United States shortly after the first of the year and it would march up Fifth Avenue in New York. We were, of course, elated, and we at once began preparations for the move and the parade." [37]

On November 19, the division was relieved from occupation duty in Berlin and began the move to the United States. The division moved first to Camp Chicago, where as many as three practice parades were conducted daily in preparation for the New York City Victory Parade. The division then moved to Camp Lucky Strike near Le Havre, France, where it was ferried across the English Channel, and billeted in British army barracks to await the trip across the Atlantic.

After celebrating another Christmas overseas, the third for some, the division moved to Southampton, boarded the *Queen Mary* ocean liner, and on December 29, 1945, departed for the United States. Lieutenant Joe Meyers was now the commanding officer of Company D. "About eighteen thousand troops were crammed into the huge vessel's bowels. Our tiny stateroom held twelve officers. We slept in canvas bunks a few inches apart and tiered four high. The open space in the middle of the room was about the size of a card table. If two occupants stood up, the remaining ten had to be in bed or outside the room. The lavatory and commode were available for use, but the bathtub was stacked high with baggage. All passengers ate two meals [daily], a breakfast of kippers and eggs and one other meal. The winter of '45–'46 had some of the heaviest weather in recorded history. Seas were so high, the open decks of the *Queen* were closed." [38]

It was January 3, and the 82nd Airborne Division was just about home. Lieutenant Meyers took in all of the unforgettable sights of that homecoming. "It was a thrilling experience to sail past the Perth Amboy lighthouse and the Statue of Liberty. Ferryboats carrying bands, fireboats, and all manner of craft greeted us as the tugboats moved the *Queen Mary* up the East River to the dock. My first sergeant was beside himself. From the deck, he pointed out his home where his wife and family were waiting to greet him. Later in the day, we debarked and moved by train to Camp Shanks. As we came down the gangplank, we were handed a small carton of cold, fresh milk. I hadn't tasted fresh milk in over a year and a half. How sweet it was!

"Upon our arrival at nearby Camp Shanks, a T-bone steak dinner awaited the troops. The following day it was more practice parades." [39]

On the morning of January 12, 1946, the 82nd Airborne Division moved by truck and rail from Camp Shanks to Manhattan to march up Fifth Avenue in the great New York City Victory Parade. As Lieutenant Meyers was getting his men formed up, "an elderly lady approached for a close-up look at my troopers. She turned to me and said, 'Why, you are only babies!'

"I remember my reply, 'Lady, those are the toughest babies you have ever seen.' We were young. I had turned twenty-three less than a month earlier. The troopers probably averaged twenty years of age. Properly trained and led, troops in the eighteen- to twenty-year age group make excellent combat soldiers. This was particularly true of young soldiers who served in volunteer units.

"It was a beautiful parade. Recorded in both still and motion pictures, the marching was the best I have ever seen. Leading D Company [up] Fifth Avenue and past the reviewing stand, ranks among the proudest moments of my thirty-year career. As we passed the reviewing stand, I heard the familiar voices of O. B. Carr and Tom McClean call out to me from the stands. Tom had recovered from the wounds he received in Holland. Stationed at the Parachute School at Fort Benning, Tom and O. B. were part of a group that flew to New York to witness the parade.

"Millions of service men and women returned to the U.S. from overseas following World War II, but I was one of the few lucky ones who marched in the Victory Parade in New York City in January 1946." [40]

Joseph Jockel had come home with the high-point men and was working and going to college at night. "I took the day off—arrived early for a good spot to watch. I can't explain my feeling as Slim Jim and his staff went by. But, when HQ 1st [Battalion] and G Company arrived, I was aghast—who were these imposters? I knew not one man or officer, where once I knew all by first name and rank. All at once, I was disenchanted and proud." [41]

Upon returning to the United States, most veterans of the 505th RCT received their discharge and got on with their civilian lives. Luis de los Santos, who had come to America illegally as a stowaway on a ship from his native Dominican Republic, served with Company D from Africa through Berlin. "Before I became a civilian, they gave me the papers to be a citizen of the United States. I was very happy." [42]

Unlike most of his fellow officers, Lieutenant Meyers decided on a career in the U.S. Army. "The following day we boarded trains and headed for army separation centers near our homes for discharge or, in my case, forty-five days of R&R (rest and relaxation). We didn't know it at the time, but the bonds of comradeship forged in combat were in many cases sufficiently strong to endure for the balance of our lives." [43]

EPILOGUE

"Invisible Pathfinders"

After the war, each man had to determine what he was going to do with the rest of his life. A few stayed with the 505th RCT, but most returned to being civilians, with many taking advantage of the greatest investment the U.S. Government ever made, the GI Bill, which gave them the opportunity to attend college. As a result, many became successful businessmen, physicians, teachers, attorneys, and scientists. The men approached civilian life the same way they did the army: they wanted to be the best at whatever they did. Bill Tucker, a successful attorney and official during the Kennedy administration, wrote: "Anyone who served with the 82nd from Africa to Berlin never really left the 82nd in spirit. No other educational or maturing processes ever equaled the impact of being an 82nd trooper. We always remembered the words: 'Never retreat. Never accept defeat.' My 82nd Airborne education has been invaluable to me in terms of taking on any tough job—and getting it done." [1]

Men courageous enough to jump out of an airplane at night, under fire, and in enemy territory weren't frightened by the challenges of starting a new business or getting an advanced degree. Even those severely wounded or injured got on with their lives, despite physical limitations. Bill Bishop had badly injured his leg in the Normandy jump and received a medical discharge. He saved his money and started a watch repair business, which grew into a successful retail jewelry business.

The regimental combat team produced great leaders, including Philip M. Hannan who served the Catholic Church, rising to archbishop emeritus of the Archdiocese of New Orleans, Louisiana. Of those who stayed in the army after the war, many were key leaders in the post–World War II era. General James M. Gavin rose to become the U.S. Army's chief of research and development, where he pioneered and developed the concept of air mobility and the airmobile doctrine, used in Vietnam and beyond. After retiring from the army, he served as the chairman of the board of the prestigious Arthur D. Little consulting firm. He was an adviser to President John F. Kennedy, who appointed Gavin ambassador to France. One of Gavin's officers, Jack Norton, rose to the rank of three-star general, commanding the 1st Cavalry Division (Airmobile) in Vietnam.

Of the enlisted men and non-commissioned officers who stayed in the army, Howard Melvin, Paul Nunan, W. A. Jones, and Horace Pearl served as sergeant majors or command sergeant majors for units in Korea and Vietnam. Elmo Bell retired as a brigadier general with the Mississippi National Guard.

ALL OF THE RETURNING OFFICERS AND MEN had at one time or another asked themselves this question: Were the terrible costs in lives, crippling wounds, mental trauma, frostbite, trench foot, and malaria worth it? Bill Tucker felt it was. "I didn't regret one minute of service as I sit here today—whether a minute of joy or defying death.

"As I look back, I often think of things we never forgot—the values that we fought to preserve, which were loosely called 'freedom.' Those values were the life-blood of our generation: honor and pride in self, family, and country; the giving and acceptance of discipline; and the moral standards of our times and our communities.

"And there are others who do not forget. Once or twice a month, when I park at a supermarket, someone, a stranger, will look my way and say, 'thank you' or give me a salute. It takes me a minute or so, but then I realize they have seen the Purple Heart registration plate on my car." [2]

Despite the hardships and loss of friends, Charles Miller, who had served with Company D, felt "it was a terrific experience for me to be in the airborne with the 82nd Airborne Division, especially the 505, and especially D Company.

"I don't know anyone in the other companies, because I was a private. I knew my squad and some of the other guys—but that was it. But our squad fought, lived, and died together.

"I am very thankful for the opportunity that I had as a young man to give what I could to my country, and I know all the other guys feel the same. There was no draft dodging among the airborne. Airborne was strictly volunteer." [3]

Reverend George B. "Chappie" Wood on the thirty-sixth anniversary of the Normandy invasion spoke these words at a memorial ceremony: "It is not warmongering to say that some things are worth fighting for. I have no time for those who say that our war dead died in vain. As long as there is someone left to remember, nobody ever dies. Wherever liberty is threatened, men will die—now and in the future. But they do not die in vain—their deeds live after them." [4]

Gus Sanders, who had served as platoon leader with Company C, didn't regard himself and the other veterans who returned alive as heroes. "If Americans today could have seen those troopers in Ste.-Mère-Église, who were shot and bayoneted before they could get out of their chutes, they would realize the price of freedom. Many of those killed had not fired a shot, and were left hanging where their chutes had caught in the trees. These were the unsung heroes of the war, not those of us who returned." [5]

Virgil Goodwin and other veterans of the regiment struggled internally with survivor's guilt. "There is one question you will ask every day for the rest of your life: 'Why am I still here?'" [6]

Most veterans, like Roy King, thankful for surviving, have looked at every day since the war as a bonus and have lived them to the fullest. "Sixty years later, do I regret anything? Of course! I cannot walk as far or remember as well. Would I change anything if I could? No! It has been a good life and I have lived it well!" [7]

The veterans have never forgotten those officers and men left behind in cemeteries who died on the long bloody road from Sicily to Germany, who will always be young in the minds of these aging veterans. On a trip to Europe in 1999, Bill Tucker and Howard "Goody" Goodson, who both served in Company I, visited the graves of their buddies in cemeteries in France, Holland, and Belgium. Tucker remembers the visit they made to the "huge American cemetery, Henri-Chapelle, in Belgium. At the cemetery, we had thirteen I Company guys to visit. Goody was in severe pain with a bad hip, which was due to be replaced, but he insisted on going to every grave with me. It was a tough job to cover all thirteen graves at that cemetery even with normal health." [8]

EVERY VETERAN WHO SERVED with the 505th RCT was a part of a unit whose legacy will live on in military history forever. Tucker felt that the "82nd Airborne was not just another of the great fighting divisions of World War II or other wars. It was an institution of immortality like Rommel's Afrika Korps or the elite wagon units of Napoleon's Grand Army." [9]

The 505th RCT did much to gain that reputation for the division. How did the 505th PIR and its supporting combat team become such a formidable fighting force? It started with leadership. Colonel Gavin led by example and expected his officers and NCOs to lead from the front. Bob Hughart had served as an enlisted man with Company F. "Our officers were up front all the time. They led the way and we followed—none of this couple of blocks behind, telling some sergeant, 'Take your squad and go this way' and his corporal to take his men and go down another street. We lost a lot of good men that way, because they were up front and saying, 'Follow me.' We'd follow them into hell and back." [10]

Arthur B. "Dutch" Schultz, who had served with Company C, felt that the officers and NCOs were largely responsible for his surviving World War II. "Men like Captains Anthony Stefanich, Jack Tallerday; Lieutenants Gus Sanders, Gerald Johnson; and Sergeants Herman R. Zeitner, Sylvester Meigs, and Elmo Bell . . . to name only a few, were largely responsible for my transformation to a combat infantryman able to do his job.

"Not only were these men superb leaders both in and out of combat, but more importantly, they took seriously the responsibility of placing the welfare of their men above their own needs. Moreover, they were not overwhelmed with their own importance. I never realized it until years later that I owed them a debt of gratitude for helping me to frame some concepts of leadership that I used in subsequent years." [11]

Gus Sanders, who had been a platoon leader with Company C, felt that the officers had the privilege of leading superb men and that there was a special chemistry between the officers and enlisted men. "Uncle Sam got the finest enlisted men he could find to make up the original 82nd Airborne, and it paid him. Our men never failed us." [12]

Ben Vandervoort knew that "mutual faith" between officers and NCOs who led from the front, and enlisted men who never let them down, had been built in the

Frying Pan and Alabama Area, and tested in Sicily, Italy, Normandy, Holland, the Bulge, and Central Europe. This was the real legacy of the 505th RCT. "No regiment in the European Theater put in as many man-to-man close-combat hours and had as many of its original members survive the war. They came home alive because they fought hard and well to do their jobs. Concern for their own safety was secondary. That was not heroics. It was professionalism. They teamed together to make a 'lucky' regiment that never lost a battle. They were magnificent and fun to be with. All of us are very proud of our regiment.

"The older paratroopers of the 1940s won't fade away. Their mutual faith and competitive spirit lives today with the airborne. And the next time America goes for broke they will be there, as invisible pathfinders, to help today's troopers scramble off the broken plays that always have, and always will, come with the airborne territory." 13

NOTES

Introduction

1. Matthew B. Ridgway, foreword to *Ready*, by Allen Langdon, Western Newspaper Publishing Co., 1986, p. xi.

Chapter 1 "As Tough And Intelligent A Group Of Fighting Men As Ever Pulled On Jump Boots"

1. Fred Caravelli, interview with author.
2. Frank Bilich, interview with author.
3. Ibid.
4. Ibid.
5. Ibid.
6. Ronald Snyder, oral history transcript, courtesy of the Eisenhower Center.
7. Edwin Sayre, interview with author.
8. Ibid.
9. James M. Gavin, *On to Berlin*, Viking Press, 1978, pp. 1–2.
10. Omar N. Bradley and Clay Blair, *A General's Life*, Simon and Schuster, 1983, p. 101
11. Gavin, *On to Berlin*, pp. 2–3.
12. Ibid, p. 3.
13. Mississippi Oral History Program, *An Oral History with Brigadier General Elmo Edwin Bell: Saga of a Survivor*, University of Southern Mississippi, 2003, p. 11.
14. Ibid.
15. Paul D. Nunan, interview with author.
16. Berge Avadanian, response to author's questionnaire.
17. Charles Copping, interview with author.
18. Ibid.
19. Anthony Antoniou, interview with author.
20. Ibid.
21. Howard C. Goodson, interview with author.
22. *Oral History with Brigadier General Elmo Edwin Bell*, p. 16.
23. Ibid, p. 17.
24. Ibid.
25. Ronald Snyder, oral history transcript, courtesy of the Eisenhower Center.
26. Goodson, interview.
27. Allan C. Barger, "People and War," privately printed, 2001, p. 10.
28. Frank Miale, *Stragedy*, Trafford Publishing, 2005, p. 6.
29. Ibid.
30. Ibid, p. 7.
31. Ibid.
32. W. A. Jones, interview with author.
33. Ibid.
34. Howard C. Anderson, written account, courtesy of Howard C. Anderson.

35. *Oral History with Brigadier Elmo Edwin Bell*, p. 41.

36. William T. Dunfee, "Parachute Infantry Training—Fort Benning, Georgia, July 1942," courtesy of William T. Dunfee.

37. Miale, *Stragedy*, p. 7.

38. Dunfee, "Parachute Infantry Training."

39. David V. Bowman, "Memoirs of a Machine Gunner," courtesy of David V. Bowman, p. 3.

40. Chester Harrington, interview with author.

41. W. A. Jones, interview.

42. Goodson, interview.

43. Dunfee, "Parachute Infantry Training."

44. Goodson, interview.

45. Dunfee, "Parachute Infantry Training."

46. Goodson, interview.

47. Barger, "War and People," p. 13.

48. Ibid.

49. Ibid.

50. Otis L. Sampson, *Time Out for Combat*, Booksurge, 2004, p. 12.

51. Nunan, interview.

52. Carl E. Thain, letter to *Static Line* magazine, May 1990, courtesy of Mrs. Carl E. Thain, p. 40.

53. Benjamin H. Vandervoort, "Drop Zone Europe," courtesy of the Army Heritage and Education Center, Carlisle, Pennsylvania, p. 1.

Chapter 2 "If You Fell Out, You Were Dismissed From The Regiment"

1. Cecil E. Prine, response to author's questionnaire.

2. Ibid.

3. Brigidere General Walter F. Winton, Jr., response to author's questionnaire.

4. Dr. Dean McCandless, "Remembering the Army," pp. 3–4, courtesy of Dr. Dean McCandless.

5. Edwin M. Sayre, interview with author.

6. Sayre, interview.

7. Paul D. Nunan, interview with author.

8. John P. Cages, written account, courtesy of the 82nd Airborne Division War Memorial Museum.

9. David V. Bowman, "Memoirs of a Machine Gunner," courtesy of David V. Bowman, pp. 6–7.

10. Frank P. Woosley, memoirs, courtesy of Frank P. Woosley.

11. Charlie D. Turner, response to author's questionnaire.

12. Otis L. Sampson, *Time Out for Combat*, Booksurge, 2004, p. 14.

13. Jack R. Isaacs, oral history transcript, courtesy of the Eisenhower Center.

14. Harry J. Buffone, response to author's questionnaire.

15. Robert W. Gillette, response to author's questionnaire.

16. Dr. David E. Thomas, letter to Alfred Ireland, September 6, 1997, courtesy of the 82nd Airborne Division War Memorial Museum.

17. Neil Droogan, response to author's questionnaire.

18. James M. Gavin, *On to Berlin*, pp. 3–4.

19. Berge Avadanian, response to author's questionnaire.

20. William L. Blank, memoirs, courtesy of the 82nd Airborne Division War Memorial . Museum.

21. Carl E. Thain, *Static Line*, May 1990, courtesy of Mrs. Carl E. Thain, p. 40.

22. Nunan, interview.

23. Norbert P. Beach, written account, courtesy of Norbert P. Beach.

24. Woosley, memoirs.

25. Ibid.

26. John P. Cages, written account, courtesy of the 82nd Airborne Division War Memorial Museum.

27. Beach, written account.

28. Cages, written account.

29. Irvin W. Seelye, response to author's questionnaire.

30. Avadanian, questionnaire.

31. Harvill W. Lazenby, response to author's questionnaire.

32. Prine, questionnaire.

33. Robert A. Fielder, written account, courtesy of Robert A. Fielder.

34. Blank, memoirs.

35. Dr. Robert Franco, letter to Al Ireland, April 19, 1999.

36. Seelye, questionnaire.

37. Gillette, written account.

38. Avadanian, questionnaire.

39. Seelye, questionnaire.

40. Joseph I. O'Jibway, response to author's questionnaire.

Chapter 3 "Africa Was A Living Hell"

1. Dr. Dean McCandless, "Remembering the Army," courtesy of Dr. Dean McCandless, p. 5.

2. Wilton H. Johnson, response to author's questionnaire.

3. Irvin W. Seelye, response to author's questionnaire.

4. Robert A. Fielder, written account, courtesy of Robert A. Fielder.

5. Matthew B. Ridgway and Harold H. Martin, *Soldier: The Memoirs of Matthew B. Ridgway*, Greenwood Press, 1956, p. 65.

6. Fielder, written account.

7. The James M. Gavin Papers, Personal Diaries, Box 8—Folder "Diary Passages, Apr–Dec 1943," courtesy of the U.S. Army Military History Institute.

8. David V. Bowman, "Memoirs of a Machine Gunner," courtesy of David V. Bowman, p. 11.

9. William H. Tucker, *Parachute Soldier*, International Airborne Books, 2nd ed., 1994, p. 12.

10. Harry J. Buffone, response to author's questionnaire.

11. Berge Avadanian, response to author's questionnaire.

12. Cecil E. Prine, response to author's questionnaire.

13. William L. Blank memoirs, courtesy of the 82nd Airborne Division War Memorial Museum.

14. W. A. Jones, interview with author.

15. Ibid.
16. Russell McConnell, interview with author.
17. Tucker, *Parachute Soldier*, p. 10.
18. McConnell, interview.
19. Daniel B. McIlvoy memoirs, courtesy of Mrs. Annie McIlvoy Zaya, p. 3.
20. Seelye, questionnaire.
21. Elmo Bell, *An Oral History with Brigadier Elmo Edwin Bell: Saga of a Survivor*, Mississippi Oral History Program, 2003, p. 67.
22. Avadanian, questionnaire.
23. McCandless, "Remembering the Army," p. 5.
24. Dr. Daniel B. McIlvoy, "Medical Detachment, 505th Parachute Infantry, 82nd Airborne Division in World War II," courtesy of Mrs. Annie McIlvoy Zaya, pp. 15–16.
25. This has previously been written as the 3rd Battalion, 504th, and 3rd Battalion 505th. General Gavin's diary entry for May 29, states "We are to put on a show for General Nogues, Governor General of Spanish Morocco on June 3rd. I pointed out the lack of coordination between the various elements and consequently was made coordinator of the entire air show. I will never learn. The object is to impress Nogues as one political step in the direction of lining up Spain on our side. We will do all that we can. Gorham's battalion is going to jump it." The "Exec's Diary—1st Battalion, 505 PIR" states on June 3, 1943 entry, "Entire battalion jumped Operation Eyewash as demonstration for Lt. Gen. Clark, CG First Army, Lt. Gen. Patton...."
26. Howard C. Goodson, interview with author.
27. Richard E. "Pat" Reid, "Chow," courtesy of the 82nd Airborne Division War Memorial Museum, p. 3.
28. The James M. Gavin Papers, Personal Diaries, Box 8—Folder "Diary Passages Apr–Dec 1943," courtesy of the U.S. Army Military History Institute, Oujda, June 9, 1943, diary entry.
29. Ibid.
30. Robert W. Gillette, response to author's questionnaire.
31. William L. Blank, written account, courtesy of the 82nd Airborne Division War Memorial Museum.
32. Harvill W. Lazenby, response to author's questionnaire.
33. Neil Droogan, response to author's questionnaire.
34. Ridgway and Martin, *Soldier*, p. 65.
35. James J. Coyle, written account, "Echoes of the Warriors," p. 59.
36. Ridgway and Martin, *Soldier*, p. 66.
37. W. A. Jones, interview.
38. Mark J. Alexander, "Personal Memories of Sicily," courtesy of Mark J. Alexander, p. 1.
39. Willard Follmer, interview with author.
40. Ibid.
41. Ibid.
42. Ibid.
43. Ibid.

44. Ibid.

45. Ibid.

46. Ibid.

47. Otis L. Sampson, *Time Out for Combat*, Booksurge, 2004, p. 46.

48. Avadanian, questionnaire.

49. Russell W. Brown, response to author's questionnaire.

50. Goodson, interview.

51. Douglas M. Bailey, response to author's questionnaire.

52. William T. Dunfee, "Sicily Invasion—Operation Husky—July 9–10, 1943," courtesy of William T. Dunfee, p. 4.

53. Ibid.

54. Bowman, "Memoirs of a Machine Gunner," p. 41.

55. Maj. Robert M. Piper, "The Operation of the 505 Parachute Infantry Regimental Combat Team (82nd Airborne Division) in the Airborne Landings on Sicily, 9–11 July 1943 (Sicilian Campaign) (Personal Experience of Assistant Regimental Adjutant)," courtesy of the Donovan Research Library, Fort Benning, Georgia, pp. 13–14.

56. Avadanian, questionnaire.

57. Ridgway and Martin, *Soldier*, pp. 66, 68.

58. Omar N. Bradley and Clay Blair, *A General's Life*, Simon and Schuster, 1983, pp. 175–176.

59. W. A. Jones, interview.

60. Russell McConnell, interview.

Chapter 4 "The Eyes of the World Are Upon You. The Hopes And Prayers Of Every American Go With You."

1. William T. Dunfee, "Sicily Invasion—Operation Husky—July 9–10, 1943," courtesy of William T. Dunfee, p. 4.

2. Irvin W. Seelye, response to author's questionnaire.

3. Major Edwin M. Sayre, "The Operations of Company A 505th Parachute Infantry (82nd Airborne Division) Airborne Landings In Sicily 9–24 July 1943 (Sicily Campaign) (Personal Experience of a Company Commander)," Infantry School, 1947, courtesy of the Donovan Research Library, Fort Benning, Georgia, p. 9.

4. Berge Avadanian, response to author's questionnaire.

5. Otis L. Sampson, "Time Out for Combat," unpublished manuscript, pp. 2–3.

6. Dunfee, "Sicily Invasion," p. 4.

7. Sayre, "Operations of Company A 505th Parachute Infantry," p. 10.

8. Raymond A. Grossman, response to author's questionnaire.

9. Raymond F. Hart, written account, courtesy of Alex Kicovic.

10. Norbert P. Beach, response to author's questionnaire.

11. William L. Blank, written account, courtesy of the 82nd Airborne Division War Memorial Museum.

12. Grossman, questionnaire.

13. Dunfee, "Sicily Invasion," pp. 4–5.

14. Willard Follmer, interview with author.

15. Harry J. Buffone, response to author's questionnaire.

16. Howard C. Goodson, interview with author.

17. Arnold G. Nagel, written account, courtesy of Alex Kicovic.

18. Michael Vuletich, written account, courtesy of Alex Kicovic.

19. Joseph I. O'Jibway, response to author's questionnaire.

20. Ibid.

21. Sayre, "Operations of Company A 505th Parachute Infantry," p. 9.

22. Dave Bullington, interview with author.

23. Sayre, "Operations of Company A 505th Parachute Infantry," pp. 9–11.

24. Robert Gillette, "The Sicily Campaign: A Personal Story of Sicily," p. 1.

25. Gillette, "The Sicily Campaign," pp. 1–2.

26. John J. Gallo, response to author's questionnaire.

27. Richard S. Aiken, letter to author, November 14, 2004.

28. Mark J. Alexander, "Personal Memories of Sicily," courtesy of Mark J. Alexander, p. 2.

29. Avadanian, questionnaire.

30. Seelye, questionnaire.

31. Douglas M. Dailey, dairy, courtesy of Douglas M. Bailey.

32. David V. Bowman, "Memoirs of a Machine Gunner," courtesy of David V. Bowman, pp. 14–15.

33. Russell W. Brown, response to author's questionnaire.

34. James J. Coyle, in *Echoes of the Warriors*, comp. and ed. by George Jacobus, n.p., 1992, pp. 59–60.

35. Alexander, "Sicily," p. 2.

36. Ibid, pp. 2–3.

37. Ibid, p. 3.

38. Coyle, in *Echoes of the Warriors*, p. 60.

39. Gillette, "The Sicily Campaign", p. 2

40. Sayre, "Operations of Company A 505th Parachute Infantry," p. 11.

41. Bullington, interview.

42. Sayre, "Operations of Company A 505th Parachute Infantry," p. 11.

43. Bullington, interview.

44. Sayre, "Operations of Company A 505th Parachute Infantry," pp. 11–12.

45. Bullington, interview.

46. Sayre, "Operations of Company A 505th Parachute Infantry," pp. 12–13.

47. Tim Dyas, written account, courtesy of Tim Dyas.

48. James M. Gavin, *On to Berlin*, Viking Press, 1978, p. 26.

49. Ibid, p. 26.

50. Dean McCandless, "Remembering the Army," courtesy of Dean McCandless, p. 6.

51. Ibid.

52. Elmo E. Bell and The University of Southern Mississippi Center for Oral History and Cultural Heritage, *An Oral History with Brigadier General Elmo Edwin Bell: A Saga of a Survivor*, The University of Southern Mississippi, 2003, pp. 76–77.

53. Ibid., pp. 77–78.

54. Joseph Gironda, in *Echoes of the Warriors*, p. 71.

55. Gus L. Sanders, questionnaire, courtesy of the Cornelius Ryan Collection, Alden Library, Ohio University.

56. McCandless, "Remembering the Army," p. 6.

57. Sayre, "Operations of Company A 505th Parachute Infantry," pp. 13–14.

58. Ibid, p. 14.

Chapter 5 "A Blazing Hell Of Mortar, Artillery, And Small Arms Fire"

1. Follmer, interview.

2. Major Edwin M. Sayre, "The Operations of Company A 505th Parachute Infantry (82nd Airborne Division) Airborne Landings in Sicily 9–24 July 1943 (Sicily Campaign) (Personal Experience of a Company Commander)," Infantry School, 1947, courtesy of the Donovan Research Library, Fort Benning, Georgia, pp. 14–16.

3. "82nd Airborne Division in Sicily and Italy, Part II—Sicily," courtesy of the 82nd Airborne Division War Memorial Museum, p. 25.

4. Ibid.

5. James M. Gavin, *On to Berlin*, Viking Press, 1978, p. 29.

6. Bill Bishop, interview with author.

7. Gavin, *On to Berlin*, p. 29.

8. Bishop, interview.

9. Russell McConnell, interview with author.

10. Bishop, interview.

11. McConnell, interview.

12. Robert Fielder, written account, courtesy of Robert Fielder.

13. Cloid Wigle, written account, courtesy of Cloid Wigle.

14. Wigle, written account.

15. Ibid.

16. Bishop interview.

17. McConnell interview.

18. Pat Reid, "Chow," courtesy of the 82nd Airborne Division War Memorial Museum, p. 5.

19. Fielder, written account.

20. Wigle, written account.

21. Gavin, *On to Berlin*, pp. 29–30.

22. Ibid, p. 30.

23. Ibid.

24. Ray Grossman, response to author's questionnaire.

25. Gavin, *On to Berlin*, p. 32.

26. Ray Grossman, written account.

27. Gavin, *On to Berlin*, p. 32.

28. Private First Class Murray Goldman, sworn statement, May 16, 1945.

29. Colonel Arthur L. Kelly, Principal Interviewer, "Interview with Daniel B. McIlvoy," March 25, 1988, American Military Veterans Oral History Project, 2000, University of Kentucky.

30. Goldman, sworn statement.

31. Raymond F. Hart, written account, courtesy of Alex Kicovic.

32. Fielder, written account.

33. "82nd Airborne Division in Sicily and Italy, Part II—Sicily," p. 26.

34. Ibid.

35. Bill Bishop, interview with author.

36. Bishop, interview.

37. Hart, written account.

38. Gavin, *On to Berlin*, pp. 30–32.

39. Jerry Huth, interview with author.

40. Frank M. Miale, written account.

41. Huth, interview.

42. Ibid.

43. James A. Rightley, response to author's questionnaire.

44. "82nd Airborne Division in Sicily and Italy, Part II—Sicily," p. 26.

45. Dr. Daniel B. McIlvoy, "Medical Detachment, 505th Parachute Infantry, 82nd Airborne Division in World War II," courtesy of Mrs. Annie McIlvoy Zaya, p. 4.

46. Dean McCandless, "Remembering the Army," courtesy of Dean McCandless, pp. 7–8.

47. Mark J. Alexander, "Personal Memories of Sicily," courtesy of Mark J. Alexander, p. 4.

48. Hart, written account.

49. Sayre, "Operations of Company A 505th Parachute Infantry," p. 17.

50. Colonel Gorham's date of death is listed in army records as July 11, 1941. Both Captain Edwin Sayre, in his monograph written in 1947, and Dean McCandless, who was with Gorham when he was killed, state that Gorham was in fact killed during action that took place on July 12, 1943. McCandless states that he found Gorham's CP on the morning of July 11 and was put on outpost duty by Gorham that evening. He states the next morning Gorham recalled him and they moved to Hill 41, where Gorham was killed.

51. Dean McCandless, "Remembering the Army," courtesy of Dean McCandless, pp. 7–8.

52. Sayre, "Operations of Company A 505th," p. 17.

53. "82nd Airborne Division in Sicily and Italy, Part II—Sicily," p. 13.

54. Fredrick W. Randall, written account, courtesy of Wheatley T. Christensen.

55. McConnell, interview.

56. Irvin W. Seelye, response to author's questionnaire.

57. McIlvoy, "Medical Detachment," p. 6.

58. Fielder, written account.

59. Sayre, "Operations of Company A 505th," pp. 17–18.

Chapter 6 "The Italians Were Something Less Than Enthused About Fighting"

1. William T. Dunfee, "Sicily Invasion—Operation Husky—July 9–10, 1943," Courtesy of William T. Dunfee, p. 9.

2. Ibid.

3. William L. Blank memoirs, courtesy of the 82nd Airborne Division War Memorial Museum.

4. Dunfee, "Sicily Invasion," pp. 9–10.

5. Col. Mark J. Alexander, "Personal Memories of Sicily (Revision 7-20-2002)," p. 6.

6. Kurt Student, Nuremburg Trials.

7. Jerry Huth, interview with author.

8. Col. Mark J. Alexander, "Italy—1943," courtesy of Mark J. Alexander, p. 1.

9. Raymond A. Grossman, response to author's questionnaire.

10. Alexander, "Italy—1943," p. 1.

11. Ibid.

12. Captain John Norton, "Pathfinder Operations—Italy 14–15 Sept. 1943," courtesy of Lieutenant General (U.S. Army Retired) John Norton.

13. Jerome V. Huth, letter September 28, 1999, to Lieutenant General John Norton, courtesy of Lieutenant General John Norton.

14. Norton, "Pathfinder Operations."

15. William L. Blank, written account, courtesy of the 82nd Airborne Division War Memorial Museum.

16. Allan C. Barger, "War and People," 2001, p. 56.

17. Norton, "Pathfinder Operations."

18. William L. Blank memoirs.

19. Benjamin H. Vandervoort, "Drop Zone Europe."

20. Mark J. Alexander, "Italy—1943," courtesy of Mark J. Alexander, pp. 2–3.

21. Spencer F. Wurst and Gayle Wurst, Descending from the Clouds, Casemate, 2004, p. 85.

22. Alexander, "Italy," p. 3.

23. Wurst and Wurst, Descending from the Clouds, pp. 85–86.

24. Victor M. Schmidt, in Echoes of the Warriors, comp. and ed. by Jacobus, n.p., 1992, pp. 198–199.

25. Berge Avadanian, response to author's questionnaire.

26. Alexander, "Italy," p. 3.

27. Russell W. Brown, response to author's questionnaire.

28. Dr. Daryle E. Whitfield, interview with author.

29. Brown, questionnaire.

30. Wurst and Wurst, Descending from the Clouds, pp. 88–89.

31. Julius Axman, as quoted in Otis L. Sampson, "Time Out for Combat," unpublished manuscript, pp. 131–132.

32. Edward Carpus, as quoted in Otis L. Sampson, "Time Out for Combat," unpublished manuscript, p. 133.

33. Earl W. Boling, written account in "Echoes of the Warriors," 1992, p. 109.

34. John W. Keller, written account in "Echoes of the Warriors," compiled and edited by George Jacobus, 1992, p. 191.

35. Julius Axman, as quoted in Sampson, "Time Out for Combat," unpublished manuscript, p. 132.

36. Otis L. Sampson, Time Out for Combat, Booksurge, 2004, pp. 103–104.

37. Ibid, p. 104.

38. Ibid, pp. 105–106.

39. Julius Axman, as quoted in Sampson, "Time Out for Combat," unpublished manuscript, p. 132.

40. Talton W. Long, as quoted in Otis L. Sampson, "Time Out for Combat," unpublished . manuscript, pp. 138–139.

41. Sampson, *Time Out for Combat*, p. 107.

42. Talton W. Long, as quoted in Sampson, "Time Out for Combat," unpublished manuscript, p. 139.

43. Alexander, "Italy," p. 5.

44. Dr. Robert Franco, letter to Al Ireland, April 19, 1999.

45. Ridgway and Martin, *Soldier*, pp. 89–90.

46. Thomas C. Goins, response to author's questionnaire.

47. James Rightley, response to author's questionnaire.

48. Frank Miale, written account, courtesy of Frank Miale.

Chapter 7 "A Scene I Would Carry With Me Always"

1. James M. Gavin, *On to Berlin*, Viking Press, 1978, pp. 73–74.

2. Robert A. Fielder, written account, courtesy of Robert A. Fielder.

3. Raymond A. Grossman, response to author's questionnaire.

4. Berge Avadanian, response to author's questionnaire.

5. Fielder, written account.

6. James J. Coyle, in *Echoes of the Warriors*, comp. and ed. by George Jacobus, p. 65.

7. James M. Gavin, *On to Berlin*, Viking Press, 1978, p. 90.

8. Avadanian, questionnaire.

9. Irvin W. Seelye, response to author's questionnaire.

10. Harold R. Thain, response to author's questionnaire.

11. Thain, questionnaire.

12. Gordon Pryne, interview with author.

13. Fielder, written account.

14. Colonel Robert M. Piper, written account, courtesy of Colonel Robert M. Piper.

15. Robert Gillette, response to author's questionnaire.

16. Russell W. Brown, response to author's questionnaire.

17. Norris S. White, response to author's questionnaire.

18. Gillette, questionnaire.

19. Avadanian, questionnaire.

20. Charles Copping, interview with author.

21. James Elmo Jones, oral history, courtesy of the Eisenhower Center.

22. Fielder, written account.

23. Jack R. Isaacs, oral history, courtesy of the Eisenhower Center.

24. "82nd Airborne Division Action in Normandy, France," courtesy of the 82 Airborne Division War Memorial Museum, p. 2

25. Matthew B. Ridgway, foreword to *Ready*, by Allen Langdon, Western Newspaper Publishing Co., 1986, p. xi.

26. Hubert S. Bass, letter to Cornelius Ryan, March 20, 1959, courtesy of the Cornelius Ryan Collection, Alden Library, Ohio University.

27. Coyle, in *Echoes of the Warriors*, p. 66.

28. Ernest R. DePaolantonio, response to author's questionnaire.

29. Roy O. King, response to author's questionnaire.

30. William H. Tucker, *Parachute Soldier*, International Airborne Books, 2nd ed., 1994, pp. 29–30.

31. Benjamin H. Vandervoort, "Drop Zone Europe," p. 3.

32. Ibid., pp. 1–2.

33. Gus L. Sanders, questionnaire, courtesy of the Cornelius Ryan Collection.

34. Ronald Snyder, oral history transcript, courtesy of the Eisenhower Center.

35. Avadanian, questionnaire.

36. Kenneth Russell, oral history, courtesy of the Eisenhower Center.

37. Ibid.

38. Snyder, oral history transcript.

39. Charles Miller, oral history, courtesy of the Eisenhower Center.

40. Dennis G. O'Loughlin, "Fierce Individualists—U.S. Paratroopers in WWII," 1977, courtesy of Frank P. Woosley, p. 187.

41. Dennis G. O'Loughlin, "Fierce Individualists—U.S. Paratroopers in WWII," 1977, courtesy of Frank P. Woosley, pp. 188–189.

42. Copping, interview with author.

43. Ralph Stout, Jr., interview with author.

44. Norbert Beach, response to author's questionnaire.

45. Tucker, *Parachute Soldier*, p. 31.

46. Arthur B. Schultz, oral history, courtesy of the Eisenhower Center.

47. Tucker, *Parachute Soldier*, pp. 31–32.

48. James Elmo Jones, oral history, courtesy of the Eisenhower Center.

49. Hubert S. Bass letter to Cornelius Ryan, March 20, 1959, courtesy of the Cornelius Ryan Collection, Alden Library, Ohio University.

50. James Elmo Jones, oral history.

51. Bass to Ryan, March 20, 1959.

52. James Elmo Jones, oral history.

53. Ibid.

54. Anthony J. DeMayo, questionnaire, courtesy of the Cornelius Ryan Collection.

55. Copping, interview with author.

56. Robert M. Murphy, interview with author.

57. James Elmo Jones, oral history.

58. Buffalo Boy Canoe, questionnaire, courtesy of the Cornelius Ryan Collection.

59. Arthur B. Schultz, oral history transcript, courtesy of the Eisenhower Center.

60. Bill Bishop, interview with author.

Chapter 8 "An Irresistible Force That Nothing Could Stop"

1. Anthony J. DeMayo, written account, courtesy of the Cornelius Ryan Collection, Alden Library, Ohio University, p. 4.

2. Benjamin H. Vandervoort, written account, courtesy of the Cornelius Ryan Collection, Alden Library, Ohio University, p. 1.

3. Hubert S. Bass letter to Cornelius Ryan, March 20, 1959, courtesy of the Cornelius Ryan Collection, Alden Library, Ohio University.

4. Benjamin H. Vandervoort, written account, courtesy of the Cornelius Ryan Collection, Alden Library, Ohio University, p. 1.

5. William J. Meddaugh, questionnaire, courtesy of the Cornelius Ryan Collection, Alden Library, Ohio University.

6. Bass to Ryan, March 20, 1959.

7. Vandervoort, written account, p. 1.

8. James Elmo Jones, oral history, courtesy of the Eisenhower Center.

9. Vandervoort, written account, p. 1.

10. Russell W. Brown, response to author's questionnaire.

11. Kenneth Russell, oral history, courtesy of the Eisenhower Center.

12. Ibid.

13. "D-Day Participant Survived by Feigning Death," *Fayetteville [North Carolina] Observer*, May 16, 1969, Section B, p. 1.

14. Kenneth Russell, oral history.

15. Cullen Clark, written account, courtesy of the Ryan Collection, Alden Library, Ohio University, pp. 2–3.

16. James J. Coyle, in *Echoes of the Warriors*, comp. and ed. by Jacobus, n.p., 1992, p. 261.

17. George Jacobus, in *Echoes of the Warriors*, pp. 239–240.

18. Vandervoort, written account, p. 2.

19. Roy King, written account, courtesy of Roy King.

20. Ibid.

21. Charles Miller, oral history, courtesy of the Eisenhower Center.

22. Don Ellis, interview with author.

23. Robert M. Robinson, questionnaire, courtesy of the Cornelius Ryan Collection.

24. Lyle B. Putnam questionnaire, courtesy of the Cornelius Ryan Collection, Alden Library, Ohio University, p. 2.

25. Jack R. Isaacs, oral history, courtesy of the Eisenhower Center.

26. Ronald Snyder, oral history transcript, courtesy of the Eisenhower Center.

27. Wheatley T. Christensen, "Normandy," courtesy of Wheatley T. Christensen.

28. Jack M. Hillman, letter to Al Ireland.

29. Clarence McKelvey, as quoted in "456th Parachute Field Artillery History," Starlyn R. Jorgensen, pp. 109–111.

30. Ray Grossman, as quoted in "456th Parachute Field Artillery History," n. p., Starlyn R. Jorgensen, p. 109.

31. Joseph I. O'Jibway, response to author's questionnaire.

32. Harvill Lazenby, response to author's questionnaire.

33. Arthur B. Schultz, oral history transcript, courtesy of the Eisenhower Center.

34. Elmo Bell, *An Oral History with Brigadier Elmo Edwin Bell: Saga of a Survivor*, . Mississippi Oral History Program, 2003, pp. 143–144.

35. John E. Wasner, written account, courtesy of John E. Wasner.

36. John J. Walsh, response to author's questionnaire.

37. Gordon Pryne, interview with author.

38. Jack Tallerday, questionnaire, courtesy of the Cornelius Ryan Collection, p. 4.

39. Neil Droogan, response to author's questionnaire.

40. Mark J. Alexander, "Normandy," courtesy of Mark J. Alexander, pp. 1–2.

41. Reverend George B. Wood, questionnaire, courtesy of the Ryan Collection.

42. William E. Ekman questionnaire, courtesy of the Ryan Collection, Alden Library, Ohio University, p. 2.

43. James A. Rightley, response to author's questionnaire.

44. Thomas C. Goins, response to author's questionnaire.

45. Leslie P. Cruise, written account, courtesy of Leslie P. Cruise.

46. William L. Blank, memoirs, courtesy of the 82nd Airborne Division War Memorial Museum.

47. Les Cruise, written account.

48. Ronald Snyder, oral history.

49. John M. Steele, questionnaire, courtesy of the Ryan Collection, Alden Library, Ohio University.

50. Christensen, "Normandy."

51. Blank, memoirs.

52. Christensen, "Normandy."

53. Norbert Beach, response to author's questionnaire.

54. Les Cruise, written account.

55. William L. Blank, written account, courtesy of the 82nd Airborne Division War Memorial Museum.

56. William H. Tucker, *Parachute Soldier*, International Airborne Books, 2nd ed., 1994, p. 38.

57. Anthony J. DeMayo, questionnaire, courtesy of the Ryan Collection.

58. James Elmo Jones, oral history, courtesy of the Eisenhower Center.

59. Ibid.

60. DeMayo, questionnaire.

61. Jack Isaacs, oral history.

62. Langdon, *Ready*, p. 56, footnote.

63. Lieutenant Colonel Raymond E. Singleton, as quoted in "Debriefing Conference—Operation Neptune," 13 August 1944, courtesy of the 82nd Airborne Division War Memorial Museum, p. 12.

64. Les Cruise, written account.

65. General James M. Gavin interview, Ryan Collection, Alden Library, Ohio University, p. 5.

Chapter 9 "A Small Unit Performance That Has Seldom Been Equaled"

1. Benjamin H. Vandervoort, written account, courtesy of the Cornelius Ryan Collection, Alden Library, Ohio University, p. 1.

2. Mark J. Alexander, "Normandy," courtesy of Mark J. Alexander, pp. 2–3.

3. Milton E. Schlesener letter to Frank Vanderbilt, courtesy of Mrs. Frankie James.

4. Ibid.

5. Gerald R. Weed, interview with author.

6. Benjamin H. Vandervoort, written account, courtesy of the Ryan Collection, Alden Library, Ohio University, p. 1.

7. Dr. Lyle B. Putnam, questionnaire, courtesy of the Cornelius Ryan Collection, Alden Library, Ohio University.

8. Dr. Daniel B. McIlvoy, "Medical Detachment, 505th Parachute Infantry, 82nd Airborne Division in World War II," courtesy of Mrs. Annie McIlvoy Zaya, p. 19.

9. W. A. Jones, interview with author.

10. George B. Wood questionnaire, courtesy of the Ryan Collection, Alden Library, Ohio University, p. 3.

11. W. A. Jones, interview.

12. George B. Wood questionnaire, p. 3.

13. Charles E. Sammon letter to Cornelius Ryan, March 21, 1959, courtesy of the Cornelius Ryan Collection, Alden Library, Ohio University.

14. Raymond A. Grossman, response to author's questionnaire.

15. William T. Dunfee, "Normandy, The Cotentin Peninsula," courtesy of William T. Dunfee, p. 4.

16. Marty Cuccio, interview with author.

17. Dunfee, "Normandy."

18. Jack M. Hillman, letter to Al Ireland, courtesy of the 82nd Airborne Division War Memorial Museum.

19. William H. Tucker, *Parachute Soldier*, International Airborne Books, 2nd ed., 1994, pp. 40–41.

20. Cullen E. Clark, Jr., written account, courtesy of the Cornelius Ryan Collection.

21. William L. Blank, written account, courtesy of the 82nd Airborne Division War Memorial Museum.

22. Weed, interview.

23. Benjamin H. Vandervoort, written account, courtesy of the Ryan Collection, Alden . Library, Ohio University, pp. 1–2.

24. Ibid., p. 2.

25. Ted Peterson letter to Cornelius Ryan, March 22, 1959, courtesy of the Cornelius Ryan Collection, Alden Library, Ohio University.

26. Weed, interview.

27. Ibid.

28. Otis L. Sampson, *Time Out for Combat*, Booksurge, 2004, p. 195.

29. Peterson to Ryan, March 22, 1959.

30. Stanley W. Kotlarz, interview with author.

31. Sampson, *Time Out for Combat*, p. 196.

32. Peterson to Ryan, March 22, 1959.

33. Kotlarz, interview.

34. Weed, interview.

35. Ibid.

36. Ibid.

37. Vandervoort, written account, p. 2.

38. Alexander, "Normandy," pp. 2–3.

39. Arthur B. Schultz, oral history transcript, courtesy of the Eisenhower Center.

40. Joseph I. O'Jibway, response to author's questionnaire.

41. Ibid.

42. John J. Dolan letter to James M. Gavin, March 15, 1959, courtesy of the Ryan . Collection, Alden Library, Ohio University.

43. Robert M. Murphy, *No Better Place to Die*, Critical Hit, 1999, p. 22.

44. Dolan to Gavin, March 15, 1959.

45. Ibid.

46. William D. Owens, written account, courtesy of the Cornelius Ryan Collection.

47. Dolan to Gavin, March 15, 1959.

48. Ibid.

49. Cecil E. Prine, response to author's questionnaire.

50. James M. Gavin interview, courtesy of the Cornelius Ryan Collection, Alden Library, Ohio University, p. 5.

51. Dolan to Gavin, March 15, 1959.

52. Ibid.

53. Ibid.

54. Gordon Pryne interview with author.

55. Marcus Heim Jr., "D-Day, June 6, 1944," courtesy of Mrs. Marcus Heim, p. 1.

56. Dolan to Gavin, March 15, 1959.

57. Ibid.

58. Elmo E. Bell and University of Southern Mississippi Center for Oral History and Cultural Heritage, *An Oral History with Brigadier General Elmo Edwin Bell: A Saga of a Survivor*, 2003, p. 148.

59. Dolan to Gavin, March 15, 1959.

60. Heim, "D-Day, June 6, 1944," p. 1.

61. Bell, *Oral History*, p. 149.

62. Dave Bullington, interview with author.

63. Prine, questionnaire.

64. Heim, "D-Day, June 6, 1944," p. 2.

65. Dolan to Gavin, March 15, 1959.

66. Bell, *Oral History*, p. 149.

67. Heim, "D-Day, June 6, 1944," p. 2.

68. Dolan to Gavin, March 15, 1959.

69. Bell, *Oral History*, p. 149.

70. Dolan to Gavin, March 15, 1959.

71. Mark J. Alexander, "Thirty-Four Days in Normandy in 1944," courtesy of Mark J. Alexander, pp. 3–4.

72. Dolan to Gavin, March 15, 1959.

73. Alexander, "Normandy," p. 3.

Chapter 10 "The 82nd Airborne Division's Undiscovered World War II Equivalent Of Sergeant Alvin C. York"

1. William D. Owens, written account, courtesy of the Cornelius Ryan Collection, Alden Library, Ohio University.
2. John J. Dolan letter to James M. Gavin, March 15, 1959, courtesy of Ryan Collection, Alden Library, Ohio University.
3. Owens, written account.
4. Robert M. Murphy, *No Better Place to Die*, Critical Hit, 2000, p. 51.
5. Cecil E. Prine, response to author's questionnaire
6. Dolan to Gavin, March 15, 1959.
7. Owens, written account.
8. Dave Bullington, interview with author.
9. Robert M. Murphy, response to author's questionnaire.
10. Robert M. Murphy, interview with author.
11. Owens, written account.
12. Prine, questionnaire
13. Prine, questionnaire.
14. Dolan to Gavin, March 15, 1959.
15. Benjamin H. Vandervoort, "Waverly Wray, Ste.-Mére-Église, Normandy – June 7, 1944," courtesy of Lieutenant General Jack Norton, p. 1.
16. Irvin W. Seelye, response to author's questionnaire.
17. Vandervoort, "Waverly Wray," pp. 1–2.
18. David V. Bowman, "Memoirs of a Machine Gunner," courtesy of David V. Bowman, pp. 41–42.
19. Vandervoort, "Waverly Wray," p. 2.
20. Vandervoort, "Waverly Wray," pp. 2–3.
21. Thomas J. McClean, sworn statement supporting Medal of Honor resubmission for Waverly Wray, March 1, 1984, courtesy of Lieutenant General Jack Norton.
22. Frank Silanskis, sworn statement supporting Medal of Honor resubmission for Waverly . Wray, March 5, 1984, courtesy of Lieutenant General Jack Norton.
23. Paul D. Nunan, sworn statement supporting Medal of Honor resubmission for Waverly Wray, March 2, 1984, courtesy of Lieutenant General Jack Norton.
24. Ibid.
25. Charles Miller, oral history, courtesy of the Eisenhower Center.
26. Vandervoort, "Waverly Wray," pp. 3–4.
27. James Elmo Jones, oral history, courtesy of the Eisenhower Center.
28. James J. Coyle, in *Echoes of the Warriors*, compiled and edited by George Jacobus, n. p. 1992, p. 263.
29. Rick Rogers, "Off to War: The Story of a Soldier in WWII—Joseph L. Comer, Co. H, 3rd Battalion, 505 PIR, 82nd Airborne Division," courtesy of Rick Rogers, p. 41.
30. Earl W. Boling, in *Echoes of the Warriors*, p. 125.
31. Stanley W. Kotlarz, interview with author.

32. Floyd West, Jr., letter to Mr. Walter J. Turnbull, Jr., April 14, 1947, courtesy of Mrs. Frankie James.

33. Coyle, in *Echoes of the Warriors*, p. 263.

34. Otis L. Sampson, *Time Out for Combat*, Booksurge, 2004, p. 203.

35. James Elmo Jones, oral history.

36. Otis L. Sampson, "Time Out for Combat," unpublished manuscript, p. 215–216.

37. Frank P. Woosley, in "Time Out for Combat," unpublished manuscript, p. 224.

38. Coyle, in *Echoes of the Warriors*, p. 263.

39. Woosely in *Time Out for Combat*, p. 209.

40. Coyle, in *Echoes of the Warriors*, pp. 263–264.

41. Sampson, *Time Out for Combat*, p. 203.

42. Earl W. Boling, in "Echoes of the Warriors," p. 125.

43. John Keller, letter to Cornelius Ryan, March 7, 1959, courtesy of the Cornelius Ryan Collection, Alden Library, Ohio University.

44. Coyle, in *Echoes of the Warriors*, p. 264.

45. Sampson, *Time Out for Combat*, p. 203.

46. Woosely in *Time Out for Combat*, p. 209.

47. Sampson in *Time Out for Combat*, pp. 204–205.

48. Coyle, in *Echoes of the Warriors*, p. 264.

49. Sampson, *Time Out for Combat*, p. 205.

50. Keller, letter to Ryan, March 7, 1959.

51. Coyle, in *Echoes of the Warriors*, p. 264.

52. Benjamin H. Vandervoort, written account, p. 6.

53. General James M. Gavin, as quoted in Allen L. Langdon, *Ready: The History of the 505th, 82nd Airborne Division*, Western Newspaper Publishing Company, 1986, p. 64.

54. Arthur B. Schultz, "Normandy Campaign, From 7 June–15 June 1944," courtesy of Arthur B. Schultz, pp. 2–3.

55. Vandervoort, "Waverly Wray," pp. 3–4.

Chapter 11   "I Would Rather Have A Platoon Of Those Men Than A Battalion Of Regular Infantry"

1. Eldon M. Clark, interview with author.

2. Reverend George B. Wood, questionnaire, courtesy of the Cornelius Ryan Collection, Alden Library, Ohio University.

3. James A. Rightley, response to author's questionnaire.

4. Russell W. Brown, response to author's questionnaire.

5. Allen Langdon states in *Ready* on page 74 that there were forty paratroopers at Neuville-au-Plain. The unit history, June 1944, of the 746th Tank Battalion states, "The flanking platoon in their movement reached Neuville au Plain, seized the town, liberating 19 American paratroopers from the 82nd A/B Div., taking 60 prisoners. In radioing back as to instructions as to disposition of the prisoners, Lt. Rainer, platoon leader, inquired as to possibility of bringing back a quantity of what he called 'fine saddle horses' which he was loath to leave in their present situation. Being refused permission, the horses were turned

loose, prisoners taken aboard the tanks, and the column returned to bivouac at St. Martin after the town had been taken over by friendly infantry. The task force closed in bivouac at 2300." http://www.geocities.com/viajero43081/history.htm

6. William T. Dunfee, "Normandy, The Cotentin Peninsula," courtesy of William T. Dunfee, pp. 6–7.

7. Dr. Daniel B. McIlvoy, "Medical Detachment, 505th Parachute Infantry, 82nd Airborne Division in World War II," courtesy of Mrs. Annie McIlvoy Zaya, pp. 12–13.

8. William H. Tucker, *Parachute Soldier*, International Airborne Books, 2nd ed., 1994, p. 47.

9. Ibid.

10. Ibid.

11. Ibid.

12. Harry J. Buffone, response to author's questionnaire.

13. Marty Cuccio, interview with author.

14. Harvill W. Lazenby, response to author's questionnaire.

15. Mark J. Alexander, "Thirty-four days in Normandy in 1944," courtesy of Mark J. Alexander, p. 4.

16. Frank P. Woosley, written account, courtesy of Frank P. Woosley.

17. Arthur B. Schultz, "The General and the Private," courtesy of Arthur B. Schultz, p. 15.

18. Alexander, "Normandy," p. 4.

19. I. W. Seelye, response to author's questionnaire.

20. Woosley, written account.

21. Alexander, "Normandy," pp. 4–5.

22. Arthur B. Schultz, oral history transcript, courtesy of the Eisenhower Center.

23. Ibid.

24. Jack M. Hillman, letter to Al Ireland, courtesy of the 82nd Airborne Division War Memorial Museum.

25. Alexander, "Thirty-four Days in Normandy," pp. 5–6.

26. David Bowman, response to author's questionnaire.

27. Wilton Johnson, response to author's questionnaire.

28. Roy O. King, response to author's questionnaire.

29. Earl W. Boling, in *Echoes of the Warriors*, comp. and ed. by George Jacobus, n.p, 1992, p. 127.

30. Boling, in *Echoes of the Warriors*, pp. 127–128.

31. Alexander, "Normandy," pp. 5–6.

32. Clarence W. McKelvey, oral history transcript, courtesy of the Eisenhower Center.

33. James V. Rodier, response to author's questionnaire.

34. Spencer F. Wurst and Gayle Wurst, *Descending from the Clouds*, Casemate, 2004, p. 148.

35. Wurst and Wurst, *Descending from the Clouds*, pp. 148–149.

36. Ibid, p. 148.

37. Allen L. Langdon, *Ready: The History of the 505th, 82nd Airborne Division*, Western Newspaper Publishing Company, 1986, p. 80.

38. Ibid.

39. Paul D. Nunan, interview with author.

40. Brown, questionnaire.

41. Wurst and Wurst, *Descending from the Clouds*, p. 149.

42. Alexander, "Normandy," p. 6.

43. Boling, in *Echoes of the Warriors*, p. 129.

44. Ibid.

45. Wurst and Wurst, *Descending from the Clouds*, pp. 150–151.

46. Jack R. Isaacs, oral history, courtesy of the Eisenhower Center.

47. Dunfee, "Normandy," p. 7.

48. William L. Blank, memoirs, courtesy of 82nd Airborne Division War Memorial Museum.

49. Isaacs, oral history.

50. Ibid.

51. Rick Rogers, "Off to War: The Story of a Soldier in WWII—Joseph L. Comer, Co. H, . 3rd Battalion, 505 PIR, 82nd Airborne Division," courtesy of Rick Rogers, p. 39.

52. Robert A. Fielder, written account, courtesy of Robert A. Fielder.

53. Clark, interview.

54. Gus L. Sanders, questionnaire, courtesy of the Cornelius Ryan Collection.

55. William E. Ekman, interview with Mike Ekman, courtesy of Mike Ekman.

56. Fielder, written account.

57. Frank Bilich, interview with author.

58. Hubert S. Bass, letter to Cornelius Ryan, March 20, 1959, courtesy of the Cornelius Ryan Collection.

59. Neil Droogan, response to author's questionnaire.

60. Bilich, interview.

61. Robinson, questionnaire, Cornelius Ryan Collection.

62. Blank, memoirs.

63. Ibid.

64. Henry Matzelle, written account, courtesy of Frankie James.

65. Sanders, questionnaire, Cornelius Ryan Collection.

66. Bilich, interview.

Chapter 12 "The Sky Is Full Of Silk"

1. Charles Miller, oral history, courtesy of the Eisenhower Center.

2. Albert Mallis, in Deryk Wills, *Put On Your Boots and Parachutes!* privately published 1992, p. 136.

3. Dennis Force, as quoted in Deryk Wills, *Put On Your Boots and Parachutes!* privately published 1992, p. 120.

4. James J. Meyers, "Proud to Be, Memoirs of Colonel James J. Meyers," courtesy of the 82nd Airborne Division War Memorial Museum and Mrs. James J. Meyers, p. 76.

5. Ibid., pp. 76–78, 81.

6. Matthew B. Ridgway, as quoted in Clay Blair, *Ridgway's Paratroopers*, Dial Press, p. 355.

7. The James M. Gavin Papers, Personal Diaries, Box 8, Folder—"Diary Passages," courtesy of the U.S. Army Military History Institute.

8. Robert Wienecke, questionnaire, courtesy of the Cornelius Ryan Collection, Alden Library, Ohio University.

9. HQ 82nd Airborne Division, APO 469, U.S. Army, 11 September 1944, "Order of Battle Summary."

10. Captain Jack Tallerday, "Operations of the 505th Parachute Infantry Regiment (82nd Airborne Division) in the Airborne Landing and Battle of Groesbeek and Nijmegen, Holland 17–25 September 1944, (Rhineland Campaign), (Personal Experience of a Company Commander)," Infantry School, 1948–1949, courtesy of the Donovan Research Library, Fort Benning, Georgia, p. 11.

11. Ibid.

12. Ibid.

13. William F. Mastrangelo, questionnaire, courtesy of the Ryan Collection, Alden Library, . Ohio University.

14. John H. Allen, questionnaire, courtesy of Ryan Collection, Alden Library, Ohio . University.

15. Clifford W. Schrader, questionnaire, courtesy of the Ryan Collection, Alden Library, Ohio University.

16. Arthur B. Schultz, written account, courtesy of Arthur B. Schultz.

17. Mastrangelo, questionnaire.

18. James L. Kaiser, questionnaire, courtesy of the Ryan Collection, Alden Library, Ohio University.

19. Russell R. O'Neal, questionnaire, courtesy of the Ryan Collection, Alden Library, Ohio . University.

20. George B. Wood, questionnaire, courtesy of the Ryan Collection, Alden Library, Ohio University.

21. William H. Tucker, *Parachute Soldier*, International Airborne Books, 2nd ed., 1994, p. 77.

22. Bill Meddaugh, in *Echoes of the Warriors*, compiled and edited by George Jacobus, n. p. 1992, pp. 353–356.

23. Schrader, questionnaire.

24. Arthur B. Schultz, "Holland Campaign, 15 September–12 November 1944," courtesy of Arthur B. Schultz, p. 2.

25. William T. Dunfee, written account, courtesy of William T. Dunfee.

26. Meddaugh, in *Echoes of the Warriors*, p. 356.

27. Dennis G. O'Loughlin, "Fierce Individualists—U.S. Paratroopers in WWII," unpublished manuscript 1977, courtesy of Frank P. Woosley, pp. 238–239.

28. Meddaugh, in *Echoes of the Warriors*, p. 356.

29. Jack Tallerday, questionnaire, courtesy of the courtesy of the Ryan Collection, Alden Library, Ohio University.

30. Salih John Siam response to author's questionnaire.

31. Fred Caravelli, interview with author.

32. Robert M. Piper, questionnaire, courtesy of the Ryan Collection, Alden Library, Ohio University.

33. Meddaugh, in *Echoes of the Warriors*, pp. 356–357.

34. William R. Hays, Jr., "A Paratrooper in WWII," courtesy of the William R. Hays, Jr. family, p. 9.

35. Meyers, "Proud to Be," p. 84.

36. Robert Franco, as quoted in *Put On Your Boots and Parachutes!* Deryk Wills, 1992, p. 127.

37. Michael Brilla, questionnaire, courtesy of the Ryan Collection, Alden Library, Ohio . University.

38. Meddaugh, in *Echoes of the Warriors*, pp. 357–358.

39. Frank Bilich, letter to Al Ireland, June 5, 1998, courtesy of the 82nd Airborne Division War Memorial Museum.

40. Daniel B. McIlvoy, Jr., letter to Clarence F. Montgomery, October 31, 1960, courtesy of . the Cornelius Ryan Collection.

41. Meddaugh, in *Echoes of the Warriors*, pp. 357–358.

42. Kaiser, questionnaire.

43. William L. Blank, memoirs, courtesy of the 82nd Airborne Division War Memorial Museum.

44. William H. Tucker, questionnaire, courtesy of the Cornelius Ryan Collection, Alden Library, Ohio University.

45. Jack M. Hillman, letter to Al Ireland.

46. Mastrangelo, questionnaire.

47. Ernest R. Blanchard, questionnaire, courtesy of the Cornelius Ryan Collection.

48. James E. McDavid, questionnaire, courtesy of the Cornelius Ryan Collection.

49. Robert A. Fielder, questionnaire, courtesy of the Cornelius Ryan Collection.

50. John T. Diffin, written account, courtesy of John T. Diffin.

51. Stanley Weinberg, questionnaire, courtesy of the Cornelius Ryan Collection, Alden Library, Ohio University.

52. O'Neal, questionnaire.

53. Harvill Lazenby, questionnaire, courtesy of the Cornelius Ryan Collection, Alden Library, Ohio University.

54. Arthur B. Schultz, "Holland Campaign," courtesy of Arthur B. Schultz, p. 2.

55. Frank M. Miale, written account, courtesy of Frank M. Miale.

56. Gordon A. Walberg, *Static Line*, February 1989.

Chapter 13 "All Of The Men Worshipped Him"

1. Daniel B. McIlvoy, Jr., letter to Clarence F. Montgomery, October 31, 1960, courtesy of the Cornelius Ryan Collection, Alden Library, Ohio University.

2. Paul D. Nunan, written account, courtesy of the Cornelius Ryan Collection.

3. McIlvoy to Montgomery, October 31, 1960.

4. James J. Coyle, in *Echoes of the Warriors*, comp. and ed. by George Jacobus, n.p., 1992, p. 318.

5. Spencer F. Wurst and Gayle Wurst, *Descending from the Clouds*, Casemate, 2004, p. 172.

6. Robert R. Hughart, questionnaire, courtesy of the Cornelius Ryan Collection.

7. Russell W. Brown, response to author's questionnaire.

8. William R. Hays, Jr., "A Paratrooper in WWII," courtesy of the William R. Hays, Jr. family, p. 10.

9. Hughart, questionnaire.

10. James L. Kaiser, questionnaire, courtesy of the Ryan Collection, Alden Library, Ohio University.

11. Walter B. Kroener, questionnaire, courtesy of the Ryan Collection, Alden Library, Ohio University.

12. Dunfee, written account.

13. Chris Zafiroff, response to author's questionnaire.

14. Robert A. Fielder, questionnaire, courtesy of the Cornelius Ryan Collection.

15. John T. Diffin, written account, courtesy of John T. Diffin.

16. William L. Blank, written account, courtesy of the 82nd Airborne Division War Memorial Museum.

17. Charles E. Barnhart, written account, courtesy of Reba Barnhart.

18. Harry Buffone, questionnaire, courtesy of the Ryan Collection, Alden Library, Ohio University.

19. Ibid.

20. Blank, written account.

21. Jack R. Isaacs, questionnaire, courtesy of the Cornelius Ryan Collection.

22. Lieutenant Harold E. Miller, combat interview, courtesy of the Ryan Collection, Alden Library, Ohio University.

23. Harvill Lazenby, interview, courtesy of the Ryan Collection, Alden Library, Ohio University.

24. Major Talton W. Long, combat interview, courtesy of the Ryan Collection, Alden Library, Ohio University.

25. Harold L. Gensemer, questionnaire, courtesy of the Cornelius Ryan Collection.

26. Richard H. Brownlee, questionnaire, courtesy of the Ryan Collection, Alden Library, . Ohio University.

27. John Lyons, response to author's questionnaire.

28. Cloid Wigle, response to author's questionnaire.

29. Brownlee, questionnaire.

30. Raymond A. Grossman, response to author's questionnaire.

31. John A. Price, reponse to author's questionnaire.

32. Arthur B. Schultz, "Holland Campaign, 15 September – 12 November 1944," courtesy of Arthur B. Schultz, p. 3.

33. Jack Tallerday, questionnaire, courtesy of the Ryan Collection, Alden Library, Ohio University.

34. Herman Alley, as quoted in "History of the 456th Parachute Field Artillery Battalion," compiled by Starlyn R. Jorgensen, p. 165.

35. Raymond A. Grossman, response to author's questionnaire.

36. Darrell P. Willoughby, response to author's questionnaire.

37. Gus L. Sanders, questionnaire, courtesy of the Ryan Collection, Alden Library, Ohio University.

38. Ibid.

39. Schultz, "Holland Campaign," p. 3.

40. Sanders, questionnaire.

41. Schultz, "Holland Campaign," p. 3.

42. Francis P. T. Dwyer, questionnaire, courtesy of the Cornelius Ryan Collection.

43. Alley, in "History of the 456th Parachute Field Artillery Battalion," p. 165.

44. Dr. Lester Stein, questionnaire, courtesy of the Cornelius Ryan Collection.

45. Harold R. Thain, response to author's questionnaire.

46. Gensemer, questionnaire.

47. Diffin, written account.

48. Diffin, written account.

49. Blank, written account.

Chapter 14 "You Fired Fast And Straight Or You Were Dead"

1. Benjamin H. Vandervoort, in *Echoes of the Warriors*, compiled and edited by George Jacobus, n. p. 1992, pp. 359–360.

2. Ibid., p. 359.

3. James J. Smith, in *Echoes of the Warriors*, compiled and edited by George Jacobus, n. p. 1992, p. 349.

4. John Rabig, in Deryk Wills, *Put On Your Boots and Parachutes!* Deryk Wills, 1992, p. 132.

5. Smith, in *Echoes of the Warriors*, p. 349.

6. Vandervoort, in *Echoes of the Warriors*, pp. 360–362.

7. James E. Keenan, questionnaire, courtesy of the Ryan Collection, Alden Library, Ohio University.

8. Vandervoort, in *Echoes of the Warriors*, p. 361.

9. James J. Meyers, "Proud to Be, Memoirs of Colonel James J. Meyers," courtesy of the 82nd Airborne Division War Memorial Museum and Mrs. James J. Meyers, p. 89.

10. Rabig, *Put On Your Boots and Parachutes!*, p. 132.

11. Paul D. Nunan, in Deryk Wills, *Put On Your Boots and Parachutes!* p. 132.

12. Gerald R. Weed, interview with author.

13. Meyers, "Proud to Be," p. 89.

14. Roy O. King, response to author's questionnaire.

15. David V. Bowman, "Memoirs of a Machine Gunner," courtesy of David V. Bowman, pp. 42–43.

16. Meyers, "Proud to Be," p. 89.

17. Donald E. Ellis, interview with author.

18. Ibid.

19. Ibid.

20. Julius Eisner, interview with author.

21. Ibid.

22. Bowman, "Memoirs of a Machine Gunner," p. 43.

23. Eisner, interview.

24. Bowman, "Memoirs of a Machine Gunner," p. 43.

25. Frank Aguerrebere, letter to author.

26. Ibid.

27. Bowman, "Memoirs of a Machine Gunner," p. 45.

28. Aguerrebere, letter.

29. Bowman, "Memoirs of a Machine Gunner," p. 45.

30. Meyers, "Proud to Be," pp. 89–90.

31. Nunan, *Put On Your Boots and Parachutes!* p. 132.

32. Vandervoort, in *Echoes of the Warriors*, p. 360.

33. Frank Bilich, letter to author, June 4, 2003

34. Paul D. Nunan, written account, courtesy of the Cornelius Ryan Collection.

35. Frank Bilich, in Deryk Wills, *Put On Your Boots and Parachutes!* p. 129.

36. Ibid., pp. 129–130.

37. Vandervoort, in *Echoes of the Warriors*, pp. 361–362.

38. Otis L. Sampson, in *Echoes of the Warriors*, p. 341.

39. Coyle, in *Echoes of the Warriors*, p. 319.

40. Earl W. Boling, in *Echoes of the Warriors*, p. 135.

41. Coyle, in *Echoes of the Warriors*, p. 319.

42. Boling, in *Echoes of the Warriors*, p. 135.

43. Coyle, in *Echoes of the Warriors*, p. 320.

44. Smith, in *Echoes of the Warriors*, pp. 349–350.

45. Boling, in *Echoes of the Warriors*, p. 136.

46. Coyle, in *Echoes of the Warriors*, p. 320.

47. Vandervoort, in *Echoes of the Warriors*, p. 362.

48. Coyle, in *Echoes of the Warriors*, p. 320.

49. Sampson, in *Echoes of the Warriors*, p. 341.

50. Coyle, in *Echoes of the Warriors*, p. 320.

51. Boling, in *Echoes of the Warriors*, p. 136.

52. Smith, in *Echoes of the Warriors*, p. 350.

53. Coyle, in *Echoes of the Warriors*, pp. 320–321.

54. Carl Beck, in Deryk Wills, *Put On Your Boots and Parachutes!* p. 127.

55. Coyle, in *Echoes of the Warriors*, p. 321.

56. Ibid., p. 320.

57. Sampson, in *Echoes of the Warriors*, p. 341.

58. Vandervoort, in *Echoes of the Warriors*, pp. 364, 362.

59. William R. Hays, Jr., "A Paratrooper in WWII," courtesy of the William R. Hays, Jr. family, p. 11.

60. Spencer F. Wurst and Gayle Wurst, *Descending from the Clouds*, Casemate, 2004, p. 179.

61. Russell W. Brown, response to author's questionnaire.

62. Hays, "A Paratrooper in WWII," p. 12.

63. Wurst and Wurst, *Descending from the Clouds*, Casemate, 2004, pp. 180–181.

64. Hays, "A Paratrooper in WWII," p. 12.

65. Wurst and Wurst, *Descending from the Clouds*, Casemate, 2004, pp. 181–182.

66. Hays, "A Paratrooper in WWII," p. 12.

67. Jack P. Carroll, questionnaire, courtesy of the Cornelius Ryan Collection.

68. Vandervoort, in *Echoes of the Warriors*, p. 363.

69. Smith, in *Echoes of the Warriors*, p. 350.

70. Donald D. Lassen, questionnaire, courtesy of the Cornelius Ryan Collection.

71. Meyers, "Proud to Be," p. 90.

72. Coyle, in *Echoes of the Warriors*, pp. 321–322.

73. Sampson, in *Echoes of the Warriors*, p. 342.

74. James M. Gavin, *On To Berlin*, Viking Press, 1978, p. 170.

75. Ibid.

76. George Chatterton, in Cornelius Ryan, *A Bridge Too Far*, Simon and Schuster, 1974, pp. 432–433.

77. James M. Gavin, in Cornelius Ryan, *A Bridge Too Far*, Simon and Schuster, Inc. 1974, p. 433.

78. Frederick M. Browning, as quoted in Cornelius Ryan, *A Bridge Too Far*, Simon and Schuster, Inc. 1974, p. 433.

79. Vandervoort, in *Echoes of the Warriors*, p. 363.

80. Boling, in *Echoes of the Warriors*, p. 137.

81. Bilich, *Put On Your Boots and Parachutes!* p. 130.

Chapter 15 "We're Not Going To Pull Back . . . If They Take Us Back, They're Going To Have To Carry Us Back"

1. James J. Meyers, "Proud to Be," courtesy of Mrs. James J. Meyers, p. 93.

2. James J. Smith, in *Echoes of the Warriors*, compiled and edited by George Jacobus, n. p. 1992, p. 350.

3. Benjamin H. Vandervoort, in *Echoes of the Warriors*, compiled and edited by George Jacobus, n. p. 1992, p. 364.

4. Charles Fergie, questionnaire, courtesy of the Cornelius Ryan Collection, Alden Library, Ohio University.

5. Robert J. Dwyer, questionnaire, Cornelius Ryan Collection.

6. Jack R. Isaacs, questionnaire, Cornelius Ryan Collection.

7. John Lyons, response to author's questionnaire.

8. James J. Coyle, in *Echoes of the Warriors*, compiled and edited by George Jacobus, n. p. 1992, p. 322.

9. Earl W. Boling, in *Echoes of the Warriors*, compiled and edited by George Jacobus, n. p. 1992, p. 138.

10. Coyle, in *Echoes of the Warriors*, p. 322.

11. Boling, in *Echoes of the Warriors*, pp. 138–139.

12. Coyle, in *Echoes of the Warriors*, p. 322.

13. Arnold G. Nagel, written account, courtesy of Alex Kicovic.

14. Abraham A. Mallis, as quoted in Wills, *Put On Your Boots and Parachutes!* p. 137.

15. James Elmo Jones, questionnaire, Cornelius Ryan Collection.

16. Northam H. Stolp, written account, courtesy of Northam H. Stolp.

17. Ibid.

18. Ibid.

19. Ibid.

20. Ibid.

21. Michael Vuletich, questionnaire, Cornelius Ryan Collection.

22. Robert M. Murphy, interview with author.

23. Ibid.

24. Ibid.

25. Bernard J. Tomardy, questionnaire, Cornelius Ryan Collection.

26. Stolp, written account.

27. Ibid.

28. Ibid.

29. Ibid.

30. Jack P. Carroll, questionnaire, Cornelius Ryan Collection.

31. William R. Hays, Jr., "A Paratrooper in WWII," courtesy of the William R. Hays, Jr. family, pp. 13–14.

32. Spencer F. Wurst and Gayle Wurst, *Descending from the Clouds*, Casemate, 2004, p. 186.

33. Ibid, p. 187.

34. Hays, "A Paratrooper in WWII," p. 14.

35. Vandervoort, in *Echoes of the Warriors*, p. 364.

36. Wurst and Wurst, *Descending from the Clouds*, p. 189.

37. W. A. Jones, interview with author.

38. Wurst and Wurst, *Descending from the Clouds*, p. 189.

39. Jones, interview.

40. Hays, "A Paratrooper in WWII," p. 14.

41. Vandervoort, in *Echoes of the Warriors*, p. 365.

42. Wayne W. Galvin, questionnaire, Cornelius Ryan Collection.

43. Robert R. Hughart, response to author's questionnaire.

44. James T. Steed, questionnaire, Cornelius Ryan Collection.

45. Smith, in *Echoes of the Warriors*, p. 351.

46. Clyde F. Knox, questionnaire, Cornelius Ryan Collection.

47. James E. Keenan, questionnaire, courtesy of the Cornelius Ryan Collection, Alden Library, Ohio University.

48. Vandervoort, in *Echoes of the Warriors*, p. 365.

49. Hays, "A Paratrooper in WWII," pp. 14–15.

50. Wurst and Wurst, *Descending from the Clouds*, p. 190.

51. Jones, interview.

52. Wurst and Wurst, *Descending from the Clouds*, p. 190.

53. Jones, interview.

54. Wurst and Wurst, *Descending from the Clouds*, pp. 190–191.

55. Ibid, p. 191.

56. Vandervoort, in *Echoes of the Warriors*, p. 365.

57. Wurst and Wurst, *Descending from the Clouds*, p. 191.

58. Kenneth Russell, letter to author, May 27, 2003.

59. Michael Brilla, questionnaire, Cornelius Ryan Collection, Alden Library, Ohio University.

60. Hughart, questionnaire.

61. Galvin, questionnaire.

62. Vandervoort, in *Echoes of the Warriors*, pp. 365–366.

63. Heinz Harmel, in Cornelius Ryan, *A Bridge Too Far*, Simon and Schuster, 1974, p. 473.

64. Ibid., p. 473.

65. Ibid., pp. 473–474.

66. Donald W. McKeage, written account, courtesy of Donald W. McKeage.

67. Ibid.

68. Meyers, "Proud to Be," pp. 93–94.

69. Stolp, written account.

70. Ibid.

71. British General Sir Miles Dempsey, as quoted in Gavin, *On to Berlin*, p. 185.

Chapter 16 "Boy, I Feel Sorry For The First Germans Those Guys Get A Hold Of"

1. James J. Meyers, "Proud to Be," courtesy of Mrs. James J. Meyers, pp. 93–94.

2. Richard H. Brownlee, questionnaire, courtesy of the Ryan Collection, Alden Library, Ohio University.

3. Raymond Gonzales, "Battle Stories," p. 3.

4. Brownlee, questionnaire.

5. William F. Mastrangelo, questionnaire, courtesy of the Cornelius Ryan Collection, Alden Library, Ohio University.

6. Gus L. Sanders, questionnaire, courtesy of the Cornelius Ryan Collection.

7. Bill Welch, "Medic Chet," *Erie [Pennsylvania] Morning News*, January 31, 1995.

8. Mastrangelo, questionnaire.

9. Mastrangelo, questionnaire.

10. Charles E. Barnhart, written account, courtesy of Reba Barnhart.

11. Barnhart, written account.

12. Norbert P. Beach, "Army Life as Remembered by Norbert P. Beach," courtesy of Norbert P. Beach, pp. 8–9.

13. Ibid., p. 9.

14. Barnhart, written account.

15. Daniel B. McIlvoy, memoirs, courtesy of Mrs. Annie McIlvoy Zaya, p. 21.

16. Russell W. Fischer, questionnaire, courtesy of the Cornelius Ryan Collection.

17. David V. Bowman, "Memoirs of a Machine Gunner," courtesy of David V. Bowman, p. 41.

18. William L. Blank, written account, courtesy of the 82nd Airborne Division War Memorial Museum.

19. Ibid.

20. Earl W. Boling, written account, *Echoes of the Warriors*, comp. and ed. by George Jacobus, n.p., 1992, pp. 142–143.

21. Meyers, "Proud to Be," pp. 96–97.

22. Ibid., p. 94.

23. Raymond A. Grossman, response to author's questionnaire.

24. Meyers, "Proud to Be," pp. 97–98.

25. Charles Kaiser, in Deryk Wills, *Put On Your Boots and Parachutes!* Deryk Wills, 1992, p. 129.

26. Henry D. Boswell, written account, courtesy of Henry D. Boswell.

27. William R. Hays, Jr., "A Paratrooper in WWII," courtesy of the William R. Hays, Jr. family, p. 18.

28. Gordon Pryne, interview with author.

29. Fischer, questionnaire.

30. Howard P. Melvin, letter to *Panther* (newsletter).

31. William E. Slawson, written account, courtesy of William E. Slawson.

32. Robert Gillette, response to author's questionnaire.

33. Dr. Dean McCandless, M.D., response to author's questionnaire.

34. Beach, "Army Life," p. 9.

35. "The Story of the 82nd Airborne Division in the Battle of the Belgian Bulge, in the Siegfried Line, and of the Roer River, Section II—Division Commander's Report," p. 1.

36. Hays, "A Paratrooper in WWII," pp. 18–19.

37. Beach, "Army Life," p. 9.

38. William T. Dunfee, "Ardennes Campaign, 'The Bulge,' December 1944, January and February 1945," p. 1.

39. John R. Jackson, response to author's questionnaire.

40. Arthur B. Schultz, "Battle of the Bulge History," courtesy of Arthur B. Schultz, p. 3.

41. James V. Rodier, response to author's questionnaire.

42. Colonel William E. Ekman, interview by Captain K. W. Hechler, courtesy of Mike Ekman, p. 1.

43. Wheatley T. Christensen, "Bulge Memories," p. 1.

44. Jack M. Hillman, written account, courtesy of the 82nd Airborne Division War Memorial Museum.

45. "Division Commander's Report," p. 1.

46. Beach, "Army Life," p. 9.

47. Malcolm Neel, memoirs, courtesy of Bob Burns.

48. Leslie P. Cruise, written account, courtesy of Leslie P. Cruise.

49. Virgil Goodwin, response to author's questionnaire.

50. Wilton H. Johnson, response to author's questionnaire.

51. Melvin, letter to *Panther*.

52. John J. Gallo, response to author's questionnaire.

53. Salih John Siam, response to author's questionnaire.

54. Beach, "Army Life," p. 10.

55. Joseph T. Jockel, response to author's questionnaire.

56. Hays, "A Paratrooper in WWII," p. 20.

57. Ibid.

58. Bill Meddaugh, written account, courtesy of Bill Meddaugh.

59. Benjamin H. Vandervoort, in *Echoes of the Warriors*, compiled and edited by George Jacobus, n.p. 1992, p. 399.

60. Ibid.

61. Meddaugh, written account.

62. Vandervoort, in *Echoes of the Warriors*, p. 401.

63. Meddaugh, written account.

64. Julius D. Axman, response to author's questionnaire.

65. Vandervoort, in *Echoes of the Warriors*, pp. 400–401.

Chapter 17 "The Krauts Are All Around Us"

1. Virgil Gould, interview with author.
2. James J. Meyers, "Proud to Be, Memoirs of Colonel James J. Meyers," courtesy of the 82nd Airborne Division War Memorial Museum, and Mrs. James J. Meyers, pp. 104–106.
3. Bill Meddaugh written account, courtesy of Bill Meddaugh.
4. Julius Axman, response to author's questionnaire.
5. Benjamin H. Vandervoort, written account, in *Echoes of the Warriors*, compiled and edited by George Jacobus, n. p. 1992, pp. 401–402.
6. Edward W. Arndt, in *Echoes of the Warriors*, comp. and ed. by George Jacobus, n.op, 1992, p. 417.
7. Meddaugh, written account.
8. Vandervoort, in *Echoes of the Warriors*, p. 402.
9. William R. Hays, Jr., "A Paratrooper in WWII," courtesy of the William R. Hays, Jr. family, p. 21.
10. Donald W. McKeage written account, courtesy of Donald W. McKeage.
11. Vandervoort, in *Echoes of the Warriors*, pp. 402–403.
12. Arndt in *Echoes of the Warriors*, p. 417.
13. Meddaugh, written account.
14. Arndt in *Echoes of the Warriors*, pp. 417–418.
15. Dennis G. O'Loughlin, "Fierce Individualists,"unpublished manuscript, pp. 309–310.
16. Vandervoort, in *Echoes of the Warriors*, pp. 403–404.
17. Donald W. McKeage, response to author's questionnaire.
18. Meddaugh, written account.
19. Meyers, "Proud to Be," p. 106.
20. Ibid.
21. Neil Droogan, response to author's questionnaire.
22. Droogan, questionnaire.
23. William H. Tucker, *Rendezvous at Rochelinval*, International Airborne Books, 1999, p. 29.
24. John R. Lyons, as quoted in William H. Tucker, *Rendezvous at Rochelinval*, International Airborne Books, 1999, p. 31.
25. Droogan, questionnaire.
26. Tucker, *Rendezvous at Rochelinval*, p. 29.
27. Dr. Dean McCandless, M.D., response to author's questionnaire.
28. Howard Melvin, as quoted in William H. Tucker, *Rendezvous at Rochelinval*, International Airborne Books, 1999, p. 33.
29. Ibid.
30. Jack R. Isaacs, written account, courtesy of John Isaacs.
31. Wheatley T. Christensen, "Bulge Memories," courtesy of Wheatley T. Christensen.
32. Raymond L. Daudt, interview with author.
33. Ibid.
34. Isaacs, written account.
35. Christensen, "Bulge Memories."
36. Daudt, interview.

37. Christensen, "Bulge Memories."

38. Isaacs, written account.

39. Daudt, interview.

40. Christensen, "Bulge Memories."

41. Chris Zafiroff, response to author's questionnaire.

42. Isaacs, written account.

43. Christensen, "Bulge Memories."

44. Isaacs, written account.

45. Zafiroff, questionnaire.

46. Isaacs, written account.

47. Christensen, "Bulge Memories."

48. Malcolm Neel, response to author's questionnaire.

49. Mississippi Oral History Program, *An Oral History with Brigadier Elmo Edwin Bell: Saga of a Survivor*, University of Southern Mississippi, 2003, pp. 204–205.

50. "Division Commander's Report," p. 7.

51. Clay Blair, *Ridgway's Paratroopers*, Dial Press, 1985, p. 468.

52. Blair, *Ridgway's Paratroopers*, p. 448.

53. William T. Dunfee, "Ardennes Campaign, 'The Bulge,'" courtesy of William T. Dunfee, p. 4.

54. Isaacs, written account.

55. Christensen, "Bulge Memories."

56. Joseph T. Jockel, response to author's questionnaire.

57. Christensen, "Bulge Memories."

58. Dunfee, "Ardennes Campaign," pp. 4–5.

59. Tucker, *Parachute Soldier*, p. 122.

60. Dunfee, "Ardennes Campaign," p. 5.

61. Millard W. Edgerley, response to author's questionnaire.

62. Isaacs, written account.

63. Zafiroff, questionnaire.

64. Christensen, "Bulge Memories."

65. S. John Siam, response to author's questionnaire.

66. John Lyons in William H. Tucker, *Rendezvous at Rochelinval*, International Airborne Books, 1999, p. 49.

67. S. John Siam in William H. Tucker, *Rendezvous at Rochelinval*, International Airborne Books, 1999, p. 48.

68. Lyons, in *Rendezvous at Rochelinval*, p. 49.

69. Siam, questionnaire.

70. Lyons, questionnaire.

71. Dunfee, "Ardennes Campaign," p. 5.

Chapter 18 "The Company I Came To Know And Love No Longer Existed"

1. James J. Meyers, "Proud to Be, Memoirs of Colonel James J. Meyers," courtesy of the 82nd Airborne Division War Memorial Museum and Mrs. James J. Meyers, p. 108.

2. V. P. Dewailly, written account, courtesy of V. P. Dewailly.

3. Meyers, "Proud to Be," p. 108.

4. Ibid, pp. 108–109.

5. Frank Bilich, letter to Al Ireland, June 5, 1998, courtesy of the 82nd Airborne Division War Memorial Museum.

6. Leslie P. Cruise, written account, courtesy of Leslie P. Cruise.

7. William T. Dunfee, "Ardennes Campaign, 'The Bulge,' December 1944, January and February 1945," p. 5.

8. Virgil M. Goodwin, response to author's questionnaire.

9. David V. Bowman, "Memoirs of a Machine Gunner," courtesy of David V. Bowman, p. 53.

10. Allan C. Barger, "War and People," 2001, p. 117.

11. William R. Hays, Jr., "A Paratrooper in WWII," courtesy of the William R. Hays, Jr. family, p. 24.

12. Barger, "War and People," pp. 119–121.

13. Russell W. Brown, response to author's questionnaire.

14. Meyers, "Proud to Be," p. 111.

15. Barger, "People and War," pp. 121–122.

16. Meyers, "Proud to Be," p. 111.

17. Mississippi Oral History Program, *An Oral History with Brigadier Elmo Edwin Bell: Saga of a Survivor*, University of Southern Mississippi, 2003, 210.

18. Ibid, p. 211.

19. Frank W. Thompson, letter to Al Ireland, August 12, 1997.

20. Joseph V. Tallett, oral history, courtesy of Joe Tallett.

21. Louis C. Scarborough, response to author's questionnaire.

22. *Oral History with Brigadier Elmo Edwin Bell*, p. 210.

23. Dave Bullington, interview with author.

24. Cecil E. Prine, response to author's questionnaire.

25. Tallett, oral history.

26. John R. Lyons, in William H. Tucker, *Parachute Soldier*, International Airborne Books, 2nd ed., 1994, p. 61.

27. Leslie P. Cruise, written account, courtesy of Leslie P. Cruise.

28. Dunfee, "Ardennes Campaign," p. 7.

29. William H. Tucker, *Parachute Soldier*, International Airborne Books, 2nd ed., 1994, p. 128.

30. Dennis Force, in William H. Tucker, *Rendezvous at Rochelinval*, International Airborne Books, 1999, p. 59.

31. Dunfee, "Ardennes Campaign," p. 7.

32. Leslie P. Cruise, written account, courtesy of Leslie P. Cruise.

33. Tucker, *Parachute Soldier*, p. 128.

34. William T. Dunfee, "Ardennes Campaign, 'The Bulge,' December 1944, January and February 1945," p. 7.

35. Tucker, *Parachute Soldier*, p. 128.

36. Dunfee, "Ardennes Campaign," p. 7. The 551st was an independent infantry battalion in reserve that was committed to the Battle of the Bulge entering combat with 840 men near

Werbomont the afternoon of December 21; on January 9, the 98 survivors of the battalion were relieved from defensive positions on the Salm River near Rochelinval.

37. Howard C. Goodson, interview with author.

38. S. John Siam, response to author's questionnaire.

39. Tucker, *Parachute Soldier*, p. 129.

40. S. John Siam, in William H. Tucker, *Rendezvous at Rochelinval*, International Airborne Books, 1999, p. 61.

41. Tucker, *Parachute Soldier*, p. 129.

42. Dennis Force, in William H. Tucker, *Rendezvous at Rochelinval*, International Airborne Books, 1999, p. 59.

43. Pat Passero, in William H. Tucker, *Rendezvous at Rochelinval*, International Airborne Books, 1999, pp. 59–60.

44. Force, in Tucker, *Rendezvous at Rochelinval*, p. 59.

45. Passero, in Tucker, *Rendezvous at Rochelinval*, p. 60.

46. Ibid.

47. Force, in Tucker, *Rendezvous at Rochelinval*, p. 59.

48. Lyons, in Tucker, *Rendezvous at Rochelinval*, pp. 61–62.

49. Harry J. Buffone, response to author's questionnaire.

50. Lyons, in Tucker, *Rendezvous at Rochelinval*, p. 62.

51. Tucker, *Parachute Soldier*, pp. 128–130.

52. Millard W. Edgerley, response to author's questionnaire.

53. Tucker, *Parachute Soldier*, p. 130.

54. Rick Rogers, "Off to War: The Story of a Soldier in WWII—Joseph L. Comer, Co. H, 3rd Battalion, 505 PIR, 82nd Airborne Division," courtesy of Rick Rogers, p. 56.

55. Rogers, "Off to War," p. 56.

56. Goodson, interview.

57. Beach, "Army Life," p. 10.

58. Siam, questionnaire.

59. Tucker, *Parachute Soldier*, pp. 131–132.

60. Walter L. Tuttle, "Sweating It Out, the Battle of the Bulge," courtesy of Troy Tuttle.

61. Dunfee, "Ardennes Campaign,," p. 8.

62. Beach, "Army Life," p. 10.

63. Virgil M. Goodwin, response to author's questionnaire.

64. Chris Zafiroff, response to author's questionnaire.

65. John R. Jackson, response to author's questionnaire.

66. Joseph T. Jockel, response to author's questionnaire.

67. Donald McKeage, "Battle of the Bulge," courtesy of Donald McKeage.

68. Meyers, "Proud to Be," p. 112.

69. Edward P. Laughlin, "Glimpses of Major General Gavin," courtesy of Edward P. Laughlin.

70. Meyers, "Proud to Be," p. 112.

71. Bowman, "Memoirs of a Machine Gunner," pp. 58–59.

72. Tallett, oral history.

73. Jockel, questionnaire.

74. Dunfee, "Ardennes Campaign," pp. 8–9.

75. *Oral History with Brigadier Elmo Edwin Bell*, pp. 218–220.

76. Meyers, "Proud to Be," p. 113.

77. Ibid, pp. 113–115.

78. Died of wounds January 13, 1945.

79. Brown, questionnaire.

80. Brown, questionnaire.

81. Brown, questionnaire.

82. Meyers, "Proud to Be," pp. 115–116.

83. Prine, questionnaire.

84. Dr. Dean McCandless, response to questionnaire.

85. Donald L. Brown, letter to Don McKeage, March 29, 1995, courtesy of the 82nd Airborne Division War Memorial Museum.

86. Jackson, questionnaire.

87. James M. Gavin, *On to Berlin*, Viking Press, 1978, p. 253.

88. Earl W. Boling, in *Echoes of the Warriors*, comp. and ed. by George Jacobus, n.p, 1992, pp. 149–150.

89. Arthur B. Schultz, "Battle of the Bulge History of Arthur B. 'Dutch' Schultz," courtesy of Arthur B. Schultz, pp. 6–7.

90. Wheatley T. Christensen, "Bulge Memories," courtesy of Wheatley T. Christensen.

Chapter 19 "Is This Armageddon?"

1. Joseph T. Jockel, response to author's questionnaire.

2. Harry J. Buffone, response to author's questionnaire.

3. S. John Siam, response to author's questionnaire.

4. Meyers, "Proud to Be," p. 118.

5. Arthur B. Schultz, "The Battle of the Bulge," courtesy of Arthur B. Schultz, p. 8.

6. Ibid., pp. 7–8.

7. Ibid. pp. 9–10.

8. Schultz, "Battle of the Bulge," p. 10.

9. James J. Meyers, "Proud to Be, Memoirs of Colonel James J. Meyers," courtesy of the 82nd Airborne Division War Memorial Museum and Mrs. James J. Meyers, p. 123.

10. William Slawson, written account, courtesy of William Slawson.

11. Meyers, "Proud to Be," p. 123.

12. Paul R. Brandt, response to author's questionnaire.

13. William L. Blank, memoirs, courtesy of the 82nd Airborne Division War Memorial Museum.

14. Wheatley T. Christensen, "Bulge Memories," courtesy of Wheatley T. Christensen, p. 9.

15. Blank, memoirs.

16. Wheatley T. Christensen, "Hürtgen Forest," p. 1.

17. Christensen, "Hürtgen Forest," pp. 1–2.

18. William T. Dunfee, "Ardennes Campaign, 'The Bulge,' December 1944, January and February 1945," pp. 10–11.

19. Russell W. Brown, response to author's questionnaire.

20. Buffone, questionnaire.

21. Christensen, "Hürtgen Forest," pp. 2–4.

22. Dunfee, "Ardennes Campaign,," p. 11.

23. Earl W. Boling, in *Echoes of the Warriors*, comp. and ed. by George Jacobus, n.p., 1992, p. 152.

24. Paul D. Nunan, interview with author.

25. Edward P. Laughlin, "Glimpses of Major General James Gavin," courtesy of Edward P. Laughlin.

26. William F. Borda, response to author's questionnaire.

27. William T. Dunfee and George R. Gist, "The 82nd Airborne Division at the Rhine and Elbe Rivers, April and May 1945—The Last Hurrah!" pp. 2–3.

28. Boling, in *Echoes of the Warriors*, p. 153.

29. James J. Coyle, in *Echoes of the Warriors*, pp. 326–328.

30. Meyers, "Proud To Be," pp. 131–132.

Chapter 20 "Fugitives From The Laws Of Averages"

1. James J. Meyers, "Proud to Be, Memoirs of Colonel James J. Meyers," courtesy of the 82nd Airborne Division War Memorial Museum and Mrs. James J. Meyers, p. 132.

2. Arthur B. Schultz, "Elbe River Campaign, 29 April – 9 May 1945," courtesy of Arthur B. Schultz, p. 1.

3. William F. Borda, response to author's questionnaire.

4. Norbert P. Beach, "Army Life as Remembered by Norbert P. Beach," courtesy of Norbert P. Beach, p. 11.

5. James J. Coyle, in *Echoes of the Warriors*, comp. and ed by George Jacobus, n.p., 1992, pp. 330–331.

6. Allan C. Barger, "War and People," 2001, courtesy of Allan C. Barger, p. 132.

7. Coyle, in *Echoes of the Warriors*, 331.

8. Earl W. Boling, in *Echoes of the Warriors*, p. 155.

9. Borda, questionnaire.

10. Clarence M. Stoll, Jr., response to author's questionnaire.

11. Schultz, "Elbe River Campaign," pp. 3–5.

12. James Elmo Jones, questionnaire, courtesy of the Cornelius Ryan Collection, Alden Library, Ohio University.

13. Frank G. Herkness, Army Services Experiences Questionnaire Continuation Sheet, courtesy of the U.S. Army Military History Institute, p. 1.

14. William T. Dunfee and George R. Gist, "The 82nd Airborne Division at the Rhine and Elbe Rivers, April and May 1945—The Last Hurrah!" pp. 6, 7, and 8.

15. Robert E. Erikson, response to author's questionnaire.

16. Jones, questionnaire.

17. Schultz, "Elbe River Campaign," pp. 7–8.

18. Russell W. Brown, response to author's questionnaire.

19. Archbishop Emeritus Philip M. Hannan, "The Camps at Wobbelin," courtesy of the 82nd Airborne Division War Memorial Museum.

20. Boling, in "Echoes of the Warriors," p. 158.

21. James M. Gavin, *On to Berlin*, Viking Press, 1978, pp. 289–290.

22. Meyers, "Proud to Be," pp. 134–136.

23. Brown, questionnaire.

24. Virgil M. Goodwin, response to author's questionnaire.

25. Arnold G. Nagel, written account, courtesy of Alex Kicovic.

26. Norbert Beach, response to author's questionnaire.

27. Joseph T. Jockel, response to author's questionnaire.

28. Allen L. Langdon, *"Ready: The History of the 505th, 82nd Airborne Division,"* Western . Newspaper Publishing Co., 1986, p. 130.

29. Meyers, "Proud to Be," p. 137.

30. Ibid., pp. 137–138.

31. Raymond A. Grossman, response to author's questionnaire.

32. Meyers, "Proud to Be," p. 138.

33. General George S. Patton, in *Saga of the All American*, compiled and edited by W. Forrest Dawson, The 82nd Airborne Division Association, 1946.

34. Gavin, *On to Berlin*, p. 295.

35. Ibid., p. 295.

36. Barney Oldfield, as quoted in William B. Breuer, *Geronimo!* St. Martin's Press, 1989, p. 574.

37. Gavin, *On to Berlin*, p. 296.

38. Meyers, "Proud to Be," p. 144.

39. Ibid., pp. 144–145.

40. Ibid., p. 146.

41. Jockel, questionnaire.

42. Luis de los Santos, interview with author.

43. Meyers, "Proud to Be," p. 146.

Epilogue "Invisible Pathfinders"

1. William H. Tucker, *Parachute Soldier*, International Airborne Books, 2nd ed., 1994, p. xvi.

2. William H. Tucker, *D Day: Thirty-Five Days in Normandy*, International Airborne Books, 2002, pp. 54–55.

3. Charles Miller, oral history, courtesy of the Eisenhower Center.

4. Dr. Daniel B. McIlvoy, "Medical Detachment, 505th Parachute Infantry, 82nd Airborne Division in World War II," courtesy of Mrs. Annie McIlvoy Zaya, p. 19.

5. Gus L. Sanders, questionnaire, courtesy of the Cornelius Ryan Collection, Alden Library, Ohio University.

6. Virgil M. Goodwin, response to author's questionnaire.

7. Roy O. King, response to author's questionnaire.

8. Tucker, *D Day*, p. 49.

9. Tucker, *Parachute Soldier*, p. xvi.

10. Robert R. Hughart, oral history transcript, courtesy of the Eisenhower Center.

11. Arthur B. Schultz, "Elbe River Campaign, 29 April–9 May 1945," courtesy of Arthur B. Schultz, pp. 8–9.

12. Sanders, questionnaire.

13. Benjamin H. Vandervoort, "Drop Zone Europe," p. 10.

BIBLIOGRAPHY

Published Sources

Bell, Elmo, and University of Southern Mississippi Center for Oral History and Cultural Heritage, *An Oral History with Brigadier General Elmo Edwin Bell: A Saga of a Survivor*, University of Southern Mississippi, 2003.

Blair, Clay, *Ridgway's Paratroopers*, Dial Press, 1985.

Bradley, Omar N., and Blair, Clay, *A General's Life*, Simon and Schuster, 1983.

Breuer, William B., *Drop Zone Sicily*, Presidio Press, 1983.

Breuer, William B., *Geronimo!*, St. Martin's Press, 1989.

Dawson, Forrest W., *Saga of the All American*, The 82nd Airborne Division Association, 1946.

Dougdale, J., *Panzer Divisions, Panzergrenadier Divisions, Panzer Brigades of the Army and Waffen SS in the West, Autumn 1944–Februray 1945, Ardennes and Nordwind*, Galago Publishing, 2000.

Gavin, James M., *On to Berlin*, Viking Press, 1978.

Kershaw, Robert J., *It Never Snows in September*, Sarpedon, 2001.

Langdon, Allen, *Ready*, Western Newspaper Publishing Co., 1986.

MacDonald, Charles B., *The U.S. Army in World War II: The Siegfried Line Campaign*, Office of the Chief of Military History, U.S. Army.

Margry, Karel, Editor, *Operation Market-Garden Then and Now*, Battle of Britain International Limited, 2002.

Marshall, S. L. A., *Night Drop*, Little, Brown and Company, 1962.

Miale, Frank, *Stragedy*, Trafford Publishing, 2005.

Murphy, Robert M. *No Better Place to Die*, Critical Hit, 1999.

Pallud, Jean Paul, *Battle of the Bulge Then and Now*, Battle of Britain International Limited, 1999.

Ridgway, Matthew B., and Martin, Harold H., *Soldier: The Memoirs of Matthew B. Ridgway*, Greenwood Press, 1956.

Ruppenthal, Major Roland G., *Utah Beach to Cherbourg*, U.S. Army Center of Military History, 1994.

Ryan, Cornelius, *A Bridge Too Far*, Simon and Schuster, 1974.

Sampson, Otis L., *Time Out for Combat*, Booksurge, 2004.

Saunders, Tim, *Nijmegen*, Leo Cooper, 2001.

Thuring, G., *Roll of Honor 82 Airborne Division World War II*, The Liberation Museum, Groesbeek, Holland, 1997.

Thuring, G.; Langdon, A.; *Yes, We Shall and Will Return 505th Parachute Infantry*, The Liberation Museum, Groesbeek, Holland, 1994.

Thuring, G.; van den Bergh, F.; Zwaaf, L.; Thuring, J.; *Waal Crossing*, The Liberation Museum, Groesbeek, Holland, 1992.

Tucker, William H., *D Day: Thirty-Five Days in Normandy*, International Airborne Books, 2002.

Tucker, William H., *Parachute Soldier*, International Airborne Books, 1994.

Tucker, William H., *Rendezvous at Rochelinval*, International Airborne Books, 1999.

Warren, Dr. John C., *Airborne Operations in World War II, European Theater—USAF Historical Studyies: No. 97*, MA/AH Publishing, 1956.

Wills, Deryk, *Put On Your Boots and Parachutes!* Deryk Wills, 1992.

Wurst, Spencer F. and Wurst, Gayle, *Descending from the Clouds*, Casemate Publishing, 2004.

Articles

Steele, John M., "D-Day Participant Survived by Feigning Death," *Fayetteville Observer*, May 16, 1969.

Welsh, Bill, "Medic Chet," *Erie Morning News*, January 31, 1995.

Unpublished Diaries, Sworn Statements, Letters, Written Accounts, Memoirs, and Manuscripts

Aguerrebere, Frank, letter to author, not dated.

Aiken, Richard S., letter to author, November 14, 2004.

Alexander, Mark J., "Italy—1943," Mark J. Alexander.

Alexander, Mark J., "Personal Memories of Sicily", Mark J. Alexander.

Alexander, Mark J., "Thirty-Four Days in Normandy in 1944," Mark J. Alexander.

Anderson, Howard C., written account, Howard C. Anderson.

Bailey, Douglas M., dairy, Douglas M. Bailey.

Barnhart, Charles E., written account, Ms. Reba Barnhart.

Barger, Allan C., "People and War," 2001, Allan C. Barger.

Bass, Hubert S., letter to Cornelius Ryan, March 20, 1959, Cornelius Ryan Collection, Alden Library, Ohio University.

Beach, Norbert P., "Army Life as Remembered by Norbert P. Beach," Norbert P. Beach.

Bilich, Frank A., letter to Alfred W. Ireland, June 5, 1998, 82nd Airborne Division War Memorial Museum.

Bilich, Frank A., letter to author, June 4, 2003.

Blank, William L., memoirs, 82nd Airborne Division War Memorial Museum.

Boswell, Henry D., written account, Henry D. Boswell.

Bowman, David V., "Memoirs of a Machine Gunner," David V. Bowman.

Brown, Donald L.. letter to Donald W. McKeage, March 29, 1995, 82nd Airborne Division War Memorial Museum.

Cages, John P., written account, 82nd Airborne Division War Memorial Museum.

Christensen, Wheatley T., "Bulge Memories," Wheatley T. Christensen.

Christensen, Wheatley T., "Hürtgen Forest," Wheatley T. Christensen.

Christensen, Wheatley T., "Normandy," Wheatley T. Christensen.

Cornelius Ryan Collection, Alden Library, Ohio University, written accounts from the
    following veterans of the division:
    Cullen E. Clark, Jr.
    Anthony J. DeMayo
    James M. Gavin
    Paul D. Nunan
    William D. Owens
    Benjamin H. Vandervoort

Cruise, Leslie P., written account, Leslie P. Cruise.

Diffin, John T., written account, courtesy of John T. Diffin.

Dolan, John J., letter to James M. Gavin, March 15, 1959, Cornelius Ryan Collection,
    Alden Library, Ohio University.

Dunfee, William T., "Ardennes Campaign 'The Bulge,'" William T. Dunfee.

Dunfee, William T., "Normandy, The Cotentin Peninsula," William T. Dunfee.

Dunfee, William T., "Parachute Infantry Training—Fort Benning, Georgia—July 1942,"
    William T. Dunfee.

Dunfee, William T., "Sicily Invasion—Operation Husky—July 9–10, 1943," William T.
    Dunfee.

Dunfee, William T. and Gist, George R., "The 82nd Airborne Division at the Rhine and
    Elbe Rivers, April and May 1945—The Last Hurrah!" William T. Dunfee.

Dyas, Timothy G., written account, Timothy G. Dyas.

"Echoes of the Warriors," compiled and edited by George Jacobus, 1992.

Fielder, Robert A., written account, Robert A. Fielder.

Franco, Dr. Robert, letter to Alfred W. Ireland, April 19, 1999, 82nd Airborne Division
    War Memorial Museum.

Gillette, Robert W., "The Sicily Campaign: A Personal Story of Sicily," Robert Gillette.

Gonzales, Raymond S., "Battle Stories," Arthur B. Schultz.

Hannan, Archbishop Emeritus Philip M., "The Camps at Wobbelin," 82nd Airborne Division War Memorial Museum.

Hart, Raymond F., written account, Alex Kicovic.

Hays, William R. Jr., "A Paratrooper in WWII," William R. Hays, Jr. family.

Herkness, Frank G., Army Services Experiences Questionnaire Continuation Sheet, U.S. Army Military History Institute.

Heim, Marcus Jr., "D-Day, June 6, 1944," Mrs. Marcus Heim.

Hillman, Jack M., letter to Alfred W. Ireland, not dated, 82nd Airborne Division War Memorial Museum.

Isaacs, Jack R., written account, John Isaacs.

Jorgensen, Starlyn R., "456th Parachute Field Artillery History," Starlyn R. Jorgensen.

John Keller, letter to Cornelius Ryan, March 7, 1959, Cornelius Ryan Collection, Alden Library, Ohio University.

King, Roy O., written account, Roy O. King.

Laughlin, Edward P., "Glimpses of Major General Gavin," Edward P. Laughlin.

Matzelle, Henry J., written account, Mrs. Frankie James.

McCandless, Dr. Dean, "Remembering the Army," Dr. Dean McCandless.

McClean, Thomas J., sworn statement supporting Medal of Honor resubmission for Waverly Wray, March 1, 1984, Lieutenant General John Norton.

McIlvoy, Dr. Daniel B., Jr., letter to Clarence F. Montgomery, October 31, 1960, Cornelius Ryan Collection, Alden Library, Ohio University.

McIlvoy, Dr. Daniel B., Jr., "Medical Detachment, 505th Parachute Infantry, 82nd Airborne Division in World War II," Mrs. Annie McIlvoy Zaya.

McKeage, Donald W., written account, Donald W. McKeage.

Meddaugh, William J., written account, William J. Meddaugh.

Melvin, Howard P., letter to *Panther* (newsletter).

Meyers, James J., "Proud to Be, Memoirs of Colonel James J. Meyers," Mrs. James J. Meyers and the 82nd Airborne Division War Memorial Museum.

Miale, Frank M., written account, Frank M. Miale.

Nagel, Arnold G., written account, Alex Kicovic.

Neel, Malcolm, memoirs, Robert Burns.

Nunan, Paul D., sworn statement supporting Medal of Honor resubmission for Waverly Wray, March 2, 1984, Lieutenant General John Norton.

O'Loughlin, Dennis G., "Fierce Individualists," 1977, Frank P. Woosley.

Peterson, Theodore L., letter to Cornelius Ryan, March 22, 1959, Cornelius Ryan Collection, Alden Library, Ohio University.

Piper, Robert M., written account, Robert M. Piper.

Randall, Fredrick W., written account, Wheatley T. Christensen.

Reid, Richard E., "Chow," 82nd Airborne Division War Memorial Museum.

Rogers, Rick, "Off to War: The Story of a Soldier in WWII—Joseph L. Comer, Co. H, 3rd Battalion, 505 PIR, 82nd Airborne Division," Rick Rogers.

Russell, Kenneth E., letter to author, May 27, 2003.

Sammon, Charles E., letter to Cornelius Ryan, March 21, 1959, Cornelius Ryan Collection, Alden Library, Ohio University.

Sampson, Otis L., "Time Out for Combat," unpublished manuscript.

Schlesener, Milton E., letter to Frank Vanderbilt, Mrs. Frankie James.

Schultz, Arthur B., "Battle of the Bulge History of Arthur B. 'Dutch' Schultz," Arthur B. Schultz.

Schultz, Arthur B., "Holland Campaign 17 September–12 November 1944," Arthur B. Schultz.

Schultz, Arthur B., "Normandy Campaign 7 June–15 June 1944," Arthur B. Schultz.

Silanskis, Frank V., sworn statement supporting Medal of Honor resubmission for Waverly Wray, March 5, 1984, Lieutenant General John Norton.

Slawson, William E., written account, William E. Slawson.

Stolp, Northam H., written account, courtesy of Northam H. Stolp.

Thain, Carl E., letter to *Static Line* magazine, May 1990, Mrs. Carl E. Thain.

The James M. Gavin Papers, Personal Diaries, Box 8, U.S. Army Center of Military History.

Thomas, Dr. David E., letter to Alfred W. Ireland, September 6, 1997, 82nd Airborne Division War Memorial Museum.

Thompson, Frank W., letter to Alfred W. Ireland, August 12, 1997, 82nd Airborne Division War Memorial Museum.

Tuttle, Walter L., "Sweating It Out, The Battle of the Bulge," Troy Tuttle.

Vandervoort, Benjamin H., "Drop Zone Europe," Army Heritage and Education Center.

Vandervoort, Benjamin H., "Waverly Wray, Ste.-Mére-Église, Normandy June 7, 1944," Lieutenant General (U.S. Army Retired) John Norton.

Voorhies P. Dewailly, written account, courtesy of Voorhies P. Dewailly.

Vuletich, Michael M., written account, Alex Kicovic.

Walberg, Gordon A., *Static Line*, February 1989.

Wasner, John E., written account, John E. Wasner.

West, Floyd Jr., letter to Mr. Walter J. Turnbull, Jr., April 14, 1947, Mrs. Frankie James.

Wigle, Cloid B., written account, Cloid B. Wigle.

Winton, Walter F, Jr., "Exec's Diary—1st Battalion, 505 PIR," Walter F. Winton, Jr.

Woosley, Frank P., memoirs, Frank P. Woosley.

Wurst, Spencer F., unpublished manuscript.

Responses to Author's Questionnaires from the Following Veterans of the Division

Cornelius Ryan Collection, Alden Library, Ohio University, questionnaires with the following veterans of the division:

John H. Allen
Ernest R. Blanchard
Michael A. Brilla
Richard H. Brownlee
Harry Buffone
Buffalo Boy Canoe
Jack P. Carroll
Anthony J. DeMayo
Francis P. T. Dwyer
Robert J. Dwyer
William E. Ekman
Charles Fergie
Robert A. Fielder
Russell W. Fischer
Wayne W. Galvin
Harold L. Gensemer

Robert R. Hughart
Alfred W. Ireland
James L. Kaiser
James E. Keenan
Clyde F. Knox
Walter B. Kroener
Donald D. Lassen
Harvill W. Lazenby
William F. Mastrangelo
James E. McDavid
William J. Meddaugh
Paul D. Nunan
Russell R. O'Neal
Robert M. Piper
Lyle B. Putnam
Robert M. Robinson

Gus L. Sanders
Clifford W. Schrader
James T. Steed
John M. Steele
Dr. Lester Stein
Jack Tallerday
Bernard J. Tomardy
William H. Tucker
Benjamin Vandervoort
Michael M. Vuletich
Bernard Weil
Stanley Weinberg
Robert Wienecke
George B. Wood

Author's questionnaires with the following veterans of the division:

Berge Avadanian
Julius D. Axman
Douglas M. Bailey
Norbert P. Beach
William F. Borda
David Bowman
Paul R. Brandt
Russell W. Brown
Harry J. Buffone
Ernest R. DePaolantonio
Neil Droogan
Millard W. Edgerley
Robert E. Erikson
John J. Gallo
Robert W. Gillette

Thomas C. Goins
Virgil M. Goodwin
Raymond A. Grossman
John R. Jackson
Joseph T. Jockel
Wilton H. Johnson
Roy O. King
Harvill W. Lazenby
John R. Lyons
Dr. Dean McCandless
Donald W. McKeage
Robert M. Murphy
Joseph I. O'Jibway
John A. Price
Cecil E. Prine

James A. Rightley
James V. Rodier
Markus Rupaner
Louis C. Scarborough
Irvin W. Seelye
S. John Siam
Clarence M. Stoll, Jr.
Harold R. Thain
Charlie D. Turner
John J. Walsh
Walter F. Winton, Jr.
Norris S. White
Cloid B. Wigle
Darrell P. Willoughby
Chris Zafiroff

U.S. Military Documents, After-Action Reports, Studies, Monographs, Statements, and Combat Interviews

"82nd Airborne Division in Sicily and Italy," 82nd Airborne Division War Memorial Museum.

82nd Airborne Division, "World War II Casualties, Decorations, Citations," 82nd Airborne Division War Memorial Museum.

Combat Interviews, Operation Market-Garden, Cornelius Ryan Collection, Alden Library, Ohio University.

Copies of Distinguished Service Cross citations and Presidential Unit citations, 82nd Airborne Division War Memorial Museum.

Copies of Distinguished Service Cross citations, maps, photos, and after-action reports, Cornelius Ryan Collection, Alden Library, Ohio University.

"Debriefing Conference—Operation Neptune," 13 August 1944, 82nd Airborne Division War Memorial Museum.

Eisenhower, General Dwight D., "Letter to Allied Soldiers, Sailors, and Airmen," 1944.

G-2 Reports, Normandy, 82nd Airborne Division War Memorial Museum.

Gavin, Major General James M., letter to Capt. John C. Westover, July 25, 1945, courtesy of the 82nd Airborne Division War Memorial Museum.

Goldman, Private First Class Murray, sworn statement, May 16, 1945.

Headquarters IX Troop Carrier Command, "Operation Market, Air Invasion of Holland," Cornelius Ryan Collection, Alden Library, Ohio University.

Headquarters 307th Airborne Engineer Battalion, APO 469, U.S. Army, 10 August 1944, "Unit History," Normandy after-action report, Brian Siddall.

HQ 82nd Airborne Division, APO 469, U.S. Army, 11 September 1944, "Order of Battle Summary," Cornelius Ryan Collection, Alden Library, Ohio University.

Kicovic, Alex, various documents, written accounts, and maps related to the Sicilian and Italian campaigns.

Marshall, S. L. A. Colonel, "Regimental Unit Study Number 5, Preliminary Operations Around the La Fiere Bridgehead, Merderet River, Normandy, An Action by Various Elements of the 82nd Airborne Division," History Section, European Theater of Operations.

Marshall, S. L. A. Colonel, "Regimental Unit Study Number 6, "The Capture of Ste.-Mére-Église, An Action by 505th Infantry Regiment of the 82nd Airborne Division," History Section, European Theater of Operations.

Norton, Captain John, "Pathfinder Operations—Italy 14–15 Sept. 1943," Lieutenant General (U.S. Army Retired) John Norton.

"Operation Market, A Graphic History of the 82nd Airborne Division," 82nd Airborne Division War Memorial Museum.

"Operation Market-Garden," after-action report, 82nd Airborne Division, National Archives.

"Operation Neptune," 82nd Airborne Division Action in Normandy, France," 82nd Airborne Division War Memorial Museum.

Orders and Reports for Operation Market, Cornelius Ryan Collection, Alden Library, Ohio University.

Piper, Major Robert M., "The Operation of the 505 Parachute Infantry Regimental Combat Team (82nd Airborne Division) in the Airborne Landings on Sicily, 9–11 July 1943 (Sicilian Campaign) (Personal Experience of Assistant Regimental Adjutant)," the Donovan Research Library, Fort Benning, Georgia.

"S-3 Journal, 505th Parachute Infantry Regiment, October 1944–16 June 1945," John Fielder and U.S. Military History Institute.

Sayre, Major Edwin M., "The Operations of Company A 505th Parachute Infantry (82nd Airborne Division) Airborne Landings In Sicily 9–24 July 1943 (Sicily Campaign) (Personal Experience of a Company Commander)," Infantry School, 1947, the Donovan Research Library, Fort Benning, Georgia.

Supreme Headquarters Allied Expeditionary Force, Office of Assistant Chief of Staff, G-2, "Weekly Intelligence Summary, For Week Ending 16 September 1944," Cornelius Ryan Collection, Alden Library, Ohio University.

Tallerday, Captain Jack, "Operations of the 505th Parachute Infantry Regiment (82nd Airborne Division) in the Airborne Landing and Battle of Groesbeek and Nijmegen, Holland 17–25 September 1944, (Rhineland Campaign), (Personal Experience of a Company Commander)," Infantry School, 1948–1949, Donovan Research Library, Fort Benning, Georgia.

"The Story of the 82nd Airborne Division in the Battle of the Belgian Bulge, in the Siegfried Line, and of the Roer River," 82nd Airborne Division War Memorial Museum.

Taped Interviews and Oral Histories, Interview and Oral History Transcripts

Cornelius Ryan Collection, Alden Library, Ohio University, interviews with the following veterans of the division:
James M. Gavin
Harvill W. Lazenby

Eisenhower Center, oral history transcripts of the following veterans of the division:

Willard R. Follmer	Charles Miller
Robert R. Hughart	Kenneth E. Russell
Jack R. Isaacs	Arthur B. Schultz
James Elmo Jones	Ronald Snyder
Clarence W. McKelvey	John R. Taylor

Ekman, Colonel William E., interview with Captain K. W. Hechler, Colonel Mike Ekman.

Ekman, Colonel William E., interview with Colonel Mike Ekman, Colonel Mike Ekman.

Interviews with author with the following veterans of the division:

Anthony Antoniou	Luis de los Santos	Stanley W. Kotlarz
Frank A. Bilich	Julius Eisner	Russell D. McConnell
Bill Bishop	Donald E. Ellis	Robert M. Murphy
David R. Bullington	Willard Follmer	Gordon C. Pryne
Fred F. Caravelli	Howard C. Goodson	Paul D. Nunan
Eldon M. Clark	Virgil D. Gould	Edwin Sayre
Charles Copping	Chester Harrington	Ralph Stout, Jr.
Mariano L. Cuccio	Jerome V. Huth	Gerald R. Weed
Raymond L. Daudt	W. A. Jones	Dr. Daryle E. Whitfield

Kelly, Colonel Arthur L., Principal Interviewer, "Interview with Daniel B. McIlvoy," March 25, 1988, American Military Veterans Oral History Project, 2000, University of Kentucky.

Ridgway, Matthew B., oral history, Part 2, U.S. Army Military History Institute.

Roosevelt, Franklin D., President's D-Day Prayer, June 6, 1944, Washington D.C., Audio Recordings, Tape # RLxA-1 74-1:1 75-5(1) RL 454, Franklin D. Roosevelt Library Digital Archives.

Tallett, Joseph V., oral history, Joseph V. Tallett.

Internet Web Pages

Cole, Hugh M. *The Ardennes: Battle of the Bulge*, U.S. Army Center of Military History, 1990, http://www.army.mil/cmh-pg/books/wwii/7-8/7-8_cont.htm

Fifth Army Historical Section, *Salerno: American Operations from the Beaches to the Volturno (9 September–6 October 1943)*, U.S. Army Center of Military History, 1990, http://www.army.mil/cmh-pg/books/wwii/salerno/sal-fm.htm

Research of the armored strength of the Hermann Göring Panzer Division during the Sicily Campaign, http://www.feldgrau.net/phpBB2/index.php

Research of the composition of German units in the Cotentin Peninsula at the beginning of the Normandy invasion, http://web.telia.com/~u18313395/normandy/gerob/infdiv/91id.html

Roll of Honor of 82nd Airborne Division, http://www.ww2-airborne.us/division/82_overview.html

Unit History of the U.S. 746th Tank Battalion in Normandy, http://www.geocities.com/viajero43081/history.htm

INDEX TO MAPS

MAP 1   North Africa 40

MAP 2   Planned Air Route of the 505th RCT from Kairouan to Sicily,
        9 July 1943 56

MAP 3   505th RCT Drop Pattern—Sicily 62

MAP 4   Sicily, 11 July 1943 78

MAP 5   Salerno, 13–14 September 1943 102

MAP 6   Airborne Plan, 82nd and 101st Airborne Divisions 6 June 1944 . .124

MAP 7   Invasion Routes to Normandy, 5–6 June 1944 131

MAP 8   505th PIR Drop Pattern, 6 June 1944 147

MAP 9   Ste.-Mère-Église, 6 June 1944 168

MAP 10   Ste.-Mère-Église, 7 June 1944 181

MAP 11   Montebourg Station and Le Ham, 8–11 June 1944 199

MAP 12   505th RCT Drive to St.-Sauveur-le-Vicomte, 15–18 June 1944 210

MAP 13   505 RCT Hill 131and Hill 95, 1–4 July 1944 216

MAP 14   Operation Market Garden, Zones of Operation 226

MAP 15   Holland, 17 September 1944 242

MAP 16   Nijmegen, 19 September 1944 262

MAP 17   Holland, 20 September 1944 285

MAP 18   Nijmegen, 20 September 1944 296

MAP 19   Movement of the 82nd to Werbomont 319

MAP 20   Salm River Defense, 21–24 December 1944 326

MAP 21   Trois Ponts, Belgium 328

MAP 22   Counter Offensive, 3–9 January 1945 353

MAP 23   Attack to the German Border, 28–31 January 1945 380

MAP 24   Hürtgen Forest, 7–16 February 1945 385

MAP 25   The 505th crossing of the Elbe River, 30 April–1 May 1945 394

INDEX

Aachen, Germany, 386, 388
Abrams, Capt. Charles, 224
Acate River, 52, 60
Adair, Gen. Allan, 280, 299, 306
Adams, PFC Thomas D., 69
Adrianson, Don, 121
Agrigento airfield, Sicily, 100, 101
Aguerrebere, Pvt. Frank, 266, 311
Aguirre, Pvt. Alfonso R., 275
Aiken, Lt. Richard S., 66
Alabama Area, 8, 32, 33, 34, 35, 44, 417
Albanella, Italy, 103
Alexander, Lt. Col. Mark J., 49, 50, 54, 66, 68–69, 90–91,
    97, 99–100, 105, 106, 107, 108, 114, 116, 145, 155,
    169, 176–177, 194, 177, 201–202, 203, 204–205, 207,
    210, 213
Algiers, Algeria, 98
Allen, PFC John H., 229
Allen, Cpl. Lewis D., 186
Allen, Gen. Terry, 73
Alley, Capt. Herman, 254, 255–256
Allison, Cpl. Dock W., 252
Almeida, Richard L., 197
Altavilla, Italy, 103
Amblève River, 322, 323, 346
Amsterdam, Holland, 227
Anderson, Lt. Guy R., 250
Anderson, Pvt. Howard C., 18
Antoniou, Anthony, 15
Antwerp, Belgium, 327
Anzio, Italy, 118, 227, 281
Appleby, Cpl. Sam, 192, 194
Arbrefontaine, Belgium, 366, 368, 370, 371, 375, 376
Ariasi, Pvt. Ernest L., 314
Arkwright, Gen. H. R., 114
Arndt, PFC Edward W. "Eddie", 301, 330, 333–334
Arnhem, Holland, 226, 227, 230, 233, 258, 280, 308
Arnone, Italy, 99, 105, 108, 113, 114
Atchley, PFC John E., 183, 194, 359, 364
August, Cpl. Francis, 108
Augustine, Pvt. Gus, 336
Aust, Lt. Henry, 207, 256
Auther, Cpl. Kenneth W. "Big Red", 186
Avadanian, Pvt. Berge, 15, 32, 36, 38, 43, 45, 52, 54, 58, 66,
    107–108, 117, 118, 121, 126
Avola, Sicily, 63
Axman, Sgt. Julius D., 109–110, 324–325, 329
Baier, Lyman L. "Lee", 308
Bailey, PFC Douglas M., 53, 54, 66–67
Bailey, Lt. Jack, 324
Baker, Pvt. Elmer J., 311, 315
Baldry, Sgt. Floyd M., 171, 175, 180, 291, 292, 293, 296, 297
Baldwin, Cpl. Lewis W., 86
Baldwin, PFC Richard R., 335
Ballard, Pvt. Robert S., 59
Bandienville, France, 151, 194
Banta, T/5 George, 89

Baraque-de-Fraiture, Belgium, 343
Barger, T/4 Allan C., 17, 22, 103, 351, 352–353, 355, 398
Barizzo airfield, Sicily, 100, 102
Barker, Lt. Edwin, 356
Barnett, Capt. Charles L., 376, 391, 405
Barnhart, Pvt. Charles E., 246–247, 309–310
Bartley, S/Sgt. Jack M., 50
Barton, Gen. Raymond O., 186, 187
Bartsch, Arnold W., 370
Bartunek, Sgt. Edward G.
Bass, Capt. Hubert S., 123, 130, 134, 135, 214, 217
Basse-Bodeux, Belgium, 320, 321, 322, 344, 346, 358, 359,
    364
Bastogne, Belgium, 319, 320
Batcheller, Lt. Col. Herbert F., 31, 33, 116, 119, 120
Bates, Cpl. James, 141, 142
Battipaglia, Italy, 103
Beach, Sgt. Norbert P., 34, 35, 59, 129, 151, 310, 316, 317,
    320, 321, 363, 365, 397, 408
Beaty, Sgt. Willie B., 339, 340
Beaver, Jim, 246
Beck, Pvt. Carl, 272, 273, 274
Beckwith, Alan D., 151
Beek, Holland, 282
Belfast, Northern Ireland, 117
Bell, Elmo, Sgt., 14, 16, 18, 44, 73–74, 143–144, 174–175,
    176, 177, 343, 356, 357, 371, 414, 416
Bellice, Sicily, 95
Bennett, Cpl. William, 351
Berg-en-Dal, Holland, 251
Bergeval, Belgium, 346
Berlin, Germany, 304, 402, 406, 409–412, 413, 414
Best, Holland, 225
Beste Breurtije, Capt. Arie, 230
Beuzeville-au-Plain, France, 151
Beuzeville-la-Bastille, France, 123
Biazzo Ridge, Sicily, 9, 59, 81, 82, 84, 86, 87, 89, 91, 93, 95
Bilich, Frank A. PFC, 10–11, 217, 218, 221, 237, 267,
    269–270, 283, 350
Billingslea, Lt. Col. Charles, 101
Birmingham, England, 119
Biscari, Sicily, 84
Bishop, Sgt. Bill, 81, 82, 83, 88, 133, 163, 414
Bisselt, Holland, 248
Bittrich, Lt. Gen. Wilhelm, 304,305
Blanchard, PFC Ernest R., 137, 239
Blank, S/Sgt. William "Bill", 32, 37, 39, 48, 59, 96, 102–103,
    104, 148, 150, 151, 212, 219, 238, 246, 248, 257, 311,
    383, 384
Blankenship, Pvt. Charles, 127, 137, 156
Bleckede, Germany, 395, 396, 397, 400
Bly, Henry, 30
Bois de Limors, 214, 215, 216, 220
Bolderson, PFC John, 173, 174, 175, 176
Boling, S/Sgt. Earl W., 110, 189, 191, 205, 211, 270–271,
    272, 273, 282–283, 287, 312, 376, 388, 390, 399, 405
Bolton, Capt. William A., 29

466

Bommar, Capt. William R., 51, 52, 60, 62
Bonn, Germany, 389, 392
Borda, T/5 William F. "Bill", 389, 397, 399
Born, Belgium, 381
Boswell, Sgt. Henry D. "Duke", 83, 313–314
Bowman, PFC David V. "Dave", 20, 29, 42, 54, 67, 183, 205, 264, 265–266, 311, 351, 368
Bowman, PFC Jasper, 121
Boyd, Lt. John H., 31
Bra, Belgium, 343
Bradley, Gen. Omar N., 13, 46, 55, 122, 208, 209, 225
Brandt, Sgt. Archie J., 59
Brandt, Pvt. Paul R., 383
Brereton, Gen. Lewis H., 225
Brilla, Pvt. Michael A., 236, 304
British Military Units
I Airborne Corps, 225
1st Airborne Division, 226, 257, 258, 280, 308
1st Grenadier Guards Battalion, 259
2nd Grenadier Guards Battalion, 259
6th Airborne Division, 129, 395
23rd Armoured Brigade, 104, 105, 114
XXX Corps, 226, 280
130th Brigade, 312
Coldstream Guards, 278, 289, 294
Eighth Army, 75
Glider Pilot Regiment, 281
Grenadier Guards, 273, 284, 301, 303, 304
Guards Armoured Division, 259, 270, 280
Second Army, 8, 225, 227, 257, 306, 395
Brown, T/4 Donald L., 376
Brown, PFC Horace H., 155
Brown, S/Sgt. Russell W., 53, 67, 108, 120, 136, 196, 209, 244, 275, 354, 374, 387, 402, 407
Browning, Gen. Frederick, 225, 280, 281, 306
Brownlee, Lt. Richard H., 250–251, 251–253, 308
Bruhl, Germany, 392
Bruuk, Holland, 246
Bryant, Pvt. H. T., 137, 156, 157
Buchholtz, Belgium, 382
Buffalo Boy, S/Sgt. Herbert J., 34, 268, 327
Buffone, Sgt. Harry J. "Buff", 31, 43, 96, 200, 247, 362, 378, 387
Bullington, PFC David R. "Dave", 36–37, 64, 70, 71, 175, 179, 357
Burbage, England, 118
Burdge, Pvt. John W., 110, 206, 329
Burdick, Bob, 389
Burghduff, Sgt. Charles L. "Chuck", 215, 293
Burke, Cpl. Thomas J. "Tommy", 109, 110, 113, 166, 287, 405
Burnett, Melvin, 313–314
Burns, Pvt. Dwayne, 219
Busa, Cpl. Frank, 171
Busch, Pvt. Jack R., 257, 311
Byers, Pvt. Kelly "Moose", 36, 37, 177, 294
Byrd, PFC Thomas, 205
Cadish, Lt. Harold O., 137
Cages, Pvt. John P., 29, 34, 35
Camp Billy Mitchell, Alabama, 32

Camp Bowie, Texas, 12
Camp Chicago, France, 408, 412
Camp Claiborne, Louisiana, 14, 32
Camp Don Passage, French Morocco, 41
Camp Edwards, Massachusetts, 38
Camp Hoffman, North Carolina, 35
Camp Lucky Strike, France, 412
Camp Quorn, England, 118, 157, 161, 222, 229
Camp Roberts, California, 17
Camp Shanks, New York, 412
Camp Shelby, Mississippi, 14, 16
Camp Wheeler, Georgia, 16
Canoe, T/Sgt. Buffalo Boy, 133
Cantrell, Carl T., 311
Capuccini airfield, Italy, 105
Caravelli, Pvt. Fred F., 10, 234
Carlson, Capt. George D., 314, 351, 352, 354, 355, 356, 379
Carnes, PFC Vernon D., 300
Carpenter, Cpl. Glenn J., 151, 188
Carpenter, Sgt. Ott, 26, 73, 90
Carpenter, Maj. William R., 351, 376, 390, 391
Carpus, Cpl. Edward B., 109, 110
Carr, Lt. Oliver B. "O. B.", 182, 222, 268, 269, 313, 379, 382, 383, 392, 413
Carroll, Lt. Jack P., 211, 277, 297, 300
Casablanca, French Morocco, 41
Case, Lt. Harold E. "Casey", 28, 115, 308, 332, 354, 356, 367, 370
Castellammare di Stabia, Italy, 104
Castelvetrano airfield, Sicily, 100, 102
Castillo, 1st Sgt. Tony, 93, 239
Castle Dawson, Northern Ireland, 117
Catawba River, 37
Cauquigny, France, 177
Cavallaro, PFC Nick, 361, 362
Cerny, Col. John, 50
Chappell, Lt. Bill "Flash Gordon", 17–18, 19
Chattahoochee River, 32, 33
Chatterton, Col. George, 281
Chaudion, Pvt. Fred A., 33
Chef-du-Pont, France, 123, 149, 151, 154, 172, 177, 188, causeway, 132, 169
Cheneux, Belgium, 327
Cherbourg, France, 8, 130, 132, 147, 156, 201, 204, 214, 221
Chester, Lt. Michael C. "Mike", 28, 115, 121, 132, 133, 293, 307
Christensen, T/Sgt. Wheatley T. "Chris", 140–141, 150–151, 318, 338–339, 340, 341, 342, 344, 345, 346–347, 377, 384, 386, 387
Christian, Lt. Charles R., 336, 347, 348, 360, 361, 362, 364
Clark Jr., Sgt. Cullen E., 137–138, 162–163
Clark, Sgt. Eldon M., 196, 214–215
Clark, Lt. George E., 31, 51, 53, 62, 338, 340
Clark, Brig. Gen. Hal, 46
Clark, Jessie, 358
Clark, Gen. Mark, 46, 98, 101, 104
Cleve, Germany, 248
Cliff, Lt. John C., 182, 194
Cobb, Pvt. Frank E., 34
Cobb, Lt. John H., 382

Cockrell Jr., Capt. James K., 214, 307
Coddington, Robert E., 151
Coffin, Cpl. Roger F., 288
Collins, Gen. Lawton, 187
Cologne, Germany, 281, 389, 390
Comer, Cpl. Joseph L., 188, 213, 363
Comiso airfield, Sicily, 69, 98, 100, 102
Comly, Pvt. Dave, 113
Comstock, Lt. Carl R., 38, 92
Conchello, Italy, 99
Conlon, Lt. Michael, 25
Connally, David G., 32
Connell, Lt. Ivey K., 68
Connelly, Capt. Matthew J., 90, 93, 117, 156
Cook, Pvt. Isaac, 249
Cookstown, Northern Ireland, 117
Cooper, Lt. John L., 312, 329
Cooperider, Lt. Claiborne, 101
Copping, PFC Charles "Chuck", 15, 121, 128, 133
Corcoran, Pvt. John P., 315
Corti, John P., 209
Cottesmore airfield, England, 123, 230, 231
Coustillac, Lt. Henry G., 373
Coventry, England, 130
Coxon, Lt. Donald, 170
Coyle, Lt. James J. "Jim", 49, 67–68, 69, 117–118, 123–124,
    138, 167, 187–188, 189, 190, 191–192, 193–194,
    243–244, 270, 271, 272, 273, 274, 279, 280, 286–287,
    390, 397–398
Craig, Pvt. Kenneth R., 350
Crawford, Lt. Col. Joseph, 76, 80, 91
Crosley, PFC Marvin L., 86
Crossman, Capt. Raymond M., 85
Crosville, France, 205
Crouse, Cpl. Richard, 287
Cruise, PFC Leslie P. "Les", 148–149, 151, 154, 320, 358–359
Cuccio, Pvt. Marty, 16–17, 161, 201
Cunningham, PFC Fred C., 215
Cusmano, Bernard A., 151
Custer, Gen. George Armstrong, 224
Cutler, PFC Richard W. "Dick", 360
D'Alessio, Lt. Col. Wagner J., 119
Daudt, PFC Raymond L., 339, 340
Davis, PFC Allen B., 196
Davis, PFC Edwin G., 350
Davis, Johnnie, 48
de los Santos, Luis, 413
Decker, Martin, 290
Degenhardt, Lt. Richard H., 231, 362
Dellien, Germany, 402
DeLong, Capt. Walter C., 148, 214
DeMayo, PFC Anthony J. "Tony", 132, 134, 152, 153
Dempsey, Gen. Sir Miles, 306
DePaolantonio, Pvt. Ernest R., 124
Dewailly, Pvt. V. P., 349
Diffin, PFC John T., 239–240, 246, 257
DiGiralamo, Pvt. Louis, 358
Dionne, Pvt. Raymond, 288
DiTullio, PFC Dominick, 160
Dixon, Sgt. John, 72

Dodd, Lt. John H., 120, 275, 300
Doerfler, Lt. Eugene, 66, 188, 190, 194, 330
Dolan, Capt. John J. "Red", 119, 169–170, 170–171, 172,
    173, 174, 175, 176, 177, 179, 180–181, 224, 307
Donlon, James A. "Baby", 383
Donovan, Lt. Thomas W., 257
Douve River, 118, 123, 205, 207, 208, 209, 210
Droogan, PFC Cornelius J. "Neil", 32, 48, 145, 217, 336–337
Dunfee, T/Sgt. William, 18–19, 19–20, 21–22, 53, 57, 58,
    60–61, 95, 96, 160, 161, 196, 212, 233, 245–246, 317,
    344, 345, 348, 351, 358, 359, 360, 364–365, 370–371,
    387, 388, 390, 401
Dunnegan, Pvt. Harold V., 155
Durbin, PFC Sam, 329
Durham, Lt. James L., 146
Dusseault, Albert A., 197
Dwyer, Sgt. Francis P. T. "Frank", 255
Dwyer, Lt. Robert J. "Guinness", 217, 286
Dyas, Sgt. Tim, 72, 75
Eastern Force, 259, 260, 263, 270
Éconquenaèuville, France, 151
Ede, Holland, 230
Edgerley, Pvt. Millard W., 346, 363
Edmondson, Lt. Robert N., 207
Eindhoven, Holland, 225, 226, 231, 233
Eisenhower, Gen. Dwight D., 98, 100, 116, 122, 128, 224,
    405, 411
Eisner, Cpl. Julius "Ike", 206, 264, 315
Eitelman, Cpl. Chick, 176–177
Ekman, Col. William E., 119, 120, 146, 154, 155, 172, 176,
    177, 180, 196, 197, 201, 202, 203, 204, 208, 210,
    216–217, 220, 223, 224, 229, 234, 235, 289, 310, 315,
    317–318, 321, 332, 337, 364, 375, 376, 379, 391, 403,
    408, 409, 410
Elbe River, 9, 393, 395–398, 400, 402, 406
Ellingson, T/5 Lloyd G., 303
Ellis, PFC Donald E., 139, 265
Ellis, Marshall A., 151
Emerick, Pvt. Ulysses S., 311
Enfidaville, Tunisia, 99
Ensley, Sgt. Frankie B., 390
Epinal, France, 408, 409
Epps, Sgt. Steve, 397
Erikson, Pvt. Robert E., 401
Escaut River, Belgium, 225
Esparza, PFC Santiago H., 249
Essex, Lt. George, 374
Ètienville, France, 123, 204
Euling, SS Capt. Karl-Heinz, 258, 303
Everhardy, John, 43
Faith, Capt. Don, 73
Faranfontoff, Pvt. Walter, 308
Farello airport, Sicily, 90
Fauville, France, 160, 162
Fellers, Col. Bonner, 13
Fergie, Cpl. Charles, 285
Ferguson, PFC Robert G., 170
Fielder, Lt. Robert A., 37, 41, 42, 82, 84, 87, 93, 116–117,
    119–120, 122, 214, 216, 239, 246
Fields, Lt. John J., 329

Fischer, PFC Russell W., 310, 314–315
Fitt, Pvt. Joseph C., 176
Fitzgerald, Cpl. Joseph, 101
Fitzgerald, Capt. Maurice J., 315
Fleet, Capt. Robert L., 29
Flynn, Jack S., 163
Folkingham airfield, England, 231
Follmer, Capt. Willard R. "Bill", 31, 50, 51–52, 60, 61, 62, 79, 119, 141, 221
Force, PFC Dennis, 222, 358, 361, 362
Formicola, Sam, 389
Forsythe, Wesley, 280
Fort Benning, Georgia, 8, 13, 17, 23, 25, 31, 33, 170, 413
Fort Bragg, North Carolina, 23, 33, 35, 36, 37, 38, 408
Fort Jackson, South Carolina, 36
Fort Polk, Louisiana, 14
Fosse, Belgium, 358, 359, 363, 364, 369
Fotovich, PFC George, 237
Francis, Cpl. Jack, 110, 113
Francisco, Sgt. Vernon L., 300, 367
Franco, Capt. Robert, 37–38, 114, 156, 161, 236
Franks, Cpl. Darrell J. "D. J.", 180
Frederico, PFC Frank G., 222, 347, 348
Freeland, Sgt. Fred "Freddie", 68, 355
Fresville, France, 198
Frey, Hans F., 359
Fritts, James C. "Fritz", 219
Fryer, Sgt. Melvin J., 129
Frying Pan, 8, 25, 26, 30, 31, 44, 170, 368, 383, 408, 417
Gagne, Pvt. Camille E., 300, 301
Gallo, Pvt. John J., 65, 321
Galvin, Pvt. Wayne, 300, 304
Gambosville, France, 163
Gamelcy, Gilbert L., 151
Garrett, PFC Louis H., 107
Garvaugh, Northern Ireland, 117
Gavin, Lt. Jack E., 239–240, 246, 257, 315
Gavin, Maj. Gen. James M., 8, 12, 13–14, 25, 31, 32, 33, 34, 35, 36, 42, 47, 48, 49, 55, 57, 65, 72–73, 76, 80, 81, 82, 84, 85, 86, 88–89, 92, 95, 101, 102, 104, 105, 116, 116, 118, 119, 122, 125, 154, 171–172, 177, 194, 216–217, 223, 224, 225, 227, 228, 239, 248, 259, 263, 280–281, 306, 314, 316, 318, 319, 320, 343, 357, 367, 368, 375, 376, 381, 389, 402, 403, 404, 406, 409, 411–412, 413, 414, 416
Gawan, Francis B., 151
Gela, Sicily, 50, 51, 60, 61, 67, 68, 69, 80, 81, 90, 93, 94, 125
Gennep, Holland, 228, 248, 249, 250, 251, 287, 288
Gensemer, Lt. Harold J., 250, 252, 253, 256–257, 288, 308
German Military Units
1st Panzer Grenadier Regiment, 79
1st SS Panzer Division, 327, 330, 336, 343
1st SS Panzer Grenadier Regiment, 327, 337
II SS Panzer Corps, 304
2nd SS Panzer Division, 343
3rd Fallschirmjäger Division, 281, 282
4th Company, 572nd Heavy Flak Battalion, 258
4th Flak Division, 282, 286
5th Fallschirmjäger Division, 281
6th SS Panzer Army, 327

9th SS Panzer Division, 278, 338, 343
9th SS Reconnaissance Battalion, 258, 301
10th SS Panzer Division, 258, 304
15th Panzer Grenadier Division, 55, 97
21st Fallschirmjäger Lehr Regiment, 282
62nd Volksgrenadier Division, 352, 366, 369,370
91st Airlanding Division, 123
406th Division, 258, 282
709th Antitank Battalion, 182, 188
795th Georgian Battalion, 187
1058th Grenadier Regiment, 149, 167, 196
1st Battalion, 182, 184, 186, 188, 194, 267
2nd Battalion, 182, 188, 194
3rd Battalion, 160
Abteilung 1, Panzer Artillerie Regiment 1, 327
Hermann Göring Fallschirm Panzer Division, 8, 55, 71, 75, 79, 81, 84, 90, 97
Hermann Göring Training Regiment, 258
Kampfgruppe Becker, 282
Kampfgruppe Euling, 258
Kampfgruppe Greschick, 282, 286
Kampfgruppe Hansen, 327
Kampfgruppe Hermann, 282, 288
Kampfgruppe Melitz, 258
Kampfgruppe Peiper, 327, 343, 346
Kampfgruppe Runge, 258
Kampfgruppe von Fürstenberg, 282
Panzerjäger Abteilung 1, 327
Seventh Army, 182, 186
Sturm Battalion, 182, 186
Gibbons Jr., Capt. Patrick J. Jr., 31, 121, 146
Gilbert, Pvt. Calvin C., 222, 336, 360
Gill, Pvt. John L., 287
Gillette, T/Sgt. Robert W., 31, 38, 48, 65, 69, 120, 121, 315–316
Giroda, Cpl. Leo T., 101
Gironda, Pvt. Joseph, 74
Goins, T/5 Thomas C., 115, 146
Goldman, PFC Murray, 86, 87
Gonzales, PFC Raymond S., 202, 308
Goodson, PFC Howard C. "Goody", 15–16, 17, 20–21, 22, 53, 62, 360, 363, 416
Goodwin, PFC Virgil M., 320, 351, 365, 408, 415
Gore, Sgt. John W., 106, 109
Gorham, Lt. Col. Arthur F. "Hardnose", 25, 26, 27, 28, 45, 48, 63, 71, 72, 79, 80, 90, 91, 92
Goronne, Belgium, 372, 374, 375, 376
Gougler, Sgt. Fredrick W., 250
Goulburn, Lt. Col. Edward H., 262, 299, 304
Gould, Lt. Virgil D., 327, 355, 379
Grace, 1st Sgt. Patrick F., 28
Grafwegen, Holland, 254
Grainville, France, 197
Grand-Halleux, Belgium, 322, 336, 338, 339, 340, 342
Grant, Pvt. John L., 350
Grantham, England, 122
Grave, Holland, 225, bridge, 227, 251
Graves, Lee G., 126
Gray, Maj. James Gray, 29, 33, 48, 49
Gregory, Sgt. Arthur L., 109

Groesbeek, Holland, 225, 227, 228, 229, 234, 235, 238, 243, 244, 245, 246, 248, 251, 256, 258, 259, 282, 286, 308, 309, 312
Grossman, Lt. Raymond A., 59–60, 85–86, 99, 117, 142, 160, 253, 254, 313, 410
Guernsey Island, 130
Guerrant, Lt. Morris P., 250, 401
Gurski, PFC Stanley, 215
Hable, Earl, 272, 274
Hadden, Robert "Moose", 241
Hagan III, Maj. William, 81, 84, 214, 216, 224
Hagenow, Germany, 404
Haggard, Pvt. John O., 215
Hahnen, PFC Billy G., 212
Hale, Pvt. Jack, 22
Hallahan, Cpl. William A., 360
Hamburg, Germany, 400
Hancock, Lt. Asa T., 309, 314
Handfield, Sgt. Louis L., 46
Hannan, Capt. Philip M., 403–405, 414
Hanover, Germany, 393
Harden Jr., Lt. Col. Harrison B., 33, 42, 50, 66, 69,
Harmel, Gen. Heinz, 304, 305
Harnisch, Oberstleutnant Siegfried, 250
Harrington, PFC Chester "Chet", 20, 309
Harris, Donald E., 373
Harris, Pvt. James R., 35
Harris, Lt. Joseph D., 23
Harris, Pvt. Kenneth L., 83
Harris, William A. "Wild Bill", 71
Harris, Capt. William J., 123, 146, 224, 272
Hart, Pvt. Alvin E., 109
Hart, Sgt. Raymond F., 59, 87, 88, 91
Hartman, Orval, 64
Haugen, Lt. Col. Orin D., 31, 33
Haupt, Lt. Walter, 356
Hayhurst, Sgt. Clarence W. "Tudy", 43
Haynes, PFC William R. "Rebel", 205, 264
Hays, Lt. William R. "Bill" or "Rusty", 235, 245, 275–276, 297–298, 300, 301–302, 314, 316, 321–322, 351–352
Hebein, Fred J., 162, 278, 330
Heggood, Sgt. Johnny F., 249, 250
Heim Jr., Pvt. Marcus, 173, 174, 175, 176
Hein, Sgt. Clyde E., 215
Heller, Pvt. Lee, 269
Helmstedt, Germany, 409
Henderson, Sgt. Bob, 201
Herkness, Lt. Frank, 400
Herman Jr., Pvt. Jacob T., 264, 279
Herresbach, Belgium, 381
Herrin, Pvt. Robert L., 161
Heumen, Holland, lock bridge, 248, 282, 289
Hicks Jr., Cpl. Howard W., 186
Higgins, Cpl. Thomas H., 92
Hile, Pvt. Arthur S., 198
Hill 110, France, 118, 123
Hill 131, France, 121, 216, 218, 220, 222
Hill 20, France, 160, 161, 187, 188
Hill 41, Sicily, 80, 91
Hill 71, France, 71, 118

Hill 77.8, Holland, 248
Hill 81.8, Holland, 243
Hill 82, France, 118
Hill 95, France, 218, 219, 220
Hill, Pvt. Jack, 110, 193
Hill, Sgt. Paul, 231, 363
Hillman, PFC Jack, 141, 161, 204, 239, 318
Hodge, Cpl. Bill, 211
Hodges, Gen. Courtney, 318, 323
Hogan, Cpl. Louis P., 286
Holcomb, Lt. Joseph W. "Little Joe", 214, 299, 300
Holtzmann, Pvt. Robert E., 161
Honsfeld, Belgium, 382
Hope, Bob, 99
Horn, Allen H., 151
Horrocks, Gen. Brian G., 280, 281, 306
Horsechief, Levi, 356
Horst, Holland, 246
Hough, Pvt. John J. "Scotty", 61
Hughart, PFC Robert R. "Bob", 244, 245, 300, 304, 416
Hughes, Lt. Marshall, 356, 367, 379
Hupfer, Lt. Col. C. G., 194, 197
Hürtgen Forest, Germany, 384–386, 388, 396
Husband's Bosworth, England, 118
Huston, Cpl. George F., 101
Huth, T/5 Jerome V. "Jerry", 89, 98, 101, 102
Ireland, Lt. Col. Alfred W. "Irish", 48, 65, 72, 73, 80, 85, 88, 153, 224, 316
Irvin, Lt. James M., 36, 143, 169, 201, 221, 224–225, 289
Irving, PFC George R., 161, 201
Isaacs, Capt. Jack R., 31, 59, 88, 122, 139–140, 153, 212–213, 225, 246, 248, 286, 338, 339, 340, 341–342, 344, 346, 347
Italian Military Units
4th Livorno Division, 97
54th Napoli Division, 97
206th Coastal Division, 97
Jackson, Pvt. John R., 317, 320, 366, 376
Jacobus, Pvt. George, 138
Jakiela, Sgt. Henry, 351
Janney, Lt. Richard M., 107–108
Jensen, Lt. Howard, 324, 329, 390
Jockel, S/Sgt. Joseph T., 321, 344, 366, 369, 378, 408, 413
Johnson, Lt. Fred W., 63
Johnson, Lt. Gerald "Johnny", 203, 205, 230, 416
Johnson, Richard L. "Mickey", 334
Johnson, Capt. William H., 50, 69
Johnson, Cpl. Wilton H., 41, 205
Jones, Alex "Jonesie", 342
Jones, Doyle T., 151
Jones, Sgt. Edward D. "E. D.", 374
Jones, Edwin, 161
Jones, Lt. Homer, 173
Jones, S/Sgt. James Elmo, 25, 38, 122, 129, 130–132, 133, 135, 152–153, 186–187, 190, 249, 289, 400, 401
Jones, Cpl. W. A. "Arnold", 18, 20, 43, 49, 55, 156, 157, 299, 300, 302, 414
Joster, Sgt. Roy, 235
Kacyainski, Lt. Edward, 50
Kairouan, Tunisia, 48, 49, 50, 58, 67, 98, 99, 100

Kaiser, Sgt. Charles J., 313
Kaiser, Lt. Col. James L., 224, 230, 238, 245, 313, 338, 342, 344, 363
Kall River valley, "Death Valley", 386
Kamp, Holland, 235, 243, 246, 251, 309, 310
Karmazin, Tony, 221
Kastrantas, Nick, 121
Keenan, PFC James E. "Jim", 261–262, 301, 390
Kellam, Maj. Frederick C. A., 117, 119, 146, 171, 173, 176, 221
Keller, PFC John, 110, 191, 193, 273, 282
Kelly, Cpl. James I., 166
Kerrans Jr., Brig. Gen. Charles L., 116
Kerrigan, Pvt. William J., 69
Ketz, Sgt. Joseph J., 33, 220
Kilrea, Northern Ireland, 117
Kilroy, Larry, 151
King, Sgt. Roy O., 125, 138–139, 206, 264, 415
Kirkwood, Capt. Robert "Bob", 37
Klee, Lt. Kurt B., 38, 68
Knox, PFC Clyde F., 107, 301
Kochanek, Sgt. Frank S., 249
Kommerscheidt, Germany, 386
Konar, Lt. Albert V., 98, 101, 102, 122
Kotlarz, PFC Stanley W., 166, 167, 189
Kouns, Maj. Charles W., 48, 50
Krause, Lt. Col. Edward C. "Cannonball", 29, 30, 33, 48, 50, 51, 58, 60, 80, 81, 84, 87, 88, 95, 96, 104, 125, 148, 150, 152, 154, 156, 160, 161, 187, 212, 221, 224, 364, 388
Krka, PFC Charles, 374
Kroener, Lt. Walter B., 62, 197, 245, 321
Krompasky, T/Sgt. Joseph W., 384
Krueger, Howard R., 302
Krupinski, PFC Ray, 200
La Bonneville, France, 204
La Fière, France, 123, bridge, 145, 146, 169, 171, 176–177, 194, causeway, 132, 147, 169, 171, 172, 177, 178
La Gleize, Belgium, 327, 346
La Haye-du-Puits, France, 8, 213, 216, 218
La Neuville, Belgium 336
La Tour, Belgium, 322, 327, 335, 337
LaBlanc, Pvt. Callies, 257
Laird, Lt. Arthur T., 59, 87
Lake Biviere, Sicily, 51, 60
Langdon, Allen L., 409
Langford, Sgt. Everette H., 146
Langford, Frances, 99
Lankford, Jules, 329
Laon, France, 408
Lassen, PFC Don, 278
Latek, Pvt. Edward J., 315
Laughlin, PFC Edward P., 367, 389
Lawson Field, 33
Laye, Pvt. Leland "Chief", 83
Lazar, PFC Paul M., 401
Lazenby, Sgt. Harvill W., 25, 36, 48, 143, 201, 240, 249
Le Ham, France, 202, 203, 204, 220
Le Havre, France, 412
Leaky, PFC Robert L., 129

Lebednick, Pvt. John, 222, 347
Lee, Gen. William, 13
Leicester, England, 118, 121
Lent, Holland, 258, 304
Leonard, Pvt. Larry W., 152, 162, 200
Les Forges, France, 162
Les Rosiers, France, 205
Lewis, Pvt. Donald R., 359
Liège, Belgium, 225
Lindquist, Lt. Col. Roy, 172
Linosa, 58
Long, Maj. Talton W. "Woody", 108, 110, 113, 114, 214, 224, 250, 369, 388
Long, Pvt. James D. "J. D.", 83
López, Pvt. Alfredo R., 367
Lord, Cpl. Richard J., 264
Loren, Lt. William H., 85
Losheim, Germany, 382
Losheimergraben, Germany, 382, 383
Lough Neagh, Northern Ireland, 117
Loughborough, England, 118
Lucero, Pvt. Gasper, 34
Ludlam, Sgt. Gerald, 83
Ludwigslust, Germany, 403, 404
Lupoli, Charles P., 348
Lynch, Sgt. Philip M., 374
Lyons, Pvt. John R. "Jack", 251, 286, 336, 347, 348, 358, 362
Lyons, Cpl. Warren "Pappy", 83
Maas River, 227, 229, 248
Maas-Waal Canal, 227, 229, 234, 235, 240, 251, 281, 282, 289
MacDonald, William A., 384
MacPhee, Pvt. Donald, 205
Magdets, Lt. Edward A., 239
Maglothin, Pvt. Willis E., 336
Mahaffey, Lt. Bob, 12
Maikowski, Ray "Mike", 345–346
Malay, Pvt. Francis, 109
Mallis, Pvt. Abraham Albert "Abie", 222, 288
Malta, 58
Maness, Maj. James T., 214, 225, 315, 344, 389, 399
Manfredi, Admiral Alberto, 96
Manhay, Belgium, 343
Marin, Maj. Albert, 224
Marina di Ragusa, Sicily, 69
Markwood, PFC Francis H., 390
Marr, Lt. John, 172
Martin, Pvt. William, 222
Martin, Capt. William C. "Bill", 379, 382, 383, 392, 398
Mason, Cpl. Daniel "Danny", 88
Mastrangelo, Lt. William F. "Bill", 212, 229, 230, 239, 246, 308–309
Matash, Sgt. Charles C., 162, 358, 363
Mattson, S/Sgt. Phillip O., 46
Matzelle, PFC Henry, 220–221, 368
Mauldin, Bill, 105
May, Lt. Robert L., 85
Mayer, Al, 48, 218
Mayers, PFC Raymond T., 289
McBride, Pvt. Charles S., 36

McCandless, Lt. Dean, 26, 41, 45, 73, 75, 90, 91–92, 316, 337, 375
McCarthy, George R., 163, 334
McClatchy, Pvt. Wesley H., 179
McClean, Lt. Thomas J. "Tom", 182, 184–185, 187, 189, 191, 192, 206, 222–223, 237, 284, 311, 313, 379, 413
McConnell, Pvt. Russell, 43, 44, 55, 82, 83, 93
McDaniel, Roy, 378
McDavid, PFC James E., 239
McGinity, Maj. James E., 29, 30, 84, 117, 119, 170, 171, 176
McGown, Maj. Hal D., 346
McGrew Jr., Cpl. Ralph H., 203
McIlvoy Jr., Maj. Daniel B. "Doc", 38, 44, 45, 86, 90, 93, 156, 197–198, 238, 243, 310
McIntyre, Sgt. Fay C., 309
McKeage, Cpl. Donald W., 305, 332, 335, 354, 366–367, 370
McKeage, Lt. Tom, 214
McKelvey, Lt. Clarence W., 141, 207–208
McKeown Jr., Pvt. David J., 69
McKinney, PFC James, 355
McLaughlin, Lt. Robert E., 170, 171
McMandon, Pvt. Bill, 269, 283
McMurchy, Sgt. William, 179
McPheeters, Capt. Archibald A., 225, 360, 362, 364
McRoberts, Lt. Neal L., 49, 108
Meddaugh, Lt. Bill, 135, 231–233, 233–234, 234–235, 236–237, 238, 272, 322, 323–324, 325, 328–329, 330, 331, 332, 333, 335, 376
Meelberg, Pvt. Eddie O.
Meigs, S/Sgt. Sylvester H., 229, 230, 253, 416
Melvin, C/Sgt. Maj. Howard P., 162, 315, 320–321, 337, 414
Mendieta, Pvt. Luis, 215
Merderet River, 123, 135, 169, 170, 173, 174, 177, 201, 204
Mewborne, Oscar, 370
Meyers, Lt. Francis J. "Joe", 28, 37
Meyers, Lt. James J. "Joe", 222–224, 235–236, 263–264, 266–267, 278–279, 284, 305, 307, 313, 327–328, 335–336, 349, 350, 354–355, 355–356, 367, 368, 372–373, 374–375, 378–379, 382, 383, 392–393, 395–396, 406–407, 409–410, 412–413
Miale, S/Sgt. Frank M., 17–18, 19, 89, 115, 240
Michaud, Pvt. Thomas J., 66
Michelman, Lt. Isaac, 155, 222, 263–264, 278, 279
Mill, Capt. Fredric L., 31, 49
Miller, PFC Charles H. "Charlie", 127, 139, 186, 222, 267, 415
Miller, Lt. Harold E., 249, 289
Miller, Capt. Robert H., 31
Model, Field Marshall Walter, 304
Monahan, Sgt. Lawrence F., 178
Montebourg Station, France, 143, 169, 196, 201, 202, 203, 220
Montebourg, France, 189, 193
Montenau, Belgium, 381
Montevago, Sicily, 95
Montgomery, Field Marshall Bernard L., 75, 225, 343–344, 395, 411
Mook, Holland, 229, 244, 252, 282, 288, 289, 290, 293, 294, 305, 307, 308
Mount Soprano, Italy, 103

Mount Vesuvius, Italy, 104
Mount, Pvt. William L., 289, 291, 292, 293, 297
Mulcahy, Lt. Patrick D., 101
Muller, William A., 278
München-Gladbach, Germany, 396
Murphy, Sgt. Edward F., 305, 328
Murphy, Pvt. Robert M. "Bob", 133, 178, 180, 293–294
Murrow, Edward R., 234
Nagel, S/Sgt. Arnold G. "Dutch", 63, 288, 408
Nancy, France, 408
Naples, Italy, 8, 98, 99, 104, 105, 106, 107, 114, 115, 125
Nealy, Pvt. William H., 206, 207, 377
Neel, PFC Malcolm, 320
Neilsen, Frederick C., 151
Neuberger, Pvt. William H. "Bill", 166, 221
Neuhof, Germany, 383
Neuville-au-Plain, France, 124, 155, 163–165, 167, 183, 189, 194, 196, 197, 221
Niepling, Larry, 303
Nijmegen, Holland, 8, 9, 225, 227, 228, 230, 233, 243, 244, 245, 248, 249, 250, 252, 259, 260, 261, 278, 281, 282, 287, bridges, 251, 257, 258, 280, 289, 305, 306, 308, 309, 314, 333, highway bridge, 227, 258, 279, 280, 304, 305, 309, Hunner Park, 258, 259, 272, 278, 297, 298, 301, 302, 303, 304, 305, Kronenburger Park, 258, 259, railroad bridge at, 258, 259, 264, 277, 283, 284, 285, 305, 307, 309, Valkhof, 259, 299, 301, 302, Villa Belvoir, 258, 259, 272, 299
Niland, Sgt. Robert J. "the Beast" Niland, 155, 166
Niscemi, Sicily, 50, 71, 80, 94
Noirfontaine, Belgium, 354
North Witham airfield, England, 122, 129
Norton, Lt. Col. John "Jack", 44, 68, 100, 101–102, 103, 155, 169, 176, 208, 224, 227, 414
Novak, Joe, 362
Nowinski, PFC Frank J., 109
Nunan, T/Sgt. Paul D., 14–15, 23, 29, 33, 185, 209, 243, 263, 267–269, 388, 414
Nurse, Pvt. Robert E., 301
Oakley, Lt. William A., 172, 173, 179
O'Dea, Lt. John, 390, 391
O'Donnell, 1st Sgt. Joseph V., 25
O'Jibway, S/Sgt. Joseph I. "Joe", 39, 63, 143, 169
O'Laughlin, PFC Dennis, 113, 127–128, 233, 334
Oldfield, Lt. Col. Arthur B. "Barney", 31, 411
Olds, Sgt. Donald H., 305, 307, 349, 350
Olsen, Ken, 374
Olson, Capt. Hugo V., 316
Olszewski, Cpl. Edward J. "Ozzie", 223–224, 368
O'Neal, S/Sgt. Russell R., 230, 240
O'Neill, Lt. Bertram L., 256
O'Neill, PFC Danny, 217–218
O'Neill, Pvt. John J., 145
Oosterhout, Holland, 259
Operation Dodger, 47
Operation Eyewash, 46
Operation Giant I, 99
Operation Giant II, 100
Operation Husky, 42, 49
Operation Market-Garden, 225, 238, 309

Operation Overlord, 116
Operation Pirate, 48
Oran, Algiers, harbor, 117
Orman, Lt. Travis, 140, 149, 212
Ospital, James M. "Jack", 89, 403, 404
Otto, Lt. John, 289
Oujda, French Morocco, 41, 42, 43, 44, 46, 48, 49
Over Asselt, Holland, 228
Owens, Cpl. Howard S., 63
Owens, Sgt. William D. "Bill", 170, 178, 179, 180, 181
Pack, Pvt. Elmer, 205
Packard, Lt. David L., 99, 109, 114, 192
Paestum, Italy, 101, 102, 103
Palluconi, Capt. Amelio D., 25
Parachute School, 17, 23, 31, 413
Parachute Test Battery, 23, 33
Parisi, Pvt. Joe, 336
Parker, Lt. Russell E., 222, 268, 367
Partanna, Sicily, 95
Passero, Pvt. Pat, 361, 362
Paterson, Capt. Charles, 253
Patrick, George, 401
Patrick, Pvt. Joe, 62
Patton, Gen. George S. Jr., 29, 46, 411
Payne, Lt. Houston, 190
Pearl Horace, 414
Peddicord, Lt. Roper R., 137, 138, 162–163
Peiper, Obersturmbahnführer Joachim, 327
Perry, Chris, 201, 342, 384
Peterman, Pvt. Harry, 275
Peterson, PFC Lenold, 173, 175, 176
Peterson, Lt. Theodore L. "Ted" or "Pete", 114, 165–166, 167, 183, 188–189, 190, 191, 194, 231–232
Petit-Halleux, Belgium, 322, 338, 342, 344, 346
Petrillo, Sgt. Michael, 63
Phenix City, Alabama, 34
Phillips, Lt. John B., 370
Piacenti, Joseph "Joe", 204
Picauville, France, 204
Pickels, PFC Harry G., 110, 112, 166, 190
Piper, Capt. Robert M., 54, 119, 120, 224, 234
Plasmolen, Holland, 249, 250, 256, 288
Polish 1st Independent Parachute Brigade, 226
Pompeii, Italy, 104
Pont l'Abbé, France, 146
Ponte Olivo, Sicily, 50
Popilsky, Sgt. Ben N., 109, 110, 279, 283, 287
Powell, Pvt. (-), 36
Prager, S/Sgt. Clarence, 161, 247
Presnell, Lt. George W., 170, 289, 307
Price, Cpl. John A., 253
Price, Lt. Lawrence M., 313, 356, 372, 379
Prine, Pvt. Cecil E., 25, 37, 43, 171, 175, 178, 180, 357, 375
Pritchard, PFC Norman, 209
Privelack, Germany, 406, 407
Prosser, Sgt. Evan W., 207
Pryne, PFC Gordon, 119, 145, 173, 175, 176, 314
Psaki, Lt. Nicholas J., 300
Purcell, Cpl. George H., 186
Putnam, Cpl. Clifford W., 301, 323

Putnam, Capt. Lyle B., 139, 156, 196, 312
Pynson, Roy L., 219, 311
Qualls, Lt. Charles K., 222, 305, 379
Queen Mary, 412
Queen, Sgt. Oscar L. "Stonewall", 119, 175, 179
Quorndon, England, 118, 120
Rabig, 1st Sgt. John H., 11, 195, 218, 222, 260, 263, 356
Rae, Capt. Robert D., 177
Raff, Col. Edson, 186, 188
Ragusa, Sicily, 66
Rajca, PFC Joe, 266
Rajner, PFC George J., 127, 218, 222
Randall, Sgt. Frederick W., 93
Ray, Sgt. John P., 137, 152
Realmonte, Sicily, 95
Reardon, Lt. William J. "Buck", 289
Reed Jr., Lt. William W., 330
Reharmont, Belgium, 356, 357
Reichswald, Germany, 227, 228, 246, 247, 250, 251, 253, 254, 255, 282, 286
Reid, Pvt. Richard E. "Pat", 47, 83
Reid, Lt. Wallace G., 256
Reinhold, SS Maj. Leo, 259
Rencheux, Belgium, 322, 376
Reynolds, Sgt. William F., 360
Rheims, France, 388, 405
Rhine River, 8, 225, 226, 308, 389, 390, 392, 395, 396, 397
Ricci, Sgt. Jim, 179
Rickerd, PFC Clyde, 211, 270, 274
Ridgway, Maj. Gen. Matthew B., 8, 41, 42, 49, 55, 73, 76, 79, 92, 93, 95, 96, 98, 100, 101, 104, 115, 116, 118, 122, 123, 125, 172, 186, 188, 208, 209, 210, 223, 224, 344, 395
Riethorst, Holland, 249, 250, 251, 254, 282, 288, 307, 308
Riffle, Lt. Warren A., 90
Rightley, Lt. James A. "Jim", 89–90, 115, 146, 196
Ringwald, Lt. Robert K., 140
Robbins Jr., Lt. Wilbert H., 46, 144, 356
Robinson, Sgt. James, 231
Robinson, Sgt. Peter, 304, 305
Robinson, PFC Robert M., 139, 218
Rochelinval, Belgium, 322, 336, 337, 338, 345, 346, 347, 348
Rockford, Pvt. Sonnie J. "Rocky", 309
Rodier, PFC James V., 208, 317
Roer River, 387
Rogers, 1st Sgt. Thomas J., 373
Rojas, PFC Frank, 374
Rome, Italy, 99, 100
Rosen, Capt. Robert H., 225, 297, 298
Rosowski, Edmund, 30
Ross, Pvt. William A., 179
Rowe, Lt. William A., 359
Roysdon, Capt. Dale A., 173, 176
Rupaner, Mark, 36
Russell, Capt. Clyde R., 69, 114, 118, 123, 187, 188, 203
Russell, Cpl. Jerome, 332
Russell, PFC Kenneth, 126, 127, 136, 137, 152, 303
Russian 8th Mechanized Corps, 403
Salemi, Sicily, 95
Salerno, Italy 8, 99, 100, 105, 236, 254, 378, Bay of, 98, 101

Salm River, 322, 323, 324, 325, 327, 335, 337, 338, 340, 343, 344, 346, 376
Salmchâteau, Belgium, 385, 392
Sambuca, Sicily, 95
Sammon, Lt. Charles E. "Pinky", 157–159, 332
Sampson, T/Sgt. Otis L. "The Mortar Artist", 22–23, 30, 52, 58, 110–113, 165, 166–167, 189, 190, 191, 192–193, 243, 244, 270, 273, 274, 280
Samsel, Lt. John E., 46
Sanchez, PFC William, 339
Sandefur, Sgt. Felix C., 198, 200
Sanders, Lt. Gus L., 75, 126, 215, 221, 255, 309, 356, 415, 416
Sanders, Capt. John H., 25
Santa Croce Camerina, Sicily, 69
Santa Margherita, Sicily, 95
Santa Ninfa, Sicily, 95
Saragusa, PFC Victor, 354
Savell, Lt. Bill, 300
Savoie, Capt. Domat L., 38
Sayre, Edwin M., Capt., 12, 26–29, 57, 58, 63–64, 64–65, 69–70, 71, 72, 75–76, 79–80, 91, 92, 93–94, 108
Scambelluri, PFC Michael A. "Scam" and "Iron Mike", 73, 74
Scarborough, Capt. Lee F., 38
Scarborough, Sgt. Louis C., 357
Schehl, PFC Lawrence J., 315
Schell, PFC Lowell, 374
Scherzer, Pvt. Merrill M. "Marty", 219
Schimpf, Lt. Emil H., 251, 289
Schlesener, Sgt. Milton E., 155, 156, 305
Schmees, Capt. William E., 123, 317
Schmidt, Germany, 388
Schmidt, Sgt. Victor M., 30, 106–107
Schneider, Pvt. Frank, 34
Schrader, 1st Sgt. Clifford W., 229, 233
Schroeder, Pvt. Bernard J., 350
Schuetzle, Sgt. Palmer F., 170
Schuler, Pvt. Francis A., 145
Schultz, PFC Arthur B. "Dutch", 129, 133, 143, 169, 194, 202, 203, 230, 233, 240, 253–254, 255, 317, 377, 379–380, 381, 382, 396, 399–400, 402, 416
Schwartzwalder, Capt. Ben, 172
Schwerin, Germany, 404
Scoglitti, Sicily, 62
Scruggs, Capt. Julius H., 31
Sebastion, PFC Julius A., 166
Seelye, PFC Irvin W. "Turk", 36, 38, 39, 41, 44, 57, 66, 93, 119, 182, 203
Shawver, PFC Lee E., 309
Sheffler, PFC David M., 33
Shelton, Pvt. J. D., 288
Sheridan, Pat, 72
Short, Lt. Albert W., 382
Shuman, James, 354
Siam, PFC S. John, 222, 234, 321, 347–348, 360–361, 363, 378
Sigler, Pvt. Clarence C., 34
Silanskis, Pvt. Frank "Barney", 185, 266
Simonds, Pvt. Donald E., 249

Singleton, Lt. Col. Raymond E. "Tex", 154
Slaverio, Pvt. John P., 155
Slavin, Ed, 109
Slawson, Pvt. William E. "Bill", 315, 382
Smith, Sgt. Alex, 88
Smith, Pvt. Gilbert C., 47
Smith, Lt. James J. "J. J.", 121, 130, 186, 187, 190, 225, 236, 260, 271–272, 273, 278, 280, 284, 300, 322
Smith, Capt. Lewis A. "Lew", 38
Smith, Lt. Roy H., 59
Smith, Sgt. Stanley S. "Smitty", 161
Smith, Capt. Taylor G. "T. G.", 123, 183, 185, 218, 223, 225, 259, 263, 269, 305, 313, 314, 331, 332, 351, 379, 391
Smithson, Cpl. Raymond D., 34, 166
Snyder, T/Sgt. Ronald, 11–12, 17, 126, 127, 140, 149, 150
Son, Holland, 225
Sonnenburg, Pvt. George, 335
Southampton, England, 318, 412
Spa, Belgium, 316, 318, 319, 320, 385
Spanhoe airfield, England, 123, 129
Sprinkle, Lt. John D., 68
St.-Martin-de-Varreville, France, 187
St.-Sauveur-le-Vicomte, France, 8, 118, 121, 123, 146, 196, 204, 205, 207, 208, 211, 212, 213, 216, 218, 220
St.-Vith, Belgium, 319, 381
Stark, PFC Roy A. 33–34
Stavelot, Belgium, 318
Ste.-Marie-du-Mont, France, 118
Ste.-Mère-Église, France, 8, 9, 123, 124, 125, 132, 134, 135, 137–139, 142, 143, 146–157, 159, 160, 162–165, 167, 169, 170, 172, 182, 183, 186, 187, 188, 190, 193, 196, 197, 201, 220, 415
Steed, Sgt. James T., 300
Steele, Pvt. John, 136–137, 149–150
Stein, Capt. Lester, 38, 66, 256
Stenfanich, Capt. Anthony M. "Stef", 221, 225, 254, 255, 416
Stenhouse, Capt. Gordon C., 38
Stillings, Ken, 389
Stiner, Pvt. Gordon M. "Stinky", 333
Stolberg, Germany, 389
Stoll Jr., PFC Clarence M., 399
Stolp, Pvt. Northam H., 289, 291–293, 294–296, 305, 306
Stoneking, Pvt. Thomas F., 289, 291, 292, 293, 296
Stout Jr., PFC Ralph, 128
Student, Gen. Kurt, 97
Suer, Capt. Alexander P. "Pete", 38, 90, 310
Suippes, France, 315, 316, 318, 320, 321, 349, 351, 379, 388
Supreme Headquarters Allied Expeditionary Force (SHAEF), 395, 404
Swarts, Pvt. Glenn C., 33
Sweeney, Lt. Alexander F., 159
Swift, Col. Ira P., 323, 331, 332, 379, 384
Swingler, Capt. Harold H. "Swede", 69, 89, 119, 161, 162, 221
Symonds, PFC Dick, 89
Synold, Frederick G., 200
Tague, Sgt. Robert M., 368
Tallerday, Capt. Jack, 103, 145, 169, 234, 254, 255, 369, 416
Tallett, PFC Joseph V. "Joe", 356, 357, 368

Taylor, Brig. Gen. Maxwell, 98, 100, 116
Taylor, Cpl. Stokes M., 333
Tepsick, Pvt. Rudy, 262
Ternent, Malcolm, 251
Thain, Maj. Carl E., 23, 33, 119, 256
Thain, Capt. Harold R., 119, 256
Theux, Belgium, 377, 378, 379, 381
Thomas, Maj. David E., 31–32, 37
Thomas, Sgt. Joseph N., 85, 141
Thompson, Sgt. Arthur M. "Tommie", 360
Thompson, Sgt. Frank, 356
Thompson, John "Beaver", 87
Thompson, Pvt. Roland M., 339
Thompson, Lt. Col. Tommy, 50, 66
Thompson, Sgt. Tommy, 33, 34
Tomardy, Sgt. Bernard J., 294
Tournai, Belgium, 225
Trapani, Sicily, 95, 96, 97
Trieber, PFC Douglas, 275
Tripoli, Libya, 74
Trois Ponts, Belgium, 9, 322, 323, 327, 330, 331, 332, 333, 335, 336, 346, 349
Trotman, Pvt. Paul C., 301
Tucker, Col. Reuben H., 36, 42, 251, 281, 327, 343
Tucker, Sgt. William H. "Bill", 43, 44, 125, 129, 152, 161–162, 198–200, 231, 238–239, 336, 337, 345, 358, 359, 360, 361, 362–363, 364, 414, 415, 416
Tumminello, Sicily, 95, pass, 98
Turnbull, Lt. Turner B., 155, 156, 163, 164, 165, 166, 167, 183, 189, 197, 220, 222
Turner, S/Sgt. Charlie D., 30
Tuttle, S/Sgt. Walter L., 364
Tuttle, Sgt. Roy M., 312
Udenbreth, Germany, 383

United States Military Units, United States Army
1st Cavalry Division (Airmobile), Vietnam, 414
1st Infantry Division, 42, 50, 51, 55, 62, 68, 73, 76, 80, 81, 90, 93, 381, 383
1st Special Service Force, 315
2nd Armored Division, 92
3rd Armored Division, 343
4th Infantry Division, 124, 162, 186, 187, 190, 198, 201
V Corps, 319
7th Armored Division, 341, 368, 380, 395
VII Corps, 123, 187, 198, 208, 214, 219
VIII Corps, 220, 319
8th Infantry Division, 386, 395, 402
8th Infantry Regiment, 187, 188, 190
1st Battalion, 187
2nd Battalion, 187, 188, 189
9th Infantry Division, 204, 205, 207, 388
12th Infantry Regiment, 187, 189
13th Airborne Division, 35
13th Armored Division, 392
16th Infantry Regiment, 53, 93, 94
2nd Battalion, 76, 79, 80, 91, 92, 93
17th Airborne Division, 8, 224, 408
XVIII Airborne Corps, 8, 224, 343, 395
XXII Corps, 390

26th Infantry Regiment, 80
28th Infantry Division, 17, 386, 387
30th Infantry Division, 327, 346, 349
36th Infantry Division, 12, 26, 101
39th Infantry Division, 95
45th Infantry Division, 42, 50, 55, 59, 79, 81, 84, 85, 88, 90, 91, 101
47th Infantry Regiment, 213
51st Engineer Battalion, Company C, 323
75th Infantry Division, 377
79th Infantry Division, 216
80th Airborne Antiaircraft (Antitank) Battalion, unit of 505th RCT, 9, Italy to Northern Ireland, 116, 117, move to Oadby, England, 118, glider landing in Normandy, 154, D-Day, 160, Market-Garden plan, 228, casualties during WWII, 405, Camp Chicago, 408
Battery A, 154, 182, 194, 228, 240, 241, 320, 329, 342–343, 381
Battery B, 154, 253
Battery C, 211, 253
82nd Airborne Division, 8, 35, 39, 41, 46, 49, 55, 81, 98, 100, 104, 105, 116, 118, 123, 129, 134, 137, 147, 153, 186, 195, 220, 224, 225, 226, 227, 228, 240, 255, 258, 281, 286, 289, 306, 309, 315, 319, 321, 322, 323, 344, 353, 356, 364, 377, 383, 386, 387, 389, 395, 402, 406, 408, 409, 411, 412, 414, 415, 416
82nd Airborne Reconnaissance Platoon, 229
82nd Airborne Signal Company, 50, 229
82nd Infantry Division, 14
86th Infantry Division, 389
90th Infantry Division, 204
101st Airborne Division, 8, 118, 129, 137, 142, 145, 147, 177, 183, 188, 203, 224, 225, 319, 411
112th Infantry Regiment, 386, 387
121st Infantry Regiment, 8th Infantry Division, 402
180th Infantry Regiment, 81
Company L, 80
307th Airborne Engineer Battalion, redesignated as airborne, 32, Naples, Italy, 105, 115, Italy to Northern Ireland, 116, 117, move to Burbage, England, 118, Market-Garden plan, 228, Holland jump, 240, Belgium counteroffensive, 371, WWII casualties, 405
A Company, 228
B Company, unit of 505th RCT, 9, redesignated as airborne, 32, assigned to 505th RCT, 35, Sicily objective, 48, Sicily plan, 50, Johnson commands, 50, 69, Biazzo Ridge, 81, 89, Italy preparations, 100, pathfinder team members, 101, 122, Salerno jump, 102, 103, move to Paestum, Italy, 103, barracks explosion, 115, Normandy preparations, 123, Normandy jump, 145, 146, Hill 131, 217, Operation Market-Graden plan, 228, Holland jump, 240, Salm River defense, 324, 336, 343, Siegfried Line attack, 381, Elbe River crossing, 396, 400, WWII casualties, 405, Camp Chicago, 408
C Company, 32, 228
D Company, 228
307th Airborne Medical Company, Thomas commands medical detachment, 31, assigned to 505th RCT, 35,

Oujda, 43–44, Sicily plan, 50, Ste.-Mère-Église, 197
307th Engineer Battalion, 32
325th Glider Infantry Regiment, 204, 228, 308, 381, 382, 383, 389, 402, 403
2nd Battalion, 201, 204
326th Glider Infantry Regiment, 35
376th Parachute Field Artillery Battalion, 228, 254, 308
401st Glider Infantry Regiment
2nd Battalion, 309
456th Parachute Field Artillery Battalion, unit of 505th RCT, 9, formation, 33, Harden commands, 33, assigned to 505th RCT, 35, Sicily plan, 42, 50, Sicily jump, 66, Sicily, 69, joins 504th RCT in Italy, 116, Harden relieved 119, D'Alessio commands, 119, battalion reconstituted, 119, Normandy preparations, 124, capture of Montebourg Station, 202, capture of Le Ham, 203, 204, Market-Garden plan, 228, glider flight to Holland, 253, 256, static warfare in Holland, 308, 310, Siegfried Line attack, 381, WWII casualties, 405, Camp Chicago, 408
Battery A, Operation Dodger, 47, Sicily plan, 50, Normandy preparations, 124, capture of St.-Sauveur-le-Vicomte, 207, glider flight to Holland, 253, 254, 255–256
Battery B, Sicily plan, 50, 53, Sicily preparations, 54, 66, Carl and Harold Thain command, 119, glider flight to Holland, 255, 256
Battery C, Operation Dodger, 47, Sicily plan, 50, Sicily jump, 59, Biazzo Ridge, 85, 86, USO show, 99, Italy to Northern Ireland, 116, 117, move to Husbands Bosworth, England, 118, battalion reconstituted, 119, Normandy preparations, 123, 124, Normandy jump, 141–142, D-Day, 160, glider flight to Holland, 253, 254, static warfare in Holland, 313, Trois Ponts, Berlin, 330, Berlin, 410
Battery D, Sicily plan, 50, Sicily jump, 66, Italy to Northern Ireland, 116, 117, move to Husbands Bosworth, England, 118, cadre for Battery B, 119
Headquarters Battery, Sicily plan, 50, Sicily jump, 66
502nd Parachute Infantry Regiment, 23
503rd Parachute Infantry Battalion, 13, 23, 27
504th Parachute Infantry Regiment, 8, 23, 25, 35, 36, 91, 93, 95, 98, 104, 118, 227, 228, 229, 248, 251, 281, 297, 312, 327, 343, 381, 383, 389, 402, 404
1st Battalion, 103
2nd Battalion, 103
3rd Battalion, 48, 50, 58, 90, 101, 299, 305
504th Regimental Combat Team, 90, 91, 93, 95, 98, 99, 101, 116
505th Parachute Infantry Regiment, actions in WWII, 8–9, formation, 23, Gavin commands, 25, Alabama Area, 32, 33, 34, joins 82nd Airborne Division, 35, first regimental jump, 36, Fort Bragg, 37, Sicily plan, 50, 1st anniversary barbecue, 52, Sicily 92, 93, 94, 95, Italy preparations, 98, 100, USO show, 99, move to beach at Paestum, Italy, 103, Naples, Italy, 104, Arnone, Italy, 114, Batcheller commands, 116, Italy to Northern Ireland, 116, 117, Normandy plan, 118, Quorndon, England, 118, Batcheller relieved, 120, Ekman commands, 120, pathfinder teams, 101–102,

132, 134, Normandy jump, 147, D-Day, 160, 162, 169, 176, 177, 196, capture of Montebourg Station, 201, 202, capture of Sauveur-le-Vicomte, 204, 210, 213, Hill 131, 216, Hill 95, Ekman letter, 220, Nomandy casualties, 221, reorganization after Normandy, 222, 224, Operation Market-Garden plan, 227, 228, Holland jump, 230, 231, 235, capture of Holland objectives, 243, 251, 257, Holland glider landings, 256, relieved by 325th GIR, 308, guards Nijmegen bridges, 308, 309, defense of Groesbeek, 309, south of Waal River, 312, combat readiness for Belgium, 318, casualties return from hospitals, 318, movement to Werbomont, 320–321, movement to Basse-Bodeux, 321–322, movement to Salm River, 322, Salm River defense, 336, 337, 338, 343, Belgium counteroffensive, 356, 366, 368, 376, 377, Theux, Belgium, 378, Siegfried Line attack, 381, 382, 383, 385, Hürtgen Forest, 386, 387, 388, Rhine River, 389–390, 392, Elbe River crossing, 395, 396, 401, 402, Wöbbelin concentration camp, 403, WWII casualties, 405, guards POWs, 406, Camp Chicago, 408, Epinal, 408, Berlin, 409–411, post war, 415, 416
Headquarters and Headquarters Company, formation, 31, Scruggs commands, 31, movement to overseas, 38, Oujda, 47, Sicily plan, 50, Sicily jump, 65, KIAs in Sicily, 69, Biazzo Ridge, 89, pathfinder training, 98, Italy preparations, 100, pathfinder team members, 101, Salerno jump, 102, 103, attack to Volturno River, 108, Long commands, 114, Italy to Northern Ireland, 116, Normandy preparations, 122, 123, 126, Normandy jump, 145–146, D-Day, 176, Cockrell commands, 214, Bois de Limors, 214, Hill 131, 217, Market-Garden plan, 228, Holland jump, 231, 239, capture of Holland objectives, 246, capture of Nijmegen bridges, 285, static warfare in Holland, 307, Suippes, 315, movement to Werbomont, 321, Belgium counteroffensive, 364, 367, Rheims, 388
1st Battalion, formation, 25, Gorham commands, 25, Frying Pan, 28, first regimental jump, 36, medical officers assigned, 38, Casablanca, 41, Oujda, 45, 49, Operation Eyewash, 46, Operation Dodger, 47, Sicily plan, 48, 50, Sicily jump, 63, 73, Sicily, 90, 91, Gorham killed, 92, Winton commands, 92, Italy preparations, 100, Salerno jump, 102, 103, screens 504th attack, 103, attack to Volturno River, 105, 106, 108, Kellam commands, 119, Normandy preparations, 121, 123, pathfinder team, 121, 122, 129, 130, 132, 133, Normandy jump, 130, 132, 142, 145, 146, La Fière Causeway, 147, 169, 170, 171, 176, 194, Alexander commands, 177, Grainville, 200, capture of Montebourg Station, 201–202, capture of Le Ham, 203, capture of St.-Sauveur-le-Vicomte, 204, 205, 207, 210, 212, Hagan commands, 214, Hill 131, 216, 217, 218, Hill 95, 218, 219, Long commands, 224, reorganization after Normandy, 224–225, Market-Garden plan, 228, 229, Holland jump, 231, 233, 234, 240, capture of Holland objectives, 245, 248, 250, defense of Mook, 289, 308, static warfare in Holland, 312, 313, Suippes, France, 316, movement to Salm River, 322, Belgium

counteroffensive, 356, 368–369, 371, Siegfried Line attack, 382, 383, Maness commands, 389, Elbe River crossing, 396, 397, 399, 401

A Company, formation, 25, Palluconi commands, 25, Sayre commands, 27, personnel assigned, 28, 1st regimental jump, 36, Sicily jump, 57, 58, 63, 64, Sicily, 64–65, 69–70, 72, 79, capture of Objective "Y", 75–76, Hill 41 attack, 91, attack to Volturno River, 108, 114–115, Dolan commands, 119, Chester commands 1st Battalion pathfinder team, 121, 132, Normandy jump, 133, La Fière Causeway, 169–172, 173–175, 177, 178, 179, 180, 181, D+1, 186, capture of Montebourg Station, 202, Bois de Limors, 215, Dolan promoted, 224, Normandy casualties, 229, Holland jump, 230, 233, 240, capture of Holland objectives, 248, defense of Mook, 289, 293, 294, 305, Dolan, Presnell, and Chester wounded, 307, Cockrell commands, 307, guards Nijmegen bridges, 309, static warfare in Holland, 314, Salm River defense, 322, Belgium counteroffensive, 356, 357, 358, Siegfried Line attack, 382, Elbe River crossing, 397, 399

B Company, formation, 25, Sanders command, 25, Frying Pan, 26, 27, 28, 1st regimental jump, 36, 37, movement to overseas, 38, 39, Oujda, 43, Operation Eyewash, 46, Sicily preparations, 48, Sicily jump, 63, Normandy preparations, 128, 129, Normandy jump, 143, 144, D-Day, 169, La Fière Causeway, 171, 173, D+1, 186, 190, D+3, 201, capture of Montebourg Station, 202, Bois de Limors, 215, Normandy casualties, 221, reorganization after Normandy, 222, 224–225, Holland jump, 240, capture of Holland objectives, 248–250, Mook 251, defense of Reithorst, 288, defense of Mook, 289–295, 305, movement to Werbomont, 320, Salm River defense, 322, Christmas in Belgium, 351, Belgium counteroffensive, 357, 365, 369, Siegfried Line attack, 382, Elbe River crossing, 400, 401

C Company, 25, Conlon commands, 25, first regimental jump, 36, Oujda 44, Operation Eyewash, 46, Sicily jump, 63, Sicily, 73, 75, Salerno jump, 103, pathfinders, 121, Normandy preparations, 126, 128, Normandy jump, 132, 133, 143–145, D-Day, 169, La Fière Causeway, 173, 174, 176, 177, 194, capture of Montebourg Station, 202, Montebourg Station, 203, capture of St.-Sauveur-le-Vicomte, 205, Bois de Limors, 215, Normandy casualties, 221, Stefanich returns, 225, Normandy casualties return, 229, Holland jump, 233, 234, 240, capture of Holland objectives, 248, 250, defense of Riethorst, 251–252, 288, clear Landing Zone "N", 253–254, death of Stefanich, 255, Riethorst, 308, guards Nijmegen bridges, 309, Salm River defense, 322, 342–343, Belgium counteroffensive, 356, 357, 358, 368, 369, 377, Siegfried Line attack, 381, 382, Elbe River crossing, 396, 397, 399–400, 402, Epinal, 408, 409, post war, 415, 416

Headquarters Company, formation, 26, Winton commands, 26, Operation Eyewash, 46, in Sicily, 75, Normandy jump, 129, D-Day, 169, La Fière Causeway, 171, 175, 178, D+1, 186, capture of

Holland objectives, 249, 250, Stefanich's death, 255, Belgium counteroffensive, 357, 375, Elbe River crossing, 400, Victory Parade, 413

2nd Battalion, Wright commands, 29, Gray commands, 33, medical officers assigned, 38, Alexander commands, 49, Sicily plan, 48, 50, Kairouan, 54, Sicily jump, 66, 68, Sicily, 90, 95, 97, Italy preparations, 99, 100, Salerno jump, 102, 103, attack to Volturno River, 105, 106, 107, 108, Vandervoort commands, 116, Northern Ireland, 117, Normandy preparations, 121, 123, pathfinder team, 121, 127, 132, 186, 225, Normandy briefing, 123, 124, Normandy jump, 130, 132, 134, 135, 139, movement to Neuville-au-Plain, 147, defense of Ste.-Mère-Église, 155, 156, 183, attack north of Ste.-Mère-Église, 188, 194, 196, 197, capture of Fresville, 198, capture of Montebourg Station, 201, capture of Le Ham, 202, 203, 204, capture of St.-Sauveur-le-Vicomte, 204, 205, 206, 207, 208, 210, reorganization, 214, Hill 131, 216, 217, 218, reorganization after Normandy, 219, 225, Market-Garden plan, 228, 229, Holland jump, 231, 233, 235, 237, 238, 241, capture of Holland objectives, 243, 244, call from British near Arnhem, 258, capture of Nijmegen bridges, 259, 278, 284, 297, 305, 306, defends Mook, 308, static warfare in Holland, 312, 313, Suippes, 317, movement to Salm River, 322, Trois Ponts, 323, 324, 331, 335, 337, 343, Carpenter replaces Smith, 351, Belgium counteroffensive, 354, 366, 370, 372, 374, 375, Vandervoort wounded, 376, Carpenter commands, 376, Theux, 379, Siegfried Line attack, 382, Bonn, 392, Elbe River crossing, 396, 397, 401, Berlin, 409, 410

D Company, formation, 29, Bolton commands, 29, formation, 30, wins best squad contest, 33, Cotton's Fish Camp incident, 34, Oujda, 42, Sicily preparations, 54, 66, 68, Italy preparations, 99, Salerno jump, 103, attack to Volturno River, 106, 108, Normandy preparations, 123, 125, 127, Normandy jump, 133, 138–139, defense of Neuvulle-au-Plain, 155, 163, 164, 166, defense of Ste.-Mère-Église, 182, 183, 186, 187, attack north of Ste.-Mère-Église, 189, 191, 192, 194, 196, 197, 198, capture of Le Ham, 203, capture of St.-Sauveur-le-Vicomte, 205, 206, 208, 209, 211, Bois de Limors, 214, Hill 131, 217, Normandy casualties, 220, 221, 222, replacements assigned, 222–223, Smith commands, 225, Holland jump, 235, 236, 237, capture of Holland objectives, 243, capture of Nijmegen bridges, 259, 260, 263, 267, 269, 277, 278, 283, 284, 305, death of Wray, 266–267, guards Nijmegen bridges, 307, defense of Groesbeek, 311, static warfare in Holland, 313, Smith promoted, 314, Carlson commands, 314, Suippes, 315, defense of La Tour, 322, 324, 327, 335, 337, Christmas in Belgium, 349, 351, Belgium counteroffensive, 352, 354, 355, 367, 368, 372, 374, Theux, 378–379, Martin commands, 379, Siegfried Line attack, 382–383, Rheims, 388, Bruhl, 392, Elbe River crossing, 397, 398, 399, Privelack, 406–407, Berlin, 409–410,

Victory Parade, 412–413, post war, 415
E Company, formation, 29, McGinity commands, 29, formation, 30, Alabama Area, 34, movement to overseas, 38, movement to Oujda, 41, movement to Kairouan, 49, 1st anniversary barbecue, 52, Sicily jump, 57, 58, 66, 67, 74, Sicily, 69, 93, Italy preparations, 99, attack to Volturno River, 106, 107, 108, 109, 110, 114, Russell commands, 114, integration of replacements, 117, Camp Quorn, 119, Smith commands 2nd Battalion pathfinder team, 121, Normandy preparations, 123, 127, Normandy jump, 132, 134, 135, 137, 138, 152, defense of Ste.-Mère-Église, 162–163, 165, 182, 183, 187, attack north of Ste.-Mère-Église, 188–191, 194, capture of Le Ham, 202, 203, capture of St.-Sauveur-le-Vicomte, 206, 208, 211, 212, Hill 131, 217, Smith commands, 225, Holland jump, 231, 233, 238, capture of Holland objectives, 243, capture of Nijmegen bridges, 259, 260, 261, 270, 271, 274, 277, 278, 279, 280, 282, 283, 284, 286, 297, 298, 300, 301, 305, defense of Groesbeek, 312, Meddaugh commands, 323, Trois Ponts, 322, 324, 325, 328, 330, 331, 332, 335, 336, 372, Barnett commands, 376, 379, Siegfried Line attack, 383, Rhine River, 390, Elbe River crossing, 397–399, victory in Europe, 405
F Company, Vandervoort commands, 23, 29, formation, 29, Fort Bragg, 36, McRoberts commands, 49, Kairouan, 53, Sicily jump, 67, attack to Volturno River, 105, 106, 108, 109, 114, Normandy preparations, 120, 123, 126, Normandy jump, 130, 134, 136–137, capture of Ste.-Mère-Église, 149, 152, defense of Ste.-Mère-Église, 156, 157, attack north of Ste.-Mère-Église, 196, capture of Le Ham, 202, 203, capture of St.-Sauveur-le-Vicomte, 208, 209, 211, Holcomb commands, 214, Hill 131, 217, Rosen commands, 225, Holland jump, 235, 236, capture of Holland objectives, 244–245, capture of Nijmegen bridges, 259, 260, 275, 277, 297–301, 303, 304, 305, Case commands, 308, static warfare in Holland, 314, Suippes, 316, movement to Basse-Bodeux, 321, Trois Ponts, 322, 324, 331–332, 335, withdrawal from Salm River, 348, Belgium counteroffensive, 351, 354, 355, 367, 370, 372, 374, Hays commands, 379, Siegfried Line attack, 383, Hürtgen Forest, 387, Rhine River, 389, Rhine River, 391, Elbe River crossing, 397, 399, 21st Army surrenders, 402, victory in Europe, 407, post war, 416
Headquarters Company, formation, 29, Fleet commands, 29, Alabama Area, 32, 1st regimental jump, 36, movement to overeas, 38, Casablanca, 41, Oujda, 43, 1st anniversary barbecue, 52–53, Kairouan, 55, Sicily jump, 58, 66, 68, roadblock in Sicily, 69, attack to Volturno River, 108, Normandy preparations, 123, Normandy jump, 139, defense of Ste.-Mère-Église, 157–159, capture of St.-Sauveur-le-Vicomte, 205, 208, Schmees commands, 214, Hill 131, 218, capture of Nijmegen bridges, 259, 263, 268, 297, 299, Suippes, 317, movement to Werbomont, 320, Trois Ponts, 324, 335, Belgium counteroffensive, 354, 366
3rd Battalion, formation, 31, Batcheller commands, 31,

Alabama Area, 32, Krause commands, 33, medical officers assigned, 38, Oujda, 44, 45, 46, Operation Dodger, 47, Sicily plan, 50, Kairouan, 51, Sicily jump, 58, 59, 60, 62, 63, Biazzo Ridge, 81, 82, 86, 93, Sicily, 95, 96, Italy preparations, 100, Salerno jump, 102, movement to Chiunzi Pass, 103, 104, Naples, 104, 105, Normandy preparations, 123, 124, pathfinder team, 122, 132, Normandy jump, 130, 132, 133, 139, 141, 142, movement to Ste.-Mère-Église, 147–148, 150, capture of Ste.-Mère-Église, 150, 154, defense of Ste.-Mère-Église, 155, 156, D+1, 187, attack north of Ste.-Mère-Église, 196, capture of Grainville, 198, 200, capture of Montebourg Station, 201, capture of St.-Sauveur-le-Vicomte, 207, 212, reorganization, 214, Bois de Limors, 214, Hill 131, 216, 218, Hill 95, 218, 219, reorganization after Normandy, 219, 225, Kaiser commands, 224, Market-Garden plan, 228, 229, 230, Holland jump, 231, 234, 235, 238, 240, capture of Holland objectives, 244, 245, 246, defense of Groesbeek, 251, 254, 286, 309, 310, static warfare in Holland, 312, 313, Suippes, 315, Werbomont, 321, movement to Salm River, 322, Salm River defense, 337, withdrawal from Salm River, 344, Belgium counteroffensive, 355, 362, 369, 370, 371, Theux, 378, Siegfried Line attack, 383, Elbe River crossing, 396, 397, 401
G Company, formation, 31, Gibbons commands, 31, Alabama Area, 32, Meyers commands, 37, movement to overseas, 39, Oujda, 43, 46, 48, Sicily jump, 59, Biazzo Ridge, 81, 84, 93, Sicily, 95, 96, Salerno jump, 102, liberation of Naples, 104, McGinity transfers to 1st Battalion, 119, Follmer commands, 119, Normandy preparations, 122, 126, 127, Normandy jump, 133, 139–141, movement to Ste.-Mère-Église, 148–150, capture of Ste.-Mère-Église, 150–152, defense of Ste.-Mère-Église, 153, 160–161, 163, D+1, 186, capture of Grainville, 200, capture of Montebourg Station, 201, capture of St.-Sauveur-le-Vicomte, 212, 213, Hill 95, 219, Normandy casualties, 221, Issacs commands, 225, Normandy casualties return, 229, Holland jump, 238, 239, capture of Holland objectives, 246, 248, death of Lt. Gavin, 257, defense of Groesbeek, 286, 309, 310, guards Nijmegen bridges, 308, static warfare in Holland, 313, casualties in Holland, 314, casualties return from hospitals, 318, movement to Werbomont, 321, defense of Petit-Halleux and Grand-Halleux, 322, 338, 339, 340, 341–342, withdrawal from Salm River, 344, 345, 346, Belgium counteroffensive, 358, 364, 377, Siegfried Line attack, 383–384, Hürtgen Forest, 385, Elbe River crossing, 401, 21st Army surrenders, 403, Victory Parade, 413
H Company, formation, 31, Mill commands, 31, Alabama Area, 34, 35, Oujda, 43, 44, 47, Mill replaces Norton, 49, Kairouan, 55, Sicily jump, 59, Biazzo Ridge, 82, 83, 87, 88, 91, 93, Naples, 104, Normandy jump, 129, movement to Ste.-Mère-Église, 148, capture of Ste.-Mère-Église, 150–152, defense of Ste.-Mère-Église, 154, 183, 188, Atchley awarded DSC, 194, capture of Grainville, 200, capture of St.-Sauveur-le-Vicomte,

213, Maness commands, 214, 225, capture of Holland objectives, 246, 247–248, defense of Groesbeek, 251, 310, Fitzgerald commands, 315, Suippes, 316, movement to Werbomont, 320, 321, Salm River defense, 322, Christmas in Belgium, 350, Belgium counteroffensive, 358, 359, 362, 363, 364, Siegfried Line attack, 384, Elbe River crossing, 397, Epinal, 408

I Company, formation, 31, Follmer commands, 31, Oujda, 43, 47, Sicily plan, 50, Kairouan, 53, Sicily jump, 57, 58, 60, Sicily, 61–62, 79, 95, 96, Swingler commands, 119, Normandy preparations, 125, Normandy jump, 129, 141, capture of Ste.-Mère-Église, 148, 150, 152, defense of Ste.-Mère-Église, 160–162, attack north of Ste.-Mère-Église, 197, capture of Grainville, 198, 200, guards causeway at Ètienville, 204, capture of St.-Sauveur-le-Vicomte, 212, 213, Normandy casualties, 221, replacements assigned, 222, McPheeters commands, 225, Holland jump, 231, 233, 234, 238, 239, capture of Holland objectives, 245–246, 247, defense of Groesbeek, 251, 253, 254, 286, Suippes, 315, 317, casualties return from hospitals, 318, movement to Werbomont, 321, defense of Rochelinval, 322, 336–337, withdrawal from Salm River, 344, 345, 346, 347, 348, Christmas in Belgium, 351, Belgium counteroffensive, 358–364, 370, Theux, 378, Hürtgen Forest, 386, 387, Rheims, 388, Rhine River, 390, post war, 416

Headquarters Company, formation, 31, Wall commands, 31, Fort Bragg, 37, Oujda, 41, Biazzo Ridge, 87, Konar commands 3rd Battalion pathfinder team, 122, capture of Ste.-Mère-Église, 150, 151, capture of Holland objectives, 246, 247, static warfare in Holland, 313, Salm River defense, 338, 340, withdrawal from Salm River, 346, Belgium counteroffensive, 365, 366, 369, Epinal, 408

Service Company, organization, 32, Sicily plan, 50, Biazzo Ridge, 85, pathfinder team, 101, 337

505th Regimental Combat Team, units of, 9, formation, 35, Operation Husky, 42, at Oujda, 43, 44, 45, 52nd Troop Carrier Wing assigned, 46, Sicily plan, 49, 50, 1st anniversary barbecue 52, Sicily drop zones 55, 62, route to Sicily, 90, Biazzo Ridge, 93, Sicily, 95, 97, 98, Italy preparations, 99, 100, Salerno jump, 101, movement to Maiori, Italy, 104, Normandy preparations, 120, 123, 128, Normandy casualties, 222, designated Task Force "A", 386, Rheims, 388, WWII casualties, 405, victory in Europe, 406, post war, 413, 414, 416, 417

507th Parachute Infantry Regiment, 118, 135, 137, 171, 172, 177, 204, 408

G Company, 172

508th Parachute Infantry Regiment, 118, 120, 135, 146, 172, 174, 177, 198, 200, 213, 218, 219, 228, 235, 246, 251, 257, 297, 318, 322, 332, 381

1st Battalion, 120, 213, 322

B Company, 172, 173

2nd Battalion, 213, 219

F Company, 219

3rd Battalion, 212

509th Parachute Infantry Regiment

2nd Battalion, 98, 401

551st Parachute Infantry Battalion, 360

Company C, 363, 364

592nd Field Artillery Battalion, 364

746th Tank Battalion, 190, 194

A Company, 206

Fifth Army, 46, 98, 100, 101

Fifthteenth Army, 389

First Allied Airborne Army, 225, 227

First Army, 316, 319, 323

Seventh Army, 46, 93

United States Military Units, United States Army Air Corps

IX Troop Carrier Command, 122, 228

50th Troop Carrier Wing, 228

52nd Troop Carrier Wing, 46, 50, 57, 90, 91, 228

61st Troop Carrier Group, 50

64th Troop Carrier Group, 50

313th Troop Carrier Group, 50

314th Troop Carrier Group, 50

316th Troop Carrier Group, 50

Eighth Air Force, 230

Urquhart, Gen., Robert F., 280

USS Frederick Funston, 116–117

USS George Washington, 405

USS Joseph T. Dickman, 116

USS Monterey, 38, 41

USS Nevada, 167

USS Thomas Jefferson, 116

Vah, Pvt. Pete, 129

Valognes, France, 153

Van Fleet, Col. James, 188

Vance, Norman J., 151

Vandervoort, Lt. Col. Benjamin H., 23, 29, 65, 72, 73, 80, 81, 105, 116, 123, 125–126, 134, 135–136, 138, 139, 190, 194, 195, 205, 206, 207, 208, 209, 210, 221, 235, 243, 244, 258, 259, 260–261, 262, 267, 270, 272, 273, 274–275, 277–278, 280, 282, 285, 297, 299, 300, 301, 302, 303, 304, 322–323, 324, 325, 330, 331, 332, 334–335, 354, 355, 373, 415–416

Vandevegt, Lt. Joseph W., 61, 162, 364

Vanich, PFC Sam, 161, 200, 201

Varenquebec, France, 216

Vargas, Richard A., 151

Varvarkis, PFC Charlie, 330

Vassar, Leon W., 358–359

Vaught, Cpl. Kenneth A.

Veghel, Holland, 226

Victory Parade, 412–413

Vielsalm, Belgium, 375, 385, 386

Villa Literno, Italy, 105, 106

Vittoria, Sicily, 59, 60, 62, 69, 80

Volturno River, 99, 105, 108, 109

Vossenack, Germany, 386

Vuletich, Sgt. Michael, 63, 293, 357

Waal River, 227, 228, 251, 281, 289, 297, 299, 303, 304, 305, 306, 308, 309, 312

Wagner, Capt. Jacob F., 224
Walas, Lt. John, 322, 323, 324, 329
Walberg, Cpl. Gordon A., 241, 333
Walheim, Germany, 388
Wall, Capt. Leolus L., 31
Wallace, S/Sgt. Robert E., 401
Walsh, Pvt. John J., 145
Walter, PFC William C., 161
Wanne, Belgium, 327
Ward, C/Sgt. Maj. Elmer, 31
Ward, PFC Wilbert, 215
Wasner, Pvt. John E., 144–145
Watts, Pvt. Roy L., 110
Weaver, Jess, 291
Wechsler, Lt. Ben L., 81, 90
Weed, Sgt. Gerald R. "Jerry", 156, 163, 165, 167, 263, 266, 327
Weinberg, Lt. Stanley, 215, 216, 217, 240, 249, 250, 288, 369
Weir, Lt. Brock M., 176
Werbomont, Belgium, 319, 320, 321, 328, 343, 344
Wereth, Belgium, 381
Wertich, Lt. Jake L., 329, 330, 333
West, Sgt. Floyd, 189
Western Force, 259, 260, 263
Whalen, Lt. Edward P., 32
Whicker, PFC Wilson N., 339
White, Sgt. Edward, 151
White, PFC Norris S., 121
Whitfield, PFC Daryle, 108–109
Wienecke, Col. Robert H., 224, 227, 318
Wigle, PFC Cloid, 83, 84, 251
Williams, Sgt. Richard V., 356
Willoughby, PFC Darrell P., 255
Wilson, Lt. William T., 68
Wingfield, PFC Jack C., 239

Winton Jr., Lt. Col. Walter F., 26, 64, 120, 213, 224
Wöbbelin Concentration Camp, 403–404
Wood, Captain George B. "Chappie", 90, 93, 114, 146, 156–157, 196, 201, 230–231, 415
Wood, Pvt. George M., 282, 283
Woods, Lt. Ivan F., 88, 141
Woosley, Lt. Frank P., 30, 34, 188, 190–191, 202, 203
Wray, Lt. Waverly W. "The Deacon", 30, 34, 54, 67, 68, 69, 99, 183–186, 195, 222, 263, 264, 265, 266, 267, 305
Wright, S/Sgt. Bonnie, 354
Wright, Earl H., 83
Wright, Capt. Frederick S., 29
Wroblewski, John, 72
Wurst, S/Sgt. Spencer F., 105, 106, 109, 157, 208–209, 210, 211, 244, 245, 275, 276–277, 298, 299, 302–303
Wyler, Germany, 251, 282
Wyngaert, Pvt. Julius A., 186
Yarborough, Maj. William P., 98
Yarchak, S/Sgt. Louis, 391
Yates, Sgt. James R., 141
Yeats, Maj. George, 194
York, Sgt. Alvin C., 195
Zafiroff, PFC Chris, 246, 340, 341, 346, 366
Zahurance, PFC Paul V., 331
Zaj, Maj. Edward A., 31
Zakrzewski, PFC Charles, 314
Zalenski, Boniface F., 151
Zeetze, Germany, 402
Zeigler, Lt. Harvey J., 85, 104, 105
Zeitner, S/Sgt. Herman R. "Zeke", 143, 144, 215, 240, 369, 416
Zhukov, Marshal Georgi, 411
Ziemski, Cpl. George S., 275
Zoromski, Victor P., 347